THE PRIMARY WAY

THE PRIMARY WAY
Philosophy of *Yijing*

CHUNG-YING CHENG

Foreword by
Robert Cummings Neville

The cover diagram is named "Fu Xi Square-Circle Diagram of Sixty-four Hexagrams." This diagram indicates two prior different orderings among the sixty-four hexagrams. This diagram is attributed to Fu Xi, the founder of Yijing Cosmological Symbols.

Published by State University of New York Press, Albany

© 2020 State University of New York

All rights reserved

No part of this book may be used or reproduced in any manner without written permission. No part of this book may be stored in a retrieval system or transmitted in any form or by any means including electronic, electrostatic, magnetic tape, mechanical, photocopying, recording, or otherwise without the prior permission in writing of the publisher.

For information, contact State University of New York Press, Albany, NY
www.sunypress.edu

Library of Congress Cataloging-in-Publication Data

Name: Cheng, Chung-Ying, author
Title: The primary way : philosophy of *yijing* / Chung-Ying Cheng, author.
Description: Albany : State University of New York Press, [2020] | Includes bibliographical references and index.
Identifiers: ISBN 9781438479279 (hardcover : alk. paper) | ISBN 9781438479286 (pbk. : alk. paper) | ISBN 9781438479293 (ebook)
Further information is available at the Library of Congress.

10 9 8 7 6 5 4 3 2 1

Contents

Foreword   vii

Preface   xi

Chapter 1
Introducing the *Yijing* (易经): Six Stages of Development and
Six Topics of the *Yijing*   1

Chapter 2
Yijing as Creative Inception of Chinese Philosophy   31

Chapter 3
Interpreting a Paradigm of Change in Chinese Philosophy   59

Chapter 4
Inquiring into the Primary Model: *Yijing* and Chinese
Ontological Hermeneutics   91

Chapter 5
Philosophical Significance of *Guan*: From *Guan* (观) to
Onto-Hermeneutical Unity of Methodology and Ontology   119

Chapter 6
Yin-Yang (阴阳) Way of Onto-Cosmic Thinking and Philosophy
of the *Yi* (易)   149

Chapter 7
On Harmony as Transformation: Paradigms from the *Yijing*   191

Chapter 8
Zhouyi (周易) and the Philosophy of *Wei* (Positions 位)   245

Chapter 9
Li (理) and *Qi* (气) *in the Yijing*: A Reconsideration of Being
and Nonbeing in Chinese Philosophy   273

Chapter 10
On the *Yijing* as a Symbolic System of Integrated
Communication   303

Chapter 11
On Zhu Xi's Integration of *Yili* (义理) and *Xianshu* (象数)
in the Study of the *Yijing*   331

Chapter 12
On Timeliness (*Shizhong* 时中) in the *Analects* and the *Yijing*:
An Inquiry into the Philosophical Relationship between
Confucius and the *Yijing*   353

Chinese Glossary   427

English Key Terms   435

Notes   437

A Bibliography of the *Yijing* in Chinese   475

A Bibliography of the *Yijing* in Western Languages   481

Works Cited   483

Index   503

Foreword

By good fortune and the kindness of Professor Chung-ying Cheng, I had the privilege twenty-six years ago of writing a foreword to his previous large volume of essays, *New Dimensions of Confucian and Neo-Confucian Philosophy*.¹ That foreword made three points. First, Professor Cheng is a very Catholic thinker within the Chinese tradition, not limited to one school such as the Confucian or Daoist, but drawing freely from all. Second, he not only is a scholar writing about the past, but even more is a working philosopher addressing the issues of our own time with the resources of classical philosophy, including Western philosophy. Third, he has one of the most splendid speculative imaginations of our time. These points remain true about the essays in these two volumes of *Creative Philosophy of the Yi*. Yet, much has happened in the intervening years to deepen Professor Cheng's philosophy.

First, he has thoroughly elaborated an interpretive method that he calls "onto-hermeneutics," or the hermeneutics of being. The essays discussing this are mainly in the volume *The Primary Way*, although the method informs nearly all of the articles of comparison in the other volume. Cheng was inspired by the phenomenology of Husserl and Heidegger in the development of onto-hermeneutics, but he applied that inspiration to the texts of Chinese philosophy, especially the *Yijing*. Husserlian and Heideggerian phenomenologies were careful to bracket out experience of value as well as commitments of existence. Heidegger was famous, or notorious, for believing that value-language already bespeaks a loss of being. Given the turns in early modern European philosophy that separated scientifically knowable facts from values, that hostility to experiential value is understandable, if perhaps misguided. Cheng's project is a radical departure from the European phenomenologists precisely because the Chinese texts do not permit a failure to recognize their articulations of the worth of things. Cheng's onto-hermeneutics is through and through aesthetic, dwelling on harmony. The method itself is extremely complicated, and these books invite its study in theory and practice.

Second, Cheng has devoted himself with single-minded energy to the onto-hermeneutical understanding of the *Yijing*. Now the *Yijing* is one of the most ancient and influential texts in any civilization, and the discovery of an older-yet manuscript of the text in 1973 sparked an industry of historical research. Yet the philosophical meaning of the text has often seemed like a Rorschach test for philosophers, especially for Western philosophers. Cheng has been determined that the philosophical interpretation of the *Yijing* not be a mere matter of speculative projection, eisegesis rather than exegesis. On the other hand, he is not willing, with so many of the historians, to leave the text as an ancient handbook for divination. With its many layers, the text exhibits extraordinary assumptions about the meaning of the world of nature and human kind. These assumptions have shaped the ways subsequent thinkers have taken the world, and they stand in many interesting contrasts with equally old assumptions in Western and Indian philosophies.

To combine these first two points, I believe that a significant achievement of Professor Cheng in these essays is to articulate the way of the *Yijing* as a *normative* way of life, a way that recognizes many of the real joints of nature and society, a way that needs to be practiced to be understood well, a way that leads to harmony in the deep senses these essays explore. To put the point more bluntly than Cheng usually does, the *Yijing* can be interpreted to provide an ethic grounded in the nature of being. This is what onto-hermeneutics does: not straight historical analysis, not objective metaphysics alone, but the establishment of a hermeneutical spiral that draws both an interpretation of the text from an interpretation of our own condition and a morally freighted analysis of our own condition from the orientations of the text. This is especially evident in Cheng's repeated and multi-contextual analyses of harmony, probably Cheng's most systematic philosophical contribution.

The third advance in Cheng's philosophy is precisely the fact that he now has a philosophical system, expressed in these essays, which extends throughout the main topics of philosophy. The system has a vocabulary, mainly elaborated from the *Yijing* and later Chinese philosophies, but that vocabulary is tested and refined for our time by Cheng's many discussions of other philosophical positions, East and West. Whereas in the volume twenty-six years ago, Cheng presented himself primarily as an interpreter, in these volumes he presents himself as a philosopher with a philosophy, and with the arguments to connect it critically with other philosophies. Irenic as always, he learns from everyone he studies. Yet he does not flinch upon discovering the limitations in other philosophies.

Two obstacles exist to appreciating Cheng's work here. The first is that systematic philosophy itself is out of fashion. Part of what this means is that specialists bristle if the philosopher is not up on the secondary literature and the discussions that are carried on in specialized working groups. Any philosopher with a system necessarily is going to have to work with the results of those specialized working groups, and cannot be internal to them all. The virtue of a philosophic system is that it thinks the ideas in comprehensive ways that specialists miss. Also, a philosophic system such as Cheng's can be used to address the fundamental practical philosophical issues of our time, something that the specialized analysis of ideas often cannot do.

The second obstacle is that Cheng has taken the language of the *Yijing* to be the core of his philosophy. The *Yijing* is an esoteric book, with esoteric language, rooted in a culture millennia away from our own. Thinkers whose intellectual paradigms come from analogies with modern science will find antiquity to be a hindrance rather than a help. Yet I recommend readers to persevere, because Cheng brings the intellectual motifs of the *Yijing* up to date. He is as aware as any modernist or postmodernist what needs to be left behind from the past.

On a personal note, I want to thank Chung-ying Cheng for his highly insightful interpretive essay on my own work, in *Comparative Essays*. His purpose there is to read me as a Chinese philosopher, and he does so by focusing on my theory of creation *ex nihilo*, which is just about the most Western notion in my thinking. I am pleased to see that he can apply onto-hermeneutics to even such a strange thinker as myself.

Chung-ying Cheng is one of the most creative and comprehensive philosophers of our time. It is our privilege to have these volumes of essays.

Robert Cummings Neville
Milton, Massachusetts, November, 2017

Preface

Although the *Yijing* 易经 has been treated usually as a divinatory text, what makes divination significant and later even transforms the practice of divination into a metaphysical insight into reality of change is a deep philosophy that I call "Philosophy of the Yi (易 Change)."[1] In this manner I have addressed the underlying fundamental philosophical visions and views of the *Yijing* in some explicit system of onto-cosmological understanding based on "comprehensive observation (*guan* 观)" of nature and "contemplative reflection" (*gan* 感) on oneself. Observation and reflection are not separable actions of mind in which concepts of cosmos and human self eventually co-emerge and become defined in relation to each other. This should thus reveal a dynamic relationship between cosmos and the human self. I believe that it is such an onto-cosmological understanding that has also inspired Confucius and through him his disciples and posterity to write a whole set of philosophical commentaries on the philosophy of the *Yijing* known as the *Yizhuan* 易传. The emergence and grounding of observation and reflection and eventually the creative interaction between them and thus between presentation of cosmos and transformation human self is what I refer as "the Primary Way" (*Yuanchuzhidao* 原初之道).[2]

History only witnessed the development of explanation of the meanings of symbolic forms of hexagrams in the *Yijing* from the time of Confucius to the present day based on partial understanding of the *Yizhuan*, but has not brought a full philosophical interpretation of the *Yijing* as a whole, including explaining how the Confucian interpretation itself comes about. To explain how Confucian interpretation itself comes about is to explain how the Yi symbols of trigrams and hexagrams as a system originally come about; it is to explain how cosmic observation and human self-reflection form the fountainhead and foundation of understanding these symbols and their practical uses. It is not simply to see how divination (*bu* 卜) in antiquity of China comes about to become a ritual of divination as a form of telling about future and decision for action. It is to see how divination is to be intelligently interpreted with regard to an emerging cosmology which one can understand. It is to see how divination is possible and how divination embodies a form of understanding which we can come to have even without divination.

The great practical value on understanding *Yi* is this: understanding change (*Yi*) enables a human person to develop his or her own creativity, transform his or her life and achieve his or her identity. It is in this sense it has presented a unity of theory and practice whereby theoretical understanding has to bring out practice, and practice must stimulate philosophical understanding. It is in this light that one could easily come to recognize that the way of the formation of the *Yijing* as a book of divination in fact enables us to realize how Chinese philosophy could be said to begin with the formation of the *Yijing* text in the beginning of Zhou around 1200 BCE. It will become easy to see how Confucianism and Daoism as two early schools of philosophy could be said to arise from this great beginning of the *Yijing*. Contemporary excavated texts dated back to the third to fourth century BCE have amply testified to this basic perception which we also read in Zhuangzi and Sima Qian.[3]

This book is written with the purpose not only to reveal the origins of Chinese philosophy in the *Yijing* philosophy, but to focus on the importance of the philosophy of change as an essential and perennial paradigm in Chinese philosophy which has special significance for understanding reality under such a paradigm. In this sense, it is not simply a matter of explicating the source, the formation and the system of underlying philosophy of the *Yijing* in its beginning, but a matter of consideration on philosophical methodology of observation, feeling, perception, and interpretation of a judgment in relation to time, location, and one's situation and position in the world. It has specifically to do with understanding man as an eternal symbol of symbols who does the observation and interpretation and who has to act with understanding and acquired knowledge of an end or good of one's life. It is to show how cosmology of nature is a natural part of humanity and hence informs human decision making and action, and at the same time, to show how action of man has to carry a reference to the world in creative transformation and becomes both creative and determined himself.

In light of the above, I have generally identified my work on *Yijing* in the last four decades as having made two main significant contributions to Chinese philosophy, as well as to philosophy overall.⁴ The first is that I have developed a philosophy of the *Yijing* as the primary way of being and becoming that anchors the entire tradition of Chinese philosophy and gives a contemporary meaning to an ancient text on the one hand, and on the other, brings the deep insights of this understanding to bear on ontology, cosmology, and even phenomenology and ethics in contemporary times. The second effort lies in my efforts to explicate the insightful visions and views of onto-cosmology and ethics in the *Yijing* philosophy from a comparative view or in a comparative context. In other words, I introduce views and insights of the *Yijing* in connection with special topics of philosophy such as metaphysics and non-metaphysics, being and nonbeing, time and timeless, essence and existence, divinity and the ultimate, science and religion, ecology and ethics. From this comparative view, I have dealt with these issues of the ultimate and change in light of Robert Cummings Neville, John B. Cobb Jr., Plato, Alfred North Whitehead, and Gottfried Wilhelm Leibniz. Thus, my first contribution is contained in chapters of this present volume titled the *Primary Way: Creative Philosophy of the Yi*, whereas the second contribution is to be contained in a forthcoming sequel volume to be titled the *Comparative Studies in Philosophy of the Yi*.

Here I hope that it is appropriate for me to recall the time when I first introduced philosophy of the *Yijing* as a graduate seminar at University of Hawai'i at Mānoa in the mid-1960s. Students thought they would learn divination; however, the were disappointed when I lectured on issues of the onto-cosmology of creativity, epistemology, and ethics of change and transformation with regard to questions of cosmic being and humanity. I must confess that I feel gratified when in later times students from the seminar eventually have been able to relate Yi 易 (change) to the *Yijing* 易经 and the *Yijing* to metaphysical and ethical issues in both Chinese and Western philosophies. In doing this seminar I was able to find and be convinced of root ideas of the change in the *Yijing* as the everlasting source of inspiration of Chinese philosophy in either Confucianism or Daoism. Whenever there are changes in time and history, Chinese philosophy tends to go back to its primary source for new guidance and for innovative thinking which are required to meet the challenges of the time and history. There is no stagnation or poverty of movement of ideas in the history of Chinese philosophy as mistakenly assessed by Hegel due to his lack of knowledge. I also find the *Yijing* to be such a system as being capable of easily relating to other traditions of metaphysics, epistemology, and ethics for a creative transformation and interaction toward a harmonized world of humanity. For example, this even happens when a Chan Buddhist monk makes out an interpretation of the *Yijing* text from a Chan-enlightenment point of view.[5] This could mean that the openness of the *Yijing* creativity is to allow human self-transcendence from human immanent creativity. The ultimate principle of the *Yijing* metaphysic is that there is no metaphysics as such, but human experience of observation and reflection would give rise to onto-generative interpretation and reinterpretation of being and nonbeing. There is a constant tackling of human creativity in Confucian ethics of human care and benevolence in facing a world of contingency as embodied in emergence, evolution, and realizable sustainability of life.

I must point out that this innovative view on the philosophy of *Yijing* is both creatively new and yet rooted in the implicit presupposition of a worldview and lifeview which makes understanding of present and future or time possible and thus provides a resource for action and realization of the nature of man. To study the book of the *Yijing* in this perspective is not simply to study the texts and its commentaries from past but to see it as a directive toward the cosmic and the human. It is to look into the economic and the ecological. It is to face reality as reality which is not merely being nor nonbeing but both. This approach to the *Yijing* is to treat it as a representation, a symbol of a system of symbols for our own philosophical interpretation from which we could also draw practical implications as there is always a goal of action of self-making and self-transformation in view. I take this to be an ever-refreshing philosophical challenge different from historical or textual consideration. However, this is not to do away with text or history of events which may be said to give rise to the judgments of divination which call for understanding and interpretation even at their historic moments. This is to recognize that we cannot simply rely on the text and history for understanding philosophy of *Yijing*: There is also dimension of reality apart from the issue of history and text in our seeking understanding and wisdom of humanity. Unless one takes this dimension into consideration, one cannot see the wisdom and attractive qualities of Chinese philosophy of the *ren* (仁 benevolence) in Confucianism, the *dao* (道 the way) in Daoism, or both in Neo-Confucianism.

Of course, we have to recognize that decades of studies of *Yijing* have been carried on in a tradition of commentary writings. These studies are important for making their own times and often hiding their insights in various wordings of notes and comments. Some even form a system of fundamental concepts and leading principles of insights into a pristine reality. We have typically the Daoist philosophy in Wang Bi's commentary on the *Yijing* in Wei-Jin Period, the Neo-Confucian philosophy in Zhou Dunyi, Zhang Zai, Cheng Yi, and Zhu Xi in their diagrams, comments and commentaries, which can be said to be eventually being guided by ideas of *li* 理 and *qi* 气. The *qi* idea dominates the interpretation of the *Yijing* in Zhang Zai and eventually in Wang Fuzhi of the seventeenth century. In recent decades, since May 4, 1919, the slogan is science or modern science. But as I have suggested on various occasions, the materialist-externalist interpretation of the change by modern physics is not sufficient. This is because the *Yi* philosophy also covers biosphere of life, cultural space of people, and moral action of an individual.

It is interesting also to see how excavated Silk Manuscripts of the *Yijing* also caused great excitement in a textual study of versions of the *Yijing* text. Apart from linguistic help, there remains the deficiency of onto-hermeneutical consciousness for a systematic understanding and integration of the *Yijing* concepts.

In recent years, Professor Yang Chengyin (杨成寅) from the Central Academy of Arts in Hangzhou has come to propound my work on onto-hermeneutics and onto-cosmology of the *Yijing* in his book titled the *Philosophy of the Taiji*[6] based on my papers on the *Yi* cosmology of the *taiji*. In 2013, Professor Yang published a Chinese book titled *Chung-ying Cheng's Taiji Philosophy of Creative Evolution*[7] based on my Chinese philosophy work and my further discussions with him. It is an irony that Professor Yang comes around to publish a book to address my philosophy of the *Yijing* before I could publish my more developed results as embodied in the present volume. This no doubt gives me a reason for quickening the process of bringing out my original thoughts on the *Yijing* at this time. I believe that my original thought stands out in recent decades as a philosophical methodology and also as a philosophical reconstruction of the implicit ontology and ethics of the *Yijing* from the time of Confucius. This, however, is not to say that my work or my approach has ignored the commentary tradition. In fact, I have not, as I have gone through the major schools of commentaries of the

Yijing in my seminar and transcendentally integrate whatever insights I have learned from the commentaries.

It is clear that one cannot grasp the essence of any such commentary unless one can effectively go back to the original text with its Confucian reflections in the *Yizhuan* and is capable of making a fusion of horizons or integration of ideas based on onto-hermeneutical thinking, namely thinking as a whole and thinking with reference to one's overall experience as source, but not based on historical textual exegesis alone. There is no escape from fundamental questions of being, becoming, and nonbeing in our understanding of the ultimate reality and the world of man when we read the *gua* symbolism calling for interpretation and illumination. It is in such situation that judgment related to a situation and the presentation of the form of the situation should become vivid and meaningful, with meaning derived from an underlying onto-cosmology and a conceivable projection of action in the future.

From this point of view, the *Yijing* is not just to be seen as a divination book but a book of living philosophical spirit. We come to appreciate the unity of substance and function, the source and system, the object and subject, and the theory and action, which are ultimately justified on the premises of the unity of heaven and man (*tianren heyi* 天人合一). We come to see how the basic views of reality and reality as explored in latter-day Chinese philosophy have found its place in a reconstruction of the *Yijing* philosophy and that we are truly justified in understanding *Yijing* as the very beginning of Chinese philosophy. In light of these polar unities in the *Yijing* philosophy, we must eventually come to an important reconciliation of the School of Forms and Numbers (象数 *Xiangshu*) and the School of Sense and Reason (义理 *Yili*).[8] Traditionally, the two schools are regarded as being antagonistic to each other, and this antagonism actually results from the extremes of the two approaches, forgetting that a living entity or a live situation, either on the level of the natural world or on the level of the cultural and social world, has both sides, the side of forms and numbers and the side of sense and reason. In fact, as we also can see, each side has two subsides, which are, respectively, forms and numbers for the former and the sense and reason for the latter. By analysis we can easily see that the *gua* (trigram or hexagram) symbolic forms have a numerical structure just as it has represented a natural form with constituent parts and relations. Similarly, the *gua* symbolic form has also a meaning and reference to be recognized and experienced by the human knower as each line and each form functioning as mediating representations for some propositional meaning or information which could be conveyed in some judgments of the *gua* as they were. These judgments form the core of the sense and reason of the *gua* symbolic form.

The formal structure with its living force of motion should convey its meaning and reference to the sense and reason of the knower or agent for the symbol form which stands for a natural form. Hence, the total meaning of a *gua* symbolic form must come from correspondent and coordinated mutual enhancement between its form/number structure and its meaning content. In fact, we have to assume that one generates the other as we see how a configuration of the lines with its motions and positions gives rise to a holistic *gua* symbol which yields its own judgments based on the structure of the lines. Hence, both *Xiangshu* 象数 and *Yili* 义理 sides cannot be ignored nor favored to an extreme, which will lead to a one-sided position, losing sight of the experience of the matter and the other side.

I have written my various essays on the *Yijing* over the course of the past twenty years. The chapters herein may have appeared in some form in various journals, but for the present volume they have undergone a conceptual revision and rewriting. Further, they are written as to relate and integrate with each other to form a whole understanding of the system of the *Yi* for better understanding and better appreciation.

In re-organizing my manuscripts, my former student, Dr. Nicholas S. Brasovan, has assisted me in preparing this volume for publication. There are others who have read this or that chapter with good feedback at one time or another. I wish to thank them profusely. I wish to particularly thank Robert Neville, who has written the foreword for this volume. We have been scholarly friends for over forty years, and I consider it a good fortune to know him from my days when I taught at Yale University in 1967 to 1968.

A final remark: I title this book *The Primary Way: Philosophy of Yijing*. For this title, I have in mind a deep disclosure of the onto-cosmology of change and transformation as we have experienced in nature and life and as being revealed in the text of *Yijing*. My approach to my subject is new and creative, as this has never been done before. For reference to the *Yijing*, I use the received standard Chinese text of *Yijing* as commented on by Zhu Xi (1120–1200) known as *Zhouyi benyi* 周易本义 (*Rooted Meanings of Zhouyi*) (Peking University Press edition, 2011). I believe that Zhu Xi worked on the same type of ancient *Yi* Text as did Northern Song Masters such as the Cheng Brothers, Zhang Zai, and even Zhou Dunyi and Shao Yong, but he had the innovation of attaching nine diagrams of the *Yi* symbols, which are the following: The *River Chart*, the *Luo Inscription*, *Fuxi Eight Trigram Order of Expansion*, *Fuxi Eight Trigram Circle* (relative orientation), *Fuxi Sixty-Four Hexagram Order of Expansion*, *Fuxi Sixty-Four Hexagram Circle with Inside Square*, *Wen Wang Eight Trigram Order of Relations*, *Wen Wang Eight Trigram Circle* (relative generation and destruction), and *Diagram of Transformations of Sixty-Four Hexagrams*. If we add the well-known *Taiji Diagram*, which is not included in Zhu Xi's book, we shall have ten most popular diagrams for the book of *Yijing* up to date. But my work in this book is not to deal with any special diagram, or for that matter with any special *gua* or hexagram. My purpose is intensively and exclusively philosophical: it is to explore and explain the ontological and methodological foundations of the *Yijing* thinking or *Yijing* as a system of onto-cosmological thinking. I shall refer one way or another to some of the diagrams, but only for illustration purpose. I shall, however, quote from the texts of the *Yizhuan* or *Shiyi* 十翼 (*Ten Commentaries/Ten Wings*) of the *Yijing*, which is composed of the following ten parts: *Tuanzhuan* 彖传 (Part 1, Part 2); *Xiangzhuan* 象传 (Part 1, Part 2); *Xicizhuan* 系辞传 (Part 1, Part 2);[9] *Wenyanzhuan* 文言传; *Shuoguazhuan* 说卦传; *Xuguazhuan* 序卦传; and *Zaguazhuan* 杂卦传. These parts are traditionally considered written by Confucius himself, but for what we have, it is better to consider them as commentaries on the *Yijing* by the first-generation Confucian disciples as inspired by Confucius, the Great Master.

Most of my quotations are to be derived from the original texts of the *Yijing*, including these ten *Yizhuan* documents, now taken to be an essential part of the *Yijing* as a book.

Apart from Zhu Xi, I have consulted many other *Yijing* commentaries, from Han to the present, including excavated texts of *Yijing* in Mawangdui and Guodian. All my text quotations are to be derived from this text with English translations exclusively made available by myself as the author. Although I used Zhu Xi's commented text as my text of reference, I do not generally endorse his view, as I have indicated in my chapter on Zhu Xi's approach. My approach is mainly and straightly onto-hermeneutical, onto-cosmological, and analytically philosophical.

CHAPTER 1

Introducing the *Yijing* (易经)

Six Stages of Development and
Six Topics of the *Yijing*

Based on my best understanding from what we know from the history on the formation of the *Yijing* tradition, I will give a theoretical reconstruction of the origin and formation of the book known as *Yijing* 易经 (*Book of Changes*), which has been acknowledged as the leading classic among all the Confucian classics (variously known as *Six Classics* or *Five Classics*) since the Han Dynasty of the first to second century BCE when a chair for *Yijing* was established in the Academy of the Court.[1] A theoretical reconstruction is a projected characterization of the content of the book with regard to what reality it is intended to represent and what truth it will bring to bear on life. It will also cover a process of development from a source in experience. It will show a point of view or a perspective aiming at reasonable understanding that addresses a vision of value and some issue of life. It will also endeavor to preserve coherence and consistency of thinking with a sense of reality.[2]

First, it must be made clear: we are dealing with a received text of the *Yijing* that has its own history after it was historically composed and formed. It was handed down to us from the Han Period. Without going into archaeological, historical, and linguistic details, the present version of the *Yijing* includes sixty-four six-line *gua* 卦 (hexagrams) as doubled from the eight three-line *gua* (*bagua* 八卦 trigrams) and their interpretations in the form of divinatory judgments. As we shall see, the line in a hexagram or trigram is called a *yao* 爻 (a line of movement). The movement is designated as either *yin* 阴 or *yang* 阳, indicating motion or rest. As there are six lines, the possibilities of combining *yin* and *yang* on each line lead to a number of 2 to the 6th power, which comes exactly to sixty-four hexagrams. Looked at this way, the sixty-four hexagrams are just a sequence of sixty-four combinations of *yin* and *yang* movements, and these movements are meant to represent the movements of change in things in the world. As to where the sixty-four hexagrams come from, we can see that the hexagrams are developed from eight trigrams by way of doubling the trigrams, as indicated in the calculation of eight trigrams multiplied by eight trigrams. This would be a natural process to take place in history as early as before the Zhou (circa 1200 BCE–771 BCE) in light of the fact that the judgments for some of the hexagrams could be dated back to even earlier times before the Zhou. Nevertheless, the system of sixty-four hexagrams with their appended judgments is reputed to be composed or edited in the hands of King Wen (文王) of the Zhou (in approximately the early twelfth century BCE). It is therefore known as *Zhouyi* 周易, or *Yi* of the Zhou, to distinguish it from the *Yi* of Shang and the *Yi* of Xia, the names of two earlier dynasties recorded in the *Liji* 礼记 (*Book of Rites*).

Apparently, the *Yijing* book (now also referred to as *Zhouyi* in the form it has come to from King Wen) is based on sixty-four types of divination represented by sixty-four hexagrams. This indicates a long tradition of divination (*bushi* 卜筮)[3] that gives rise to the symbolic representation of the divination in a system of symbols. Without archaeological, historical, and linguistic details, it suffices to say that after exploring excavated bronze utensils and silk and bamboo inscriptions, little doubt remains that the practice of divination is well rooted in the beginning of agriculture in early China.[4] That it could begin at that juncture is because people had reached a settled form of life and thus could acquire a system of symbols through learning that would be adequate for representing human situations together with a background understanding of how things originate and relate in processes of development as well as in an experienced actuality of world. It is a matter of constructing a useful system of cosmology with cosmogony and cosmography that would serve the purpose of promoting and enhancing agricultural land-farming according to knowledge of seasons of time. Besides, people have also developed a method of making fair composition of a representation (namely *gua*) of the human situation and a method of applicable interpretation models for the symbolic representation of human situations.

In light of recent textual research and archaeological findings, the antiquity of the *Yijing* is not to be doubted. The pertinent question is in which way the practice of divination is conducted and how prediction and interpretation are to be made before the book is formed and how early the book can be said to have been first developed. To answer this question, one must first understand how the book is organized.

The original text of the *Yijing*, known as the *jing* 经, is comprised of a system of sixty-four symbols, hexagrams analyzable in eight times eight (8 x 8) combinations of subsymbols (*gua*, trigrams), each of which has a name describing or indicating what the symbol stands for. Each symbol, called an iconic-indexical symbol, is to be attached to a judgment (*ci* 辞) as result of general prognosis and valuation for a given situation to which the symbol applies, and which is determined by divination. Each line of the hexagramatic symbol is further numerically named and given an individual prognosis and valuation for action. All else in the form of comments and explanations on either the whole symbol or lines of the symbol are called commentaries (*zhuan* 传). These commentaries are traditionally known as the *Yi Commentaries* (*Yizhuan* 易传) or "Ten Wings" (*Shiyi* 十翼), and are composed of the "*Tuan* 彖 Commentaries" (two parts), the "*Xiang* 象 Commentaries" (two parts), the "*Wenyan* 文言 Commentary," the "*Xici* 系辞 Commentaries" (two parts, entitled "*Xici Shang* 系辞上" and "*Xici Xia* 系辞下"), the "*Shuo* 说 Commentary" (also known as the "*Shuogua* 说卦"), the "*Xu* 序 Commentary," and "*Za* 杂 Commentary." They are generally regarded as composed by Confucius or his first-generation disciples.

The *Yijing*'s complex organization supports a finding that the book is the result of a process of evolution from the very beginning of the use of cosmic symbols for understanding and participating in natural processes to the final abstract and abstruse formulation of a comprehensive system of cosmology, culture, and ethics. The final formulation would have taken place in a later era when philosophical minds and reflective reason became most active. As such, the *Yijing* book probably went through six stages of development with regard to its being interpreted by human researchers.

Stage 1: Comprehensive Observation and Natural Cosmology

The first stage of development of the *Yijing* is that of the Comprehensive Observation (*guan* 观) of the natural world or natural cosmology.[5] This stage likely began during the late Neolithic period (6000 BCE–2000 BCE),[6] during the time of the domestication of sheep. Legend has it that the first of the great noble emperors, Fuxi 伏羲 (2952–2386 BCE), used *guan* to observe and to understand the world. The *guan* stage probably continued until the founding of the first Chinese dynasty, the Xia Dynasty, which arose from a succession of sage-kings and ultimately was founded by the Great Yu. According to legend, this dynasty began around 2100–2000 BCE and continued until 1600 BCE.

During this time, early ancestors of Chinese people, having spread out over the central plains along the Yellow River, experienced climate changes and seasonal changes in different geographical locations. It may not escape from the sagely among them that climate and terrain may make tremendous differences to the lives of people. The right combination of climate and land could mean harvesting and flourishing of life, whereas a weather disaster such as drought and flood could cause famine and destruction despite efforts made by man to survive. The world was a totality and seen as a whole, with human beings an essential and vital part of it. *Guan* was the panoramic overview or comprehensive observation of the entire natural world. So, for example, the people of this time would see the evening sky as a whole. However, in addition to seeing the totality of the world, the ancient Chinese also became aware that changes take place over a span of time. However, changes did not occur over the same period of time for all objects. Some changes may be so small that the naked eye could not observe the actual changing event. Some changes may be so large and take place over such a long period that, similarly, the naked eye could not observe the actual change. Nevertheless, the ancient Chinese were aware that changes occurred and that these changes followed patterns or cycles. As a result, the people began to formulate cycles of years, days, and even day and night to reflect the changes observed in nature. Thus, the *guan* showed people that change of all types—changes of forms of life, changes of time, changes of life, and changes of habits of growth—happen over differing periods of time.

Stage 2: Relating Present to Future and Making Divination

By the time of the Huangdi 黄帝 (Yellow Emperor) (2697 BCE–2598 BCE), it may be conjectured that an early civilization, complete with agriculture, settlements, and political organization had arisen. With these developments came the need to think about, plan for, and act with an eye toward the future. However, action with regard to the future requires knowledge in order to be successful. In the absence of observable knowledge about the future gleaned through the use of *guan*, one must make predictions. The method used to glean information about the future was called divination.

The practice of divination requires one to read burned cracks in the tortoise shell or oxen bone as signs signifying a certain message emanating from the objective situation in nature with reference to the situation at hand. Such a reading requires a background reference in which the signs can be described as messages and as advice. Divination practices allowed the diviner to interpret knowledge from what he knew about a good or fortunate omen and what he knew about a bad or misfortunate omen. As such, the original good and bad must be understood in terms of fortune (*ji* 吉) and misfortune (*xiong* 凶), disaster (*huo* 祸), blessing (*fu* 福), danger (*li* 厉), blame (*jiu* 咎), and regret (*lin* 吝). The valuation system of divination gradually developed into a general theory of good and bad according to which, whatever leads to fortune, security, praise, and hope for more of the same is considered good, namely that which is to be desired, whereas whatever leads to misfortune, danger, blame, and regret is considered bad, namely that which is to be avoided.

This association of human feelings and desires with events and actions reflects and reveals how the ancient human came not only to discover the world as relating to his human personal self but also to discover the human personal self as relating to the world around him. This theory further leads to the presumption and understanding or belief as to how good and bad could be based on abilities and mental dispositions, which could in general generate those things that are called good and those that are called bad. Those abilities and dispositions formed or given are then regarded as virtues 善德 and vices 恶德 relative to social and political relationships established and developed in a community.[7] Necessary action required to achieve the good and to avoid the bad would be called the duty, or what ought to be done. As a result, the moral development of the community presupposes a moral sense of what is good and bad in reference to fortunes and misfortunes. The use of fortune words and misfortune words and the like reflects an early development of the human community in which the individual person comes to have a moral relevance of fortunes and misfortunes and hence to reflect on what to do in terms of virtues and duties.

This was the period of *buci* 卜辭 (divination statements), in which advice and admonitions on what needed to be done to secure the good (the fortune) and avoid the bad (the misfortune) were given in concise phrases and sentences, or even records, engraved on the tortoise back shells or oxen shoulders. In this period, the results of interpreting or judging signs regarding their factual meanings and moral requirements for action were known as *buci* 卜辭, or divinatory judgments. These judgments were recorded in oracle bones from 2000 BCE to 1200 BCE. The *buci* likely lasted at least until the Zhou Dynasty.

Stage 3: Formation of the Trigrams and Hexagrams on the Basis of Number Theory

In the later part of the divination period, probably during the projected period of 1200–1100 BCE, in the Zhou dynasty, the *bagua* 八卦 system arose. This systemization was based on a cosmology formed around the notions of *yin* and *yang* and resulted in the production of sixty-four hexagrams with correlating names and judgments. Diviners began to organize the results of cracks into groups and assign to them either the number three or six. The number three appears to have been used because it correlates to the observed relationship of heaven, earth, and man. The number six was used because it doubles the cosmology of the three. Thus, the *bagua* system was based, in part, on an elaboration of and systemization of the diviner's cosmic symbols (heaven, earth, and man) in correlation with the divination judgments. Use of an odd and even number likely refers to *yin* and *yang*, with the odd number referring to the sign standing for *yang* and the even number referring to the sign standing for *yin*. The distinction of *yin* and *yang* appears to be the natural result of *guan*, for as one observes, one comes to see how the natural and cosmic changes always have the alternation or succession or combination of the *yin* and *yang*, that is, the shady and the lighted, the soft and the firm, the rest and the movement.[8]

In addition, odd numbers likely corresponded to straight, solid signs or lines and even seemed to correspond to broken or crooked signs or lines on the bones. The reason appears to lie in the natural working of the mental association of the broken line as signifying a twoness and the solid line as signifying a oneness.[9] Of course, other explanations are possible, be they historical or theoretical. But one cannot ignore that there is a natural simplicity in associating a solid line with a primary odd number, which is oneness, and in associating a broken line with a primary even number, which is twoness. Hence, the so-called *shuzigua* 数字卦 hides a reference to seen forms or shapes of cracks of the divination on the bones; it also implicitly introduces a principle of correlation of the numbers to the shapes.[10]

The *bagua* system arose in part because of the increasing complexity of human relationships and human actions as culture and knowledge required a more sophisticated representation of the human situation in the human lifeworld. Yet, this more sophisticated system of human situations was still thought to be derived from natural situations of the trigrams. This thinking provides an insight into the nature of human development and the natural evolution of the world, as explained below.

Stage 4: Reflection on Human Life and Discovering the Human Situation

Legend has it that in the twelfth century BCE, King Wen of Zhou (周) was imprisoned by the tyrant King Zhou (纣) of the Shang Dynasty (1600–1100 BCE). King Zhou (纣) believed that King Wen was building his own fiefdom into a large power that would threaten the central rule of Shang. During his imprisonment, King Wen developed an extended cosmology of sixty-four *gua* based on the *bagua* system, but this system was a more abstract system of signs that could be only partially interpreted by or correlated with what is observed in nature.

In the categorization of the life activities, typical incidents with their evaluations based on history or experience have been sorted into six levels or sorts. Each level was to be later assigned to the six lines of the *gua*: some with obvious justification, some without obvious justification. The line judgment can be assumed to give both explanation and justification of the line meaning. But more often than not, the line judgment is assumed to derive its judgment of meaning and hence interpretation from the meaning of the line as perceived in the context of the whole *gua* and in reference to a given situation as identified or to be identified.

The above leads to the realization that we should sort out our social lives according to their importance and values in order to be represented, not in a simple system of cosmology but in an extended system built on this cosmology. We will call this later system a "cosmo-humanological system." It is actually intended as the sixty-four hexagrams (*zhonggua* 重卦). If one were to analyze the sixty-four names of the sixty-four *gua* for the understanding of the important items of basic human situations that also embodies the basic values of life and action such as indicated in the names of the sixty-four hexagrams (*Tun* 屯, *Meng* 蒙, *Shi* 师, etc.), one would find no order to them; instead, they form arbitrarily selected categories of the natural world of the trigrams. But this natural world is meaningful because it can form resonance with human needs and respond to human actions; thus, it requires understanding and evaluation. It may yield an emergent picture of what people were most concerned with when making divinations. They are the categories of potential action and potential decision.

Stage 5: Exploring Meaning of Change and Human Virtue through Confucius

From the time of King Wen's imprisonment (approximately twelfth century BCE) until the end of the Han Dynasty (206 BCE–220 CE), Chinese scholars continued to expand on King Wen's system incorporating the cosmo-humanological system. During the sixth century BCE to the fourth century BCE, the *Yi Commentaries* (*Yizhuan* 易传), or *Ten Wings*, were produced. The *Ten Wings* focused on the basic alignment of meanings and relations of meanings that interpretation of the symbols and judgments achieved through a dynamic and yet close consistency with an underlying cosmic picture or image. Yang Xiong 杨雄 (53 BCE–18 CE), working during the Han Dynasty, later attempted to create a system that reflected a well-constructed understanding with self-conscious and explicit principles of construction. The driving force behind his work was to reconcile the name-image of the *gua* with the cosmic basic meanings of the *gua*. Indeed, this effort to sort out, to classify and organize, relative to given images is still the most tantalizing and challenging work of the *Yi* scholar today.

In the system, some correlations are well made, such as *Qian* 乾 for *tian* 天 (heaven), *Kun* 坤 for *di* 地 (earth), *fengdi* 风地 for *Guan* 观, *dilei* 地雷 for *Fu* 复, whereby the natural forces of the trigrams form to give rise to the meanings of the human situations. By combining the forces of nature's purposive activities with the actions of human persons, this system appears to make the natural forces conscious. Thus, all the hexagrams have obvious "human" meanings achieved in terms of the basic meanings of the cosmic "natural" symbols of the *bagua* 八卦. The basic meanings I here refer to are a retrospective insight in the *Shuogua* 说卦 of the *Yizhuan*: the *dong-jing* 动静, *gang-rou* 刚柔, *yin-yang* 阴阳 observation on the phenomenal level. But there are also *gua*, which are not so well interpreted and appear to be randomly associated (for example: *Huoshan* 火山 ䷷ for Travel (*Lü* 旅), *Leize* 雷泽 ䷵ for Return of the Maid (*Guimei* 归妹), *Shuilei* 水雷 ䷂ for Difficult Beginning (*Tun* 屯), *Shanlei* 山雷 ䷚ for Nourishment (*Yi* 颐), and *Shanfeng* 山风 ䷑ for Clearing Ills (*Gu* 蠱). Some others, such as *Tianfeng* 天风 ䷫ for Encounter (*Gou* 姤) and *Zehuo* 泽火 ䷰ for Reform (*Ge* 革), may also appear ambiguous.

Stage 6: Deepening Insight into the Onto-Cosmological in Philosophy of the Dao

The final period of the development of the *Yijing*, which follows the periods of systemization and correlation, occurred when, having established the *bagua* system, the users critically reflected on the system. This was a time of analysis, adjustment, correction, and totalistic interpretation. This was a time when the relationships among man and heaven and earth become explicitly articulated and exhibited, argued and discussed. As such, our traditional notion of philosophy, as it related to the *Yijing* specifically, occurred primarily at this time. In addition to a period of philosophical analysis and interpretation, one also may see this as a period of standardization of texts and elaboration of symbolic and numerological meanings. Standardization coincided with the beginning of Han Dynasty in the second century BCE to the later Han period in the third century.

During this period, the lines of each *gua* are individually and collectively commented on. In doing so, it became clear that certain principles must be followed during the divination process. For example, the fifth position is better, and the third position is not so good.[11] Hence, a later observation from the *Xici*: a line that occupies a third position tends to signify misfortune over fortune, whereas a line that occupies a fifth position tends to signify a higher degree of success and a lesser degree of failure.

In addition, necessary adjustments and corrections were made in order to achieve consistency and efficiency (so the *Yijing* could be used as a divination book). Meanwhile, the symbolism of the *gua* and its lines become more clearly projected and articulated in meaning relative to the *yin-yang* theory of cosmic force. The *yin-yang* system was capable of assigning meanings of the five powers (metal, wood, water, fire, earth) and their associated qualities regarding generation and destruction or balancing to each *gua* relative to other *gua* and to each line of the *gua* relative to the lines of the same *gua* and sometimes to relevant lines of other relevant *gua* in the system of *gua*.

Against these six stages of the development of the basic philosophy of the *Yijing*, we see that the *Yijing* is not simply any text invested with personal understanding but has received significance and funds of meaning from both the sagely and the common. The commonness of the meaning in the classic text is well described by the *Zhongyong* 中庸: "common people have used them and yet may know them." "For the ordinary things the common people all know them, but for the most profound even the sagely may not know." It is important that we move to certain important aspects of the theory and practice of the *Yijing* as we have generally described above. And these aspects that would contribute to a philosophical understanding of the *Yijing* is that with which this book has been engaged. They cover nine topics that represent nine aspects of the philosophy of *Yijing*: namely, the interpretive in understanding the *Yi* symbolic use and the reality as conveyed by such symbols. Then we can speak of the methodology of *guan* as a source and foundation for making possible such interpretive or hermeneutical approach. Then we have to see how a system of things could function as a system of communication so that we understand how the system bridges over the gap between the objective and the subjective. After the observational methodology, we must examine how hexagrams as natural symbols stand to natural forms on the one hand, and how they stand to overall meaning of harmonization on the other hand. Then we can see the system when accordingly understood stands to present three more unities and harmonizations that confront human beings and human culture, the position of location or space, and the use of time. Through these we come to see how the *Yijing* have developed its philosophical theory of positions and timeliness as two essential activities of man that carry both moral and political meanings. With this understanding, the traditional schism between form and number approach and the onto-generative approach of meaning and reason can be reconciled. Finally, we come to the unity of *li* and *qi* as two constitutive elements of ontological foundations of *li* and *qi* and principle or being and nonbeing.

Six Topics in *Yijing* Primary Philosophy

Corresponding to the six stages of development, we shall discuss the following six topics: (1) comprehensive observation as a way to conceive of the cosmology of changes; (2) the logic of divination and the philosophical and ethical foundation of the practical; (3) transformation of the *Yijing* into a philosophical treatise; (4) *Yijing* interpretation as a basis for decision making and action; (5) Confucius and *Yijing* in Confucianism; and (6) the *Yijing* and Daoism, Buddhism, folklore, and the modern sciences.

Topic 1: Comprehensive Origins of the *Yijing* and Cosmography of *Yi*

How do we conceive *Yi* (change)? I suggest the approach of "comprehensive observation" (*guan*), which consists of observing things and their changes, distant and near, up and down, left and right, on both macroscopic and microscopic levels, over a long period of time, and in a comprehensive and integrative manner. Why this approach? I suggest that *Yi* is a comprehensive phenomenon pervading all our experiences of nature, our lives, and our selves. What we can observe is a myriad of things in change and a myriad of relationships of things in change. But we need to observe their hidden dimensions and their underlying unity and source in change. Hence the *Xici Commentary* speaks of "*guan qihuitong* 观其汇通 (observation of [their] meeting together and interpenetration)" (*Xici Shang* 12). If we are confined to what we see, we can speak of "observing the forms [of things]" (*guan xiang*), and we can also speak of "observing the motions and movements of things" (*guanbian* 观变).

We could distinguish between perception and observation of what we experience as large and small, and outer and inner. We could distinguish what we observe as what other people could all observe from which each person merely perceives without the understanding or ground for assuming that other people must have the same perception.[12] Even as an outer experience, *Yi* differs from our experience of pure physical motions of microscopic objects or physical movements of macroscopic objects. *Yi* focuses on both absolute (self-oriented) and relative (relation-oriented) qualitative change of one state to another, not simply the change of space and time in the motion (*dong*) of an object. The change of space and time in the motion of an object, however, is to be explained as a consequence or a part of the phenomenon of qualitative change, whether on the macroscopic level or on the microscopic level. To observe qualitative change on the macroscopic level is called "observation of large changes" (*guanbian*), which leads to "penetrating understanding of large changes" (*tongbian*). This is explained in terms of the dynamics of the dark and the bright (*yin-yang*). In the *Shuogua Commentary* it is said: "Observe changes (*guanbian*) amidst *yin-yang* and establish *gua* (visible forms of change-situations) therefrom" (section 1).

To closely observe qualitative change on the microscopic level is called "*qiongshen zhihua*" 穷神知化 (i.e., by close observation of subtle changes one comprehends transformations) (*Xici Xia* 5). The so-called subtle changes (*shen* 神) are the unpredictable and creative changes from being to nonbeing and vice versa, and this leads to "knowledge of the minute inceptions of things" (*zhiji* 知几) (*Xici Xia* 5). One can come to this comprehension by way of observing visible changes (*guanbian*) in nature and the world and pondering over small changes. Hence, the combined terms "*bianhua* 变化" and "*zhihua* 知化" suggest a comprehensive notion of changes inclusive of large and small, visible and invisible, and movements and transformations, all in a framework of interrelation and integration of things and events.

The notion of *Yi* no doubt includes reference to changes in an inner sense of self-motivation and in a sense related to human life situated in the life world of humanity and nature; hence, it is related to human feelings and human evaluations as motivations. This is largely reflected in the naming of sixty-four hexagrams developed from the eight trigrams. For illustration, if one considers and analyzes the meanings and significations (denotation, extension, connotation, intension, intentionality, and significance) of any of the following hexagrams by its name: *Meng* 蒙 ䷃ (Obscuration), *Song* 讼 ䷅ (Litigation), *Wuwang* 无妄 ䷘ (Unexpectedness), *Xian* 咸 ䷞ (Feeling), *Jiaren* 家人 ䷤ (Family), *Kui* 睽 ䷥ (Separation), *Jian* 蹇 ䷦ (Difficulty), *Jie* 解 ䷧ (Resolution), *Sun* 损 ䷨ (Decreasing), *Yi* 益 ䷩ (Increasing), *Gou* 姤 ䷫ (Meeting), *Jing* 井 ䷯ (Well), *Ding* 鼎 ䷱ (Tripot), *Ge* 革 ䷰ (Reform), *Guimei* 归妹 ䷵ (Marrying Maid), *Lü* 旅 ䷷ (Travel), *Jie* 节 ䷻ (Restraint), *Zhongfu* 中孚 ䷼ (Inner Faith), *Jiji* 既济 ䷾ (Completion), and *Weiji* 未济 ䷿ (Incompletion), one can easily see how observations of large and small things in nature could be conceived as a whole, with an inner core and an outer shell, each of which is represented by a trigram. Together, they form a hexagram where one could grasp the relevance of the constituent trigrams for the formation of the hexagram as indicated by its name. On the other hand, the name for the hexagram is given in view of the emergent quality of the complex of natural events and the forces they represent in certain combinations, which lead to observations and identification of large and small things in human life and human situations. Consider the hexagram *Xian* 咸 ䷞ (feeling), which is composed of a lake above and a mountain below. One may see the lake as representing the natural feeling of joy and the mountain as representing the natural feeling of stillness. The resultant combined sign gives the image of joy in stillness that is a feeling emerging from the harmony of the lake and the mountain or extending the notion to a human situation, the inner harmony of the young maid with the young lad when they are together. One may use one's natural and yet free play of imagination to construe the meaning of the other hexagrams, which are given here for the vivacity of images that they generate.

To observe the inner world of human life, one must consider the activities and functions of *gan* (feeling) and *tong* (penetrative understanding). The activity and function of feeling is clearly reflected in the thirty-first hexagram, *Xian* ䷞, and the activity and function of observation of outer nature is clearly reflected in the twenty-first hexagram of *guan*. I have argued that *gan* and *guan* are two aspects of the methodology of "comprehensive observation" and that the resulting activities and functions of such activities is "interpenetrative and comprehensive understanding" (*tong* 通). The latter is composed of understanding both the outer world of things (*tong tianxia zhigu* 通天下之故) and understanding the inner world of the human mind (*tong tianxia zhizhi* 通天下之志) (see section 10 of *Xici Shang*). When a person is able to do this, the person is a sage (*shengren* 圣人). The *shengren* is a perfectly virtuous person capable of listening to people and articulating and acting on what good way of life should be followed. He has both intellectual and moral wisdom and thus is capable of guiding people for their well-being. The concept of the *shengren* is often used as an ideal model or standard for emulation and aspiration.

Regarding the first stage of *Yijing*'s development: although question remains as to whether there existed a legendary culture hero named Fuxi who invented the system of *gua* or *Yi*-symbols on the basis of his observations of nature and things in nature, there is no doubt that the eight basic symbols known as *bagua* are significant symbols for some of the most notable natural phenomena a human being would normally come across and observe in nature. These phenomena are heaven and earth, fire and water, lake and hill, and wind and thunder. Persons would further observe how these natural phenomena are powers and processes of change and transformation, which would account for the creation and destruction of things and life forms.

These natural phenomena can be then conceived in a form or framework in which all things are to be located, and all changes are to take place. Finally, the person would observe that these things and life forms found in nature are governed in some sense. They participate in some sense in the basic processes of nature. Hence, insofar as persons can experience these processes and powers in certain correlated ways, all things far and near (including cultural, technological inventions and human activities) could be related to these basic processes and powers.

Clearly, it would take a long time to make these observations, which are assumedly comprehensive in scope and insightful in depth. These observations would lead to an understanding of the world with a unity of vision—a totality of scope—to be seen also in a network of linkages and relations as well as a multitude of relevant concrete references and identifications. This would be the end of achieving understanding of the world as it is given to us. This observational process is called "*guan*" (comprehensive and contemplative observation) in the *Xici*, and the resulting vision of the world is a cosmography of well-placed and well-related powers and processes, namely a dynamical picture of the natural world in which things are to be situated.

One may ask questions about the nature of *guan* in relation to the formation of the early symbolic system of cosmography of the *Yijing*. It is safe to say that *guan* is both a process of observation and a method used for observation in order to achieve a totalistic, holistic, relational, and perspective oriented understanding of the whole of nature. As a process of observation, it accompanies a mentality of detachment and an attitude of mind, described as tranquility and receptivity. *Guan* is a naturalistic attitude of seeking understanding and learning things without forcing a prior theoretical model on nature and without letting one's emotions and desires stand in the way of understanding the world.

It is not quite phenomenology of the conscientious "bracketing-off" in a Husserlian sense, nor is it an objectivist methodology of attempting to capture the essences of objects in exclusion of the feeling and perceiving mind. *Guan* perhaps can be described as a natural attitude of seeing the natural world in terms of their overt and minute changes and relationships on the basis of our general experiences of nature. Hence, the resulting cosmic image, view, or vision, also known as *guan* (outlook or view), is both globally dynamical and individually rich in meaning. This allows for possible correlations and analogizing with other observations of things including human and cultural matters. We may thus call the *guan* a natural phenomenological observation versus rational scientific observation.

The natural and cosmic system of *gua* constitutes and provides such a background reference that can be called the "cosmic map" against which one could check on the location and relationships a given sign has signified. It can be conjectured that the cosmic map of the *gua* becomes the divinatory reference manual in a period from the beginning

With regard to the question of how a number comes to be written as it was originally written or is now written, one must answer by pointing to the power of free play of imagination as a human faculty that gives to many inventions and that allows to escape absolute and full determination and control of nature. Eventually there was a mix of forms and numbers, and the new signs for *yin* and *yang* were born.

Historically speaking, the method of *guan* has been well cultivated in both the Confucian and Daoist traditions. Chinese Buddhists even adopted *guan* in a merger of meanings between comprehensive observation and inner meditation, as conveyed by the Sanskrit terms *dhyāna* and *samādhi*. But *guan* as a way of reaching for deep and complete understanding of reality originates in the *Yijing*. In the text of the *Yijing* one even could identify and name the twenty-first hexagram of wind above and earth below as a special symbol of *guan*. As this symbol iconically and indexically suggests, one must maintain an upright and central position in order to overview or observe the world. Given a background of comprehensive observation and reflection on experience one has including one's understanding, one may easily see how the system of symbols as the cosmographical picture of the world is constructed on the basis of a comprehensive observation of an observer who does not suffer from his preconceptions or biases.

Topic 2: Logic of Divination and Ethical Foundation of the Practical

Much in vogue is the view that the *Yijing* began as a book of divination, and should be seen essentially as a book that one may consult in terms of its divinatory judgments and symbolism. There is no denial that *Zhouyi* has been used as a book of divination, as alluded to in the divinatory practices recorded in *Zuozhuan*.[13] In this sense, Zhu Xi (1130–1200), the well-known Chinese neo-Confucian scholar, is correct in identifying the book as formed from the practice of divination. But, on the other hand, one must recognize that if there is no underlying cosmic map to which diviners could refer for constituting or deriving meanings, how could it be used as a book of divination? Zhu Xi recognized that before King Wen, Fuxi observed the universe and added his insights to the interpretations in the *Zhouyi*. King Wen followed Fuxi, making divinations based on Fuxi's observations. In this sense, in order to be meaningful and fruitful as a guidebook in making practical decisions toward beneficial results and avoidance of harm, we have to recognize that divination must presuppose formation of a cosmic map.

There is no denial that divination has been practiced since the Shang Dynasty (1600 BCE–1100 BCE),[14] and it was common practice until the late Spring-Autumn Period (800 BCE–300 BCE). The question is not simply whether one divines, but why one divines and how one understands or interprets the results of divination. In general, the reason for the practice of divination is that people are worried about the future and cannot or do not know what the future holds; therefore, they cannot determine what action to take. Divination allows people to glimpse the future, thus providing a guide for present action.

Based on the rich materials of oracle inscriptions and the twenty-two recorded divination cases found in the *Zhouyi*, one can see the following: (1) one should not divine if one does not have a momentous or urgent problem at hand; (2) one divines after one has exhausted all one's knowledge and still cannot decide what to do; (3) one divines for the purpose of relating a historical precedent to the present situation or for the purpose of identifying one's position in the scheme of things; (4) a reasonable interpretation has to be given for the recommended action or actions; and (5) one has to make a choice or a decision in light of acceptable interpretations. Hence, divination neither implies determinism nor fatalism; instead, it presupposes the co-determining abilities of the human person for the future, which is significant for the person. We may call this understanding of divination "co-determinism by human interpretation and human choice."

Thus, divination is one type of use to which the *Zhouyi* is put, but the *Zhouyi* cannot be seen merely as a book of divination. Its rich and hidden cosmological significances not only make it possible to be rediscovered or reconstructed metaphysically in the *Yizhuan*, but these significances also allow the book to be used for other pursuits of life and in various fields of study, including medicine and military strategies. This explains why by the time of Confucius (551 BCE–479 BCE) and Xunzi (300 BCE–230 BCE) one need not divine to make moral or practical judgments or decisions on the basis of the understanding of the *Zhouyi*, because one had, or could have, sufficient knowledge base for making both rational and intuitive judgments. The rational judgment is one derived by virtue of some conceptual or empirical connection, whereas the intuitive judgment involves a mental grasp of a whole situation and thus leads to an image of a situation and its potential transformations. The book of *Yijing* is henceforth read and interpreted as a book of profound wisdom and cosmic and ethical insights.

As a matter of common sense, we can assume that the future is uncertain and holds many possibilities, such as one sees in weather changes. On the other hand, common sense also tells us that there are certain established trends and tendencies governing certain future events. This also means that those future events concern us because they are important to us and relate to serious purposes we wish to attain or to serious situations we want to avoid. Hence, we value some future events as beneficial (*ji* 吉) and others as harmful (*xiong* 凶), and obtaining a particular result often depends on which actions we choose. If there is no other way to know or assess a future event relative to one's purpose at hand, divination becomes important because it provides a certain (albeit randomly chosen) representation and articulation of actuality and implicit reference to a history and a future for one's given concern. Moreover, divination also provides an occasion to reflect and deliberate over one's future and one's action regarding the future with one's insight into the present situation. In other words, divination provides a means by which we can assess and understand our concern. That divination relies on a method that would provide a form of randomness as well as use of certain meaningful rules means that the result of the divination must be related to a given situation, or to a given purpose, in order to yield an understanding of both the present situation and the future event. This is why interpretation of the resulting *gua* (hexagrams or trigrams) is required and experience and expertise are needed. In short, divination can be seen as a method of anchoring the future in the present so that one clearly understands existing alternatives and assesses their consequential values before taking appropriate action.

Given the above analysis of the need and justification of divination, we can appreciate both the significance and the limitation of divination and understand why divination as a practice would wither out in the light of the philosophical understanding of the system of the *gua*. We also can understand how the very logic and process of divination would in a way contribute to the rise of the elaboration of the hidden cosmology and its application by understanding the system of *gua* by way of philosophical reflection and interpretation.

Divination is not philosophy, but there is an underlying philosophy or logic to divination. The underlying logic of divination is that one should see divination as underscoring both the limitation of the human condition and the freedom of human decision for action. On the one hand, a person is limited by his situation and even by his own purpose, and the future is not dictated by his wishes; on the other hand, a person can seek knowledge of the future or a way of understanding the possibilities of the future and thus make his own decisions. Divination provides a way of revealing one's limitations in one's lifeworld; at the same time, it provides a way of changing one's situation by acting on it appropriately.

One issue that pertains to the relevance of divination and the rise of the *Zhouyi* is the discovery of the "numerical hexagrams" (*shuzi gua* 数字卦) recorded on bones, pottery, and bronze objects by way of using the odd numbers 1, 5, 7, 9 and even numbers 6, 8 in the shape of ancient Chinese numerals. This appears to indicate that *Zhouyi* arose as a matter of sorting out "numerical hexagrams." Logically speaking, however, the understanding of the *gua* as relevant for a given situation still requires reference to a map of the reality, which I have suggested earlier as the cosmography conveyed in the *"bagua"* system. Further, the evolution of the numerical hexagrams would converge to represent the *gua* as composed of the *yin-yang* lines, which surprisingly correspond to the even and odd numbers 1 and 8. This should suggest that numbers are substitutions for the lines of hexagrams, which convey the images of the odd and even numbers.

Topic 3: *Yijing* as a Symbolic System of Interpretation

Methodologically speaking, in the historical evolution of the texts, four factors have contributed to the transformation of the *Yijing* into a philosophical treatise in the form of the commentaries. First, one must reflect on the system of the symbols as a whole in order to see how it captures the world-reality as a field of changes and transformations. As I have explained, this system of symbols can be seen as precisely arising from an effort to understand world-reality in the first place. To understand the texts philosophically is to rediscover or disclose the underlying cosmography of world-reality by way of *guan*. To realize this is also to discover a method of understanding world-reality even as it is presented to us now. Hence, the second factor, or step, in philosophical transformation is to confront directly the world-reality of natural phenomena (and processes) so that one can have a meaningful grasp of possibilities for understanding and action.

The *Xici* says: "Consequently, the superior man in residing observes the (natural) images and contemplates the judgments attached to the symbols for these images, whereas in action he observes their changes and contemplates the divinatory processes" (*Xici Shang* 2). A "superior person" cannot read a *gua* without referencing an actual image of the world for which the *gua* stands. The superior person reflects on the whole system of symbols and how each and all stand for the world-reality of changes. It is in this way that profound insights arise in the representation, reformation, and theoretical elaboration of the cosmographical picture therein.

The third factor is more hermeneutical than onto-hermeneutical, yet it depends on the onto-hermeneutical interpretation. Here we refer to the reconciliation of the symbolic meanings of the hexagrams with meanings of the original judgments (*ci*) attached to them. In a sense, the judgments are the first or original individual interpretations of the symbols (or images of the symbols) apart from cosmographical meanings they derive from the underlying system of cosmography. That these judgments are attached is basically a matter of contingency for different cases of divination, even though we must allow the efforts of an early thinker such as King Wen to sort out those judgments by way of correlation and classification, which gives rise to the formulation of the first system as a whole.

Because of this contingency of correlation, there exists a tension between the symbols and the judgments. In order to resolve this tension, two primary schools of interpretative philosophies of the *Yijing* arose in the history of the development of the discourses on the *Yijing*: the Image-Number (*Xiangshu*) School and the Meaning-Principle (*Yili*) School. Each can be further divided into subschools, namely the Image

School and the Number School for the former, and the Meaning School and the Principle School for the latter. But we must note that in actuality no school is exactly occupied with one of the four dimensions (so we may call them) to the exclusion of the other dimensions. In fact, these individual schools are more reductionist than exclusionist in their interpretation of the symbols and judgments. That is, each school would establish principles of interpretation on the basis of one dimension and then interpret other dimensions by reducing them to the terms of the chosen dimension.

As an historical note, we might mention that in the early Han Dynasty (206 BCE–220 CE) we see the rise of Image-Number School (*Xiangshu* 象数) in scholars such as Meng Xi (50 BCE) and Jing Fang (79–37 BCE). In fact, the Image-Number School flourished (even over-flourished) during the entire Han Era, until Wang Bi (226–249 CE) of the Wei-Jin Period (220–420) undertook a Daoist metaphysical critique of the Image-Number School and gave rise to the *Yili* (Meaning-Principle) School. One sees that in Wang Bi the principle of the *dao* dominates the meanings of the language, and this no doubt led to the rise of the meaning and principle-oriented interpretation and commentary on the *Yijing* in Cheng Yi (1033–1107), one of the founders of the Neo-Confucianism in Northern Song period (960–1127). It is not until Zhu Xi (1130–1200) that we see a synthetic approach to the interpretation of the *Yijing* by admitting *Xiangshu* as an element of interpretation.

After Zhu Xi, there was a tendency to move over to the *Xiangshu* considerations, as many *Yijing* scholars in the Qing Dynasty (1644–1912) did, and also a tendency to transcend *Xiangshu*, as one finds in Wang Yangming (1472–1529) and Jiao Xun (1763–1820). In modern times, there appear to have been many meaning-oriented studies, particularly in light of the 1973 discovered Mawangdui Silk Manuscripts of the *Zhouyi*. In stressing practical use for individual purposes, there also appears to have been a contemporary revival of the *Xiangshu* studies in both China and Taiwan. But the key problem is still how we can resolve the tension between *Xiangshu* and *Yili*, which actually exists in the original texts of the *Yijing* up to this day, and integrate them in a holistic theory of understanding of reality and its representation in a system of symbols.

It should be clear that a balanced and unified approach to the interpretation of the *Yijing* as exhibited in my work on *Yijing* and its underlying methodology of onto-hermeneutics is essential for understanding the philosophical deep structure of the *Yijing* text and the source of insights of observation for constructing such a text or for applying divination as a useful practice of deciding one's place in the world and possible action for changing it. This means that we must integrate Image-Number and Meaning-Principle as four dimensions of the *Yijing* philosophy of world-reality—namely, the perceptive experience, the rational organization, the language of understanding, and the onto-cosmology of world-reality.[15]

We now come to the fourth factor of philosophical interpretation, which is the factor of making human decisions and human action. With regard to this goal, the need for interpretation is practical, and interpretation is to relate a present situation to a given symbolism that has its primary and associated meanings as established by experiences so that one can make relevant decisions for actions. The momentum for decision making comes from people's need to act because we want to or have to act in a situation. We may also say that it is the situation that calls for our decision making and action.

The need for decision and action, therefore, reflect the ontological status of our situated state of being, which is in turn a matter of changes and transformations of the world. Our actions are parts of the changes and transformations of the world, which are required for attaining our goals, which would increase our being, or avoiding harms and disasters, which would diminish our being. Understanding is therefore necessary for making correct decisions relative to our specific goals. In other words, one must understand a given situation by placing oneself in a world picture in which one's action and choice would be rhetorically, if not rationally, justified.

There are two considerations for this practical concern of interpretation: one is to understand the situation relative to one's problem or problems so that we can acquire a reason for acting one way or another. The second is to assess the quality and consequence of one's actions. Neither of these considerations would hold if there were no understanding of the situation: this means that interpretation of the situation is a necessity for decision making and action in the first place.

Regarding the validity of interpretation of a given situation in the *Yijing*, there is the obvious problem of identifying the nature of the situation either by divination or by knowledge. In the absence of knowledge divination substitutes as the practice has it. But when knowledge can be established, there is no need for divination. Even in the case of knowledge, it is an interpretation of the situation in light of a relevant worldview or cosmology that gives us the needed knowledge. Or one may say that there is a tacit interpretation that applies. In the *Yijing* texts, this tacit interpretation becomes explicit in the *Yizhuan*. Once knowledge is established, one can make a choice and decision as to what to do in a situation.

Further, there is valuation of the situation, and in the *Yijing*, valuation goes together with knowledge of a situation. Categories of valuation include the following: suspicious (*ji* 蠱), small error (*lin* 吝), regret (*jiu* 咎), perilous (*li* 厉), and misfortune (*xiong* 凶). Of course, we can also state the absence of any of these features in a situation. The point is that these categories of valuation identify the nature of a known situation for the purpose of decision making and action. One must make a decision for a proper form of action in order to compensate the badness of a situation or to ride on the goodness of a situation. Here we see the duality between the situation as the given necessity and the human action as the positive power of balance and transformation. One is position (*wei* 位), and the other is movement (*dong* 动), as represented by the line (*yao* 爻).

The key principle for decision and action is to strive for maximum unity or harmony of the position and movement, or situation and action. Although the *Yijing* texts normally hold that one should strive for unity and harmony, one has the freedom of will not to seek these, but instead to act on one's volitions and face the consequences. In this sense, the categories of valuation mentioned above are not those of moral values, although they coincide with a moral life if one persists in acting toward maximum harmony consistently. In other words, one would have to see harmony as a norm for the whole and general goal of life, only tolerating disharmonious and yet morally right actions on individual occasions.

This requirement of course reflects the underlying cosmic picture of the whole universe. It is in this sense that morality has an ultimate cosmological significance: it is what would contribute to the ultimate goodness of the universe. It is precisely what is meant to act morally, which literally is to act according to the way (*dao*) of heaven and earth or to act so that one would "cherish and embrace primal harmony" (*baohe taihe* 保合太和). But there is again no denial of freedom of will, for what freedom of will comes to is nothing but the independent power to act and transform according to its own internal decision in light of knowledge. This freedom of will is creativity with consciousness of choice of the person rooted in the cosmic source or the *dao*.

One must recognize the realism of axiology together with realism of human existence in the *Yijing* philosophy. There also is a sense of the deep link between the universe and the human person reflected in the sense of a deep link between creative changes of the universe and creative action of a person. The whole function of interpretation of the *gua* is for enlightened understanding of such a link and an enlightened action or orientation of life, in light of such a link, so that both universe and the person would maintain a sufficiency of creative advance and transformation. Morality as free human action toward a vision with understanding of a situation is just an aspect of such an onto-cosmological process.

Topic 4: Interpretation as Basis for Decision Making and Action

As we have seen, divination gives rise to a need for interpretation, and interpretation of a symbol requires appeal to a cosmic map or cosmography. There is no reason why the practical need of divination prompts the theoretical or contemplative cognition of the world-reality that would in turn satisfy a practical need. As an individual, one may raise the question as to which is more primary: the practical or the theoretical. As a matter of fact, both the practical and the theoretical cannot be separated; they are interdependent. When we reflect on the rise of the system of the *gua* as symbols for interpretation of reality, however, we must realize that world-reality has been already presented in this system of symbols by way of "comprehensive observation" so that each symbol could be interpreted relative to a given situation as identified in divination. The interpretation can be conceived as a procedure of applying the *gua* to the situation and at the same time appealing to the sign and hence the whole system of *gua* for generating meaning. The meaning is generated in the reflection of the diviner in full view of the creative tension arising between the situation and the sign. It is the result of resolving the tension by producing a unity of the *gua* sign and the situation according to the understanding of the diviner. But this meaning must be seen as a dynamical force not only for revealing a view or a vision of what the situation is about or what it has in its charge for self-realization but as a need for action as inspired or guided by the vision. This is the tension of knowing and action, which is a different order of tension that exists in the symbol as applied to situation with its implicit presuppositions about reality. The tension between the knowing and action is one that requires transforming the known into a factor leading to action.

Topic 5: Confucius and Philosophy of *Yijing* in Confucianism

The *Yijing* is grounded in, and at the same time laid the groundwork for, the notion that the value of harmonization as benefits and harms to a person can be transformed into moral values of good and bad, right and wrong. However, it was Confucius who undertook the final step of the explicit transformation of cosmological thinking into moral consciousness and moral reasoning in an effort to define and develop the human person. First, Confucius (551–479 BCE) recognized the universality of humanity, which he called the virtue of *ren* 仁 (benevolent love) and attributed to every human being. He further recognized the necessary social ordering and harmonizing principle, which he called the *li* (proprieties) and which have been instituted for the maintenance of humanity and creation of human civilization.

With regard *li*, one can detect two avenues by which Confucius developed his insights: (1) general observation and general reflection on humanity and (2) historical understanding of human society. Since it was in the beginning of the Zhou Dynasty that resources for these insights, if not the insights themselves, were formulated in the basic texts of *Zhouyi* 周易 and *Zhouli* 周礼 (which are composed of the *Zhouguan* 周官 and *Yili* 仪礼 [ancient Chinese ceremonies and rites]), one may say that Confucius inherited both these insights and has made them explicit in his dialogues with his disciples.

Ren and *li* thus formed the foundation and fountainhead of the Confucian corpus of thinking in Confucius's effort to reform and transform the society and individuals of his times. Perhaps it is the lack of such insights in the general populace that made him acutely aware of the need for articulating them and accentuating them. This should explain why Confucius devoted a career of over forty years to teaching after he was disillusioned with the politics of his native state, Lu. But more than that, this also should explain the profound and deep unity underlying his philosophy of humans and society. When Confucius says, "To overcome oneself and restore the practice of proprieties is benevolent love" (*keji fuli wei ren* 克己复礼为仁), he has fused the two notions *li* and *ren* into one unity of two differentiated aspects.

The Confucian *Analects* appears as a body of diverse dialogues and conversations between Confucius and his disciples. But underneath there are Confucius's feelings for *ren* that provide a thread of unity for his thinking and his vision of humanity. His basic ideas of *ren* and *li* in unity lead to other ideas of polar contrast and polar complementariness such as we find in the various notions of virtues and human relationships. Eventually, what emerges is an intense interest in contemplating the way of the heaven (*tiandao* 天道), rooted in the way of change and constancy in the *Yijing*. Confucius says in the *Analects* that "Heaven does not speak, and simply lets four seasons rotate and all things grow" (*Analects* 17.19). This numinous feeling of heaven as a silent providing power underscores the creativity of the *taiji* or the *dao* in the *Yizhuan*. It is also linked to his (perhaps earlier) notion of *tian* as a power being capable of endowing an innate virtue in him and also capable of sustaining human culture in the world. In the latter instance, one may argue that *tian* is a source responsible for the rise of *ren* and *li*. Hence, this *tian* is not Daoist *dao*, which manifests itself more in nature than in man, but the *dao* of the *Yizhuan* from which human values and human cultures arise and flourish.

It might be suggested that this understanding comes into being because Confucius devoted himself to the study of the *Yijing* since the age of fifty. Although his famous statement in the *Analects*, "Given more years to study the *Yi*, by the age of fifty I would then be free from big mistakes" (*Analects* 7.17), has been subjected to a philological critique by Ouyang Xiu (1007–1072) in the Song Period (960–1279), the critique itself appears basically groundless, because in the larger context of knowing the *tianming* 天命, the interest in studying the *Yi* and even the actual study of the *Yi* by Confucius are now evident facts.[16] This leads to a useful hypothesis that the *Analects* is a work largely based on Confucius's responses and reflections on the way of human persons that are perhaps dated to before he was fifty years of age, whereas after age fifty, and particularly in the later period of his life, Confucius may have engaged himself intensely in the study, reflections, and teaching of the *Yi*.

Confucius treated the age of fifty as a crucial time of critical self-understanding in man, and this critical self-understanding was derived from knowledge of the mandate of heaven (*tianming*), which can be described as knowing the limitations of human life as well as apprehending the potentialities of one's human nature. To fulfill oneself by realizing one's potentialities within one's limitations in life *is* to fulfill the *tianming* for oneself. This suggests that one comes to know both the natural tendencies of things, which is the way of heaven (*tiandao* 天道), and the moral disposition of oneself, which is the way of man *rendao* 人道. One also comes to know that one should model oneself after the way of heaven for its continuous creativity and productivity.

This explains how a relatively large body of statements on *Yi* has been listed as direct quotations from him in various parts of the *Xici* and other sources. Recent findings in the Mawangdui *Yijing* silk texts make it amply clear that in his later years Confucius engaged in enthusiastic discussions on the *Yijing*, seeking individual as well as general understanding that leads to interpretations of meanings of diverse *gua* in the *Yijing*. Based on this understanding, Sima Qian's (145 BCE–86 BCE) (*Prefect of the Grand Scribes of the Han Dynasty*) statement that Confucius completed the commentaries on the *Yijing* is not totally without grounds. But, more historically speaking, it is Confucius's several disciples and their own disciples that actually composed and edited these Confucian commentaries as originally inspired by Confucius.

Once we see how this implicit reference to the *Yi* cosmology of creativity and timely moral action in the *Analects* became developed and conceptualized in the formation of the *Yizhuan*, we are able to see how an explicit philosophy of the creative *tiandao* (way of the heaven and the self-cultivating *rendao* become established in other later Confucian writings after Confucius. I mean specifically the *Doctrine of the Mean* (*Zhongyong* 中庸) and the *Mencius*, in which one finds specifically how an onto-cosmologically rooted unity of persons and heaven could become transformed into a socially and politically meaningful unity of the way of persons and the way of heaven. From this, one can easily come to see how the *Yijing* in its philosophical aspects becomes actively involved with and engaged in the development of Confucianism. Ever since Confucianism was established as the mainstream ideology and philosophy in the Han Dynasty, the *Yijing* has been known more as source of cosmic wisdom than a book for mere divination.

The rise of Neo-Confucianism with *Yijing* as its guiding principle in the Song period was no accident. The challenges from Buddhism and Daoism, both as a metaphysical and a practical philosophy or religion, makes the *Yijing* a challenge to itself. Could the *Yijing* philosophy satisfy the requirement and need for theoretical presentation of truth of change and at the same time provide a practical alternative for solving the ultimate questions of life and death as well. The focus is now not just on understanding the categories of being and nonbeing as *wuji* 无极 (ultimateless) and *taiji* 太极 (great ultimate) but as principles of constitution of rationality (*li* 理) and creative movement of something experienced as real, namely the vital force (*qi* 气). This understanding makes it possible to apply the philosophy of the *Yijing* to moral cultivation of self and political regulation of society. Thus, we can see how the tradition of *Yijing* is not only the origin of Chinese philosophy, but becomes the very ground of Confucianism and Neo-Confucianism. In contemporary Neo-Confucianism, however, this spirit of onto-cosmological thinking seems to retreat from outside observation and come to concentration on mind speculation, yet in a deeper sense it still serves as a source of inspiration for absorption, observation, harmonization and integration with regard to new challenges from modern science and Western philosophical thoughts. For example, Zhu Xi (1120–1200) has observed how shells found on the top of mountain indicated how earth has changed from ocean to land and hills.

Topic 6: The *Yijing* and Daoism, Buddhism, Folklore, and the Modern Sciences

Our five topics covered above do not exhaust how the *Yijing* as a philosophical cosmic sign book is related to other philosophical schools beside Confucianism and Neo-Confucianism. Insofar as the *Yijing* is the primary origin and source of Chinese philosophy, the close relevance of the *Yijing* for Daoism is not to be forgotten. It must be maintained that the notion of the *dao* could emerge from the comprehensive observation of the cosmos and nature at large in a relatively early period, but this may actually have come to be written down in a relatively later period. This should explain how we could have two philosophical positions regarding the notion of the *dao*, the Daoist notion of the *dao*, which states that the *dao* is unspeakable, and the *Yizhuan* notion and essentially the Confucian-Neo-Confucian notion of the *dao*, which states that "Alternation of one *yin* and one *yang* is called the *dao*." Perhaps, the *Yizhuan* notion of the *dao* is an answer to the Daoist notion and may have come into existence later. But this may simply imply that Laozi (sixth century BCE) and the Daoists may have responded to an even earlier notion of the *Dao*, which was conceived and spoken of by even earlier philosophers. If we contemplate the world of things and things in the world, do we come to some notion of the way that things form and transform, interrelate and interact?

Both Laozi and the *Yizhuan* recognize the source nature of the *dao*. In regard to describing the workings of the *dao* and its true identity, however, it seems clear that language cannot make any articulation simply because it is primarily made to refer to individual things and things in fixed categories; thus, its function is not even to illuminate the *dao*. One must use language to allude to things beyond language, not to describe them. In this respect, there does not really exist any contradiction between the Laozi view and the *Yizhuan* view. The real difference is a matter of how the onto-cosmology of the *dao* is to be applied to human life and action, where one would see a difference of the Daoist and the Confucian philosophies. The *Tuan* 彖 and *Xiang* 象 *Commentaries* are no doubt Confucian in orientation, urging participation and action on the part of the human person, in contrast with a position on enjoying nature and leading a life of spontaneity and inaction from the Daoist point of view.

It is indeed possible to write a Daoist commentary on the *Yijing* texts of symbolism and judgments, as was done in the Ming era. But the point here is that it is actually necessary, not just possible, for the *Yijing* to inspire the Daoist view of the source of things in the world and it actually can be seen as providing all the basic elements of a naturalistic cosmology or even naturalistic ethics. It might be said that the *Yijing* has inspired and enriched the Daoist views of the world and continues to do so up to the present. On the other hand, we have to recognize that Daoist classical writings no doubt in one way or another reflect and even expand a *Yijing* point of view in the direction of naturalness and non-action (in Laozi) or roaming (in Zhuangzi), particularly in the arena of human person and human government in a time of social and political disorder in which the pro-active principle of creativity in heaven and earth must be left alone.[17]

The relation of the *Yijing* philosophy to modern science is external and theoretical rather than internal and historical as in the case of Confucianism and Daoism. How and why the *Yijing* philosophy applies to modern science is due to the abstract mathematical structure of the *Yijing* symbolism on the one hand, and the abstract theoretical nature of modern science on the other. One can easily see how the primary interpretation of the *Yijing* symbolism as a system of *yin-yang* forces operate in various systems of science, which could then be seen as systems of *Yi*-symbolism on different levels of reality. This explains how Leibniz was surprised to find that the *Prior-Heaven Diagram of Hexagrams* (*xiantiantu* 先天图) attributed to Fuxi 伏羲 confirmed his system of binary numbers.[18]

For modern biology, again, it is the natural system of DNA that could be expressed by the sixty-four *zhonggua* 重卦. Perhaps one could eventually formulate a system of quarks or subquarks in modern elementary physics based on the binary system of the *Yi* symbolism. All of these suggest that a deeper link of the scientific system with the underlying philosophy of the *Yi* and its symbolic forms must be researched on the basis of experience and experiment for identification and interpretation. However, serious studies of these kinds have yet to be started.

As to how the *Yijing* has been and could be related to Buddhism, I have observed in the book's Preface how Chan Buddhist Ouyi Zhixu has made a Chan-enlightenmental interpretation of the meaningfulness of the *Yijing* System. This shows that any deeper understanding of reality could incorporate a perspective on creativity of change and transformation and vice versa. But this is not within the scope of discussion of this book, nor are matters to do with any intellectual or folkloric application of *Yijing* in daily lives of people, such as medicine and geomancy.[19]

CHAPTER 2

Yijing as Creative Inception of Chinese Philosophy

Historical Background and Theoretical Presupposition

The *Yijing* as a classical text of Chinese philosophy dated back to the beginning of the well-known Zhou dynasty (circa 1200 BCE). Although we lack complete information as to how the *Yijing* was created, it is obvious that this text was formed on the basis of a long history of observation of the changes in nature and is formed for the purpose of making proper judgments and conducting appropriate human action in light of an understanding of future occurrences of events that would affect the life of an individual or destiny of a nation. As mentioned in the *Xici* 系辞, it was Fuxi 伏羲 who made comprehensive observations of the heavens and earth and examines things near and far, and then "began to invent the eight *gua* 八卦 (eight trigrams), so that we may reach and understand the powers of the divinity (*shenming* 神明), and classify-record the facts of ten thousand things." The importance of this description is that the *gua* were not arbitrarily created but invented in light of comprehensive observation of things above and below, and the goal of this observation is to understand nature and describe kinds of things in nature so that we may relate to them and thus respond to them as part of our efforts to develop as individuals. Fuxi need not be a single person but might refer to a tribe or group of people who developed a special concern for nature and for using nature in the development of man.

According to the *Historical Records* of Sima Qian, it was King Wen (Founder of Zhou) who emended the eight *gua* system of Fuxi into the sixty-four *zhonggua* 重卦 (hexagrams) system during his imprisonment by Jie Zhou 桀纣, the last King of Shang. The significance of this expansion lies in his ability to integrate forms of change with judgments on the changes from concrete cases of divination from a long past that may cover two previous dynasties over 800 years, the Shang 商 and the Xia 夏. But the practice of divination may exist well beyond 2000 BCE if one stretches the imagination. Hence, we can speak of *Zhouyi* 周易 (Yi of Zhou as established by King Wen 文王 about 1200 BCE), versus *Shangyi* 商易 (Yi of Shang, from circa sixteenth century BCE to twelfth century BCE) and *Xiayi* 夏易 (Yi of Xia, from circa twentieth century BCE to sixteenth century BCE), of which we have only fragments of records in *Shangyi* (known as *Guizang* 归藏), or just mention the name *Liangshan* 连山 for *Xiayi*, as stated in the *Annals of Lu State* (*Autumn and Spring of Lu*) and later historical writings.

Divination is an essential part of the main corpus of the *Yijing* tradition insofar as the *Yijing* is understood as a practical art for guidance of human action. But the *Yijing* tradition of divination has the characteristic of basing one's judgment about future action on actual observed trends of events in nature, not on conjectured wills of deities who may dominate religious or shamanistic beliefs of a people. Although there are shamans in antiquity in China, we notice that *wu* 巫 (shaman) and *shi* 史 (history-recorder) came into being at about the same time, and eventually it was *shi* who dominated in later history. It is fair to say that history must be the basis for predicting and knowing the future. In divination we are concerned with the future in light of the past and present, and a diviner must be a person who could interpret a present event for the future action in light of past history. But again we may also note that the diviner must develop a comprehensive corpus of knowledge and insights so that he can construct his analysis of events and prediction of the future not only on the ground of factual history but in light of and in reference to his comprehensive understanding of events and the nature of the cosmos in general. That is why general and comprehensive observation of things at large in the manner of Fuxi is equally important for interpreting results of divination.

It is in terms of this understanding that we can see how the *Yijing* as a text has embodied and presupposed a development of a cosmic view of the world in which human beings live and hence embodied and presupposed an awareness of the needs of humans in their engagement with and dealing with the natural environment. It is not only that humans must engage and deal with the natural environment, but that they must engage and deal with a human environment that arises from political, economic, and social activities of humans. Humans are born in the middle of cultural and human environments and hence must engage and deal with other humans in both cultural and personal contexts.

What is intended in the *Yijing* is that an individual can solve her practical life problems against a comprehensive system of observations of nature understood as composed of heaven, earth, and humankind. In this sense, the *Yijing* is not merely a text dealing with divinatory judgments, but one that contains and presupposes a system of human understanding of nature: of heaven, earth, and humankind. In this sense the *Yijing* is both practically oriented and theoretically contented for both action and understanding of an individual. One may see how this theoretical content is hidden in the practical judgments of divination as people normally use the text as manual for divination without reflecting on its theoretical content. One may fail to notice that it is this theoretical content that leads to its practical use in the present form or format of judgment making under a series of sixty-four *gua*. Yet as soon as we become aware of the underlying and the presupposed preunderstanding of nature (heaven and earth) in relation to humankind as formed in a long history of observation and practice, we must celebrate the *Yijing* as the very beginning of Chinese philosophy as I have claimed in my previous articles as early as 1987.[1] I have also claimed that *Yijing* and the tradition of "comprehensive observation of changes" (*tongbian* 通变) it represents forms the very source of inspiration for later development of Chinese philosophy throughout history of Chinese philosophy as we may see.[2]

One might question whether the reflective understanding of nature in relation to humans in the *Yijing* text could be said to be philosophy in the proper sense of the word. If "philosophy" means inquiry into the truth of the matter for whatever topic or theme that is important and meaningful to us as human beings and which may have a practical bearing on our form of life and our decision on action, then no doubt what is presupposed and preunderstood in the text of *Yijing* is precisely what philosophy is about. Without such philosophical activity there is no way in which a deep descriptive account of change as cognized and experienced by an observer could be given. What the *Yijing* author(s) has focused on in nature reflects a philosophical interest to find out how change takes place and how we may deal with change. It is both a practical and theoretical concern with the practical built on the theoretical and the theoretical guided by the practical. This concern no doubt overlaps with the Socratic concern with finding out the correct meaning and reference of a concept in order to resolve a doubt for understanding and making a decision for action.³ Yet it must be also recognized that they have radically different ways of seeking philosophical understanding, one by sagely discovery and the other by critical dialogue.

It is interesting to note that when we read through the original judgments (*guaci*), many concepts or ideas involved remain tacit or implicit and thus call for a definition and clarification that could have actually taken place with Confucius's conscientious effort to seek their meanings and their implication for action. This means that the writing and eventual development of the *Yizhuan* 易传 as the comprehensive commentary on the *Yi* Texts (forms and judgments) are not accidental but a great task and achievement for responding to queries related to the underlying philosophy of the *Yi* Text in the fifth to fourth century BCE, during which period Confucius had more time for study and reflection for himself and his disciples in regard to ancient classics in his home state Lu. From this point of view, the *Ten Wings* (*Shiyi* 十翼)—particularly the *Commentary on Judgment* (*Tuanzhuan* 彖传), *Commentary on Text and Words* (*Wenyan* 文言传), *Commentary on Images* (*Xiangzhuan* 象传), and the *Appended Statements Great Commentary* (*Xici Dazhuan* 系辞大传)—must be considered as explicit elucidation of the underlying philosophy of the *Yi* as conceived from ancient divinatory practice with implicit understanding of images and symbols referring to a cosmic reality of change and explicit judgments of the action to be taken. In all these commentaries we see concepts are explicitly defined according to ordinary understanding, concepts created on the basis of deep experience and insights into reality, statements, and judgments of what cosmic reality is and what we can learn from them.

It is obvious that almost all of these commentaries have their central philosophical concerns that can be described as onto-cosmological, cosmological, ethical, environmental-ethical, philosophical-anthropological, and political-philosophical. Although the language expressing them is succinct and compacted, one can approach them if one masters the language and at the same time has profound experience of life and reality. Indeed, on this basis, one could find them most insightful and penetrating as a philosophical account of reality and a philosophy of man. In this sense, we must conclude that the *Yizhuan* becomes the explicit source and beginning of Chinese philosophy in all its aspects, and this means that the *Yijing* or the *Yi* Text contains the implicit onto-cosmological insights of Chinese philosophy that are uncovered by broad reflection and long-term reflection of Confucius and his disciples, just as the *Yi* Text itself was formed based on the reflections of King Wen and other early sage kings (philosophically minded rulers) on divinatory practice. In the last analysis, we see that even in the practice of divination, the primary philosophical activities of making onto-cosmic discovery, doing onto-hermeneutical interpretation, exercising moral judgment on action, engaging in philosophical reflection, and providing justification are clearly present.[4] With this being said, my thesis that the *Yijing* is the beginning and source of Chinese philosophy, which is composed of major schools of philosophy such as Confucianism and Daoism, can be easily explained and justified.

Five Levels of Onto-Hermeneutical Formation of the *Yi* Text

Based on the above analysis, we may now see how the *Yijing* text embodies five strata or layers of understanding and interpretation of reality (nature) that can also be conceived as five levels or stages of development. These five levels are (1) observation (*guan*), (2) symbolization (*xiang*), (3) systematization (*tong*), (4) divination (*bu*), and (5) interpretation (*jie*). These five levels, or stages, can be described and explained in terms of certain key concepts or key words in the *Yijing* or *Yizhuan* texts.

The insights of ontological understanding in connection with using and interpreting human symbols and language is actually developed and presented in the Chinese philosophical tradition as early as the formation of the *Book of Changes* (*The Book of Yi*, or the *Yijing*) text and consequent formation of the commentaries of the *Yijing* text known as the *Yizhuan* 易传 (*Commentaries on the Yijing*, which since the early Han times has become part of the *Book of Changes*, commonly known as the "Shiyi 十翼" ["Ten Wings"]). It is in my reflection and research on the origins of the *Yi* Texts and the rise of the *Yi* commentaries that I came to an ontological-hermeneutical understanding that led to the formation of the general concept of onto-hermeneutics, and to the *specific* concept that Chinese hermeneutics has its primal model in the onto-hermeneutics based on the formation of the *Yi* Text and the transformation of an intimate understanding of the *Yi* Text into the philosophical system of the *Yizhuan*. The *Yizhuan*, in turn, discloses or illustrates the onto-hermeneutics of the *Yijing*.

In the following section I develop my understanding of a *Yi*-based onto-hermeneutics consistent with an understanding of the texts of the *Yijing* and an interpretation of the *Yijing* texts in terms of the *Yizhuan* philosophy of onto-cosmology. We may point out that the very understanding of the *Yi* Text in light of the *Yizhuan* and vice versa is a required procedure for any genuine understanding of the *Yi* Text as well as the subject matter of the text.[5] It can be considered as the very foundation and process in which both the text and event could be illuminated. Thus, one also must consider how the original *Yijing* texts were formed in the encounter of an original position or situation in which an individual must interpret this world-reality of change and henceforth register his understanding in a system of symbols and a form of language. It must be recognized that the *Yijing* is formed as a system of symbols intended to refer to and represent the world-reality based on comprehensive observation (*guan*). This system of symbols has been used to divine the future for the purpose of seeking correct and propitious action.

In the first stage, "observation" here means "*guan* 观," or "comprehensive observation," which is the name of the twentieth hexagram. This is a key concept I use here to identify the very foundation of the formation of the *Yi*-symbols in light of both this *Guan gua* (hexagram) and the *Xici Commentary* of the *Yizhuan* (*Yijing Commentaries*), as we shall see.

Second, symbolization is the process of imaging (*xiang* 象), in light of which an image or likeness of an event or a situation is formed. All trigrams and hexagrams are images or symbols that either iconically or indexically stand for real situations in nature or life. Although the *Yi* Text does not employ the word "*xiang*," the use of the *gua*-symbols is a manifest action of imaging iconic and indexical representation. It is a public image to be hung up for anyone to see; hence, it is called the *gua* 卦 (the form hung up). It is in the interest of capturing the spirit of imaging that the largest systematic interpretation of the *Yi* Text among all the commentaries, the *Xiangzhuan*, was written.

In the third stage, the systematization of the *Yi*-symbols (*gua* 卦) together with their names and appended *gua* judgments and line (*yao* 爻) explanations (*ci* 辞) are what makes the *Yijing* a text, a book (*shu* 书), and a system of ordered sequence of *gua* forms. Although we do not know precisely when such systematization is made, we can understand how King Wen could have come to organize the *gua* and their judgments and explanations into the present ordered sequences of *gua* and the *Yi* Text known as the *Zhouyi*. He must have already acquired a vision of onto-cosmological nature in its creative development that consists in the formation of the *yin-yang* forces in interactive actions that lead to both differentiation of things and integration of things. He must have come to understand a philosophy of creative changes in the networking and interconnections of events in the world that is a process of formation and transformation of things. There is no better term than *tongbian* 通變 (penetrating or understanding changes) to indicate this understanding that inspires systematization of forms and images.

Fourth, divination stands for practice of divining a present situation or condition with milfoil stalks (*shi* 蓍) in order to produce an image of the present situation, the significance of which can be interpreted in light of signs as revealed in cracks of burned oracle bones (tortoise back shells and oxen shoulder bones) (*bu* 卜). To speak out the meaning of the divination is then called oral divination (*zhan* 占). There is also the ancient word *zhen* 貞, which suggests divination using sea shell or tortoise shell. The word *zhen* suggests a shell has been fixed with a divination judgment. The words *zhen*, *shi*, and *zhan* have appeared in the *Yijing* Texts, but we know that the general practice of divination (*bu*) has been recorded in "divinatory judgments" (*buci* 卜辞) traceable to circa 2000 BCE.

Finally, interpretation stands for two basic concepts in the *Yi* Texts, namely the concept of clarification or illumination (*ming*) and the concept of resolution (*jie* 解). In the *Tuan*, *Xiang*, and *Xici* commentaries, the word "*ming*" is used to clarify a belief, an argument, a punishment, an administrative policy, the meaning of a time, and the moral implication of fortunate and misfortunate (*ji* and *xiong*). It is clear that *ming* is to interpret and explain in the German sense of "*Auslegung*" so that a point, a truth, a fact and a value can be made clear. But when we face a *gua* situation, we also wish to find a way out or a way of resolution. The interpretation of a *gua* situation faces the demand that we can make an informed decision on action in light of the understanding of the situation, and the action will bring out a relief and resolution of the debacle present in the situation. Hence the relevance of the concept of *jie*, which stands for resolution out of difficulty.

Given the above explanation we can see the following correspondences of stages or levels of formation of the *Yi* Text as follows:

Observation	*guan* (observation) / *cha* (inspection)
Symbolization	*xiang* (image) / *gua* (trigram) / *yao* (lines)
Systematization	*shu* (writing) / *ci* (diction; judgment) / *yan* (language)
Divination	*bu* (divination) / *zhen* (turtle shell divination) / *shi* (milfoil stalk divination) / *zhan* (oral divination)[6]
Interpretation	*ming* (clarifying) / *jie* (dissolution; explanation)

Although we speak of five stages of the development of the *Yi* Text, we can see that actual divination plays a central role in the systematization of text, because it is whereby hexagram judgments (*guaci*) and line explanations (*yaoci*) are generated to illuminate the *gua* symbols, in such a way that correlating adjustments could be made in order to preserve a fundamental mode of understanding in terms of observations of *yin-yang* forces and their alignments. During a long process, each stage or level could feed back to enrich or rectify the earlier stage or a presupposed level in order to achieve an organic totality of interrelated parts.[7] Here we have a primal form of onto-hermeneutic understanding that consists in presenting a message of reality from rereading a given description in light of new experience and confrontation with reality. This onto-hermeneutic understanding is therefore a matter of an onto-hermeneutic circle or integration of parts and the whole of experiences of a situated state of reality or event. It is a circle because a circulation of attribution and regulation of meaning in light of experience and understanding of a given situation in the world-reality is presupposed. It is not simply a matter of a hermeneutic circle alone, which consists in inter-determination of meaning of terms in a holistic text/context of understanding in which reference to a dynamical reality or any reality is not made or assumed.

We may ask how the *Yi* Text becomes formed as a result of onto-hermeneutic understanding and thus embodies an onto-hermeneutic understanding that leads to formation of an epistemology-oriented methodology and an onto-cosmology or *benti*-ontology of this universe and thus functions as a perpetual source and inceptive foundation of Chinese philosophy and its development. To answer this question, one must look into how the formation of earliest *Yi*-symbols and names could be explained in terms of human experiences of the world that contains nature (heaven and earth), humans, and their interactions. It can be seen that trigrams are developed as an organized set of symbols to stand for salient natural events and processes and structures of nature as we have observed them. There are eight trigrams (*bagua*), which suggest eight major and dominant natural phenomena and processes by our observation. These major processes are considered central to our understanding of nature and are treated as a basis for formation and constitution of all other concrete events and processes of nature.

The eight phenomena/processes as represented by the trigrams are also observed to be derived from even more basic forces or processes that correspond to our experiences of the general and pervasive qualities of the world. Hence we can speak of our experiences of *yin* 阴 (shady) and *yang* 阳 (bright), *gang* 刚 (firmness) and *rou* 柔 (softness), *dong* 动 (motion) and *jing* 静 (rest), and relative qualities such as empty and substantial, potential and actual, progress and regress, and up and down as basic dimensions of events such as fire and water or structures such as lake and hill. Even heaven and earth can be said to be observed to have those features that we normally experience in actual feelings and concrete situations. Based on those experiences of qualities of events and things, we may reach a more generalized notion of *yin* and *yang* as preserving force and advancing force that can apply to all experiences of qualities in their polaristic contrast and dynamic interdependence. This is what the Daoist has done by introducing the concepts of *de* 德 (the virtue) and *dao* 道 (the way). They can be also described as signs of order and vitality titled *li* 理 and *qi* 气 in the Neo-Confucian philosophy of the Song-Ming period. Insofar as we can be said to experience *de* and *dao* or *li* and *qi* in reality, we also can be said to experience *yin-yang* qualities such as dark and bright, soft and firm, moving and still etc. Such contrast and interdependence of *yin* and *yang* eventually leads to the positing of a single primary source of them that is called the *taiji* 太极 (the great ultimate). Hence, it is said in the *Yizhuan* that "Change has *taiji*, from which two norms (*yin* and *yang*) arise" (*Xici Shang* 11). All things can be said to arise from *taiji* by way of *yin-yang* polaristic complementing operation and are sustained as existing by the *taiji* as the inexhaustible source of creativity.[8]

Now, given the primary symbols of experiences of reality, the eight trigrams can be said to be composed of these primary symbols in terms of certain internal *de-dao* and *li-qi* relationships. These trigrams further combine into larger configurations of sixty-four hexagrams by way of binomial expansion that would logically capture structures and vitalities of natural events and processes in the world. The binomial expansion gives us a reason to think that all things in the world must be related in both rational and vitalistic ways. Of course, we need not to stop at sixty-four hexagrams, but for empirical reasons the set of sixty-four hexagrams comes to represent a stable, meaning-generating and hence usable set of basic human conditions, which we can commonly and normally understand and manage or act on with both reason and will. Here we see how a principle of epistemic and regulative simplicity is implicitly at work: the system of sixty-four hexagrams is simply considered a representation of reality at a level consistent with our needs and capacity of understanding.

The system of sixty-four hexagrams forms a web of interrelated meanings that reflect interrelatedness of things and transformation of events in human experiences. It is up to the human mind, the interpreter of symbols, to make out tendencies in those changes and transformations by interpretation of emerging meanings in human situations for regulative and pragmatic action. But simultaneously as also an intended objective description of natural and human-social processes, formal and logical rules could be given as these are ways in which a human mind would regulate itself. From this understanding we see a system of image-forms-symbols being formed in the process of our observation, reflection, and interpretation of nature. Needless to say, this system is formed in a long-range process of observation, reflection, and interpretation, which is comprehensive in scope and layered in structure and need not be confined to the experience of a single person, but could cover accumulated experience and invention of science and technology in a culture and its tradition.

As the formation of *Yi* symbols requires correct adjustment to reality and achievement of an operative system that could represent an open totality of nature and life at a significant time, we may mention five basic epistemological principles for explaining how the *Yijing* system of *yin-yang* symbols functions in a dynamic and creative process toward representation of reality and nature. They are the (1) Principle of Comprehensive Observation, which ensures openness and continuity of observation from both a minute and holistic points of view; (2) Principle of Systematic (or organic) Consistency and Simplicity, which requires the whole system of observations be organized in cogent and coherent experiences and concepts of mutual support; (3) Principle of

Polaristic Opposition and Complementation, which shows how creativity of production and individuation of things could take place; (4) Principle of Creative Unfolding and Development, which allows and invites new experiences of nature and reality in a growing and expanding process of life-realization; and finally (5) Principle of Understanding in Human Consciousness and its Creative Self-Regulation, which points to the emergence of human consciousness and its inherent power of creative decision and action based on understanding of nature. These five epistemological principles in working together also define and provide a methodological understanding of the Yi-thinking. It can be said to represent the methodology of Yijing philosophy as a way of ontological thinking, not just as a way of experiential knowing.

Benti-Ontology as Onto-cosmology of the Yi

Apart from the epistemology and methodology that define the mode of Yijing knowing and thinking, the Yijing has initiated an onto-cosmological tradition by providing an onto-cosmological model of reality that has influenced the whole posterity of philosophers in the long history of Chinese philosophy. How do we understand this onto-cosmological model of reality? The answer is by looking into the mutual defining relationship between source-origin and substantial development of reality we may come to think of reality as representing a benti 本体, namely root-body, source-reality, or onto-cosmos. How do we understand this concept of root-body, source-reality or onto-cosmos and its reference? In the first place, we must recognize that all the changes we have observed must have an adequate source or ultimate origin so that changes could happen and continue. This is what the term "ben 本" indicates. The etymology of this word is both iconic and indexic as it shows it to be the underground root of a tree.[9] The ultimate source or ultimate origin is called taiji 太极 in the Xici, but in the Yi Text is referred as the yuan 元 (the ultimate source).[10] This ultimate source manifests itself in two modes of being, namely in yin and yang, and thus has two dimensions that are respectively referred to as Qianyuan 乾元 (the source power of Qian 乾) and the Kunyuan 坤元 (the source power of Kun 坤), the former of which is the moving and creating power and the latter of which is the preserving and sustaining power. But we must also regard the two as belonging to each other and forming a holistic unity that suggests an underlying source for its differentiation into the *yin* and the *yang*, corresponding to *Qian* and *Kun*. This is precisely the great ultimate (*taiji* 太极) as the ultimate beginning of existence and hence the inceptive creativity. It can be conceived that this inceptive creativity as oneness must generate two modes of being, namely the *Qianyuan* and the *Kunyuan* as mediums for the creative differentiation and individuation of things. Hence, we can see the root source of being and existence as a matter of a unity differentiated into duality and eventually into diversity. One could wonder what this differentiation means: is it a matter of ontological manifestation in a Spinozain sense, or a matter of cosmological generation in a Whiteheadean sense? The Chinese word being used for relating *taiji* to two norms *yin* and *yang* is "*sheng* 生," which means generating or, better, giving birth to.[11] In other words, it must create itself into a body of *yin* and *yang* and reality of parts that we can call the *ti* 体 (the body, the organic wholeness of the hidden and the manifest). As being cannot but creatively generate things of existence, we see how ontology of being must be described as onto-cosmology; that is, what exists must generate a thing or things capable of generating new things. Hence, for the *Yijing*, ontology of being is a natural matter of onto-cosmology—a matter of a source (source-being) giving rise to things in a process of generation from *ben* to *ti*. I take it to be a matter of creativity from the source to things, including creativity from nonbeing to being insofar we can identify nonbeing such as *wu* 无 as the source of being *you* 有 as held by Laozi or Wang Bi.

In light of this creative activity of the *taiji*, one can see how every consequent event can be said to derive from it and become parts of a whole that have many levels and organization and may be subject to many ways of description. But we must note that all events and resulting state of being form one body (*yiti* 一体) in the universe even though there are indefinite numbers of individual things and events in the universe. To say that they form one body is to say that they are organically related in one way or another in a process of subprocesses of generation that we as human beings could even experience and observe. Although the *Yi* Text did not explicitly mention this concept of *ti*, it is implied and thus is implicit in the formation of the eight or sixty-four hexagrams system that has all the qualities of forming one body and thus exhibiting one body of interrelated differences and identities on different levels. Typically, there are levels of being from the great ultimate as the starting point to two norms, then to four forms and then to *bagua* and eventually to sixty-four *gua* as shown in Shao Yong's "Diagram of Ordering of Sixty-Four Hexagrams."[12] Each hexagram of the sixty-four *gua* has its internal constituent lines that also form a body of interdependency of two trigrams, the upper and the lower, the inner and outer. But they can be also read as a form of six interactive lines of force.

It is obvious that the initial differentiation of *yin* and *yang* from the *taiji* forms the elementary *ti* that is composed of two lines, the *yin* and *yang*, based on one unity of the great ultimate. *Ti* could get more complex when we come to higher and higher levels of complexity of things. In this sense we see that the fundamental nature of *ti* is unity in diversity and diversity in unity in a process and action of creativity. As such, what constitutes one body is that it is an organic whole and that it has internal parts relative to external environment. In other words, the body is a body because one can speak of what is internal or inner of the body (within the body) and what is external or outer of the body (without the body). While there is basic coherence within, it still is subject to internal changes of the body. While internal changes are related to external changes, they are still different. A body must interact with other bodies or things so that it may develop and grow and realize its potential in a given environment. As we have noted, this process of internal-external interaction is essential for changes and transformations both internal and external. Finally, we must note that for the cosmic body, although there is no sense of speaking of outer and inner, there is still the sense of whole universe that contains changes within. In this sense, we can speak of the cosmic body with its elements in a developing state of indeterminacy. With this explanation of *ti*, we can easily speak of *benti* as source-body, source-reality, origin-body, or onto-cosmos, so that we may identify a body with its originating source.

From the *Zhouyi*'s point of view, the universe or cosmos forms a *benti* by itself since we can consider it as a coherent whole with interrelated parts even though we may not be clear about what is external to it. In this cosmic *benti* there is no external limitation and yet there is inexhaustible inner force as its source. We may indeed interpret "ontology" in its open context as study of the being as ultimate source and the study of the ultimate source (*benyuan* 本源 or 本元) as study of being, but since the ultimate source is a creative power for the creative development of the universe and nature, the study of being as the ultimate source and the study of ultimate source as being is thus also the study of being as generative becoming and the study of generative becoming as being.

Hence, we can speak of this universe as onto-cosmos or a *ti* of being as generative becoming and generative becoming as being.

Given this notion of ultimate source-reality, which we call the cosmic *benti*, we see that there is no boundary between the inner and the outer, the *Yizhuan* speaks of "Changes has no body and creativity (divinity 神) has no direction" (*Xici Shang* 4). On the other hand, for the human being, the *benti* is his own emerging and self-realizing self that is rooted in cosmos and that grows and develops in its interaction with external world. What is emphatically emphasized is that the unity of self comes from efforts of the individual in unifying or integrating the inner with the outer, as said in the *Zhongyong*.[13] The basic view involved is that the human being has creativity rooted in the cosmic creativity and that should be cultivated conscientiously by the human individual so that the potential of individuation could be fully realized and at the same time the creative differentiation of cosmic reality (cosmic *benti*) could become more richly realized in a unity of difference.

In this sense of *ti*, the *Yizhuan* speaks of an individual maintaining his correct and position and dwelling in his own body (*zhengwei juti* 正位居体, from *Kun Wenyan*). It is when a person has developed and cultivated himself into an integrative unity of mind and body and maintained his own creative force that we can speak of his *benti*, as such. For the concept of *benti* refers to a creative source and a creative process of self-development and self-formation with a person's initial transformative power as a part.

What is the significance of the *benti*? First, it gives rise to the onto-cosmological understanding of universe and the human being. Thus, we can speak of onto-epistomology, onto-ethics, and onto-aesthetics in which the inner versus outer issue could be resolved in a unity of the inner and outer. We must note that *ben* is not a cause, but a source, that *ti* is not substance in Aristotle but organic unity in the *Yijing*. It is not transcendent as there is no real separation between the *ben* and the *ti*, but a generative unity between them. It is not pure immanence either as there is always creative action and efforts to be made to transcend one's self in one state of being or one stage of becoming. The *ben* is conceived as powerful source of creativity without exhaustion, and the *ti* is conceived as both basis and result of actualization and achievement that exhibit the creativity of the *taiji*, the ultimate source and the ultimate creativity. Hence, it is not substance nor any essentialist thing based on the Aristotelian or Platonic metaphysics.

The most important feature of *benti* for humans is that we can rest with powers to improve and cultivate ourselves so that we can properly be said to be creative. It is on this basis we can speak of developing ourselves into moral beings, for example, through referring to a model or paradigm of onto-cosmological creativity.

Ti-Yong and Three Meanings of Yi

With *benti* clarified, we may now introduce the idea of *ti-yong*, which is based on the concept of *benti*. First of all, one can see that the notion of *yong* 用 is essential to the understanding of divinatory judgment, for the purpose of the divinatory judgment is its usefulness (*yong*) in making pragmatic decisions. But *yong* as a verb is not just its usefulness for human action toward a purpose. It is the actual functioning and agency that comes from our understanding and engagement. Ontologically speaking, *yong* is the activity of the *ti* or body that gives rise to new events while fulfilling a virtual capacity for creativity. In the statement, "Do not use the hidden dragon" (*Qianlong wuyong* 潜龙勿用), what is meant to be conveyed is to avoid making hidden energy function at that stage of development because it would serve no purpose. Hence the so-called *yong* or function is the power inherent in a body that could become creatively constructive for a purpose in a context of appropriate conditions. In divinatory judgments, there are many statements of "to use" *yong* 用 and many statements of "not to use" *wuyong* 勿用, each of which is based on consideration of how a body or *ti* fits in with the circumstances and time. In this perspective, the whole universe is a matter of the *yong* of the cosmic body, and the creative results of the *yong* are the actual content of the universe that contributes to the development and transformation of the *benti*. We can thus see how the notion of *ti* is rooted in *ben* and realized in *yong* and forms a process of creative development of the actuality of heaven, earth, and man. We can illustrate the process of continuous refeeding and reinvigorated creative activity of the cosmos as follows:

ben → ti → yong → ben → ti → yong → . . . .

It is clear that we may also apply this model of creative action and regenerative action to the human *benti*, so we can also speak of the ben-ti-yong 本-体-用 development of the individual. What is referred to as the self-cultivational (xiuji 修己) process in Confucianism is precisely an embodiment of such a cosmic process of creation and regeneration. This is because a human has her own benti and hence her yong of benti, briefly identified as the ti-yong relationship. Both the Yijing Xici and the Zhongyong remark that for ordinary people life functions with their inner power, and yet they are not aware of this (baixing riyong er buzhi 百姓日用而不知). The reason we need to become aware of our benti is that we need to know and preserve our inner powers and cultivate them and then make proper use of them for their realization and realization of human life. Hence, the benti-cosmology has important ethical and moral implication for development of the human self as benti and tiyong process of actualization and achievement.[14] It is a process through which the human benti or the human self could be extended to include others and be identified with heaven and earth of total onto-cosmic existence in terms of its incessant creativity.

The use of the Yi for the purpose of yong in action is served by knowledge and understanding that could be first induced by divination in a framework of understanding. As to the use for making utensils or other tools, one can point to the xiang 象 or image system in the Yi. The xiang images come from observation of nature and the world; it is where our human understanding first begins. With each xiang one could design something useful either for oneself or for the common people. According to the Xici, many of the useful inventions from the past are inspired by identifying the relevant gua. This suggests that images of the gua carry deep human purposive meanings as they could stimulate the human mind toward making designs for technical and cultural inventions.

Given a deep understanding of the cosmic benti that presents this world as a variety in unity and a change in constancy, a theory of three meanings of Yi as content of the cosmic benti has emerged in the work of Yiwei Qianzuodu 易纬乾凿度 and repeated in the writings of the Yi Text commentator Zheng Xuan (郑玄) in the later Han period. We must note that this articulation of three meanings of the Yi also reflects three underlying principles of the Yi in the Yizhuan.[15]

First, there is the nonchange (buyi 不易) of change in the sense of change as a constant activity. It is said in the Xici that "The life-creativity of life is called the change (Yi)" (Xici Shang 5). What makes life-creativity possible is the source of life that is constant and that is abundant without limitation and that is creative of things according to the principle of *yin-yang* differentiation and re-differentiation, compounding and re-compounding. As this is the nature of the *taiji* that stands for the source of life-creativity, one can see how the constancy in change is in fact the creativity of the *taiji*. There is another sense of the constancy that follows from this creativity principle, namely the world as actuality is constant. Although things come and go, the actuality of the world as indicated in the ways of heaven and earth always remains actual. It is the constancy of the *dao*, which represents the co-creation, alternation, and interaction of *yin* and *yang*, resulting in the formation of the mutual positing of heaven and earth. From heaven and earth, we come to the four seasons, and from the four seasons we come to eight phenomena of nature. In between, we discovered the five powers. All these have certain constancy relative to a deeper constancy that is ultimately the creativity of the *taiji*. In this sense, we may speak of a hierarchy of constancies in terms of which concrete events and individual things take place, endure for certain time, and then vanish with other events and other individuals to take their place. This is a constancy of cosmology rooted in the constancy of the ontology of *taiji* and *dao*.

One may raise the question of whether we can conceive a still deeper reality from which the ontology of *taiji* or the ontology of *you* (Being, as resulting from the statement "Yi you taiji 易有太极") would have to arise. Neither the *Xici* nor the *Tuan* has explicitly discussed this issue. But in the *Xici Shang* 12, it is mentioned that the *Qian* and *Kun* are sources of change and that if *Qian* and *Kun* are destroyed one would not see change anymore. Hence, there is the possibility of the vanishing or destruction of the world as we know it. Whether there is a primal state of *wu* after destruction is not mentioned. However, it is in the *Daodejing* that the state of *wu* (void and nonbeing) is focused on as the origin of *you* (Being). Two interesting points have also been mentioned in the *Daodejing*, the first being that the *dao* that gives rise to all things follows the naturalness (*ziran*), suggesting some state of the natural as being the *wu* and vice versa. The second point is that the *wu* and the *you* mutually generate each other (*youwu xiangsheng* 有无相生), suggesting a mode of *yin-yang* complementation and unity. From these points, it appears that the constancy of *you* 有 in *taiji* must imply a constancy of the *wu* in the *you* and the constancy of *wu* in *ziran* must also imply a constancy of *you* in *taiji*. This turns out to be the view presented in Zhou Dunyi's treatise "*Taiji tu shuo* 太极图说" (Discourse on the Diagram of the *Taiji*). Concluding from this exploration, it seems clear that the constancy of the *Yi* should not exclude the constancy of *wu*, or in other words, it should include the constancies of both *you* and *wu*. It would then lead to the view that these fundamental constancies are a must for the changes in the world and also for the nonchanges in the world, and therefore is a necessity by the logic of the matter.

The second principle of *Yi* is the principle of change and transformation (*bianyi* 变易 or *bianhua* 变化) among things. It pertains to what we experience as changes in life and death, formation and destruction of things and growth and movements in space and time. These changes certainly can be regarded as in-changes (or intra-changes in an individual being), between-changes (interchanges in nature) and out-changes (exchanges in human activities) we find in many levels of existence of things including ourselves as human beings. It is obvious that in all these changes there are individuations of both forms and matter of contents. One can see that all these changes have different sources of moving forces, which must be ultimately derived from the *taiji*. It is made quite clear by Shao Yong in his diagram on how sixty-four *gua* are founded on a hierarchy of forms that go back to the substratum of the *taiji* 太极 and *wuji* 无极 (the nonultimate). The *Yijing* as a book on change deals primarily with the forms of change in this sense and examine their relationships of origination formation, dependent formation, sector transformation and mutual transformation so that we see how changes follow a certain dialectical pattern of change and nonchange. One must learn from these forms and transformations as given in the *Yijing* Texts in order to know changes in our life experiences, just as we need to take lessons from our life experiences of the changes to appreciate how the forms of change in the *Yijing* are derived and how are they related and how given proper conditions how predictions and decisions could be made for the fulfillment of one's life and value.

Apart from these aspects of change, there are two essential elements in change that we have to take seriously: (1) the creativity of human beings and (2) the contingency of the events in life and nature. For the creativity of human beings, it is necessary that we must know what change is and what we are as human beings and make efforts to master our own existence and nature so we can remain free and capable of acting. It is from freedom of our life and activity of our capacity that we could become creative in participating in the creative advances of nature or heaven and earth. This is a central point made by the Confucians in the study of the *Yi*. In the *Xici* there are places in which this topic of human creativity has been discussed. For example, it cites from Confucius:

What does Yi suggest to us? It suggests to us to explore in things in order to form purposive activities (*kaiwu chengwu* 开物成务), so that we may integrate with the great way of the world. Thus the sage uses his knowledge of the change to comprehend the feelings and desires of the people under heaven and to achieve the great deeds under heaven and to dissolve the great doubts under heaven. (*Xici Shang* 11)

The important message is that an individual can become creative in knowing and identifying with the creativity of heaven and earth. Thus, the *Qian Wenyan* states, "To unite with heaven and earth in their virtues, to unite with sun and moon in their brightness, to unite with the four seasons in their ordering and to unite with spirits and deities in their powers of bringing good fortunes and bad fortunes," and such a person is called the great man (*daren* 大人) or the sage (*shengren* 圣人).

Regarding the question of contingency, we see that we have no way to determine beforehand when exactly we shall die or when exactly we were born. The change on its minute level is subtle and even beyond human perception. Perhaps it is because we do not know the conditions of the change so that we do not know details of change. Hence, one may suggest that if we do come to know those conditions, we shall be more certain about what and when and where a change will take place. But we must not forget that there is a deeper sense of contingency, namely what is to happen may depend on the whole universe, and we have an open universe in the making. This means that anything could happen, and until it happens we cannot and no one else could know what will have to happen. It is in this sense of deep contingency that the Yi says: "The spirits have no directions and the Yi has no substance." It is in this sense that the way of change is indeed unpredictable (*bukece* 不可测) and unknowable (*bukezhi* 不可知). Mencius states that "to be sagely and unknowable is called the divine" (7A25). In this sense, the contingency is in essence the same thing as the creativity of the *taiji*. It is perhaps with reference to this deep contingency or creativity that divination becomes an opportunity for learning and knowing something new each time. This contingency is no doubt equally reflected in the randomness of the happening of the changing lines of a hexagram, which determine the *zigua* 自卦 from the *bengua* 本卦. It also remains a metaphysical question as to whether the deep contingency of change is a matter of necessity of change.

Finally, we come to the principle of *jianyi* 简易, or simplicity of change. The word "*jian* 简" apparently suggests the easy and simple way in which the change is recorded on the bamboo pieces, which simplifies the method of recording at the time of early Zhou. But simplicity is also a direct experience of life and we can sometimes see among different possibilities which one embodies the actuality the easiest and the quickest. Apparently, simplicity in an ontological sense is the world of *Qian* and *Kun* in togetherness, which create the world without any obstruction. Subsequently, our understanding of the world and things could also be made simple and easy if we understand the ways of *Qian* and *Kun*. Thus, it is said in the *Xici Shang* 1:

> *Qian* acts in the easy way; *Kun* functions by simplicity. Acting in the easy enables people to understand easily and functioning by simplicity enables people to follow through. Easy understanding then leads to closeness, easy following then leads to efficiency of work. Closeness results in long endurance while having efficient work results in great achievement. Long endurance is the virtue of the talented, whereas great achievement is the deed of the talented. Hence, the abilities of easy doing and simple following embody the principles of the world. Once these principles are practiced, the world-order of right positions will be obtained.

This statement shows how simplicity and easiness are the ontological qualities of *Qian* and *Kun* and how they give rise to an epistemology of understanding in simplicity and easiness and a political economy of worldly achievements and deeds. In *Xici Xia* 1, the same assertion on the simplicity of *Qian* and easiness of *Kun* as attributes of their activities is made. From this, it is further concluded that all moving forces (such as reflected in the lines of a *gua*) and all forms of things are to be understand as projection of simplicity and easiness in being and becoming. From this, one may infer that the model of onto-cosmological development and exhibition in the *Yi* Text forms a model of simplicity and easiness in explaining and understanding. We may further infer that the philosophy of *Yi* is regarded as the most logical explanation of change, whereby the world of change must function from a principle of simplicity. This means that for the *Yi* philosophy, logic, and reason must be founded on the principles of the *Yi*, which includes all the basic statements of the world formation, such as "the *dao* is the alternation of *yin* and *yang*" and "the *Yi* has an ultimate."

One should not forget that in claiming simplicity and easiness, the *Yi* Text is also comprehensive and inclusive of all the *xiang* and their changes. It is simple and yet most comprehensive because it neglects nothing and ignores nothing. It is an onto-cosmology of all beings, which includes the unity of being and becoming as demonstrated in the explanation of the creativity principle that unifies both constancy and contingency. Now we come to see that one reason for this unity is the need for simplicity. In light of this need, nonbeing, being and their relationships are well integrated in a simple system of being and understanding at the same time.

With the three principles of change so described and interpreted, one can and must learn that the human way of life could achieve a comprehensive content and fulfill its potentiality by following and embodying the ways of heaven and earth. But this following is also a matter of creative development according to deep and simple understanding of being and becoming as the *Yi* Text suggests. It is a cosmic education with both profound ontological and profound moral significances. To make human activity creatively meaningful, I have further added on two more principles of the onto-cosmology of the *Yi*, namely the Principle of Exchange (*jiaoyi* 交易) and the Principle of Harmonization (*heyi* 和易).[16]

Remarks on Diversification of *Yi* into *Xiangshu* 象数 and *Yili* 义理

An important characteristic of the *Yi* philosophy is its involvement with images and numbers. Images are forms in which we envisage events and situations so that we can have a total meaning of events and situations. As they are found to be representable in terms of *yin-yang* lines of change, odd and even numbers naturally become significant. Besides, a holistic understanding of the process of change within sixty-four hexagrams requires consideration of numbers. This no doubt involves our reflection on the observed relations among images with regard to their formation and transformation. The representation of heaven and earth in diagrams indicating positions and directions—such as *River Chart* (*Hetu* 河图) and *Luo Script* (*Luoshu* 洛书)—also involve numbers. Hence numbers become symbolic of image-meanings and vice versa. To use numbers to make divination and hence to form a *gua* may start very early in the history of *Yijing* development. Although we could appropriate and explore into numbers for telling about the future, one cannot ignore judgments of divination to be made for actual life purposes and in terms of real experiences and knowledge of nature and humanity. How such judgments and their relating principles are analyzed and related is not simply a matter of images and numbers.

Yet it is clear that one cannot ignore images and numbers for intuitive understanding as well as ways of transformations among hexagrams and thus real human situations. In the early study of the *Yi* system in the Han period, the school of images and numbers dominate because they want to identify symbolic meanings for judgments through numbers of lines and *gua*. It is by focusing on the Daoist wisdom on contemplation on true meanings of words that images and numbers are dismissed. However, this is also a radical move, for it is a fact that hexagrams can be said to be generated by numbers and their representation in numbers are important for understanding inner and outer relations of the *gua*. It is not until Zhu Xi that both judgmental meaning and implication on one hand and images and numbers are mutually supporting each other and thus complementing. Philosophy of *Yi* as having these two sides must maintain a balance and integrative position for integrating the *Xiangshu* and *Yili*.

Remarks on the Rise of Daoism and Confucianism

As the source and origin of Chinese philosophy, the philosophy of *Yijing* has given rise to two major schools of Chinese philosophy: Daoism and Confucianism. For Daoism, it is obvious that the *dao* describes the way and process of change and transformation of things in nature. The creative function of *dao* even carries a broader meaning than *taiji* as creative source, for *dao* may also refer to nonbeing apart from being. In the *Daodejing* 道德经 one sees a similar dialectics of development as to what one finds in the *Yi* manuscripts. But there are two main differences in Daoism from the philosophy of *Yi*: one is its relative detachment from images and forms as it concentrates on how things arise by the spontaneous or *wuwei* 无为 action of the *dao*. In this sense, Daoism is more retrospective rather than prospective, more inner-looking than outer-looking like the *Yi* philosophy. Although things can be said to rise by the *dao* according to Laozi, and as Dao cannot be positively identified as it goes beyond our language and knowledge, the voidness of the *dao* suggests a more negative approach to *dao* and change which is from voidness to being. This may eventually lead to the notion of *wuji* 无极, which is essential for completing a full position of creative arising, resulting in a more complete redescription of onto-cosmology of *wuji* that is the essence of Zhou Dunyi's onto-cosmology in the Song period.

The direct successor from the *Yijing* is Confucianism. Not only did Confucius read and explore the *Yijing* text early in his life, he came to derive a full disclosure of the inner meanings of the system of Yi divinations in the natural birthings of things as natural creativity of nature. In addition, he sees in Yi divinations the development of virtues such as *ren yi li zhi xin* 仁义礼智信 that are to be performed in timely manner and as a matter of self-control for both justice and harmony of relations. This has been made clear in my discussion of the formation of the *Yizhuan* that is inspired by Confucius's teaching and thinking about the Yi tradition. The Confucian spirit of seeking positive understanding and self-transcendence and self–discipline fully represents philosophy of the Zhouyi at its best. Suffice it to say that the whole system of Confucian onto-cosmology and moral philosophy that I call onto-ethics is more or less a redevelopment and exploration of the Yi meanings. From Confucius to Zisi to Mencius and then to Xunzi there is nothing that cannot be related to the Yi tradition.

After the classical period, the philosophy of *Yijing* was further explored and absorbed in the Neo-Confucian philosophy of the Song Ming, and Yi way of thinking and its *benti*-ontology and onto-cosmology have led the Confucian mainstream of Chinese philosophy. Apart from achieving a distinctive philosophy of *li* and *qi*, the philosophy of *Yijing* as a way of thinking (as onto-hermeneutics) has brought Confucianism into closer contact with both Daoism and Chinese Buddhism. In this connection we may also mention that Chinese Buddhism is transformed into Chinese Buddhism from Indian Buddhism by fundamental points of *benti*-ontology, which gives rise to the notions of original nature and Buddha nature that are essential for many Chinese schools of Buddhism.

Remarks on Comparison with Heraclitus, Whitehead, and Dewey

For better understanding, it is useful to make a brief comparison of the *Yijing* philosophy of change to that of philosophers of change in the

Western tradition. Although one may not claim that philosophy of change is the mainstream of Western philosophy, we can see that the pre-Socratic philosopher Heraclitus (circa 500 BCE) enjoyed a special status in his highlighting a philosophy of flux that influenced notions of change in the Western tradition and its search for a solution. For Heraclitus, change is made possible by strife between natural elements such as fire and water. The world is a state of conflict that gives rise to all things. Heraclitus observed that one cannot put one's foot into the same river. But he did not develop a coherent theory of the states of change nor explain how a contradictory pair of elements could become complementary and harmonizing functions of reality. In this sense, Heraclitus made change a mystery that remains unresolved apart from the approach of transcendence above phenomenal change-events. In contrast, the philosophy of *Yijing* has comprehensively and systematically developed a system of change based on onto-cosmology of change and has even provided a way of dealing with changes for our human growth and development. Change is more rationally treated than poetically confronted in Heraclitus.

In contemporary Western philosophy, the most remarkable philosopher to deal with change is undoubtedly Alfred North Whitehead (1861–1947). In *Process and Reality*, Whitehead formulated a philosophy of change in which polaristic unity of the mental and the physical in any actual entity was asserted and a principle of creativity for many becoming one was introduced as an ultimate. He did not consider nature as an open totality that can be experienced or described in a system of symbolic signs. Neither did he explicitly consider the other side of a creativity that consists in creativity of one becoming many in terms of duality of the creative and the receptive or preservative. The last chapter in his book developed a philosophical theology in which God is conceived to have two natures that account for innovative changes of the world. But Whitehead does not wish to face the problem of creation from nothingness and lacks an underlying unity to derive from the two natures of God. In the philosophy of the *Yijing*, the problem of being and nonbeing to be mutually generated is recognized. In comparison there is no dualism of the real and the ideal but a duality of *yin* and *yang* in the Yi philosophy, even though both take immanence seriously. For Yi philosophy, there is a continuous of transcendence with immanence in the continuing creative move from *wuji* to *taiji*, but Whitehead would return to a dualist doctrine of transcendence in the form of eternal objects. There is of course no such commitment to eternal objects in the philosophy of change in *Yijing*.

Finally, we need to mention the pragmatic American philosopher, John Dewey (1859–1952). Dewey in his 1925 book *Experience and Nature* observed that the world is precarious and perilous because of its contingency and becoming. He stressed that this is what we have experienced, and our experience has reached deep in the changing character of nature. He advocated continuous reconstruction of human knowledge and a pragmatic solution to any philosophical problems, which he titled instrumentalism. There is a particular relativism in Dewey's philosophical understanding of change that requires different approaches in different times.

Conclusion

We often speak of the *Yijing* way of thinking and describe it as characterizing the basic mode of Chinese philosophical thinking. But characterizing the *Yijing* way of thinking can be difficult, as there are many aspects of the *Yijing* way of thinking to be integrated into an ontological unity experienced by the sage or a well-cultivated individual. In our analysis, we have demonstrated how the *Yijing* arises from a process of observation together with an act of integration of observation and feeling in the observer into a comprehensive and penetrating understanding. The feeling of a person toward a given situation must be explained as the natural reciprocation and interaction between the *yin* and *yang* forces at work, which leads to the person's direct experience of dynamics of a unity in duality. Then each step in the five steps described above could also be regarded as realizing or exemplifying a relevant but partial approach and access to understanding reality. Apart from comprehensive observation and direct and simple penetrating feeling, there are also understanding and thinking of reality by way of images. But so-called "images" are actually form-objects or process-events, which we may refer to as overt and ostensible (observable and feelable) phenomena in the world. Hence, they are not arbitrary mental fabrications but things couched in the thickness of world-reality.

As our experiences of things as images (*xiang* 象) can be said to be based on our feelings (*gan* 感) as responses (*ying* 应) to things that affect our perceptions or sensations and feelings in concrete contexts, they are related to our cognitive language on the one hand and to our idea-intentions of the mind on the other. Even though Wang Bi has argued that once one reaches images one can forget language whereas one can forget images once one reaches ideas in mind, there is no necessity of doing this Neo-Daoist transcendent thinking in the larger tradition of onto-cosmological and onto-hermeneutical thinking of the *Yijing*. Instead, one can see how events or things in the world on one side, image-language or symbols for naming and describing them in the middle, and mental activities in our ideas or feelings on the other side, form an ontological-hermeneutical circle and a creative unity of understanding and thus each of them cannot be logically separated. It is in this sense we can speak of a genuine ontological understanding or interpretation of reality. This understanding or interpretation of reality is no doubt always rooted and supported individually and collectively by a history of comprehensive observations, individualized feelings and holistic penetrating syntheses, which should eventually lead to an organically interrelated image of things.

From this point of view, we can see how the *Yijing* thinking is largely a dynamic, dialectical (as a dialogical and negotiating process), interactive and integrative process of thinking and understanding, neither fixing on objects as essences nor insisting on reducing things or presentations to the Husserlian phenomenological pure ideation. A critical study of the *Yi* Text has shown how the Chinese way of understanding and thinking does not focus on anything essentialistic *simpliciter* nor follow simply phenomenological methodology. Instead, it rather consists in letting reality speaking to us and in our learning from reality in concrete and yet context-transcendent and yet context-inclusive contexts. It can be therefore characterized as focal, contextual, trans-concrete, interrelated, and dynamic.

It would be no doubt useful and rewarding to show how the Chinese onto-cosmology in the *Yi* Text and the onto-hermeneutics model in the *Yizhuan* have shaped and contributed to later developments of the Chinese philosophical tradition. The onto-hermeneutics of the *Yijing* has functioned as a primary model in *benti*-ontology and onto-cosmology, but also functions as a primary model in form as well as in formless spirit. It is not so much a following, or imitating, or simulating as a genuine inspiration and a call for thinking and understanding in creativity that has guided and inspired the development of the long tradition of Chinese philosophy. In this sense, the *Yijing* provides an emancipating force toward an onto-cosmological thinking in face of an onto-cosmological reality.

We can point to the history of Chinese philosophy and show that the major trends of the development of the history of Chinese is guided, inspired, sustained, and enriched by this primary model of onto-cosmological and onto-hermeneutical thinking, knowing, understanding, and interpreting in the *Yijing*. To make our points, we can cite many telling examples: in the Han Confucianism of Dong Zhongshu, in the Wei-Jin Neo-Daoism of Wang Bi and Guo Xiang, in the Sui-Tang Chinese Buddhism of Tiantai, Huayan, and Chan, in the Song-Ming Neo-Confucianism of Zhou Dunyi, Zhang Zai, Shao Yong, Cheng Brothers, Zhu Xi, Lu Xiangshan, Wang Yangming, Wang Fuzhi, and finally in the mid-Qing textual Confucianism of Dai Zhen. Both the changing and unchanging elements, both identity and difference, both closure and openness, both conservatism and creativity, both tradition and modernity and even postmodernity can be so illuminated and illustrated. Even with regard to twentieth-century Chinese philosophy, one could not achieve a good and deep understanding without seeing it in light of such paradigms of ontological thinking and understanding in the *Yi* tradition. It remains a task to be accomplished in the future. In the spirit of cosmic education, it remains ever more a challenging and rewarding task to be accomplished.

CHAPTER 3

Interpreting a Paradigm of Change in Chinese Philosophy

Introductory Remarks on a Paradigm of Change

The phenomenon of change concerns many issues. We will first review how Greek philosophy starting with Heraclitus viewed the matter and then explore the response of Chinese classical philosophy. Heraclitus (535–475 BCE) offered his concept of change as a way of understanding reality. In his *Fragments*, he stated that everything is in a state of flux and claimed that no one can step into the same river twice. Heraclitus apparently explains change in terms of power of fire. Perhaps due to fire's power of generation and destruction, fire is considered to account for creation and destruction of things and in this sense fire is regarded as the natural cause of change. In a deeper sense, Heraclitus may have explained change or interchange of fire and all objects of nature as resulting of balancing of warring opposites such as cold and warm, or dry and wet, or path up and path down. The result of such balancing is called justice (*dike*) or perhaps harmony, but this overall justice or harmony does not prevent individual things to become what they are not such as the warm becomes cold and the cold becomes warm. What makes this justice and harmony possible is some hidden principle vaguely referred as "the word," or *logos*.

Heraclitus does not explain how *logos* works except to indicate that harmony is kept like a strung bow with its strung string in lyre. One may wonder whether *logos* maintains balance of things through a change of opposites or retains change through balance. What is important to note is that he would allow such a principle of balance or harmony to work among changes and thus may assume that *logos* functions like a law of nature or even the *taiji* and the *dao* of the *Yizhuan* or the *dao* of the Laozi and Zhuangzi. It is essentially a principle of unity with dynamical power of creating opposition and harmony at the same time. If an individual wants to lead a life of justice and harmony, she requires insight into the nature of this principle and must develop the wisdom of applying the principle of *logos* to follow it as it is given in nature. She must achieve a common measure and balance among conflicting forces of reality and life in a world that is both cosmic and chaotic (acosmic).

From this, we can see, among other things, that in some dominating aspects Heraclitus is much like Zhuangzi. Zhuangzi speaks of a reality that is "one moment living and another moment dying, one moment dying and another moment living, one moment agreeable, another moment disagreeable, one moment disagreeable and another moment agreeable."[1] Zhuangzi explicitly affirms that the "*dao* penetrates all things in unison" and that this oneness may be considered a harmony which sustains all opposing forces and yet makes them subject to an overall highly tight and strung interdependence on their own.[2] A human being must know the *dao* in a world of change so that he can identify with it to achieve inner peace and tranquility. That means that he should "affirm what is not affirmed, assert truth of what is not asserted true" and remain without arguing and debating. In this respect, we can detect a similarly pessimist or passivist mood in Heraclitus as in Zhuangzi. This is one reason I select Zhuangzi for immediate comparison with Heraclitus.

Although we do not have his philosophy in full, and though it is hard to decipher the full meaning of the fragments we do have, Heraclitus no doubt grasped one essential trait of change: change cannot be held back, and as such there are always new and fresh experiences of a new reality. Not only can we not step into the same river twice, but no *same person* can step into the same river twice.[3] Quine and others reject this position: we *can* step into the same river twice because we can characterize the same water and the same person under identifying concepts of divided reference. But this point does not negate the original insight of Heraclitus, namely that reality is sequence of fleeting moments that are experienced as such. We still can speak of having no basic essence, for things in nature necessarily are subject to change from what it is to what it is not. Hence a thing is both itself and not itself—a contradiction of the law of identity.

Aristotle rejects Heraclitus's denial of the law of identity and develops the view that change (*kinesis*) is a matter of real movement to be physically identified as locomotion in space, growth or diminution in quantity or alteration in property and quality, all to be explained in terms of his four-causes theory. Among the four causes, I believe that Aristotle would have to identify efficient cause for change in natural changes of form and matter of a living thing toward an end (*telos*), for change is to change into actuality of a thing with its proper form which satisfies its internal end. We can speak of a teleological theory of change for living things. But whether the whole world is to be seen as organic and living is a metaphysical question for Aristotle. Perhaps for nonliving things in nature change is merely movement following laws of nature to be determined by empirical inquiry. In general, change is seen as activities of things from a potential state of matter to an actualized state with form. Even locomotion of objects could be viewed as forms of realization of substantial potentiality. It is obvious that Aristotle does not stress the process of change as a macroscopic and cosmological principle in which all things are involved. The reality is a world of well-ordered hierarchy of sorts of things or substances with internal movements determined by relevant corresponding forms and ends. Since individual things are logically describable in terms of universal concepts, the law of identity is to be maintained at all costs.

In later Greek philosophy, one may see that the Heraclitean *logos* becomes God as an immanent principle in Stoics and finally appears as a transcendent principle in Christian Gospels as God who creates the world and orders the changes of the mundane according to some moral plan. In this manner, the Heraclitean model of change becomes completely transformed into providence of a supernatural power and loses its touch with empirical observation. In modern times, we can point to both Hegel and Whitehead as inheriting from Heraclitus a dialectical point of view on change, but they have devised two different principles and two positive plans for answering the question or issue of change: how is change to be described and explained? For Hegel, the *logos* or rather the idea or spirit (*nous*) is regarded as the ultimate reason for change in reality and change follows a dialectical pattern of thesis, antithesis and synthesis. The ultimate goal is to achieve comprehensive inclusion of all beings in an infinite order achieved by the movement of the Absolute Spirit. The net result is that Hegel has made our experience of change a matter of a subjective form of reasoning on the part of the Absolute Spirit and thus loses touch with change in an open world of experience.

As for Whitehead, in his book *Process and Reality* (1929), we see a grand synthesis of Plato, Aristotle, and Hegel in a generalized scheme of Heraclitean change. There is ultimately the great ultimate (called God) that comprehends eternal objects as innovative forms on the one hand, and implements change by way of a process of ingraining and concrescence on the other. There arises the metaphysical principle of creativity that explains how singularity and multitude of beings are possible and how things interpenetrate and interfuse by way of mutual "prehensive" feelings. It is interesting to note that Whitehead eventually came to see any being or actual occasion as a bipolar existence so that change can be ultimately explained or understood as reciprocal creative activities between the primordial (the subjective) nature and the consequent (the objective) nature of God. It is this eternal God that orders things through a creative process of change of many into one and one into many. At a time between Hegel and Whitehead, John Dewey speaks of the precariousness of reality in his book *Experience and Nature* (1925), noting the stable and the unstable in our experiences of nature. He could be closer to a philosophy of change if he focused on the creative nature of change apart from his concern with transactional relationships between the human and nature based on the human's own creativity, which is rooted in the creativity of nature.

From this brief review of traditional Western concepts of change, we come to see several important issues and problems of change. We see that, in Greek philosophy, there are polarities of change recognized, but they have not come to an ultimate synthesis in a macroscopic metaphysical philosophy of heaven and earth and their creativities for change and transformation. We see also that *logos* is conceived as arbiter of strife of forces but not necessarily and explicitly recognized as source of creation and sustenance. The question is why positive generative aspects of change toward life and positive creative forces of *yin* and *yang* are not equally stressed. Although Heraclitus approaches Zhuangzi in many respects, Zhuangzi may not negate a creative positive cosmology of Laozi. A major difference in Laozi and Zhuangzi is that in Zhuangzi humanity appears to have lost its creativity as co-creative partner of heaven and earth, as one finds in Laozi. In other words, Zhuangzi has taken a more receptive and passive posture than has Laozi.

Then, in Aristotle, we come to see a cosmic universe as a closed-in system of teleology controlled by reasoning of forms and ends, which seem to fence off or cone off a self-creative new world of open adventures. Finally, in the premodern to modern world of Europe, we come to see a creeping-in transcendent theology of a moral God for the accounting of change. This has been subjectified in Hegel's dialectical account of human history and objectified in Whitehead's process metaphysics. In neither is the process of naturalization of natural changes as both organic and inorganic changes made the dominating theme, although the scope no doubt has enlarged to include all we know about the world. In light of all these issues, we can now develop a more experiential, more comprehensive, and more human-involved and experience-directed philosophy of change in the texts of *Yijing* and *Daodejing*.

If one insists on raising the question as to why there is no similar development in the Western tradition, the answer is that there is an early foreclosure on comprehensive observation in a premature or predisposed theory of change as strife and harmony without relating further to another deep ecological source of nature and life. In other words, from my own understanding of Greek philosophy from Heraclitus to Aristotle, we must take into consideration the strong influence of Plato and Platonism, which looks down on change and takes off to a world of eternal forms perhaps under the influence of Pythagoras and Parmenides.

In the following I shall present the philosophy of change from the *Yijing*, *Yizhuan*, and *Daodejing* points of view with my integrative interpretation based on quoted texts from these three classics. I shall concentrate on five major points: (1) How is *Yi* (creative change) in *Yijing* to be understood, identified, and articulated in a system of *gua* or as a system of patterns of transformation? (2) How does macroscopic observation provide the base or foundation for understanding both cosmic change and human change as rooted in cosmic change? (3) How do we understand the order of the world as a result of action of principles of creativity and sustainability from a deep source of change? (4) How does philosophy of change become moralized in Confucius through the *Yizhuan*? (5) How does the *Daodejing* come to recognize a self-rooted Dao on the principle of creative change as creative voiding? Given answers to all these questions, we shall see how reality as a process of change produces an open universe of ever-renewing and ever-self-ordering with polarity and bipolarity on different levels. We shall also come to understand the facilitating role and value position of humans in a *yin-yang* and *dao* cosmos of change and creativity.

Yi in the Form of *Gua* System as Patterns of Transformations

The first important question is how should one come to understand change (*yi*) in the beginning of Chinese philosophy? Without a doubt I would say that one must take the original texts of *Yijing* and its Confucian commentary *Yizhuan* seriously. Despite the form and the language, one must see the organization of the hexagrams and their judgments as motivated and directed by a single vision of reality that gives meaning to the divinatory practice and makes divination a method for understanding human ends and desires in a world of contingent changes. One must see how vast and long-term observation gives rise to a single vision of unity of changes with basic patterns of change that eventually are organized into a system of *gua* (trigrams/hexagrams symbols of patterns of change and transformation).

With this system of symbolic forms, we are further enabled to see and experience change on different levels. We come to see how the natural world and natural changes affect us and our lives, and at the same time how we could also change the natural courses of change in our own world of human relations and self-sustenance from our own participation in changes. We see how patterns of change and transformations share a common and basic pattern and structure of movement, which we may identify as *yin* and *yang*. What are the *yin* and *yang*? In terms of their etymology, *yin* and *yang* are shadows and lights that one experiences on a mountain side and river bank. They are the most elemental experiences we have as human beings in relation to nature qua heaven and earth. But this elemental experience contains the pattern of change and transformation from opposition to supplementation to mutual transformation. They are not separable but form a unity of opposing forces and momentum as we watch how sunlight gives rise to darkness of night which eventually gives rise to broad daylight.

We also see how comparable forces or features similar to *yin* and *yang* can be said to manifest *yin* and *yang* once we understand *yin* and *yang* as deeper principles underlying phenomena of change. Those similar principles are soft and hard, rest and motion, having and not-having, and hence being and not-being.[4] This opposition of forces by absorbing relevant features of experience into our experience of *yin* and *yang* eventually makes *yin* and *yang* categories for explaining any relevant opposites in any major areas of experience. Hence, it is said in *Xici Shang* 5 that "conjunction and alternation of *yin* and *yang* is called the *dao*." The *dao* is the way how things are formed and transformed. This means that the world of things and their changes is a matter of movement of *dao* in terms of interacting functioning of *yin* and *yang*.

The *yin* and *yang* principles can also be extended to cover principles of virtues, as we can see how correspondences can be established between them. The second section of the *Discourse Commentary* (*Shuogua*) of the *Yijing* says:

> In the antiquity the sage creates the book of symbols of change for the purpose of conforming to the principles and reasons of nature and necessity (*xing-ming*). Therefore he established the principle of *yin* and *yang* for heaven, established the principle of soft and hard for earth, established the principle of benevolence (*ren* 仁) and righteousness (*yi* 义) for man.

Since *ren*, or benevolence, is a soft attitude in comparison with righteousness, *ren* is considered a principle of *yin* in contrast with *yi* as the principle of *yang*. But later in other contexts one can see that *ren* is considered *yang* whereas *yi* is considered as *yin*. This means that the *yin* and *yang* principles must be understood as norms or standards with meanings that other concepts must conform to in their multifarious applications and determinations. To acquire such meanings, one must form a whole onto-cosmological system of understanding bearing on the world as we experience in which *yang* becomes the principle of *Qian* (乾), the principle of power and creativity, whereas *yin* becomes the principle of *Kun* (坤), the principle of receptivity and preservation. Under such a system, we understand *ren* not merely as a principle of soft love and care, but as a principle of creativity and life giving, and hence it naturally takes on the dynamic quality of *Qian* or *yang*.

Similarly, under such a system, *yi* becomes a principle of preserving order of existence and has the quality of *yin* or *Kun*. This means that natural principles of change could be used as norms and standards of change could be used for understanding changes in human domains of moral activities. We shall explore this in a later part of our discussion. What is important to note here is that the formation of the *gua* (卦 trigram / hexagram) system as descriptions of patterns would naturally lead to perception of such as prescription of standards or norms for the purpose of providing a basis for justification for understanding and explanation of human behavior in the world. Such a moralization of nature took place in the middle of systematic inquiries into the nature of change by Confucius and his disciples in early fourth century BCE after the Yi Text had been used for divination for at least over 700 years.[5]

The question is how do we reach such a descriptive-prescriptive system of changes in *gua* in the first place? Ultimately, how can we come to see the world of change as a comprehensive unfolding of a diversity of things, including such places as heaven and earth and all that is between heaven and earth, as a continuous transformation of discrete phenomena, such as four seasons of the year, and as orderly presentations of all of the natural elements? It is not enough for us to see the elemental forces of *yin* and *yang* in interplay, but to see all possibilities of changes that could fall into an order or orders of changes. In other words, the *gua* system must embody principles of formation and transformation of *yin* and *yang* that would apply to all such possibilities of change.

Of course, in order to achieve this vision and understanding in a symbolic system, mere experience of individual things is not enough; one needs a process experience and understanding that would invoke intellectual insight into change as a process that we can generalize and quantify over all things in terms of the interplay of *yin* and *yang*. It is in such insight into change we come to the binary representation of all things in a structure of 2 to the *n*th power of forms based on *yin* and *yang* as two comprehensive numbers, 0 and 1. Although numbers or present-day numerals are not used, the signs of solid line and broken line such as "—" and "- -" serve the purpose of identifying *yin* and *yang* and give the *yin/yang* the capacity to represent all things and situations as directed combinations of solid and broken lines. The resulting system therefore has the following five features:

1. It is generative of all combinations of *yin* and *yang* and hence representative of transformations in a given situation or a state of affairs.

2. It is individually exclusive in the sense that any combination is unique on its own with its historical transformation background and anticipated possibilities of change.

3. It is collectively inclusive: all things in the world are theoretically included in such a system as all things are

either there or not there namely as *yang* or as *yin* or any sort of synthesis of the *yang* and *yin*.

4. It is an open system with both extendibility and reducibility as we can identify different levels of change orders in terms of the orders of 2. The present system of sixty-four hexagrams is just a convenient one we choose and develop on the basis of broad experience with a practical purpose.

5. It is an interpretive system that interprets reality on a chosen level of interpretation based on experience. In order to make interpretation adequate to the needs of explanation and prediction we need to introduce formal and informal rules of interpretation which are consistent and which can be a matter of induction and local insight. In other words, the system of *gua* is suggestive of ways of interpretation which are available in one's experience of the situation.

These five features should enable us to see how a system of *gua* comes to represent possible patterns of change and transformation that are also derived from interrelations on the level of basic alternations of *yin* and *yang*. Hence, any hexagram or *gua* in six lines is established on the basis of *yin-yang* interactions and would naturally give rise to descriptive forms by observation or to prescriptive forms by reflection. The whole system of *gua* is intended as descriptive forms but can be used as prescriptive forms that govern situations of human experience by interpretation and understanding. That we are able to do this is due to our ability to see and oversee things in the long and overall process of understanding by observation and feeling that the *Yijing* describes as *guan* (观) and *gan* (感). Traditional accounts have not paid attention to this important process of understanding and thus leave explanation of the rise of the *gua*-system in a vacuum. For our purposes, it is necessary that we understand this process as the epistemological foundation and source for understanding change as a system of transformations and formations that are taken for granted. It is this process of understanding change through observation and feeling that marks the primary difference in the Chinese philosophy of change as compared to the Greek view and the modern Western view.

Guan: The Macro-Epistemic Principle of Understanding Change

What, then, is the *guan* (观) as comprehensive observation? It is to look over all things in the nature and world in an extensive and comprehensive way so that we see things as a whole and as belonging to a whole as much as we can observe.[6] All things are emerging from this whole and presented in the whole. At the same time, one observes the rich differences of things and even their unique places in the whole scenario of things. Here we have the famous statement from the *Yizhuan* in reference to *guan*:

> In ancient time when Baoxi (Fuxi) reigned over the world, he observed the images in the sky comprehensively, he also observes the laws of things on earth comprehensively. He observes the patters of birds and beasts with regard to fitting in with their localities. He takes in things close at hand, and things far away. Consequently, he starts to draw out the eight trigrams, for the purpose of articulating his understanding of the powers of the divine, and expressing the state of affairs of a thousand of things. (*Xici Xia* 2)

Three matters emerge in this manner of comprehensive observation: namely, relationships of things in concrete locations and times, such as four directions and four seasons, and formations and transformations of things in time and space. Things are not only in a whole but also in a changing environment in which things also change. One sees the object, but one sees it in a connected background of all other things. Finally, one sees things in emerging patterns of order that are embedded in an even more generalized order of rise and decline that conforms to the ways in which the *yin* and *yang* interact. In fact, one will see how the *yin* and *yang* interact as two opposite sides of a unity that exhibit many possibilities of relationships and dependencies or interdependencies.

Since *guan* is an open process of experiencing the world, it does not lead to dogmatic beliefs. It is not the phenomenological reduction *á la* Husserl because it does not *bracket out* anything and does not lead to noetic images, but rather to phenomenal forms called the *xiang*. On the contrary, *guan* is to *bracket in* all things that one experiences and that one is capable of experiencing through observation. It yields to any presentation of phenomena in the world in a holistic manner and links it to the whole world of things, both things in space and things in time present and past. *Guan* does not privilege any observation over any other, but lets all observations fall into a holistic order in which differences and transformations are accommodated. Neither does *guan* separate space from time, and changes are observed as moving relations. This means one can see things over a long period of time and thus attain a more complete picture of the world of things.

The only thing we have not had experience of is the future: that is, we cannot experience future *qua* future and must wait for it to happen or else make it happen according to our action. Of course, we can imagine the future and make plans for the future. For making things happen in the future, we must know things present and past, and we must know ourselves and our abilities and their limitations. In this regard, we can see how an individual might witness how she could change the course of some change through her own action, and she is also able to see in what mode she is capable to initiate her own action. This again means that an individual is not only capable of observing the changes of the world but is capable of contemplating changes she could initiate as a human body or as a human person in the middle of things in which she is situated as an observer. Hence, *guan* is totalistic and inclusive of the whole of things, including objective things and humans complete with their relationships and actions.

This process of *guan* with comprehensive coverage endures a long time and thus requires a mind of calm and detachment. Perhaps one could also say that the ability to observe comprehensively leads to a mindstate of tranquility that makes comprehensive observation possible. In such a state of mind, the world is presented in one's *guan*, and the resulting *guan* hence can be said to lead to the formation and thus defining of a human self from contemplative or reflective perspectives. We may refer to this emerging self as the contemplative self.

In this process of comprehensive observation, we come to see a deep objectivity of things in their relations and changes, while at the same time we see a deep subjectivity of ourselves as humans, which allows us to see things in their deep objectivity. It is in this manner that we may come to see how we can contemplate the future directions of movements of things and how we can adjust ourselves or arouse ourselves for a feasible course of action toward a realizable goal. It is in this manner that all the symbolic forms of *gua* represent both objective patterns of change and subjective courses of action. There emerges in this understanding by *guan* a reflective unity between the subject of my person as a human agent and the world object as part of the whole. My selected course of action would naturally coincide with the open futurity of the world of things. The will in myself and the will of the future would have to converge in order to make things happen. Hence, this stance of *guan* presents an important insight into the onto-generative or onto-cosmological order of things because it underscores our basic native ability to know: it is not intellectual intuition focusing on a transcendent object but an empirical and yet intellectual grasp of the whole of experience, as much as we can make out, intended to cover all things in the world.

This is a form of macro-epistemology that has very important methodological significance; that is, *guan* is both epistemological and cosmological and as such is rooted in an onto-cosmological understanding that is part of the onto-cosmological scene and hence is reflective and self-observing. A human being is part of the universe, and his perceptions and understanding are therefore part of the universe. It is in light of these cognitive activities that he comes to see the universe as a whole and how his understanding stands as revealing the nature of changes of the world.

We may now see how it is through a state of reflective tranquility induced by *guan* between the world and the mind that one becomes innovative or creative. Although the texts did not establish a necessary link between *guan* and scientific knowledge and technological invention, it does not exclude such possibilities. In the *Xici* of the *Yizhuan*, after describing the process of *guan*, a list of inventions on the basis of reflection of the trigramatic symbols is given. Accordingly, the hexagram *Li* 离 gives rise to fishnet, the hexagram *Yi* 益 gives rise to plough, the hexagram *Shihe* 噬嗑 gives rise to market. One can see that invention includes concrete utensils and abstract institutions as well. In fact, the whole second section of *Xici Xia* describes how human civilization with cities and governments arises from learning from reflections on the results of *guan* and the suggestiveness of *gua* symbols reflecting *guan*. All these convey the impression and understanding that it is in the deep and comprehensive observation of nature (heaven and earth) that humanity steps into the orderly development of tool use and the rise of a whole civilization. This indicates that human language and thinking and reasoning together with its creative and productive activities are founded or derived from understanding of nature based on comprehensive observation. The *guan* could be finally described as interactive understanding between humans and the world. When we experience the nature and change of the world, we also come to experience the creative talents of ourselves as human beings.

World-Ordering: Creative Principles of Onto-Cosmology

The most important principle of change in the world as revealed by the *guan* epistemology is the principle of *yin-yang* alternation. As the basic modes of perceived pattern, *yin-yang* distinctions, relations of their mutual completion and mutual enhancement, and their generation by opposition and eventually their joint production of novel things in the world are among the most brilliant observations of the *Yijing* initiators. It must be said that it is only in the context of enduring observations across the whole macroscopic magnitude of heaven and earth that the *yin-yang* pattern is to be seen as so fundamental that one has to say that it governs both creation of heaven and earth and transformation of all things under heaven. In this sense, we have to see *yin-yang* principle as a *principle of creative co-creativity* as it involves an insight into the creative activities of the *yin-yang* movements in things. The *yin-yang* principle is thus not a matter of bipolarity but of bipolarization—a way of realization of reality such as exemplified in the quantum physical phenomenon of "vacuum polarization."

As the *Yizhuan* defines it, *yin-yang* is to be seen in soft-hard, bright-dark, moving-rest distinctions and relations. These are subtle movements of nature, but they form a relation of dependency and generation and hence embody the impulse of creation and production as we see in the relationship of heaven and earth, sun and moon, male and female, and the rotating seasons. It is a matter of observation and analogous reasoning that we could identify the *yin-yang* relationship in the quantum world and biological sphere apart from the macro-phenomenon world of material things.

In the *Yijing* we see the fundamentality of the principle of *yin-ying* polarity in the first two hexagrams of *Qian* and *Kun*, which have been described through translation as the Creative and the Receptive.[7] These translations are basically correct except that we must understand that the receptivity of *Kun* is also part of the cosmic creativity I refer to as co-creativity. That is, one has to see creativity as a phenomenon in the *Yijing* as involving many levels and many aspects of change. Thus we may call *Qian* the positive creativity, whereas we may call *Kun* the receptive creativity, for it is in *Kun* that we find provision of nutritive elements and support for substantiating impulses of the *Qian* that provides initiative motive power for creation. The togetherness and mutuality is to be explained in the notion of the great ultimate (*taiji* 太极) one finds in section 11 of the *Xici Shang*.

The importance of introducing the concept of *taiji* is that it points to a source of all the changes starting with the generation of the *yin-yang* as represented by the hexagrams of *Qian* and *Kun*. One must notice that the concept of *taiji* is formed on the basis of all the changes observed by the sages, which could be used to explain the generation of all changes. In this sense *taiji* is the principle of ultimate creativity underlying the principle of creative co-creativity of the *yin-yang*. It inspires and enables the sage to be perceptive and be creative as well. It would become a foundation for the capacity of understanding of sage in regard to his understanding of the wishes of people and thence would provide plans for developing human deeds of culture and achievements and lead people out of doubt.[8] In this sense, *taiji* is also the *dao*, which not only alternates between the *yin* and *yang* but penetrates into all things and human plans and actions.

It is said in *Xici Shang* 11 that "the Changes have the great ultimate, which generates the two norms [of *Qian* and *Kun*]. The two norms generate four images (*xiang* 象) and the four images generate the eight trigrams." This statement is intended to describe the symbolic texts of the *Yijing*, which reflect the patterns of generation of changes, but it can be also understood as a description of the cosmogonic process of reality, which becomes the foundation of the well-known discourse on the *taiji* written by Zhou Dunyi (1017–1073) in the Song Period. It shows that there is an ultimate beginning that leads to the differentiation of beings by way of polarization, which moves on to produce all things in the world. Two points must be quickly noted: first, the polar differentiation indicates that all things are deeply related and united, like the *yin-yang* in a whole, and in this sense *taiji* is also the uniting and integrating principle. One sees that in the formation of the *gua*, it is the principle of integration of the lines of movements that produce individual situations and, for that reason, events and things. Second, the *taiji* is a continuous creative force and hence the sustaining force for the process of multiplying things. One notices insight into such a character of continuing and sustaining creativity in statements such as "The creativity of creativity (*shengsheng*) is called the change" (*Xici Shang* 5), and "*Qian* and *Kun*, are they the nexus of the change? When the *Qian* and *Kun* are ordered, there is the ultimate and whole creativity (*Yi* 易). If *Qian-Kun* are destroyed, there is nothing to present the ultimate and whole creativity. If the ultimate and the whole creativity cannot be seen, the *Qian* and *Kun* would be extinguished" (*Xici Shang* 12).

One can see how the creativity of creativity—namely, the ultimate creativity of the whole, which is *taiji*—is conceived as the ultimate foundation and fountainhead of the changes and orders of things in the world. Here we see a philosophy of cosmology in creativity presented in the texts of *Yizhuan* (apart from *Xici* there are the important texts of *Tuan*, *Xiang* and *Shuogua*, and *Xugua* and *Zagua*) based on observations and interpretations of the *Yijing* as well as the actual observation of the natural reality as presented by the symbolic forms and system of the *Yi* Texts. This philosophy of creative cosmology is not just a theoretical interpretation of the texts but the result of experience of actual observation of reality as described by the texts, which in a sense were made possible by the use of divination which requests one to confront a changing universe and a changing world of life.

Because the *taiji* is ever present in the generation of things in the world, this universe is not a completed order of things independent of changes or time and space. It is ever creatively generated and remade or retrieved, as described by Zhuangzi. It is a universe full of creative life with its creative potential to develop or encounter difficulties. It takes a creative insight into the whole process of changing to resolve difficulty and produce innovation. Insofar as the human mind and intelligence are able to comprehend the world, its directions and potential of change, the human individual is also capable of making creative changes and resolving difficulties of life, which will be discussed later. For now, I want to note the *taiji* as the origination of being of things and *dao* as the procession of advance of things: whatever comes into being is a contribution to the becoming of the world as continuous origination and sustenance.

There is no separate being from beings as creatively generated in the whole process of becoming of things. Even when we do our own thinking, this thinking cannot be separated from our experience of life and reality as activity. Hence, there is no separate metaphysics of being from the cosmology of origination and evolution. It is thus important to see ontology as a reference to being in the context of actual becoming, so we must speak of cosmo-ontology (being as emerging from cosmic changes) in reference to onto-cosmology (cosmic changes initiated by origination of being) and vice versa. The term "onto-" must refer to the originating function of *taiji*, whereas "cosmology" refers to the realization and presentation of polarity of *Qian* and *Kun*. In this manner, we may simply come to speak of an "onto-generative cosmology" based on a "generative ontology," distinct from ontology as traditionally conceived in the West.[9]

With this understanding of onto-cosmology, we must note that we can still speak of the invisible *dao* and the visible *qi* (器 utensils or things) without thinking of them as separate or separable. The whole world of things is the whole world of the *dao*, and the whole world of the *dao* is involved and penetrated through and through with all things (as well as each individual thing) in the whole world of things. With this understanding, it is humans who are able to cultivate the *dao* for inducing and transforming *qi* and for developing *qi* to push forward the *dao*. The *Xici* describes this as "to transform (*hua*) and make a controlled decision it is called the change (*bian*), to move and promote it in action it is called going through (*tong*)" (*Xici Shang* 12).

Concerning the question of transcendence, we must distinguish *transcendence simpliciter* as a separate position from *transcendence as continuous creation*. One must also distinguish the absolute transcendence we would never know and the relative transcendence of moving into different and higher stages of development. Although the onto-cosmology of *taiji* and *Qian-Kun* is not a philosophy of transcendence as a separate position, it may be asked whether it may have a source beyond the reach of all things but that serves as the condition of the emergence of the *taiji* itself. This is the idea of *wu*, or emptiness, as introduced in the *Daodejing*. It is said in the *Daodejing* that "the *dao* gives rise to one, one to two and two to three and three give rise to all things" (chapter 42) on the one hand, and that "all things under heaven are born from being (*you* 有) and being (*you*) is born from emptiness (*wu* 无)" (chapter 40), on the other. One may see that if we take oneness and also *you* (being) as referring to a state of the *taiji*, or even as a function of the *taiji*, we may feel that there is a prior state before or leading to *taiji*, which is *wu*. In this case, do we have a transcendent state apart from the *taiji*? The answer is that we need not conceive in this way, for the *dao* or the *wu* are still to be experienced or embodied in the oneness of being and the *taiji* as a source even though we can also conceive it as an aspect of the *you* or the *taiji*.

In essence, we may speak of two ways of conceiving the relation of *taiji* as *you* to *dao* or to *wu*. In one way the *wu* is an aspect of functioning of *taiji* that gives rise to *you*, whereas *you* is another aspect of functioning of *taiji* that gives rise to *wu*. In this sense, all things are subject to both being substantiated and being emptied and there is no priority of *wu* before *you*, as indicated by Laozi's statements "*you* and *wu* mutually generate each other" (chapter 2). In another way, we may see that *wu* or *dao* subtly provides momentum of change and transformation of things and therefore in one sense it is the independent condition and source of *taiji*, and in another the underlying and immanent foundation and resource of the *taiji*. We may call this relationship "immanent transcendence" or "transcendent immanence" in order to indicate the seeming paradoxical functioning of both and neither between the *taiji* and the *dao*: *taiji* is the source aspect of the *dao*, and *dao* is the process aspect of the *taiji*, as I have discussed elsewhere.

We have no space to detail on the symbolic system of the *Yi* as given in the received texts of *Yijing*. What needs to be remarked on is the logical nature or mathematical nature of such a system that embodies potentially infinite possibilities of transformations of one state to and from another. Although in the actual *Yi* Text, only sixty-four *gua* are presented, there are potentially infinite *gua* on different levels of configuring the reality. These are needed because our experience of change and transformation based on the long process of *guan* as overseeing and being overseen as whole or as parts of the whole makes necessary the requirements of presentation of such elevating and ascendable complexity in such a way. It is ingenious of the authors of the *gua* to devise such a way of symbolic representation that reflects changes we experience and changes we could experience on a practical level.[10] Each presentation of a situation in a *gua* involves a special configuration of lines with special features of position, direction, and movement. This gives rise to the numerology of the *Yi*. Many scholars from Han on have focused on numerology for the purpose of predicting or calculating events for political or personal purposes. But they may commit a fallacy of losing sight of the changing reality as one must experience in one's own person. With this changing reality and with the changing circumstances of one's life, it is only fit to explain and predict changes not simply on rigid forms and numbers but in light of living forces of reality. This means we must go beyond numerology to understand change, and hence that to understand change involves a reconstruction of one's experiences of change in light of the onto-cosmology of *taiji* and the *dao* as symbolized in the *gua* system.

To understand change is therefore a matter of integration of experiences in both form and content based on observation. This shows how deep and wide observation could become the source of understanding of patterns of nature and natural inclinations of human beings. One comes to see that it is through *guan* we are able to establish an order of nature and an order of myself as a knowing and acting person. It is through such a process that human reason for knowing is born and human wisdom for action emerges.[11]

In connection with the issue of *taiji* and transcendence, we need to explore a little into the significance of *Tuan* 彖 *Commentary* on the *Qian* hexagram. It says, "Great is the *Qian* as the originator, all things depend on it for their beginning." Then it says how the way of the *Qian* (*Qiandao*) changes and transforms so that all things will find their natures with their destinies well placed and thus cherishing and preserving the primordial harmony (*taihe*)" (see *Qian Tuan Commentary*). In the *Tuan Commentary* for *Kun*, there is mention of the *Kun* as the originator that all things would depend on for living. The commentary also mentions how Kun follows submissively the *Qian* power as the leading power. Most significant in these two commentaries is that *Qian* and *Kun* are apparently two functions of the *taiji*, and as such they must function together to preserve primordial harmony. What is primordial harmony? It is the source from which both *Qian* and *Kun* come and thus the ultimate reality behind the two. Is it the *taiji* itself, or something underlying *taiji* that proves the creativity of the *taiji*. In either case, we see what is behind *taiji* is to be realized in *taiji*, which may receive a title such as *wuji* in Zhou Dunyi's discourse on *taiji* or *Taixu* in Zhang Zai's essay *Zhengmeng*. It is something intimately connected with *taiji*, but it is at the same time the source of infinite creativity for *taiji*, and it can be preserved in the supreme harmony of *taiji*'s creative activities and productions; hence, it acquires the title "supreme harmony" (*taihe* 太和) in Zhang Zai.

In light of the above, we come to see the world as not just a random process of arbitrary and contingent movements, but as a creatively regulated world of events and things interconnected both internally and externally. It is indeed a world of contingencies, but it need not be regarded as always perilous and "precarious," as John Dewey has claimed.[12] It is a world of deep harmony with creative tensions among transforming forces of things and events. It is a world of creative harmonization from which human beings can learn and develop thorough understandings and active participations. It is in this light that we can speak of the creative principles of world ordering: namely, the *taiji* principle of origination and the *dao* principle of accomplishing. In essence, these two principles can be seen as embodied in the principle of *yin-yang* and function on the basis of conjunction and alternation, opposition and complementation, being and nonbeing. We could, on the other hand, see all reality as an open field of creative forces sustained by the ultimate creativity of creativity (*shengsheng* 生).

Thus far we have answered the question of how we can rely on *guan* as a way of discovering the patterns of change and how such a discovery shows us we are involved in and confronted with a reality that is neither fleeting nor static, but is rather a world of changes with nonchanges that can be revealed in patterns of stability and ways of transformation among things as well as our own selves. We found that *guan* shows a world capable of being molded and changed by ourselves, but also a world in which we need to change and transform ourselves in light of the world of things. This leads to the answer to the second question, namely the question concerning the position of human beings in the world of changes. It is a question related to a need to explain why human beings are capable of achieving great deeds and making creative changes in the world.

Confucian Moralization of Change and Creative Cultivation of Humanity

It is important to point out that *guan* has an implicit aim of practical action. For one could assume that as a biological species, humans must act according to their understanding of the world in order to survive and to avoid harm and extinction from inutile passivity. Accordingly, they must discover early on that only through viewing and observing the world as a whole[13] can they know how to identify, orient, and transform themselves by transforming their environment and acting in accordance with each other, or the group or community as a whole. But there are many things out of sight of individual persons, and the most important concern is the future since future means possibilities of change and transformation. In order to act, one must find one's location in the whole scenario of the world as determined by *guan* and our feelings toward it.

To find one's location in the world of change is the reason divination was invented. In my explanation of divination,[14] I have pointed out time and again that divination in an advanced stage must depend on a map of locations to be presented by the *guan* understanding and hence by a map of possibilities captured in the *gua* forms.

Since the future is not determined and holds multiple possibilities of development, there is worry, misgiving, and even anxiety over one's fortune to come. Hence, divination becomes a tool for identifying directions among possible actions and can serve as a guide based on a comprehensive overview and appraisal of a situation against a background of the whole scenario of the world. The more comprehensively and more coherently the relationships of things are revealed in a world vision, the better the ground for making such divinatory decisions will be. On the other hand, with the practical needs for divination, one requires larger and deeper observations of the world and examinations of the self and their interactive relationships. Hence we can also say that *guan* contributes to the development and the use of divination as a practical tool for advising us about what to do in the future, whereas the continued practice of divination contributes to our understanding of the world and of our own selves as practical agents in an increasingly fuller and richer picture of the world as full of the possibilities of change. In the end one can see how *guan* eventually surpasses divination and leads to an independent worldview in terms of which one can cultivate oneself for adaptation and transformation without use of divination.[15]

As the world is seen in a process of generation and development, human beings are naturally seen as parts of the world of heaven-earth-and-man and therefore are also involved in a process of generation and development. But with human intelligence and capacity to know, human beings could bring changes and transformations through self-conscious efforts and actions. It is in this spirit that we see how divination has been invented and how a philosophy of change based on results of divination is developed. What is essential to this process of development is the understanding that both world and man are contingent on each other and could expect to co-determine each other in the formation of a more determinate world and a more determinate human self. With understanding, the divinatory judgments for *gua* and lines of the *gua* are written with the presupposition that human beings can change the world, just as the world can change human beings.[16]

Interpreting a Paradigm of Change in Chinese Philosophy   79

Both the world situation and the human self have potentiality for development, and there is no end to a continuing transformative process of both the world and the human self. It is in the actual encounter between the world and the human self both the world and the human self become determined and defined. This means that at any time the polarity of world and human beings can be discerned such that the human being knows his potentiality and his limitations so that he could make a choice for his development. The point is that there is no absolute freedom, just as there is no absolute determination. It is in recognition of this limitation and potentiality of human beings that we can adjust to the world and can also make attempts to reach our best at different times of our lives.

It is interesting to note that many of the *gua*, if not all the *gua*, are named after certain contemplated actions to be performed by the human person. For example, the twenty-fourth *gua*, the *Fu* 复, which sees no problem of going out and coming in, carrying no blame of the arrival of friends: "Repeat many times the same way, so by the seventh day there is return and there is advantage in doing some action." This judgment can be seen either as specifying certain sorts of activities or as specifying no specific action at all in a period of seven days. Hence, the human person can do many types of things within this general framework. Another *gua*, the forty-ninth *gua*, the Ge 革, observes that one acquires faith upon the completion of a task: "This shows the prosperity of the originating source and it is advantageous to persevere." There can be many actions that can bring back faith on completion, and this implies that one could start reform and revolution in a given situation. This means one must see such reform or revolutionary action as a task to complete in order to find a new identity of faith. We can indeed try out many *gua*, including the first *gua*, the *Qian* 乾, where one is advised to start with a task that is prosperous with effort and through which one can attain a good result through perseverance. In the lines of each *gua*, different stages or types of action can be attempted or avoided. There are possibilities for maneuver created by a situation and at the same time limited by the situation. Each individual is encouraged to recognize her situation and to find potential advantages, or to avoid potential disadvantages, through potential action or nonaction.

One may question whether there is real freedom of human will in regard to this philosophical purview of the relativity of human action and an identifiable configuration of a situation of change. The answer is twofold: (1) there is no imaginative freedom or absolute freedom in any sense independent of choice; and (2) there is no absolute choice of anything apart from a concrete and real situation of change. Freedom requires the openness of space allowed in a situation as well as the potential ability to make choices and to follow through with regard to a self-designated end concerning the whole life. In this sense, we have freedom at any point of our life given that (1) we are presented with different possibilities, both objective and subjective possibilities, in a world of change, and that (2) this world of change is creatively developed through the interaction of the subject with the object and through interaction of the whole with the part.

Another point to be observed is that the human situation and human abilities are considered as derived from natural situations in the onto-cosmology of change and the evolutionary transformation of nature. Although the world is highly contingent and highly creative, there is also a high degree of freedom in human choice and human self-transformation. In the Confucian commentaries (the "Ten Wings"), we see clearly how the hexagrams are given both a naturalist and a humanist interpretation. It is obvious that the *Yijing* authors in forming the sixty-four hexagrams saw them as emerging from the primitive eight trigrams of natural forces. This could mean that humanity is regarded as a creative development from nature. There are thus two approaches to understanding humanity: (1) the naturalistic and hence more reductive approach, and (2) the humanistic and more moralistic approach. In the *gua* judgments, we can perceive how the former implicitly identifies a naturalist environment for the latter, which identifies what issue or problem a human person may face in this life in such a naturalistic environment. The dual aspects of a situation are first brought out in the *Tuan Commentary*.

Apart from this, there is in the *Xiang Commentary* another form of contrast: the naturalist description of a situation and a moral lesson to be drawn from reflecting on the situation. How is this possible? The answer is that given the naturalist description of a situation, such as the *Qian gua*, one can reflect on the situation in one's mind and identify human capacities and desires with eminent features of the situation, which would give a positive human meaning to human action relative to a human end. One can command oneself to pursue such an end or to form a rule of action which would enrich one's life or improve and strengthen it.[17] Thus for the *Qian* case, the *Xiang Commentary* says that [since] the heaven moves vigorously and ceaselessly, the self-ruling person (*junzi*) should likewise strengthen himself without cessation. This goes for all sixty-four of the *gua*, in which the *Xiang Commentary* always performs the action of moral normalization of a natural process with the implicit assumption of a corresponding humanization of the natural process. Such being the case, one sees how an individual can have free action and free choice on the level of human emergence, which leads to moral attribution and moral action. This may be regarded as another form of creativity: the creativity of meaning and significance derived from a given holistic observation of change outside the individual and from a given holistic reflection and feeling inside the individual.

We can thus see how cosmic changes might take many creative turns that lead to the naturalization of the contingent, the humanization of the regulative, and the moralization of the norm. One may even see this as both a matter of natural evolution and a matter of human evolution. The human being has from the very beginning participated in the cosmic creativity; therefore, he has within himself a natural creativity of advancing himself to the level of moral creativity. Thus, we must see (1) that moral creativity is a matter of natural creativity just as our moralization of nature is also a naturalization of our morality, and hence (2) that our ethics and morality are derived from and based on an onto-cosmology of creative formation and transformation. Nevertheless, we cannot simply say that the universe we confront is a moral universe, as people tend to see in reading *Yizhuan*, given that the thrust of *Yizhuan* as a collective work of Confucius and his disciples lies in realizing the deep harmony of the world of change together with realizing the deep harmony of our nature, which brings out morality of good from such realization. In other words, the universe of change is a creative universe from which we have learned and from which we will continue to learn in order to achieve our identity as moral and intelligent human persons. As Confucius sees it, this moral creativity of a person should lead to a development of collective world of humanity in terms of *ren* and *yi*, as mentioned above.

Immediately following the statement on the *dao* as an alternation of *yin* and *yang*, the *Xici* says: "What is inherited from the *dao* is good, what is completed in *dao* is nature" (*Xici Shang* 5). This means that because human beings are emergent from the *dao*, the nature of the human being is good, and so-called human nature (*xing*) is a natural creative result of cosmic change. In the holistic context of understanding, what is called "good" is no other than what leads to fuller and more prosperous and firm development of human nature. One may even suggest that to be naturally developed and capable of realizing the nature is good. "Good" is therefore what brings out the potential of creativity with which one can realize one's intrinsic end and utilize the possibilities given in a situation. This does not deny that good can be a matter of realization in a series of progressive pursuits in one's life which becomes eventually confirmed as the ultimate end or value of the person. It is in this sense that good is to be seen as great deeds achieved or a great virtue accomplished. The virtue (*de*) is the capacity for bringing out the creativity in a person, and it is also the power to renovate and reinvigorate the human person in realizing its end given in his nature. In this sense, we can see how human beings are related to the cosmic reality of heaven and earth as two sustaining polar powers of cosmic creativity:

> The great man is one who joins his virtue and power with heaven and earth, joins his illuminating light with sun and moon, joins his orderly action with the four seasons, joins his ability to achieve good fortune and avoid misfortune with spirits and deities. What is thus determined by *a priori* performance even heaven cannot violate. What happens afterwards must just follow the timely determination of nature (heaven). These are the norms which heaven would not violate. How could man violate them? How could spirits and deities violate them? (*Qian Wenyan* 乾文言)

From this quotation we can see that in the full development of the human creativity there will be ultimate harmony in the world of change, for it is in human creativity that the creative harmony of change will be fulfilled, just as heaven and earth will transform this world of things into an ultimate state of supreme harmony. It must be noted, however, that harmony is not an abstract idea but much more a concrete term referring to a state of prosperity and well-being suitable for sustaining life.[18]

The ultimate harmony is therefore the primordial state of prosperity and well-being, which can be continued and developed or be discontinued and destroyed. It makes good sense to say that the stipulation of the *Qian* as *yuan* (元 origination) / *heng* (亨 prosperity) / *li* (利 advantage) / *zhen* (贞 perseverance) are forms and ways of indicating the presence of a primordial harmony. Here we must also note that it is on the basis of this original and ultimate harmony that we can speak of the *ji* (吉 auspicious), *xiong* (凶 inauspicious), *huo* (禍 misfortune), *fu* (福 fortune) which characterizes the language of early morality. What is revealing is that the misfortune, the fortunate, the auspicious, and the inauspicious are the early experiences of morality, as morality is to be considered most relevant to realization of human life. In this context, one can see how harmony 和 is related to the state of the auspicious and fortunate, and disharmony to the state of the inauspicious and misfortune.[19]

Once we see how *ji* and *xiong* lead to creative prosperity and destructive privation, we can say that one is morally good and the other is morally bad, namely in the sense in which the morally good is universally desirable and life-preserving, and the morally bad is universally undesirable and life-destroying. We may even mark out emotions associated with these two states and use them for identifying these two states. It is in this fashion that we come to transform these two premoral states into indexes for desirable states of what is morally good and undesirable states of what is morally bad.

We can also see how this idea of moral good and bad extends to others in the same community given that their well-being can positively affect us and their ill-being can make us feel insecure and doubtful about our future. In essence, whatever gives us feeling and hope for well-being is good, and what renders us deprived and despairing is bad. It is in this sense that we come to realize *good* as a rich and thick concept that can apply to many things in life.[20] We finally come to an idea of supreme good (*zhishan* 至善), which extends to all people under heaven in realizing the state of universal well-being as a state of universal harmony that would be considered the realization of the primordial harmony as a source. It is in light of this moral understanding that we come to see morality as realization of the *dao* in the participation of *dao* by means of individual *de*. It is not accidental that the Chinese term *dao-de* 道德 as composed of both *dao* 道 and *de* 德 is used to stand for morality. That we are capable of performing actions of *daode* is considered the creative power of creativity (*shengsheng*). It is this power that is experienced as the essence of defining the change and transformation of both the cosmos and man.

Confucius comes to realize the creative power of creativity when he speaks of *ren* 仁. For him, *ren* is both *dao* and *de* and hence the *de* from *dao* and the *dao* realizing the *de*. We can see this realization of the *dao* and *de* in his explanation of *ren* as a deep experience of humanity as creativity.

Confucius did not define "will" nor the "good" that the will can will. But in his reflections we see what a person could will, and that in his willing, a person becomes what he is, and his willing confers worth on actions done accordingly. Confucius says: "Is *ren* remote from me? If I desire *ren*, then *ren* is here" (*Analects* 7.30).[21] This important statement shows that the desire of virtue based on no physical desires nor pertaining to any particular interest can be said to be a will in the Kantian sense of free will and good will; however, such a desire (will) has as its object in *ren*, which is not to be exclusively defined but rather be explained through reference to Confucius's own words. What is *ren*? Though there are many meanings, the most significant is the following: "Yan Yuan asks, 'What is *ren*?' Confucius replies: 'To discipline oneself (*keji*) so that one could practice *li* is *ren*. If for a single day one is able to discipline oneself and practice *li*, the whole world will return to *ren*. To do *ren* comes from oneself, how could it come from others?'" (*Analects* 12.1).

It is clear that to discipline oneself (*keji* 克己) is to control one's desires and emotions and thus to reach a state of intellectual and spiritual freedom, where one is not bound by one's physical desires so that one can freely practice the *li* which are rules or maxims of what the right thing to do is. In this sense, *ren* does not depend on any other condition than one's willing. In other words, it is the good that does not depend on any other things but only on the will of oneself.

Ren is not an empty word—it represents an ideal of harmony that one can reach through acting according to the rules that makes harmony possible. Although one can bring harmony to the whole world by acting on good will, the world is subject to change. Therefore, in order to sustain goodness in the world, it is necessary that one cultivates oneself without cessation; and this should enhance the possibility that the good will prevail over the whole world. Here we may conclude that the Confucian moralization of cosmic changes provides both a base and a challenge for the self-cultivation of the human agent. The realization through comprehensive observation that the world of change is a world of creative generation of life could be said to have inspired Confucius with the idea of *ren* as the source of universal humanity, which can be realized only in a world of creative change with a devotion to self-cultivation of one's self in emulation of cosmic creativity.

Renovative Insights from *Daodejing* on Cosmic Changes

In the *Daodejing* 道德经, we see a vivid description of how harmony develops from forces of formation and transformation: "All things hold *yang* and shoulder the *yin*, and they reach harmony by the pushing and pulling of the *qi* 气" (*Daodejing* 42). Here, Laozi focuses on the actual processes of reaching harmony and indicates that harmony is achieved naturally by activities of the *yin* and the *yang* forces. It is a state of balance and integration through mingling and conjoining, not free from a sense of conflict and impact as active *qi* shows. For Laozi, what is important in change is this process of struggling for an equitable resolution. It is specifically realized that, because there are many conflicts, we come to value harmony and that, because we lost the *dao*, we come to speak of benevolence and righteousness. What he sees in the world is the result of an underlying force called the *dao* which gives rise to a multitude of things.

In this sense change as formation and transformation of things must be regarded as deriving from as an underlying force as such. Thus, he says: "The *dao* produces one, one produces two, two produces three, three produces the ten thousand things" (DDJ 42). Here we see a parallel statement similar to the *Yizhuan* speaking of the *taiji* producing two norms and two norms producing four images and four images producing eight trigrams. But here we deal with a more abstract metaphorical description: the one stands for the *taiji*, the two stands for *yin* and *yang*, and the three stands for productivity of the *yin-yang* from which all things arise as a matter of fact. In this regard, Laozi could be said to transcend the *Yijing*'s symbolic system of trigrams and hexagrams in seeking a more metaphorical expression of the onto-cosmological insight of origination and development. With this formulation of the origin of the world, we see several important insights of Laozi regarding change as a factor of reality.

First, in identifying the one with the *taiji*, Laozi has freed *dao* as the ultimate concept or notion which refers to the ultimate reality. *Dao* produces the one and should not identify with the one, similarly for what is produced by one, etc. In this sense, *dao* is not being but instead the void (*wu*) that is emptied of being. As empty, *dao* is regarded as the inexhaustible source of being of heaven and earth and everything, as we can see from section 6 of DDJ: "The spirit of valley never dies, it is called the profound female. The gate of the profound female is the source of the heaven and earth. It lasts and endures invisibly, and there is inexhaustibility of its power in use" (DDJ 6). This suggests that it is because of its being void it is capable of producing all things. Hence, we have to think of the *dao* as both empty and not empty and this makes the *dao* inconceivable and unspeakable in concepts.

This is precisely what the first sentence of the DDJ suggests: "the *dao* which can be spoken of is not the constant *dao*." The constant *dao* is that which gives rise to change, and yet is itself not the change just because it is the change. In this regard we have a notion of change in *dao* which transcends all the symbolic system of forms in *Yijing* and yet contains a dialectics of development by self-transcendence and self-denial. *Dao* is both *you* 有 and *wu* 无 and in order to give rise to *you* it has to constantly *wu* (DDJ 40). We can see *you* and *wu* as verbs of making being and making nonbeing, namely as *you-ing* and *wu-ing*. It is through self-denial of *wu-ing* that we have continued *you-ing* by integrating both the *you* and *wu* which is equal to denial of *you* for *wu* and denial of *wu* for *you*.[22]

That *dao* gives rise to *you* or the *taiji* is considered a matter of spontaneity (*ziran*) by Laozi. Laozi specifically speaks of the *dao* as "following the *ziran*" (DDJ 25). But what is *ziran* 自然? It is occurrence without specific reason or specific cause. As a concept, *ziran* is the natural state that supports all other states but is not supported by any state. It is just what it comes to be spontaneously without any specific cause. The idea of *ziran* is further explained by nonaction (*wuwei* 无为) which means that there is no effort nor intention for such action. We may therefore express this idea of *ziran* as self-existence and self-presentation or self-occurrence of anything. We have to understand it by accepting it as it is but not by relating any other concepts. In this sense of *ziran*, we see how changes can come naturally and whatever change presents are also natural emergences which we should accept and accommodate as parts of our life.

With this *ziran* described as *wuwei*, Laozi comes to see creation of all things in the world as a result of *dao*'s nonaction which can be described as: "Give birth to but not having it; nourishing without holding one, growing it without dominating" (DDJ 10 and 51). In this sense, Laozi wishes to reach for a state of *dao* (or ultimate reality), which is prior to all events and which will lead to all events with no desire to possess or control. A world of change is thus supported by *dao*, which will naturally resolve in harmony and peace without any strife and effort. Hence, one may say that *dao* is constantly actionless, and yet because of this nonaction it has acted on all things.

Finally, we should come to know *dao* in another respect: "To return to the origin is the movement of the *dao*, weakness is the function of *dao*" (DDJ 34). Although the *Yizhuan* speaks of the *taiji* as the great ultimate from which all things are derived, there is no suggestion that all things return to the origin. It is Laozi's insight that all things will return to its origin. It is said, "All things emerge together, I shall watch their reversion. For all teeming things, each will return to its root" (DDJ 16). This could mean that all things will return to the state of *wu* because *wu* is the source from which all things are generated. This means that all the changes in the world could be seen as both generative and degenerative, both moving forward and moving backward, both substantiating and emptying. This is not to say that change must be circular or cycling; rather, the creative activities of the *dao* consist of two phases: coming and going, which could be seen as mutually generating each other so that new life will forge out in such a way that the universe is constantly renewing itself. This could be also seen as a new way of understanding or interpretation of the meaning of the *gua* of Completion 既济 and of the *gua* of Incompletion 未济. The Completion indicates a return to the source whereas Incompletion suggests an ongoing form of life.

With this Daoist insight and new understanding of change, Laozi envisions a new role for the sage in regard to how to govern his people. The advice is nonaction: one will do nothing so that everything will be done of its accord. This is to apply the *dao* to the case of political rule. In fact, to follow the *dao* is to let things emerge without guiding them, to give rise without having them, to nourish without domineering, and to complete without claiming credit (DDJ 2 and 10). In this fashion, it is trusted that the *dao* will spontaneously enable each person to complete his living potential without interference from outside forces if one is one with the *dao*. It is to reduce the conflict of competing forces to the minimum, or perhaps to the nonbeing of the *dao*. For the individual human being, Laozi suggests the motto of "reaching for the ultimate of void and abiding by the ultimate tranquility" (DDJ 16). This is indeed a far cry from the Confucian positivism in the moralization of change for the purpose of self-actualization and self-fulfillment.

Concluding Remarks: Truth and Trust in the Change

From the above analysis of the idea of change in the Chinese tradition, we see how a profound paradigm of change (yi 易) has developed and undergone three basic stages of transformation in the formation of the onto-cosmology of formation and transformation of things. In the formation of the *Yijing* philosophy of change, one sees that comprehensive observation of changes provides a source and inspiration for an understanding of both world and the human self in deep harmony and consonance of mutual responsiveness. This leads to the Confucian transformation of the laws of nature into moral challenges of human renovation and moral understanding. It forges the relation between the cosmic and the human in a much challenging way. Finally, we witness the Daoist view on transformation of change which leads to a detached and yet inclusive point of view.

Change is an inevitable fact and part of life; it is up to each individual to transcend local change and devote oneself to the collective and social transformation of the people as a whole. In all these aspects the Yi paradigm of change stands out conspicuously in the world against a background of Western philosophy of change beginning with Heraclitus and Aristotle and continuing with Hegel, Whitehead, and Dewey that can be fruitfully compared with the philosophy of Yi.

The importance of Yi in the Chinese tradition lies in the fact that reality is experienced as an open process with deep creativity and comprehensive scope which the human person must learn in order to become what he can become. In such a learning process, it is not only that the truth of the cosmic that becomes presented but that the truth of human existence also becomes realized. There is no other way of understanding such truth than experiencing and embodying the principles of change which have been called the principles of creativities in the original *Yijing* text and the interpretive Confucian *Yizhuan*, in both Confucian reflections and in Laozi's speculative insights.

No less important is the unique message from the Yi paradigm of change that the truth of the cosmic and the truth of the human existence are based on deep experience of reality and yet lead to a trust in the human person, and consequently the trust in the cosmic as carrier of the truth of change, namely the truth of formation and transformation as realization of creativity in both the forms of change and the trust of the human in the cosmic and the reverse. We see that the *Yi* Text first assures us that originating leads to prosperity and that prosperity leads to advantage and perseverance in trust and faith. Then we read in the *Daodejing*: "The Way as a thing is merely there and yet not there. In being there and being not there, there is the form. In being not there and being there, there is the thing. In being dark and profound, there is the subtle something. This subtle something is most real and true, and that is where trust lies" (DDJ 21).

CHAPTER 4

Inquiring into the Primary Model

Yijing and Chinese Ontological Hermeneutics

The Question of Chinese Ontological Hermeneutics

Hermeneutics is often thought to be a modern Western concept that focuses on studying the methods (in a broad sense) and principles of hermeneutical interpretation of texts and the related subject matter embodied in the texts. During the beginning of the nineteenth century, early hermeneutics was cultivated as a set of principles of interpretation of texts by thinkers such as Friedrich Ast.[1] It was not until the middle of the twentieth century that Hans-Georg Gadamer developed hermeneutics into a philosophy of humanistic understanding without specific reference to texts.

Hermeneutics—or philosophical hermeneutics, as Gadamer called it—is simply a philosophical exploration into how understanding arises in a human subject in reference to a subject matter. Gadamer argued that all human undertakings in the humanities and sciences belong to the domain of philosophical hermeneutics. In his book *Truth and Method* (1960), Gadamer inquired into the major fields of human understanding, such as art, history, and language, as well as science and practical and moral philosophy. Gadamer's major thesis was to establish the "universality of hermeneutical experience." For Gadamer, hermeneutics is a universal discipline bearing on human understanding and interpretation, although human understanding and interpretation occur in historically situated concrete contexts.

Habermas objected to Gadamer's position.[2] For Habermas, scientific knowledge is considered a reflection of reality without involvement of subjectivity that is bound with hermeneutical experience and interpretation in language. I believe that Gadamer made his strongest and perhaps most important point during his encounter with Habermas: even in scientific constructions, we cannot escape raising questions that are hermeneutical in nature. Thus, even scientific construction could be questioned in the interest of an understanding based on an effective historical reflection of its finitude and open-endedness.

As I see it, this leads to an urgent need to develop a hermeneutics from an even more profound basis or root, namely, hermeneutics as a way of understanding the world both phenomenologically and ontologically at the same time. This no doubt implies that we must concentrate on how our use of language to describe a given phenomenon may open up to an understanding that goes beyond the present form and meaning of the language. This new understanding, nevertheless, could feed back to enrich the meaning of the given form of language. In other words, language becomes creative when our minds become creative as energized by our encounter with the language of texts as well as our experience of the world.

There is no doubt a strong hermeneutical tradition in the history of Chinese arts and humanities inclusive of literature, history, and philosophy. But how to characterize this important tradition becomes itself a hermeneutical issue. This is because our understanding of what constitutes a hermeneutical understanding is hermeneutical. In other words, our understanding is subject to different interpretations and is therefore subject to different changes in interpretations under different circumstances and from different perspectives. However, all interpretations, no matter how different, are founded on some underlying paradigm or model of understanding reality and truth. Perhaps it is in the nature of interpretation and understanding that an appeal to an understanding of reality and truth always is made. This understanding of reality and truth is simultaneously the source of meaning and the driving force for seeking understanding. Without such a reference, no understanding and no interpretation can be made.

Thus, we can speak of the Chinese hermeneutical tradition as basically *ontological*. To understand and to interpret is to appeal to this underlying ontological hermeneutics (onto-hermeneutics), or the onto-hermeneutical understanding of reality, for the actualization and validation of a specific interpretation in a specific situation that we encounter in our understanding. As such, we have both elements of change and elements of constancy in the hermeneutical tradition, which are integrated to give rise to many philosophical and ontological hermeneutical texts.

To characterize this singular phenomenon of ontological interpretation of a text in a situation, we may use the words of *Yiwei Qianzuodu* 易纬乾凿度[3] in its description of the concept of change (*Yi*): "Change is change (*bianyi*), no change (*buyi*), and simplicity (*jianyi*)."[4] This suggests three stages and three levels of hermeneutical understanding: on the surface there are received texts, which reflect a given understanding of a subject matter that is open to interpretation; then there is the subject matter of which interpretations can be made or are required to be made; and finally there is the ultimate source from which interpretations are made and in view of which justification of interpretation is made.

How we describe this ultimate source is interesting to examine. In my reflections, it can be identified as a primary model or way in which any interpretation is to be made. This ultimate source also can be identified as the preunderstood or presupposed experience of the ultimate reality in the hermeneutical tradition. Thus, it may be suggested that the Chinese textual and philosophical hermeneutical tradition frequently changes, but some standard of reality and truth remains basically unchanged. The way in which the tradition accommodates changes conforms to the need for minimally preserving the underlying structure of the tradition. A resulting question, therefore, is what are the unchanging elements and changing factors in the Chinese hermeneutical tradition and what factors could link the two and integrate them into a systematic, unified understanding or vision of understanding in an ontological hermeneutics.

If we can speak of an ontological hermeneutical tradition, can we speak of developing an ontological hermeneutics for the tradition? In this case it should be asked: what is ontological hermeneutics? Is it a closed concept hidden in the hermeneutical tradition or an open concept to be constructed from the tradition? This last question is very important because it suggests that the very notion of ontological hermeneutics must presuppose an antecedent or a correlated notion of an ontological hermeneutic tradition and vice versa. One cannot obtain without the other, and they form what I would later refer as an onto-hermeneutic circle. In a philosophical exploration then, hermeneutics should not be confined to a mere phenomenological account of the hermeneutical practice, but instead could be established as a theoretical construction or reconstruction of the ways and means in which a hermeneutical practice and tradition has been carried on and implemented. This notion of hermeneutics also could ascend to the level where ontological reference to both the subject and the object in a unified experience of the ultimate reality requires clarification. Ontological hermeneutics or onto-hermeneutics is precisely such a way of understanding or interpreting in which reference to the ultimate reality is implicitly presupposed or is explicitly made.[5]

Based on this broad preunderstanding of hermeneutics, we can see how an ontological hermeneutics arises from a hermeneutical tradition first as a theoretical reflection and second as a metaphysical or ontological reflection and justification of such reflection. In this light, one also can see how a hermeneutical tradition could change with time and history and yet retain its fundamental identity or integrity in reference to reality, for this reference to reality is the ultimate way to provide the identity and integrity in a context of changes according to time. In light of this and the above understanding of hermeneutics as a broad open concept, we come to see how a variety of forms of hermeneutical understanding and a variety of historical developmental patterns have been embodied in a single cultural tradition.

There need be no surprise that the Chinese ontological hermeneutical tradition should give rise to a theory of Chinese ontological hermeneutical understanding or a Chinese ontological hermeneutics; this is just like the Chinese philosophical tradition giving rise to a theory of philosophical understanding or Chinese philosophy. This is not to deny that there are common traits and even common principles shared by both Western hermeneutics and Chinese hermeneutics. But the temporality and historicity of each construction also provide a basis for exhibition and the sustaining of a difference. Again, this is not to say that contributions to a universal or universalizable onto-hermeneutics could not be made from each theory and each tradition. As a matter of fact, it should be recognized that it is only on the basis of difference that a contribution to a totalizing or integrative theory could be fruitfully made.

Chinese hermeneutics may be considered vastly different from Western hermeneutics. In light of the theoretical and abstract nature of modern and contemporary hermeneutics in the West, one can readily see that Chinese literary and philosophical traditions may not have anything systematically comparable to the hermeneutical theory in the West.[6] This vast difference may cause some scholars, when confronted with the problem of Chinese hermeneutics, to feel at a loss because they are not able to identify a Western pattern of hermeneutical understanding in a large Chinese context; hence, they are tempted to declare that there is no way to talk of Chinese hermeneutical theory with regard to understanding and interpretation of Chinese traditional literary and philosophical texts.[7] Yet, it is evident that the development of Chinese humanities is marked by a strong ontological hermeneutical tradition in the sense that a concrete and direct practice of ontological hermeneutical interpretation is heavily engaged. Hence, it is meaningful to speak of the Chinese ontological hermeneutical tradition in Chinese learning even without any systemized formulation of Chinese ontological hermeneutics or onto-hermeneutics.

This position is apparently acceptable insofar as there is no theory of interpretation proposed throughout the long Chinese philosophical tradition. But this does not mean that hermeneutics as a self-conscious form of proposing and justifying interpretation is not consciously entertained by Chinese minds in their activities of interpretation. The way that Chinese scholars and philosophers did their interpretative work conscientiously and persistently suggests that they have a hermeneutical preunderstanding, and they could have theoretical hermeneutical insights even though they may not have systematically formulated them afterwards or beforehand. This means that this scholarly effort is based on an abiding awareness of some basic hermeneutical issue as a heritage and as a challenge.

Hence, one may simply argue that the very way Chinese hermeneutics functions is different from its Western counterpart and that the two traditions represent two different modes of understanding and interpretation, which need not to be conceived as immediately incompatible or incommensurable. Further, one need not be reduced to the other or made to substitute one for the other.[8]

Here we come to something that harkens back to both Plato and Heidegger on the one hand, and the *Yijing* on the other; it is that which I have chosen to call "onto-hermeneutical."[9] In this light, the movement from tradition of *exegetical* interpretation to philosophical interpretation and to onto-hermeneutical interpretation represents a process of emancipation from a given tradition, a text, and a given form of language so that the tradition, the text, and the form of language could be renovated and enriched. In the West, such emancipation has taken the discipline of philosophical hermeneutics beyond exegesis. Now we can do the same for Chinese philosophical and ontological hermeneutics in bringing out the principles of understanding beyond exegetical practice. We also can look forward to embracing and incorporating methodological insights of exegesis, the subject-oriented reflective insights of the Gadamerian philosophical hermeneutics, as well as the analytical constructive theories of scientific and logical knowledge into an integrated theory of human understanding relative to our interpretation of human existence and reality. This we may title the onto-hermeneutical or ontological hermeneutical enterprise.

Rise of the *Yi* Text from *Guan* and *Xiang*

In the following I shall concentrate on the key processes of observation, divination and interpretation in the construction of the primary model of interpretation in the *Yi* Text formation as the foundation and beginning of the Chinese hermeneutical tradition.

How does the *Yi* Text or *Yijing* arise and form itself?[10] To answer this question one needs to look into how the formation of earliest *Yi*-symbols and names could be explained in terms of human experiences of the world, which contain nature, the individual, and interactions between nature and the individual. It seems obvious that the trigrams, as an organized set of symbols, stand for salient natural events, processes, and structures of nature as we observe them. There are eight trigrams (*bagua* 八卦) because there are eight major and dominant natural phenomena and processes that have been observed as central to our understanding of the natural reality. Not only are they central to our understanding of nature, they are observed and considered to be foundations and resources for all other concrete events and processes of nature.

The eight phenomena-processes, as represented by the trigrams, also are observed to be derived from or constituted by even more basic forces or processes that correspond to our experiences of the general and pervasive qualities of the world. Hence we can speak of our experiences of *yin* (shady 暗) and *yang* (bright 明); *gang* (firmness 刚) and *ruo* (softness 柔); *dong* (motion 动) and *qing* (rest 静); empty and substantial, potential and actual, progress and regress, and up and down as basic dimensions of events (such as fire and water) or structures (such as lake and hill). Even heaven and earth are said to be observed to have those features that we normally experience in concrete feeling and actual situations. Based on those experiences of qualities (qualia) of events and things, we may reach more generalized notions of *yin* and *yang*, which can apply to all experiences of qualia in their polaristic contrast and dynamic interdependence.

These notions of qualia-experiences could be said to be represented by the ancient *yin-yang* symbols: — — and ———. These symbols indicate experiences that are open to distinction, differentiation, and classification into further similar types of experiences. Additionally, a principle of relativity is built in, for example, whatever is soft is relative to a chosen standard of softness on a scale of comparison. In this way, these two generalized qualia symbols are primary symbols of experiences of reality; they register our experiences of the world in whatever way we happen to experience, such as locally, regionally, globally, particularly, generally, this moment, this period, or this era. As primary symbols of qualia, they also are iconic and indexical; they represent some configurable features of reality with a sense of impact or force. In fact, the symbols can be explicitly described as signs of the movement and the nature of *qi* or natural vital force. Insofar as we can be said to experience *qi*, *qi* is a natural substance-process of reality. We experience it in terms of our qualia-experiences such as dark and bright, soft and firm, moving and still.[11]

Now, given the primary symbols of experiences of reality (*yin-yang*), the eight trigrams can be said to be composed of these primary symbols in terms of certain internal *qi*-relationships. These trigrams are further components of larger configurations of events and processes; we can build from them by way of certain natural and logical principles. Sixty-four hexagrams are thus constructed as a sequence of correlations and oppositions resulting from holistic thinking. Of course, we need not stop at sixty-four hexagrams, but it seems that for empirical reasons the set of sixty-four hexagrams represents an adequate set of basic human conditions that we can understand and manage with ease. Here we see the Principle of Simplicity at work, which we find in the "threefold meaning theory of the *Yi*" in the *Yiwei* 易纬 works of the late Western Han. The Principle of Simplicity holds that it is rational and useful to describe and handle reality in the simplest way we can, without losing sight of the totality and the comprehensive scope of all things and events. In other words, what are presumed as changing and nonchanging must be represented in the simplest system of signs we can devise so that we can read meanings of signs and act on our understandings of situations.

The system of sixty-four hexagrams is precisely such a system. It can be said that it is a representation of reality at a level consistent with our needs and capacity of understanding. On the other hand, the system also contains subsystems such as that of eight trigrams. In this sense, insofar as eight trigrams form primarily a system of natural symbols, the sixty-four hexagrams form primarily a system of human-natural symbols that can be given both naturalistic meanings and human or humanistic meanings, including psychological meanings as their extensions.

As a system, we need also to remark that the eight trigrams and sixty-four hexagrams are organically interrelated to form a web of networked meanings. This is a reflection of the interrelatedness of things and events in human experiences. One thing leads to another by way of transformation and change and there are many forms of change and transformation. In these changes and transformations new meanings and new situations are realized. It is up to the human mind, the interpreter of symbols, to make out meanings and tendencies in those changes and transformations. But as an intended objective description of natural and human-social processes, formal and logical rules could be given, for these are ways in which a human mind could self-regulate. All in all, we see the system of image-forms-symbols formed in the process of observation of nature and in the experiences of organizing our observations on nature and ourselves. This system is formed during a long process of natural and historical observations that need not be confined to a single person or time. On the contrary, what is involved in the organization of observations belongs to a group of people and is intertwined with the progress of culture and technology.

Based on my own archaeological observations, I propose that the process of observation pertaining to the formation of the *Yi* trigrams and hexagrams may well have begun in the late Neolithic period when we see the invention of fine tools from jade and animal bones.[12] It is also the time when sheep became domesticated and nomadic tribesman began to settle down to raise cattle and cultivate fields. In this light we can then justify the story of Fuxi. This is because the name "Fuxi" 伏羲 suggests that sheep have been domesticated. The story is one of a culture hero who, among other achievements, had engaged in observations of nature and invented the system of primary symbols of our experiences of nature; consequently, as culture and community evolved in more advanced and sophisticated forms, he invented the system of eight trigrams and possibly the sixty-four hexagrams.

We may quote from *Xici* to describe this process of comprehensive observation as a source of inspiration for the formation of the *Yi* symbols:

> In the ancient time when Fuxi reigned in the world, he observed heavenly forms upward and observed regularities of

earthly things downward. He observed the patterns of shapes and habits among birds and beasts and their fitting environments on earth. He gathered information from nearby things as well as from distant objects. Consequently he started to make the eight trigrams for the purpose of penetrating into the powers of the divine and the clear and in order to sort out things according to natures (true states) of the ten thousand things. (Xici Xia 2)

Based on what I have described above, the creators of the Yi symbols took a naturalistic approach to the question of the formation of Yi symbols. This naturalistic understanding leads us to stress the importance of *comprehensive observation* (*guan*) and the consequent contemplation of organic relationships of things in nature and in our social and cultural lives. The formation of Yi symbols also did not occur at one single time, but required a long period of time to allow for adjustments and to achieve a neatness and simplicity that would cover the totality of nature and life at the same time. We see that it is the Principle of Comprehensive Observation and the Principle of Simplicity at work that leads to the choice of the *yin-yang* symbols as a basis for the formation of the eight trigrams.

What is noteworthy is that the Yi symbols were designed to capture the subtle and minute changes of the world/reality as well as the resulting overt large phenomena of the world. It is intended to be both comprehensive and exhaustive so that no small change will be ignored. It is also intended to register the internal changes within a situation or process as well as external changes in an open context of relationships. Hence, there is also a third principle at work: the Principle of Dialectical Development. This principle indicates how the system of symbols and its interpretations or implications of meaning (both connotative and denotative) are expandable in insofar as persons have experiences of nature and life in a growing and expanding process. It is this principle that leads the development of eight trigrams into sixty-four hexagrams with the subject matter of the eight trigrams fully incorporated in the structure of the sixty-four hexagrams.

The Practical and Logical Relevance of *Bu* (Divination)

Now we may consider the philosophical significance of divination in the formation of the interpretation of the symbols of the Yi Text. Although we have no idea how divination started, we could speculate on the basis of the *Yizhuan* to illustrate how divination started as a desirable practice toward seeking well-being of the individual. In one passage it is said, "The flourishing of the *Yi* (symbolism), was it at the time of middle antiquity? The author of the *Yi* symbols, did he have a profound anxiety" (*Xici Xia* 6)?

As we have reason to believe that the *Yizhuan* was formed in the hands of the first generation disciples of Confucius, what was referred to as middle antiquity must refer to a time of flourishing of human civilization that could be anytime from the Yellow Emperor (twenty-seventh century BCE) to the beginning of the Xia Dynasty (2100–1600 BCE). What is more important to notice is the implicit statement on the (existential) feeling condition of the creator of the *Yi* symbols. The profound anxiety (*youhuan*) here means worry and misgiving about an uncertain future that may prevent the fulfillment of the well-being of an individual. That future is uncertain because the world reality is subject to change and transformation, and we do not know when, where, how and what change may take place. This uncertainty no doubt reflects our deficiency of knowledge of nature. It also reflects our unconscious misgiving about the complexity of the human condition and human mind.

What is assumed as desirable is to have knowledge of the nature of a given situation; what is also desirable is a trust in the virtues of human agency. If we have any understanding of what a given situation may involve and implicate, as well as how things may move in a field of dynamic forces, we are able to adjust our action to avoid disasters and to pursue benefits. The question is whether we can ever come to know this. Even though an individual may have acquired a rich experience of life, and a community may have accumulated a wealth of wisdom on what to do under certain conditions, there are still other conditions and situations where and when we are at a loss. That is to say, one is not always certain as to what to make of a situation, or as to what would be the right action to take, or the right decision to make. Hence, the uncertainty and indetermination of the future is a real thing for us to inquire into; it is a real issue for us to deal with.

In light of this analysis, it seems clear that divination is adopted as the art of understanding the future by understanding and interpreting what a given situation is and what it holds for us in terms of good and bad, good fortune and misfortune. In order to make divination meaningful, one must appeal to God or spirits for revelations or to find a logical or scientific way to read the future. In the case of the divination using the *Yi* Text, there is no mention of appeal to God or spirits. In fact, in the very development of the *Yi* symbolism as an onto-cosmology that reflects states of nature and hence states of human lifeworld: appeal to God or spirits are rendered unnecessary. It is assumed that one can simply read the *gua* in order to understand a situation.

The crucial problem of divination becomes one of deciding which *gua* to choose to represent a given situation. How to choose it (and how we justify our decision) becomes the central difficulty to be overcome. There is no direct reply to this question. The only answer is that by following an established method of divination one would naturally come to a *gua* that would be a symbolic representation of the present situation relative to our question or goal of inquiry. But one can still query why such a method of divination might yield a correct answer. We may ask what distinguishes one method from another in its ability to yield a correct *gua* or a picture of the present world.

In the *Xici*, we have a description of a procedure on how to form a *gua* by manipulating milfoil stalks in a certain ordered way. It is interesting to note that this procedure is founded on the onto-cosmology of the *Yi* philosophy: there is the *taiji*, and *taiji* gives rise to two forms of *yin* and *yang*, which would generate four seasons and then the days of a whole solar-lunar year. It is by calculating numbers of the milfoil stalks in their mimicking the cosmic generation process that one comes to define a *gua* line by line. But still one can ask why this decision procedure must yield a true image rather than a false one. Here a diviner may have to appeal to some naive faith that this process will reveal the reality of a situation and one must trust one's virtuous action to deal with the situation. To make this come true is to fulfill the helping power of the divine (*keyu you shen yi*).[13] The quote from Confucius says, "If one knows the ways of change, could he know the doings of the divine" (*Xici Shang* 9)?

In fact, the logic of divination consists in probable knowing under restrictions of a given situation. This logic would say: if one genuinely does not know a situation and one must make a decision, then to decide one way or another would have the same probability. To divine is to find a point of contact with reality so that one may make a relevant decision in light of some induced interpretation of a situation. The *gua* yielded by the divination provides an aid for anchoring oneself in a situation so that one can relate or organize all relevant information around the *gua* in order to achieve a reasonable answer and make a responsible decision on action. Divination, therefore, becomes a practical way of fulfilling oneself in certain critical conditions of life. To divine is to find a way of justification for understanding and action. The logic and morality of the situation require one to generally adopt the wisdom of doing things with caution, patience, consultation, and readiness to respond to changes in accordance with faith in virtues and trust in a natural order of complementation, reversal and balance. In this sense, divination becomes a way of negotiating one's understanding of a situation, a way of reflection and a way of rallying one's spirit and intelligence. Divination becomes a matter of practical understanding and a process of developing one's practical wisdom.

There are two other ways in which divination is to be justified. One has to do with the doctrine of "feeling and response" (*ganying*). In section 10 of the *Xici Shang*, it is said, "The *Yi* system is without thought and without action. It is still and without motion. But [once it is put to divination] it will have direct feeling and thus will penetrate to the causes of all things. If it is not a most divine thing, how could it do this?"

It is clear that the direct feeling must come from the diviner using the *Yi* system, and the feeling must be based on recognizing the nature of a situation. This way our foresight and insight into the changes of the situation could be manifested. But how could a diviner come to possess such a divining (foreknowing) power? Of course, he must know the given situation in a certain way; he must know what to divine for, and he must have a way of telling the future trends by relating the moving forces in a situation. But there is still no guarantee that his judgment will be foolproof. But what then is required is he must be warranted in formulating judgments about future trends of a given affair and about what good and bad might result. In order to do this, according to the *Yizhuan*, what is most essential is the ability to see minute and inceptive forces of change in a given situation and the related ability to draw correct conclusions in light of knowledge of the situation. It appears that what is relevant is understanding and experience of similar cases in the past. One can learn from trials and errors of the past, knowledge of the relationships among things and forces in the world, and the way things normally develop according to principles of dialectics of change as disclosed by the total system of the *Yi* symbols.

This then leads to a second way of divining the future *via* the concept of sage (*shengren*) in the *Yizhuan*. It is the sages who have come to have an understanding of the people, their ambitions and their desires, and an understanding of the numbers and dialectical changes in light of how all things move in a total system. It is in this way that the sage will be able to detect and determine which situation is which and identify the image of a situation without divination. It is said:

> The sage has seen the complex things in the world and imaged them in forms and symbols. Thus those forms and symbols are called images (*xiang*). The sage has witnessed the movements of things and observed how things meet each other. In performing a proper ritual, he can append his judgments of fortune and misfortune to lines of the *gua*. This is called judgments (*ci*) to the lines (*yao*). To tell the most complex things without disliking them; to tell the most subtle movements of things without confusion; to imagine before speaking; to reflect before acting: It is in imagination and discursive thinking that the sage can detect and make changes. (*Xici Shang* 8)

Although a proper ritual is mentioned, here one sees only small appeal to divination. Perhaps one can see divination as a ritual that the sage must experience for its ritualistic importance. But what is actually required is that that the sage has a genuine and sincere way of understanding things. And this way consists in observation, minute perception, simulation, reflection, and discursive thinking, not in blindly following a ritual. One can further see that in the *Xici*, for the most part, the authors are arguing for taking the way of changes directly and using the *Yi* symbols as tools or mediums to fathom the subtle changes. It even suggests that the reason we can tell changes is that things are imaged in the symbols, things at large must change according to large principles while particulars of change in a concrete situation require close monitoring and awareness. The action of divination is to discover what minute beginnings of change things in a situation could have. It is advised therefore that "a superior person at rest will contemplate an image-form (of a situation) and study its judgment, and in motion will observe the changes of the image-form and study its divination" (*Xici Shang* 2). So far, the divination could provide a clue for the future in the absence of evidence to the contrary, and it provides an occasion to reflect on one's capabilities and their limitations; hence, it provides an occasion to cultivate and nourish one's virtues of patience, persistence, perseverance, and good faith.

Of course, what is assumed here is that the *Yi* Text has been systematized and a correlation of meaning between form-images and judgments are aligned; hence, it represents an ideal manual for reference when needed. With familiarity with such a system one can make educated guesses and inferences by way of association of experiences and analogical-metaphorical understanding.

Systematization and Interpretation

In order for the sage to recognize the true nature of a situation, the *Xici* has developed an explicit onto-cosmology, as explained in chapter 3, where the being as source of creative development of the world to explain and justify the existence and meaning of the *gua* was disclosed. This onto-cosmology is essential and effective for understanding the depth of meaning of the *Yi* symbols so that one may even say that it is hidden in the mind of the inventor of the symbols of the *Yi* Text. The following statements from the *Xici* largely indicate how this onto-cosmology is conceived and how it becomes a basis for global interpretation:

1. "One *yin* and one *yang* is called the *dao*" (*Xici Shang* 5).
2. "Therefore, the *Yi* system has its *taiji* (the great ultimate). The *taiji* produces two norms. Two norms give rise to four forms, and four forms produces eight trigrams. The eight trigrams determine what is fortunate and what is misfortune. By considering the fortune and misfortune great deeds are produced" (*Xici Shang* 11).
3. "The creative (*Qian*) and the receptive (*Kun*), are they the source and resource of the *Yi*? When *Qian* and *Kun* are presented in order, the way of change is established therein. If *Qian* and *Kun* are destroyed, there is no change to be seen. If one cannot see the changes, there is extinction of the *Qian* and the *Kun*" (*Xici Shang* 12).
4. "What is above form is called the *dao*, what is within form is called the vessel" (*ibid.*).

The *Yi* symbols and the *Yi* Text, which embody the *Yi* System, have all the above ideas hidden or present in their images, judgments, and interrelationships. These ideas become explicit as if emerging from the *Yi* Text. But being explicit and articulated as a philosophy of reality and cosmology makes a difference, namely, the onto-cosmological philosophy of the *Yi* becomes itself a system and an object of understanding, thinking or consideration. It is a movement from phenomenology to cosmology and ontology or onto-cosmology, for it recognizes changes are parts of the ultimate reality. Of course, it takes a human mind to make this happen. But the point is that unless the substance of the thought is implicit, the explicit statement could not easily arise as a result. In the words of the *Xici*, "the language of judgment is such that it designates what it designates" (*Xici Xia* 3). It is because the *Yi* symbols have designated what they have designated, and the authors of the *Yi* Text have indicated what they have experienced that the authors of the *Yizhuan* are able to bring out the subject matter of the *Yi* symbol system and formulate the underlying onto-cosmology.

This onto-cosmology is further developed in the *Tuan Commentary* (*Tuanzhuan*), which has focused on the *Qian* 乾 (creative) and *Kun* 坤 (receptive) as two creative sources and brings out their onto-cosmological significance. *Qian gua* (creativity) is to stand for the *Qian yuan* (source of creativity), and *Kun gua* (receptivity) is to stand for the *Kun yuan* (source of the receptive). As such, *Qian* and *Kun* become two primary forces that give rise to all forms and eventually give rise to all things. They themselves no doubt form a unity that would stand for the *taiji* (the great ultimate), as it is said that the change between *yin* and *yang* requires a source that is to be called *taiji*. This seems to be an elaboration of the *Xici*'s basic idea of the alternation of *yin as receptive* and *yang as creative*. The *Wenyan Commentary* follows the *Tuan* in elaborating the moral side of the creative power of *Qian* and *Kun* as two creative origins. There is also the *Xiang Commentary*, which strives to preserve the form-image side of a *gua*. The *Xiang Commentary* also introduces the principle of moral implication and projection as a principle of interpretation. It is in the *Xiang Commentary* that all *gua* are seen and rendered to give moral instructions. This means that any image or *gua* will naturally carry a moral meaning; it is up to the individual to make this moral meaning clear and relevant.

Here we see the composite nature of the notion of *Yi*. This notion contains interplay, interformation, and an interpenetration of form and activity, intention and reference of language, understanding and what is being understood. The *Yi* emerges as a creative force in both nature and humans (feeling and human mind), which leads to the formation and transformation of both things and persons. As a result of comprehensive understanding this same *Yi* also gives rise to a symbolic system (a text) for representing and understanding formation and transformation of things in *Yi*. Thus, any reference to the term *Yi* may suggest a primary experience of change, the experienced form and process of change, the force of change by itself, and the symbolic text representing the change based on our experience of change. All these meanings and references, however, are integrated in the comprehensive notion of change, which I refer to as the onto-cosmology of *Yi*.

The onto-cosmology of the *Yi*, as I have discussed elsewhere, bears on the theoretical understanding of *Yi* as the ultimate and primary nature of creativity and as reality. This reality is further simultaneously presenting itself as a cosmogony and cosmography of things and individuals. It also is disclosed in the understanding of nature and reality as both being and becoming, as both the ultimate and the beginning, as both nonchange (or constancy) of change and change of constancy, as both permanence and motion, as both oneness of a comprehensive power (creativity) and myriad of things from such a creative power. This onto-cosmology of *Yi* is first formulated in the *Tuan Zhuan* of the hexagram *Qian* and hexagram *Kun*, which gives creative power to all things and individuals. It is also discursively presented in the *Xici* and other commentaries of the Confucian School after the fifth century BCE. In the 1973 Mawangdui Silk Manuscript it is suggested in the *Ersanzi Wen* 二三子问 (*Several Disciples Asking*), *Xici* (*the Appendix*), *Yizhiyi* 易之义 (*Meaning of Divination*), and *Yao* 要 (*Essentials*). We may simply call this onto-cosmology of *Yi* the "Onto-cosmology of Proto-Creativity," for we can conceive *Yi* as simply creativity-from-creativity and even further creativity of creativity.

With the onto-cosmology of the *Yi* system thus formulated, one can interpret any given *gua* not only in terms of its judgment but also in terms of all the judgments of all *gua*, for *gua* are themselves seen as correlates and complements of each other in an ordered system. Moreover, one could interpret the judgments in the terms *gua* form as well. Whether one takes forms as the primary reference or takes the judgments as the primary reference, one could make an interpretation of a given situation in light of the underlying philosophy. One need not appeal to divination as a means of identifying a situation. One could probably identify a situation in light of the onto-cosmology of the alternation of the *yin* and *yang* in the *dao*, whereas one can also identify the *dao* as a system of changes governed by return, reversion, reciprocity, opposition, mutuality, complementation, and continuous creative creativity (*shengsheng* 生生). What I mean by identification is a situation to be formed by divination or by projection of understanding from experience. It is something involved with one's insight into one's relation with the world and others as well as one's own self-understanding in relation to the world. In a presented *gua* symbol such as the *gua* of *Tun* (Initial Settlement with water above thunder), one is confronted with a great position for development and yet with early difficulty to be overcome with plan and work. When attempting to understand life and reality, not only can divination be brushed aside as something unnecessary, the whole system of the *Yi* Text, along with its symbolism and its judgments, can be set aside. For one can directly appeal to one's own observation, intuition, experience, and enlightenment to determine what reality is and what the meaning of a situation is in the light of totality of reality.

Wang Bi 王弼 (226–249), a Daoistic interpreter of the *Yi* System, is one who began this line of thought and paved the way for a full era of Song and Ming Neo-Confucian philosophers to follow suit and flourish. One also may observe that in the *Yizhuan* such a tendency toward metaphysical explanation at expense of divination is mixed with efforts to interlink philosophical interpretations with readings of the lines and structures of the *gua*. For Confucius it is clear that moral cultivation requires an onto-cosmological philosophy, but not specifically a system of images and symbols and a procedure of divination. On the other hand, it must also be said that it is by reflection on the implicit and embodied onto-cosmology in the symbols of the *Yi* that one comes to directly confront and experience the changes of the reality. It might still be asked whether or not in the absence of the formulation of the *Yi* System a vivid and penetrating understanding of reality as onto-cosmology is possible.

Considering the coherence and consistency of the system of the *gua* in the *Yi* Text, now we could even suggest that the *Yi* Text begins with an image of nature and cosmos, which reflects our comprehensive understanding of reality.[14] It is only on the basis of such a developed or developing image of nature that we are able to make practical use of the image or system of symbols together with their underlying understanding. In this sense, one must not say that the book of the *Yijing* is merely a book of divination. Instead one must assert that the *Yi* Text develops as a result of cosmic understanding. It provides a cosmological interpretation or description of our observations of nature and an ontological reference to the forces and origins of changes. Hence, it is a book of onto-cosmological understanding, which nevertheless lends itself naturally to the use of divination. As indicated above, in the formation and systematization of the *Yi* Text, divination is recognized as playing a central role in the quest for correlation of form and meaning, theory and action, symbol and reference, and fact and value. In other words, divination is recognized as an essential process or stage of the use of the symbols that enables the book to grow, develop, and at the same time awaken the diviner to be conscious of the underlying principles of onto-cosmological understanding directly based on our natural experiences of reality.

This is not to say, however, that the *Yi* Text has not been used for divination for a long period, or that its origination may not link to some practical need and anxiety pertaining to controlling one's future. We have seen how the primary *yin-yang* symbols of the *Yi* are onto-cosmological in nature, even though they can be manipulated in the accruing of meaning for the *gua* and the *yao* (lines) in the *gua*. Without the primary onto-cosmological meaning of the *yin-yang* symbols, no manipulation of images of the *gua* and of movements of the *yao* can be justified. It is in this sense that the systematization represents both a natural need for interpretation and a process of making rational and reasonable interpretation of the *gua* and the *yao*.

The systematization also implies a need to justify itself. Here we see again a subtle process at work, namely, the comprehensive observation continually at work leading to the actual formation of an organic system of symbols. With the system once formed, however, one needs to know whether it suggests or reveals a reality that we can understand or contemplate. To come to this step, of course, a person must undertake the task of inquiring into the hidden reality in the *Yi* Text and advance his experience as a basis for a new interpretation of the *Yi* Text, not as a text but as a document or a symbol presenting the reality that the inquirer confronts. This person here, we know, is Confucius in his later years after the age of fifty. It is in light of this inquiry that an explicit onto-cosmology will emerge to form an explicit philosophy as articulated in the *Yizhuan*. This is how the *Yizhuan* itself was formed.

In our discussion we make use of only the *Xici*. But the same principle of interpretation, in light of the totalistic understanding of the *Yi* symbolism and its reference to reality, is discussed and used in other *Yizhuan* commentaries. One can see the *Shuogua* 说卦 (*Discourse Commentary*) as a systematic explanation and interpretation of the symbolic forms against a background of dynamic understanding of the eight *gua* as natural forces. These *gua* are interrelated in a circle of complementary oppositions as well as in a circle of mutually generating five powers (*wuxing*). An analysis will show that what are known as the pre-heaven diagram and post-heaven diagram are first suggested in the *Shuogua* 说卦:[15]

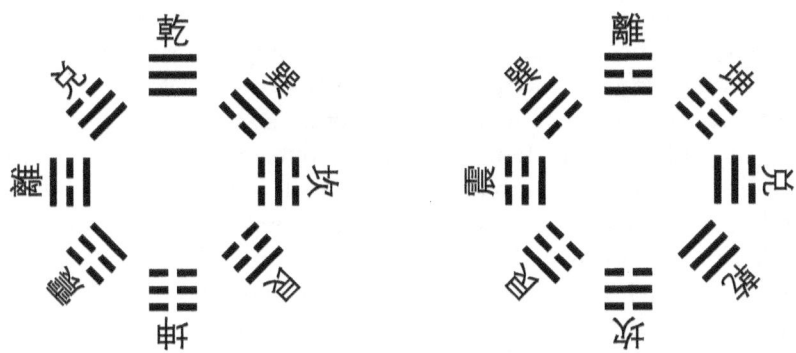

The Pre-Heaven Diagram of *Bagua*   The Post-Heaven Diagram of *Bagua*

These two diagrams are highly significant, for they capture the systemic features of the *gua* system, and to produce the system requires a deep observation and thinking. Here we see that the Principle of Organic Holism has been used as a principle of interpretation. By merging the theory of five powers with the eight *gua* system it also can be shown how understanding could creatively develop if we can integrate the two systems into one. There is also the principle of extension of images by likeness. But this could be overdone, for many of the images may only be shown to remotely relate to the primary image of the *gua*.

One sees in the *Xugua* 序卦 (*Sequence Commentary*) an effort to show the rationality or empirical validity of the order and sequence of the *gua* based on the principle of balance and creative generation. In the case of the *Zagua* 杂卦 (*Miscellaneous Commentary*), an attempt to illustrate the meanings of all *gua* in contrast or in some essential and abstract manner is made. The principle of interpretation is again holism of meaning.

Now, in light of our analysis of the divination process, and the interpretation involved in understanding reality and applying the *Yi* symbols (trigrams and hexagrams), we may distinguish between the formation of the Yi symbols and the Yi system of judgments. This distinction is based on divinatory practice and the formation of the Yizhuan 易传 understanding of the Yi Text. It is obvious that the formation of the Yi symbols and Yi system of judgments involves the primary situation of interpretation and understanding, where understanding of reality is an unconscious interpretation of the natural events of the world. The primary situation involves the use of primary symbols, which directly reflect an experience of reality. In the Yi Text it also reflects a comprehensive observation (*guan*), which leads to interpretation of a whole organic system of events and processes as well as a holistic system of interpretation. This involves internal adjustments in terms of levels of differentiation of symbolism as well as a basic correlation between symbols and names, on the one hand, and making judgments and drawing moral lessons, on the other hand. This primary model is based on the projection of balanced feelings of truth, method, experience and reason. It requires the whole person to react to the world as a whole and to individual situations in particular.

In the formation of the *Yizhuan*, the authors were responding to a given body of texts of symbols and their judgments. To a great extent, *Yizhuan* commentary, such as the *Xiangzhuan* 象传, responds to the *gua* and the situation of the *gua*, as illustrated by the *Tuan Commentary* 象传. What needs to be stressed are two important points: first, in responding to the symbols and texts of the judgments in the Yi Text, the *Xiangzhuan* also responds to the open-ended meaning and content of the *gua*. Second, in addition to responding to the meanings of words and paradigms, it also responds to the real situations, which the commentaries have suggested. Hence the situation of interpretation in the *Yizhuan* is highly selective and always integrative. The *Yizhuan* must respond to the Text and the live situation as indicated by the Text.

Original Position of Onto-Interpretation and Eight Primary Principles

The individual must open herself to what is taking place in the world. She must have an understanding of the world-reality in terms of the onto-cosmology of change. It may take a sage (a person who has comprehensively observed the world and deeply reflected on what has been observed) to do this, but again the Yi Text has made available the result of such an observation and reflection so that others who are not necessarily sages could rely on such a profound and comprehensive understanding of world-reality. Specifically, a diviner would have to assume having such an understanding so that she can make a divinatory judgment on the basis of such an understanding. What is called a "divinatory judgment" (*guaci*) is essentially a normative interpretation of a given situation based on such an understanding relative to a specific purpose. The specific purpose would require and enable the diviner to see the situation in an evaluative and practical or even moral perspective, which means she must draw some judgment of values (propitious, risky, or good and bad, in terms of impact of harm or benefit) in light of her understanding of the situation. It would also enable her to give some practical admonition on actions to be taken. Hence the content of divinatory judgment would normally have three components: (1) interpretative description of the situation against the background of the onto-cosmology of the *gua*; (2) the evaluation of the situation from the perspective of a specific purpose or motive that motivates the divinatory inquiry; (3) and the specific action to be taken or avoided. It is also understood that the value of a situation or change depends on the action to be taken, and this means that the values in a *guaci* could be conditional on the action to be taken. Take for an example the *guaci* 卦辞 of the *Kun* 坤:

> *Kun*: Fundamentally prosperous, it is advantageous to be firm as a female horse. The superior person has to do something, but he may lose his direction first, and then find his mentor or leader. In the Southwest, he will gain a friend, but in the Northeast, he will lose a friend. It is propitious to be firm in being stable.

Although the *guaci* (divinatory judgment) did not give a description of the situation, the *gua* symbol and the name *Kun* have suggested what a basic situation it is as against the onto-cosmography of the change. The *guaci* has concentrated on the values of the situation and practical advices given to the person who initiates the divination: namely it answers his worries and questions. The statement "in the southwest, he will gain a friend, but in the northeast, he will lose a friend," can be understood as the conditional sentence: "If one goes southwest, he will gain a friend, and if he goes northeast, he will lose a friend." It is clear that the situation is an open and nondeterminate one, as most times are, and it is up to the person concerned to make a choice and decide on an action. What we have learned from this divining situation is that a situation has its openness even though it has its restrictions and has provided a framework for understanding and action.

The so-called openness means opening of some possibilities under the restrictions of the given situation. A situation is always a process of change or a transition in transformation in the context of all other situations as provided in the onto-cosmography of the *guan*.

On the other hand, the engaged person, whether he is the diviner or a third person who initiates a divinatory inquiry, is always free to make his choice or his decision concerning action. The person is not totally determined by the situation. But knowing the situation, the person would know what the enlightened decisions to make are. In addition, there is another implication to be drawn—namely, the engaged individual is ideally self-cultivated so that the individual would have better mind and better moral and intellectual resources to meet the needs of a situation. Both Confucius and Mencius have stressed the importance of self-cultivation, which presupposes the existence of free will (in some sense) and has the practical significance of meeting the needs of a situation.

Our description of a divining situation shows that one must use a method of divination to arrive at an image of a given situation; this image of course is the *gua* of the situation. The *gua* reflects the situation for us to understand and make judgment. Hence, one can see the importance of divination. But is there an alternative to divination for the determining of a given situation? The answer is positive. In fact, the Yi Text has provided the category of "Feeling" as such an alternative. The thirty-first *gua* is called *Xian* 咸, which means simply *gan* 感 (feeling). This *gua* is composed of lake above and hill below, which suggests a dynamic harmony, or harmony in action, as illustrated by the relationship of a young woman and a young man in a bond of feeling of love and care. Hence, this image of a situation is one of creative production and peace and suggests a good *yin-yang* interaction between the above and below. In a sense, the large universe is bonded in such a creative feeling of interaction and reciprocal regard so that all things can prosper. In the *Xici*, this relationship of creative feeling is described as "feeling and response" (*ganying* 感应), in terms of which a penetrating understanding of causes and reasons is possible.

With this understanding of the power of feeling, a person well experienced in *guan* is considered capable of sensitively responding to a situation with his profound feeling about his situation and therefore could come to describe the situation in the form of a symbolic image. Again, to have a feeling is not to abandon perceptual observation and conceptual understanding; instead, perceptual observation and conceptual understanding could provide a framework for the occasioning of a feeling. Feeling in this sense is the connecting and interactive factor between two natural objects; thus, it indicates the actual communication or sharing of two states of being. Hence, a proper feeling represents and leads to an insight or understanding of some unknown situation. Based on recognition derived from the feeling, one could come to configure one's situation with all factors considered. This is like constructing an image or model of one's position in the world, which can be put to the test in view of one's actual experience and in light of one's historical existence. This is also like formulating a theory of a natural phenomenon in which the cause and nature of the phenomenon are explained and made available to confirmation and corroboration. If what is constructed and formulated comes to reflect or disclose a reality, one may be said to have a penetrating understanding or comprehension (*tong* 通).

From being capable of observation to being capable of feeling, and from being capable of feeling to reaching comprehension, one may be said to be capable of generating a *gua* without using divination. It is to be noted that it is in the reflection on the meaning of the *gua*, and perhaps on the meaning of the divination, that divination was transcended and transformed into knowledge, enlightenment, and creative understanding.

The way in which one generates a *gua* with one's creative understanding is one place where one can be said to have made a creative or a creative-ontological interpretation of the situation. This interpretation is creative because it takes one's feeling and mind to achieve an understanding, and it is ontological because it presupposes experience of a reality to be identified by observation, feeling and comprehension. As this situation is both ontological and interpretative, we may also call it onto-hermeneutical. Another way of looking at the matter is that one must have first developed or possessed an onto-cosmological understanding of reality. One may apply this onto-cosmological understanding to a situation to generate a specific understanding of the situation, so long as the situation is within the scope of the preunderstanding of onto-cosmological understanding.

Whereas divination relies on a particular method of divination to generate such an onto-hermeneutical understanding, observation-feeling-comprehension generates such an understanding without appeal to any divination. As divination can be dispensed with in this mode of generating understanding in terms of a *gua*, Confucius could say, "I do not need to engage divination" (*Lunyu* 13.22).[16] Xunzi also states that there is no need to do divination to achieve knowledge. As a matter of fact, one can have knowledge of a situation with divination and without necessarily generating a *gua* for understanding. But this does not mean that one can dispense with a preunderstanding of an onto-cosmological reality in having knowledge or understanding the reality of a situation. This does not mean that one need not engage the reality of a specific situation for specific understanding of the situation. There is always the element of seeing, observing, feeling, reflecting, or comprehending the reality of the situation together with a prior understanding of reality in general. Once one has reached such a nondivinatory understanding, one can come to produce a judgment of the situation by the use of language.

This use of language is to describe the situation as one sees it. Language is, further, used to draw practical evaluation of the situation relative to one's descriptive understanding. This is just like what one does while producing judgments with divination. To divine is to have knowledge of a situation with future implications for evaluation and action. This is how interpretation as understanding is always ontological, and there is no better place to recognize this ontological engagement than to generate an interpretation or understanding of the situation. The origination of *gua* in feeling and comprehension provides a primary model in terms of which understanding as creative interpretation becomes possible.

It is perhaps because of the possibility of this creative interpretation in the primary situation of divinatory judgments or in the generation of nondivinatory comprehension (*tong*) that all other interpretations are possible. Here let me first present the primary situation of creative interpretation in both the divinatory and nondivinatory way:

Yi 易: understanding of change ← *guan* 观 (observation)

|

Xiang 象: perception of specific situation ← *bu* 卜 (divination) or *gan* (feeling)

|

Gua 卦: symbolic representation ← *tong* 通 (comprehension)

|

Ming 名: naming ← *zhi* 指 (identifying use of language)

|

Ci 辞: judgment ← *yan* 言 (descriptive and prescriptive use of language)

If we generalize to a broad situation of creative interpretation and understanding—a situation in which we need to appeal to the onto-cosmology of the *gua* system—we derive the following:

> General understanding of reality → Specific perception of a situation → Symbolic description of the situation → Reflective evaluation of the situation → Determinative prescription of action → Reinforced and reformulated understanding of reality

Now we can come to the generation of the Confucian *Ten Wings*, which are general interpretations of the *gua*-situations with reference to the *Yi* Text. It should be noted, the *Ten Wings* do not exclude reference to a preunderstanding of reality and a conceptual engagement with the reality of a specific situation. We may see that the Confucian *Ten Wings*, as general interpretations of the *Yi* Text, were made after thorough discussion initiated by Confucius and continued by his disciples. Better still it can be presumed that Confucius has led and inspired his disciples in a thorough discussion of the *Yi* Text and came to reach a general understanding and interpretation of the *Yi* Text, based, in no small part, on their preunderstanding of reality. The *Ten Wings* are the cumulative results of such discussion and inquiry.

Here, my focus is on the dynamics of creative interpretation or onto-hermeneutical interpretation and understanding of the *Yi* Text, not on the dating or the historical verification or authentication of the *Ten Wings*. Further, my focus is not on the temporal ordering, philosophical importance, or implications of the *Ten Wings*. I consider them all as being produced at about the same period of time. I consider them to be inquiries into different aspects of the *Yi* Text from different but related points of view. Their difference is the difference between topical focus, and they share a commonness not only in originating from the Confucian discourse, but also in illustrating the same onto-cosmological understanding of change generated by a long background of *gua*.

We may now generalize this process of generating creative interpretation and onto-hermeneutical understanding in the language of the *Ten Wings* (in particular the *Xici*). We may regard this process of generating creative interpretation as the Origin of the Interpretation or Understanding (*Yuanchuan* or *Yuanjie*).

1. Observation (*Guan*) and Feeling (*Gan*)   Observation
2. Comprehensive interpenetration (*Huitong*)   Comprehension
3. One *Yin* and One *Yang* is called the *Dao*   Symbolization
4. The *Yi* has its *Taiji*   Systematization
5. Establish the Images (*gua xiang*) to image ideas   Divination
6. Attach judgments (*ci*) and exhaust language (*yan*)   Interpretation
7. Observe images and formulate with judgments
8. Observe changes and play with divination

We can see that each step leads to the other, and the final step also merges or goes back to the first step. This is how an onto-cosmological circle was completed and yet ceaselessly circulates in an open process of comprehensive understanding and creative interpretation. We may call these eight processes the eight primary principles of interpretation in the *Yi* tradition.

In this sense, the *Tuan Commentary* (two parts) is intended to illustrate the onto-cosmological beginning or cosmogony. We see the *Xiang Commentary* (two parts) as intended to draw moral lessons on cultivation of the individual in light of the understanding of a situation. We see *Wenyan Commentary* as developing the moral and cultural implication of the first two *gua* in metaphysics of cultural and moral values. We see the *Shuogua Commentary* as a logical effort to sort out the origins of *gua* and their philosophical significance. The *Shuogua Commentary* may represent a pre-hexagram background of the metaphysical or onto-cosmology of the eight trigrams and their extended application by way of imaging. We see the *Xu Commentary* as a treatise to focus on the meaning and reason of the sequence of *gua* in a systematic coherence. We see the *Zagua Commentary* as also a short treatise to focus on the meaning of *gua* as contrastive polarities so that an order of development of the *gua* can be understood. Finally, we see the *Xici Commentary* as efforts made to bring out a synthetic and comprehensive understanding of the onto-cosmogony and onto-cosmology of the changes together with their application to cultural inventions and moral cultivation. It is the work of interpretation from many hands in the Confucian school. This is the formation of the multi-dimensional understanding of the primary model in the *Ten Wings* of the *Yizhuan*.

With this short description we can now present the production of the *Ten Wings* as the result of efforts to interpret the *Yi* Text in a creative way after the Primary Model but in a reflective and integrative way transcending divination yet still incorporating divination. But what is important to understand is that in the modeling of the Primary Model one can see the engagement with reality and reflecting on reality while dealing with the text of Yi are done at the same time. There will be no such interpretative results if one only focuses on the *sache* (facts) of the text, which means here the large reality of change as reflected in the onto-cosmology of the Yi Text.

There are two observations to be made. First, one needs to see here that the production of the Ten Wings follows the Primary Model of Creative Interpretation with a reference to the Yi Text. It is through the Yi Text that the attention of the authors of the Ten Wings is brought to the onto-cosmology of change. Hence, the Ten Wings are creative interpretations as well as onto-hermeneutic interpretations. Second, it is clear that the production of the Ten Wings is the production of an explicitly philosophical Yi Text, which is eventually incorporated into the primary Yi Text and since the Han is considered integral to this original Yi Text. It is on the basis of this new comprehensive text of the Yi that future creative interpretation and onto-hermeneutical interpretations are carried out. These can be illustrated in both the development of the Xiangshu (Images-Numbers) School in the Han times or in the Yili (Meanings-Principles) School in the Song/Ming times.

The turning-point in Wang Bi (226–249), who in his commentary on the Zhouyi daringly wipes out the Xiangshu approach in favor of a creative void (*wu*) for understanding the ultimate, also illustrates how an onto-cosmological and onto-hermeneutical approach could make a difference, even though it is conducted within the tradition and paradigm of onto-cosmological understanding generated by *guan*. But it is through this tradition that philosophers, common people, and scholars of history and literature are brought to engage and confront a reality of creative change and hence are able to continuously draw inspiration for new meanings to give to old texts in the literary and philosophical tradition in Chinese civilization.

CHAPTER 5

Philosophical Significance of *Guan*

From *Guan* (观) to Onto-Hermeneutical Unity of Methodology and Ontology

When the question arises as to how the original set of trigram symbols came to be, the suggested answer from the *Xici* commentary on the *Yijing* is that Fuxi observed (*guan*) the heavens (*tian*) and looked down at the earth, and he considered things afar as well as pondered things close by so that he was able to invent the eight trigrams.[1] In this chapter I do not intend to discuss whether the legend of Fuxi is reliable or how the *Xici* commentary came to suggest this legend. Instead, I want to consider how this suggested process of designing or inventing a system of eight trigrams (*bagua*) is logically plausible and philosophically significant.

To look over heaven above and earth below, as well as to consider things afar and things close by, is indeed a logical way to design a generalized system of description of all things between heaven and earth in symbols. In fact, there is no other reliable way to discover what is shared in common among things, namely, the basic processes or structures of things in nature. In order to achieve the actual system of *bagua*, one must deeply understand nature as it is. This will enable one to make a dynamic presentation of nature in a meaningful and suggestive system of symbols (such as the *bagua*), where the symbols are reflective and even explanatory of heaven, earth, and all processes of natural constitution and transformation therein. That this is possible hinges on how we understand *guan*. To understand the process of *guan*, we must analyze and examine the use of *guan* in the text and commentaries of the *Yijing*.

The reason we choose to focus on *guan* as a basis for ontogenesis (the process of formation in a deeper logical sense) of the *Yijing* worldview is further prompted by various paradigms in which *guan* is spoken of in the *Xici* and other commentaries. The *Xici* speaks of *guan* in the following basic paradigms:

1. "The sage designs the *gua* (trigram/hexagram) forms in order to *guan* (oversee) phenomena and append judgment" (*Xici Shang* 1).

2. "In residing, the superior person *guan* (oversees) phenomena and contemplates their judgments; in movement he *guan* the changes and contemplates their divinations" (*Xici Shang* 2).

3. "[The sage] looks up to *guanyu* (look over) patterns of heaven; looks down to get an overview of the patterns of earth, and thus knows the reasons and causes of the dark and the bright" (*Xici Shang* 4).

4. "The sage has something to see among all things in the chaos under heaven and proposes a description of their matters, so that positions and relations (*wuyi*) can be represented symbolically. Thus, this is called the symbols (*xiang*). The sage has something to see among all movements under heaven. He *guan* (oversees) their connections and interpenetrations so that he can perform rites in accordance with them. [The sage] also appends judgments on what is propitious to do and what is not. This is called 'line of movement' (*yao*)" (*Xici Shang* 8).

5. "The way of heaven and earth is essential for correctly presenting and overseeing forms (*zheng guan*); the way of the sun and moon is essential for attaining oneness (*zheng fu yi*)"[2] (*Xici Xia* 1).

6. "In the ancient times when Baoxi (Fuxi) reigned over the world, he looked up to *guan* (survey) forms in heaven and looked down to *guan* norms on earth. He *guan* (observed) patterns of birds and beasts and what circumstances on earth befit them. He took in things close to his person

and took in things far from him as well. Thus, he began to design the eight trigrams (*bagua*) in order to comprehend the powers of the divine and to classify the types of movements of ten thousand things" (*Xici Xia* 2).

7. "The one who knows to *guan* the judgments of a *gua*, he would think through over half the way" (*Xici Xia* 9).

These paradigms demonstrate that *guan* is essential in order for a person to understand forms and activities in the world. *Guan* is the basis for forming a picture of the things in the world in a totalistic framework: a framework indicated by the system of *bagua*. We may say that the *bagua* result from the sage's activities of *guan*. But we also may point out that once sages designed the *bagua*, they could observe more facts about things and their corresponding movements. Thus, the process of *guan* is to identify forms from actual observation of things and to apply form to things in order to better understand them. In order to get forms of the world so that we may apply them to things, one must be very careful and thorough about one's observations; further, one must be careful and thorough in reflecting on these observations in order to arrive at the correct forms. As we shall see, these forms must come out naturally from astute observations that capture totality, relationships, and possibilities of change, such as diminishments, expansions, and various kinds of transformation. In this sense, we can see the *bagua* as a dialectical and dynamic representation, resulting from the process of *guan*, and we also can see *guan* as a continuous open process of verifying the forms and movements of things.

The term "forms" (*xiang*) has the double-edged meaning of "presentation" (*xian*) and "representation" (*shi*), as well as "discovery" and "invention." *Guan* has the meaning of looking for *xiang* (forms), and *xiang* are precisely what are capable and worthy of being looked for. Besides, *guan* gives rises to "establish" the forms as images (also *xiang*) so that forms are inventions as well. In this sense, *guan xiang* can be said to be a process in which the forms of things and forms of seeing things coincide, and in which the object and subject co-determine what look a thing has or how a thing presents itself. Neither subjective idealism nor objective materialism makes knowledge possible. Rather, a "pre-established harmony" (to use Leibniz's term) makes our *guan* of *xiang* (forms) as well as the presentation of *xiang* to *guan* possible. This pre-established harmony, which we may refer to as the *dao*, even makes the *xiang* capable of being observed (*keguan*). *Guan* always will serve the purpose of creativity, such as creation of cultural systems or making of utensils or invention of techniques, as described in *Xici Xia* 2. In this sense, the discovery of *xiang* as forms makes invention of *xiang* as images possible; this invention of *xiang* as images is, on the other hand, an inspired discovery of objective forms that would fulfill our wishes for subjective value creation. Thus, it is said,

> The sage establishes the *xiang* (as image) to fulfill his intention (for value fulfillment). [The sage] designs the *gua* to fulfill his sense of veracity and falsity (*qingwei*). [The sage] appends judgments to fulfill what is beneficial to people, and promotes the study of this in order to fulfill creativity (*sheng*). (*Xici Shang* 12)

This suggests that *guan* as both discovery of forms and invention of images is the infinite source of meaning, inspiration, and motivation for all important cultural and civilizational activities. *Guan* is what gives meaning to a sage's quest for his own place and role and status in the world. In fact, it is *guan* and its profound uses that only a sage is capable of cultivating; in this sense, *guan* is what makes a sage a sage. Anyone who cultivates *guan* is not only able to see forms in actuality, but is also clear about what is past and anticipates what is to come. Such a person is able to uncover the minute and the subtle and illuminate the hidden and the obscure. What is required from this person is the ability to discriminate among things and to give them proper names, to make correct descriptions in language and proper evaluations in judgment.[3]

In the *Discourse Commentary* (*Shuoguazhuan*) we have the following paradigms:

> [The sage] *guan* (observes) changes among *yin* and *yang* and establishes the system of *gua*, develops thoughts in light of firm and soft and produces the lines of movement (*yao*), harmonizes the *dao* and the *de* (virtue), and thus introduces orderings (*li*) among meanings (*yi*). He would exhaust all orderings, and fulfill individual natures of things to reach for the unchanging way (*ming*). (section 1)

In the *Sequence Commentary* (*Xuguazhuan*), it is said, "When things are large they become something worthy of being seen (*keguan*). Thus the *Guan gua* was offered. Any thing which is worthy of being seen has something to match with (*he*); therefore, the *Shihe gua* was offered." In the *Miscellaneous Commentary* (*Zaguazhuan*), it is said, "The meanings of *Lin* and *Guan gua* are such that either I approach (*yu*) things or things present themselves to me."

We may thus conclude that *guan* in the *Yijing* describes and defines a methodology (from the view of rational consciousness) and a process of observing, knowing and understanding things in the world as well as the world of things. Accordingly, *guan* can be said to have the following characteristics:

1. It sees or oversees things *in* a totality; it purports to see and oversee the totality *of* things; and it sees and oversees things or a thing *as* a totality. *Guan* is totalistic or integrative seeing.

2. It sees and oversees things in a dynamic manner in terms of their movements and ruling tendencies or potentiality to change or transformation. *Guan* is dynamic seeing.

3. It sees and oversees things as places or positions in a context of relevance and meaningful relationships. *Guan* is positional or organic-contextual seeing.

4. It sees things with specific reference to time as time is the most profound motivating force and most comprehensive scope and context in which things are located. Time is also the source of both creative transformation and forced change. To understand a thing is to understand the place of the thing in time. *Guan* is temporal or transformative seeing.

5. It sees things in interaction with one another tending toward conflict or harmony within themselves. This conflict or harmony leads to the coming into being of new things and the going out of being of old things. *Guan* is interactive seeing.

6. It sees things in specific interaction with individuals in reference to their meaningfulness for value creation, civilization, and other useful practical activities. *Guan* is evaluative and inventive seeing.

7. It sees the original source of activities of things and persons and thus their mutual interpenetrations (*huitong*) leading toward understanding the onto-cosmology of the world. *Guan* is *onto-cosmological* seeing.

8. It sees things in a network of levels and dimensions as described in all the above points; moreover, *guan* sees things with understanding based on harmony and coherence of discovery of creativity in the objective. *Guan* is onto-hermeneutical seeing.[4]

It is thus clear that *guan* is an infinitely rich concept that cannot be identified by any single activity of observation; as it is observation on many levels and from many dimensions, there is no specific point of view to be named as such. Any specific point of view is self-limiting and self-confining, and hence is to be called a *guandian* (literally: point of view). But *guan* is not any single point of view, for it is *all* points of view—that is, it is a viewing from all points. Alternatively, we could state it in the negative: *guan* is a viewing from no specific point of view at all. Rationally speaking, however, if we call *guan* a methodology of seeing and understanding things in the world and the world of things, it is still a point of view, namely the point of view of no point of view. It is a self-correcting, self-negating, and self-transcending point of view. In this sense, *guan* is what I have identified as onto-hermeneutical thinking or simply onto-hermeneutics. For simplicity it can also be called "comprehensive observation."[5]

As a final remark on the nature of *guan*, it is not simply phenomenological experience or observation as defined by Husserl, for it is not understood in the Husserlian sense of perception by bracketing out preconceptions, nor is *guan* a reduction to some rationalized eidetic consciousness through "free imaginative variation" of intellectual thinking.[6] Rather, it is to experientially fathom and sort things out in an understanding of totality according to one's capability of achieving. Things present themselves in a natural simple manner. There is in fact more affinity with Heidegger than with Husserl. Heidegger speaks of ontological phenomenology or phenomenology as ontology by which he is able to investigate the actuality of totality of things and beings.[7]

Heidegger's investigation leads to a nonessentialist interpretation of Being and *Dasein* within the scope of the horizon of time. In this sense, ontological phenomenology is similar to the process of *guan*, for it wishes to scan and survey all the beings-in-the-world without pinning them down to any transcendental ultimate essences. However, as we shall see, although Heidegger's project yields many useful results which can be compared to the process of *guan*, and which also can be used to enrich the inventory of *guan* as an open overview of the world, Heidegger has not given any clear identification or description of the method of phenomenology as ontology; that is, he has not shown how it is the same as ontological phenomenology, as the process of *guan* would suggest.

Insofar as the ontological and phenomenological must mutually define each other in a totality of things and beings, we have what I have described as onto-hermeneutical understanding. In the process of *guan*, one must reach an onto-hermeneutical understanding of the totality of things and beings; this understanding maintains that viewing things and beings gives rise to a view of things and beings that in turn makes the viewing possible. To be more specific, in the process of *guan*, one achieves a view or overview as one views and overviews the world or a situation, and the viewing process is also an enhanced outcome or result of viewing; that is, the viewing is part of what is being viewed, and what is being viewed is also a part of the viewing. In this process of interpenetration of viewing and what is being viewed, there is a reciprocity and circulation of vital energy or creative force between the viewing person and the world. In the *guan* process, the subject of the viewing is identifiable with the activity of viewing, which is again identifiable with the object of viewing, for it is the fact that the object is viewable that makes the viewing possible as viewing. Thus, one can recognize *guan* both as a method of viewing and the resulting view or overview of the viewing process. The methodological aspect and the onto-presentational aspect in the process of *guan* cannot be separated; they naturally fall into unison and oneness because their interdependency dialectically forms a unity.

What then is the philosophical significance of *guan*? In light of the above, let us try to explain this so that we see *guan* as a presentation and illustration of the onto-hermeneutical process of understanding the world in reality and its consequent achievement of formation of the trigram and hexagram systems.

When we hear sounds, we are not merely hearing sounds. Sounds are not simply data given to us. We hear things about the world and we also hear from relationships that exist between us and the world of things. In hearing, the mind, the heart, the body, and nature (or spirit) all come to work.[8] On combining these different levels we come to understand the meanings of sounds as sounds; again, we do not merely hear sounds (as simple sense data). The meaning of "sounds as not merely sounds" is conveyed by the Chinese concepts *jingjie* and *Yijing* (world infused with a level of projective understanding).[9] When a sound is heard, it reveals a *jingjie* of one sort while concealing *jingjie* of the other. Each sound, or group of sounds, either hides or reveals such a world of projective understanding. If we do not hear anything, then we come to know and understand a nonspecifically outstanding or presented world: the world of profound silence, a world in which no sound sounds out. In such a world, whatever sounds naturally occur form a basic accord that is aptly expressed by the Chinese idiom "*wanlai wusheng*" (The ten thousand sounds are quiet).[10] Can we hear or sense such a world of quietude or silence? Yes, apart from the Daoist tradition, even the Neo-Confucian Cheng Yi comes to speak of it: "All things when seen in contemplation naturally appear to have a manner of stirring of life."[11] This is because individuals can vitally respond to the invisible formation of things with their hearts and bodies in their contemplation of things.

As in the case of hearing, seeing is multileveled with respect to sensation, perception, mind, heart, nature, and spirit of a human being. Hence, reality can be disclosed and hidden (or withdrawn) in seeing as well. The concept of "*jingjie*" (境界 mind vision) applies to the other senses as well; these senses are then absorbed into a process of contemplation. Hence, we may regard *guan* as composed of the natural unity of all senses: seeing, hearing, touching, tasting, smelling, and feeling. This being said, however, *guan* is more clearly related to the visual sense in the etymological formation of the term. The Chinese character for "*guan*" contains the radical "*jian*," or "seeing," which is explicitly visual.[12] In fact, the Chinese language is primarily a visual image language, which deepens or elevates the language of heart and mind to the language of nature and principle through natural understanding and self-cultivation.[13]

Further Explanation of *Guan* in Connection with Heidegger's *Aletheia*

Scientific objectivity depends on nonscientific subjectivity; we need to transcend and integrate both. Relativity or relativism can be resolved into a concrete situation that is neither absolute nor relative. This invites us to consider how an objective, universal worldview is possible although it must be derived from the subjective individual. This is possible because the subjective individual can transcend his subjectivity by cultivating his *guan* to a point that it will not be biased by any scope, level, or perspective, thereby accepting a position of centrality and rectitude. In this connection, we can take a lesson from Heidegger's concept of the presencing of Being as the basis of beings and the disclosure of *aletheia* (truth) as understanding.[14]

Heidegger suggests that Being shows itself as "presencing of beings which are present."[15] While the presence of beings is disclosed, Being as "presencing of beings" is often concealed. When we look at beings merely as beings or things, we do not see the Being. It is as Aristotle says: "for as the eyes of bats are to the blaze of day, so is the mind of our soul to things which are by nature most manifest of all."[16] But with effort and concentration, perhaps, we can see the Being of beings while yet seeing beings. On the other hand, while we see the Being of beings, we may overlook beings whose presencing is Being. In this sense, the Being is disclosed while beings become concealed.

The Chinese Chan Buddhistic understanding offers two other possibilities of seeing: we can either see both Being and beings at the same time, or we can see no Being and no beings even if there *are* both beings and their Being. As Chan Master Linji 临济 says in the motto of "Four Pieces of Stuff" (*Siliao jian* 四料简): "Sometimes, (I) take away a person (being) without taking away the world (*jing* 境 as Being); sometimes (I) take away the world (*jing* as Being) without taking away the person (being); sometimes (I) take away both the person (being) and the world (*jing* as Being); sometimes (I) do not take away the person (being) nor the world (*jing* as Being)."[17] Here one can see that the alternation of disclosure and concealment presents a dialectical relationship relative to the enlightened mind—the mind that has no separation from the truth of Being and Being of truth.

Heidegger wishes to inquire into the metaphysical ground of all ontological concepts and principles, namely, the Being (which, from the standpoint of the *Yijing*, may be regarded as *taiji* or the great ultimate, which is to be discussed later) qua ground for all beings to which those concepts and principles apply. He finds Human Existence (namely *Dasein*) and time (or temporality in all its connected ecstasies) to be the very disclosures of Being, and from these disclosures Being is understood as ontological difference. Presumably, he finds this by his own native ability to see or view (*guan*), which he calls "philosophical phenomenology" (PP) or "ontological phenomenology" (OP), which is a phenomenology not reduced to consciousness by eidetic reduction in the style of Husserl, but which, on the other hand, reveals the ontological structure, state, and process or activity of Being-in-the-world, or the existence of *Dasein* (Being-I or a human being) and knowing the world.[18] We may, therefore, identify this PP or OP as the *guan* of which the *Yijing* speaks. It is not any specific or relative viewing; rather, it is a natural, Being-inspired disclosure of Being (in the form of a self-reflection and cross-examination of self and things). In this sense, Heidegger may claim a self-consistency of applying his method to explain and justify the existence of his method. This method must be methodologically self-fulfilling and self-defining, as a presencing of Being, which can lead to disclosures of the Being of all beings, specifically the Being of *Dasein*. In a word, this is what I call the method of "onto-hermeneutics," which first makes its appearance in the activity of the *guan* in the *Yijing*.

Onto-Hermeneutics of Being

"Onto-hermeneutics" means interpretation based on and from the standpoint of ontological or onto-cosmological understanding or understanding of being-in-the-world. It is also interpretation for ontological or onto-cosmological understanding as well as interpretation toward ontological or onto-cosmological understanding. Therefore, it is simultaneously of, for, and by ontological or onto-cosmological understanding. Hence, one needs a beginning in ontological or onto-cosmological understanding whether by way of Heidegger's "meditative thinking" (*Gelassenheit*) or by the *Yijing* way of *guan* (contemplative observation).[19] No beginning, however, is absolute, for a beginning must assume something beyond itself and therefore will form a circle with it. To begin is not only to move forward but to move backward as well. It is to treat time as a circle of understanding of being that again forms a circle with non-time on a higher plane or in a deeper sense. As an interpretation we need to see language itself as being full of creative potentiality for revealing as well as concealing reality or that which is to be understood. Hence, a creative use of language in directly confronting reality is important. An effort in all its seriousness and genuineness makes a beginning of understanding possible.

In the original text (*jing*) of the *Yijing*, there is the "presencing of Being" in every concrete situation of life. In every concrete situation of life is hidden the "presencing of Being," which is the Way of Transformation (*Yi bianhua zhi dao*, or *yi yin yi yang dao*, or *tiandi zhi dao*). This is conveyed by the composition of a hexagram as a situation of life from two trigrams as two situations of nature—more specifically, a unity of the trigrams as two situations of nature, or a unity of the *yin* and the *yang*. While reading the hexagram, one can focus on one, the other, or both trigrams in the hexagram in many ways.

The basic meaning of the hexagram is derived from the *yin-yang* relationships of the trigrams and their component lines.[20] But it is not always possible to see the language meaning of a hexagram from the language meaning of the trigrams. This is why the image (*xiang*) of a hexagram is very important, for in the image one can detect the presencing of the trigrams as a background, base, and ground. Is a trigram an instance of the Presencing of Being? Yes, one may see the eight trigrams as symbols that are regarded as the presencing of the Being when they are used. But even here we do not really have a *direct* Presencing of Being, for the trigrams are composed of three basic lines (*yao*), each line representing *yin* or *yang*, respectively. The direct presentation of Being, therefore, should be seen as alternation-transformation-comprehension-opposition-complementation of the *yin* and *yang*. *Yin* and *yang* in this complex intimate relationship of interdependence present the ultimate form of Being. This form actually is not a real form; it exists only in the forms of things or situations. It is also necessary to point out that the *yin* and *yang* form a unity that functions by way of alternation, transformation, comprehension, opposition, and complementation. In this way, the Being in the *Yijing* light is more indeterminately and dynamically conceived than Being in Heidegger.

One must see Being in the discovery of meaning beyond the symbolic presentation and name of a hexagram. The way to do this is, again, to rely upon *guan*. As explained earlier, *guan* or *xian* (appear), is to look carefully into the overall and extensive presentation of things. It is in the act of *guan* that world presents itself, and we can also say that in the presentation of the world we realize our *guan* action. This does not mean there is no world of things when there is no *guan*; nor does it mean that when we have *guan* there must be objective presentation. The human being looks into himself by reflecting and realizes the feeling or image of his own reality as the creative self. Therefore, for example, in hexagram *Fu* 复 it is asked, "In *Fu*, does it present the heart-mind of heaven and earth?" (复, 其见天地之心乎?) The world of heaven and earth could reflect my observation by presenting the activities of a reviving spring that appeals to me to be the spirit and mind of what I experience in my self as the generation of vitality of life. The heart-mind of heaven and earth is the heart-mind of myself that is realized in the presentation of the heaven and earth in the Fu symbol and judgment, and vice versa. This no doubt can be regarded as a matter of spontaneous unification of the subject and object through a vibrant experience and feeling of my heart and mind. It is also a matter of onto-generativity or onto-creativity of both the subjective and the objective in a moment of openness of *guan*. Thus, one can similarly discover new meanings in the images of the hexagrams: *Bi* 比 ䷇, *Xian* 咸 ䷞, *Heng* 恒 ䷟, *Dazhuang* 大壮 ䷡ (in terms of *ke jian* or "It can be seen that"). When the *Tuan Commentary* speaks of the "*shiyi*" 时义 (timely meaning) or "*shiyong*" 时用 (timely function) or just the "*shi*" 时 (timeliness) of a *gua* 卦 (such as *Gou* 姤 ䷫, *Ge* 革 ䷰, *Jian* 蹇 ䷦, *Guai* 夬 ䷪, *Kan* 坎 ䷜, *Yi* 颐 ䷚, *Sui* 随 ䷐, and *Yu* 豫 ䷏), it speaks of Being as presenced in a concrete situation that can be said to result from the activity of *guan*. In fact, we may even suggest that the possible development of the *Yi* Text (symbolism and judgments) into philosophical discourses (*Zhuan* or *Ten Wings*) presupposes the activity of *guan* as the activity of discovering new meanings and disclosing new world structures of a given situation based on the presencing of Being therein.

In the *Yijing*, *guan* can thus be said to be a natural capacity of preunderstanding, which implies a natural attitude of openness to things. It can be likened to the *Gelassenheit* of Heidegger in which the Being of beings or things will be experienced as being shown. One may say that it implies a general perspective of Being, for it provides a way of illumination that makes things seen and discovered. It is a general principle of ontological difference at work. To make explicit this principle, one can say that one sees or views (*guan*) things from the perspective of Being, which should be identified with *dao*, as we shall see later.

In yet a different sense, *guan* is a viewing from a specific perspective. Hence, one may have *guan* from different perspectives; therefore, *guan* is a projection of perspective onto things, which reveals things relative to this perspective. It is in this sense that we may speak of a specific *guan*, or a relative *guan*, namely, *guan* from a specific or relative point of view as defined by a being, state, or level of reality. In Shao Yong's foreword to his *Jirangji* 击壤集, it is said:

> To view (*guan*) nature (*xing*) from (the perspective of) the *dao*, to view mind from (the perspective of) the nature, to view the body from the point of view of mind and to view things from the point of view of the body, these serve well the purpose of ordering (*zhi*) beings, but are still not off from harm. These would not be as good as viewing the *dao* from the *dao*, viewing the nature from the nature, viewing the mind from mind, viewing the body from the body and viewing things from things. In adopting this way of viewing (*guan*), even if one wishes to do harm, is this possible? If so, thus, to view family from family, to view a nation from a nation, to view the world from the world, the merits of this can be consequently known.[21]

To view X from Y requires one to know Y and thus a self-knowledge of the viewer's position or his point of view, and to view X from X naturally requires one to step out of one's given point of view and to focus on a thing disregarding the ontological difference. It is in this way that a thing is seen in a natural light without drawing a specific conclusion. In this way, the Being of a thing is allowed to come out so that its being can be affirmed. In the relative way of viewing, however, what is viewed shows its Being only in contrast and in relation to another being. This other being, then, discloses some aspects of the Being of the viewed, while, at the same time, it hides other aspects of the Being of the given being.

One may now see that the systems of trigrams and hexagrams respectively present two systems of perspectives on two levels. Each trigram, or each hexagram, is a way to look at or view (*guan*) the world; further, one may equally say that each has its being presented in a specific light so that the world has its Being presented in a specific way. As there are two levels of presentation, the trigrammatic and the hexagrammatic, the world has its Being both presented and hidden at the same time. A level is essentially a level of disclosure as well as a level of concealment of Being. The transformation of these diagrams (*gua*) then indicates the transformation of views according to the transformation of the world.

It is on the basis of this onto-hermeneutical method that Heidegger is able to speak of the transcendental structure of human existence and the facticity of the world of beings. It is on the same methodical basis that the legendary *Yijing* founder, Fuxi, can be said to have discovered the eight trigrams of nature. Revealed in the process of this method are not simply the eight forms, but also their interrelationships, their symmetric oppositions and line-form complementarities, their interdependencies, and their various transformations. What is revealed is time in all its phases: the beginning, the middle process, the ending, and the returning, which just is beginning in the ending. The whole process of time-being thus forms a creative circling. What is revealed is a vertical sense (as opposed to a horizontal sense) of derivation, growth, and development, which is not found in the transformational interrelationships described above. It is found, however, in the tracing to the origin, or source; it is found in the ingression of the origin into the levels of individual events by differentiation. This process reveals a vitality and creativity of life; tracing to the origin reveals vitality and creativity of thinking inspired by the method of *guan*. Indeed, this method and process is one of onto-hermeneutic reflection on the eight forms of trigrams, and it is from such a process that the concept of *taiji* came into being.

Onto-Hermeneutics of *Taiji*

One may ask whether we can have a *guan* of a diagram (*gua*) in a non-relative sense. The answer is affirmative, but this means that one must trace the diagram to its primary origin. This means that the ultimate, or absolute, view must come from the original source: the source from which all diagrams are derived by differentiation. This is the view from the point of the *taiji* (the great ultimate). From this point of view, we may then speak of viewing a thing from the thing itself, for this is the primary way in which the Being of things is disclosed. *Taiji* 太极 is where Being comes to disclose all beings in the world. To view the world from the point of view of *taiji* is to transcend all points of view. It is to see things in the offing or before things are things. It is to also see the in the context of background, grounding of their differences. But to view things from this point of view of *taiji* is not to eliminate all differences among things, nor is it to see no such differences. But to see this as arising from nondifference is to see all possibilities of differences. In this sense it is a dynamical way of seeing things. In order to achieve the dynamism of this seeing, one must return to the source, the *taiji*, and one must see things as beginnings from the same source. One must do this by way of contemplation, or even meditation. Hence, *guan* can be justifiably called "contemplative observation." (There is another sense of contemplation or observation, as already above, namely, to respond to things not only without the senses, but without heart and mind.) To contemplate is to give full play to oneself as an integrated entity toward an integrated response in the form of creatively thinking out and articulating a view.

To spell out the full significance of *guan*, we may therefore conclude that *guan* is *comprehensive, contemplative* and *creative* observation. These three characterizations of *guan* carry explicit reference to comprehension and comprehensive coverage, as well as interactive contemplation with full interplay among sense experiences, feelings, intellect, and creativity. We may even say that *guan* is creative observation based on comprehensive and contemplative observation, but which, once it is established, will lead to more comprehensive and contemplative observation. There is even a circle among the three: comprehension and contemplation lead to creativity, which in turn leads to more comprehension and more contemplation, which further forms the foundation for more creativity.

The formation of the *Yijing* symbolism in trigrams and hexagrams, even in naming the trigrams and hexagrams, as well as attaching or writing out judgments for the individual *gua* 卦 and *yao* 爻 (lines), clearly fits in with this pattern and process of *guan* as comprehensive, contemplative, and creative observation. Devoid of any such single component activity both the symbolism and the interpretation of the symbolism would not be possible. We may indeed regard the formation of the symbolism as the primordial creation of a creative mind based on a vastly comprehensive, profoundly contemplative observation and understanding of a universal reality both outside and inside. Even the very possibility of divination (*zhan* or *bu*) and its interpretation has to depend on the actuality of *guan* as a comprehensive, contemplative and creative action. The symbolic system of the *Yijing* can therefore be said to be a great *guan* 观 (great overview) based on onto-cosmological reality and yet presenting the onto-cosmological reality as such.

The Greek Disclosure of Being and *Guan* in the Yijing

Heidegger wished to find the first disclosure of Being in the beginning of Western philosophy, namely, in the form of Greek philosophy. That is why he took an interest in the fragments of pre-Socratics such as Parmenides, Anaximander, and Heraclitus. His thesis is that in those pre-Socratic philosophers one could find the language of Being, in particular, in the Greek words of *emenai* (to be), *to eon* (being), *tois* (things), *ousi* (beings), *ta panta* (everything), which eventually become represented in Platonic writings by the terms *to on* (Being) and *ta onta* (beings) or *ta eon* and *t'eonta*.[22] According to Heidegger, when Plato uses the words "*ta onta*," he means "a world of ideas (*eide*)," which, in opposition to "what is not (*me on*)," is taken to mean "what truly is, truth, or reality, which is independent of time and space." But for Heidegger, the first meaning of "*ta onta*" is "the actuality of presence, or existence in the present, as opposed to the past and the future." Hence, the original meaning of "*ta onta*" corresponds to the German word "*die Anwesenheit*" (presence in time) taken along with "*die Gegenwart*" (presence in space). The combination of the two words suggests to Heidegger the *coming to presence* of whatever presents itself, namely the Being of beings or the *eon* of *eonta*. This also means that the presence of a being brings Being with it, which further brings forth beings, all in virtue (and by way) of time.

Time is in the nature of beings from Being, and it is also in the Being of beings. Time is the essence of Being as source of beings, whereas beings are vehicles of Being. It is in this sense that Heidegger's notion of Being is actually the same as *dao*, which signifies the source in the aspect of bringing forth things and changes or transformations, namely the change aspect of the *taiji* mentioned in the *Dazhuan* (Great Commentary) of the *Yijing*. We may indeed title this source of beings "Being-time," and we may title the process of being or issuing beings "time-being," or alternatively, "*taiji*" and "*dao*" (two powerful ontic terms designating the ultimate of being and time).

For Heidegger, the Greek thinking in its beginning confronts Being (via *guan* in the *Yijing's* terminology) by focusing on its power of bringing out beings in human language: it is through human language that beings come to be named beings and become known. Hence, language is the foremost and first form in which Being reveals itself as Being. Since language is a human discovery or invention, one may infer that it is the first characteristic way of realizing human being as Being. It perhaps can be regarded as the first transcendental representation of the Being-time based on the reflection of *Dasein* as *Dasein*, through which Heidegger can criticize all other rigid forms of representation of Being and reinstate the vitality of self-knowing as an existing subject at present and in the presence of Being. For the Greeks, this is first known as *logos*, as mentioned in Anaximander's and Heraclitus's fragments. In other words, *logos* (propositional rationality) is the first disclosure with its specific concentration on the gathering power of Being in beings in ancient Greek philosophy.

Equally important in Greek thinking on being is the disclosure of Being as *moira* (necessitation) in the fragments of Parmenides, which suggest the fateful or logically necessary identity of Being of thinking and thinking of Being in which beings are seen as "presencing of Being." In this sense, we may see *moira* as Being-time in which time is only seen in the form of Being and thereby assumes no existence in any form.

Another important concept from the pre-Socratic fragments is *aletheia* (unconcealment), which means uncovering or disclosure of beings in whatever form Being is concealed. In this sense, *aletheia* brings the *logos* and *moira* to bear on each other, for *logos* brings out beings in human language and *moira* obliterates beings in human thinking. Both are forms of *aletheia* and thus take two forms of realization: the Being to beings and beings to Being, or Being to and from beings and Being to and from, beings via thinking. Perhaps a naturalistic reading of *aletheia* is more appropriate here, yet one still cannot forget the logical point that human thinking is a reflection of ontological difference which leads from beings to beings but which could intend to achieve ontological identity by bringing beings to Being.

In the naturalistic sense of *aletheia* in the form of Being leading to beings, one can speak of the differentiation of the *dao* into ten thousand things (*wanwu* 万物) and the formation of the world of beings in which *Dasein* is one among them. In this process we can also observe that each being has its own principle of being that we can call the nature of a thing or being, namely what makes it so and what maintains its being as being in a specific way. Individual nature (*xing* 性) in this sense is not separate from the *dao*, for it receives its confirmation and substance from the *dao*; more importantly, it thus constitutes a way in which the Being or the *dao* can be seen or disclosed by *guan*.

For Heidegger, what is important is that the Greek notions of *logos*, *moira*, and *aletheia* all indicate that beings manifest themselves as being present, because they issue forth from Being in a process of time; moreover, time indicates an activity or process of natural disclosure (*aletheia*) in which Being as the presencing of what presents itself as disclosed or concealed. This, for Heidegger, is the essence of understanding the truth of Being, though he has not come to discuss how this comes to form a structure and how this can be used once the structure is formed, as in the case of the *Yijing*. The Greeks simply lost focus on this matter and neglected the once primary and fresh vision and meaning of Being or *eon*. Instead, they sought something else based on an interest in seeking the transcendence of a world of ideas. The turning-point could very well be Socrates, whose desire to transcend and eternalize, in a *daimon* spirituality and to definitize in definitions of things, turns our thinking from onto-cosmology of Being to philosophizing about human identity and its self-interest in ideas or ideology.

According to Heidegger, this ideological turn of thinking leads to seeking a substance idea for explaining everything else, and the seeking cannot be stopped because no result of the seeking can satisfy the human mind as *Dasein*. In such seeking, Being is reduced to one being among others and becomes a present entity variously named as idea, energy, *actus purus*, reason, will, and will to power or spirit of God.[23]

The great difference between the Greek beginning of Western metaphysics and the Chinese beginning of Chinese metaphysics is the ability to continue and develop original insights into Being-time and time-Being: whereas Socrates, Plato, and Aristotle came to develop an atemporal world of ideas that led to a transcendent religion and mechanistic science (all beginning by an act of transcendence or self-transcendence of Being and time in Socrates and Plato), the Chinese developed the *Yijing* by way of systematic observation of the world. This development is made possible by the *guan* way of thinking, inspired by Being and time, which enriches life as life. At the same time, however, the *guan* way of thinking obliterates the abstract world of ideas, logic, and beings merely understood as beings, viz., the world depicted by mechanistic science. In the *Yijing* philosophy one thus finds the home of the fundamental metaphysics of Being and time (the house of Being and time) and their union in which the disclosures of Being in beings and beings in Being are dynamically and continuously possible.[24] In a word, this is the world of the symbolic forms called *xiang* 象.

Through his study of Anaximander and Parmenides, Heidegger appears to come to appreciate and confirm the profound relevance of time for Being, for it is in these pre-Socratic philosophers that Being is seen to issue forth beings in the mode of presencing (coming to presence) that leads to presentation in the present. In this sense, being is being present, which is self-presentation as well as coming to presence. This means that being present, self-presentation, and coming to presence among other beings are internally interdependent and organically interwoven. They are the three aspects of time-being and being-time, the unity of which should be provisionally named "dao," which, otherwise, is unnamable or unthought.

The Heideggerian idea of the "unthought" (*das Ungedachte*) or the "unthinkable" (*das Unvordenkliche*) and Laozi's idea of the "unnamable" (*feichangming*) are similar and perhaps speak to the Same, that is, the Ultimate. In the *Yijing* text, it is the totalistic unity and coherence of the symbolic system that speaks to this Same. In the *Yizhuan*, it is the terms "*Yi*" (transformation), "*taiji*," and "*dao*" that collectively and respectively convey the ultimate as the ultimate. In the Neo-Confucian system of the Cheng Brothers and Zhu Xi, this "ultimate" receives the name of "*li*," whereas in Zhang Zai it receives the names of "*taixu*" and "*taihe*."[25] In later Heidegger, the term "appropriation," or "*Ereignis*," is given to naming this Ultimate as the Same.[26] This also means that time and Being form an inseparable relationship of mutual definability and interreference in understanding (and therefore finding meanings in) actual instances of beings. There is no time without Being and no Being without time. Thus, Being can be said to be an aspect of time just as time can be said to be an aspect of Being. Perhaps, the best way to describe this relationship is the rich, multimeaningful statement of Cheng Yi: "The substance and the function come from the same source and there is no gap between the manifest and the unmanifest." (See Cheng Yi's own preface to his *Yichuan Yizhuan*.)

Substance (*ti*) and Function (*yong*) in *Guan*

As "substance" (*ti* 体) and "function" (*yong* 用) are used in Chinese philosophy to define a rich variety of relationships that are organically interrelated and mutually enriching, to see the relationship of Being and Time in this web is useful for both illuminating and explicating purposes. One can see *ti* and *yong* in relationships of state/act, substance/functioning (or operating), cause/result, source/offspring, rest/movement, essence/

form, and inner/outer. As we can see, all these categorical relationships characterize a relation of source or root or ground to development, embodiment and state of being which can be described as that of complementary opposition and mutual enhancement. The most intricate of all these is that *ti* and *yong* can be regarded as mutually subject-centered and reciprocally object-focused. This a matter of exchangeable focusing and centering is possible because they share a common source and root from which both spring forth and from which it acquires the power and impetus of mutual enhancement and interchange.

Many polarities of action and movement are found in time or the time-process of being (which is the coming to presence), for example, approach and withdrawal, emergence and evanescence, disclosure and concealment, appearing and disappearing, rising and falling, coming and going, living and dying. Thus, it is in the nature of time that polarities as such come into being; they present time's manner of being. This explains how the Greek view (*guan*) the world of beings before the abstraction of ideas from the world takes place. In this regard, the Greeks share with the *Yijing* their discoveries of polarities of qualities of beings or simply the polarities of beings, polarity being a mode of presence of Being as time or time as Being. However, when Socrates comes to seek rational definition and thus metaphysical essences of beings via reason or *logos* as a transcending force, the world of such an ontological or ontic understanding is lost and withdrawn. This is seen by Nietzsche as the tragedy of "the death of God," which is coeval with the birth of reason or *logos* as a power toward the eternity of ideas and norms. *Logos* becomes the revealing power of human language for Being and Time become transformed into a power of concealing Being and a methodological fixation on beings as beings. To recover or to rediscover Being, one has to go beyond Socratic rationalization of Being and time so that Being and time can be differently confronted with freedom by and in the human existence.

For the *Yijing*, there is no such rationalistic turning and there is no seeking of essences of things or beings in terms of the beings themselves, but all beings are seen and taken to involve a totality of presentation and presence of beings that reveal their ground as Being or *dao*, or alternatively *taiji*. Hence, the *Xici* commentary states: "One *yin* and one *yang* is called the *dao*"; moreover, "There is *taiji* in change (*Yi*): The *taiji* generates the two norms (*yin* and *yang*), the two norms generate the four forms and the four forms generate the eight trigrams" (*Xici Shang* 11). In this presentational display of Being, not only are all things brought about in interrelated forms, but also all forms can be traced to their historical or temporal beginnings along a process of differentiation and integration. Thus, Being is always seen as a temporal process of rising and falling, coming and going, resting and moving, or the presentational display of up and down, right and left, active and passive, ruling and the ruled, and so on, which also implies a process of time-bound transformational interpenetration. There is no static and fixed relationship but always an exchange and interchange against a background of creative unity.

All these polar relationships, whether horizontal display/transformation or vertical display/transformation, are to be revealed in the basic presencing of Being in the form of the *yin* (the shade) and the *yang* (the light), the form of *gang* (firm) and *rou* (soft), or in the form of *dong* (movement) and *jing* (rest), all of which reflect Being's movements of opening (*pi*) and closing (*he*). In his manner, then, the disclosing and withdrawing (or hiding) in the Heideggerian understanding of Being can be explained by the *yin* and *yang* of *dao*, whereas the term "*aletheia*" in early Heidegger stresses the alternation and simultaneity of disclosure and concealment of Being in beings, and *ereignis* in later Heidegger stresses the function of creative appropriation or making of things or beings become most relevant.

In the *Discourse Commentary* (*Shuogua* 说卦) it is said:

> (The sage) views (*guan*) changes in *yin* and *yang* and thus establishes the trigrams; (sages) develop their viewing, resulting in terms of firm and soft and thus generate the lines of trigrams; (the sage) harmonizes these changes and transformations in terms of *dao* and *de* (the virtual powers and natures of individual beings) so that an order of correctness and rightness can be implemented. He is to exhaust the rational understanding (*li*), fulfill nature (*jin xing*) in order to reach for identification with the ultimate (*dao* or *tian*) (namely, reaching for the destiny, *zhi ming*). (section 1)

In this context of fundamental ontological understanding, *li*, *xing*, and *ming* are all different forms of manifestation of *dao* or Being, each of which serves the purpose of illuminating the substance and function of Being. One may even suggest the resemblance of *li* to the *logos* of Anaximander, the resemblance of *ming* to the *moira* of Parmenides, and finally the resemblance of *xing* as the realized and revealed nature of human existence to the *aletheia* of Heraclitus. But there is an important difference: the *ming* in the *Yijing* understanding of Being does not suggest death as an object of anxiety; on the contrary, *ming* implies a reconciliation with extinction or death without anxiety (*angst*) and a return of the individual being to Being or *dao* as the ultimate, under the spur of the sense of misgivings (*youhuan*) about one's loss of understanding and failure in emulating the *dao* or *tian*.

To conclude, we see how the *guan* method of seeing and thinking in the *Yijing* brings out a cosmo-ontological and humanological presentation of beings (things) against a background and in the context of presence of Being (*dao* or *taiji*, the two being conveyed by the term "*Yi*"). In the *Yijing*, this presentation and presence are well sustained and thus materialize into a systematic presentation of symbolic forms and polaristic structures: they are direct results of sustained *guan*, rather than the outcome of a transcendental conceptual analysis or a short-term intellectual intuition of mind. *This is how onto-hermeneutical thinking works.* Along with this presentation is the realization and understanding of the natures of the presentation in relation to the observer, or the viewer, which are to be described in terms of *li* 理, *xing* 性, and *ming* 命 or *logos*, *aletheia*, *and moira*. These notions form a unity of understanding of Being in human existence, namely, *Dasein* in Heidegger, but in the *Yizhuan* the unity is to be manifested in a viewing person entitled "sage" (*shengren* 圣人).

Whether we use *li*, *xing*, and *ming* or *logos*, *aletheia*, and *moira*, we must see *guan* as capable of invoking deep feeling and understanding from a person pertaining to the experience of the totality and ontological significance of a situation. In this sense, that which is presented as viewable (*keguan* 可观, as distinguished from *suoguan* 所观), must already be an embodiment of truth and value so that it may inspire an understanding and a feeling of truth and value. Hence, there is reciprocity between the viewer/observer (*guanzhe* 观者) and that which is observed and observable: the viewer can give rise to value in a specific situation just as the viewable can give rise to value in a deep observing self. We may say that that this is possible due to the underlying unity of a felt polarity between the viewer and the viewable, which is to be disclosingly realized in the process of viewing.[27] One can see that this unity of feeling in fact can be explained as arising from the polarization and its consequent unity between the view and the viewable in a common field. Because of the dynamic nature of viewing process, there is an exchange, not a fixation, of *yin* and *yang* roles between the viewer and the viewable. The achieved state of viewing is therefore one of total presentation of a situation in which the viewer becomes enhanced and enriched in her ability to reach for the *dao* and for a more cultivated self toward making better judgment and action in life.

Analysis of the *Guan-Gua* 观卦 ䷓: *Guan* as Based on Centrality (*Zhong* 中) and Rectitude (*Zheng* 正)

Fortunately, we have a *gua* named "*Guan*," the twentieth *gua* with wind above and earth below, which can lend itself to an onto-hermeneutical understanding of viewing in view of the totality of things and beings, namely in view of the *dao* or the *taiji*. The term "*guan*" does not appear in other *gua* except with one occurrence in the twenty-seventh *gua* named Yi in which "*guan*" appears in the sentence "Forsake your divine tortoise, but look at (*guan*) my face, while I am eating." In this occurrence, the meaning of "*guan*" is just the same as the "*guan*" in the *Guan gua*. In order to effectively and meaningfully interpret and understand *Guan-gua* (*gua* #20), we shall follow the flow of the *gua* and register the essentials.

First, the name "*guan*" apparently is derived from a scene where a bird looks at its surroundings. Even today there is the water bird called *guan*, which must carefully scan fish in water to survive. Hence, *guan* suggests a state of constant awareness, alertness, and watchfulness so that one can not only find one's place in the world but can act from one's understanding of the world and one's position in it. In this case, one might think of *guan* as "a bird's eye view" in its comprehensiveness and watchfulness. We also note that the *Guan gua* corresponds structurally to the trigram Gen 艮 (*gen*), which means stillness as exemplified by a hill. The symbol of a hill means that there is a framework or manner as well as movement and dynamism, just as there is a solid hill that has wind blowing over its land. When we understand *guan* as a process of comprehensive, contemplative, and creative observation, we can appreciate how dynamic creativity is fermented and comprehended in a still and profound contemplation, as suggested by the trigrammatic form of Gen and the hexagramatic content of the *Guan gua*.

Second, with regard to the *gua*-judgment of *Guan*, we begin with the idea that it is possible for one to perform oblation in sacrificial rites without making actual offerings if one has a reverent heart. This judgment suggests that in the contemplative observation of the *guan* one can participate in a ritual situation with sincerity and serious attentiveness without being engaged in the actual performance of details of the ritual. What counts is the presence of a genuine heart that feels and comprehends reality by "feeling and response" (*ganying* 感应) to the overall viewing.[28] As the trigrammatic composition indicates, this is likened to wind moving over the land in the *Xiang Commentary*. The *Xiang* thereby suggests that this analogy of *guan* would inspire sage rulers to make their rounds throughout their respective countries in order to know how people feel and to know what they need, so that the ruler can respond by adopting an enlightened policy of education and edification. However, to be successful, the rules require a genuine heart that understands realities through feeling and responding to that which is being viewed, that is, the rulers' subjects. This indicates a reciprocal interaction as suggested in the relationship between the viewer and the viewed.

Third, we are led from the above to the important question of what conditions one has to meet in order to achieve the reciprocating relationship in a genuine overall observation of a situation. The answer is well provided for by the *Tuan Commentary* on the *gua* that conforms with our explanation of the standpoint of *Guan*. The *Tuan* says: "The great view is from above, it is conforming and penetrating: one should maintain a state of centrality and rectitude when viewing the world" (*Tuan* judgment of *Guan gua*). Although the great view could be above and the viewer can look up to the view, it is far better to look from above so that one will have an overview like wind over land. The point is how we could achieve such a view from above. The answer is as suggested: maintain a position of centrality and rectitude. Hence, the key notions for understanding the great view (*daguan* 大观) are *zhong* (centrality) and *zheng* (rectitude). But then what are *zhong* and *zheng*? To answer this question, we must temporarily leave our discussion of *gua*.

Both *zhong* and *zheng* are to be realized in an individual person, and by extension they are realized in the position that an individual occupies.[29] But there is also a fundamental difference between *zhong* and *zheng*: whereas *zhong* refers to the central position an individual occupies among all positions, *zheng* refers to the state and posture of the individual independent of position but which could be expressed in external features and internal attitude. *Zhong* also could express something inside or internal to an individual, but what makes the individual have the *zhong* quality is his/her relation to other individuals; it is the relation from which he/she is able to relate to others without effort and from which he/she is to derive strength and goodness by nature.

The terms "*zhong*" and "*zheng*" can be used as verbs, which means an individual can realize *zhong* and *zheng* by achieving an ideal goal or ideal state of value that one should not turn away from. Ontologically speaking, we must see *zhong* as the most desirable position of being, that is, the source of cosmic creativity, while we must see *zheng* as the most desirable state in which one can maintain one's position of centrality or one's virtues in a situation which is not *zhong*. Thus, we can see the possibility of having *zhong* without *zheng*, and vice versa. If one has the position of centrality without having the state of rectitude, one has to strive for rectitude in order to fulfill one's potentiality for bringing benefits to oneself and others. On the other hand, if one has rectitude without centrality, one would not be in a position to achieve optimum efficacy of influence and benefiting, but nevertheless could maintain one's integrity even in times of adversity. The most desirable state for an individual (or anything) to have is both centrality of position and rectitude of state. Such a position would be the source of efficacious virtues, which is to say virtues that can benefit others as well as oneself.

Along these lines, the *Wenyan Commentary* makes the point, "Great indeed is the creative (*Qian*). It is firm, powerful, central and correct (*gang jian zhong zheng*). It is pure and quintessential essence (*chuncui jing*)." In this passage one can see that the *Qian gua* represents both the creative source of all things and firmness and powerful strength. Hence, it is appropriate to regard the primordial creativity of what the *Qian* stands for—namely, *dao* or *taiji*—as the ultimate manifestation and fulfillment of centrality and the state of rectitude. One may thus say that anything that has the fitting position and is in a state to be creative has the position of centrality and the state of rectitude. In Song Neo-Confucianism, Zhu Xi observed that everything is *taiji*.[30] It is from the view that everything can be creatively effective, and this makes it possible to say that everything can be in a central position and a state of rectitude. Of course, this may be because everything has its nature derived from and based on the primordial source of creativity, namely the onto-cosmological *taiji* or *dao*. This also means that anything that maintains its position and state of centrality and rectitude must maintain its link and identification with the ultimate source of being and becoming.

In the earliest texts of the *Yijing*, *zhong* is seen as designating the occupation of the central line of the trigram; hence, it is seen as occupation of the second and fifth lines of the hexagram. But if one asks what constitutes the centrality of the whole six-line hexagram, the answer is that this centrality falls up the middle two lines of the *gua*, namely, the third and fourth lines, which are regarded as the most difficult, even risky, lines in the whole *gua*. But these two lines do stand for human and for what a human may have understood and what he decides to do. Such a person must consult the central line of the upper trigram, which is the fifth line, or power line, of the hexagram and the central line of the lower trigram, which is the second line, or hope line, of the hexagram so that a balanced understanding and decision for action could be made. As interpreted, anything attached to those central lines has the initiating power to reach out for creative influence. *Zheng*, however, is not attached to line positions; rather, it is given to the quality and nature of a force occupying a line.

The quality of the force occupying the line is generally regarded as in a state of rectitude if it fits with the quality of the line in terms of *yin* and *yang*. If a *yang* force takes place in a *yang* line or a *yin* force takes place in a *yin* line, the situation is fitting and becoming and hence is in a state of rectitude, otherwise it is not fitting, not becoming and hence not in a state of rectitude. Accordingly, this would decrease its power to be creatively effective. This is quite understandable because a force has to be reinforced by its *situ* and hence requires the *yang* force to go with the *yang* position and the *yin* force to go with the *yin* position. This is what would be the basic operational meaning of rectitude. By extension, an individual would always have to ask whether one's own qualities befit one's surroundings and the role one is meant to play. If they are befitting, the individual is in a state of rectitude, and if not, she is not. This test would make *zheng* an intrinsic requirement of the creativity of an individual, which would nicely contrast with the extrinsic requirement of such in the notion of centrality or *zhong*. Hence, in the hexagrams *zhong* does not entail *zheng* nor *zheng* entail *zhong*.[31]

The *Tuanzhuan* always admonishes persons to maintain *zheng* and from this firmness (*zhen* 贞), even if one does not have the strategic position of centrality, to exercise creativity (even in a place of weakness and in time of adversity).[32]

It is relevant to mention that in later developments of Confucianism, *zhong* and *zheng* each becomes internalized as a state of the original (human) nature and consequently the state of the heart-mind of a person. This is the philosophy of centrality (*zhong*) and harmony (*he*) in the

Doctrine of the Mean (Zhongyong). In this philosophy zhong and zheng must be cultivated as virtues for one has to cultivate one's nature and heart-mind to retain original centrality and rectitude and to remove the contrary from obscuring or obstructing the nature or the heart-mind in a person. Hence, zhong and zheng can be developed as virtues of a person.

With regard to he: he can be considered an extension of zhong when zhong interacts properly with outside circumstances. Zheng is not specifically mentioned except in reference to the Confucian sayings on "rectifying oneself" (zheng ji 正己) or "correct target" (zheng hu 正鵠) or "rectifying names" (zheng ming 正名). The Zhongyong speaks of "Being orderly, serious, in centered and correct are sufficient for (a person) to achieve and maintain dignity and respectability." But again this is not an elaboration to require zheng as an independent requirement for being creatively interacting and participatory in the large world.[33]

One may remark that when the Zhongyong 中庸 thematizes the onto-cosmological importance of "fulfilling centrality and harmony" (zhi zhonghe 致中和), it has reintroduced zhong and consequently he 和 (harmony) as onto-cosmological qualities, which are to be seen in when "heaven and earth become well-positioned and ten thousand things become nourished." The Confucian internalization of zhong and zheng as virtues has a good consequence: one can see and cultivate the virtues of zhong and zheng within oneself; moreover, zhong and zheng are not only foundations for moral or virtuous action but are an adequate basis for the overseeing or comprehensive observation and understanding of the world.

We may now return to an analysis of the lines of the Guan gua, which has the configuration ䷓. We can see how each line is characterized in reference to the quality of zhong in position and the quality of zheng in state. We also see how zheng increases as one goes up the figure and in combination with the zhong position and how this indicates different views of different qualities. The first line (closest to the bottom of the figure) is named "Child's View" (Tong guan 童观). It is conditioned and confined by its position (beginning and yang) and state (yin). There is no blame for small persons (xiao ren 小人), as the small person has limited resources. For a superior person, however, a child's view would be a problem. Both the superior person and the child should act as will befit expectations.

The second line is named "Peeping View" (Kui guan 窥观), which is characterized by yin (although zhong) in a lower position and yin (zheng as befitting the position) in state as well. It describes the view of some people in some situations such as women peeping hidden behind doors. This view does not befit a superior person, or any person, when confronted with a normal situation.

The third line shows a change from the previous views in both *zhong* and *zheng*: as it becomes part of the central position in the whole hexagram, but does not quite attain a state of rectitude. It is at a critical stage or level of transformation and hence requires and prompts a view, which would help to make decisions to move forward or to step backward in one's life. This, of course, is within one's rights, and it is even an obligation and hence relies on our deeper understanding of the way. The important point about "view" in this line is that *guan* is practically oriented: it is not simply to overview one's decisions to move forward or to step backward—it is to view the world and one's life in order to move forward or step backward. The fourth line being *zhong* on the upper side and *zheng* for the conformity of position and state in *yin* says in its judgment that it is time to see the light of a country (*guan guo zhi guang* 观国之光); this also means it is advantageous to visit a ruler and become his guest of honor. This requires the person at this position to take initiative in making the visit and thus acquire a relevant view. This implies that there is a propitious scenario worthy of the exploration. Without the inherent positional centrality and the state-rectitude, one would not have the view or the ability to develop the view.

When we come to the fifth line, we normally come to an upper (or great) centrality posing for great overview of the world and self; this calls for a state of rectitude to achieve what is potentially a great view. It happens that in this *gua* the fifth line occupied by the *yang* force (namely, 9-5) has a built-in power and rectitude by experience and convention as a line such as 9-5 or 6-3 refers a position with its inherent quality of *yin* or *yang* given in the whole situation or environment of the *gua* or symbolic form. Hence, it is high time to examine one's life (which must be worthy of being viewed and has something valuable to offer for viewing) with a goal to refine it, and also to achieve freedom from doubts regarding whether to move forward or backward as in the case of the third line occupied by a *yin* force (namely, 6-3). The *Xiang* for this 9-5 line says that to look over my life is to look over people (*guan min*); to look over one's life is to view the virtues of people in order to foster self-improvement for a rule based upon self-examination.[34] I propose here to explain the second *guan* as "show" (*xian* or *shi*). Hence, to examine my life is to show people my life so that, as a ruler, I have nothing to hide and nothing to be ashamed of, and perhaps, instead, I have something to present as an exemplary model for people to emulate. This is the way to become a responsible and trustworthy person in high position.

Coming to the sixth line, one comes to the last portion of one's life, or to a stage or level where one does not have great power or should not have it. As upper-9, it is neither formally *zhong* nor formally *zheng*, yet it does enjoy a high position and presumably has passed through many interesting experiences. It is thus the time to look over one's life objectively, detached and impartial. To do this is also a form of cultivating one's virtue, and this is no doubt a worthy way of establishing a worthy view from which to view oneself and everything else.

To conclude, we can see how the *Guan gua* has illustrated the dynamic and dialectical nature of *guan*. Specifically, its *tuan* message has provided us with a fundamental principle, the principle of *zhong zheng* 中正, for understanding and evaluating the *guan* as a process and even a method for understanding and evaluating the world, life, and reality.

CHAPTER 6

Yin-Yang (阴阳) Way of Onto-Cosmic Thinking and Philosophy of the *Yi* (易)

Introductory Remarks

When reading the history of Chinese philosophy, one will inevitably ask when and how Chinese philosophy originated. The answer to this question is that Chinese philosophy as deep thinking on the nature of the world and the nature of human self has its origins in the formation of the *Yijing* (易经 the *Book of Changes*) as a text at the beginning of the Zhou Dynasty in the early twelfth century BCE.[1] The *Yijing* was known first as the *Zhouyi* (周易), which suggests that the method of knowing changed in the time of Zhou. The name also suggests that it deals with all changes (易 *Yi*) in the world, covering both natural changes and changes introduced through human action. Before the *Zhouyi* it is believed there was the *Yinyi* in the Yin Period (circa 1600 BCE) and the *Xiayi* in the Xia Period (circa 2000 BCE).

To say that the beginning of the formation of the *Zhouyi* is the beginning of Chinese philosophy is an important proposition in light of the contemporary findings on matters related to the history of the text known as the *Zhouyi*, and also in light of the influence of the *Zhouyi* on the development of Chinese philosophy. It is through the disclosure of philosophical insights embodied in the texts of the *Zhouyi* that the book was transformed from a text of divination into a text of philosophical wisdom, which can be variously described as philosophy of the *Yi* or the onto-cosmology of *Yi* or the *benti* (本体) ontology of the *Yi* (易的本体有论).[2] This transformation is essential for understanding how the

Zhouyi could be regarded as forming a system of ideas or views about the world and ourselves as human beings. We must first explain how the *Zhouyi* can be said to contain philosophical insights in the sense of presupposition and preunderstanding.

In order to understand the *Yijing* essentially as a book of philosophical wisdom that was developed and used as a book of divination, we must know what it concerns and how it is to be understood as a book of primordial philosophy. In simple terms, this text concerns the genesis of the onto-cosmological world (nature) in terms of the movement and rest of *yin* and *yang* forces at the most basic level. The idea is that the world is composed of activities of *yin* and *yang* forces that systematically form world-situations in which we find ourselves. This understanding has the potentiality for explaining all things in their formation and transformation. It is also congenial with incorporating human beings as part and parcel of the onto-cosmological process of reality-realization. This has the benign consequence to the effect that a human being could actively change the world. This understanding also forms the core of thinking in the formation of the image-forms (trigrams/hexagrams *gua* 卦) and *yao* (爻 six lines that structure each *gua*) in the *Yijing* text. One may indeed regard the *gua* as symbols for situation-making configurations of living forces (*vis viva*) of change (namely, the *qi* 气) and the *yao* as symbols of the living forces of *yin* (阴) and *yang* (阳) natures.[3] Normally a broken line signifies a living force of *yin* and a solid line signifies a living force of the *yang*.

As we shall see, the capacity to change naturally causes us to regard our *yin* and *yang* experiences of nature as revealing creative forces of *yin* and *yang* in natural reality. At the same time, the terms *yin* and *yang* retain their phenomenological meanings in terms of our experiences of light and dark, motion and rest, hardness and softness, and so on. Not only could *yin-yang* be regarded as living forces of nature, they can also be treated as qualities of things, and qualities of things could be experienced and described also as a matter of *yin* and *yang* forces, namely as creative forces of the *qi*. It is interesting to note that the original texts of *Zhouyi* did not mention *qi*, and it is not until the writing of the *Yizhuan* that the term *qi* was used. But this is not to say that experiences and understanding of *qi* as living forces may not begin with the observation and experiences of the *yin-yang* forces in process of change in reality (nature).

Yin-Yang Way of Onto-Cosmic Thinking

Although the original Yi Text rarely mentioned the *yin* and *yang*, we must assume that they are taken for granted insofar as our experiences of nature and ourselves are concerned. Yet a distinction between experience of *yin* and experience of the *yang* must be made. This no doubt gives rise to the statement in the *Xici*: "Alternation of one *yin* and one *yang* is to be called *dao* (道)." (*Yi yin yi yang zhi wei dao*.)[4] Hence, we normally assume that we know what the *yin-yang* model of thinking stands for. But in actuality we may not really know what *yin* and *yang* are or how these two words are used in the Yi Text. In asserting that "the alternation of one *yin* and one *yang* is to be called *dao*," we must notice the use of the term "*zhiwei*" (之谓 "is to be called") in distinction from the term "*weizhi*" (谓之 "is called"). The former indicates a real definition that consists of an insight into the nature of things that leads to the definition of a thing in light of the insight, whereas the latter indicates a conventional definition that consists in identifying a use of language of description by convention. In light of this distinction, one can see what is said as "*yi yin yi yang zhi wei dao*" is a reflection of insight into reality of change by the author of the *Xici*. Along the same lines, we may also identify the similar insightful real definitions in various sections of the *Xici*. We have the following assertions:

> To be abundant is to be called great deed; to renew oneself is to be called sagely virtue. To be creative of creativity is called the change. To form an image is to be called Power (乾). To follow is to be called Receptivity (坤). To explore into the numbers is to know the future and is called the future is to be called divination. To comprehend changes is to be called an event. In the exchanges of *yin* and *yang* there is unpredictability and this is to be called the divine." (*Xici Shang* 5)

In contrast, we see how the author of the *Xici* illustrates the use of "*weizhi*":

> The benevolent (仁者) sees it and call it the benevolent, the wise (智者) sees it and calls it the wise. . . . Thus the closing of the gate we call it *Kun* (坤), the opening of the gate we call it the *Qian* (乾). One closing and one opening we call it change (变 *bian*). Going and coming without limit we call it

going through (通 *tong*). To present we call it the form-image (象 *xiang*). To form we call it vessel [器 *qi* i.e., come to have a function to be used] to manufacture and make use of we call it to follow [法 *fa*, a norm or a model]. To be constantly and generally used in and by people we call it the divine. (*Xici Shang* 5, 11)

One can see the distinction between what is characterized as "*weizhi*" and what is characterized as "*zhiwei*" in the following way: the assertions in terms of the former reflects a deeper cosmological experience, whereas the latter is intended to describe what has been conventionally identified in the use of the language by people. Hence, I suggest the distinction between them as reflecting a movement of understanding from common experience to insightful experience in the formation of a cosmological ontology or onto-cosmology of reality as experienced by the early *Yi*-thinkers.

In connection with this understanding, we must come to face the question of how the *yin-yang* model of thinking is epistemologically justified and the question of how this model leads to a philosophy of onto-cosmology of change embedded in a system of image-forms (*gua*) in the *Yijing*. I shall first describe how the *yin-yang* way of thinking is conceived and formulated. I shall then introduce three principles as the foundation on which our experiences of *yin* and *yang* become consolidated in a system of onto-cosmology. Then I will introduce some methodological principles of understanding and interpretation that would unify the division of the *Xiangshu* (象数) and *Yili* (义理) schools for an integrative approach to this philosophy of change in the *Yijing*. We shall note the stages of how this transformation took place.

Yin-Yang Way / Model of Onto-Cosmic Thinking

To understand the world, we must observe the world. To understand the human self, we must reflect on the human self. It is from this point of view that the beginning of the *Yijing* must be traced to the process of observation and reflection as revealed in the formation of the *gua* system. The world on which human observation focuses presents itself as a world of changes. It is a world of things in change and a world of change in which things emerge. When a person observes the world thoroughly and without missing any form of change, she is said to be engaged in "a comprehensive observation" (观 *guan*) of the world, as described in the *Yizhuan* for the *Zhouyi*. This effort to make comprehensive observation leads to the following results:

1. One observes that changes in the world always take the form of one *yin* and one *yang* in a relation of reciprocity and resonance. This experience comes from observation of the shine of light together with the darkness or shade that forms the background of the light. Hence the word "*yang*" originally means the lighted side of a hill in the South whereas the word "*yin*" means the shaded side of a hill in the North. It is then generalized to mean a contrasting correlation between the light and the dark. The phenomenological observation also indicates that whenever there is *yang* there is *yin*, and where there is *yin* there is *yang*. Besides, we could experience the *yang* as the visible and the *yin* as the invisible or the *yang* as the formed and the *yin* as the unformed. Hence what is *yin* could be experienced as what is given as the invisible preexisting background of a thing whereas what is *yang* is hence experienced as what is given as the visible thrust of formation of a thing. In this sense *yin* and *yang* are to be understood phenomenologically in dynamic context of alternation or correlation. The alternation of one *yin* and one *yang* as a process of *dao* no doubt contributes to our understanding of the *dao* as both the source-origin and the creative process of the *yin* and *yang*. For it implies that *yin* and *yang* are to emerge as a related pair of forces and states of becoming through the agency of the *dao*. Earlier Laozi (老子) in *Daodejing* (道德经) has suggested that "the *Dao* generates one, one generates two and the two generates three. The three generates all things. All things bear the *yin* and hold the *yang*, and reach harmony by dynamically mixing [the *yin* and the *yang*]."[5] Laozi may come to the notion of *dao* through reflecting on the origin of all things. One may also come to see the *dao* through a process of becoming by way of *yin* and *yang* alternation. It is in the *Xici* that one finds how the becoming of the *yin* and *yang* is defined as the *dao*.[6]

Another effect of this is that many other qualities of things could be intuitively and generally identified as *yin* and *yang* as extended qualities of *yin* and *yang*. Even things and life forms could be by intuitive association and experience identified or classified as *yin* and *yang* in action. Thus, the qualities of motion (动 *dong*) and rest (静 *jing*) could be said to be matter of *yang* and *yin* as motion is more a thrust of force like a ray of light whereas rest appears to be a background for the motion that remains not so noticeable. Similarly, we can see hardness (刚 *gang*) and softness (柔 *rou*) as more or less a matter of *yin* and *yang* because hardness in the sense of larger resistance and/or thrust of force is more *yang* than *yin*, whereas softness with smaller resistance and tolerance is more *yin* than *yang*. When an object is more dominated by *yang* qualities, it is a *yang* thing; when an object is more dominated by *yin* qualities, it is a *yin* matter. In light of this extended consideration, the whole world of things and changes can be regarded as evolved from forces of *yin* and *yang*. It is in reference to this *yin-yang* analysis that Chinese medical art is able develop a system of diagnosis, medication, and medical care based on the *yin-yang* relationships of interaction, reinforcement, overcoming, submission, balance, and harmonization.

Epistemologically, we must also observe that *yin* and *yang* forces could be experienced as a matter of degrees of contrast and therefore as a relation rather than as a quality. In other words, under certain circumstances the *yin* quality is only relatively *yin* in contrast with a *yang* quality, whereas it is identified as a *yang* quality in contrast with a *yin* quality, such as in the case of hardness and softness. This relativity of *yin-yang* distinction must be justified in a context or situation where degrees of *yin* and *yang* could be experienced and identified. This is not to say that *yin* and *yang* do not have objective reference in the context of an onto-cosmology founded and supported by comprehensive experience of things in the world. This means that we must be reminded of contexts of identification of the *yin* and the *yang*. We must distinguish between our judgments of *yin* and *yang* based on our limited experience and special ends from our understanding of *yin* and *yang* as cosmic forces and states of becoming.

2. Through observation and experience we can see that *yin* and *yang* are related in many intimate reciprocal and interactive ways: *yang* can be said to bring out *yin*, just as *yin* can be said to bring out *yang*. In effect, this interaction suggests that *yin* and *yang* must arise at the same time from a primordial source of activity and creativity, known as *taiji* (太极 the great ultimate). Since *taiji*, like the *yang* force, may need a background support, analogical thinking may lead to the understanding of absence of *taiji* as basis of *taiji*. This leads to the notion of *wuji* (无极 the nonultimate), which cannot be positively identified as such but which can be said to give rise to the sustainable matrix of the creativity and action of the *taiji*.[7]

The relationship between *yin* and *yang* can be also seen as mutually supporting, mutually transforming, mutually balancing, mutually enhancing and mutually furthering for the new. In a deeper and extended sense, one can see that *yin* and *yang* stand in a relation of the indeterminate and the determining whereby the *yang* may be said to arise from the *yin* just as motion starts from the rest, and vice versa. This mutual origination that leads to both the determining and the indeterminate is called the *dao*. This leads to the formulation of onto-cosmology of be-ing from non-be-ing, which exhibits the principle of unlimit creativity of the *dao* of generation: the generation of the world by way of generation of *yin-yang* forces or *qi* (气). In other words, as *yin-yang* becomes a growing complex system, a diversity of things would arise by way of the generative functioning of the *yin-yang* forces of creativity based on both the creativity of the *taiji* and the creativity of the *wuji*. Diversity and complexity still retain the positive relationship of enhancing, supporting, and complementing the *yin-yang* forces on the one hand; on the other hand, there are always negative relationships of opposition, resistance, tension, and balance in the *yin-yang*. These two kinds of tendencies will further function as agencies of formation and transformation of things toward the new. In this sense, the *yin-yang* relationship is creative and productive: it is creative because it leads to new possibilities of realization, and it is productive because it is generative of new things. It is in light of these generative and productive changes that the change is called *Yi* in the broad sense of creative change, which incorporates all kinds of changes, including no change, simple change, differential change, and integrative change: all to be explained by way of interchange and exchange of the *yin* and *yang* forces.

3. With this generative and creative relationship of *yin* and *yang* in view, reality of the world is seen as a matter of constant renewing and refreshing, creation and re-creation. It is said that "to produce the productive is called the *Yi*." This is the most important principle for the formulation of the ontology and cosmology of the *yin* and *yang* forces after the principle of the alternation of the *yin* and *yang*. We may note that both the principle of alternation (co-creativity) and the principle of productivity (or creativity) have two aspects: the phenomenological and the onto-cosmological. The phenomenological aspect refers to our experience and observation of the phenomena of the *yin-yang* as human experiences of reality, whereas the onto-cosmological aspect refers to

the objective reality of the world that we must acknowledge because our observation and ourselves as human beings are part and parcel of the world. The union of ontology and cosmology in onto-cosmology of the *taiji* and *wuji* or of the *yin* and *yang* is a matter of internal linking of the *yin-yang* from the *taiji* and the *taiji* from the *wuji*.

We may now summarize what has been developed thus far: as *yin-yang* forces are revealed in *yin-yang* experiences by us, *yin-yang* indicates both objective moving powers and the human experiences of the objective at the same time. The term *yin-yang* has two further connotations: *yin-yang* as qualities of things or simply as types of things. The world is both differentiated and integrated by an open and comprehensive system and an ongoing process of the *yin-yang* forces as experienced by the human person. In a like manner, *taiji* and *wuji* are equally established as powers of creativity and co-creativity as well as principles of *yin-yang* interchanges and exchanges as rooted in the *taiji* and *wuji*. When we come to the symbolic texts of the *Yijing*, one will note that the threefold meanings of *yin-yang* as experiences, as creative forces of nature, and as qualities of things are all to be symbolized by the *yao* lines of the *gua* in the *Yijing*. We must distinguish all these types and levels of the meanings and reference of the term *yin-yang* as applied to the texts of the *Yijing*. We finally come to see the *yao* lines as providing a symbolism of the *yin-yang* forces, qualities, and aspects and of human beings and their experiences.

Three Principles of Onto-Epistemology of the *Yi*

Thus far we have given a description of the formulation of the onto-cosmology of the change in terms of the *yin-yang* experiences and *yin-yang* forces. Now we come to three fundamental principles of onto-epistemology for the onto-cosmology of the *yin-yang* thinking. The three epistemological principles for the experiencing of the *yin-yang* dynamics are the principle of comprehensive observation (*guan*), the principle of reflective response (感 *gan*), and the principle of integration of the two, all of which are explicitly suggested in the *Yijing* text itself, unlike the implicit embodiment of onto-cosmology of change in the *Yijing* text.

The first principle is directed to the outer world; the second principle is directed to the inner feelings of the human person; the third principle brings the two together so that we have a view on how the world and human being are to be related in a creative process of interaction.

It is easy to see how one needs to open one's eyes and mind to see and feel the world as comprehensively and as objectively as possible. To engage in comprehensive observation is to let the things and events present themselves so that *guanzhe* (观者 the observer) would notice the particularities of things as outstanding and unique and yet embedded in a process of change and transformation. It is to see all things as related or interrelated (relations as part of observable reality) and to form a totality, a whole. Thus, it is said that Fuxi (伏羲) in antiquity had comprehensively observed the forms in the sky and norms on earth. He even observed the polished exterior of birds and beasts and how they relate to the environment. He would also take things near and far in order to be comprehensive in scope so that he could devise a system of eight forms. With this system of eight forms (八卦 *bagua*) understood in relation to each other, he was able to understand the power and potential of the creative and the illuminative as these forms become a reflection of not only the changing events and situations of nature but vectors and tendencies of living forces in nature. Although terms like *qi*, *yin*, and *yang* have not been used in the *Zhouyi* texts of judgments, their presence and emergence in the *Yizhuan* says a great deal about the underlying and hidden cosmological feelings and ontological experience in the symbolization and judgmental thinking of the early *Yi* diviners.

The reason a *Yi* thinker needs to be creative and illuminative is that he could apply what he understands without too much risk. In the *guan* hexagram, observation is conceived as an enlarging and therefore an open process from which *yin* and *yang* could be observed. It is a process of moving from smaller scope of observation to a larger scope of observation, from observing what happens in one's own life to what happens in the life of man in general. As I have discussed in my essay on *guan*,[8] *guan* forms the foundation for understanding the whole system of changes in nature and also provides an orientation from which one may determine and come to know a system of positions in which the observer is located. Not only does the world become known as a system of changes, we come also to see how the world changes and how things change in the world. *Guan* is comprehensive and nonreductive and therefore preserves the natural scene of reality from a truly macro-phenomenal point of view. Hence, the *Tuan Commentary* on the *Guan* hexagram remarks that "One comes to have a great view of things from the above, and things will become compliant and penetrating. This is also to see the world (under heaven) from the centrality that is a measure of correctness." It is in this central position that heaven is said to make a difference to the four seasons and that the sage is able to offer his teachings with the whole world in unison.⁹

On the principle of reflective resonance, it is to be noted that this principle requests an understanding of our inner feelings. This is due to our self-introspective observation. But the principle would require that this self-introspective observation should be conscientiously made, and that the inner activities of one's mind and heart could be made to bear on one's intention and goal. Apparently, this principle is deeply seated in *Yijing* because *Yijing* itself speaks of resonance (感 *gan*) and response (应 *ying*). In the *Xici* it is said that the milfoil for divination is such that it is without thoughts and without actions and hence remains unmoved. But it is through feeling (*gan*) that it comes to comprehend the causes of things in the world.¹⁰ It is clear that for the authors of the *Xici*, feeling (*gan*) could be an avenue not only for superficial perception but for penetrating understanding. It is in this sense of feeling that we can speak of the supreme experience and understanding of reality (the *dao*) and its principles (*li* 理) as the moving of the invisible spirit-vitality (*shen* 神) of *qi*. It is important to note that this feeling is not confined to the ordinary feeling in our sensation and emotions but has something to do with one's deep perception and insight into reality.

In order to have a deep perception and insight into reality, which we may call "spiritual feelings" (神感 *shengan*), one must further reflect on what he ordinarily feels in heart and mind so that he can feel deeper and become enlightened on what is inside himself that forms a response to that which would become disclosed or unveiled in light of the feeling. This explains how one could "know the reasons / causes for the dark and the bright," and "know the reasons for death and life and the transformations of things and floating spirits."¹¹

The basic principle of this feeling is always one of *yin-yang* correspondence and resonance. Hence, the feeling must be seen as a response to a reality that causes the feeling and yet at the same time reveals itself as the cause so that the feeling would recognize it as the cause. But, again, this recognition is not simply a matter of identifying an object; rather, it is also a way of acknowledging a common source to which the resonance and response can be accounted and in terms of which conflict will be resolved and a harmony will be formed. In this sense, this resonance is creative for both heart and mind transformation and transformation of the natural course of events through the actions of the person motivated by his feelings. Perhaps a few simple examples will illustrate: during a storm, one experiences the feeling of fear. In child abuse, one experiences feelings of anger. In serving one's parents, one experiences a feeling of joy. All of these feelings may come naturally, and on reflection they reveal a deeper relation of oneself to others and the world, and one also sees how the world should be or should not be acted on. One also comes to see and reject wrong ways of approaching others and the world, as one comes to see and appreciate the right ways of approaching others and the world. Further reflection may lead to a fundamental insight into the natural law of storms, the value of non-violence, the love in humanity. All in all, the principle of feeling is a dynamic and dialectic principle that calls on us to search for a deeper self and a deeper reality of the world, and to quest for a reconciliation and consonance between the subject and the object through mutual transformation and interaction.[12]

In the Yi Text there is the Xian (咸) hexagram that depicts a situation of dynamic feeling on one's body. It is to be noted that the word xian (咸) means feeling (gan 感). Etymologically, the two words are related in that the word xian may originally have the feeling gan as its core meaning. It may be considered the short form for the word gan or the original form of gan since gan has added the radical heart to the word xian to become gan. But in light of my explanation of the gan-ying (感应) relationship as dynamic accord between the subject and object, I have come to the following explanation of the relationship between the two words: the word xian already means uniformity and accord, and it is the uniformity and accord of an army in guarding. In order to stress the deeper sense of feeling toward its cause in resonance and accord, this word was borrowed to indicate how the mind could feel a sense of unison and accord with its object and cause of feeling. The Xian gua is actually used to illustrate this situation of concrete sensation of feeling in such a way that this initial feeling of closeness could advance to a more intimate relationship with the object and cause of the feeling. Eventually, the subject and the object could become united into oneness.[13]

Given the above analysis of the two principles, it is natural that we should come to see how these two principles should unite to form a whole picture of our understanding of the world of change. The observation principle is outer-directed, as observation is outer-directed, and yet it requires the inner feelings of the human person to be open and objective and centrally placed. On the other hand, the feeling principle is an inner-directed, as feeling is inner-directed, and yet it requires the outer observation of the human person to be aware of what is being disclosed and revealed so that a deeper truth and reality could be identified and felt. The combinatory use of the two principles must be complementary and beneficial to each other, and this would be beneficial to the development and transformation of the human person in his mind and heart interaction. This enhances the understanding of a deeper definition and identification of the human person in an onto-cosmic context. In this context, both the scope of the observation and the depth of feeling must reveal and disclose the larger reality of the cosmos and the deeper source of reality in which the outer and the inner are to be found. The openness of the process of observation and reflection also assumes that nothing is to be left out and the genuine sense of change will be preserved so that a more comprehensive observation and a more extensive reflection will take place. This no doubt would lead to the formation of the system of forms that are historically formed in a process of the organization and reconciliation of many factors of experience by such an ideal person whom one could call the sage or the sage-king. It is in this process of synthetic collation that one sees the preservation of the fundamental experiences of the *yin-yang* and the extended qualities of *gang–rou* and *dong-jing*, whereas the three pairs could further lead to more complex notions of *yin-yang* in concrete things and concrete situations such as heaven and earth, male and female, individual and society, power and virtue, creativity and receptivity, or being and nonbeing.

In the interests of methodology, we may call the combinatory use of the observation and feelings the principle of comprehensive integration (*tong*). This principle is inherent in our experience of reality as an open, ongoing, dynamic process of change, for there is nothing to be unnecessarily excluded insofar as we see the *yin-yang* of the experience in totality. Yet the world as the process of change will constantly bring up new things that are open to our observation and reflection, hence in order to preserve the original sense of reality in totality and oneness when we are confronted with simple phenomena, we must integrate all our relevant experiences on *yin-yang* into a comprehensive unity. To integrate is not to reduce experiences of differences to homogeneity, but to establish a framework of open unity with maximum diversity of experiences interrelated into a wholeness. Both Daoist and Confucian philosophers have seen the necessity and meaningfulness for this effort toward comprehensive integration. In the *Daodejing*, Laozi speaks of the oneness of heaven, the oneness of earth, and so on, yet everything will remain unshackled by the *dao* because *dao* does not dominate nor possess. Similarly, in Confucianism, the ideal value is harmony and harmonization. One must harmonize all differences into a harmonious unity in which everything will have a proper place and a better opportunity for self-realization and self-transformation. Hence, Confucius speaks of a moral person as "achieving harmony and yet preserving differences." In this sense, the principle of comprehensive integration is also a principle of universal harmonization. It is principle of co-creativity for the formation of a large world.

We may further note that the principle of observation leads to the discovery of a multitude of differences in the world. This may be regarded as a disclosure of the functional differentiation of the reality as we observe in the world. On the other hand, the principle of feeling leads to reconciliation and harmonization of the differences and hence a principle of onto-cosmological integration. The possibility of comprehensive integration is a methodological principle inherent in both processes of comprehensive observation and profound feeling, as both are founded and premised on the onto-cosmological integration of our understanding rooted in our deep feelings of ourselves with regard to the world. The deeper feelings of humanity must find response and resonance in the unity and affinity with the world. This is generally referred to as the union of heaven and man in one (天人合一 *tianrenheyi*), but more specifically it should be better spelled out as "the union of heaven and man in their creative powers" (天人合德 *tianrenhede*) as indicated in the *Wenyan Commentary* of the hexagram *Qian*. For the latter suggests that it is because of presence of creative powers (such as comprehensive observation and deep feelings) in man that man can reach a union with the primordial creativity of heaven and earth. Thus, one must not see the principle of comprehensive integration as simply a matter of onto-cosmological integration, but as a matter of extensive differentiation that embodies the functional differentiation as a natural creative process.

With this understanding, we finally come to see how the onto-epistemological principle of comprehensive integration becomes methodologically a principle of interpretation and understanding in regard to the multitude of beings in the world as well as in regard to the multitude of assertions in a textual discourse. To do so is to interpret by means of concepts or use of language against a background of established observations and feelings. Hence, we can see how an onto-epistemological principle from the *Yijing* makes our conceptual integration and discursive understanding of the world and our human selves possible.

"*Yi*" as School of *Yin* and *Yang* and "*Yi*" as Onto-Cosmology of Change

In Zhuangzi's *Tianxia* chapter (庄子天下篇), Zhuangzi summarizes on the general features of the ancient canonical texts in the following way:

> The *Poetry* is to speak of the human aspirations, the *History* is to speak of affairs and events, the *Rites* is to speak of human conduct, the *Music* is to speak of harmony, the *Changes* (Yi) is to speak of the *yin* and *yang* exchanges, and the *Spring-Autumn* is to speak of the proper titles and ranks. (名份 *mingfen*)

The *Yi* here clearly refers to the tradition of understanding of nature and human events in terms of exchange of *yin* and *yang* forces. Specifically, it refers to the *Yi* as a text just as other texts of the humanistic tradition from the past.

With this understanding of the *Yi* as a text of *yin-yang* discourse, traditional explanation of the meaning of *Yi* begins with focusing on the formation of the character *Yi* in the Chinese in reference to understanding of the *yin* and *yang* forces. But the word *yi* written 易 is nowhere explained in the original texts of the *Yijing*. What the term *yi* originally is intended to mean and refer to and how it became the name for a conceptual system of judgments of divination become fundamental questions. *Shouwen jiezi* (说文解字) of Xu Shen (许慎 circa 58–147 CE) in the early Han explains the word *Yi* as designating a lizard with its head and four legs. This idea may come from interpreting the shape of the word engraved on bronze in the early Zhou time. It is apparent that this word is used to designate the book of *Yijing* or the system of divinations in a later time, when ideas of the *Yizhuan* were first inspired by Confucius (551–479 BCE) in the later part of his life, for it is in the *Yizhuan* that the word *Yi* is used to identify generally the system of divinatory judgments and the practice of divination. In fact, it is used to refer to four aspects of the practice of divination for the purpose of understanding and predicting the future. Hence, it is said in the *Xici*:

> The *Yi* has four ways of the sage: for those who wish to speak would appeal to the judgments, for those who favor action would appeal to changes; for those who wish to manufacture would take *xiang* (象 forms of the *Yi* phenomena) seriously, those who wish to do divination takes the divination seriously. (*Xici Shang* 10)

In actuality, the use of the term *Yi* is even broader in scope than this passage suggested, because it is used to refer to the activities of heaven and earth and for that matter, the powers (and virtues) of heaven and earth in formation and transformation of things in the cosmos. Hence, it is said that "to generate that which generates is called the *Yi*" (*Xici Shang* 5).

Shuowen also indicates that the word *Yi* is formed from the two words "sun" and "moon" and thus represents the *yin* (shade) and *yang* (shine) of nature. But in all oracle bone inscriptions of the word *Yi* 易, the lower part of the word does not suggest a moon shape. Hence, the meaning of the word 易 cannot be said to derive from the composition of the words standing for sun and moon. We must find another explanation.

After considering all aspects of the formation of the word *Yi*, I find that the best explanation is to be found in *Yi* as indicating and representing the appearance of the sun and clouding of the sun by floating clouds. The second part of the word therefore could be easily identified as the vital force *qi*. Hence, the word *Yi* is a term to indicate free changes of *qi* and hence can be said to be the way of opening and closing, dark and bright, motion and rest, firm and soft. As *qi* is one of the ancient terms appearing in the oracle bones, to use *qi* to explain the *Yi* is more reasonable and more conforming to the actuality and experience than the static combination of sun and moon.

As we take the shining and shading experience as the primitive experience of change, we can see that change consists in changing from shining to shading of the light or in changing from shading to shining of the light. But we also see that shining and shading may coexist for a period of time before there is complete shading or complete shining as clouds may move one way or another. We also come to see that this kind of change occurs naturally and constitutes a natural course of events in the world. We further notice that changes of this sort take place against a background sky and space that may contain other things but that may appear not changing against the moving clouds and events of shining and shading. But this is not to say that they may not change from one state to another state. What we come to see for the moment is that there is change marked by shining, which we may call the *yang* (literally sun shining on the hill), and there is also the change marked by shade, which we may call the *yin* (literally shadows over the hill). We notice that it is by removing the cloud over the sun that we come to have the shining, and it is by moving the cloud over the sun that we come to have shade. The results of shining and shading, which are respectively brightness and shade, can be also called *yang* and *yin*. We can see that it is the relative constancy of no-change that marks out relative changes of *yin* and *yang* and their manifestation against the background of no-change. With all these in view, it is no surprise that *Yi*, or change, is eventually given three meanings by Zheng Xuan (郑玄 127–200). He says: "There is one name of *Yi* which contains three meanings: first, simple change (简易 *jianyi*); second, changing into something else (变易 *bianyi*); third, nonchange (不易 *buyi*)."[14]

We can see that all three aspects of change actually come from the *Xici* of the *Yizhuan* as inspired by Confucius. In the *Xici*, it is said that "the *Qian* leads the great creation, the *Kun* completes the creation of things. *Qian* leads by the simple quality of changing (*Yi*), the *Kun* is capable of completing by simply following."[15] There is a unity of the initial change and the completive action, which is intended by the term "*Yi jian*" (易简), literally completive action of change. Hence, it is said to be the condition and cause for obtaining of the order (*li*) of the world in which everything will be well positioned and related. In this sense, it is evident that the term *Yi jian*, which literally refers to bamboo pieces for recording and writing, indicates an easy and simple way of recording and writing, easier than earlier forms of recording such as using knots of strings. *Jian* (简) could therefore suggest the beginning of writing and invention of symbols for indicating not just objects but concepts of human minds as well. But the point of speaking of *yijian* or *jianyi* as a principle of change is that it indicates evolution to a more advanced stage of development of culture and knowledge through inventive power of human minds. To be simple and easy (as the term *jianyi* suggests semantically) is to go beyond a given form of experience to a higher form of experience that integrates the earlier forms of experience in a new form of experience with greater scope and greater unity and hence greater simplicity. This new form of experience requires intelligent use of mind for organization, interrelation and comprehensive integration. In this sense, the idea of *yijian* or *jianyi* is one of rational ordering and ontological rooting.

Concerning the *bianyi*, the notion of qualitative and quantitative change is conveyed; it is change that pervades all the changes of the world that give rise to the order of things. It is indicated in the emergence of natural phenomena of the sun and moon, the wind and rain, the hill and the river, the thunder and lake, and the heat and cold in the four seasons. It also is evidenced in the emergence of the male and the female as two genders of living species. In the words of *Xici* and *Shuogua*, we can see qualitative change as the emergence of *yin* and *yang*, as two alternating and interacting forces and forms of things that we can experience. As I have discussed earlier, *yin* and *yang* refer to the bright and the shady aspects of the reality we experience and hence our experiences of such. From the root meanings of *yin* and *yang* we come to see how *yin* and *yang* on the one hand are to be identified as qualities of things that emerge or occur as a result of change and our experiences of them, and on the other hand the natural objects and events that we can identify in nature such as sun and moon, heaven and earth, hill and lake, wind and thunder, water and fire. It is obvious that this extended notion of *yin* and *yang* must retain the basic pattern of the nature of *yin* and *yang* as qualities of things and as forces of change. In these senses, the qualities of softness and firmness and moving and rest are introduced as extensions and exemplifications of *yin* and *yang*. These new qualities can be further combined and synthesized into ideas of powers that exhibit these qualities with special functions of production, preservation, transformation and realization. In this fashion, we must note that the content of *yin* and *yang* as two primary onto-cosmic categories of reality become extremely rich and complex. This has the consequence of making it difficult to identify the exact reference of *yin* and *yang* in many concrete things and situations, although the basic meanings of *yin* and *yang* have remained phenomenologically and intuitively basic and constant because our basic experience of the *yin* and *yang* remain the same.

It is in light of this combination and synthesis that the powers of *Qian* and *Kun* were introduced as the primary powers of production and transformation of things in the world. Hence, in the *Xici* it is said that "the *Qian* is such that when it is at rest, it is concentrated and when it is moving it goes straight, hence it eminently produces things. The *Kun* is such that when it is at rest, it is closed and when it is moving it is open, hence it vastly produces things."¹⁶ That there is motion and rest is a matter of experience and observation. Motion and rest pertain to the nature of *Qian* and *Kun* and can be identified as belonging to the distinction between *yang* and *yin*. As *Qian* and *Kun* could be said to be moving and at rest, one can infer that there are *yin* and *yang* in *yin* and *yang* and consequently *yin* and *yang* form an embedded order of levels or hierarchies of *yin* and *yang*. *Qian* and *Kun* would allow such a hierarchical order of *yin-yang* to be formed. As noted, an extended notion of the *yin* and *yang* is firmness (*gang*) and softness (*rou*). It is said in *Xici Shang* 1 that "when the *gang* and *rou* mutually interact, we have the changes." Although *gang* and *rou* may refer to solid and broken lines of a *gua* (trigrams or hexagrams), the rudimentary meanings of firmness and softness are still derived from our experiences of things in nature and natural events. Then the question arises as to whether *gang* and *rou* could be referred to as correlates of *yin* and *yang*. The answer is affirmative, as we see how the *Shuogua* refers to the "*yin* and *yang* as the way of establishing the way of heaven" and to the "*gang* and *rou* as the way of establishing the way of earth." Hence, we can see *gang* and *rou* as *yang* and *yin* on earth.

It is through a similar analogy that *Shuogua* refers to "*ren* (仁 benevolence) and *yi* (义 righteousness) as establishing the way of man." As heaven, earth, and man form parallel processes of the cosmic world, they share a common pattern of polarities of the *yin* and *yang* relationships that resonate with one another. But one must see *yin* and *yang* as capable of being realized in many different characters, in different situations and on different levels of things. Hence, *yin* and *yang* could refer to the most basic features of all the extended *yin* and *yang* qualities, and hence refers to the specific features of things in their concrete relationships. One can then see how *ren* is like *yang* in the enlightening and productive power of *ren* and how *yi* is like *yin* in the disciplining and distributing powers of the *yi*. Hence, *ren* is comparable to *yang* as *yi* is comparable to *yin*. One may even extend the *yin* and *yang* paradigm to description of the contrast between the *xiaoran* (小人 the small man) and the *junzi* (君子 the superior or moral man). In doing so, we have advanced from description of nature in *yin* and *yang* to description of human qualities and moral qualities of human persons in *yin* and *yang*. We may argue that our experience of the *yin* and *yang* as an open process of distinction making and contrast-making allows such a development. One must make the development clear by recognizing the importance of powers of metaphorical extension and functional analogy in our experiences of *yin* and *yang*.

In light of the above analysis, we may represent the *yin* and *yang* relationships in these principles:

1. *Yin* and *yang* as two basic onto-cosmo-logical categories of reality (being and becoming) give rise to further *yin* and *yang* in a hierarchical differentiation and branching that could be unlimited. One can speak of a *yin*-series of qualities and a *yang*-series of qualities in our experience of the world.

2. *Yin* and *yang* will have to be realized and recognized in different qualities to be described such as movement and rest, firmness and softness, progress and retrogress, and so on and so forth.

3. Concrete things can be said to be formed from different combinations of qualities from the *yin*-series and the *yang*-series.

It is in light of these three principles that we can speak of *yin* and *yang* as pervasive and basic categories of identification and description and therefore considering and thinking of natural events and human affairs as related and even correlated experiences of the same basic qualities and powers of nature and humanity. These three principles also show the complexity of the thoughts and discourses of *yin* and *yang* in ordinary language and in the system of forms of trigrams and hexagrams that introduce a logical order in such a thought and speech.

In light of the *Xici* and *Shuogua*, we may further present and exhibit the following characteristics of the relations of the *yin* and *yang*: (1) mutual dependence in a relation of initiation and completion, (2) differentiation of their relations into two different functions that can be described as opposition and yet complementation, (3) rooted in a basic unity between the two and sharing a common source from which the two arise. These three characteristics make *yin* and *yang* a dynamic unity of a process of origination, differentiation, sustenance, complementation and completion. But one must also note that any result of completion is the beginning or origination of a new process as well. It is in this sense that we must speak of the creative and co-creative creativity of the *yin* and *yang*. (4) One must also understand the *yin* and *yang* as an open process that can be embedded in and related to other processes as time passes. The openness and complexity of the process make the changes in *yin* and *yang* essentially unpredictable, as suggested in *Xici Shang* 5. We thus speak of the subtleties of the divine (*shen*). The *shen* is conceived as a supreme form of creative and co-creative change that innovates, renovates, and transforms and that can be experienced but cannot be fully describable in common language.

In reference to the divinatory process, four words can describe the process as being divined from a situation: *yuan* (元 origination), *heng* (亨 prosperity), *li* (利 benefiting), and *zhen* (貞 sustaining, hence stability and firmness).[17] One may see that my analysis of the *yin* and *yang* has included the four stages of ideal change and articulated the nature of prosperity and benefit, and even sustainability in terms of real functions of change, namely *yuan* as origination, *heng* as complementation or integration, *li* as achievement, and *zhen* as completion. After the completion of *zhen*, origination would start a new process. In reality, new processes constantly emerge and old processes constantly fade. Processes interweave and interact and lead to more branching and / or merging of processes. This is how the change as *bianyi* works. In light of fading of the old and the rise of the new, we may consider *li* as a turning-point toward difficulty, conflict, or simply weakness. Only a few hexagrams indicate or identify the explicit presence of such a turning. It is because of such a turning that we must sustain and persevere to the final stage of completion, as described as *zhen*. That said, we may now regard the process of change as a dialectical process consisting of five stages of becoming: origination, integration, achievement, differentiation, and completion by sustaining toward a larger integration after a new origination. The process is referred to as "arising from sustaining" (貞下起元 *zhenxia qiyuan*).

Finally, we come to see the relevance of nonchange: in the *Xici*, we can see at least four forms of constancy. First, we have the constancy of the *dao* that consists in the interchange and exchange of *yin* and *yang*. Then we have the constancy of continuous productivity of change, referred to in *Xici Shang* 5 as the creativity and co-creativity of creativity (生生 *shengsheng*). There is also the constancy, or nonchange, of the *taiji*, which is the source of all changes. When the *Xici* says that the "*Yi* has *taiji* and *taiji* produces two norms (*yin* and *yang*) and two norms produce four forms (*yin* and *yang* of the *yin* and *yang*) and four forms produce the eight images (the *yin* and *yang* of the *yin* and the *yang* of the *yin* and *yang*)," the *taiji* remains an undefined concept, but in context it clearly refers to a source of production of changes. Whether *taiji* is the *dao* remains unclear until Zhu Xi comes to assert that *taiji* is the principle (*li*) of the *dao*, which is the alternation of *yin* and *yang*.[18] Clearly, as *li*, *taiji* must remain constantly *taiji*, although it must give rise to the two forces of *yin* and *yang*. In this sense, *taiji* is not unlike the unmoved mover in Aristotle's metaphysics. But as *taiji* is also *dao* in the sense that it is constantly self-realizing and realizing what is indeterminate of the *wuji*, we must see the *taiji* as both moving and not moving, and thus not like the unmoved mover in Aristotle at all. *Taiji*, then, is indeterminate and indeterminable by all changes, and yet it embodies all changes as its body, whereas it has its roots in the infinite potentiality of giving rise to creative changes in all things. *Taiji* is not just an unmoved mover but a moving force moving together with all things.[19]

There is also the constancy, or nonchange, of the orientation of heaven and earth, or of other relationships that give rise to the structure and space framework and order relationships in the world. It is the constancy of well positioning (定位 *dingwei*) of heaven and earth and everything between heaven and earth.[20] There is also the constancy of values in the world of humanity. The ideal values from virtues such as *ren* and *yi* suggest that they are the norms that must hold up and be conformed to, and as such they are also the objects for us to emulate and embody in our minds and actions. It is clear that Confucius emphasized these latter two forms of constancy. It is also to be recognized that for Confucianism, as for Daoism, the constancy of *dao* is the basis for all other constancies as it is also the basis for the changes in the world. It is also to be noted that with the contrast between change and constancy we see the possibility of extension of the *yin* and *yang* notion to this contrast. We can come to see that change as a whole is *yang* and constancy as a whole is *yin*. This leads to a contrast between *wu* (无) and *you* (有) in the mode of *yin* and *yang*, as first initiated by the Daoist Laozi.

For Laozi, *wu* (nonbeing) is more fundamental than *you* (being), which arises through creative action of the supreme *yang*, or *Qian*. It is in Daoism of Laozi that we see *yin* as *wu* acquiring a fundamental onto-cosmological significance. On the other hand, the Confucian thinkers take the *yang* and *you* so seriously that they regard the *taiji* and then *Qian yuan* (乾元) as the source of all things without asking how *taiji* arises.

This problem remains unanswered until Zhou Dunyi, in his essay *Taiji tu shuo* (太极图说 *Taiji Diagram Discourse*), asserts that "the ultimateless (*wuji*) and then the great ultimate (*taiji*)." This assertion no doubt carries the implication that the *wuji* that can be read as the ultimate *wu* and hence the supreme *yin* is more primary. On the other hand, Zhu Xi interprets the *wuji* as an aspect of *taiji*, namely the infinity aspect of the *taiji*. However, we can suggest the following way of reconciliation: *you* and *wu* as *yin* and *yang* mutually give rise and condition each other and thus form a unity that is both *wu* and *you* and hence can be said to be both *wuji* and *taiji*. We may indeed regard this as the fundamental onto-cosmological principle of being from nonbeing. We may call it the principle of creativity of co-creativity. It is in this understanding that both Daoism and Confucianism could find their unison, and yet they could also differ by developing and focusing on different aspects of the same ultimate reality of being-becoming-nonbeing.

At this point, I wish to introduce the notion of *yao*, which is translated as "line of change." As the word indicates, change takes place when the *yin* and *yang* meet and cross each other, which means that change could be conceived as the interplay of two forces: the *yin* force that comes to play when the *yang* comes in to play. When the shine shines, the shade shades, and there is always the shade because of the shine. *Yang* and *yin*, like shine and shade, are intrinsically connected in the creativity that gives rise to the interplay marked by the initiative force of *yang* and the receptive force of the *yin*. This source of creativity is referred to as the *taiji*, the ultimate source of change that unifies and provides the unifying ground and momentum of the *yin* and *yang* as manifested in shine and shade. Hence, the *Xici* asserts that "the change has *taiji*," in the sense that *yin* and *yang* have *taiji* as its grounding and ultimate source. Here we can see that the term *Yi*, or change, can refer to the entire phenomenon of change as we experience and observe it but is to be explained by a system of the initial momentum of change that is indicated by the term *yao*, the line of simple change. As indicated in the concept of *yao*, *yao* captures the simple meaning of change, namely the meaning of the interplay and interchange of the two forces of *yin* and *yang* from the same source called *taiji*. It is understood by Song philosophers that this idea of *taiji* is presupposed in the formation of the whole system of sixty-four *zhonggua* (重卦 hexagrams) as standard forms, or *gua* in the *Yijing*.

Once change takes place, we shall have the resulting changed state from a prior state, called *bianyi* (perhaps better described as transformation). That change and transformation take place requires a background of nonchange to be otherwise identified. Hence, the three dimensions of change are actually one event: it is analytically three but synthetically one that is to be experienced by us as oneness as well. It must be maintained that this unity of three meanings of change is a result of reflection of our deep experience of change, and that this reflection takes place when the human mind has undertaken to understand the change as both a large and small phenomenon of our experience of nature and of ourselves. This recognition is important because it leads to the development of the original text of Yi as a record of change through practical divination, and also leads to a philosophy of change in the later commentaries of the Yi Text, as inspired by Confucius.

As the three meanings of Yi are basically derived from the Xici, in a recent publication I have added two more basic component meanings of Yi to the meaning of Yi—namely, the meaning of exchange (交易 jiaoyi) and the meaning of harmonization (和易 heyi).[21] It is highly important to recognize the necessity and significance of this addition, which is actually an act of completion, because these two aspects are actually present even more implicitly than the other three features in the Xici, but unfortunately remain unnoticed. They are nevertheless essential for understanding the functions and efficacy of the Yi as onto-cosmic change. I first introduced the idea of jiaoyi, which means trading or exchange, but also means intercourse or interchange. In Xia 2 of the Xici, it is said that people gather to exchange goods, and after such trading they return home. But in the Tuan Commentary, jiao (交) simply means linking and having exchange between two forces, such as heaven and earth. It is maintained in the Tuan of Tai hexagram that it is when heaven and earth interchange that all things in the world become interconnected, which is of course a propitious condition for producing good and creation of life. Similar ideas are found in the Xiang Commentary, and even in the line judgment of the Dayou (大有) hexagram. These sources show how relevant the concept of jiao or jiaoyi is. I have pointed out that whereas bianyi is more a vertical concept, jiaoyi is more horizontal in referring to the common behavior of making exchanges or trading. When an exchange takes place within an underlying unity, it is interchange. Hence, I take jiaoyi as an independent aspect of the Yi action.

As for harmonization, it is important to see that change leads to the continual enrichment of life of diversity in harmonization or in a process of mutual adjustment and harmonization, as this is indicated in the root idea of "preserve and conserve the primordial harmony" (保合太和 baohe taihe) in the *Tuan Commentary* on the hexagram *Qian*. This aspect of *Yi* also reflects the natural purposefulness of the cosmic change, which can also be described as the natural tendency of natural events. The *Tuan* on *Qian* says: "The way of *Qian* changes and transforms so that all things will find their natures formed and their positions established (各正性命 gezheng xingming). [Hence] to preserve and conserve the primordial harmony is conducive to fulfillment in firmness (乃利貞 nai lizhen)." This suggests that it is on the condition of the primordial harmony among all things that things will remain prospering and furthering on, and hence conforming to the idea of the creative co-creativity of the ultimate. For nature to lead to primordial harmony is a natural tendency, whereas for human beings it should be a principle of moral development for human individual and human community if human beings are to be free from war and destruction. In this sense, preservation of primordial harmony or harmonization toward the primordial harmony is a teleological requirement for the survival and flourishing of humanity.

We can also see that the primordial harmony (太和 taihe) is the source and goal for the *Yi*, which is further inherent in the *yin-yang* relationship and creation of things and life. From all this discussion of harmonization as a function of the *Yi*, we can legitimately speak of *heyi* (*Yi* as harmonization) as forming an independent characteristic of the *Yi* concept. Hence, we may conclude that there is a total of five senses of *Yi*, or that *Yi* has an open structure that allows us to interpret changes in these five senses that are themselves related and well coordinated.

Characterization of *Yi* as Onto-Generative Cosmology

As indicated above, in the *Xici Commentary* of the *Yizhuan* of the *Zhouyi* we witness the emergence of the two basic concepts that characterize the ultimate reality that the human person has experienced. As we have seen, these two basic concepts are respectively that of the great ultimate (*taiji*) and that of the way (*dao*). Both concepts are derived from the human experience of the formations and transformations of things in nature that are referred as the *bianyi* or *bianhua* (change), but in a sense represent a general characterization of and a deeper insight into the general nature of change in terms of the *yin* and *yang*. We know that the sixty-four hexagrams are then generated from the doubling of the eight trigrams generated from the three-time self-differentiation into the *yin* and *yang*. This process of generation is remarkable in establishing a cosmogonical picture of the rise and development of reality as a world of events and things, as well as in providing a cosmographical way of thinking to be symbolized in systemic structures of trigrams and hexagrams. This process of generation we may also call the *dao*. Again, as we have seen, the sustaining source of this process of generation that provides ceaseless creative power is called the *taiji*. The *dao* is *taiji* insofar as *taiji* is considered a process of change, whereas the *taiji* is *dao* insofar as *dao* is considered as a source or origin of change. We may therefore speak of two aspects of the same thing: namely, the process aspect and the origination aspect of *taiji-dao*. Together they refer to the same thing: the totality of the reality of creativity, change, and transformation, which we have called ultimate creativity, or *taiji-dao*.

We may call this cosmogonic and cosmographical way of thinking and description of reality and world the "ontocosmology of the *taiji* and the *dao*." The "onto-" part of the term "ontocosmology" suggests the meaning of the *taiji*, and the "-cosmology" part of the term suggests the meaning of the *dao* where *taiji* represents the ultimate source of *yin-yang* changes and the *dao* represents the process of such changes. Since it is this theory of the *taiji* and the *dao* that forms the backbone and mainstream of the metaphysical thinking in the 3,200-year history of Chinese philosophy,[22] we should regard it as the fundamental theory of reality and creativity in Chinese philosophy, often referred to as the *benti*-ontology of the *dao* and *taiji*.[23] Confucius in his late age studied and voiced his comments and reflections on the *Yijing* and led to the writing of the *Yizhuan* by his followers, since regarded as a Confucian classic, perhaps even the leading one. Although one may regard *Yizhuan* (commentaries on the *Zhouyi*, written down in the fifth to third centuries BCE) as Confucius's own onto-cosmological reflections on reality and human creativity, the central ideas and views of it, as I have argued, could be still seen as basically implicit in the contexts of the original *Zhouyi* texts and symbolism.[24]

This means that the onto-cosmology of the *taiji* and the *dao* is not just Confucian but an articulation of the ancient Chinese way of thinking, observing, and interpreting reality. However, in order to distinguish it from the later *Yijing*-inspired Daoist approach to reality in the Daoist School of Laozi (around the middle of the sixth century BCE; exact dates are uncertain) and Zhuangzi (ca. 370–300 BCE) and its elaboration of the philosophy of the *dao*, we may refer to it as the "Onto-Cosmology of the *Yi*," since this theory is suggested and more or less explicitly formulated in the *Yizhuan*, particularly in the *Tuanzhuan* (彖传) and *Xici* portions of the commentaries.²⁵ I distinguish this onto-cosmology of *Yi* in the *Yijing* from the onto-cosmology of the *dao* in Daoism of Laozi and Zhuangzi. I call the former the *dao* of the *Yi* (易之道 *yizhidao*) and the latter the *Yi* of the *dao* (道之易 *daozhiyi*).

In order to understand the "Onto-cosmology of the *Yi*" as the fundamental Chinese theory of reality and creativity, we should take note of the following characterization of the metaphysical way of thinking based on our experience and insights into change, which at the same time constitutes the substance of wisdom on reality and life of the human person. The understanding of this provides an insight into the nature of reality at any given moment and in any given situation. Consequently, it provides guidance for choosing appropriate action if action is called for and an inspiration for self-disciplining and self-cultivation of oneself toward better moral development.²⁶

1. *Reality as inexhaustible origination*. We can trace the beginning of the presentation and development of the world reality to the beginning of a root source. This root source, called "the great ultimate" (*taiji*), is the absolute beginning of all things, but it is also the sustaining base for all things even at present because all changes of the world are based on it and contained in it. In this sense the *taiji* is in fact the primordial and inexhaustible source of the creative and transformative force of all changes and is conveyed by the notion of "creativity of creativity" or "generation of generation" (*shengsheng*) in the *Xici*. In this sense of reality, reality is not something stationary or static underneath a world of fleeting phenomena, nor a world of forms or ideas reflected in a world of imitations or veiled from a screen of illusions or delusions. Neither is it something accessible only by abstraction of human thinking or revelations of a transcendent God, as in Christian theology. Reality is concrete, vivid, and holistic not only in the sense that all things are interrelated within a whole as originally defined by the oneness of the *taiji*, but also in the sense that changes and nonchanges underlying the changes are organically part and parcel of the same thing, and there cannot be strict demarcation or bifurcation between appearance and reality. In this sense, changes and the constant and continuous regeneration of things in reality are constitute reality.

Any scheme to divide or separate reality will serve only a limited purpose and will be rendered inept by confrontation with reality. This means that all theories of reality share with reality the nature of change and must be subject to the continuous challenges of an ever-developing and becoming process of formation and transformation. Therefore, we may understand the *taiji* as not just primary origination but as constant or ceaseless origination, which explains creativity in the sense of creative change. In a Whiteheadian spirit, we may say that the world is in the making and is constantly and forever in the making. It is not only that many become one by increasing one, but also that one becomes many by increasing many. In this sense, the ultimate source of creativity is both one and many.

2. *Reality as a polar-generative process*. When the *taiji* gives rise to things in the world, it does so by bringing in a whole of polarities, the positive and the negative or the *yang* (the brightening/the moving/the firm) and the *yin* (the darkening/the restive/the soft). These polarities are subcontraries that exist simultaneously and are conspicuous on a specific level. They are also simultaneously contraries that are hidden on more concrete levels of things. In this latter sense, they are identifiable with the *taiji* because the *taiji* as the source of all changes is always hidden under all things. The generation of new things occurs on the basis of the coexistence and interaction between polarities.[27] Unlike Whitehead's postulation of the rise of novelty from pure ideas, novelties in this model derive from internal dynamics of the becoming of world, from which a division into the *yin* and the *yang* and a combination of the *yin* and the *yang* are the basic ways to give rise to new things. The novelty of things is inherent in the very source of the world itself, and it is also inherent in the creative potential of a thing that requires the interaction of forces to bring about.

3. *Reality as multi-interactive harmony*. An individual thing or an individual class of things always has two sides: the *yin*, which pertains to its stationary state of existence and its receptivity to the outside world (it is its given nature), and the *yang*, which pertains to its dynamical state of developing its propensities in its interaction with the outside world. As the *yin-yang* polarities are definitive of individual things or individual classes of things, that a thing must interact with the outside world is in the nature of the thing itself. It is in this process of interaction that a thing fulfills its potentialities of nature and runs its course of bounded

existence. It is in maintaining itself as a given nature that we can speak of the "centrality" (中 *zhong*) of a thing, and in properly taking and giving with other things we can speak of "harmony" (*he*) between or among things.[28] There could be noncentrality and disharmony in the formation and transformation of things, which would be a problem and a crisis for its identity and its survival in the world of reality as things. Hence, there naturally arises the natural disposition of a thing to maintain its own centrality and to reach harmony with other things. But in the case of humans, these two aspects of existence must be cultivated in order to enhance and realize the fulfillment of the human propensity and creative potentiality.

It is said: "One *yin* and one *yang* are thus called the *dao*. To follow it is goodness and to complete it is nature" (*Xici Shang* 5). How do we understand this in reference to individual things? The *dao* is how things come into being and how they grow and develop in the process of time, whereas the process of one *yin* and one *yang* is made of the alternation, conjunction, and mutual interaction of the positive and negative forces and positive and negative activities of the individual things that result in formation and transformation of things.

4. *Reality as virtual hierarchization*. The world comprises many levels, each of which is a combination of the *yin* and the *yang* forces or activities of such in things. For the *taiji* and the *dao* model of cosmogony and cosmography (and hence onto-cosmology), there are genuine general features of the *yin* and the *yang*, which are understood as rest/motion, darkness/brightness (or invisibility/visibility), softness/firmness, closedness/openness, retrospective propensity / prospective propensities, and other such properties. Although these properties are basically described in phenomenal and experiential terms of human persons, there is no reason why they could not be described in a logical and scientific language of abstract and primary properties. Perhaps one could identify the *yin* and the *yang* elements or processes in the genetic code and the theory of subelementary particles, as many people have done. Similarly, there is no reason why the values and emotions and intentions could not also be described in the language of the *yin* and the *yang*. In this light, the *yin* and the *yang* should be regarded as neutral and variant functions or operators that act to generate relationships and changes. The important point is to remember that, as there are levels of simplicity and complexity of structures and activities in a scheme of things in being and becoming, so there are levels of the *yin* and the *yang* in the world of reality.

On the highest and most general level, there is the "great ultimate" (*taiji*). On the second level, there are the *yin* and the *yang*. On the third level, there are the Four Forms. On the fourth level are the Eight Trigrams. This can go on forever *ad infinitum*. But individual things must be seen on an individual level of the *yin* and the *yang*, which represent a complex hierarchy of levels of the *yin* and the *yang* as well as a complex world of *yin-yang* interactions.

This means that the individual thing or person is only understood and acts in a context of a field and web of forces; in this context, one is still capable of making a creative impact on, and a contribution to, the formation and transformation of the world. When the *Zhongyong* (*Doctrine of the Mean*) speaks of the human person as capable of participating in creative transformations of heaven and earth and forming a triad with heaven and earth, human creativity becomes a vehicle and a mode of cosmic creativity that has been deeply embedded in the existence of a human person because the source of human existence could be traced to this creativity of the ultimate reality.

5. *Reality as recursive (not like a circle but like a spiral) but limitless regenerativity*. Although the commentaries of the *Zhouyi* have not mentioned the recursive and regenerative nature of the *Yi*, the presentation of nature in eight trigrams and of the world in sixty-four hexagrams in the original symbolism (in hexagrams) of 1200 BCE and appended judgments of divination clearly suggest that nature is a process of both collective and distributive balance, and functions as a process of return and reversion, as suggested by the rotation of seasons and celestial cycles. The interesting thing to note is that once we are able to represent the world in a collectively inclusive and individually exclusive enumeration of stages or facets, these stages and facets will have to recur as patterns or forms of understanding or existential characterizations on a special level. It is clear that we are able to limit our understanding and characterizations to a special level or particular domain and then work out or design some definitive categorical system of description or projection. This is why we could use the eight trigrams and sixty-four hexagrams at the same time—because they belong to different levels of relevance and meaningful description.

What is implied in this description of reality is that reality is both limited and limitless: it is limited on a specific level of description that serves a human purpose; it is limitless because any specific level of description could serve a purpose in only a limited way, as it can be transcended or abandoned for a higher or more specific level of description. We may say that there are virtually unlimited numbers of levels of description, just as theoretically there could be an unlimited number of systems of scientific knowledge in the progression of scientific inquiry. On each level of description there is the recursion of the finite categorized reality. This is so because it is in the nature of change that the world of reality must be regeneratively represented. This may be called regenerative recursion that is no doubt a form of cosmic creativity. It is this regenerative recursion that gives stability to the process and may be called structure of the process.

In the *taiji* and the *dao* model of reality, what is shown in the symbolism of the *Yi* is a regenerative recursion by reversion—namely, the stage of the *yin* must revert to the stage of the *yang* in order to realize creative change and vice versa. It is in the process of time that the *yin* and the *yang* are interacting by alternating. One could thus expect that reaching the limit of the worst would mean a return to a better condition. Although in practice it is difficult to know whether one has reached the worst, or how long the getting better will last, it is nevertheless possible to conceive of reality as an alternation between more beneficent or more advantageous at one end and more maleficent and more disadvantageous at another relative to a human position on the same level as a natural process of change, as in *Zhouyi*.

6. *Reality as organismic totality*. From the above description, is it clear that the world of reality in the model of the *taiji* and the *dao* is totalistic in the sense that all things are included and there is nothing beyond it. It is said that "the *Book of the Change* is extensive and all-comprehensive. It contains the way of heaven, the way of man and the way of earth" (*Xici Xia* 10). For the early Chinese, the world of reality was confined to heaven, earth, and ten thousand things among which the human person stands out as the most intelligent and the one capable of forming a tripartnership with heaven and earth. Everything in this reality comes from the *taiji* and follows or embodies the *dao*. Hence, there could not be anything outside this world of reality with the *taiji* and the *dao*. This implies that there is no transcendent being outside this world and in fact nothing is to be conceived beyond the world of the *taiji* and the *dao*.[29] When we come to Laozi, we find that even when the notion of emptiness or void (*wu*) is introduced, what the term *wu* stands for is part and parcel of the universe of the *dao*. The *dao* in Laozi is simply enriched by something called the void or nonbeing (*wu*). Similarly, when Zhou

Dunyi (周敦颐 1017–1073) speaks of the ultimateless (*wuji*) giving rise to the great ultimate in his well-known essay *Discourse on the Diagram of the Great Ultimate* (*Taiji tu shuo*), he is simply extending the *dao* to cover both void and nonvoid.

There is no break between the void and the nonvoid; hence, one does not have a transcendent nothingness or emptiness apart from reality. In this nontranscendence we do not speak merely of immanence but also of totality as derived and sustained from a source. Immanence refers to values and powers inherent in the things themselves, but totality refers to all the interrelated parts of all things in reality based on a source of creativity. The reason things belong or hang together is that in the ultimate reality all things are not simply contained but rather are all interrelated, or even interpenetrating. Yet it is still to be recognized that the ultimate source of creativity is in each and every thing, and yet at the same time is an ultimate, which is not identical with each and everything. In this sense, there is immanent transcendence for each and everything. It is in the organismic nature of the totality as immanent transcendence that not only can there not be any object "outside," but all things exist together by way of mutual support or even mutual grounding as provided by the ultimate source of creativity. This is how the transcendent immanence of Heaven in the nature of humanity leads to an interminable exchange between, as well as a unity of, humanity and heaven in the direction of development, elevation, enrichment, and fulfillment.

Integrating the *Xiangshu* School and the *Yili* School

Over the last several decades, the success of Chinese archaeological findings has included the 1973 discovery of the Silk Manuscripts (帛书 Boshu) of the *Yijing* and the 1997 Bamboo Inscriptions Manuscripts (竹简 Zhujian) of the *Yijing*. Since the Silk Manuscripts of the *Yijing* are radically different in their ordering of *gua* from the received version, scholars have come to see that there is no unique or absolute ordering of the *gua* for interpreting a system of *gua* or for use of divination. It is obvious that the Boshu order is generated like Jing Fang's (京房) "Diagram of Eight Palaces" (八宫图), with eight palaces arranged according to a formal procedure with an overall plan of positions in the sequence. On the other hand, the *guaxu* (卦序 order of the hexagrams) in the received version does not appear to follow any formally designed plan and hence is open to explanation on grounds other than a formal one. In fact, it calls for more than a logical explanation in terms of opposition (反 *fan*) and reversion (覆 *fu*), and hence allows more space for historical or philosophical interpretation. The *guaxu* of the Silk Manuscripts renews a few scholars' interests in the school of *Xiangshu* in the Han, because the difference between the two *gua* orders suggested a distinction of the two approaches to the meaning of the *gua* for understanding a situational reality in divination, by way of looking into the configuration of the lines of the *gua* or by way of contemplating the actual process of change in a human situation with a human purpose.

On the side of the Boshu and Jing Fang (77–37 BCE), the reference and meaning of the *gua* is assumed to be found in the numerological relations of the lines in *gua* and the images suggested by the lines as previously assigned or associated. On the other hand, the received version could be regarded as requiring query into meanings of the *gua* in reference to external events or onto-cosmological theories. But, as a matter of fact, even for the received version the images and numbers could be regarded as crucial for the meaning of each *gua* and no reference need be made in regard to what goes beyond them. This is because the *gua* is made of lines that can be seen as occupying significant positions and also be significantly related. This means that each *gua* is an organic unit that represents a situation and contains a message for the future in the divination. But how to identify this situation and retrieve such a message poses the fundamental question for divination. For the *Xiangshu* approach, the answer is that one can find the present situation and the message for the future right in the images and numbers of the *gua*. This leads to search and design for a system of interpreting the images of the lines and their relationships within the same *gua* and also with reference to transformations by formal variations to another *gua*. We may speak of the following types of positioning and their transformation: centralizing (*zhong*), fittingness or correctness (正 *zheng*), succession (承 *cheng*), overriding (乘 *cheng*), matching (比 *bi*) and responding (应 *ying*).[30] These may be regarded as conventions governing the interpretation of the line meaning so that one could reach an interpretation of the *gua* message. But these conventions are still based on the human experiences of positions and forces in the positions close and far. Then there is another set of conventions for generating related meanings of the gua or each line in the *gua* in terms of opposition and reversion that would shed light on the meaning of one by the other. There are other similar operations that could be relevant: the transposition (of the *gua*) and the nuclear expansion (互 *hu*). For other system-relative operations, in order to preserve the order, one can speak of the *Eight Palaces Diagram* (*Bagong Diagram*) and other setups such as fly-hide (飞伏 *feifu*), situation to respondent (世应 *shiying*), twenty-four seasonal times, and twelve grand forms. With these mechanisms introduced, one can assign any meaning to a *gua* or a line for a person to arrive at by way of these means. No doubt this would appear arbitrary and contrived. But this is precisely how the *Xiangshu* School comes to interpret the meaning of the *gua*. Interestingly, one can see the constraint of meanings of a *gua* or a line in a *gua* as provided by the judgments of the *gua* or the line. Consequently, interpretation becomes a matter of arriving at the judgments from looking into the number relations and image relations of the *gua* or line. The ingenuity of doing so is sometimes most surprising.

The great problem with the *Xiangshu* School lies in its lack of attention to the actual environmental factors and contexts of the divination. It also has trouble with using the prior meaning of a *gua* or line judgment to devise a series of moves that conform to those functions. Yet it must be admitted that for the pure *Xiangshu* School approach one must know the formal structural meaning and meaning from associations with images and numbers or number operations, because the images and times revealed in the analysis of the *gua* or line could be used to devise a judgment for the *gua* and line. To compare with the primitive contexts of divination, this *Xiangshu* model would have to ask the interpreter to close eyes and ears to outside matters and concentrate only on what has been presented in form by itself. In this spirit, one could ask simply whether such a *Xiangshu* form would be truly relevant or illuminating. The answer is no.

The failure of the *Xiangshu* School is a failure of not meeting the standards of experience and rationality as embodied in the five principles of interpretation suggested above, but for those who could believe it, it remains an ingenious skill of analysis and associative reasoning. Before the *Xiangshu* School was well developed in the Han in the hands of Jing Fang, the question of how divination by *Zhouyi* could be effective often arose. If we look into the logical side of the divination, we can easily see that we must satisfy two requirements to make the divination of the future work. First, we need a cosmic map that provides a detailed guide on how things may develop and how reality could be described, against which we could identify the present situation of the diviner or the concerned. Second, we must find a way of identifying the present situation. This quest is not just for a method of divination but a way of reading and interpreting the result of divination, be it tortoise bone cracks or hexagrams. In order to get the correct result that can provide rational warranty and credibility, the two questions have to expand into five questions, which I outline in the following paragraphs.

1. Do I have an adequate description of the cosmic reality including all their laws of change? Attempts to answer this question may lead to scientific investigation, or it may lead to an ontological theory of cosmic change and epistemology of change that can be relied on to answer questions of interpretation and application.

2. Is my method of capturing the present situation or state of becoming adequate to the goal of doing so? How do I justify my method of identifying the present situation when the problem at hand is not a matter of obvious physical signs as index or icon, but as symbols to be interpreted psychologically, historically, theologically, or philosophically? One may appeal to revelation or the workings of *shenming* (神明 divine spirit) as a base. But then we must know how the *shenming* or spirits works in matters of divination or related activities.

3. With a text like the *Yijing*, we must read the lines and forms as produced or identified. What are the best ways of reading and interpretation? Do we limit ourselves to the intrastructures and relationships of numbers of the lines so that I can retrieve some useful message of the situation or do I also consult the philosophy underlying the forms on a different level? In other words, could I also consult the judgments that have been made as an indication of meaning and significance or some other views in order to draw specific judgments of the given divinatory result? The parting of ways takes place when there are those who rely more on general rational understandings and deliberative meanings of judgments disagree with those who primarily use numbers and images for interpretation, sometimes even at the expense or in neglect of judgments or general understanding.

4. One needs to press for the purpose of divination for knowledge of the future and the warrant of such knowledge in correspondence to the future. This leads to a general question of the ontological status of the future and time: is the future determined and fixed for us to know? Or is the future indeterminate so that my presumed knowledge and action will make a difference? Hence, we may question as to whether divination gives us an empirical disclosure of the future or some possibil-

ity or possibilities of the future for us to choose from. For the *Xiangshu* School, the future is most often regarded as revealed in the numbers and images and therefore divination becomes a matter of divine revelation that should command belief and trust. But for the rationalist, prediction pertaining to the future is always a matter of careful assessment to be evaluated and used for its relevance, not for its certainty. It is a matter of circumstantial evidence and judgment based on consideration with the assumption of the validity of the cosmic map, the prediction method, the model of interpretation, and the evaluation of probability and credibility in a context of both history and experience.

5. Finally, one must face the problem of making decisions as to what to do, and this no doubt involves questions of value, valuation, and evaluation. It involves the overall commitment of the concerned or the diviner in a given belief system and a standard for rational justification. It also involves the philosophical understanding of moral values as to whether they are reducible to questions of utilities or whether they remain independent and have a source independent of divinatory process.

Historically, it is assumed that by the time of Confucius that method of divination and the ways of interpretation were well developed and that "the diviner" had become an official profession or appointment. But with Confucius we also come to a rational consciousness that would question the practice of divination and yet wish to separate the wisdom of the judgments of the divination from such practice. In this sense, Confucius is not a skeptic but a philosophical thinker who wishes to see oneself as capable of making relevant reasonable judgment of knowledge and value based on common experience. This no doubt means that by the time of Confucius common sense and knowledge of nature and society have been greatly advanced, and there is no need to resort to divination for important decisions of life and state. We may therefore see the time of Confucius as the time of *post-divinatory rational consciousness* that is both historically rooted and future directed. What distinguishes Confucius, among other things, is his awakening and belief of innate understanding (知 *zhi*), which may result from deep and frequent reflection on oneself and a wide and vast learning process. It is on the basis of this innate understanding that Confucius comes to the desire for human heartedness (仁 *ren*) and sees it as source and arbiter for all other virtues including rites, righteousness, integrity, and other forms of wisdom. It is in this context of understanding that Confucius comes to make a radical revolution in the study of change (*Yi*) (which we may also call a Copernican type of revolution): study of change is to develop one's wisdom and prudence as well as moral judgment of life situations and action based on facts and experience rather than on external *shenming* or the authority of the diviner. This is vastly different from seeing divination as revealing the judgments of a diviner by appeal to the power of *shenming*,[31] or by appeal to the validity of a divination method.

With this revolutionary understanding of divination, Confucius had undertaken a strong interest in reinterpretation of the *Judgments* of the *Yi*, which we may call a prudent-moral (善恶 *shan-e*) interpretation rather than a good fortune–misfortune (吉凶 *ji-xiong*) interpretation of the *Yi* Texts and *Yi* judgments. In doing so, he did not appeal to the lines of the *gua* but only to the general meaning and general judgment of the *gua*, and commented on many of the *Yi gua*. Given the time framework for his devotion to the study of *Yi*, it is likely that in his mature years he had gone over all the *gua* judgments and all the line judgments of each *gua*, although what has been preserved in the received version of the *Yijing* and other classical texts does not cover all the *gua*, nor does it cover all of the lines for each *gua* on which comments are given.[32]

In the Silk Manuscripts one finds records of conversations of Confucius with his disciples on the nature of divination. In the record titled *Yao* (要篇 *Essentials*), Confucius makes the following statement in answer to his disciple Zigong's question whether he believes in divination. "I have made divinations a hundred times and seventy percent are correct. Regarding my divination on the Zhu Liangshan, I follow what most diviners would say." He also said:

> Regarding use of the *Yi* Text, I put aside the divinations. I observe what concerns virtue and righteousness (德义 *deyi*) in them. [There are three types of people], those who divine and reach the numbers [for interpretation], those who understand the numbers and reach for virtues, and those who abide by the virtue of humanity and act on the principle of righteousness (仁守之而义行之 *renshouzhi er yixingzhi*). Those who divine and yet do not reach for the numbers, they are called the shaman; those who use numbers and yet do not reach for virtues, they are called historians (史 *shi*). With divinations of the shaman and historians, one may wish to reach for an ideal state but have not reached them. One may like them, but one also need to criticize them as not quite right. If the

posterity criticizes me, perhaps the cause may be my view on the *Yi*? I merely seek virtues in them. One may say that I and the shamans and historians share the same route but reach different goals. A superior man seeks happiness in his virtuous conduct, therefore he would not offer many sacrifices. A superior man seeks good in their practice of *ren* and *Yi*, therefore they do not engage in many divinations. Did I therefore put divinations on a secondary place?[33]

What is said here is highly important for the Confucian revolution of the *Yi* divination and interpretation. First, Confucius does not absolutely reject divination, and has actually engaged in practicing divination. But he sees divination as only a step toward reaching numbers and then reaching virtues. He still regards divination and reaching numbers as important, as they are the occasions that provides an understanding of a given situation and given problem. But he would not stop at the stage of reaching conclusions on *jixiong* and went to seek virtues to perform. That is, he would regard the results as revealing a problem of the human individual and therefore calling for his own self-examination so that he could correct them or find a way of improving his virtues. He would follow the virtues, not the advice on fortune and misfortune.

Although Confucius did not deny the relevance of divination and divinatory interpretation as a source for moral reflection, there is a deeper criticism of divination on the part of Confucius: namely, that divinations may not always be accurate. For him, only a portion (70 percent) is correct. Although 70 percent is a large percentage, there is of course no guarantee that divinations will be accurate. Confucius then said that in seeking virtues one may have fewer divinations. This means that there are independent ways of reflecting on one's moral conduct, which need not be a matter of divination. Divination is to identify a present or future state of affairs, and then draw judgments on fortune or misfortune regarding what has been predicted. But we may not need divinations because we can independently examine the represented state of affairs and their tendencies and use induction and learning from the past to know the future. Hence, it is not necessary to consult divination. This is how Confucius started his Copernican revolution in the reading of the *Yi*.

Confucius says: "If one lost one's virtues, one moves to the divine spirits; if one is remote from wisdom and strategic thinking, one would be busy with divinations" (489). It is a revolution that leads to a thorough humanist and rationalist reflection of human activities and knows them from an empirical and rational point of view without any mediation from divination. With the increase of our knowledge and the ability to do self-determination, divination can be completely dispensed with. In actuality, by the time of the late Warring States Period, Xunzi (荀子) was able to assert that one need not do any divination.

With the Confucian revolution in a new approach to the meaning of the Yi Texts, one could still wish to know how one reads texts and interprets its judgments. In general, Confucius takes self-reflection and learning as the solution to human problems, including problems on how to act under uncertain circumstances. If one learns by experience and if one thinks by reflection and self-criticism, one would find one's answer and one's way. Confucius has suggested the combination of the two approaches, thinking and learning: "To learn without thinking is dangerous; to think without learning is empty and fruitless." A more concrete way of seeking a correct understanding of the texts, including the texts of the Yi, is provided by Mencius. In rejecting Gaozi's approach to budongxin (不动心 nonmoving of one's mind and heart by external things), Mencius says, "It is fine that if one does not gain truth in one's mind, one need not seek it in the vital forces. But it is wrong that if one does not find truth in what one speaks one will not seek it in one's mind" (2A2). He also suggests: "[Therefore], for those who interpret the Poetry, one does not detain one's understanding of what is said (辞 ci) from what is said in (文 wen); further, one needs not to detain what the ci is intended as the truth of the matter (旨 zhi). One uses one's understanding (意 yi) to trace back to one's intended point (志 zhi)" (5A4). The subtle distinction made among wen, ci, yi, and zhi is highly important: they represent different levels of articulation of one's intended message. It takes a careful mind and insight to reach the true point of a text. We may still regard this as a method of interpretation, but with his method of interpretation, one need not resort to external authority or divine spirit for understanding the moral import of the judgments of the Yi Text, or even the matter of truth of what is presented or presented in the forms of the gua.

Perhaps it is through this new approach to interpretation of the Yi Text, as started by Confucius, that the hidden intelligence and presupposed understanding of change becomes gradually uncovered and expanded in various Confucian disciples' writings. We have no reason not to believe that the whole set of essays known as *Yizhuan* are inspired by the Confucian revolution in reading the *Yi* Texts. The *Yizhuan* can be seen as reflecting a Confucian spirit of seeking to accommodate divinatory practice, and yet go beyond it in order to reach a fuller understanding of the cosmic map of reality. In order to see how human beings could learn from the cosmic map, one must also decide what is to be done or ought to be done in light of one's moral consciousness as a human person and as a member of the human community. Both the appended essays from the Boshu *Yijing* and the Bamboo Inscriptions of the *Yijing* in 1993 (referred to as the Bamboo Manuscripts of the *Yi*) have given ample testimony to the strong likelihood that it is the youngest disciple of Confucius (also his grandson) Zisi (子思) and others who have actually expanded this onto-cosmic-moral consciousness for a philosophy of human persons, including self-examination of the human self and a systematic understanding of the cosmic map for understanding the *Yi* Texts and its import for moral self-cultivation and political, moral, institutional development for a virtuous rule.[34]

The formation of the *Yizhuan* has had the consequence of influencing scholars of the *Yi*, particularly those who have followed the tradition regarding the *Yi* Text as a book for divination. With the new revolution in the *Yi* philosophy by Confucius and his school, the traditional scholars—perhaps including the shamans and historians—wished to vindicate their many years of divination practice, so, they started to find new ways of more sophisticated numerology and image associative reasoning (such as even based on parts of the *Yizhuan*) in order to make divination appealing and attractive. Given the atmosphere that *Yi* was used as a divination book and saved as a divination book from the burning in the Qin period, those efforts turned out to be very successful. They would and should explain how the Han *Yi* becomes highly developed in the field of *Xiangshu* despite the Confucian revolution in the *Yi* Text tradition. Although both the *Hanshu* (汉书) and the *Shiji* (史记) record a lineage of the inheritors of the *Yi* from Zixia, the disciple of Confucius, in practice of the *Yi* most of the inheritors and transmitters seem to be versed in numbers and images.[35] In fact it becomes a dominating feature of the New Text School (今文经学派) on Classics. Hence, we have *Yi* specialists like Meng Xi (孟喜), Jiao Yanshou (焦延寿), and eventually Jing Fang who offered highly elaborate systems of interpretation in numbers and images to the total neglect of judgments and language, not to say use of one's own self-examination and learning from both past and present.

This engrossment with the *Xiangshu* continued for a long period—perhaps from the latter half of the first century BCE to the time of Wang Bi (王弼 226–249). During this period, the *Xiangshu* application of the *Yi* degenerated into superstition in many ways and created a sense of fatalism that is unhealthy for development of humanity and the political rule. In light of this, Wang Bi came forward to start a new approach to the interpretation of the *Yi* as inspired by the Laozi's *Daodejing* (道德经), which ended up in rejecting the School of the *Xiangshu* and established a long tradition for philosophical understanding of the *Yi* Text. It must be recognized, however, that the work of Wang Bi's *Commentary on Zhouyi* is in a sense a return to the Confucian tradition of seeking virtues and righteousness of the *Yi* judgments; in another aspect, however, it goes beyond the Confucian tradition in promoting a Daoist understanding of the *Yi* reality that goes beyond both language and thinking. But one must acknowledge that Wang Bi's works on *Yi* has reopened the way toward a new wave of *Yili* understanding of the *Yi*, which one will find in the works of the Song and Ming Neo-Confucians, including Zhou Dunyi, Chen Yi (程颐), Zhang Zai (张载), Shao Yong (邵雍), Zhu Xi (朱熹), and others.

Conclusion: Philosophical Reflection on Development of Philosophy of *Yi*

In light of my description of historical developments of the philosophy of the *Yijing*, we cannot fail to note various features and various problems and issues in such a development. The most important is that the development itself could be regarded as a dialectical, one that is a matter of onto-cosmological or methodological renovation in human consciousness encountering a changing world. There are limits and limitations of the human consciousness that seeks a comprehensive theory for capturing the process of creative change in reality whereas there is no limit to such creative change in reality. The core idea is to face the change and transform oneself in order to meet the changes by shaping oneself not only as an agent of change but as an entity of being with individuality and cosmic vision. Any system of philosophy of change that prevents one from seeing the change and responding in creative thinking would lapse in a limitation and enclosure and therefore defeats the purpose of understanding the future and totality of change by an individual human in an open manner. This happened in the *Xiangshu* approach in the Han, and also happened in some *Yili* systems in the Song and Ming periods. The limitation of a system may reflect a cultural state of a time and its political environment in that time. But changes will set in so that a new scenario of problems would prompt new changes in experience and theory. With this understanding, we may briefly characterize the historical development of the *Yi* philosophy in the following crucial stages and look for a future of new development:

1. Formation of *Zhouyi* text from early practices and reflections on divination (from Fuxi 伏羲 to King Wen 文王 of Zhou 周) that constitutes a dialectics-oriented system of symbolic understanding of changes open to integrative interpretation for the purpose of adaptation and action.

2. Discovery of humanity and radical revolution in interpretation of divination toward moral consciousness and moral transformation of man in Confucius and the early Confucian School (from Confucius to the end of the Warring States Period); an effort to integrate the divination and moral cultivation into a primary philosophy of creative change.

3. Elaboration of the numerology and images of *Yi* system for prediction and control (from the beginning of Han 汉 to End of Han); wide application of the *Yi* system in medicine and politics, lapsing in contrived superstition.

4. Purification of the schools of *Xiangshu* (象数) for an open and unmediated understanding of change (from Wang Bi to the end of the Tang Period 唐); the rise of neo-Daoism and Chinese Buddhism and their impact on *Yijing* interpretation toward passivism.

5. Resurgence and prominence of an onto-cosmological approach to *Yi* philosophy in neo-Confucianism (from Song 宋 to Ming 明 Periods); philosophical systems of *Yili* (义理) formed issues on integration and later lapsed into subjectivism and idealism.

6. Return to textual studies of the *Yijing* through the Qing 清 Period to the present day; new discoveries of *Yijing* texts

and other cultural relics; unconscious searching for new ground for philosophical interpretation.

7. A new philosophy of Yi against its historical background and its concern with an open future and creative creativity; onto-hermeneutical renovation on the neo-Confucian model in accordance with the principle of comprehensive integration and comparable understanding in global and cosmic contexts.

A new approach to the philosophy of the *Yijing* must presuppose a critical understanding of such a historical development of the *Yijing*. It should also see the limitations and dangers of exclusive *Xiangshu* or exclusive *Yili* approaches. It must recognize that images and numbers and even diagrams and charts are merely representational and symbolic tools for the understanding of the nature of reality and its creative changes, and this includes a reflection of the human person as part of this process of creative change of reality. No tools are perfect, and no tools need dominate our thinking and experience on the change of reality; however, insofar as they are facilitating an understanding, they are part of the system of understanding, though not the ends or goals of understanding.

On the other hand, analytical reflection and creative interpretation based on insights into experiences of changes and truths of being and becoming should lead to a systematic formulation of our understanding of the onto-cosmic reality of nature and humans in their mutual interaction and in their impact on transformation of the human individual as a moral entity. Such a philosophical understanding is identified as both onto-cosmological and onto-ethical (hence, the system could be considered onto-cosmo-ethical), which is a characteristic of Chinese philosophy in general and a characteristic of both the Confucian-Neo-Confucian and the Daoist-Neo-Daoist philosophies in particular.

We may also hold that the philosophy of the *Yi* as understood in the above not only provides a historical and genetic basis for understanding the nature of Chinese philosophy in its historical forms, it also constitutes the core spirit of Chinese philosophy that by its own nature of confronting changes in reality forms the creative force for future development of Chinese philosophy and global philosophy of humanity because of its openness, creativity, and integrative dialectics toward harmonization.

CHAPTER 7

On Harmony as Transformation

Paradigms from the *Yijing*

The Greek and Chinese Notions of Harmony

"Harmony" has a rich intuitive meaning in common usage. It suggests concord, accord, attunement, agreement, togetherness, and peaceful contentedness. How does the word "harmony" attain such a rich variety of meanings? Why does this variety of meanings suggest a common core of reference or at least a family resemblance to one another? The etymology behind the term "harmony," from the Greek word "*harmonia*," seems to explain the primal or basic model of its meaning: harmony is the agreement of musical notes that create a perception of internal togetherness and mutual support among the individual notes.[1] But then, how and why this model of meaning extends to apply to other experiences or observations remains to be explained.[2]

To answer this question, one can focus on aspects of the basic meaning of musical harmony via analytical reflection, including (1) musical harmony is a totality of parts; (2) each part of the totality is related to other parts in the totality; and (3) all parts contribute to the formation of the totality in the sense of wholeness. In the second aspect, the relation of each part to the other parts in the musical harmony is one of support and recognition, not of destroying or overcoming. Further, the relation of each part and all parts to the whole are similarly describable as one of support and recognition so that the formation of the whole implies also the explicit realization of an implicit order internally present in the parts.

This analytical reconstruction of musical harmony, however, is not complete without also mentioning (4): relating parts to totality in music is a dynamic process consummated in the movement of time. In mentioning time, one cannot ignore the spatial involvement inherent in musical harmony because in producing a piece of music, the locations of the sounds and the relations of locations in space make a difference. Hence, one must recognize musical harmony as a four-dimensional totality exhibiting an order of mutual support among its notes and realizing itself (the totality) in an explicit process of time and with an implicit reference to space.

Given the above analytical characterization of musical harmony as a basic model of harmony, it is not difficult to see how this model of harmony applies to the other human experiences of harmony in mathematics, physics, and daily life. The experience of musical harmony awakens our common-sense notion of harmony as an agreeable totality of agreeable parts. We experience this sense of harmony in color, numbers, movements, natural objects, manmade things, human behavior, human writing and poetry, human thinking, emotions, design, management, and organization. Harmony, in other words, is both internally and externally real. Our experiences enable us to recognize the four-dimensional structure of harmony. Our perceptions enable us to identify the concrete harmony in diverse experiences of concrete things and events. Our thinking mind enables us to create an image and design of harmony in a general sense; it even enables us to make an effort to realize them. The real inner and outer world of human beings contains the world of harmony as real as well as ideal. All of our experiences of harmony endow upon the term "harmony" a variety of family-resembling meanings in our use of the term itself. Why this is so is now obvious: all concrete harmonies share the same core of the harmonic structure and yet form different harmonies characteristic of each concrete individual situation.

Harmony is deeply rooted in ourselves and in the world. Despite his assertions that "War is the common condition of things," and, "All things come to pass through the compulsion of strife,"[3] Heraclitus recognizes this deep-rooted harmony. He says, "The hidden harmony is better than the obvious," and elsewhere, "There is a harmony in the bending back, as in the case of the bow and the lyre."[4] As Wheelwright observes, there is no need to see a conflict of positions in Heraclitus: Heraclitus speaks of the strife of things in the world of flux, and yet he asserts that beneath this world of strife, there is a harmony hidden from the obvious. Heraclitus appears to suggest the importance of the positive role of strife, for it is through strife that things come to pass. He also seems to suggest that from the viewpoint of the *logos*, or wisdom, even strife is a form of bringing out or fulfilling the hidden harmony. In this sense, strife is only the *contrariety* and *relativity* of things in change and transformation; it is a mode of harmony. This notion of strife will be made more explicit later in the notion of strife or conflict in the *Yijing*.

In Chinese, the concept of harmony is conveyed by the term "*he* 和," an ideograph indicating the conjoining of grain with the mouth. Etymologically, this appears to suggest the origin of the concept of harmony (*he*) in the gustatory experience of food.[5] Thus, it is natural to see how a pre-Confucian scholar/minister, Yan Ying, in the seventh century BCE described *he* precisely in terms of well-concocted food.

> Harmony is like making soup: [one has to use] water, fire, sauce, vinegar, salt, and plum in order to cook the fish and the meat; one has to heat them with firewood. The cook will mix (harmonize, *he*) them, and reach for a balanced (*zhi*) taste, [He does this] by compensating what is deficient and releasing, or dispensing, what is excessive. When the master eats, his heart/mind will be purified.[6]

In fact, this concept of harmony is not simply applied to the taste of food, but also to the hearing of music and pleasant sound. Thus, Yan Ying continues:

> The sound is like the taste. It is founded on one *qi* (vital force), two styles (*ti*), three types (*lei*), four instruments (*wu*), five sounds (*sheng*), six measures (*lu*), seven notes (*yin*), eight winds (*feng*), and nine themes (*ke*). These things mutually complete one another [to produce music]; [it is also founded upon] purity/impurity; smallness/bigness; shortness/lengthiness; speediness/slowness; sorrow/joy; firmness/softness; lateness/ forwardness; highness/lowness; inner/outer, and inclusiveness/ non-inclusiveness. These matters complement one another [to produce music]; when the superior man hears this, he will calm his heart/mind. When his heart/mind is calmed, his virtue (*de*) will remain harmonious.[7]

The important point to observe is that harmony of sound in good music is often made of various elements on different levels, or of different kinds, which are nevertheless related to one another in virtually supportive and mutually strengthening relationships. What is even more significant is that harmony (*he*) created in sound as well as in taste is intended to bring *peace* and *harmony* in the mind of the superior person (*yi ping qi xin* 以平其心). So, he or she will do things harmoniously (得和 *de he*) and thus conduct a fair and harmonious government, which leads to the peace of the people. As these implicit conceptions of harmony demonstrate, harmony is considered both a quality of things and a quality of perception; it is both a quality of mind and a quality of judgment and conduct. Things, perception, state of mind, judgment, and conduct can share the same structure and quality of harmony; they, then, can be linked together or caused one by the other.[8] This recognition is indeed important, as we shall see in the philosophy of the *Yijing* and in Confucian philosophy, for the realization of harmony in the world through realization of harmony in the person and vice versa.

To summarize, the relationship of external and internal harmony can be expressed in the following diagram:

$$\text{External Harmony} \begin{Bmatrix} \text{Music} \\ \text{Food} \end{Bmatrix} \text{Internal Harmony} \begin{Bmatrix} \text{Mind} \\ \text{Virtue} \end{Bmatrix} \text{External/Internal Harmony} \begin{Bmatrix} \text{Government} \\ \text{People} \end{Bmatrix}$$

As the above discussion shows, both the ancient Greek notion of harmony (*harmonia*) in music, and the ancient Chinese notion of harmony (*he*) in music and in food, share the recognition that harmony results from different elements being related in an appropriate way to give rise to a totality of wholeness and this further leads to the experience of agreement and unison. Exactly how different elements are related in order to have this result may depend on what the elements and the resulting whole are; certain principles governing the relationship have yet to be explained, if it is explainable at all. Besides, one must account for the existence of strife as the opposite of harmony in the world to resolve this opposition; consequently, one must resolve the strife itself if harmony is to reign as the ultimate order of the world.

Distinction between Harmony and Identity: Confucian System versus the Moist View

In his discussion of harmony, Yan Ying distinguishes harmony from identity (*tong*): harmony means interdepartmental complementation for things and intersubjective supplementation for people, because if there is no such complementation for things or supplementation for people, there would be no production or completion of a totality in either case. Identity, on the other hand, entails no such complementation or supplementation because there is no existence of *different* elements or *different* views or values. In other words, harmony admits disagreement and difference in unison, but identity admits no disagreement and difference. Yan Ying's explanation of the difference between identity and harmony in regard to the relation between the ruler and the ministers is again highly instructive:

> [The principle of harmony in food preparation] also applies to the relation between the Ruler and his Minister. The Ruler sees what is right, yet he may fail to see what is not right; thus, the Minister should point out what is not right, so that he may complement/complete what is seen right by the Ruler; [on the other hand], if the Ruler sees what is not right, he may yet fail to see what is right; thus the Minister should point out what is right so that he may complement/complete what is not rightly seen by the ruler. In this way the government is smooth and without mistake, and the people will have no disputes.
>   [In regard to Liang Jiuju (a Minister to the Ruler of the state of Qi)], where a Ruler sees what is right, Ju also concurs. Where the ruler sees what is not right, Ju also rejects. This is like [in making food] to mix water with water, but for taste, who would care to eat the food? This is also like playing the same tune on the same harp; who would care to listen to such music? The undesirability of seeing identity between Ruler and Ministers lies precisely here.[9]

Yan Ying perceives harmony as the completion of a whole by different parts, whether those parts are perceptions or judgments. From this it follows that difference in judgments and perceptions need not be destructive *disagreement* that undoes the totality underlying the disagreement; instead, whatever disagreement there is should be constructive toward realizing the underlying totality. A distinction therefore between antithetical/antagonistic and nonantithetical/nonantagonistic disagreement can be made: the former leads to a totality in which the disagreeing parties become equal members and coexist to complement each other; the latter leads to no such totality, or perhaps even to the destruction of whatever underlying totality there is, and thus to the destruction of one of the disagreeing parties, or both of them. In this sense, the former defines harmony in a dynamic sense, whereas the latter defines the opposite of harmony, strife, in a radical sense. Under this view, strife means the irresoluble conflict, the cessation of which is the destruction of the conflicting elements. One must again note that conflict may be resolved into harmony when the conflicting elements *evolve* into different things or different states of their existence through a natural force that integrates or unifies them into a totalistic system. In this case, harmony remains, for there is still a whole of differences, which complete the whole and complement each other. This, as we shall see, remains the basic insight of the philosophy of the *Yijing*.

Harmony, then, is the absence of strife or conflict, but not the absence of difference, whereas identity is not only the absence of strife and conflict but also the absence of difference. As such, there are two kinds of strife: one kind leads to harmony, the other to identity. The latter is strife in the radical sense; the former is strife in the relative sense. Consequently, there are two types of ontology and two types of dialectics: for radical-strife-ontology, all strife in the world is only radical strife, and the radical strife is the basis and ground for the dialectical changes in the world; hence, we will have a dialectics of strife and identity. For the relative-strife-ontology, on the other hand, all strife in the world is only relative strife, and the relative strife is the basis and ground for the dialectical change of the world. It is through the transformation of things that strife leads to harmony. Hence, we will have a dialectics of harmonization. We shall see that the philosophy of the *Yijing* illustrates both this ontology of harmony and this dialectics of harmonization.

In the philosophy of Confucius in the *Analects*, the doctrine of harmony represents an approach to harmony *par excellence*. The world is seen as chaotic because *dao*—the supreme and ultimate harmony—does not prevail. But does this mean that *dao* is completely missing from the world? No. One might quickly point out that the reason Confucius sets out to reform the world is precisely his conviction that there is the *dao*, even if temporally not prevailing, hidden in the hearts/minds of rulers and people, who may be "awakened" to its presence, allowing harmony and order to be brought into the world.

Here, I call the *dao* the "supreme harmony" because the Confucian conception of the *dao* is precisely the conception of a total order in which everything and every person under heaven will have its, his, or her proper place in proper time. Moreover, all things and all persons form a relationship of mutual support and complementation so that an organic unity results. One need only point to Confucius's stress on virtues as the basis of action and his formulation of the doctrine of "rectifying names" (*zhengming*) as the foundation of human relationships and social order for support. In his vision, only when things and persons fall into proper places in a whole order and relate to each other in a supportive manner will harmony result. His stress on *ren*—love based on humanity—enables an individual to embrace the whole and to relate the higher parts (such as ruler) to lower parts (such as people). His stress on *yi* (righteousness and justice) is no less insightful; it enables each individual to relate to other individuals in concentric systems of relationships without upsetting the balance or the stability of the system. *Yi* is to do justice while taking into consideration time, place, relationship, goal, value, and the total underlying harmony of the society. Hence, *yi* is an individualistic principle based on totalistic consideration.[10]

The Confucian *li* (propriety and ritual) bespeaks the importance of the smooth maintenance of relationships so that every individual also may learn from every other in order to enrich and perfect oneself. *Li* is a social order derived from a sense of harmony cultivated in an individual and objectified through common consciousness displayed in the social behavior of individuals. Hence, *li* is a social harmony that integrates all different persons in the same community while allowing for individual differences. It therefore becomes the form and the discipline that captures the best results of the application of *ren* and *yi* in a society.

Finally, Confucius shows that he has faith in the perfectibility of man through self-cultivation. This no doubt reflects his conviction, and perhaps his perception, that there is a deep and hidden harmony in the virtue of humankind, a harmony that can be cultivated, awakened, and fulfilled. Persons are able to become agents of transformation that will transform an external, chaotic world into a harmonious order of *ren*, *yi*, and *li*. This perception or conviction is so profound that it may be used to define what the genuine Confucian position is. His perception and conviction are equivalent to the cognition of a natural structure of goodness and self-sufficiency founded in harmony, shared by human beings and the world. This is the concept of *dao*; moreover, it is also the concept of human nature (*xing*), as is made amply clear by the *Doctrine of the Mean* (*Zhongyong*) as well as the philosophy of Mencius.

In light of this Confucian philosophy of the human being, one can see how Confucius apprehends and advocates harmony as a basic virtue for the superior person (*junzi*). Thus, Confucius says: "The superior man lives in harmony (*he*) with others, but does not cling to identity (*tong*) with others; the small man clings to identity (*tong*) with others, but does not live in harmony with others."[11]

This means that the *junzi* may disagree with others and yet still treat them with respect and as important players in obtaining the greater good. The *junzi* may, therefore, thrive on this disagreement by making disagreement a source of fruitful and creative relationship. The small person's attitude in clinging to others by identity, on the other hand, is basically sterile and results in selfish partisanship. This passage also shows that *he* and *tong* are two different states of relationship between persons. But in order to achieve the state of *harmony* in human relationships, one must cultivate a state of harmony in mind and behavior. Thus, all the basic Confucian virtues such as *ren*, *yi*, *li*, and *zhi* (wisdom) are ideas and norms for developing a harmonious personality of an individual; when cultivated and realized, these virtues become the very ingredients of the harmony of mind and the harmony of social behavior. They further serve to articulate harmony as a natural and internally integrated state that follows from the obtaining of these virtues. Thus, Confucius says:

> The use of the proprieties (*li*) has its precious value in achieving harmony. What is good about the way of previous sage-kings (*xianwang*) is precisely this: All things small or large, follow this principle. [But one must also note that there is something which cannot be thus done; namely,] if one only knows to strive for harmony *for the sake of* harmony *without* the restraint of proprieties, that is where something cannot be done.[12]

Why is it not right if one only knows to strive for harmony *for the sake* of harmony *without* restraint of proprieties? The answer is that harmony must be constituted by the order of proprieties in order to qualify as being genuine harmony; the sense of harmony in a person without guidance of virtues, such as *li*, leads only to false harmony, resulting in an unstable and nonenduring relationship or in an unstable and shallow character. This point simply brings us to a heightened understanding of harmony as an ordered state of mind or relationship and thus as necessarily constituted of *li* and other virtues. From this understanding that harmony can be realized as a foundation of stability and natural strength, we see that people and society in a state of harmony are inevitably stable and peaceful and thus can be productive. There should be no worry about the *poverty* (*ping*) or *fewness* of the people in a state. Hence the Confucian statement: "Having equally distributed wealth, there is no poverty. Being harmonious in relationship, there is no fewness of people; being secure and stable, there is no danger of downfall."[13] Later, Mencius even declares that among the three important things for a state, the climate (*tianshi*), the natural resources (*dili*), and the human harmony (*renhe*), the climate is not as important as the natural resources, and natural resources are not as important as human harmony.[14]

Mencius's notion of harmony is clearly illustrated by his description of Liu Xiahui as the "sage of harmony" (*sheng zhi he* 圣之和) in contrast to Bo Yi as "the sage of purity" (*sheng zhi qing* 圣之清) and Yi Yin as the "sage of responsibility" (*sheng zhi ren* 圣之任). Mencius says:

> Liu Xiahui was not ashamed of an ill-named ruler, nor did he decline the offer of a small position. When he was appointed, he did not hide his abilities and always behaved according to the way. When he was neglected, he made no complaint. When he encountered hardship and poverty, he did not have self-pity. When he was with his fellow-villagers, he enjoyed himself so much that he did not wish to depart. [He said:] "You are you and I am I; even if you undress and put yourself by my side, how could you taint me?" Hence, learning of the way of Liu Xiahui, a ruffian will become tolerant and a mean person amiable.[15]

Liu Xiahui has the virtue of harmony simply because he is able to tolerate differences and even accept bad situations that are unworthy of his service or company, yet at the same time, he preserves his own identity and purity. In doing so, he also is capable of transforming the bad into the good, the unworthy into the worthy. This concept of harmony is consistent with the concept of harmony developed by Yan Yin and Confucius, and also has all the conceptual elements of harmony we shall formally develop and illustrate in the philosophy of the *Yijing*.

One important development of the concept of harmony (*he*) in classical Confucian philosophy occurs in the writing of the *Zhongyong* (*The Doctrine of the Mean*). In this development, harmony is both a state of mind and a state of things, both an act of doing things by a person and a result of such doing. In particular, *he* is considered to be rooted in human nature (*xing*). As human nature is derived from the "mandate of heaven" (*tianming*), it is thus rooted in the ultimate reality of heaven. Human nature, as the foundation of human heart and mind, will articulate itself in feelings of the heart and judgments of reason in response to things and events of the world in a process of interaction with things in the world. Given this understanding of human nature, the question becomes how one may realize one's feelings and reason in a way that preserves the original equilibrium of human nature, and at the same time nurtures a growth and fulfillment of a person's nature. In order to do this, one must let out one's feelings in proper measure, with proper intentionality, and with proper restraint relative to an event or situation in the world. If one can do this consistently, one is said to have achieved *he*.

He is, therefore, the state of resonance and consonance between a person and the world in a responsive interactive relationship. *He* permits the difference of feelings and realizes this difference in different contexts. In such realization, one will not lose sight of the fundamental equilibrium in oneself nor create a disorder in the world, which would be likely if the equilibrium in oneself were lost. *He* is moreover supposed to restore a state of disorder to a state of order, and restore a state of insufficiency to one of sufficiency. In this sense, *he* is not simply a principle of heart-mind (*xin*), but a principle of nature (*xing*). *He* is the way heaven orders and benefits things. Thus, the *Zhongyong* says:

> When the feelings of joy, anger, sorrow, and happiness are not elicited, this is the state of equilibrium (centrality *zhong*). When these feelings become elicited, and at the same time follow proper limitation of nature (*zhong jian*), this is called *he*. Equilibrium is the great basis of the world, *he* is the way whereby an order of all things is attained. If a person succeeds in reaching *zhong* and *he*, then heaven and earth will

be well-positioned and all ten thousand things will be well nourished.¹⁶

As we shall see, this concept of *he* is highly recognizable in the *Great Appendix* (*Xici*) of the *Yijing*. This suggests that by the time the *Zhongyong* and the *Xici* were written, under the influence of the Confucian school, the concept of *he* had acquired a deepened metaphysical significance. *He* is not simply a state of nature, nor simply a state of mind, but a creative process of harmonizing the world by the mind, which results in a better state of the world. This is captured in the statements used to describe the profound and sagely wisdom and virtue of Confucius:

> He is like heaven and earth upon which nothing is not held up and under which nothing not covered. He is like the alternating movements of the four seasons and like the alternating shining of the sun and the moon. All the ten thousand things are naturally nourished without harming each other. Things go their parallel ways without obstructing one another. The small virtues are like tributary waters, moving without stop. The great virtues are so wide and dense that they allow things to grow and produce without end. This is how heaven and earth are great.¹⁷

This description of the greatness of heaven and earth is a description of harmony in the Confucian perspective with both a human and a metaphysical reference.

If the philosophy of Confucius and Mencius can be described as the "philosophy of harmony and harmonization" (*shang he*), the philosophy of Mo Di, a late contemporary of Confucius, can be described as the philosophy of identity and identification (*shang tong*). We have seen how Confucius makes the distinction between *harmony* and *identity* in the *Analects*. Yet when Mo Di teaches his doctrine, he specifically singles out the concept of *tong* as his central teaching: all people should follow heaven and should identify their will with the "will of heaven" (*tianzhi*) so that there is no difference in the conception of justice and righteousness (*yi*) nor is there disagreement or dispute over the words and meanings of sages. Mo Di wishes to see a society ruled by the central doctrines of one truth in universal love and universal righteousness. He tries to argue for this on the basis of the activities of heaven. In this regard, he differs significantly from the Confucianists not only in the contrast between *tong* as a principle of elimination of difference and *he* as a principle of comprehension of differences, but also in the contrast between seeing heaven as a divine source of life and power and seeing heaven as a creative principle of the manifold of things that should coexist in harmony rather than in identity. In the *Liji* (*Record of Rites*), the Confucians speak of the ideal of "great unity" (*da tong*) in the well-known chapter on the *Li yun* (*Evolution of Li*). But this ideal of "great unity" means universal harmony rather than universal identity. Hence, the "great unity" is actually a state of great harmony.

Notably, however, in the Neo-Moist Canons (*Mo Pian*), four kinds of identity are distinguished, and the concept of identity (*tong*) is thus defined for four different kinds of identity:[18] (1) the identity of one thing referred to by two names (*zhong*), (2) the identity of belonging to the same body (*ti*), (3) the identity of grouping together in the same space (*he*), and (4) the identity of belonging to the same class (*lei*). Given these distinctions, it is evident that not all identities are exclusive of differences. In fact, identity of belonging to the same body (*ti tong*) is quite compatible with the notion of *he*; indeed, it basically exemplifies the same structure of *he*: integration of differences as parts (*jian*) in a unity of totality.[19]

Resonance among Harmony (*he*), Centrality (*zhong*), and Unity (*yi*)

In our discussion of *he* as a state of harmony between mind and world, we have referred to the equilibrium of mind as the requisite foundation for *he*. This equilibrium or centrality of mind (*zhong*) is important because it gives a starting point for the realization of *he*: *zhong* is the state of nondifferentiation of human feelings, which under proper conditions will differentiate into different feelings. In this sense, *zhong* is not the same thing as identity where no difference is to be allowed, potentially or actually.

In fact, one might say that *zhong* indicates the *proper positioning* of a state of mind for a person in a context of relationships among different things: this state or position will enable the mind, or the person, to reach out to different things for the purpose of harmony. Hence, the concept of *zhong* can be spatially or geometrically conceived as well as qualitatively conceived. In the spatial sense, *zhong* is the middle position between two points on a line, neither to the right nor to the left. In the qualitative sense, *zhong* is the mean between the excessive and the deficient, and thus neither inclined toward excessiveness nor inclined toward insufficiency. The first sense of *zhong* is well illustrated in the notion of central position of lines 2 and 5 in the hexagrams of the *Yijing*.[20] The second sense of the *zhong* is illustrated many times in the *Shang Shu* (*The Book of Documents*): "Neither insufficient nor excessive, all must follow the righteousness of the King."[21] This is the *zhong* that Confucius refers to in the *Analects* as "neither excessive or insufficient."[22] In both these senses, *zhong* is a state not dominated by a dogma, and thus not subject to the restriction of a specialized differentiation described as an excess or as an insufficiency. In this sense, *zhong* is a generalized state of being which is the beginning of all things. But this is only one aspect of the meaning of *zhong*. There is yet a deeper aspect to be explained in the following.

As the *zhong* mediates extremes and differences, it should be able to generate differences and integrate them into unity. This is first suggested in the statement of Lu Xing: "To govern the people, [the ruler] should not deviate from the middle (*zhong*) in listening to the two sides in a litigation, and should not be prejudicially bent to either of the two sides in the litigation."[23] The reason a ruler, or judge, should not lean toward either side of the litigating parties is that he should make fair and correct judgments that are acceptable to both parties and to the people at large. He is to maintain a position above the two sides and yet reach out and influence them. In this sense, by recognizing difference and yet integrating the differences in unity, *zhong* becomes a way to realize *he*. The spirit with which Confucius speaks of seeking knowledge by "questioning two extremes and exhausting their possibilities."[24] It can also be said that it is in this sense that Yao urges Shun to "hold steadfast to the *zhong*" (*yunzhijue zhong*) [in administering the government], and Mencius praises Tang for the fact that Tang holds steadfast to the *zhong* and seeks to establish the worthy without being bound to any prejudice."[25] In this sense, *zhong* also becomes a supreme virtue and supreme way for realizing harmony and goodness for oneself as well as for others.[26] He suggests the middle position between the extreme egoism of Yang Chu and the extreme of altruism of Mo Di as the desirable way to relate oneself to the world, and mentions Zi Mo, the Confucian, as holding this middle position. But he also comments that if one holds steadfast to the *zhong* without an ability to adapt to individual and changing circumstances, then "to hold steadfast to the *zhong*" becomes "holding steadfast to the oneness" (*yi*). This means that *zhong* is *oneness* (*yi*) with adaptability; it is capable of concretizing a principle and applying itself to different situations; in contrast, *yi* is *zhong* in rigidity and thereby violates the very meaning of *zhong*. But this also suggests that the notion of *zhong* could include the notion of *oneness*, which should mediate between two extreme positions and produce the most desirable course of action.

This discussion of *zhong* should shed light on the relation of *zhong* to *he*. In one sense, *zhong* is the foundation of *he*, where differences are not generated. In another sense, *zhong* is the state of *he* where differences are organized and integrated, and in this sense *zhong* is the way of harmonizing differences and producing a unity necessary for the total integration of differences as parts. This analysis also brings out two senses of unity (一 *yi*). In one sense, unity is the static state of *oneness* without adaptability, which, while transcending the differences, is incapable of integrating the differences. In another sense of unity, however, as we shall discuss in the philosophy of the *Yijing*, unity is creative and productive of differences (as its parts), without losing the unifying ground and principle, while at the same time maintaining unity among differences even under changing circumstances. This creative unity, in distinction to the stationary unity, is the basis for producing and strengthening harmony as a system of integrating differences.

To summarize our discussion of the notions of *he*, *tong*, *zhong*, and *yi*, we may articulate their relationships in the following network:[27]

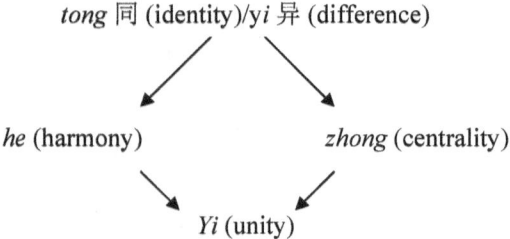

"Oneness" (*yi*) is the underlying unity among all parts in a totality, which gives relevance and relationship to the parts in the totality. Of course, there can be many types and even many degrees of unity in a totality. The unity could be a prevailing thread linking all parts; it could also be an interrelatedness among all parts, a functional interdependence that contributes toward the overall balance, and thus stability and strength of the whole. Further, the unity could be thoroughly fused in a well-formed network of relationships, which can be best described as a state of interpenetration among parts and whole; here, the wholeness of parts and partiality of whole are equally present.[28] The first type of unity is to be clearly found in any hierarchical structure in nature, society, government, or architecture. The second type of unity is to be found in biological systems and is often referred to as an organic system. The third type of unity is basically conceived in the metaphysics of Huayan Buddhism, Zhu Xi, and Wang Yangming as representing the true nature of reality.[29] Unity is to be strived for by an individual who seeks enlightenment or the understanding of reality. For these systems, a world of things is not normally seen as interpenetrating, and therefore a lack of unity is apparently the case. How to reconcile the true order of unity in a reality that apparently lacks unity is often the fundamental question that many philosophers attempt to settle, or for that matter may fail to settle. A deeper and more challenging question is how to reconcile all different types of unitary order as if they are layers or levels of order in a totalistic and unitary system.

Confucius has remarked to his disciple, Zeng Shen, "My way is threaded with unity."[30] In making this remark Confucius referred to the corpus of his teaching as an underlying unity of truth. Zeng Shen perceived this unity of truth as the way of loyalty (central-mindedness, *zhong*) and compassion (like-mindedness, *shu*). This is correct but not quite complete. Unity (oneness, *yi*) in the Confucian teaching is oneness, not twoness: an ultimate principle must be focused on. In the Confucian *Analects*, there is no concept better than *ren* (humanity) that can qualify to act as this principle of unity.

In light of this consideration, one may draw the correct conclusion that *zhong* and *shu* are two aspects of *ren*, and all other virtues and norms are to be integrated into this system of oneness, one centrality with two manifestations. On this basis, one can also show that the Confucian doctrine of *ren* demonstrates a highly integrated structure of interdependence, which Confucius has projected to be the *ideal* development and realization of the nature of man, and consequently, can be said to reflect a highly integrated system of human and social reality, which would exemplify an ideal state of harmony. How oneness (unity) contributes to harmony appears to be well illustrated by the Confucian perception and teachings, as well as what these teachings have achieved.

In Mencius, oneness (*yi*) is also counted as an important power to be achieved in order to further achieve order and harmony in the world. When King Xiang of the State of Liang (*Liang Hui Wang*) asked, "How can the world be ordered and stabilized?," Mencius replied, "The world is to be ordered and stabilized on the basis of oneness" (*yi*).[31] Mencius did not elaborate on this idea of oneness, but from his philosophy it is clear that this oneness again is no less than the principle and virtue of *ren*. He has indicated this by replying to the second question of King Xiang: "Who is capable of unifying the world?" Mencius answered, "Only he who does not indulge himself in killing people can unify (give oneness to) the world."[32] "Not to indulge in killing people" is a manifestation of *ren*. The so-called oneness of the world is no more than the unity of all people who become related to one another and to their ruler in the bond of humanity and love, justice and righteousness, morality and respect, truth and wisdom: all being manifestations of *ren* as well as manifestations of the goodness in the nature of man. Again, it is clear that the unity of the world in Mencius bespeaks a state of harmony, which is to be constituted by the realization of the nature of man and the realization of the nature of all things.

In the *Daodejing*, it is said that the *dao* gives rise to oneness.[33] Without going into detail on Laozi's philosophy of *dao* and *de*, it suffices here to indicate that the *dao*, as the primordial unity, in order to give rise to the manifold of things, must give rise to the unity of things in the beginning. The unity (oneness) of things, as we shall see, coincides to a large extent with the concept of the *taiji* in the *Yijing*. It is the source of vitality and life in things as well as the sustaining base for the differentiation of things in a process of change. Indeed, Laozi even points out that it is only when things possess and maintain this oneness that they become the *best* of what they are. Hence, it is said:

> Heaven acquires the oneness so that it is pure, Earth acquires the oneness so that it is peaceful; the spirit acquires the oneness so that it is subtle; the valley acquires the oneness so that it is full of life; the myriad things acquire the oneness so that they are flourishing; the dukes and kings acquire the oneness so that they become leaders of the world. They all become what they are because of acquisition of oneness.[34]

The oneness is the *dao* in its activity of producing things and the world.

Four Grades of Harmony versus Four Grades of Strife

With all our discussion of the notion of *he*, *tong*, *zhong*, and *Yi* in the classical Chinese philosophical resources, we are now confronted with the problem: how do we systematically interpret the concept of harmony in light of this discussion? That is, how do we arrive at a theoretical understanding of harmony so that all insights from the above discussion can be incorporated and can be extended to a comprehensive explanation of reality and experience that may even lead to significant uses in practical life? To answer this important question, we must first recall that harmony in the sense of Greek *"harmonia"* and in the sense of Chinese *"he"* always involves different elements, and that these different elements work together and support one another as parts of a whole to make a unity of the whole possible. Harmony is the experience, the perception, as well as the reality of this unity of a whole together with the interrelationship of its parts. But it is left undecided as to how these parts are related in order to be related in harmony. In other words, the logic of the harmonious relationship is left unspecified and unaccounted for. However, if we examine the possible relationships of two different things or two parts of a whole, we can easily identify the following possibilities of relationships.

The first possibility is that two different things, or two parts of a whole, can be minimally related in terms of logical consistency; that is, it's possible that there exists no incompatibility between two things. Consider a pen and an orange on a table: are they related any more than sharing the table and being placed side by side? Unless another relationship can be invested in them, they are related in a state of logical conjunction and noncontradiction. There need not be any support or significant relationship between them, nor, of course, are they dependent on each other for their individual existence. If there is any harmony between them, their harmony is the minimal co-presence without contradiction or contrariety. Perhaps many things exist in this relationship of irrelevance and individual self-sufficiency. This form of harmony, if it is harmony at all, perhaps can be illustrated by the *Daodejing*'s statement: "The people [in the idealized community] do not interact with each other from birth to death."[35]

A second possibility is that of a material relationship. Different things certainly can be better related than merely related by logical consistency or logical compatibility when they become interactive with each other.

In this sense, two different things can have a material relationship as well as a logical relationship.[36] This material relationship can be simply a physical influence between two different things or a subatomic, atomic, or molecular interaction between them.[37] These relationships need not add or detract anything from the two different things, but the two different things are related through interactions between them thereby forming a common field of co-existence. However, the two different things are still far from being actively supportive of each other.

A third possibility is that the interaction between two different things involves mutual support in the increase of internal coherence of the relationship between them. The mutual support of two things means that each contributes to the other in its growth and fulfillment and thus enables two different things to form a relationship of fruitful interdependence. The family relationship between husband and wife illustrates this relationship as well as any other socially organized group or community relationship that serves the purpose of mutual strengthening and enrichment. Such a relationship could be described as organic, as it is in the organic body that different organs become interdependent such that each functions well independently. This would be a higher degree of harmony between two things.

A fourth possibility occurs when the interdependence becomes interpenetration in the sense that the parts of a whole are more interfused and the whole becomes actively participating in the parts as the parts do in the whole. In this case, the relation of harmony will become more productive and creative in the sense that a new order of differentiation resulting in unity takes place, without, at the same time, losing the ground of the unity governing the parts of the original whole. During this creative interpenetration, harmony reaches its ideal state as suggested in the human experience of harmony in music or food. This state of harmony is creative because it is dynamic: it always involves change and transformation in the process of time as illustrated in the production of life.

In light of the above, we have now defined four grades, or four modes, of harmony that, in comparison with one another, are different in degree of coherence of relationship between their parts and wholes. The more coherently the parts and whole are related, the more harmony there is. Indeed, in the ideal sense of harmony intended by the Greek term *harmonia* and the Chinese term *he*, no relationship qualifies as harmony other than the close-knit interdependence and perhaps even interpenetration among the parts and the whole. The Chinese Hua Yan Buddhist philosophy of totality and the Neo-Confucian philosophy of *li* (principle) and *qi* (vitality) also contend that reality is harmonious in this ideal sense and that all disharmony or strife is mere appearance.

With the above schematic characterization of harmony, we also can describe the lack of harmony, and consequently, the nature of strife, according to the negation of the four grades of harmony. First, we can recognize that the loss of harmony in a realistic sense must *not* result from simply negating one grade of harmony to the exclusion of other grades of harmony. On the contrary, strife and the lack of harmony derive from negation of all grades of harmony in the above characterization—that is, if all the above grades of harmony are recognized as modes of harmony at all. The reason is simple. The negation of grade-four harmony (interpenetration) still has left the other three grades of harmony viable. The negation of grade-one harmony (logical consistency) entails negation of other higher-grade harmonies and thus becomes equivalent to the negation of all harmonies. The result of such a negation is logical inconsistency or logical incompatibility of the form: $\sim(A \wedge B) \Rightarrow (\sim A \wedge B) \vee (A \wedge \sim B)$, assuming that A and B are two different systems or two subsystems of a larger system.

If we construe strife as the opposite of harmony, then in the light of the preceding discussion strife becomes the logical inconsistency or incompatibility between two different things, each of which leads to the negation of the other thing, and therefore "contradicts" the other by not being able to co-exist with it. If strife means exclusion and elimination as an end, it is precisely due to this end that the two things at strife war against each other. We could define the first grade of strife as a case of logical inconsistency or incompatibility, which implies eliminating the existence of one thing at the expense of another. A second grade of strife may be defined as difference in indifference, which one often finds in the classical example of social alienation. A person, or a class of people, is alienated from society and *vice versa* if there is neither mutual concern nor any significant interaction between the two. In fact, hostility may be said to be potentially present in the relation of alienation: when the hostility breaks out in the open: each side has the intention to destroy or diminish the other such as the case of husband and wife in divorce. Then we have the third grade, or mode, of strife. Finally, when two sides maintain communication and interaction, but still intend to resist or actually do *resist* moving to a higher form of closer interaction, we may be said to have the fourth grade/mode of strife. It is evident that these grades/modes of strife corresponding to types of decreasing degrees of support relationships are among the last four relationships in harmony.

Harmony as Unity of Opposites

Given the above analyses of harmony and strife, it is pertinent to ask how full and ideal harmony can be constructed and how strife can be reconciled with harmony if strife is as real as harmony. At this point, we can bring in the *Yijing* notion of interpretation in order to provide a deeper analysis of the possible relationships among parts of a whole. For this purpose, we have to look for the condition and the basis for the interpenetrating relationship in the case of ideal and full harmony. The philosophy of the *Yijing* suggests that the very condition of interpenetration of things in a whole is the unity of opposites. This proposition regarding unity of opposites is to be understood in a twofold way: it is only in the genuine *opposites* that unity is to be found; and it is only in the genuine unity of things that the opposites are found. Thus, unity and opposites go hand in hand, and each becomes the condition for the existence of the other. In fact, we can assume that all differences in a unity are opposites, which need not be related to each other as opposites on one level or another. When and only when those unrelated opposites become genuinely related as opposites do they form a unity and thus form a harmony in a creative sense. A good example to illustrate this is the case where we have a group of men and women who could be sorted out as compatible and fitting couples, but before they are sorted out in one way or another, they remain unknown to each other as ideal partners. Therefore, in this group, men and women cannot be said to form a unity as harmony. But once they are sorted out as compatible and fitting couples, they form a group of couples that can be described as harmonious unity. Of course, here we assume that couples of men and women are examples of opposites.

To a certain degree, Heraclitus recognizes that opposites form a unity. However, he does not explain the principle of such unity itself. His assertion that "Cool things become warm, the warm things grow cool" is significant.[38] It shows that opposites can mutually transform into one another, and one may therefore suggest that their unity is their mutual transformability. Heraclitus also asserts that "war" is the common condition and that "strife is justice and all things come to pass through the compulsion of strife."[39] But what is called "war" or "strife" is simply the apparent incompatibility, and hence the mutual transformability, of the opposites. It is due to the strife of things that Heraclitus conceives change to be possible. He further infers that without strife, and hence without change, all things would cease to exist.[40] The paradoxical conclusion drawn from this is that things exist because of the conflict and strife among them, and hence because of their being opposite to each other. Yet, things will perish from conflict and strife. Conflict and strife conduce to both the existence and perishing of things, and hence, the change and transformation of things.

Nowhere, however, does Heraclitus explain how strife conduces to existence, and how strife conduces to perishing. He fails to see that it is due to the power of unity that two opposites in unity give rise to existence of things, and it is due to the power of the opposition that two opposites in a unity give rise to the perishing of one or the other opposite, or they give rise to the mutual transformation between the two. He fails to focus on, or perhaps even fails to see, the unity side of the two opposites and for that matter, fails to recognize the genuine nature of genuine opposites. Are warm and cool generally opposites? If they are, they must form a unity that leads to the existence of things. That cool becomes warm, or warm becomes cool, in some situations would mean the production of life and activity such as the recovery from illness and growth in animal life. In other situations, this transformation from one opposite to the other in which the conjunction of opposites is formed would mean the cessation of life and thus the perishing of a given thing. But in this sense, the conjunction of opposites should be more appropriately described as a *disunity* rather than unity of opposites.

Heraclitus focused explicitly on the disunity (strife) and transformation of opposites and failed to state the "principle of *unity*" as part of the process of change. In fact, one may point out that in change and transformation of things there are both *unity* and *disunity*, but then the very presence of change and transformation in existing things should presuppose a unity of unity and disunity, and thus should underscore the unity of opposites as a productive and creative principle in a metaphysical sense. We may indicate this relationship in the following diagram:

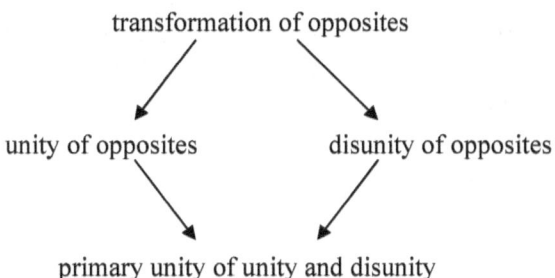

With an analysis and critique of the Heraclitean concept of strife and his implicit thesis of "disunity" of opposites, we may return to the philosophy of the *Yijing* as a source for formulating and providing a comprehensive theory of harmony and strife, in which harmony is metaphysically founded and fundamentally illuminated, and strife can be given a proper place and clearly explained. The very importance of the *Yijing* philosophy consists in its recognition of change (*bian*) and transformation (*hua*) as constitutive of reality[41] as well as in its insight that change and transformation primarily take place because of *unity* instead of disunity of things. Even disunity and strife should contribute to the unity of things on a deeper level. This is because again, in the *Yijing*, all differences between things come from a unity, which is interpreted as creative, whereby differences are interrelated and become interrelating, interpenetrating and inseparable. On this basis, not only all differences are explained, but also the nature of their differences as differences; the possibilities of strife and perishing are properly recognized and explained. This is again because a well-entrenched concept of creative unity, hence a metaphysical notion of harmony, is developed. In this sense of harmony, conditions of consistency, relationship, mutual support, and interpenetration are reaffirmed and a basic model for relating differences in harmony (*via* harmonization) can be constructed. Accordingly, ways can be developed for explaining significances of strife in harmony as well as for transforming strife into harmony.

Harmony and the Primary Unity of Opposites

Although the thesis of unity of opposites has been discussed in philosophy in many contexts, no attention appears to be focused on the unity of opposites as an essential requirement for full harmony, and on the primary unity of opposites that provides for the unity of opposites as a metaphysical foundation. The reason a unity of opposites is essential for harmony is that differences must be integrated into mutual support and mutual complementation. But there is no better integration in this sense than integration of opposites in unity, where differences become opposites and complement each other.

Here we presume that the unity of opposites has the following five basic meanings:

1. Opposites are differences that are not incompatible nor inconsistent, and therefore need not be contradictory. They are differences that are opposite in the sense that they possess contrary qualities occupying opposite positions in a continuum. Hence, opposites are polarities belonging to a totality.

2. Opposites, considered by themselves, are initially exclusive, but they become complementary when considered as parts in a whole through process of integration.

3. The underlying whole of the polar opposites integrates opposites into a relationship of interdependence in which each opposite has a function defined relative to the whole as well as relative to the other opposite.

4. The mutual restraining of opposites reflects self-limitation of the opposites in the whole, but this self-limitation at the same time opens new opportunities for expansion and realization of potentiality in each. In other words, they become both limited and extended in the whole formed by their unity and togetherness.

5. The unity of opposites is always presupposed in their differences and opposition, and it can be said that it is from this presupposed unity that their differences and opposition can be maintained.

The last point brings out the problem of the primary unity of opposites. One may ask: how is this primary unity of opposites possible? The simple answer is this: unless the unity of opposites is primary, there will be irresoluble difficulty in explaining oneness in terms of multiplicity or in explaining multiplicity in terms of oneness. In other words, one would have to take a Parmenidean position of immutable oneness, or one must take a Democritean position of myriad atoms in permanent motion. In either position, one cannot account for the given phenomenon of change in the world, which involves simultaneous unity and multiplicity. There is neither an *a priori* reason why there must be a prior unity defying multiplicity, nor an *a priori* reason why there must be a prior multiplicity without unity; moreover, experience does not give any reason to argue *either* way. On the contrary, an open acceptance of experience leads us to see oneness in multiplicity and multiplicity in oneness.[42] Modern philosophy beginning with Hegel already stresses the importance of one whole in conjunction with many elements. Contemporary philosophy and contemporary science, including physics and biology, also are awakened to the givenness and hence the importance of whole and holographic structures. What is needed is actually to focus on the reality of *change* as a given phenomenon before one quickly flies into the sky of abstraction.

The primary unity of opposites is founded on the following two observations. First, the unity of opposites is phenomenologically primary, as the meaning of unity of opposites is derived from observations of relationships in time and in space in which parts are *opposite* in quality and yet complement each other to form a whole totality. The four seasons of a year, the day and night of a whole day, the color orange and color blue of a full spectrum, and the family of male and female persons, not only are capable of being perceived as a totality with mutually exclusive and at the same time reciprocally complementary parts or aspects, but they are indeed perceived as such. Such perception is natural and spontaneous as in practical life. They need not be learned, nor do they need to be taught. It is part and parcel of our lifeworld and life experience. This perception seems to embody a lesson for integration of knowledge and experience on a higher plane. If we do not see things as unity of opposites in a totality of wholeness, and thus as different approaches to different aspects of the same thing, or if we are carried away by a singular linear way of thinking losing sight of other possible ways of thinking, we will lose sight of the totality, and we will find ourselves consumed by *paradoxes* and *puzzles*.

Paradoxes and puzzles sometimes require that we make certain subtle distinctions in order to resolve them such as in the case of logical and semantic paradoxes. At other times, paradoxes and puzzles require us to synthesize and integrate distinction and differences to form a perception of the whole in terms of unity of opposites, which lies behind the distinctions and differences, such as in the case of paradoxes of *waves/particles* and "action at a distance" in quantum mechanics. In the latter case, the paradox is only resolved by *perceiving*, not only *positioning* the dual quality of wave and particles forming one whole process, and thus *perceiving* the whole process of the photon phenomenon as having dual qualities of waves and particles. This is a perception forced on us by nature; when incorporated with other perceptions of similar kind, this perception seems to take on a naturalness and spontaneity of its own.

In the philosophy of the *Yijing*, the most direct and natural experience of opposite duality and its complementarities comes from the observation of the totality of opposition and complementation of darkness and shade (*yin*) and light and bright (*yang*). Hence, the doctrine of *yin* and *yang* becomes the primary phenomenological basis for all other *yin/yang* relationships of unity of opposites. With this background of understanding, all unities of opposites should be ultimately justified in terms of the *yin/yang* paradigm and should be eventually perceived to have this *yin/yang* relationship of opposition and complementarity in a highly integrated totality of wholeness.

Second, the unity of opposites also is ontologically primary in the sense that it is from and through the unity of opposites that all things can be understood to arise. The phenomenon of change and transformation is not understood as a mere process of ordering, integration, and growth, nor is it understood as a mere process of disordering, disintegration, and decay. Instead, it is understood as an alternation of order and disorder, integration and disintegration, growth and decay. This alternation suggests a totality and a unity that has two opposite aspects which complement each other. Understanding of this is both experiential and theoretical. It is experiential because there could be genuine consciousness of experiencing the underlying reality that manifests these two *aspects* of change. It is theoretical because this experience of the unity of opposites suggests a way of thinking that makes the conception of an underlying reality an ontologically relevant and ontologically fruitful idea. With this ontological understanding based on this experience, the unity of opposites is seen not only to be regularity of description but a principle of explanation: It explains why and how unity gives rise to opposites and why and how opposites give rise to unity. As a principle of explanation, unity can be regarded as the primary source of life and order. Hence, unity becomes creativity, and creativity becomes unity. Since all alternations of opposites can be conceived as having an underlying unity, this underlying unity can be conceived as the primal and ultimate source and basis for all alternations of opposites.

Further, it can be seen that unity as a creative principle gives rise to differences and preserves an order of differences by creating all differences as essentially opposites. Unity as a creative principle is also creative in the sense that in producing differences it preserves the creativity of unity at the same time. The only way this is possible is the way in which differences created by unity are opposites that complement each other to form the unity. This also means that unity *per se* has the potentiality of creating opposites, and opposites have the potentiality of forming unities. There is therefore a higher-order unity, the *unity of identity and difference*.[43] If there is still difference from this unity, the progression to still higher-order unity would follow until we reach the supreme unity of opposites, which is productive of all opposites. If the unity is conceived as mere identity and opposition is conceived as mere difference—unity as unity without difference, and opposition as opposition without unity—then the opposition between the identity and difference will form a unity, which is the unity of identity and difference. Such is the meaning of unity implicit in the creativity of all opposites, and such is the meaning of creativity implicit in the unity of opposites. Hence, ontologically, unity and opposites must be one in a most primary sense, and unity of opposites must be a creative principle both self-explanatory and explanatory of all opposition and unities in reality. With this understanding of the unity of opposites as a creative principle, we see that the unity of opposites is *primarily ontological* and *ontologically primary*. We may even proceed to explain all creative activities as resulting from the opposites-creating activity of unity on the one hand, and the unity-forming activity of opposites on the other. This is also how harmony can be ultimately defined.

Harmony conceived as a relationship of integrating differences as parts in a whole, can be conceived as a unity of opposites and opposites in unity. There are essentially two types of harmony based on this conception of harmony: (1) harmony resulting from explicit differentiation of unity without losing unity, and (2) harmony resulting from explicit integration of differences without losing the oppositional nature of differences. In the latter case, it is important to point out that for differences to be integrated into a unity and formed into harmony, the differences must be transformed or understood as transformed into opposites in the first place. Harmony can therefore be regarded as a principle of transforming differences into opposites and integrating opposites into unity. Hence harmony is a principle of integration.

On the other hand, harmony can be regarded as creating opposites and transforming opposites into different orders of different unities. Hence, harmony also is a principle of differentiation. In this sense, harmony can be conceived simply as both a unity of opposites and a differentiation in unity. Harmony, then, contains and presupposes a unity of opposites as its ontological principle. As such, it is the principle whereby the unity of opposites as a primary ontological principle becomes fully realized as both unity and opposition. In harmony, both the product and result of unity of opposites act as a creative principle and as a productive process.

Thus, we can have harmony in the three phrases presented as follows: It is clear that harmony as a creative principle indicates that the creative

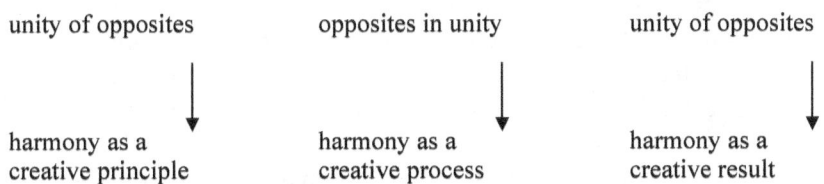

principle works to bring harmony in its creative action, which is of course different the harmony realized in a crerative process.

The philosophy of the *Yijing* is founded on the insights of both the phenomenological and ontological primary unity of opposites as a creative principle and process. Without too much detail, we can now describe how the *Yijing* conceives the unity of opposites as a creative principle provided for all things in nature, including human beings. Specifically, the *Yijing* refers to this principle as "primary unity" (*taiji*)[44] or the "creativity of creativity" (*shengsheng*).[45] On the basis of this principle, the *Yijing* also explains how differences of things arise and how—when all differences are well oriented and well positioned (*wei*)—they become mutually supporting and complementary opposites. After opposites are formed, there is always equilibrium or centrality (*zhong*), and there is always a new unity (*yi*) of things. On the basis of attainment of centrality and unity, development of new differences and opposites will ensue and thus a creative advance to a new order of unities will follow. This is the change and transformation that exhibits the creative potentiality and creative activity of the primary unity of opposites. In both the process and the product of this change and transformation, harmony will be realized in the full sense, and harmonization will be achieved to the full extent. In the following, I will characterize five major stages of harmonization and their corresponding aspects of harmony in terms of the paradigms of the primary unity of opposites from the *Yijing*, which may not coincide with the five meanings of the unities of opposites.[46]

We shall begin with *unity as creativity*. The primary unity of creativity, which manifests in the alternation of opposites, is the universal totality that integrates the opposites, which also is called *dao* in the

Yijing. Thus, *dao* is defined as "the alternation of *yin* (shade, soft, rest) and *yang* (bright, firm, motion)."[47]

The *dao* is what makes the alternation of opposites, *yin* and *yang*, possible. This process leads to the creation of the world as an ordered structure. Hence, one can specify the world in terms of the spatial relationships of heaven and earth, which are opposite and complementary to each other, as well as in terms of the temporal relationships of winter and summer, which are again opposite and complementary to each other. These relationships form a totality of a whole world in which the unities and totalities take place. This process is referred to as "creativity of creativity" (*shengsheng*).[48] The primary unity that gives use to this process is called the "*taiji*" (the great ultimate).[49] Hence, it is said that the *taiji* gives rise to the polarity of *yin* and *yang*. Notably, when this polarity arises, there is still unity of the totality that enables each polarity to act as a unity and hence give rise to a second level polarity of *yin-yang*. This process can be continued; along these lines, the rise of eight trigrams, and eventually that of sixty-four hexagrams, can be explained.[50] This indicates how the *primary unity* of the *dao* is unlimited in its activity, how its creativity is renewed in new unities produced, and it is how unity is re-affirmed in each new creative activity of the *dao*.

The following structure of division indicates the unbounded nature of creativity in unity and creativity of the *dao*, primary unity of opposites:

the primary unity

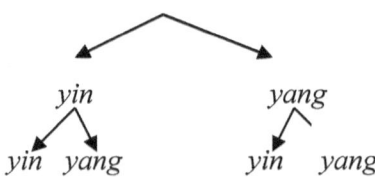

The above shows that creativity takes two directions to accomplish and to perpetuate. In the downward or forward direction (if we look at the diagram sideways), we can see the creative division of opposites, whereas in the upward or backward direction we can see creativity as *bian* (*chuanghua*) and penetration (*tong*). In the *Xici Shang*, it is said, "the closing door is called *Kun* and the opening door is called *Qian*. One closing and one opening is called *change*. The incessant coming-and-going without ending is called *penetration*."[51] Here, the closing door can be interpreted as the upward or backward movement of unification and the opening door can be interpreted as the downward or forward movement of division. *Tong* is the penetration through which a dynamic process of unifying all creative divisions—hence, the interpenetration of unity and division—will take place. In this sense of penetration, the primary unity of opposites can be explained; moreover, it is in this sense that the ultimate and final unity of all unities of opposites, which would themselves be unities, can be articulated.

To express the creativity of the primary unity of opposites, there is no better passage than the *Tuan Commentary* on the *Qian* and *Kun* hexagrams:

> The great is the origin of creativity (*Qian yuan*). It is the source from which all things originate and hence [it] commands heaven. By the moving of clouds and the showering of rain, different things acquire their forms. [The sage] understands the beginning and end (of this creativity), and thus completes the six positions in time in the hexagram [for a structured unity of the different stages and aspects of a whole phenomenon in relationship] and rides on six dragons (referring to the different phases of creative advance of the primary unity) to command heaven. The way of *Qian* (creativity) changes and transforms things and positions all things according to their nature and necessities (*xing* and *ming*). [Consequently,] the great harmony (*taihe*) is accomplished and sustained. Thus it is propitious for holding to the creativity of unity. [In regard to people,] the Sagely King also stands out among all ordinary things, and through his creative unification enables the ten thousand nations in the world to reach peace and tranquility (*ling*).[52]
>
> Supreme is the origin of receptivity (*Kun yuan*). It is the source from which all things derive their life. It follows and cherishes heaven in conformity. The *Kun* is powerful so as to hold all things, and its virtue matches that of *Qian* without limit. It comprehends expanse [of space] and is capable of developing [the power of *Qian*]. Thus under its influence all things become prosperous.[53]

The *Qian* and the *Kun* are each an aspect of creativity. They thus form the primary unity of opposites that gives rise to all things.

One should not separate the *Qian* from the *Kun* in understanding the concept of the *taiji*, the primary unity of opposites. Hence, the order of all *gua*-symbols (hexagram-symbols) is arranged in a sequence of unity of opposites following one after another. All *gua*-symbols come in pairs that are related as opposites by inversion or reversion. Thus, for example, *Qian* (Creativity ䷀) and *Kun* (Receptivity ䷁) are related as opposites by inversion, and *Jiaren* (Family ䷤) and *Kui* (Estrangement ䷥) are related as opposites by reversion. Whether by inversion or reversion, opposites are opposites in the sense that they are polar differences and complements of one another; in this manner, they form a true totality of a whole in life or in the world.

Even considered alone as a source of creativity, *Qian* or *Kun* is a unity of its own: namely, a unity of different lines in different positions that correspond to each other in various relationships of polarity and unity. In other words, as in the *Kun* symbolism, in the *Qian* symbolism an interpretation of meaning in terms of various unities of opposites, or the lack thereof (and hence a need for complementary opposition in other *gua*) in the *gua*-structure is not only possible, but it is necessary for understanding the ontological meaning of *Qian*. As we shall explain, each *gua* represents a situation or relationship of harmony, lack of harmony, or even disharmony, that is to be interpreted or transformed through a process of harmonization inherent in the creative movement of the primary unity of opposites, that is, the *taiji*.

Differences as Opposites

In the creative division of the *taiji*, differentiation takes place. This difference, however, always takes the form of polar contrast and complementary opposition. This idea is contained in the *Yijing* statement quoted earlier: "One *yin* and one *yang* is called the *dao*." One can interpret this statement as comprehending two forms of complementary opposition: spatial conjunction and temporal alternation. Both, however, exhibit the structure of the unity of opposites, which implies the differentiation of *dao* into opposites. But then the question inevitably arises: can we interpret all differences as opposites and therefore as forming unities? This question becomes critical in light of the fact that in the world's multitude of things, and the human world of perceived situations, we encounter strife, conflict, and incoherence among differences. In fact, as we have already discussed, there could be harmony of different grades; it need not be the case that all differences are complementary opposites that form creative unities. On the contrary, there could be logical incompatibilities, inconsistencies, indifferences, alienations, or unrelatedness among different or similar things. How do we then interpret differences as opposites? In particular, how do we *see* or *realize* harmony amidst disharmony? The answer to this important question is to explain first how opposites are often seen to exist as *differences only*; after understanding this, we must then explain how differences can be seen as opposites as well.

Even though differences are *created* as opposites, they are only opposites on different levels and in different totalistic contexts. In other words, apart from the primary unity of opposites, all other unities of opposites are formed only when the total spectrum of differences is taken into consideration on a specified level of ontological or perceptual differentiation. The more differentiated things are, the more specific the level of ontological or perceptual differentiation is, the more different things could exist without being immediately related in a unity of opposites. This is for the simple reason that a difference (whether a quality or a thing) needs to form a unity with another difference, which is its opposite, and yet there are more different things that are generated than merely two appropriate opposites. This latter generation occurs on a level beyond the primary unity of opposites and its immediate differentiation into opposites which should form a unity as a totality. Hence, a unity of difference is formed only when the differences qualify as opposites. When differences are not opposites, they cannot form unities, yet they must be related in one way or another. This explains why we can have harmonies of different grades, as we have defined. This also explains why we could even have strife, disharmonies, or antiharmonies of different grades, as suggested earlier.[54]

Again, we also must point out that apart from the primary unity of opposites (the *taiji*), all individual different things (or all differences after differentiation of the *taiji*) are individually insufficient as a perfect unity *per se*. Any individual thing needs other different things (or differences) to perfect it for the potential and actual interest of integration and unity. This again suggests a metaphysical ground for change and transformation in things and their interrelatedness. Even different things may not contain opposites; they may still form a link or a medium for reaching a unity of opposites—that is, for relating to an opposite—that would form a unity with a given thing. In this sense, different things can perform a function of *mediation* in virtue of their differences. Also, even though for a given thing only one from many different things could form a unity of opposites with it at a time for a specific purpose, all other remaining things could also form unities of opposites at the same time or at other times for many different purposes. When all different unities are formed, they can all together form a unity of opposites in totality, the members of which are themselves unities of opposites, and so forth and so on.

There could be unities of opposites of different orders, depending on levels of differentiation. For the understanding of this, the following three points are made: (1) for anything in a total group of differences, we can define the total group as a collectively exhaustive and individually exclusive group of differences related to a level of differentiation. As opposites are conceived and defined in the system of *gua*, there is always one and only one opposite for some thing. For example, the opposite for *Qian* ䷀ is *Kun* ䷁, and the opposite for *Kan* ☵ is *Li* ☲. (2) All different things in a totality (a total group of differences) on a level of differentiation can form appropriate unities of opposites, and there is no different thing that has no appropriate opposite with which it can form a unity. (3) The totality of different things or differences on a level of differentiation can always form a unity of opposites of a higher order based on unities of opposites formed within the total group of differences. Therefore, the primary unity of opposites is primary because it contains all other unities of opposites on lower levels, and this unity is the first unity of totality and the ultimate totality of unity at the same time.

The above points relating to the theoretical structure of differences as opposites are all presented in the texts of the *Yijing*. Although no explicit formulation was made until the Neo-Confucian philosopher Shao Yong (1011–1077), and although Shao Yong himself did not recognize the profound significance of his formulation, we cannot deny that the perception of unity of opposites and its primacy is clearly laid out in formation of the symbolism of the text. A presentation of the relationship of the opposites, *yin-yang*, as an ontological process of creative division and unification will immediately illuminate and illustrate these important points regarding the formation of unities on multiple levels of differentiation. Consequently, it should bring to light all other points relating to the relationships of differences on the same level. Consider the diagrams presented, with —— standing for *yang* and — — standing for *yin*.

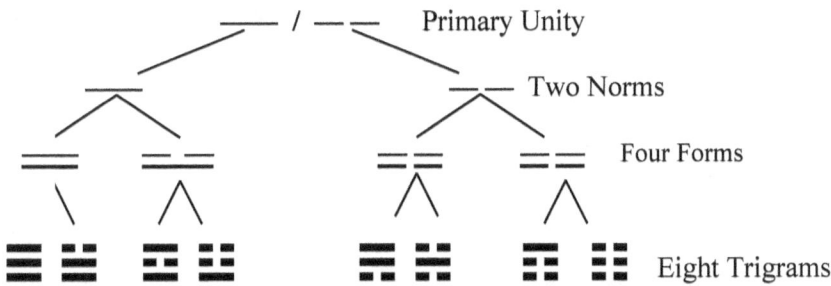

On the level of the primary unity, there is creativity of one unity that provides a source for the creative division into other levels of reality. On the level of the two norms (*liang yi*), one can easily see how the totality of two norms forms a unity of opposites. It is in the totality of differences that the unity of opposites is to be formed. On the level of the four forms (*si xiang* 四象), one can see that there are two unities of opposites (太阳 ⚌, 太阴 ⚏), (少阳 ⚎, 少阴 ⚍), which together form a higher order of unity that is the totality of the two unities. Similarly, for the level of eight trigrams, one can also see that there are four unities of opposites (*Qian* ☰, *Kun* ☷) (*Li* ☲, *Kan* ☵) (*Dui* ☱, *Gen* ☶) (*Xun* ☴, *Zhen* ☳), which together form a set of unities of opposites of a higher order [(*Qian*, *Kun*), (*Kun*, *Qian*)], [(*Li*, *Kan*), (*Kan*, *Li*)], [(*Dui*, *Gen*), (*Gen*, *Dui*)] [(*Xun*, *Zhen*), (*Zhen*, *Xun*)], which together form a unity of opposites of a still higher order, and which exhaust the totality of individual differences of hexagrams on that level of differentiation. This unity of the totality of unities on the level of the eight trigrams is often represented by the Fuxi diagram of eight trigrams.[55]

On the level of four forms, although one can form two unities of opposites, which together form a higher order unity of opposites, it is also logically possible to see the arrangement of opposites in the following way—(⚌ ⚏) and (⚎ ⚍)—which together form a unity of opposites according to their *yin-yang* positioning. The two individual unities of opposites are formed with each form in the unity linked to a form in the other in such a way as (⚎ ⚌) (⚍ ⚏), in which we can see interpenetration of unities in a large unity, which is the totality of individual differences. Similar arrangement of interpenetration for the eight trigrams can also be made: [(☰, ☷) (☱, ☶)]; [(☲, ☵) (☴, ☳)]. When the trigrams double to sixty-four hexagrams in the *Yi* Text, the same points and principles hold for the formation of unities of opposites in terms of totalities and interpenetrations.

Positioning *(wei)* and Centralization *(zhong)*

The *Xici* says:

> Heaven is lofty and the earth is low. This is the way in which the creative (*Qian*) and the receptive (*Kun*) are determined. When the low and the lofty are displayed, the noble and the lowly are positioned. There is constant order in movement and rest. Hence the firm and the soft are fixed. Tendencies of change (*fang*) are developed according to different kinds of things, and things are distinguished according to the kinds to which they belong. In virtue of this, good fortune and ill fortune are generated. Celestial bodies form in the heaven, natural objects form on earth; consequently, there is change and transformation.[56]

From this important passage, we see that what is significant in the creative division of the primary unity is that the qualitative opposites form complementary relationships for all natural things in the world, including the spatial and temporal relationships. The spatial relationship is derived from the opposition of high and low, and the temporal relationship from that of movement and rest. All other things between heaven and earth and their concrete relationships are generated from the qualitative opposition of the firm and the soft. This generation and the tendency to seek relationships gives rise to change and transformation. The generative unity of opposites provides an order for all the different things in the universe.

In this universal order, everything, small or big, has its proper place and position. It is through this placement and positioning (*wei*) of things in the total order or system that all things become what they are and become related to other things. The placement and positioning of a thing is how a thing is oriented with respect to other things. The principle for this orientation—placement and positioning—is again how a thing is placed in a proper place and a proper position. Whether or not a place or a position is proper is determined by whether its nature (generally conceived as *yin* or *yang*) is recognized as fitting into the corresponding place or position (also generally conceived as *yin* or *yang* in relative distinction) in the totality of the whole system. Hence, the concept of *wei* is a concept of correct relationship according to the unity of opposites in a system; it is a concept of one simple thing fitting into a whole system of distinctions, which constitutes the total scheme of different things.

Again, as the symbolic system of the *gua* is designed to reflect this concept of placement and positioning in the totality of a system, this symbolic system no doubt can be used to illustrate this concept of placement and positioning: a hexagram (*gua*) has a six-line structure, each line of which is a place or position, which is either *yin* or *yang* according to its being numbered odd or even.

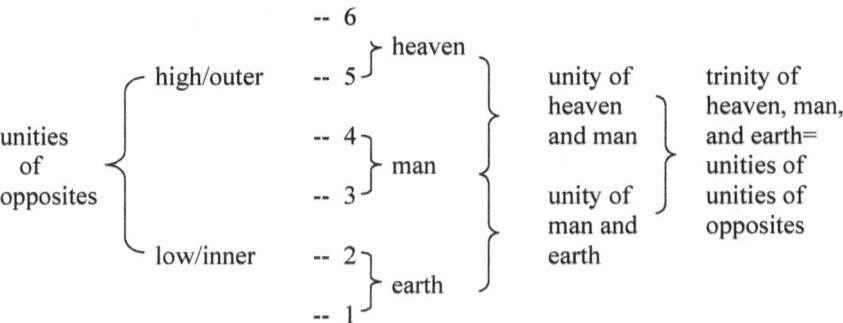

Hence, a hexagram (*gua*) can be seen as an essentially balanced system of opposites (as places or positions) in which different unities of opposites can be constructed. It is in this system that the spatial terms "high" and "low" become meaningful. When the qualitative terms *firm* and *soft* are to be *placed* or positioned according to the places of high and low, it is readily seen that the *firm* should pair with the "high" or the "odd" position and the *soft* with the "low" or the "even" position. Similarly, the absorption of "movement" into "high" and "firm" and the absorption of "rest" into "low" and "soft" would be a matter of placement or positioning.[57]

We can, then, distinguish two senses of placement or positioning for individual things: in one sense, all things are already *placed* where they *are* in the totality of *positions* in the system of the *dao* (the totality of things with intrinsic harmonious placement as reflected in an abstract hexagram *gua* system). In another sense, all things need not be *properly* placed where they are actually placed, because whether or not a *yang*-line that indicates a quality of a situation or a person occupies a *yang* or *odd* position is not determined before actual experience. There are simply two possibilities for a *yang* quality: the odd position, which *befits* it or the even position, which *misfits* it. The notion of placement or positioning (*wei*) in the *Yijing* is precisely developed on the basis of this recognition of the lineup or non-lineup of a quality with a position. When a quality befits a position, the situation is defined as "obtaining a proper position" (*dang wei* or *de wei*) and the position for the quality is referred to as "correct" (*zheng*). On the other hand, when a quality misfits a position, the situation is referred as "not obtaining a proper position" (*bu dang wei* or *bu de wei*) and the position for the quality is referred as "incorrect" (*bu zheng*). Since there are two positions in the structure of the hexagram (*gua*) that are in the middle, one for the upper trigram and the other for the lower trigram, these two positions are specifically referred to as the central (*zhong*) positions (*wei*). Obtaining a central position is called "obtaining the central" (*de zhong*), and not obtaining a central position is called "not obtaining the central" (*bu de zhong*).

The "correct positioning" or "proper placement" (*de wei*) of a quality is important for giving identity to the quality in question. But one may wonder why the "central placement" or "centralization" (*de zhong*) is important for a quality. In order to understand this, one must recall what was said earlier about the meaning of *zhong* as a moral principle of behavior as well as a cosmological principle of development. As either principle *zhong* provides a solid and stable foundation and a constant source of activity. In this sense *zhong* is very much like the primary unity in which all differences are unities without separation. In a central position a state of affairs or a thing is such that all differences related to it are activated and balanced so that a unity can be found. If we conceive two extremes of an action as opposites, then unity is to be achieved through *zhong*. One might even state it better: it is through the uniting force and mediating power of *zhong* that a unity of opposites could be created from the two extremes, a unity that would therefore differ from either extreme. In this sense, *zhong* is the principle of mediating and harmonizing two extremes by transforming them into a new entity represented by the integrity of the central position or the mean course of an action. It is in this sense that *centrality* is a profound principle of placement and consequently the profound principle of unity through placement. That the *Yijing* stresses the importance of *zhong* is indeed neither accidental nor arbitrary, for it is the principle through which unity of differences in a whole structure is to be realized. Again, one can simply look at a trigram and be reminded as to how the trigram presents a unity of opposites through the mediation and uniting power of the central position:

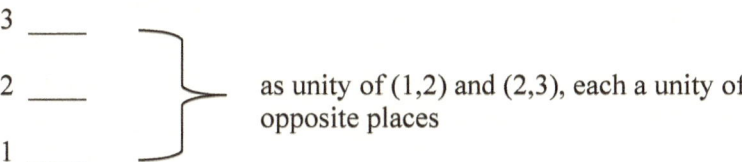

For understanding the principle of proper placement and central positioning (centralization), we can cite the third hexagram, *Qian* (influence), as an illustration. In *Qian*, the first line and the top line are not centrally placed. Both the second line and fifth line obtain a position of centrality. The second line also responds to the fifth line in resonance, and hence enhances and reinforces the harmonious nature of the *gua*, thereby bringing goodness with their presence.[58]

On the basis of the above discussion, two further points related to consideration of positioning and centrality must be mentioned. First, all hexagrams in the *Yijing* provide a study of the problem of placement, the relationship of things in their placement. Through their relative placement, all things are related in a network of mediating interaction, disharmonious opposition, or harmonious complementation.[59] Hence, the harmony and disharmony of a thing in a situation depends, to a great extent, on the internal structures of placement. Second, since all different things are to be related in a larger framework of relationships provided by the totality of things, how one thing or one situation, as represented by a structure of *gua*, relates to another or other things or situations, as represented by other *gua*-structures, also leads to more complicated considerations of interstructural or intersituational placement relationships. How to harmonize a thing or a situation in the context of other things or other situations—namely, how to achieve harmony for a thing or situation in a framework potentially involving all things on a level—is a matter of achieving unity of opposites through proper placement in the intersystematic relationships of things. This last consideration leads us to the concept of harmony as transformation.

Harmony as Transformation

We have seen harmony as both a matter of creative unity of differentiation and as a matter of mutual relationship in placement. But both creative unity of differentiation and mutual relationship placement are related to transformation as a process of development, interaction, and movement. For the creative unity of differentiation, it is clear that the primary unity of opposites gives rise to a totality of opposites in unity by way of self-transformation: the totality of opposites in a unity is a realization of harmony in the full sense of the term. Further differentiation of the totality of opposites based on the creative momentum and power of the primary unity leads to different strata of totalities of different things, each of which, in relation to its totality, could be harmonized by relating to another in a unity as already explained. But this process of relating is not a simple matter when a manifold of things and situations takes place. In other words, the totality can admit a multitude of differences, and not all different things must be related in a natural process of growth and development. A thing by itself also may change its inner structure through its interaction with other things, and therefore may confront new contexts of relationships with other things. This happening can again be considered due to the inner and inherent creative potential of the primary unity, which sustains the actual change of all things through change in their relationships and their consequent inner structures.

From this, we can readily see two forms of transformations: the transformation of things through the self-transformation of the creative source—the primary unity—and the transformation of the interaction of things *via* their relative relationships in the totality of things. The first form of transformation can be called *vertical transformation*, and the second form of transformation can be called *horizontal transformation*. Again we can illustrate this distinction by referring to the structure of the differentiation process of the primary unity in the *Yijing* philosophy.

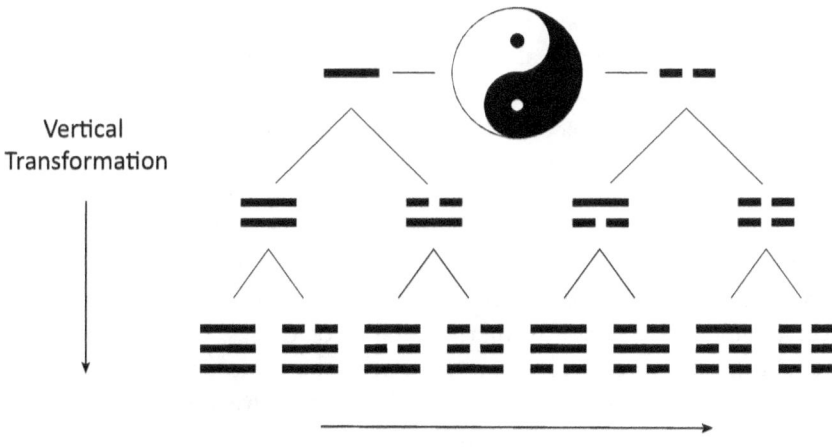

The transformation from the *taiji* to the sixty-four hexagrammatic situations is a matter of *vertical transformation*; the interrelationship, interaction, and mutual transformation among all the sixty-four hexagrams is a matter of *horizontal transformation*. As for the *vertical transformation*, we see how totalities on different levels of ontological differentiation relate to each other, and how they differentiate as well as integrate. These differentiations and integrations readily follow and exhibit the principle of one dividing into two and two unifying into one. Hence the statement, "When expanded, the totality fills all six directions and when contracted, the totality returns into one single unity" (Cheng Yi's *Preface to Zhongyong*). With this vertical transformation, we can see how harmony is achieved, thereby completely satisfying the requirement of the unity of opposites. In this sense harmony is the initial and infinite creativity of the primary unity, and it is the harmony of the totality of things. Metaphysically, the whole universe is basically a harmony if one understands the whole *universe* as a *whole* universe.

After things are differentiated into a multitude, each thing has an identity of its own, and yet, it is placed in the structure of the totality without necessarily relating to things in the totality in an immediate unity of opposites. Hence, even in the contextual harmony of the totality of things, there need not be a *harmony for an individual thing*. The *harmony for an individual thing* depends on how it is related to other things in *time*, *space*, and *quality*. In order to reach for a harmony, the individual thing is involved in a process of transformation; in other words, transformation among different individual things in terms of their *time–space–quality* relationships are a necessary requirement for obtaining the harmony for an individual thing. We may also present this point in a metaphysical mode consistent with the recognition of the universal change and transformation of all things. Because of the *need* for harmony for an individual thing in a totality, there arises change and transformation in reality. One may also explain the existence of lack of harmony, or strife, and discord as the condition that individual things have when they have yet to find their harmony in the totality of things, and hence as the condition of change and transformation in the horizontal sense. In light of this interpretation of disharmony and strife, we need not consider them as "bad" or "evil" nor consider them as simply contradictory to harmony. In the context of change and transformation, disharmony and strife fulfill a function of inducing and encouraging development and integration, and hence satisfy a need for reaching *harmony* for individual things. Consequently, disharmony and strife fulfill the need for achieving harmony of the totality on a level. In fact, one may regard disharmony and strife on one hand, and harmony and unity on the other as *opposites* to be mutually harmonized in a larger unity; but relative to this larger unity, disharmony and strife will lose their negative meaning and will transform themselves into a relationship of complementary opposition, and hence they will form a unity.

One must distinguish these two *senses*, and hence the two *types* of transformation: the *vertical* and the *horizontal*. The vertical transformation is always harmonious as it exhibits the creativity of the primary unity. This is the ontological or metaphysical transformation. The horizontal transformation need not be always *harmonious*. When it is harmonious, it becomes lined up with the vertical transformation, and hence becomes a movement of creative integration and differentiation. Namely, it becomes a process of producing a new totality of differences without losing unity; it is what activity of unity (or harmony) means, which defines the nature of primary unity. But when it is not harmonious, it simply means that there is no harmony to the individual thing and the transformation is the necessary result of such a lack of harmony as well as a result of need and search for harmony. Hence, horizontal transformation is indicative of lack of harmony (in the full sense), or of lack of individual creative unity—that is, to act as a primary unity—and is indicative of an inner creativity to achieve harmony in the totality. Therefore, horizontal transformation is both negative and positive in meaning. It exhibits by itself a unity of opposites and presents a *harmony* or *harmonization* of its own. Without this understanding of transformation, we would see *harmony* only as transformation in the vertical sense, namely in an ontological sense in which harmony is seen to produce a unity of opposites in a creative process of the *taiji* creativity, and we would not see *transformation* as harmony as well. Here transformation is understood in both vertical and horizontal senses.

In the horizontal sense, transformation is phenomenological and worldly. It belongs to the daily world of events and situation. It is where conflict, confrontation and strife occur as experience shows us. Although there is much congruity between the horizontal and vertical transformation, they are closely related in terms of the totalistic consideration of the structure of things and the whole process of transformation. In a deeper sense, all things have corresponding complements in the totality to which they belong. It is in this deeper and logical sense that the vertical and the horizontal transformation coincide. One can thus regard the horizontal transformation as simply the ideal way in which the vertical transformation is to be fulfilled. To see the mutual differentiation and ultimate unity of the vertical (ontological) and horizontal (phenomenological) transformation is precisely the crux of the dialectics of harmonization.[60]

The *Yijing* makes a distinction between change (*bian*) and transformation (*hua*), even though in the *Xici* "change-transformation (*bianhua*)" is used as if it is a single term. The distinction is conveyed in the statement "to transform and *order* the transformation is called the change (*bian*)" and the statement "to transform and order the transformation consists in change (*bian*)."[61] In these statements, it is clear that transformation is the subtle and natural change that takes place in things, and change (*bian*) is transformation into an order, or according to an order, inherent in things or introduced by the participation of persons and is, therefore, the *conspicuous* transformation of things. *Xici* also describes *bian* as "one closing and one opening," (*yihe yipi*) signifying the movements of the primary unity of the *dao*. As such, *bian* contains the creativity of the primary unity and is made possible by the underlying unity of things in the *dao*.

On this ground, the *Xici* speaks of the "change-penetration" (*biantong*) apart from "change-transformation" (*bianhua*), where *tong* (penetration) is defined as "the incessant process of coming-and-going without end (*wanglai wu qiong*)" or as "pushing through and doing a thing" (*tui er xing zhi*),"[62] again stressing the possibility of personal participation on the human level. Hence, "*biantong*" is the thorough achievement of creative change and the opening of a new vista of change. The whole process of transformation/change/penetration (*hua/bian/tong*) indicates the open-ended process of creative transformation in the order of things, necessarily producing both a new momentum of change and a new order in things.

The more important distinction between a *vertical* transformation and a *horizontal* transformation is more subtly made in the *Xici* of the *Yijing*. The *Xici* says that "[The way of change] changes what is suitable to change (*wei bian suo shi*)."[63] This implies that change is a natural tendency inherent in the nature of things, and it belongs to the network of relationships among things. The *Xici Xia* also says, "When the way of change is such that a thing reaches a dead end, it will change; when change takes place, it will penetrate; when change penetrates, then it will last."[64] This passage further describes change as a result of difficulty or deadlock. If conflict or strife is a difficulty or a deadlock (*qiong*), then change is necessary. This passage also describes change as penetrating and lasting, and this implies that change is thoroughgoing and will change the whole system in which it occurs; the results of changing then will last as it establishes a new order of unities. In both these descriptions, the horizontal transformation is focused upon. On the horizontal plane, things are not fixed in relationships once for all, and there is much need for adjustment for better and smoother relationships of a more unified and harmonious order. Thus, change must take place according to need and what is required in a situation. Similarly, only on the horizontal plane are there conflict, strife, and deadlock.[65]

The meaning of vertical transformation is found in the following statements: "When heaven and earth are well positioned, the way of change [*Yi*][66] becomes activated within. The original nature [*zhengxing*] [things shown in the primary unity] will last and last [*cuncun*]. This is the gate to [understanding] the way and righteousness"; "When celestial bodies are formed in heaven and all shapes of things are formed in earth, then there is seen the change and transformation [*bianhua*]."[67] In both statements, the placement of things is said to be well secured in a well-organized relationship, and it may be said that this implies that a harmony already obtains. Yet it is stated that only when things are well ordered and placed in the totality of things will change and transformation hold sway. This means that achieved harmony will induce transformation and change in a vertical sense: the transformation is purely creative as based on a prior obtained state of well-placedness and harmony. This also means that harmony itself is a creative force for creating new unities or differences.

Dialectics of Harmonization

In the above, I first analyzed and then synthesized the concept of harmony in terms of the philosophical framework of the *Yijing* and its paradigms. Through this philosophical reconstruction a theory of harmony has also been developed. The basic assumption of this theory of harmony is that harmony exists in the depths of the structure of reality and reveals itself at different levels of differentiation of reality, whereas the differentiation of reality is considered to be a necessary characteristic of harmony. Harmony is also dynamic and temporal, and therefore always entails, or presupposes, a process of development and interaction, organization and reorganization. Hence, the theory of harmony is at the same time a theory of harmonization, and the *metaphysics of harmony* is at the same time a *dialectics of harmonization*, for the process of reaching harmony is a creative as well as an ordered quality of harmony. In other words, harmony is part of harmonization as harmonization is part of harmony. They are two aspects of the same reality. The philosophical statement that transformation unifies nonchange (*buyi*), change (*bianyi*) and simplicity (*jianyi*) applies most appropriately to this dialectical process and metaphysical reality of harmony and harmonization. In fact, I have analyzed the *nonchange*, the *change*, and the *simplicity* as three aspects of transformation in terms of the unity of opposites as well as the interaction of opposites in unity.[68] The *nonchange* would be the *primary unity* of opposites and the vertical transformation of creativity; *change* would be the horizontal change of appropriation and deappropriation; the *simplicity* would be the horizontal transformation as regulated in the framework of vertical transformation, or *bianyi* in the framework of *buyi*.

As a *dialectics of harmonization*, the theory of harmony has exhibited itself in the differentiation between vertical transformation and horizontal transformation and in their basic and ultimate unification. In this differentiation/unification, strife and harmony, conflict and resolution, and war and peace are all admitted as real possibilities, and each acquires a proper place in the scheme of things. In order to see how the theory of harmony described above—unity as creativity, differences as opposites, centralization of positioning (placement), and harmony as transformation—develops as a dialectical process of change and harmonization, we can identify the following six stages of this process:

A. Unity as creativity and creativity as unity

B. Differentiation: vertical and horizontal

C. Relating by placement and positioning

D. Transformation as harmony (horizontal)

E. Centralization and integration of differences into opposites

F. Harmony as transformation (vertical)

I make a distinction between *transformation as harmony* in D and *harmony as transformation* in F. This is done in order to underscore the distinction between the two, whereby the *horizontal transformation* in reaching harmony is a harmony in virtue of the ontological reality of the totality of opposites in unity, and the integration of differences accomplishes a unity of opposites to thus become creative in the vertical sense; that is, the integration of differences is capable of producing a new horizon of reality.

With this explanation, we have the dialectical process of change and harmonization symbolized as follows:

A → B → C → D → E → F

We could regard "C → D → E → F" as designating a process where differences become the source of conflict, strife, disunity, and lack of harmonization; at the same time, we can regard this symbol string as representing a process where harmonization is at work. Conflict and strife lead to placement and positioning; placement and positioning lead to centralization and integration into opposites; finally, centralization and integration lead to unity and harmony. This process is thus a process of transformation *toward* harmony as well as a transformation *from* harmony. In light of this consideration, the whole dialectical process of change and harmonization is basically threefold:

unity ↔ differentiation ↔ transformation

When transformation reaches the goal of harmonization, having harmonized and integrated all differences into unities of opposites, we return to the original state of primary creativity in which a new level or new horizon of reality will be produced.

The simplified dialectics of harmonization may appear similar to the Hegelian dialectics of thesis–antithesis–synthesis. However, the appearance is essentially illusory. The triadic form of the dialectics of harmonization does not contain the Hegelian logic and metaphysics as its content. I have elsewhere explored this important difference between the dialectics of harmonization and the Hegelian dialectics, which I call the dialectics of conflict.[69] A second difference is found in the complexity of the transformational stages in the dialectics of harmonization, which, as we have explained above, involves many considerations that are different from, and not necessarily consistent with, the consideration of double negation (negation of negation) and sublimation/sublations (die Aufhebung). These many considerations belong to the unique tradition of the Yijing as a way of thinking and organizing experiences. Even for the stage of unity as creativity and the stage of differentiation, it is more complicated (but without losing structure) than mere assertion and mere negation, or contradiction (but again, it is not necessarily inconsistent with these). Hence, we must recognize the dialectics of harmonization as a unique but powerful way of thinking deeply rooted in the human mind as well as in the nature of understanding of things by mind. The process of the *dialectics of harmonization* can therefore be presented as follows:

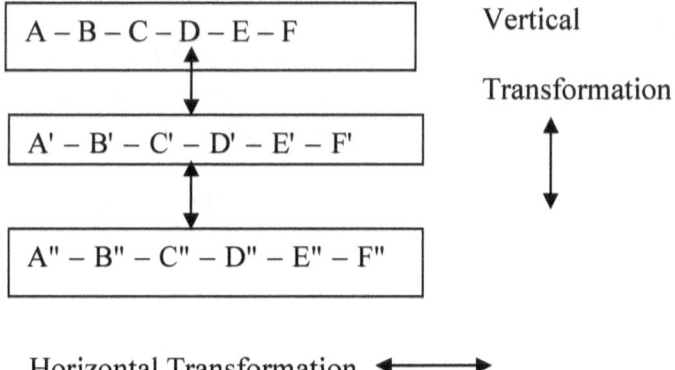

Thus, when transformation is seen as harmony in this process of harmonization, harmony can be seen as transformation as well. Moreover, any attainment of harmony is a creative opening of a new horizon of reality; conversely, any realization of a new horizon of reality provides a new example of the attainment of harmony.

The dialectical process of harmonization as developed above is based on the overall observation and experience of nature at large. This is one of the important sources of the insights of the *Yijing*. As such, this dialectical process of harmonization implies or presupposes a cosmological philosophy of nature and humankind's experience of nature. In fact, it can be considered as an implicit philosophy of nature. One might therefore even see the *metaphysics of harmony* of nature[70] and the *dialectics of harmonization* as two aspects of the same thinking.[71] As persons are part and parcel of nature, the *metaphysics of harmony* and the *dialectics of harmonization* can indeed apply to people and what is related to people, namely, to the relation between persons and the world, between persons and their environments, between persons and their situation.

Timely Application (*shizhong*)

Consider a person alone: a person is an overall organic unity of his or her body, perception, feelings, and mind, each of which has relative unity of its own. How this organic unity of a person also sustains the unity in body, unity in perception, unity in feelings, and unity in mind remains an important and difficult question. Yet it is often the case that, only when one's unity in perception, in feelings, and in mind is sustained, can one enjoy a state of harmony within oneself. Moreover, only when such a state of harmony within oneself is reached is one able to develop into a higher order of self-realization in the sense that one is capable of becoming truly creative. To sustain one's unity and develop creativity, one requires a process of self-cultivation (*xiu sheng*), a process stressed by Confucians since Confucius.

Confucians, including Confucius, Mencius and Xunzi, recognize that the process of self-cultivation involves both correct understanding (theory) and correct practice (action). Valid self-cultivation is always found in the unity of theory and practice, and understanding and action. Hence, to sustain harmony and unity in oneself, one must achieve unity of understanding and action. But there will be no unity if there is no correct understanding of one's position and relationship with others in the world, and there will be no unity if there is no correct action following correct understanding.

To see what correct understanding consists of, we must see how one is to sustain one's own personal unity by sustaining the unity between oneself and others in the various situations one finds oneself placed in. In order to develop or even to sustain unity, one must relate to others or the world in a dialectical way; one must understand or be aware of the following: (1) how others (or the world) orientate themselves toward one's own person; (2) how to complement others and the world/situation so that no alienation or conflict arises—if conflict or alienation does arise, one must understand how to reduce it so that a harmonious relationship can develop; (3) how to conduct oneself so that one's actions elicit a desired situation of unity and harmony. Through realization of unity, unity between humankind and the world can be sustained, and ultimately the unity within oneself as a person will be sustained or achieved.

The entire text of the *Yijing* is developed with a view to provide correct understanding and correct action for a person in the course of life or in the process of self-cultivation. This is made possible by the development of the *metaphysics of harmony* and the *dialectics of harmonization* implicitly present in the *Yijing* text.[72] This means that *correct understanding* and *correct action* emerge in light of the framework of the *metaphysics of harmony* and *dialectics of harmonization*. The key idea for harmony engendering a correct understanding and correct action is to understand one's positioning. In other words, with correct understanding—understanding one's position in a situation at a given time—one can act correctly at the right time in the right place. Correct understanding and correct action are required for achieving unity and accord between oneself and the world, and this will enable one to fulfill oneself. One must note that correct understanding and correct action are not always conducive to one's immediate advantage or interest, but nevertheless they will always contribute to one's total growth as a person. One must also note that to act according to one's circumstances is not to act without principle; on the contrary, it is to act with a principle that will bring out the harmony and unity in the circumstances, and thus contribute to the unity and harmony between the agent and the world at large.

Confucius used the term "timely application" or "timely action" (*shizhong* 时中) to describe how a superior person does the right thing at the right time in order to achieve the state of unity (*zhong*) and harmony (*he*). He says: "The superior man follows the doctrine of the mean, whereas the small man contradicts the doctrine of the mean; when the superior man follows the doctrine of the mean, he does things in terms of timely action; that is, he acts with timeliness. When the small man contradicts the doctrine of the mean, he does things without any restraint or fear."[73] The *Doctrine of the Mean* (the *Zhongyong* principle) consists in the doctrine of centrality (unity) and harmony, which we have covered earlier in the chapter. It also consists in doing things neither in excess (*guo*) nor in deficiency (*buzhi*); this activity is taken so that a person not only contributes to the centrality and harmony of things but also exhibits constancy of such centrality and harmony, which a person also will find appropriate and meaningful for her life. The constancy (*chang*) and appropriateness (*yi*) of one's action explains why one's timely action (*shizhong*) is both a universal principle and a specific performance; it also explains how "timely action" means to do things fitting into a time (*zhongshi*).[74]

Without going into more detail into the notion of "timely action" as suggested by Confucius, one can see that timely action is an extension and application of the *metaphysics of harmony* and *dialectics of harmonization*. To act with timeliness is to do the right thing at the right time in order to achieve unity, centrality, and harmony. This is precisely what the *Yi* Text is intended to suggest. As I have elsewhere explored the relation between the Confucian philosophy of "timely action" and the concept of time and timeliness in the *Yi* Text, I will now confine myself to a brief analysis of "timely action" in the *Yijing* so as to show how timely action fulfills unity and harmony for a person during the course of personal growth: that is, how "timely action" *harmonizes* the relation between people and their world, whether at peace or in crisis.

The concept of *time* plays an important role in the *Yijing*. For the *Yi* Text, time is the concrete process of creative change in the world and is best illustrated by the rotation of seasons. As seasons exhibit a total harmony, so time is essentially a process of harmonization among all things, whereas time is conceivable as part and parcel of change and transformation. The *metaphysics of harmony* and the *dialectics of harmonization* completely apply to our understanding of *time*.[75] To follow time and exhibit the virtue and power of time is then called "timeliness" (*shi*). Here, the term "*shi*" refers to time in concretion as specifically achieved by a person. "*Shi*" also can be used as a verb, as in "*shi erhou xing*" (act after one *times* time right). In regard to "timing time right," "timeliness" can be explained as "right timing of an action." This notion of "timeliness" is well expressed throughout the Yi Text in terms of how concrete goodness, virtue, unity, and harmony can be cultivated and achieved, and how calamity, anxiety, evil, and misfortune can be avoided and prevented.

The idioms and paradigms of time or *timeliness* are illustrated by the following nonexhaustive uses of the term "*shi*" in the *Yijing* Texts:

1. The six positions are accomplished in *time* (*liu wei shi cheng* 六位时成). (*Qian Tuan*)

2. Become cautious because of *time* (*yin qi shi er ti* 因其时而惕). (*Qian* 9-3)

3. For advancing virtue and organizing one's deed, it is desirable to do things on *time* (*jin de xiu ye, yu ji shi ye* 进德修业, 欲及时也). (*Qian* 9-4)

4. The *time*, forsake it (*shi shi ye* 是时也). (*Qian, Xiang*)

5. To advance with *time* (*yu shi xie xing* 与时偕行). (*Qian, Xiang*)

6. To reach the ultimate with *time* (*yu shi xie ji* 与时偕极). (*Qian, Xiang*)

7. It is appropriate to hold firm to an implicit order: this is due to *time* (*han zhang ke zhen, yi shi fa ye* 含章可贞, 以时发也). (*Kun* 6-3)

8. To obey heaven and move with *time* (*cheng tian er shi xing* 承天而时行). (*Kun, Wenyan*)

9. To act out of prosperity for fitting *time* (*yi heng xing shizhong ye* 以亨行时中也). (*Meng, Tuan*)

10. To respond to heaven and to act with *time* (*yin hu tian er shi xing* 应乎天而时行). (*Dayou, Tuan*)

11. How great is the import of *time* in *yu* (*yu zhi shi yi da yi zai* 豫之时义大矣哉). (*Yu, Tuan*, and also see *sui, dun, gou,* and *lü* for their *Tuan*)

12. How great is the function (use) of *time* in *danger* (*xian zhi shi yong da yi zai* 险之时用大矣哉). (*Xikan*, see also *Gui* and *Qian*)

13. How great is the *time* in *Yi* (*yi zhi shi da yi zai* 颐之时义大矣哉). (*Yi*, see also *Xie* and *Ge*)

14. The world follows *time* at any time (*tianxia sui shi* 天下随时). (*Sui, Tuan*)

15. To observe the order of heaven and discern the changes of *time* (*guan hu tian wen yi cha shi bian* 观乎天文以察时变). (*Bi, Tuan*)

16. The *time* nourishes all things (*shi yu wan wu* 时育万物). (*Wuwang, Xiang*)

17. The soft arises because of *time* (*rou yi shi sheng* 柔以时升). (*Sheng, Tuan*)

18. "Stop when *time* requires stop, advance when *time* requires advance" (*shi zhi ze zhi, shi xing ze xing* 时止则止, 时行则行). (*Gen, Tuan*)

19. To ebb and to tide according to *time* (*yu shi xiao xi* 与时消息). (*Feng, Tuan*)

20. When heaven and earth mutually restrain each other, the four seasons take place (*tiandi jie er si shi cheng* 天地节而四时成). (*Jie, Tuan*)

21. Misfortune because of worst *time*-missing (*shi shi ji ye* 失时极也). (*Jie*, 9-2 *xiang*)

The essence of "timely action" is expressed clearly by the motto in the *Tuan* judgment of the *Gen gua*: "Stop when time requires stop, advance when time requires advance." As time in this context means all the relationships of things in which one is situated, it is obvious that to be timely one must understand correctly one's position and act according to what the position dictates. One cannot have correct understanding unless one understands the totality of things (even in a relative sense) and their relationships; further, one cannot act with time unless one relates to the totality of things in an appropriate way. Hence, time signifies the whole structure of harmony as well as the process of harmonization. One's understanding signifies one's understanding of the structure of harmony in things; and one's action in time signifies a process of harmonization in things and in oneself. We may therefore express the "timeliness of action" or "timely action" as follows:

Totality of things   → Process of harmonization

Correct understanding → Timely action

Because timely action is based on understanding of the *metaphysics of harmony*, which deals with totality of things and their relationships, and the *dialectics of harmonization*, which fulfills the process of harmonization, timely action can aptly be called the "timely application of time."

In the *Xici Xia*, it is said, "to change and penetrate (*biantong*) is to follow time (*qu shi*)."[76] Only when one follows *time* (and hence follows a correct understanding of the relationships of things and their potentiality for harmonization) and acts accordingly can one change and transform toward harmony. Change and transformation follow the intrinsic principle of "changing according to what is suitable" (*wei bian suo shi*).[77] Hence, to act with time and to cultivate the virtue of "timely action" and the sense of timeliness, one must cultivate understanding and mastery of the *dialectics of harmonization* as the inner logic of change and transformation.

Finally, it is to be pointed out that all the *gua* in the Yi Text may be seen as symbolic of different *moments* or *modes* of *time* in the dialectical relationships of things, and thus they require different modes of action on the part of a person to harmonize. From this point of view, one can see how all *gua*, *Tuan* judgments, and *Xian* admonitions provide counsel, prescribe norms for actions, and formulate most penetratingly Confucian virtues in action.[78]

Conclusion

In this chapter I have explored the metaphysics of harmony and the dialectics of harmonization in light of the philosophy of the *Yijing*. I have specifically clarified and discussed the concepts of harmony (*harmonia*) in Greek, harmony (*he*) in Chinese, and related concepts of unity, differentiation, centrality, and placement. I have shown how harmony can be conceived as a unity of opposites, which, in their turn, may be unities of opposites. In this definition of harmony, we could have harmony on different levels and in different contexts with different relationships. In this connection, I also have explained the nature of the "primary unity of opposites" referred to as the *taiji* and argued for the primacy of the "primary unity" (*taiji*). We have further harmonization in terms of the following aspects of reality: (1) creativity as unity; (2) differences as opposites; (3) placement as centralization; and (4) harmony as transformation.

I have elaborated the concept of harmony as transformation. In light of the distinction between "vertical transformation" and "horizontal transformation," there are two types of "harmony as transformation": (1) "harmony as transformation," which is "vertical transformation," and (2) "harmony as transformation" for "horizontal transformation," which I also label "transformation as harmony." Hence, harmony can be seen from a transformational point of view just as transformation can be seen from a harmonizational point of view. From the terms of the unity of both these views, I develop the *dialectics of harmonization*, which, as I have shown, consists in a relatively creative process of unity/differentiation/transformation.

A third kind of transformation has been introduced in connection with my exploration into the notion of "timely application" or "timely action" (*shizhong*). This kind of transformation in accordance with "timely complication"—or for that matter, constituting "timely application"—is an application of *dialectics of harmonization* to the cultivation or self-cultivation of a person in terms of harmony *within* and harmony *without*. The harmony *within* and harmony *without* cannot be separated, but must form a unity in order to give true harmony to the person. But, again, harmony is to be seen and achieved through a dialectical process of harmonization. In this vein, we discussed the process of harmonization for a person. We also explored the meaning of "time" or "timeliness" in connection with "timely action" in the *Yijing* Texts. Although more must be done to explain the role of heart-mind and reason in correct understanding and action, it may be said that the heart-mind constitutes a third kind of "transformation as harmony" or "harmony as transformation" apart from the vertical and horizontal transformations in things of nature, where neither human will nor human understanding are taken into consideration.

We have taken a realistic metaphysical point of view by treating harmony and harmonization as real processes of reality, but we have not ignored the reality and necessity of strife and conflict. We further have attempted to explain harmony in understanding and action and their unity on a human level. Implicitly, human freedom, or human free will, and human participation in events of nature, and hence human creativity, are here affirmed. This third type of "transformation as harmony," or "harmony as transformation," also can be expressed as an intersection of the vertical and horizontal transformation based on a person's creative participation or creative co-participation in the "primary unity of heaven and earth."[79] This is symbolically expressed as follows:

As a final note, in elaborating the *dialectics of harmonization*, we have not touched on the problem of the comparison of this dialectics with other dialectics in comparative philosophy. In previous work, I explored the differences between this dialectic and the *dialectics of conflict* represented by Hegel and Marx on the one hand, and this dialectic and the *dialectics of negation* represented by Madhyamika Buddhism on the other.[80]

CHAPTER 8

Zhouyi (周易) and the Philosophy of *Wei* (Positions 位)

Introduction: Unity in Multiplicity and the Notion of *Wei*

The importance of the notion of *wei* (position/positioning) in Chinese society and Chinese culture cannot be underestimated. Although human societies and human cultures in general have well-understood "positions" in social, economic, and political contexts, in Chinese society and Chinese culture, "positions" are not simply understood as social and political positions or positions in a given system of valuations such as the academy. Instead, they are understood on a much deeper level, namely on an onto-cosmological level,[1] whereby the valuations of human individuals are projected onto positions in relation to heaven and earth. Simultaneously, the nature and function of heaven and earth[2] are imprinted onto the individual. Hence, the concept of *diwei* (positions on earth) suggests an analogy to a position with reference to any given position in a system of (human) activities.[3] But the single term "*wei*" has its specific significance: it refers to a positioning in the primary onto-cosmology, which should underlie any other constructed or developed system, for it is most fundamental and has everything to do with the very existence of a thing and its worth. In this sense, *wei* can be said to define the worth and *raison d'être* of anything, particularly those of the human individual.

However, as the world of reality is in constant flux, which can be creative in both a macroscopic and a microscopic sense, bringing a new scenario or a new alignment of forces, the positions (*wei*) of things and persons no doubt must accordingly receive new orientations in the contexts of new configurations. A person must be aware of this and act according to his position in a context where positions are understood to be vested with a dynamic force, a perspective, and a potentiality relative to the world and things in the world. In this sense, considerations of position become extremely important because they are not only tied up with the good and bad fortunes of a person, but with what the person has become and can become. One must consider the world as a whole and oneself as a whole in order to assess one's meaning of life and potentiality for value achievement. In this sense, we could say that the life of a person is shot through and through with considerations and issues of positioning of one's life in a world of reality onto-cosmologically understood. Positions become a person's destinies, or the grounds and fields on which one may fulfill the roles that one has found for oneself, as well as fulfill oneself as onto-cosmologically rooted in life and the world of reality.

Onto-cosmology of Positions as Positioning

This onto-cosmological orientation of positions no doubt comes from the *Zhouyi*. This notion is first explicitly described in the *Yizhuan*, which expresses a common theme found in the Confucian and the Daoist tradition of positioning the human person in the world of reality and in the world of humanity.[4] As the *Yizhuan* has had great influence on later Chinese philosophy, particularly in the development of Confucianism, and as it also reflects a synthesis of the main traditions of ideas in the "axial age" of China, I shall use it as the basis for the elucidation of the philosophy of *wei* in order to show how *wei* is to be understood in interpreting the meaning of *gua* (hexagrams), and consequently how it also has been evaluated in Confucianism and Daoism as a guide for human decision and action.

I shall first describe the philosophical understanding of *wei* in the onto-cosmological system of the *Yizhuan*. Then I shall demonstrate how this system is already implicit in the original symbolic texts of the *Zhouyi*. We shall see how this would give grounds for the development of Confucianism, and how Daoism and Chan Buddhism have strived to modify it in a philosophy of the *Dao* and a philosophy of the void or emptiness in which the highest position would be the position of "no position" (*wuwei*).

The opening statement of the *Xici* of the *Yizhuan* is, "Where Heaven is noble and earth is low, the creative and the receptive are fixed; when the low and the high are displayed, the noble and the humble are also positioned" (*Shang* 1). Although this statement describes both the actual cosmological structure of reality and the symbolism of such a structure in the trigrams or hexagrams in a spatial paradigm of high and low, what really differentiates the high and low are the inherent powers and functions in the spatial positions. Without such understanding of the powers, values, and functions inherent in positions, what meaning could one assign to the high and low in space? That is why high and low could give rise to, and be affiliated with, the distinction between the noble and lowly. In the case of the high and noble, we find the designation of the power of creativity (*Qian* ☰), and in the case of the low and lowly we find the designation of the power of receptivity (*Kun* ☷). For the *Xici* authors, the power of creativity consists in initiating and generating the world of things like heaven and is hence seen as high, whereas the power of receptivity consists in preserving and nourishing things like earth and is hence seen as low. Both powers are necessary for making the world as well as for positioning heaven and earth and all things in the world. The positioning of these in fact amounts to the formation and transformation of the world and all things in the world toward order, balance, and harmony; hence, such positioning is equivalent to creating, sustaining, or maintaining a dynamic equilibrium of the reality in creative change.

In other words, we can see that it is for the onto-cosmological explanation of the world that the positioning of things in the world in its creative change is realized as an internal ordering of a textured whole in the making. In the *Zhongyong*, there is the idea of "well positioned-ness of heaven and earth" by way of realization (*zhi*) of centrality (*zhong*) and harmony (*he*). There are two possible interpretations. In the first, if a person has achieved centrality within and harmony in his relations with the world, the state of the world will present a centrality and a harmony, which is understood as the well positioned-ness of heaven and earth. In the second, the relationship between heaven and earth is an example and illustration of centrality and harmony in which all things are well fitted and well positioned (*wei*) together. Human beings should learn from the centrality and harmony of heaven and earth.

The term *wei* is intended to describe the standing up (*li*) of a person, which means that a person establishes herself in the world by accomplishing a virtue.⁵ In short, positioning is a holistic and dynamic concept of worldmaking in an onto-cosmological sense. Hence, an explanation of such worldmaking and a characterization of onto-cosmology is in order. We shall do this in five steps.

First, one observes that things in the world are constantly newly formed and transformed and in this sense are in a process of creative change. In order to see how the positioning of the high and the low takes place, the *Xici* suggests that the power of creativity (*Qian*) and the power of receptivity (*Kun*) form a holistic relationship of "moving and rest" (*dong-jing*) from which comes also the holistic relationship of "firmness and softness" (*gang-rou*) and the holistic relationship of "initiating and following" (*zhu-cong*).⁶ Things are formed and distinguished by their natural kinds through these relationships. One also may say that it is these relationships that determine the distinction between the power of creativity and the power of receptivity. For what is creative is moving, initiating and firm in its action, and what is receptive is restive, supportive, and soft in its action (and hence preserves and nourishes). These relationships also are known as the relationship of *yin* (darkening) and *yang* (brightening). Obviously, *yin* and *yang* are terms for natural phenomena indicating shade and light, which are then affiliated and correlated with the negative and the positive components in a process of generation (*sheng*), change (*bian*), and transformation (*hua*) of things in the world as widely experienced by human beings, namely, the phenomena of moving/resting, initiation/support, firmness/softness, and their polarities and reciprocations in nature. In this fashion, we can see *yin* and *yang* both as simple experiences of creative change in the world and as global forces or powers composed of the polarities of moving, initiation, and firmness on the one hand and resting, support, and softness on the other; hence, they are known as *Qian* and *Kun*. We can simply say that the powers of creativity and receptivity pervade onto-cosmological sources of creative change in things as exemplified in the two aspects of *yin* and *yang*.

Although there is no pinning down of the ontological status of the *yin/yang* in the *Xici* and other commentaries of the *Zhouyi*, it seems clear from other classical sources such as *Shangjunshu* or *Laozi* that *yin* and *yang* could be seen as two basic forms of the vital force or energy known as the *qi*, in contrast to outward patterning (*li*) and principled ordering in intelligible and rational thinking.⁷

Second, one observes that the relationship of *yin* and *yang* or *Qian* and *Kun* is internal to a process of creative change and hence is one of dynamic equilibrium, resonance, synergistic harmonization, and ceaseless interchange and exchange of energy. It thus forms a unity and whole of oneness in which *yin* and *yang* become two aspects or two components. As a matter of logical reflection as well as a matter of comprehensive observation (*guan*), one can speak of the oneness of the conjunction and alternation of the *yin* and *yang* as the *dao* (the way). Hence, it is said, "One *yin* and one *yang* is called the *dao*" (*Xici Shang* 5). As dynamic synergy, interchange and exchange of one *yin* and one *yang* are considered to be the necessary and sufficient conditions for the formation and transformation of things; further, one will see the relationship of *yin-yang* or *Qian/Kun* as two moments of a process of creative productivity (described as *shengsheng zhi wei Yi*), namely as "gate-closing" (*he hu*) and "gate-opening" (*pi hu*). Why closing and opening? It is as if the creation and flow of energy require this onto-cosmological switching in rhythmic release. It is therefore said:

> One closing and one opening is called change. Coming and going without exhaustion is called penetrating through (*tong*). Being presented, it is called the forms (*xiang*). Being shaped, it is called the utensils (*qi*). To utilize it for human purpose, it is called the norm (*fa*). When being used for human needs by people it is called the divine (*shen*). (*Xici Shang* 11)

The inexhaustible change is therefore the same as the Way; it is an inherent creative movement and an inexhaustible source of value and utility for human purposes.

In this sense, onto-cosmological reality is potentially a field and process of value generation, for it not only gives rise to humankind in the two sexes ("The way of *Qian* forms the male person and the way of *Kun* forms the female person" (*Xici Shang* 1), but also gives rise to circumstances and opportunities that would benefit or harm, enrich or impoverish human persons. In this sense, we may speak of the powers of creative change as values or disvalues of life or human life. But whether it benefits or harms, whether it enriches or impoverishes, again depends on the positioning of things and persons in the world. For we may regard the way of *yin-yang* as having created a world of interplay of powers in the positioning of things, as things have their powers and functions in the positions they have in a unity of the whole process-reality in accordance with the way of *yin-yang*.

Third, how does the *yin* and *yang* as a unity of the *dao* and as an inexhaustible source of change give rise to all things as we know them? Here we must return to the one, unified, inexhaustible source of change, the *taiji* (the great ultimate). In the *Xici*, it is said, "Creative change has the great ultimate, which generates the two norms (*liang yi* or *yin/yang*). The two norms give rise to four forms (*si xiang*) and the four forms to eight trigrams (*bagua*)" (*Shang* 11). This procedure and process not only gives an ordered way for the generation of things in a cosmogonic sense but also gives a way of understanding the world of things as internally ordered and organismically interrelated. Further, it presents the world as it is now in an orderly way no matter how multitudinous it is. In both the cosmogonic and the cosmographic sense, the world is a world of well-positioned things and processes in a hierarchy of levels with reference to an organic unity of interrelated positions. Positioning is essential to this process and procedure of generation, and we would not understand the positions of things without understanding their positioning in this process and procedure.

Before we move to describe how this process as a procedure secures the positioning of things when they are generated, we need to point out that it is on this understanding of the *taiji* as the primordial source and fountainhead of creative change that we have come to have a full-fledged cosmogony of things in terms of their source as well as their process of creative change, which is the *dao*. Both the notions of *taiji* and *dao* are essential to the cosmogony of things; in light of the process and procedure of polaristic generation we also see how both notions transform the cosmogony into a cosmography, which presents a map or picture of the world with its positioning of things internal to it.[8] Further, it is in light of this notion of *taiji* and the *dao* of *yin* and *yang* that we can see how an even more detailed cosmology is derived in the *Taiji tu shuo* (*Discourse on the Diagram of the Great Ultimate*) of Zhou Dunyi (1017–1073).[9]

We also want to note that it is in light of this internal ordering of the *taiji* that the following statement from the *Xici* becomes crystal clear: "When the easiness [of *Qian*] and simplicity [of *Kun*] obtain, the patterning of things, and the principles of their patterning in the world, would also obtain. Once these obtain, there is completion of positioning in the world as thus formed" (*Shang* 1). Because the generative formation of things in the world is a process of self-organization and self-positioning of all things at the same time, this positioning is inherent in and coeval with the formation of all things in the context of all things. Hence, no thing whatsoever can exist without a cosmogonic and cosmographic positioning of the thing.

Fourth, as positioning of things is a matter of creative formation of the open universe from the very beginning, it is not only an expression of power and function of the source and the way, but a realization of value in the sense of goodness. "To succeed [in the deeds of creating life] is a goodness (*shan*). But that which will complete the deeds [in individual things] is nature (*xing*)" (*Shang* 5). Here, "goodness" indicates a state of value such as creation of life and its internal and external harmonization, which is not confined to merely moral goodness but which can be reflectively determined as desirable.[10] Positioning provides both a basis and an occasion for the development of a thing's goodness. In fact, it is through positioning of things that things become individual things in goodness. We may indeed regard positioning as a principle of individuation which conforms to goodness: things are individuated in terms of their natures; or one may say that natures (*xing*) are formed when things are positioned in the formation and transformation of primary harmony of the world. Their positioning in a sense gives rise to their individual natures because it is how things are creatively formed; as such, they receive creative potentiality from the source, the *taiji*, and this is precisely how their natures are to be regarded as good.

Natures are individuating forces, but also they are tendencies or propensities, which are disposed toward an inherent balance and completion of things. They are active forces that can creatively respond to circumstances for preserving and developing their identities. In this sense, they inherit from the source and are sustained by the source. They also constitute the world of reality and participate in the transformations of the way. Under highly optimal conditions, the transformation can be a matter of level and quality, not just a matter of meeting inner needs and fulfilling inner capabilities. It can be a matter of realizing the creative functions of heaven and earth so that a larger life and greater form of value can come into existence such as in the preservation of culture and of human community. This is then the succession of the goodness of the source, for it is the development and fulfillment of a universal condition for the completion of individual natures among human persons. It is a matter of the higher development of the human person based on his participation in the life productivity of heaven and earth. Here we see this state of accomplishment of goodness in the words of the *Doctrine of the Mean* (*Zhongyong*), a work that was written in the same period as the *Yizhuan* and which belongs to the same group and generation of Confucian disciples.[11]

Without engaging in an exegesis of this text, one still may see that the fulfillment of one's nature is a matter of taking the initiative to develop or preserve one's capacities in accordance with an understanding and a vision of the universal harmony of things. This point is well understood in both Confucianism and Daoism and is essential for achieving a unity of humans with heaven and earth. But, this again requires that one benefit others so that one provides a guide and an inspiring example for the fulfillment of the natures of others. Further it requires that one make it possible to improve the surroundings as a means of maintaining and nourishing a community and a culture. This improvement is described in the *Yizhuan* as "expanding life" (*guangsheng*) and "enhancing life" (*dasheng*) and "opening things so that they are used for higher values and functions" (*kaiwu chengwu*). This means that goodness is the result of the creative activity of human nature. This creative activity of human nature contributes to further development and the development of others as well as contributing to the creative development of a sustainable culture, which preserves and promotes the original and primordial values inherent in the source. In this process, the *dao* can be said to become a universal life-sustaining harmony and life-productive equilibrium in the order of well-positioned things. This leads to the recognition that human virtues are forms of self-development of natures and the bases for achieving value and goodness.

Fifth, the reason a person should understand the way of heaven and earth is that one should develop oneself to match heaven and earth; in understanding reality in terms of creative change, one would thus develop capacities, and hence virtues, to achieve harmony on a higher plane. This is basically the idea of "enlarging the way" (*hongdao*) in the Confucian *Analects* (15.29). But as we can see in the *Yizhuan*, the purpose of life is to overcome difficulties and hardships and achieve an influence that can be described as similar to the way of heaven, namely, to enable creative formation and transformation of things without extremities and without waywardness. This is to consciously cultivate oneself toward becoming a sage person of comprehensive virtues. This sagacious ability is described in the following:

> He [the Sage] is like heaven and earth and hence will not violate them. He has wisdom of knowing all things and his way of acting helps the world. Therefore, he does not go to an extreme. Even doing things in exceptional circumstances, there is no diversion from rectitude. He enjoys the principles of heaven and understands the destiny of heaven. Therefore he has no worries. He is capable of settling in a land, and cultivates benevolence among the community. He is capable of loving. (*Xici Shang* 4)

What is stressed in the *Yizhuan* but not in any other Confucian texts is that a person should observe (*guan*) the large and the small of things so that one may come to know and appreciate the subtle and various kinds of change, and thus perhaps be able to divine with sensible and insightful interpretations. In such onto-cosmological understanding one finds oneself capable of acting with benevolence (*ren*) and wisdom (*zhi*); for *ren* is no more than the comprehensive ability to produce life and be creative, and *zhi* is no more than the ability to achieve results conducive to a purpose. In this sense, the human person participates in the creative activities of heaven and earth and is a part of nature that functions naturally in the sense of exhibiting *ren* and *zhi*. Thus, we can speak of heaven and earth having the virtues of great abundance of life (*fuyou*) and ever-refreshing vitality (*rixin*). One can also see that there is the trinity and hence the unity of heaven and the person: namely, in their interacting functions and virtues, heaven, earth, and the person could be a dynamic whole and one integrated system. Thus, Cheng Yi says: "Heaven and earth have no mind in accomplishing transformation of things, but the sage (the one who achieves understanding of heaven and earth) has a mind, and thus refrains from acting on his own (*wuwei*)."[12]

From the positioning of heaven and earth there ensues the great function of creativity and receptivity from which life and world are born. The dynamic movements of heaven and earth are derived from this potential energy inherent in the positioning of heaven and earth (we may indeed call this the positional energy). Similarly, when a person achieves the great virtues of heaven and earth, she is said to occupy the position of heaven and earth and hence is as creative as heaven and earth are. One sees here that virtues are inherent in positions; and if one has achieved virtues one can be said to have achieved a certain positioning, or be said to have overcome the limitations of one's given position and have transformed oneself into another position. In other words, we could see the following scheme of transformation of positions:

positioning → onto-cosmological understanding → virtues → new positioning

What we generally understand as a "situation" or state of affairs is simply an unrecognized and undisclosed positioning in the scheme of things, which is itself rooted in the onto-cosmological structure of the world. One could look into and understand this structure and hence achieve inspiration for imitating nature or heaven and earth, which is then the very beginning of virtues. We shall see that the whole world of reality is to be represented in a structure of positions as manifested in the matrix of the *taiji*, and this structure also is to be seen as a sequence of stages in a process of creative change. All individual things are, therefore, both positioned and staged, and they belong simultaneously to a structure and a process that is one at the same time and in the same place. (This is to say that time and space or place are interpenetrating and inseparable as one, as the *taiji* and the *dao* are inseparable. We may indeed speak of the source aspect or the *taiji* aspect as well as the time aspect or the *dao* aspect of the same thing.) Thus, a situation in which a thing finds itself is both a position and a stage that constitutes, confines, and defines the thing. How we understand the situation of the thing, or for that matter how we understand the thing, requires our understanding of the position of the thing in the whole structure of the world as well as its stage in the process of change. In theory, the co-determination of the thing in its process aspect and structure aspect also goes along with the creative force exhibited in the structure and process of the thing itself because the thing is part and parcel of the whole structure and the whole process.

In the case of a human individual, we have seen that understanding the world of reality is a way to reflect on the virtues of heaven and earth inherent in oneself and hence to initiate creative transformation of oneself; in turn, this would lead to the related positioning of oneself. In a sense, this is to fulfill as well as to overcome one's own positioning (in space and time) and to realize the *taiji* and the *dao*. We can see that all Confucian virtues could be understood and interpreted as inherent or actual powers of transformation of one's positioning, so that one may realize the potentiality of creativity inherent in a situation and elevate oneself to a higher and higher plane until reaching the unity of human and heaven which is the original and primordial positioning of heaven and earth. On the other hand, any situation or positioning can be interpreted as containing a virtue in terms of which one could overcome and transform that situation. One must understand, or have the ability to understand, that a situation is always a positioning, and hence a positing of power and function from which a virtue or ability to act creatively can be derived.

Now we have described the onto-cosmological understanding of the world of reality (or for that matter the onto-cosmology of reality) in which positioning of heaven and earth as symbols of creative exchange and interchange of nature is first conceived as the basis for the origination and development of the world of creativity. From this original positioning, the world of things is derived and thus positioned. To exist is to be positioned in the structure of the configuration of the *taiji* and the process of creative change of the *dao*. On this ground, the world is to be symbolized in a system of symbols called *gua*, or "signs to be hung up," which symbolizes the whole structured configuration of the world as well as the process of change in the world. In this symbolization, it is clear that the positioning of things is exhibited in their mutual relationships of up and down, before and after, right and left, backward and forward, with a constant reference to the totality of reality and the total creativity and openness of the process. Symbols, like the things they stand for, are given meaning and individuated by a totality (in this case, a totality of symbols) and its potential openness of transformability, and hence their positioning is also so defined and individuated, which gives it both a place and a power to change positions in the totality of a system. Such is the onto-cosmological meaning of positioning and its resulting positions in the world of reality.

Positioning in the Symbolic System of Manifest Forms (*gua*)

We have explained how the system of *gua* arises from a process of comprehensive observation (*guan*) and reflection on things. We have also explained how each *gua* could be regarded as representing a positioning that is the constitution and definition of the thing. Hence, the whole system of *gua* represents a whole world of reality in which each individual thing receives its positioning, and this means that each thing is constituted and defined in terms of its position in the universal and whole configuration of reality. This is very clear from the constitution of the *gua* itself. If we take the *bagua* system, for example, it is clear that each *gua* is constituted in terms of three lines representing a mix of *yin* and *yang* forces. Thus, we have a sequence of the eight forms: ☰ ☱ ☲ ☳ ☴ ☵ ☶ ☷.

The question is: how do we order them? If we did not have onto-cosmological insights, we could not know how to choose one order over another, and we could not know how to justify the existing order in the *Fuxi Diagram*. But with such insight, we would arrive at the ordering of the eight forms in what is known as the *Fuxi Diagram*. The *Shuogua Commentary* actually describes the relationships in terms of the polar unities of opposites of the eight trigrams: "Heaven and earth are fixed in positions (*dingwei*), mountain and lake interact with vital force (*qi*), thunder and wind are struggling closely with each other, water and fire do not harm each other." Thus, we have the formation of the eight trigrams.

The *Fuxi Diagram* demonstrates that the positioning of the *Qian* and *Kun* and other forms determines the constitution of the forms; conversely, we can say that it is the positioning of the forms that gives rise to the constitution of the forms. Positions are potential or virtual constitutions, and constitutions are explicit positions of the forms. What is important are the relationships exhibited in the diagram among all the forms, which determine their positions and constitutions. By extension, via known methods of powering by two, we can see how the *bagua* system could be expanded into the system of sixty-four forms and thus embodying sixty-four positions or constitutions of individual things or events in the whole world of reality. These are known as sixty-four *zhonggua* (double trigrams or hexagrams). We know that this can be expanded infinitely or indefinitely. This extendibility is a feature of the symbolic system that reflects the differentiation and integration processes of reality. Now we can see not only that positions in the formation of *bagua* can be ordered in a circle to suggest a process of circulation and feedback, but also that it can be arranged or ordered in a hierarchy of levels of being. Thus, we can construct the following diagram of the hierarchical ordering of the forms in the same fashion as Shao Yong has made it:

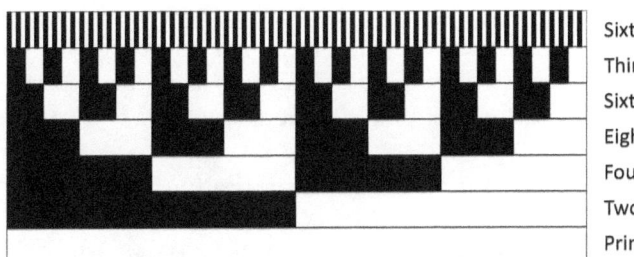

	Sixty-four Gua (Hexagrams)
	Thirty-Two Gua
	Sixteen Gua
	Eight Gua (Trigrams)
	Four Forms
	Two Norms
	Primary Unity (Taiji)

From this diagram we can see that there are four layers of world-being (for we can take a view of the world from the point of a given level). On the highest level we have *taiji*, which is unity of *yin* and *yang* in its inseparable or undifferentiated state. Its inherent power would give rise to the second level of world-being, which then constitutes the world of *yin* and *yang*, as two basic categories or movements of the world. In a similar move of self-differentiation, we come to the third level of four norms and the fourth level of eight trigrams. In this process of differentiation one can see that there is a natural ordering of the levels of being as well as a natural ordering of the forms on the same level. Hence, we have a hierarchical ordering in which we can also see how the primary *yin* and *yang* must occupy a position at the top of the hierarchy, whereas other forms on lower levels can be seen to be derived from them. There is no real positioning of higher and lower between the *yin* and *yang* as powers of creativity; only when *yin* and *yang* become incorporated in or identified with a world of our understanding, do we see the order of high heaven and low earth from a human point of view. But even so, as we see from the *Fuxi Circle*, there is no absolute distinction of higher and lower apart from suggesting a relationship of creative interaction and interdependence.[13] We could further note that on the *bagua* level the ordering of the eight trigrams is the basis for the ordering of the *gua* in the *Fuxi Circle* as shown earlier. This shows how the *Fuxi Circle* is not arbitrarily proposed, but proposed on the strength of a pristine insight into the dialectical differentiation of things from a single source.

We must observe that there are other ways of configuring the positions of *gua* in describing the world-reality. For example, there are the

Post-Heaven or *King Wen Diagram*, the *Hetu* (*River Chart*) and the *Luoshu* (*Luo Script*), which are based on an empirical-metaphysical theory of five processes of reality (*wuxing*) or based on the harmonic representations of dynamic balances of forces being observed to function one way or another.[14]

In the *Shuogua Commentary* we also have the suggestion as to how the *King Wen Diagram* (or *Post-Heaven Diagram*) is formed on the principles of mutual generation of the five powers (*wuxing*). It is said:

> The power of the ruler issues from the *Zhen* (arising: wood). Things become ordered and regulated at *Xun* (entering: wood). It meets other forms at *Li* (brightening: fire). It engages itself in war at *Kun* (receiving: earth). It finds happy words to say at *Dui* (enjoying: metal). It engages in war at *Qian* (creating: metal). It belabors itself at *Kan* (falling: water) and finally, develops the language for truth at *Gen* (resting: earth).

This amounts to a "positional" description of the Five Powers (as indicated in my parenthetical references) and their mutual generational relationships.

In regard to the three diagrams above, we can define and characterize a form or a positioning (*wei*) as follows. First, a form is constituted by yin and yang lines (indicating that a position is constituted by yin and yang forces). Second, a form belongs to a system of forms on a level of representation (indicating that a position belongs to a system of configurations of positions on a level of differentiation of reality).

Third, a level of representation can be generated from integration and differentiation of the primary forms of yin and yang. This indicates that a position could be moved from one level to another through change of the whole configuration of the world by integration and differentiation of the yin/yang forces of the *taiji*, which is the inexhaustible source of creativity. The shifting of levels can be understood both epistemologically as a matter of cognition or onto-cosmologically as a matter of creative integration and differentiation based on the source. It is a vertical movement of the *dao* that can be described in *Laozi* as a going-back or return (*fu*) when simplifying, and as birth or generation (*sheng*).

Fourth, on a given level, forms can be ordered in a progression as if in a forward movement or in a backward movement as shown in the *Fuxi Circle*. This indicates that positions are dynamically transformable

Zhouyi and the Philosophy of *Wei* (Positions)   259

in a process of creative change on a horizontal plane that would have the forward-positive progression described as positivity (*zheng*) and a backward-negative regression described as reversion (*fan*). The *Fuxi Circle* shows that *zheng* would naturally lead to *fan*, and *fan* by way of its own *fan* would lead to the original *zheng* form.[15]

Finally, on a given level, there are many ways in which forms can be related or interrelated. They can be related as reverse (*cuo*) such as from ☷ to ☰, transposition (*yi*) such as from ☳ to ☶, or converse (*zong*) such as from ☱ to ☴, and in the case of sixty-four hexagrams, even as nuclear interface (*hu*) such as from ䷀ to ䷁. Hence, there are basic transformations according to these forms.[16]

In light of the above, we must remember that a given position has its positioning in the course of the development of the *taiji* and in the structuring of a level or synchronized world. As a result of the intersecting of time and space, the position has a historical background as well as a contextual foreground for its identification. But the actual formation and possible future transformation is not simply determined by these two factors but also by its own endowed or vested vitality directly derived from the source. In this sense, the very constitution, and its inherent capacity, also determines its possible transformation. Hence, we need to look into the internal structure of the form of a position in order to appreciate the creative potentiality of that position. Again, this internal structuring of the positioning can be further described in the language of positions or positioning.

As a *gua* form is formed of lines of *yin* and *yang*, those lines (*yao*) would represent or actually occupy positions in a *gua*. Thus, in the double trigram or hexagram we have six lines of *yin* and *yang* and six positions in the *gua* structure. The question is what those lines would represent or show. The answer is that each of them represents a state of the constitution of a situation or a stage of the development of such a constitution, and hence a position of a given state of affairs. If we consider the whole *gua* as a symbolic representation of a development of a situation, then each line would represent a state or stage of such a development, or the whole situation at a certain time period or occasion. Since a situation in fact is a position in the world of reality, this means that the *yao* lines in fact represent positions within a position. The complex of the *gua* positioning would of course determine the function and potentiality of such a position.

By the same token, as a situation of a *gua* itself is a position within the framework of the onto-cosmological process and structure of reality, which is a positioning itself, the positioning of heaven and earth in creative interaction, we would then have a situation in which the *yao* lines are positions in a *gua* position, which is again a position among a sequence of positions representing the cosmic order of things. This nested or embedded position is relevant as a framework or a system (not just history) for the reading of the full meaning or the full development of a *yao* position, just as a *yao* position is important for the understanding of the formation and transformation of a *gua* position.

According to the *Xici*, *yao* is where one will find the initial movement in a situation, and it is an index of any change (*Shang* 8). In this sense, it is a symbol for the incipient movement or change of any circumstances, which an observant person must take care to see in order to understand the direction and nature of change of a situation. It is said:

> As a text the *Book of Changes* is all comprehensive. It bears on the way of heaven, the way of persons and the way of earth. Having the three powers or ways (*sancai*) and doubling them [because of the alternation between *yin* and *yang*], there come the six lines. The six lines are nothing else than the ways of the three powers. Due to the changing movement of the *dao* there come the *yao* (or the lines of movement, namely traces from movement of the *dao*). The *yao* have their gradations [higher or lower positions]. That is why we recognize things (*wu*). The mixing of things gives rise to patterns (of orders or organizations, *wen*). Because *wen* could be well-positioned or ill-positioned, therefore come the fortunes or misfortunes (for a person). (*Xia* 10)

From this one sees why and how a hexagram is actually formed: it represents the powers of heaven, human, and earth: with heaven on the top, human (or person) in the middle, and earth on the bottom, each in double lines symbolizing the conjunction of *yin* and *yang*, or *gang* (firmness) and *rou* (softness), as mentioned in the *Shuo Commentary*. The *yao* positions therefore are displayed in each *gua* in the form of the combination of selected *yao* lines of the following:

```
9-6  ─────────        6-6  ──  ──
9-5  ─────────        6-5  ──  ──
9-4  ─────────        6-4  ──  ──
9-3  ─────────        6-3  ──  ──
9-2  ─────────        6-2  ──  ──
9-1  ─────────        6-1  ──  ──
```

The above shows how the relationships between heaven, humans, and earth are formed. One can also see how one person could move from the earth position to the heaven position. Now it also is clear that there is a distinction between the *yin* and the *yang* in each of the tripartite powers, resulting in the first line being an odd number fitting for the occupation of the *yang* force, and the second line an even number fitting for the occupation of a *yin* force. The same rule holds for the third/fourth lines and the fifth/sixth lines. In this arrangement, the *yao* positions are those lines to be occupied by the *yin* and *yang* forces, so that each line could be named according to the number of the position and the nature of the force occupying it. Using number 6 to represent *yin* and number 9 to represent *yang*, we could have the *yao* positions named as "First-6 (beginning)" or "9-First"; "6-Second" or "9-Second"; "6-Third" or "9-Third"; "6-Fourth" or "9-Fourth"; "6-Fifth" or "9-Fifth"; and "Top (Sixth)-6" or "Top (Sixth)-9." It is in the nature of the *yao* positions "First-9," "6-Second," "9-Third," "6-Fourth," "9-Fifth," and "Top (6)-Sixth" that they are befitting because the odd or even natures of the positions are occupied by corresponding *yang* or *yin* forces. In these we have cases of "correct positioning" or "matching positions" (*dangwei*) or of "obtaining the positions" (*dewei*). These are cases of "correctness," or "rightness" (*zheng*).

These are called "right," or "correct," because these positions would enable the powers of *yin* and *yang* to function naturally and properly within the context of the *gua*. On the other hand, in cases of "First-6," "9-Second," "6-Third," "9-Fourth," "6-Fifth," and "Top-9," one would expect an internal disharmony between the position and the force occupying the position; hence, they are considered to be cases of incorrectness or non-rightness (*buzheng*), and also are called "not matching a position" (*budangwei*) or "losing a position" (*shiwei*). Besides these, a *yao* position is also described as being central (*zhong*) or noncentral (*buzhong*), indicating whether the line is in the middle of the lower/upper trigram or not. In this fashion, we see how "9-Fifth" is a position of both correctness and centrality (*zhengzhong*) because the *yang* occupies a middle position of the higher trigram on a *yang* line. One must realize that the paradigms of *zhengzhong*, *zheng*, *zhong*, *dangwei*, *budangwei*, *dewei*, and *shiwei* are well developed and much used in the *Xiang Commentary* on the *yao* lines. They are sometimes used in the *Tuan Commentary* on the *gua* and in the *Xiang Commentary* on the *gua*.[17]

Then there come the paradigms such as "respond/answer to" (*ying*) or "pair/match" (*bi*) and "succeed/inherit" (*cheng*) or "ride/override" (*cheng*). The Han Dynasty *Yijing* authors used a rich vocabulary to describe the nature and potentiality of a *yao* position. In these descriptions, a *yao* position becomes fully specifiable in reference to its line position, its quality, the relation between the two (correctness or incorrectness), its position relative to the trigram substructure, its position relative to other *yao* lines in terms of *yin-yang* correspondences across a line, or same-quality pairing, overriding and succeeding between two neighboring lines. The basic concern that motivates these forms of description of a *yao* position is to detect harmony, balance, and potentiality for creativity or creative change toward goodness rather than badness. We can see that a *yao* position is a concentration of many relational and qualitative forces, and is always contextualized in a framework of a *gua* and thus in a way mimicking how an actual position in a person's life is restricted and influenced by many factors in one's life and actions.

We also must note that, as described, the *yao* position is a potentiality of power confined by the structure of a larger situation, and manifests itself as a state or stage of the structure as a process. In this regard a *yao* position is actually a time-position (*shiwei*), changing from line to line according to the progression of time. Each line's meaning is enhanced or disclosed in this progression of time in the framework of a *gua*, which itself could change to another *gua* if the *yao* position has changed its quality such as in the case of line-change (*yaobian*). In divination, when there is the *yaobian* there must be a *guabian* or change of the *gua*. Independently of divination, we may interpret this *gua* change as a function of the *yao* change and this simply means that the whole context is conditioned and changes in accord with the changes of its elements. But again, the changes of the *yao* lines take place within a configuration of the *gua* and hence are simultaneously confined in a *gua* as a whole context or framework. We should further remember that a situation in life or the world can always be represented by a *gua*; the actual state of the situation in a process of time is only to be represented by a *yao* position in the *gua* and this is so because a *gua* is not simply to be conceived as a structure or configuration of forces but also as a process of development or creative change to be realized in a process of time.[18]

We may now formulate the logic of *yao* positions in the following fashion:

1. A *yao* position is an index of creative movement and potentiality for such a movement. It is generated in time and therefore to be considered as a time-position (*shiwei*).

2. A *yao* position is a multidimensional vector of change as confined within the framework structure of a *gua*.

3. A *yao* change nevertheless determines the change of the *gua* and hence the quality and the nature of the situation as a whole.

4. The strength or lack of strength of a *yao* position lies in its quality and relational support, hence it could lead to goodness or badness, fortune or misfortune.

5. A *yao* position has its inner creative force derived from the system of *gua* and reflects the contingencies of actual occasions.

With the *yao* positions thus understood, we see that any *gua* could be interpreted accordingly. A *gua* is a structural configuration of a process of change in six stages, or six positions. If a *gua* applies to a situation, the *gua* will shed light on the situation in terms of its structure-process nature. In fact, we could simply regard a *gua* as a description of a hypothetical situation in which a person finds oneself. Thus, we can see how the six *yao* positions could characterize some main features in the present and/or predict some events in the future. In light of this characterization, one could make corresponding admonitions regarding decisions to be made or actions to be taken. The nature of a *yao* position provides for the possibilities of creative change, and there is no enclosure of a position arising from its underlying onto-cosmological background or positioning. Hence, moral decisions toward free actions or participation from the individual person are real and genuine choices.

As an illustration, we may explain the *yao* positions in the *Qian* hexagram (☰). First, we must note that the *Qian gua* occupies a central and supreme position among all the sixty-four hexagrams. Its *gua* position is determined by its composition for creativity and action; namely, it is the symbol for the all creative and all active sources of power and energy, because it is made of six *yang yao* lines. Although the *yao* positions of 9-Second, 9-Fourth, and 9-Top (or Sixth) are not quite correct (*zheng*), the total strength of the *yang* lines gives the whole *gua* an optimistic and sanguine quality. Hence, the *gua* itself as a whole is judged as highly positive in values and confidently characterized by the words "*yuan heng li zhen*" (originating, prosperous, advantageous, firm) of the *guaci*. But if we look into each of the six *yao* lines, or positions, we find that each has its positive contribution to make, yet individually each must be judged according to its position in the context of the overall positivity. In the first line (9-First) position, we see it characterized as "Hidden dragon, do not use it." As the *Qian gua* is considered the symbol for pure creative power of heaven and hence describable as the Chinese dragon (*long*), the first *yao* is therefore the first manifestation of the creative power and hence a first state or first stage where the *long* appears. But from the point of view of the whole *gua*, this first position represents a hidden state of the *long* and at this position the *long* cannot do anything yet. Therefore, the advice is not to use this position for any purpose. Not to use it is to leave it alone, to let it further develop itself and to wait for the right time. Hence, this *yao* position carries a message of patience and caution in both a description and a prescription in light of the structure of the whole *gua*.

In the second line (9-Second) position we see it characterized as "See the dragon on the field. Advantage to see the great man." In this position, the creative power of heaven has stirred and hence presents an opportunity for some form of action. The great man could be the fifth line (9-Fifth) position, which has a natural resonance with the second line position because they all share the feature of being in the middle of a trigram. In comparison with the fifth line, the second line is not only less advanced in its positional potential but not *dangwei* (fitting by positions), whereas the fifth line is where the creative power of heaven reaches its highest point and its positioning is one of *dangwei*. Hence, we find the prescription to seek friendship and advice of the great man. Following the same logic, in the third line (9-Third) position, the judgment runs as "the superior man is firm and active throughout the day and he has a sense of misgiving in the evening. Dangerous but no blame." The description in this judgment is not direct; it reflects the situation as one requiring active engagement but careful control. This is because the creative power of heaven has reached a critical point where extreme caution must be exercised during a transition of no centrality.

The third line being noncentral is in fact always unstable, particularly when it is occupied by a *yang* or *gang* force. In becoming 9-Third it can be rash and foolhardy and there jeopardize many desirable factors. Hence, there is the implicit advice on self-caution and self-warning. Perhaps in light of this, the *Wenyan Commentary* on this line also says that the superior man is active and concerned so that he wishes to advance virtues and cultivate his actions. This means that the superior man is able to exercise care in time and thus has no arrogance in a higher position and no anxiety in a lower position. With this, even a position may carry an instability and there is no blame on the person. In fact, the person in that position may counterbalance his bad position with his good virtues and this means that a person can overcome his weakness with strength from his virtue. If, on the other hand, the third line is 6-Third, it would be unstable through its weakness, exhibited by the absence of both centrality (*zhong*) and correctness (*zheng*). If support from *cheng* / *cheng* / *ying* are weaker still, this position will tend or lead to great danger and possible destruction. For example, one sees in the 6-Third *yao* position in the *Bi* hexagram precisely such an unfortunate state. In the *Wenyan* Commentary on the third line of *Qian*, it is said that one is devoted to advancing virtues so that "one will not be arrogant when reaching high position and will not be worrisome when occupying a low position" (*ju shangwei erbujiao, zai xiawei erbuyou*).

In the fourth line (9-Fourth) position we are told implicitly that the dragon could jump around in the deep water and there is no blame. The dragon has passed a critical period and is in a preparatory stage for assuming a greater role and for exercising greater power. In the fifth line (9-Fifth) position we reach a point of supremacy of power described as "Flying dragon in sky" with the prescription of "Advantage to see the great man." Why still say "Advantage to see the great man"? Because when a person who consults the *Yijing* is not yet in power, he could go seek the great man in power. If this person is already in the position of power, it is useful to see another great man (even one at the 9-Second according to Zhu Xi) for resolving a difficulty or achieving a larger deed. Now we come to the top line (Top-9) position, where the power of dragon has reached the highest point and become overdue. Hence, there would be regret if one exercises whatever power one has for a purpose not befitting one's position. The judgment "Dragon at extreme high point. Regret" (亢龙有悔) describes the situation and prescribes implicitly no action and self-control, as a Daoist would do. Such is the nature of this *yao* position in the *Qian*. A Confucian interpretation is different: it is said in the *Wenyan Commentary* that "[The dragon on the top line] is noble and yet without position, high and yet without people; the able person is in the lower position and [this position] has no assistance. Hence there will be regret upon action."

In line with what we have said about the *gua* positions, no position lasts permanently in the process-reality of the *dao*. Hence, in time, a new situation will develop in which any given position will naturally change, and if we are able to know it, we would be able to use a *gua* to describe it and also to find out what would be the describable action or decision to take. It is possible that at the moment when one comes to know one's situation, it is a situation that is about to turn into another situation. Although there could be many possible situations into which a given situation may turn, according to the system of sixty-four *gua* (on a 2 to the sixth power level of onto-cosmology or the *taiji* world), there are sixty-three possible *gua* into which a given *gua* could transform itself. How does this transformation take place? Theoretically, it can be shown that any *gua* could transform into any other *gua* by a sequence of operations such as reversion, conversion, and transposition. In fact, we allow both full and partial line-to-line reversion (to change a *yin*-line to a *yang*-line and vice versa). With such limited operations of reversion, conversion, and transposition, a given *gua is* able to yield any other *gua* in the system. This means there is a potential equivalence between all the *gua* in light of the basic movements of change, which would transform an old configuration of energy alignment into another one. Sometimes the change is unnoticeable because it is gradual and slow: this is the *hua* aspect (transformation or the unnoticeable change, whether quantitative or qualitative) of the *bianhua*. But when the transformation is accomplished, it is the *bian* aspect (change or the noticeable change, whether quantitative or qualitative) of the *bianhua*. Because when one *yao* line changes its nature, the whole *gua* configuration changes and becomes another *gua*, it can be said that when one line changes, the *bian* is already present. Hence, the quantitative change of *hua* must be less evident than the *yao* line changes, and this is indicated as the *ji* (incipient change) in any movement. A person must have wisdom to notice the *ji* of a movement so he can be prepared for, or can participate in, the movement.

Imagine we could extend vertically the world line into a higher power of 2, say 2 to the 100th power, so that we could see each line of the new *gua* form. Does that mean that the *ji* (minuscule) movement of a situation could be caught in such a form? The reply is both yes and no. Insofar as a line change does impact a *gua* form change, it is a *bian*. But, then, we may not notice this form change, in which case the line change can still count as a *ji*. Perhaps we could see *ji* as relative to our perception and knowledge and therefore it can be unnoticeable or noticeable, depending on our ability to perceive and know. This means that we could even think of the *yao* line change in the sixty-four *gua* system as a *ji* change which, when noticed, becomes what is known as a line change in a *gua*. But we may not notice it taking place, and thus we may not know what new situation we will be in, even though we have known the present situation we are in.

From what we have said about the relativity of perception of *ji* and the relativity of the extension of a world level, we could imagine the nth power of two approaches to infinity; then it is imaginable that all resulting situations or positions remain very closely similar and approximate in time and space, or space-time. We shall have a situation that approximates a continuum in which any small difference would be hard to detect and the world would be seen as a connected whole. Imagining it thus, we can say that the world of reality is one in which the infinite power of 2 is infinity, or infinity of infinity (allowing transfinite numbers) and thus forms a densely ordered class of things and events. But this world is still not separable from the level of reality in which we notice the sixty-four changes or any other convenient changes on convenient levels congruent with our abilities of perception, thought, and action. In this way, we are able to see that the wisdom of understanding reality is to approach reality as it is or as it is in transformation, and to perform our own action on whatever level we feel necessary, and competent to perform.

A further lesson one may draw from this thought experiment is that even on the level of sixty-four *gua* there is discreteness as well as continuity among all *gua*. There is a question in this case as to how we could logically order these *gua* in an order reflecting and measuring our understanding of the process of reality formation and transformation.[19]

The Nature of Divination with Regard to Positioning

In connection with this discussion of the nature of real change in the world, we may make a remark on the nature or function of the art of divination (*bu/shi/zhan*) in the ancient period in China. As archaeology of *buci* (divined judgments) has proven, divination has been practiced since the time of Shang (Yin) (1766–1122 BCE). The *Zhouyi* could be the most advanced and newest method of divination developed by the founders of the Zhou (1122–481 BCE). The method of divination must be separated from the manual of consultation to which the result of divination is to be compared for basic identification or interpretation. This manual, formulated with a symbolism of the *gua* with *yin/yang* lines, would function like a map of the world, whereas the method of divination would function like an indicator or locator, which would identify a *gua* when it is used.[20]

How good, efficient, or accurate the method of divination is as a tool for predicting or foretelling the trends or situations of the future for a person with regard to a specific or general purpose is a question separate from the question of whether the symbolism is adequate in comprehending or reflecting the reality of world in process. It is possible that the method is not accurate, whereas the symbolism and its underlying understanding of the world are adequate to our best experience. On the other hand, we could have a good and accurate method yet lack a good or adequate map to make correct identifications. Of course, a method of divination cannot be totally separated from its map because the method has to presuppose the map in its operation as well as in its projection or identification of a result. The result must be set in the language of the map so that it can be said to be a divination relevant to the map.

Even the way of divination could be formulated as a reflection of the map in the first place, as is the case of the Zhou method of divination as described in Zhu Xi's *Zhouyi benyi* (*Original Meanings of Zhouyi*). In a sense, we could regard the method as a dynamically manageable or calculable process of operations of the theory; and the theory would be identified as the result of using a specific form of method or procedure. But it is also the case that the theory could be the result of using many methods, and has evolved into an adequate picture of the world, whereas any one method would eventually be outgrown and become inadequate. New methods have to be devised to match the theory, just as at some other time a new theory will have to be developed from a new method.

Once we have made the distinction between method and theory, we can see that in the practice of Zhouyi divination there is a way of identifying the yao (line) change and hence introducing a gua change. When such a yao (line) change takes place in a given gua, we have what is known as the bianyao (changed line), and the changed yao will cause the change of the gua accordingly. We then have the biangua (changed gua) resulting from the original gua. Thus, we could have Qian ䷀ changed into Gou ䷫ (with trigram Qian ☰ above and trigram Xun ☴ below) if we have the bianyao on the First-9 position. The same Qian ䷀ could become the Dun ䷠ (with Qian ☰ above and Gen ☶ below) if we have two bianyao on the first and second line positions. Which position or positions would have the bianyao is to be determined by the system of divination that consists in a procedure of calculating numbers by manipulating the milfoil stalks. My purpose in speaking of the bianyao is not to describe the method of divination (for which there are many books), but to point out that the system of divination allows any combination of bianyao to happen. This means that any gua could yield any other gua, due to the number and order of bianyao being introduced. This no doubt conforms to the nature of creative change in which any form could become any other form and any situation could change into any different situation (of course, still relative to a system of interpretation for human world affairs).[21]

We now come to some important generalizations on the *yao* positions from the *Xici*. In section 9 of the *Xici Xia* it is said with reference to the *yao* positions:

> Two and Four have the same deed and yet different positions. They are good at different things. Two has more approbation, but Four has more fear. This is a matter of closeness. The way of the soft is not beneficial to the distant. Its essence is for no blame and its function is for the soft to occupy the middle. Three and Five have the same deed and yet different

positions. Three has more misfortunes, and Five has more achievements. This is a matter of being noble or lowly. For these positions, the soft is dangerous and the firm will win.

This is a useful and insightful observation on the function and value of the *yao* positions as borne out by the judgments of the *yao*. Indeed, one may regard this as an indication of the natures of these *yao* positions from which the judgments receive their explanations. Now the question is: what about *yao* positions on the first and sixth lines? In light of what has been said about the other positions, my answer to this question is that the first position is sometimes associated with approbation and sometimes with fear. This is because it could develop into either the second line or the third line state. This is borne out by actual first line *yao*. Similarly, the sixth position is sometimes with approbation and sometimes with fear, perhaps depending on how it is acted on, whether with self-control or with presumption of power.

Conclusion: *Wei* from Confucianism to Daoism and Buddhism

An important distinction between Confucian philosophy and Daoist philosophy is that Confucianism considers morality, society, and even political concern as essential aspects of a person. For Confucius, a person may not be in a position or in a time to contribute his talents to government, but one is nevertheless never not in a position to care for one's community and cultivate one's morality, which is inevitably society oriented. On the other hand, Daoism does not consider any of the three as essential for the cultivation or the well-being of the individual. Laozi and Zhuangzi had their own ideas of what constitutes a good government and a good society. But the basis for their thinking is that the *dao*—as an onto-cosmological process of reality—should always be the guide. To follow the *dao* is to be natural, spontaneous, and not to seek to act; in this way, one is bound to reject both Confucian morality and conventional society as ultimately essential to well-being and a good life.

This essential difference between Confucianism and Daoism is clearly reflected in the Confucian affirmation of consideration of "position" (*wei*) and the Daoist disregard of such consideration. For Confucianism, *wei* is always a relation of ranking high or low in government, society, and even morality. Hence, we see that the *Zhongyong* (section 20) speaks of the "the grading of love according to kinship and the ranking of respect according to virtue" (*qinqinzhisha, zunxianzhideng*) as the source from which the rites (*li*) arise. The onto-cosmology of the *Yizhuan* could be considered to provide a metaphysical foundation for the consideration of *wei* in the political, social, and moral sense, so the reference to *wei* is thus necessary and important. But for Daoists, it is precisely because of the onto-cosmological nature of the world that one could transcend both state and society and concentrate on seeking the *dao* and acting according to the *dao*. They would not pay any, or much, attention to a discourse of *wei* even on a cosmological plane. From this point of view, we could see that the *Yizhuan* is much more a Confucian work than a Daoist work, although there are views on the nature and process of reality that could lend support to the Daoist view on the *dao* and vice versa.[22]

CHAPTER 9

Li (理) and *Qi* (气) in the *Yijing*
A Reconsideration of Being and Nonbeing in Chinese Philosophy

Three Strata of the *Yijing* and Logic of Divination

The *Yijing* is a profound book and should be understood as such. As it has been used to serve a divinatory purpose, and to a large extent developed from the divinatory practice, it has been regarded as essentially a divination book.[1] But this view is mistaken on two counts. First, the divination judgments constitute only an early portion of the book, which is itself based on a philosophically meaningful symbolism, and which provides a foundation for a deepening growth of philosophical significance. The whole *Yijing* might be said to consist of three large strata of work: symbolism, divination judgments, and explicitly philosophical commentaries. The development of the *Yijing* into these three strata endows the book with a philosophical significance, which can only be accounted for in terms of a root metaphysical insight embodied in the original symbolism.

Second, the very practice of divination associated with the *Yijing* has its own philosophical and metaphysical significance and need not be explained on the basis of superstition or mysticism, as is commonly assumed.[2] However, a rational and philosophical interpretation of the presuppositions of the divinatory practice, according to which divination already presupposes a rational as well as an empirical understanding of the world, is possible. Divination, then, results from a ritualistically appropriate and psychologically satisfying process of practical decision making under circumstances that rule out knowledge, yet invite and warrant speculation. One might say that the whole divinatory process is an exercise in subject-objectification and object-subjectification for the purpose of preparing the individual to act rightly and adjust correctly.[3] Understanding the divinatory process in this way can be called a matter of philosophizing about divination.

One might indeed see the long philosophical tradition of the *Yijing* as an ongoing effort to achieve a full understanding of reality. Understanding the *Yijing* this way adds to its richness and profundity. Precisely in this spirit, the *Yijing* was a source of its inspiration for the Neo-Confucian movement culminating in Cheng Yi and Zhu Xi, who, along with other Neo-Confucianists, interpreted it in terms of the *li*, *qi*, and other concepts. For these thinkers, then, the *Yijing* became the supportive base and fermenting ground for developing the notions of *li*, *qi*, *xin*, and *xing*.

We have seen in previous chapters a full-fledged analysis and synthesis of the multidimensional wisdom and pluraphasal (multiphase) dialectics of the *Yijing*,[4] which includes an adequate account of the philosophy of divination. Now I shall inquire and explain how the Neo-Confucian philosophical categories of *li* and *qi* could be developed from the rich resources of the *Yijing*, and how difficulties involving this *li-qi* scheme in the Neo-Confucian philosophy of Zhu Xi can be overcome in light of a closer understanding of the metaphysical visions of the *Yijing*.[5] To achieve this goal, I shall first briefly present the Neo-Confucian view of *li-qi* in Zhu Xi and the Cheng Brothers (Cheng Hao and Cheng Yi) to locate the difficulties of bifurcation, dualism, and the downgrading of *qi*. Then I shall show how the *Yijing* philosophy can be mined for an adequate reconceptualization and redefinition of the *li* and *qi* categories and how the *Yijing* further provides an adequate perspective for the understanding of *li* and *qi*. This approach is quite different from that of Zhu Xi and others who used *li* and *qi* of Neo-Confucian philosophy to illuminate the *Yijing*. I shall then delineate how in this new light of the *Yijing*, the main difficulties of Neo-Confucianism may be avoided. Finally, I shall reconsider the question of being and nonbeing in the philosophical wisdom of the *Yijing* in order to suggest the way in which being and nonbeing should be related in the light of this philosophy. I also shall make some historical remarks on the great chain of being and nonbeing and on Daoism.

Li and *Qi* as Understood in Neo-Confucian Philosophy

The notions of *li* and *qi* are not much mentioned as correlative metaphysical concepts in earlier Neo-Confucians such as Shao Yong, Zhou Dunyi, and Cheng Mingdao. In their commentaries or treatises on the *Yijing*, these scholars did not refer to *li* for an explanation of the evolution of *yin* and *yang* forces and their differentiation into five powers; nor did these scholars use *li* in understanding ultimate categories of reality such as *dao* or *taiji*. The central dominant concepts in Shao Yong's *Huangji jingshi* are "*yinyang, dongjing, gangru, bianhua, ganyin*, and *tiandi*." Even when *li* is mentioned by these early Neo-Confucians, it is basically treated as an object of knowledge and mind. Unlike *qi*, *li* is not here given an independent cosmological position. Thus, Shao Yong says, "Among all things in the world none does not have *li*. What is called *li* is what can be known after close investigation."[6] *Li* is indeed in all things but does not play the so-called worldmaking role of *qi* as in the *qi* of *yin-yang*.

Similarly, in the *Taiji tu shuo* (*Discourse on the Diagram of the Great Ultimate*) and *Tongshu* (*Book on Comprehending the Yi*), Zhou Dunyi neither ontologizes nor cosmologizes *li*. For Zhou Dunyi, the basic concepts that have cosmological and ontological significance are *wuji, taiji, dongjing, cheng*, and *yin-yang* (which are referred to as the two *qi*). *Li* (principle/reason) is used by Zhou Dunyi to refer to a proportionate relation and interaction in the sense of *li* (propriety/ritual).[7] Thus he says, "*Yin* and *yang*, when balanced (*li*), become harmonized."[8] Even Cheng Mingdao emphasized that we "see the vital appearances of heaven, earth, and living things,"[9] but do not "exhaust the *li* (*qiong li*)." He further speaks of "*li* of heaven, earth and ten thousand things" and "heavenly *li*." He even says, "Life is what is called *xing* (nature). *Xing* is *qi, qi* is *xing*. This is what life is all about."[10]

With Cheng Yi, *li* comes to be considered essential in the constitution of things. Cheng Yi says, "What is at the heart of things is *li*; what is at the heart of treating things is *yi*."[11] When he says, "The *li* in the world is such that if it ends it will begin again. Thus, it is everlasting and inexhaustible,"[12] *li* is not simply described as the constant way of the world, but it is identified *as* and *with* the constant way of the world. Consequently, he says: "Shrinking, stretching, coming and going are only *li*,"[13] and "The *li* of creativity (*shengsheng*) will come naturally and will not end."[14] In contrast to Mingdao, he asserts, "Nature (*xing*) is *li*."[15]

In the case of Zhang Zai, his philosophy of cosmogony centers around the idea of *qi* (vital force) which is described both as *taihe* (the ultimate harmony) and *taixu* (the ultimate void), an idea which corresponds to the *taiji* in the *Yijing*. He says, "*Taixu* has no forms; it is the original substance of *qi*."[16] In fact, for Zhang Zai all things in the world such as Heaven, Earth and all qualities in humankind such as *xing* and *xin* are due to the "transformation of *qi*"[17] (*qihua*). He does speak of *li* and *qiong li*; however, *li* is nothing but the intrinsic and inherent order and pattern naturally produced by *qi* in the process of *qihua*. In this case, *li* does not therefore occupy an autonomous ontological position in the separation from things, nor does it possess a generative and creative function like *qi*. As we shall see, this point is very important for an understanding of the meaning and position of nonbeing in the philosophy of the *Yijing*. Zhang Zai has, in my view, more than any other Neo-Confucian, preserved the metaphysical insight of the *Yijing* and made most clear the metaphysical distinction between the Confucian concept of original substance (*benti*) or reality, which is *taixu*, and the Daoist and Buddhist conceptions of such, which is *wu* (void) or *kong* (nothingness or emptiness).

Zhu Xi, alone, perhaps under the penetrating influence of Cheng Yi, made *li* a cosmological and ontological principle of being and not just an epistemological principle of knowledge. For Zhu Xi, not only is *li* a principle correlative to the principle of *qi*, which is constitutive of all things, but also it comes to assume in time the supreme position of being the ultimate principle or foundation of reality, method, order, humankind, and values. Rather than take cues from the texts of the *Yijing* to explain the concept of *li*, Zhu Xi used *li* to explain basic entities and processes in the *Yijing* such as *taiji*, *dao*, and *huidong* (universal change). In his *Zhouyi benyi*, Zhu Xi even explained *forms* (*xing*) in the *Yijing* as "the resemblance of *li*."[18]

That Zhu Xi considers *li* to have an explanatory function, which itself does not need explanation, is highly significant. This means that to him *li* is the most fundamental metaphysical category. Thus he says, "*Taiji* is only a *li* . . . *Taiji* is only a supreme good and best reason (*daoli*) . . . *Taiji* is the ultimate *li*."[19] He even describes the *wuji* of Zhou Dunyi as an attribute of *li*. According to Zhu Xi, *wuji* is only a term referring to *li* in virtue of *li*'s formlessness, limitlessness, and self-sufficiency. He says, "Zhouzi [Zhou Dunyi], being afraid that one seeks *taiji* beyond *taiji* therefore speaks of the *wuji*; once called *wuji*, one cannot force oneself to seek it as the *li* of being (*you de daoli*)."[20] On this basis,

Zhu Xi defends the Zhou Dunyi position of "*wuji er taiji*" (the ultimateless and then the great ultimate) against the attack of Lu Xiangshan.[21] Lu Xiangshan thinks that the ultimateless stands for *wu* (void), and hence has Daoist implication. For Zhu Xi, on the other hand, the ultimateless indicates the unlimitedness and infinity of the *taiji* and need not be Daoist oriented. My view on this is simply that there is a reason to believe that Zhou Dunyi has integrated both the Daoist and Confucian view of the ultimate reality. The key point, in fact, is the idea of emergent creativity indicated by the Chinese term "*er*."

Li, for Zhu Xi, represents the ontological ground of things, the ultimate constitution of things, and is what makes things things and what things follow in their being things. He says, "As for all things in the world, they have their reasons for being what they are and have laws they follow. These are the *li*."[22] In Zhu Xi's writings, the independent ontological status that *li* acquires is shown by his understanding of *li* as something existing prior to all things. Thus he says, "If one considers the matter from the viewpoint of *li*, one will see that even when there are no such and such things, there are *li* for these things. There are also *li*, for which there are no such and such things."[23] In the *Yulei* 语类 of Zhu Xi, one can see that Zhu Xi has come almost explicitly to the position that *li* exists independently and prior to *qi*, the other metaphysically constitutional principle in his philosophy.

Although he affirms, in general, that under heaven there is no *qi* that has no *li*, nor *li* that has no *qi*, he considers *li* as more basic than *qi*; his reason is that *li* is above forms (*xing er shang*). He asks, rhetorically, "From the point of view of a distinction between above forms and under forms, is there no distinction between before and after?"[24] And on several occasions in the section on *li* and *qi* in the *Yulei*, Zhu Xi states with seemingly philosophical conviction that if we want to infer the origins of *li* and *qi*, we must say that "*Li* is before, *qi* is after."[25] This kind of statement suggests not only a logical priority, but also a metaphysical priority of *li* before *qi*. The distinction between before and after is clearly not intended to be a logical but rather a cosmological distinction. Thus, we have the following exchange:

Xu asks: "Before heaven and earth are distinguished, are there many things?"

Zhu Xi answers: "There is only the *li*."[26]

For Zhu Xi, *li* even assumes the metaphysical status of *taiji*. *Li* is the ground principle of the constitution of things. *Qi* is affirmed to be the principle that gives rise to the forms of things, just as *li* gives rise to the nature (*xing*) of things. However, he does stress the creative worldmaking power of *qi*, that is, *qi*'s capabilities of condensation and dispersion, in contrast to *li*'s "properties of unfeelingness, lack of calculation, and inactivity."[27] Yet, if *li* has been identified with *taiji* and *dao*, there arises the question of whether *li* may not actually possess creative agency. Regarding this identification, the least we can say is that Zhu Xi does not sufficiently work out the role, status, function, and significance of *li* and consequently that of *qi* and *li* in their relationships. In fact, his views on the priority question of *li* and *qi* and his treatment of *li* as an ultimate category of existence and explanation inevitably burdens him with the charge of dualism.

The charge of dualism against Zhu Xi consists in pointing out that Zhu Xi has bifurcated the nature of things into *li* and *qi* as principles of independent ontological status in such a way that their relations become difficult to understand. A consequence of this dualism is found in the explanation of human existence. Zhu Xi holds that humans have the nature of *li* (*xing* or *yili*), which forms the root of virtues and the nature of *qi* (*qizhi*), which in turn form the essence of desires and habits. This also leads him to separate mind into *daoxin* (mind of *dao*) and *renxin* (mind of person). This view of human existence and mind naturally leads him to an axiological disparagement and degradation of human desires, which to him can be controlled only through the strengthening of the heavenly *li* and weakening of the *qizhi*. This view further results in a moralistic distortion of the true image of persons.

I consider the dualism of *li* and *qi* and the disparaging distinction between *tianli* and *qizhi* to be fundamental difficulties in the philosophy of Zhu Xi. I believe these difficulties perhaps result from an insufficient and wrong-headed interpretation and understanding of the philosophy of the *Yijing*, which deals with the problems of creativity, or nature and evolution of things, as well as the essence of human morality. I suspect that Zhu Xi did not consider the *Yijing* in its own light, with the result that the principles of *li* and *qi* and their relationships fail to emerge with a coherent structure. On the contrary, Zhu Xi came to his commentary on the *Yijing* with predetermined concepts of *li* and *qi*, as the commentary was written in his forty-eighth year, by which age he was fairly deep into his academic career.[28]

The difficulties in Zhu Xi's philosophy with *li* and *qi* vanish as these concepts and their relationships are formulated and redefined in the light of the *Yijing*, which allows them to function as more adequate categories of existence and explanation in a system of metaphysics, epistemology, and theory of human nature. Only after this understanding is achieved may *li* and *qi* be used to further illuminate the philosophical profundity of the *Yijing*. I consider this undertaking to be both an exercise in hermeneutical analysis and an exercise in philosophical integration based on profound experience and profound thinking. Accordingly, it has a wide range of metaphysical significance, one which concerns the question of being and nonbeing and their relationships in philosophy in general and Chinese philosophy in particular.

Using the *Yijing* to Understand and Reconceptualize Notions of *Li* and *Qi*

How do the concepts *li* and *qi* prevail in the *Yijing*? As I indicated in the opening paragraph of the chapter, the *Yijing* has three main strata—symbolism, divinatory judgments, and philosophical commentaries—all developed in a sequence of historical time, under the guidance of its own internal logic of growth and development in time. Thus, the very development of the *Yijing* bespeaks of the profound significance of the unity of nature and humanity in the unity and growth of time. We can regard the symbolism as providing an inductive-empirical metaphysics consisting of a dynamic system of symbols that represent major interrelated events and phenomena of cosmological significance. The divinatory judgments (*tuanci* and *yaoci*) can be said to provide an evaluative metaphysics prescribing a sequence of decision-inducing, situation-describing, practical statements aimed at correct guidance of practical decisions and actions. This metaphysics is complicated and seldom correctly understood in rational terms. For this reason, it requires a separate consideration for its proper understanding. Here it suffices to point out that embodied in the dynamic system of *Yijing* symbolism is a system based on the inductive-empirical metaphysics. The metaphysics also presupposes a well-developed system of categories of evaluation for human well-being, as indicated in terms such as *ji* (good fortune), *xiong* (ill fortune), *hui* (resentment), *lin* (difficulty), *qiu* (blame), *li* (danger), and *yong* (benefit). Further, this metaphysics of divination grows out of the metaphysics of symbolism, just as the third type of metaphysics—namely, the explanatory metaphysics of the great integration embodied in the Commentaries—grows out of both. The explanatory metaphysics of the Commentaries, demonstrates that a profound observation and experiences of life naturally gives rise to an explanatory scheme based on profound reflections. Against this background, we shall see that *li* and *qi* are embodied in the dynamic system of symbolic trigrams and hexagrams, called the *gua*. The system's efficiency was tested in the practical metaphysics of divinatory judgments, but it finally emerged with conceptual and explanatory clarity in the *Ten Commentaries*. We shall discuss the meaning, content, and reference of *li* and *qi* on these three levels: symbolism, practical metaphysics, and explanatory metaphysics.

If we consider the formation of the eight trigrams closely, we discover that this system of symbolism satisfies the following conditions:

1. The system gives a descriptive representation of major processes and phenomena of the natural world. This representation is intended to be observationally complete, which is to say, complete as far as human observation of nature is concerned.

2. The system of symbolism demonstrates deductive reducibility to oneness and unity.

3. The system shows an unlimited creative generation and extension to differentiation and multiplicity.

4. The system maintains an internal interrelated structure among all its symbols.

5. The system exhibits relationships of complementarity, opposition, symmetry, reversion, order, and balance.

6. The system combines the concreteness of particularity with the abstractness of generality in both empirical and conceptual suggestiveness.

Satisfying the above conditions, which are discovered in analysis of the system itself, the system of symbolism that arose is the one most capable of representing and showing the fluid quality of change (*bian*), transformation (*hua*), and movement (*dong*) open to our observation and experience on a large scale. Indeed, the system is a highly ingenious way of representing and showing change, transformation, and motion in their totality and in their fundamental structure. Although the system is basically formal, it nevertheless produces a dynamic quality through the external, internal, inductive, and deductive relationships of its symbols.

The very extension of eight trigrams to sixty-four hexagrams indicates the potentiality of the dynamic order of change, transformation, and motion. The extension also indicates the degree of particularity of reality open to our experience, observation, and conceptual representation. In fact, there is no limit to this expansion as it has infinite possibilities. Thus, we can speak of levels or structures of being relative to degrees of differentiation and particularity. On the other hand, this system of symbolism could reduce and return into the single unity of oneness. Through the reduction to four forms (*si xiang*) and two norms (*liang yi*), the unified system might be identified with what the term *taiji* denotes. Although what we have explicitly formulated as adequate conditions of this system were not recognized at the time of the formation of this system itself, on close examination, these conditions and characteristics present themselves. For, if we examine the *Ten Commentaries* of the *Yijing* that constitute an explanatory metaphysics, we find that it is precisely these conditions and characteristics that are made clear and explicit by Confucius and his followers.

Although there is no actual deduction in the original system of eight trigrams, the following statements from *Xici* bear out the conditions and characteristics of the symbolism and certainly should not be regarded as arbitrary observations:

> Alternation of one *yin* and *yang* is called the *dao*. . . . The creative generation of creativity is called *Yi* (change) (*Xici Shang* 5).

> Consequently, the *Yi* has the *taiji*, which generates the two norms. The two norms produce the four phenomena. . . . The four phenomena produce eight trigrams (*Xici Shang* 11).

> The eight trigrams form a sequence wherein forms (of Nature) are found, thus they are thereby doubled and lines of movement (*yao*) are found within the double trigrams. (*Yao* is the imitation of the movement in the world.) (*Xici Xia* 1).

The ultimate justification of these conditions and characteristics, however, must be said to consist in the long-range, deep observation and experience of change in reality and change as reality. For, it is with such a long range and a totalistic context of time that these conditions and characteristics of change in reality and as reality are revealed. One might therefore speak of a "primordial and profound feeling and insight into change" (PPFIC), establishing itself as the most basic premise of *understanding* reality. This PPFIC is what leads to an effective representation of the symbolism. Thus, the symbolism should be regarded as providing conceptually abstract yet concretely suggestive descriptions that mirror reality based on PPFIC. Indeed, we may characterize the symbolism in a way conforming to change, so that the symbolism can be seen to embody and manifest the transformation and movement of change. This change (*Yi*) is a process of creativity, or creativity in process of transformation, that has the characteristics of creativity (*Yi*), constancy (*buyi*), and simplicity (*jianyi*), as suggested by the Han commentator on the *Yijing*, Zheng Kangcheng (127–200).[29] These three characteristics are found in the structure and dynamic quality of the system. As *Yi* is a unity and a source of creativity, it is referred to as *taiji* or *dao*. As *Yi* is a multitude and process, it is the activity of *yin* and *yang* and multifarious forms of ten thousand things. The dynamic quality and the quality of simplicity are exemplified in the oneness of this unity, multiplicity, source, and process. This is aptly expressed by Zhou Dunyi in the following statements: "Five powers are one *yinyang*; *yinyang* are one *taiji*; and *taiji* is originally *wuji*."[30] Here, the *wuji* can be said to refer to the constancy and simplicity of the *taiji*.

The substance of the dynamic quality represented in the symbolism can be labeled "*qi*," whereas the pattern and structure of the substance, which realizes the substance in its fullest development (change, transformation, movement), can be labeled "*li*." In other words, we can regard the two sets of qualities, which exist side by side in the symbolism, as the set of qualities such as change (*bian*), transformation (*hua*), and movement (*dong*), and the set of qualities such as patterns, forms (*xiang*), and order, as representing two aspects of the same unity, namely the whole and ultimate source of *change* (*Yi*). We may define *qi* as substance of the first set of qualities and the *li* as substance of the second set of qualities. These two substances are one, as these two sets of qualities are never separable. But, if change and its dynamics are more pertinent to the common understanding of *qi*, then the ultimate of change and the process of change are more aptly called *qi* or the transformation of *qi* (*qihua*). However, *qihua* does not separate itself from the forms so that *li*, as form, is an inherent quality of *qi* to be brought out in the process of change. The inseparability and unity of the two are clear in this system of symbolism. We may, therefore, conclude in light of the above that *qi* is *Yi* (or *hua*) and *li* is *xiang*, or more conservatively speaking *Yi* is *qi* and *xing* (physical form) is *li*. As such, *li* and *qi* and their relationship become clear from an understanding of the structure, function, and dynamic of the symbolism of *gua*.

The eight trigrams of the *gua* are used to represent the major forms and patterns of the natural world, when this world is already conceived through observation and experience as a well-ordered whole of interrelating and interacting forms. Thus Heaven ☰, Earth ☷, Thunder ☳, Wind ☴, Water ☵, Fire ☲, Mountain ☶, and Lake ☱ constitute the natural referents of the eight trigrams. But the eight trigrams do not just represent concrete natural events and forms; they also are principles and qualities of the natural processes and structures. In this regard, they are known as *Qian* (strong), *Kun* (soft), *Zhen* (movement), *Xun* (entering), *Kan* (falling in), *Li* (travel in pairs), *Gen* (stop), and *Dui* (joy). These are qualities that reflect the main experiences of change in reality and should be understood in reference to one another. Through these representations and references, not only do natural events and objects become interrelated, but the world of humans and the world of nature become interrelated as well.

In regards to the question of the relationship between *li* and *qi*, *qi* is precisely what constitutes the order and organizational patterns of the natural process of change, and *li* is the end product of the natural process of change. No *li* can be apart from *qi*; but in the case of *taiji*, *qi* may have *li* reduced to the simplest form of formlessness and indeterminacy. This is the form of creativity (*Yi*). Thus, *li* is thus only the internal structure and implicit pattern in the *qi* process; it cannot be the creative agent by itself as suggested by Zhu Xi.

As the above discussion indicates, when we come to the level of divinatory evaluation, we find that *li* and *qi* have reached a more differentiated and more comprehensive structure of meaning. The recognition of *li* and *qi* and their distinction can be said to consist in affirming the referential meaningfulness of the *gua* forms (the hexagrams) and their names, and at the same time establishing the evaluative judgments of caution, warning, and fortune relative to a given situation under the propitious conditions required by the divinatory ritual. Simply stated, this is the total situation of experience (presenting the events and things one encounters in one's life and career) and is thus the configuration of forms, which yet do not form an order or order themselves relative to the individual who divines. Thus, it is the life situation in the course of development and change that poses a problem for the individual. On the other hand, *li* is a deep understanding of the problematic life situation and an insight into the ways of meeting the situation so that a propitious order will ensue or chaos can be avoided. Again, *li* is not separate and separable from *qi*, but is generated from *qi* only when *qi* exists. In the evaluative judgments of divination, this is quite clear. The problematic configuration of a life situation itself evolves into a nonproblematic configuration by allowing change of a given life situation. However, the given situation gives rise to its reorientation and thus may be said to create or realize a resolution potential. *Li* is *qi*'s potential for rational satisfaction of order and novelty, which is thoroughly determined in the evolution and creation of a new situation.

In terms of the actual judgments of evaluation in divination, *li* can be said to be the natural forces that the situation suggests and the values that the situation induces; therefore, *li* can be said to be the reasons for the evaluation. *Qi*, on the other hand, is what produces the situation, the forms and values. In other words, *qi* is what enables a new situation in form or values to be produced and is the agency for change, transformation, and movement. Thus, *qi* is the underlying creative power of a situation that sustains or changes the situation and that gives humans free will and power of determination under given circumstances. Thus, given any *gua* and its judgment in the *Yijing*, we need to know what the *gua* represents or means to us, and why it is judged the way it is or why a course of action is advised or not advised. Generally, the Commentaries on the images of the *gua* (*Xiangzhuan*) render the implicit reasons, forms, issues, and courses of action explicit. For example, take *Li gua*, the images, name, and judgment of which are as follows:

> *Li* (fire, light, sun-moon as source of both): It will be an advantage to be firm and correct. [The situation and the right attitude] will bring success. Keeping cow (or cherish a cow-like docility) brings good fortune.[31]

Li is the *gua* obtained by the divining individual. But what is the meaning of this *gua*? What is the meaning of the judgment of this *gua* as it was given in the ancient practice? To understand its meaning is to understand its form, value, and rationale. But one cannot understand the *li* (principle) of these *gua* unless one also understands the particular situation one encounters and the forces that bring about this situation. Moreover, one must also understand the real possibilities for change and transformation or maintenance of the situation, whereby the course of action may become meaningful. To understand the constitutive background and particularity of the given situation and to understand the real possibility of change and the agency for such change is to understand the *qi* of the situation. Again, as the forms, values, and reasons for actions and their embodying situation are not separate and separable, *li* and *qi* are not separable. They are merely two aspects of the total situation involving an objective reference and a subjective relating of background context of causes and effects, and a moving tendency potential of agency and change within a range of possibilities. These two aspects may be referred to simply as form (*xiang*) and change (*hua*) or movement (*dong*), but form and change are one and are always one in the context of the evolving situation. As such, it is not conceivable that they are independent of each other. Further, it is not conceivable that the reality of life is separate and separable from real open situations of life.

Both *Commentaries* on *Judgment* and *Form* give the following elucidation and explanation of the *Li gua*. *Tuan* says: "*Li* means being attached to. The sun and moon have their place in the sky. All the grains, grass, and trees have their place on the earth. The double brightness (of the two trigrams) adheres to what is correct and the result is the transforming and perfecting of all under the sky."[32]

Xiang says: "The trigrams for brightness, repeated, forms *Li*. The great man, in accordance with this, cultivates more and more his brilliant (virtue) and diffuses its brightness over the four quarters (of the land)."[33]

The significance of the *Tuan* and *Xiang* statements on *Li* is that they explicitly elucidate the forms, values, and advisable courses of action, while they simultaneously justify the understanding of a situation as provided. They may be said to give the *li* of the situation, which is implicit in the situation until it is made explicit by the *Tuan* and *Xiang* statements.

Throughout the sixty-four *gua*, we find the same pattern of judging evaluation relative to a particular situation and the same *Tuan* and *Xiang* evaluations of the following structures:

Gua (symbol, name)

Gua Judgment

Tuan Judgment: explanation and justification of judgment

Xiang Judgment: elucidation of form and what a great or superior person does in accordance with it

The *li* of a *gua* is found not only in the explanation of meaning and justification of a judgment, but also in the elucidation of form and what a great or superior person does accordingly.

What should be specifically noted is that the elucidation of form in the *Xiang* statement is always couched in terms of the forms of nature, the original archetypes of human observation and experience of natural environment. This is significant for the following reasons. First, it shows that *li* can be said to have forms of nature and cannot be separate from the order, prehension (*gan*), and responsive (*yin*) relationships of natural manifestations of *qi* (or *qihua*). Second, it is important to note that the course of action in a judgment is actually explained and justified in accordance with the principle that a person should act in accordance with nature—*li* of human action is derived from *li* of natural movement. Consequently, *li*, in a fuller sense, is the accord and unity one achieves between humanity and nature. Therefore, *li* is the ideal form to be obtained by the power of human beings. This point is very important because we shall see that it provides a way of correcting and removing the Neo-Confucian view of the cultivation of persons by maintaining a strict control on their desires and temperaments, resulting from a biased understanding of *li-qi* relationships.

A close study and analysis of the sixty-four *gua* and their appended *Tuan* and *Xiang Commentaries* suffice to convince us that *li* is an inherent quality of *qi* and gradually takes shape in the evolution of natural or human situations, which is to say, a structural presentation of a situation in the light of human understanding. *Qi*, on the other hand, can be said to be the situational matrix from which *li* emerges: it is the context of change and the agency of configuration identified as the *Yi*. Not only can *li* not be separate from the *qi*, *li* is in fact a self-differentiation and self-transformation from the *qi*. In other words, order, pattern, form, and structure are not imposed from outside; instead, they are born inside the *qi*. Order and pattern are the end results of the organizing activity of *qi* and form and structure are the end result of the constituting activity of *qi*.

Using the *Yijing* to Avoid the Difficulties of Neo-Confucianism

When we recognize reason and principles in things and our planned conduct, it can be said that we only project our innate sense of order into things or follow the order emerging from a given evolving situation. There is no occasion that should lead us to even guess that *li* can be independent and autonomous or exist prior to *qi* and to all existing things. In other words, our examination and analysis show that *li* and *qi* always form a unity and whole, and their distinction consists in recognizing that *li* is an activity of *qi* and the end product of *qi* activity. That is, the activity of *qi* is naturally to order, organize, structure, and harmonize: hence, it is *li*. As *qi* is unlimited in its agency and power to change, any given form and order are steps and media for furthering a new order and form. The infinite creativity and agency for transformation are characteristics of *qi*. Its unity and differentiation into a rich order is good, just as creativity and change are good. These points are brought out only when we come to the philosophical commentaries of the *Xici* and *Shuoguazhuan*, which integrate the *li-qi* relationships and provide a coherent metaphysics of change, transformation and movement. The *Xici* and *Shuogua* leave no doubt that the ultimate and original substance of reality is nothing but the creative force of change (*Yi*), which manifests itself in the ordering and structuring activities of *yin* and *yang*.

Both *yin* and *yang* are the two primary states or two primary aspects (forms) of the *qi* creativity, and there is a wide empirical basis for their understanding. The *yin-yang* activity leads to other opposite and complementary forms of activities or attributes that are essential for the constitution, stratification, and differentiation of things in the world. *Yin-yang* activity is indeed a worldmaking (activity). But the very important understanding of the *qi* creativity is that no matter how great the differentiation and stratification of things in the world, the activities of *qi* form one unitary whole—it begins with a unity of formless creativity and ends with a unity of order and harmony. But the ending and the beginning also form a unity leading to more order and harmony with an underlying agency that allows for more change. This is shown by the following diagram:

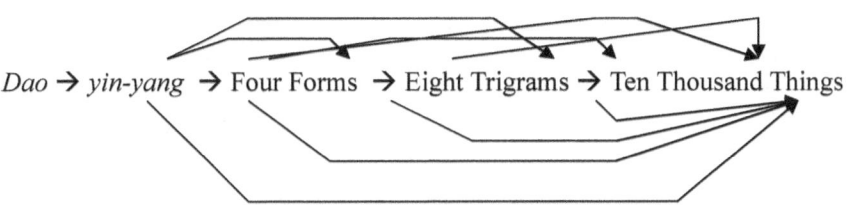

Dao → *yin-yang* → Four Forms → Eight Trigrams → Ten Thousand Things

The unity of yin and yang is called "dao" and "taiji" by the Xici. The following passage in the Xici gives a clear articulation of the qi creativity, which incorporates the activity of ordering the structuring which is the li. "The alternation of one yin and one yang is called dao. What succeeds is good. What accomplishes is nature . . . To generate the generating power is the Yi. To form forms is called Qian, and to follow and imitate is Kun." The Xici continues:

> Thus closing [the door] is called Kun; opening [the door] is called Qian. The alternation of one closing and one opening is called change. To pass from one into another without ending is called the course of things (qi). Therefore the Yi has the great ultimate which produces the two principles. These two principles produce the four forms, which then produce the eight trigrams.[34]

One might say that the alternation of yin and yang is the qi or the qi activity. The goodness and nature of qi creativity, which makes change and formation of things possible, may be called li. But in this regard li is simply the creative ordering power and activity of qi. The taiji is nothing but the qi, which in virtue of its own nature and of its own accord gives rise to differentiation of things. The very formation of the eight trigrams summarizes the process and capacity of the qi creativity. In the Shuogua, it is stated:

> In the ancient time when the sages made the Yi, it was with the design that its figures should be in conformity with the principles (li) underlying the nature and destinies of things and men; with this view they exhibited in themselves the way of heaven, called yin and yang, the way of earth, called the weak (soft) and the strong (or hard), and the way of men, under the names of benevolence and righteousness.[35]

Here again the Yi exhibits its qi creativity, which is described as the alternation of yin and yang, soft and hard, kindness and justice. Here, li, as a pattern or order of nature of things and humans, is mentioned; li is the order of heaven, earth and humans, and it is only to be seen and generated in the process of qi creativity.

The first paragraph of the *Shuogua* in fact describes how the sages come to understand the *li* of things and humans through the ordering activity of justice and virtue. It implicitly shows how humans should make an effort to understand *li* by following the ordering activity of *yin* and *yang*. It states:

> [The ancient sages contemplated the changes in the alternation and complementation of] *yin* and *yang* and thereby formed the eight trigrams. They developed [the principles of] strong and soft and thereby formed the lines of the trigrams. They harmonized things and men by following the *dao* (the way) and the *de* (virtue) and *put things in order* (*li*) by according with righteousness. Thus they *thoroughly understood the principles* (*qiong li*), fulfilled the nature of all things (*jin xing*) and reached the state of embodying the mandate [of Heaven] (*zhi yu ming*).

In this context, to thoroughly understand the *li* is to contemplate changes of *yin* and *yang* and to apply and develop the relationships of hard and soft. Further, such understanding requires that one harmonize things through the way and the virtue, which are norms for achieving unity and accord among things and persons; moreover, the harmonization serves as a norm for achieving community order. The end result and goal in this is clearly the fulfillment of nature and the embodiment of destiny in an individual. Therefore, by inference, *li* is nothing other than principles of changes of *yin* and *yang*, relationships of soft and hard in the objective world, and virtues such as love and righteousness in human conduct. There is nothing suggestive of its ontological status and independence, for it is an inherent order and ordering activity of *qi* embodied in *yin-yang*, soft-hard, and the harmonious relation between society and individual.Since Zhu Xi wished to interpret the *Yijing* with his *li-qi* distinction and metaphysical concept of *li*, he referred to *li* many times in an attempt to interpret or explain major, crucial passages in the *Great Appendix* (*Xici*). But very often he misleads readers into thinking that *li* and *qi* are two separate things. In interpreting the statement, "The alternation of one *yin* and one *yang* is called the *dao*," he says, "The alternating movement of *yin* and *yang* is *qi*. The principle (*li*) of this is the so-called *dao*."[36] This interpretation apparently separates the qi of the yin and yang from the li of dao. In fact, the alternation of yin and yang is the dao and hence is the li. As yin and yang are nothing but their alternation, the alternation of yin and yang is the creative activity of the qi.[37] Although there is a difference between qi as substance and its creative activity, the difference is one between subject and predicate, or between substance and attribute. Consequently, li does not have an independent metaphysical status, but is evolved and revealed only in the activities in the qi. The differences of things due to li in all things thus are actually unified in the primordial unity of qi.

In light of the Xici, we may indeed identify the Great Ultimate (taiji) as qi instead of as li. This was also borne out by earlier commentators on Zhouyi. For example, Zheng Xuan says, "Taiji is the fine harmonious undifferentiated qi."[38] Kong Yingda says, "Taiji refers to the undifferentiated oneness of the original qi before heaven and earth are distinguished. It is the original beginning and the original oneness."[39] Oddly, Zhu Xi ignored this fundamentally important recognition. The only explanation for Zhu Xi's dualism perhaps can be said to be that in his over-zealous effort to make a distinction between li and qi he loses sight of this ontologically primary reality of qi as the source of li. In other words, Zhu Xi fails to see the metaphysical and logical character of the distinction between qi and li. Metaphysically speaking, qi is the source and substance of creativity and li is the ordering and differentiating activities of the creative qi. Li is the way in which the creativity of qi is shown in concrete things. Logically speaking, qi is always the subject, and li is the predicate or attribute of qi. There is no subjectless li, as there is no attributeless qi. Throughout the Xici, it is clear that the change, which is qi creativity (or qihua), is constantly active and constantly productive of concrete things. Qi is thus the worldmaking process of energy, movement and the end product of such worldmaking process. Its creativity is shown in the cultivating of yin and yang, soft and hard, movement (dong) and rest (jing), shrinking and stretching (gui and sheng), and opening and closing (he and bi). As the creativity of Yi is constant and boundless, the produced world is under constant change and transformation and this leads to more differentiation and more concrete things. The Xici thus describes not only how the sages formed the gua, but how the sages prompted the beginnings of civilization, culture, and institutions for the benefit of humanity.

To summarize, we may identify qi with change, transformation, and movement. Further, we may also identify it with the life creativity (*shengsheng*) and all the things in the world in the process of change, transformation, and movement. On the other hand, we may identify *li* with all the specific forms of change, transformation, and movement. *Li* is ordering, differentiation, balancing, harmonizing, unifying, classifying, relating, and organizing activities of *qi*. In this sense, *qi* is aptly called by Zhang Zai *the* harmony (*tai he*).

Insofar as *qi* is the infinite source of change, rich differentiation and activities, it cannot be identified with any specific thing. Moreover, any specific thing does not have significance until it is located amongst other specifically formed things, which as a whole are the products of the creativity of *qi*. Since *qi* lacks specific forms, but is revealed only in the change, transformation, and movement of things, it is indeterminate and indeterminable. In this sense, Zhang Zai aptly calls *qi* the great void (*taixu*). If we can speak of *li* for *qi* in the state of *taixu*, we can say that *li* is the *li* that *qi* does not have a specific *li*, and it will remain in indeterminacy. We may call the *li* the indeterminate *li*, just as we can regard the *qi* as indeterminate *qi*.[40] In this sense, *qi* is only the movement (*dong*), never the form (*xiang*), and *li* as the product and specific movement can be contrasted relatively with the *qi*. In another sense, however, the ultimate *li* is the *li* that *qi* is never formed; in this sense, then, *qi* can be also called *wuji* (the ultimateless). Zhu Xi treats the term "*wuji*" as indicating the ultimate nature of the *taiji* beyond which nothing can be sought as opposed to existence of the infinite, but this is not the void in the Daoist sense.[41] Zhu Xi is philosophically right in this interpretation, although his own conception of *Taiji* as *li* is mistaken.

The *Yi* conception of the *taiji* is that *taiji* is the ultimate one source of change and the constancy of change itself. The *taiji* is not further limited by other attributes and is not produced from the void or the infinite. The *taiji* is the void and the infinite, but is at the same time the change, transformation, and movement. While Zhou Dunyi's statement "*Wuji er taiji*" can be given a simple interpretation by saying that being is born out of nonbeing in some sense, it nevertheless can be interpreted in such a way that it accords perfectly with the conceptions of *qi* and *li* developed from the *Yijing*. The statement indicates merely that *qi* is the indeterminate, formless source of change and order, and that it is because of this that it gives rise to all forms, things and specific activities. This is the highest and ultimate form of creativity: the *qi* creativity.

There is, finally, another matter we must mention in describing *qi* in light of the *Yijing Xici*. *Qi*, through its ordering activities, may produce all variety of things in order, yet it starts with the simple activities, the basic forms of activities such as differentiation and alternation of *yin* and *yang*, soft and hard, rest and movement: these are simplest in our observation, experience and conceptual understanding. The complexity, difference, and order of things arise through the constancy of the simplest activities. This is also an attribute of the creativity of the *qi*. In this light, we may call *qi* the ultimate simplicity (*taijian* or *taiyi*). This inherent simplicity and easiness of *qi* change can also be said to be the *li* of *qi*. When one sees things in terms of *qi*-change, one can see how things come to be and not to be in a natural order of simplicity and easiness. We can, therefore, also see that nothing cannot be understood in light of the activities of *qi*, namely the activities of *yin* and *yang*, hard and soft, rest and movement. Thus, the *Xici* says:

> The power of *Qian* (symbol for heaven) directs the beginning of things by way of its being easeful. The power of *Kun* (symbol for earth) fills its role (of completing things) by way of its being simple. Being easeful it is easy to know; being simple it is easy to follow. Being easy to know, it is easy for it to have close followers. Being easy to follow, achievements are ensured. Having close followers one can last long. Having achievements, one becomes great. Lasting long one attains the virtue of the sage. Being great one consummates the deeds of the sage. When one understands the easefulness (of *Qian*) and simplicity (of the *Kun*), (one understands) all the principles under heaven. When one understands all the principles under heaven, one achieves the right position amidst all things.

Here "the principles under heaven" (*tianxia zhi li*) are evidently premised on the attributes of easefulness and simplicity of the *Yi* or *qi* creativity in the alternation of *yin* and *yang*. They are evidently conceived to ensue in a harmonious integration of an individual within and with the *Yi* or *qi*-creative order of things.

In the above we have explicated the concepts of *li* and *qi* and their relationship in light of the symbolism, divination judgments and commentaries in the *Yijing*. I did more than a hermeneutical exercise on the meanings of *li* and *qi* as two fundamental categories, pertaining to the modes of being and nonbeing, for I have also called attention to the primordial experience of the ultimate reality in the notion of *qi* and its creativity from which *li* as pattern and ordering activities develop. It seems to me that the *Yijing* captures the primordial experience and perception of the ultimate reality and has successfully formulated it in its symbolism, applied it in its divinatory judgments, and explicated and systematized it in its commentaries. If Fuxi, King Wen, Duke Zhou, Confucius, and his immediate disciples are historically responsible for the development of the various strata of the *Yijing*, what they did was to live through the root perception and experience of *Yi* process and make an effort to illuminate these. The *Yijing* presents a unitary whole of the root insight into the reality that allows creative differences and evolution, and simultaneously provides a creative identity of all differences and evolutionary possibilities in the unity of *Yi*, *li*, and *qi* themselves. Time is the form of this *Yi* unity.

In the context of such an understanding, we can see immediately that the metaphysical dualism or dualistic tendency in Cheng Yi and Zhu Xi's metaphysical system has neither historical foundation in the *Yijing* nor theoretical basis by itself. As we see how *li* and *qi* should be conceived and related in the philosophy of the *Yijing*, the difficulties of Zhu Xi's ontological bifurcation disappear. The solution to such difficulties in the ontological status of *li* and its relation to *qi* in terms of logical and temporal priority is simply to redefine and re-conceptualize them so that there are no such difficulties. Our redefinition and re-conceptualization through a philosophical analysis of the *Yijing* makes it amply clear that *li* is only a property of *qi*, an end product of *qi* creativity, as well as an ordering activity manifesting the creativity of *qi*. There cannot be a bifurcation or separation between the two (*li* and *qi*) in any sense whatever.

The philosophical understanding of the *Yijing* makes possible an enlightened critique of Zhu Xi's anthropological metaphysics. The judgments and commentaries of the *Yijing* make amply clear that goodness and righteousness and other virtues come from understanding the change and creativity in nature of things, and from the consequent effort to cultivate a harmonious whole with heaven and earth and all things, embodying our understanding of *Yi* in our life and practice. The criterion for goodness and righteousness is found in people's relations with the total reality of order and harmony that results from the unity and reality of *qi* and *li*, and not simply from suppression of something conceived as irrational nature (*qizhi zhi xing*) at the expense of something conceived as rational nature (*yili shi xing*). The *qi* and *li* in a person are originally one. In order to cultivate the human person, this unity must be cultivated, which necessitates a proper appreciation of elements of *qizhi* (vital faculties) in one's human existence. Even a moral weakness of a person cannot be simply blamed on human desires, which are considered a form of *qi* creativity. The problem of evil and moral weakness is not a problem of human desires by themselves, but a problem of developing an integrated personality and intelligent and righteous mind in accord with the large universe and humanity at large.

The ultimate ground for goodness and moral strength comes from the effort of persons to see and embody the creativity and unity of *Yi* or unity of *li* and *qi* in the larger universe. Thus, the *Wenyanzhuan* says of the *Qian gua*:

> The great man is one who identifies himself with the virtue of heaven and earth, the brightness of sun and moon, with the orderly sequence of the four seasons, and the good and bad fortunes of the spirits (*guisheng*) [substances of *qi* in transformation associated with things in past and future]. He may precede heaven and heaven will not act in opposition to him, he may follow heaven but will act as timely as would heaven. If heaven will not act in opposition to him, how much less will men? How much less will the spirits?[42]

Toward Unifying Being and Nonbeing in Chinese Philosophy

Given the above reorientation of the *li-qi* philosophy in the context of the *Yijing*, what can be said about the problem of being and nonbeing in Chinese philosophy? Being and nonbeing, in the sense of "*you*" and "*wu*," respectively, in the Chinese language, are the most conspicuous considerations throughout the long history of Chinese philosophy. Being in the sense of "*you*" is things (*wu*) and affairs (*shi*) in the world; nonbeing in the sense of "*wu*" is simply the absence of things and affairs in the world. When there are things and affairs, they can be seen, heard, and felt; when there are no things and affairs then no specific things and affairs are seen, heard, and felt. Yet this does not mean that the world is nothingness or reality is not existent. A detailed analysis of common usage of the terms "*you*" and "*wu*" and idioms involving "*you*" and "*wu*" will reveal that to the Chinese mind, if we can use this general term at all, there are always concrete references for the terms "*you*" and "*wu*."

Philosophically speaking, the Chinese mind maintains an outstanding perception of the world that would include both being and nonbeing as concrete, experienceable states of the real. This perception and consequently the associated conception of the world and reality has two important characteristics: (1) The world and reality are not in any way opposed to the subject-mind of man as are opposed the objective and the subjective in modern Western philosophy. The sense of reality and the world is thus not determined by cognition alone nor confined to recognition of objects. The sense of reality and the world in its refined sense is the sense of the unitary and participatory interaction between humans and reality. In other words, the sense of reality and world includes the sense of human existence and a sense of human participation in the world and human efficacy in the transformation and consummation of things in the world. (2) *You* and *wu*, as two states of reality, are not independent of each other; in fact, they are relatively determined by each other; in other words, they are opposite, complementary and generative to each other in our understanding of happenings in the world. (See *Daodejing*, chapter 2, where Loazi speaks of the mutual generation of being / *you* and nonbeing / *wu*.)

These two points are no doubt based on the general perception that reality is a process of change, transformation, and movement that cannot be described as simply *you* or simply *wu*, but can be described only as the interpenetration and mutual dependence of *you* and *wu*, which is the highest grade of harmony, according to the discussion in chapter three. Not only are change, transformation, and movement seen as characterizing relations of *you* and *wu*, but the very experience of life generation and production of novelty and variation in the world also are seen as resulting from the intricate contrariety and differences, identity and complementarity, of *you* and *wu*. In this sense, being and nonbeing form a dynamic whole and unity which can be said to give rise to things in the world and which enables generation of life and novelty through change and transformation. Even time is understood as no more than a process of concreting of things and life, and cannot be conceived really independent of such.

Given these characteristics of the Chinese vision and perception of reality, it seems clear that reality in the Chinese experience is an experience and vision of creative unity exemplified in the unity and totality of life as an everlasting process of productive transformation. Reality for the Chinese experience is an open wholeness that begins with a pristine unity and harmony which it preserves and presents in the process or change and transformation. The experience of change and transformation is very deep and profound. In this experience: life, time, transformation, harmony, wholeness, unity, relativity, and humanity all become interfused and interwoven. The net result of such an experience is the philosophical vision of change or *Yi* presented and presupposed in the constant creativity of *dao*. *Dao* is being, but it also reveals the ultimate reality of a unity of being and nonbeing. For how do we know *Dao* or the Great Ultimate if we do not understand the world of things (*qi*)?

Against this background of understanding of being and nonbeing, the Chinese mind cannot accept a concept of absolute being, that is, the concept of being to the exclusion of nonbeing, nor a concept of absolute nonbeing, that is, the concept of nonbeing to the exclusion of being. Or to put it another way, the indigenous philosophical wisdom developed in the tradition of the *Yijing* cannot recognize the validity of the concept of being to the exclusion of nonbeing. The very experience of reality as change and creativity in Chinese philosophical phenomenology does not permit the evolution of such views and concepts. This explains why Chinese philosophy has, from the very start, rejected a *Hīnayāna* (*Theravāda*) approach by which reality is conceived as nothingness (Sanskrit: *śūnyatā*) or extinction (Sanskrit: *nirvāna*) in an absolute sense. Moreover, this explains why *Mahāyāna* Buddhism introduced from India into China eventually developed into forms of thinking that embody a metaphysics of unity of being and nonbeing as shown in the philosophical writings of Tian Tai, Huayan, and Chan.

Notably, the understanding and interpretation of being and nonbeing in Chinese Buddhism requires much philosophical sophistication, attention, and understanding of indigenous Chinese philosophy, such as the metaphysical wisdom of the *Yijing* and that of Daoism, a doctrine I shall briefly touch on later. I shall simply assert that "nothingness" (Chinese: *kong*; Sanskrit: *śūnyatā*) in Chinese Buddhism is a reality seen both as being and nonbeing, both as transformation of being into nonbeing and transformation of nonbeing into being. Logically speaking, nothingness is an open system of unobstructed and unlimited possibilities. The Chan Buddhist philosophy has particularly stressed this form of understanding reality and even developed techniques of cultivation for making this understanding possible. The state of self-realization, which incorporates this understanding, is known as enlightenment or illumination (*wu*). *Wu* is a state whereby the original unity and harmony of being and nonbeing are achieved and consequently the original sense of opposition, and yet complementarity, between object and subject is achieved.

In light of this understanding, perhaps a Chan master would not only reject attachment to being, to nonbeing, to being of nonbeing, to nonbeing of being, to nonbeing of nonbeing, but also would reject the rejection of such rejection. The world or reality will appear as it is, yet what a richness and what an emptiness of the appearing reality! We also might suggest that the difference between the indigenous Chinese view of unity of being and nonbeing and the Chinese Buddhist view is a matter of styles of experience. The Chan Buddhist philosophy requires validity of immediate perception and immediate understanding. The *Yijing* on the other hand would require a more thoroughgoing process of absorption, mediation, and participation. The former is more perceptually oriented, whereas the latter is more life action oriented. Metaphysically speaking, the former seems to stress the "form of completion" (*jiji*); the latter seems to stress the "state of incompletion" (*weiji*) in the *Yijing*. *You* and *wu* and their relationship cannot be understood without understanding these basic experiences and cannot be explained apart from the context of these experiences. In fact, one might say that *you* and *wu* emerge from these background experiences and assimilate these experiences as their quintessence. One might thus say that *you* and *wu* are two states of reality, which as a whole and through their interactions preserve and present the whole reality as harmony, change, transformation, and life generation. To be brief, *you* and *wu* can be regarded as two forms of creativity, which is the essence of reality in Chinese experience and philosophy.

With this discussion as a background, one can see that the *Yijing* has developed and presented the view that reality is the interchange of *you* and *wu*, and it always preserves the whole on the one hand and always produces life and novelty on the other. As the whole reality is *taiji*, *you* and *wu* in their relative positioning and movement are *yin-yang* forces or states of the *taiji*. As a process, reality is the change (*Yi*) or transformation (*hua*) itself, which is described as creative creativity (*shengsheng*). As we have shown, *taiji* is *qi*, not *li*, and change is the transformation of *qi*. *Li* thus can be said to be relations and structures inherent in the creativity of *qi* and manifestation of such creativity in concreteness.

In light of this interpretation, *you* is the creative movement of *qi*, and *wu* is the unlimited source energy of *qi*. *You* also is the product of pattern and order (*li*) in the world; *wu* is the continuing transformation for production of pattern and order. Perhaps for simplicity we can explain *wu* in terms of the indeterminate *qi* and *you* as the determinate form of *li*. But in making this interpretation we must be aware that the sense of reality in the sense of *taiji* is one that is not limited to this relative contrast of *qi* and *li* or *wu* and *you*. In the ultimate wholeness, unity and harmony, creativity, *qi* and *li* are one, and cannot be confined to a specific process or specific product. In this sense, the *Yijing* states that the "Subtleties of change have no limit and the change (or creativity) has no substance" (*shen wu fang, Yi wu ti*).[43] Further, in this sense, one can also understand the statement of Zhou Dunyi: "The ultimateless and yet the great ultimate" (*wuji er taiji*), which means the following: Creativity cannot but be creative; it must arise from the *wuji*, yet it is not to be exhausted by the process of transformation. The first statement points to the fact that the concrete world of things manifests the infinite source of creativity, or that *you* manifests the *wu*, the delimitation of *you*:

wu ← you

The second statement points to the fact that the unlimited reality of creativity manifests, cannot but manifest, a process of change and production of life—or that *wu* manifests *you*, the determination of *wu*:

wu → you

To understand that *you* and *wu*, or *wu* and *you*, are one and yet are not one, and yet are oneness of their identity and difference is the only correct way of understanding what reality is.

The *Xici* also says, "What is above forms is called the *dao*, what is within forms is called *qi* (vessel)." *Dao* is the limitless and substanceless creativity of *Yi* or the indeterminate energy of *qi*, whereas the world as we see it everyday is the manifestation and product the form of incompletion (*weiji*).[44] Thus the former presents the completed product of understanding; the latter presents the incompletable process of creativity, which is the core idea of the *Yijing* as we have seen, and from which involvement with society and humanity is possible. One also may say that the *Yijing* view is more cosmological than ontological, and that the Chinese Buddhist view is more ontological than cosmological.

In light of the *Yijing* tradition, it also is clear that reality, in the absolute sense, which is developed in Greek philosophy, Christianity, and modern European philosophy, be it rationalist or empiricist or be it metaphysical or scientific, is not acceptable. The absolute view of reality involves a search for reality behind a surface of common sense, a veil of change and appearance, or a layer of variegated differentiation. Parmenides developed the notion of the immutable being that is devoid of any motion and sensation, and that can be approached only through contemplation of thought. This Parmenidean being is a good example of the absolute being in Western philosophy, which also is exemplified, in various degrees, in Plato's world of ideas; Aristotle's notion of the unmoved mover, or matterless form; the Christian theological notion of godhead; the Cartesian-Spinozan-Leibnizian view of substance; or the Hegelian notion of absolute spirit—all of which are part of the classical physical philosophy of matter, space, and time.[45] Even the most Eastern-minded Heidegger does not fully appropriate the rich creative dialectics of the interpenetration of being and nonbeing and their co-creativity as the basis for understanding being and nonbeing.

To return to the concepts of *li* and *qi* as fundamental categories of being and nonbeing, we may mention that some of the Neo-Confucian philosophers do have adequate understanding of the relation of being and nonbeing, in terms of their understanding of the *Yijing* and in reference to *qi*. One passage from Zhang Zai is specifically significant: "To know that the void (*xu kong*) is *qi*, then one knows that the phenomena of *you* and *wu*, hidden and manifest, subtle transformations of human nature and destiny, the penetration into oneness without bifurcation are the condensation, dispersion, and outgoing and incoming, the forming and de-forming of *qi*. If one is to be able to infer where these phenomena come from, one must deeply understand the philosophy of the *Yijing*."[46]

Zhang Zai's insight into the nature of *qi* is also an insight into the relation of being and nonbeing and an insight into the philosophy of creative change in the *Yijing* as we have already explained. What is interesting to note is that in his effort to reject an absolute notion of nonbeing or nothingness, he rejects not only the Buddhist ontologization of nonbeing but the apparent thesis of Daoists: "The being (*you*) is born out of nonbeing (*wu*)" ("*You sheng yu wu*").[47] However if we realize that in the best form and in the deepest sense the Buddhist and the Daoist also may reject the view attributed to them or held by their followers,

Zhang Zai might be construed as showing to what extent the Buddhist and the Daoist might be misunderstood and to what an extent the correct vision of reality incorporating the unity of being and nonbeing and their transformability should be maintained.

Mingdao says: "Within heaven and earth there is merely a *gan* (feeling) and *ying* (response), what other things are there?"⁴⁸ Yichuan says: "There is no inception of movement and rest; there is no beginning of *yin* and *yang*. If not the one who knows the *dao*, who else can see this?"⁴⁹ Mingdao also says: "The beginningless and expansive *dao* has no beginnings of anything, yet the ten thousand things are already complete within it. Not yet responding to it is not something prior to it; responding to it is not something posterior to it."⁵⁰ These statements also suffice to testify to the insightful view of being and nonbeing and their unity in light of the philosophical tradition of the *Yijing* as we have expounded.

Finally, the metaphysical view of being and nonbeing in the Daoist philosophy of Laozi remains to be illuminated. Again, as I do not have space for a full discussion of the Daoist metaphysics, I shall confine myself to some salient points on the Daoist view of being and nonbeing as revealed in the text of the *Daodejing*. In the first place, I wish to stress that the view that Laozi considers *dao* as simply nonbeing or void and the view that for Laozi and also for Zhuangzi being is generated from the nonbeing or void are both mistaken. *Dao* cannot be identified simply with nonbeing, nor being made a matter of derivation from nonbeing. A close reading of *Daodejing* will reveal that *dao* comprehends both being and nonbeing, and that *wu* (void) and *you* (being) are both derived from the uncategorizable *dao*, even though they have different names, or for that matter, possess different functions in relation to each other and in relation to nature and man. To understand this is to understand the profoundest nature of *dao*. The second chapter of the *Daodejing* says explicitly: "Therefore *you* and *wu* mutually generate each other, the difficult and the easy mutually accomplish each other, the long and the short mutually form each other, the high and the low mutually slope each other; sounds and tones mutually harmonize each other, and before and after mutually follow each other."⁵¹

The metaphysical point here is clear: *you* and *wu* give rise to each other in the unity of *dao* that comprehends both and yet remains unlimited by either. *Dao* permits creative transformation of being into nonbeing and vice versa, and permits an endless and effortless transformation of such. This feature of *dao* as the creative source of all is manifested in statements of chapter 4:

Dao is invisible yet its function and usefulness are infinite. It is so deep that it looks like the ancestor of the ten thousand things. It does not show its sharp edge, and yet resolves all entanglements of things; it is soaked with light and fused with dust. It is so pure that it seems to vanish yet it exists: I do not know its origin but only that it appears before any source!

Chapter 5: "Void and yet not exhausted, the more it moves the more it gives." Chapter 6: "The spirit of the valley does not die; this is called the Profound Female. The Profound Female is the root of heaven and earth. It lasts everlastingly and its functioning is inexhaustible." Chapter 7: "Heaven and earth are long living. The reason why heaven and earth are long living is that they do not exist for themselves; thus they can last long." All these chapters seem to suggest that *dao* as the ultimate reality is not simply *wu* nor simply the source of *you*, but is a state of unity of both and the transformation of both. Chapter 16, chapter 21, and chapter 25 also indicate how this ultimate reality of *dao* is to be understood or seen, and it was referred to in fact as *huanghu* (the Chaos) or the great (*da*), the passing (*shi*), the distant (*yuan*), the reversion (*fan*). This only shows that *dao* could be understood beyond the simple categories of being and nonbeing and defies description in conventional language of being and nonbeing.

Although in chapter 40 it is said that "All things under heaven are born from *you* and *you* from *wu*," and in chapter 42 it is said that "*dao* gives birth to oneness, oneness to twoness, twoness to threeness, and threeness to the ten thousand things," the principal point of the author of the *Daodejing* in making these statements is still that *you* and *wu*, *dao* and the ten thousand things are a unity and whole. The *wu*, in particular, being part of the *dao*, though it gives birth to *you*, is no doubt simultaneously given birth to by the *you*, for the ultimate principle of the *dao* is that "The *dao* always does nothing so that everything is done" (chapter 37). The very nature of *dao* makes all things, *you* and *wu*, come of its own accord ("The ten thousand things are to be self-transformed," chapter 37) and come all together and go all together. ("The ten thousand things arise all together, I thus contemplate their return," chapter 16.)

In view of this understanding of the Daoist view of the *dao* as the ultimate reality, it is not too difficult to conclude that the Daoist view of being and nonbeing essentially supports and reinforces the view of change (*Yi*) and transformation (*hua*) in the philosophy of the *Yijing*.

CHAPTER 10

On the *Yijing* as a Symbolic System of Integrated Communication

Introduction: Content and Goal of Communication

Communication is a common experience of daily life and a social necessity for humans. Although it has been described on many levels of social organization and relative to different purposes, its content and ideal goal does not seem to be sufficiently specified, particularly when its content and goal are seen as related to each other. What I intend here perhaps can be conveyed by raising two critical questions concerning communication. First, what sort of thing is communicated when communication takes place between people or between groups of people? Second, what difference does it make to people as agents of communication? If we can answer these two questions with some degree of adequacy, we will be clearer about the nature of communication and will, therefore, make better use of communication.

An obvious answer to the first question is that *all* sorts of things can be communicated between people or between groups of people, including ideas, concepts, facts, values, norms, knowledge, feelings, and so on. All of these can be important contents of communication. To communicate these is to exchange them between persons or transfer them from a person who possesses them in some sense to another person who did not possess them. Communication, therefore, can be regarded as a learning process, a process of proposing, asserting, denying, and persuading, or a process of settling an issue.

According to J. L. Austin's insight into the use of language, language can be constative or performative.[1] This means that use of language can be a statement of fact or constitute a speech act accomplishing a task other than statement. In this regard, we can see language use as a speech act capable of having many functions including stating, commanding, agreeing, and so forth. Thus, the speech act can be seen as having three aspects: namely, using the language form, intending to do a task, and doing the nonlinguistic task. Hence communication, like the use of language, but not simply like the use of language, can be said to have three corresponding functions or forces: namely, an illocutionary (or nonsymbolic) function/force, a perlocutionary (or per-symbolic) function/force, as well as a locutionary (or symbolic) function/force. The illocutionary function/force is the *direct* meaning impact on the hearer (or recipient of communication), the perlocutionary function/force is the resulting state of mind of the hearer, and the locutionary function/force is the surface meaning of the *communication* medium. Using this Austinian analysis of communication enables us to see that communication presupposes, for all its success, that for any individual in any social context, agents of communication must be able to appraise and understand what is intended to be communicated and what is not. Further, the agent also must be able to appraise and understand what difference communication makes or fails to make. The theory further presupposes that the agents of communication are cognitively sound in that they are capable of distinguishing between the content and goal of communication and between success and failure of communication of a content for a given goal.

Three Types of Communication

At this point, we may distinguish three types of communication. The distinctions concern how much organization of the content of communication is involved, as well as how much participation and understanding the agents of communication have achieved from receiving the communication.

The first type of communication is communication whereby facts are communicated and the recipient of the communicated message becomes impressed by or informed of the communicated facts. Here, I mean by "fact" anything that is commonly accepted as fact in a normal community under average circumstances. Facts are, on the one hand, distinguished from concepts or abstract knowledge and, on the other hand, from norms or values. Although "fact" is a complex concept, which is subject to philosophical analysis, one preeminent feature of a "fact" in common sense is that anything is a fact if it is considered a part of the real objective world and the listener does not question its credibility as such. Several criteria of *factuality* of a fact can be suggested: (1) a fact is objective; (2) a fact is easily recognizable as objective; (3) the credibility of a fact consists of producing objective evidence, which leads to recognition of the fact. In communication, facts are to be reported, recorded, and broadcast or transmitted as items of information. Thus, people or a person can be informed of facts as a result of the communication of facts.

The informational or factual mode and pattern of communication corresponds accordingly to the *communication of facts*. Such a pattern is an objective mode of communication with stress on objectivity, uniformity, and consensus of community. We might suggest that when anything is communicated as an item of information, it *becomes* a fact. The mode of communication in terms of information defines the nature of the content of the communication; it defines how the content of communication is to be taken or received by the recipient—just as the content of the communication as appraised by the community sets the way or the mode in which the content of communication is to be accepted or taken by the recipient of the communication. This leads to the conclusion that *fact* and the informational mode of communication are mutually definitive of each other. The paradigm for this mode of communication is that "I am informed of the fact that 'p,' where 'p' is any description of a fact or anything intended as a *fact*." The informational mode of communication, being so entrenched in human experience, is a common and basic mode of communication.

When communication is in the informational mode, the item that is communicated is always self-explanatory and meaning-complete by itself; that is, it needs no other items to establish its communicability. This means that a fact is by nature self-explanatory and complete in meaning by itself.[2] Contrary to facts, concepts are neither self-explanatory nor complete in meaning by themselves. Instead, a concept requires other concepts to complete or complement its meaning, and therefore takes form with other concepts. A system of concepts, when applied to what is understood as reality or facts, becomes knowledge. As to how and under what circumstances concepts apply need not concern us here for our understanding of concepts, what is important is that concepts can be regarded as a deeper, more general, more enduring, and more objective description of reality. In this sense, concepts form a system of knowledge or a corpus of knowledge and thus represent a more organized view of facts. Further, concepts as objects of communication can be linked to or rooted in our *intentions* or *beliefs*, and therefore can be basic for action and become a richer source of meaning than items of information or isolated facts.

In light of the above characterization of concepts, we come to the second mode of communication: the conceptual or systematic mode of communication. The content in this mode of communication is concepts that either explicitly or implicitly form a unity and an interdependence. Even when one single concept is actually communicated, other concepts will ensue by presupposition or by implication if communication is to achieve success. The goal of communication in this mode is to be expressed by the paradigm, "I know that such and such is the case and I know why." Note that in this conceptual mode of communication the recipient is not only informed of a fact that is linked to a proposition, but is aware of reasons that amplify the meaning of the fact or a proposition expressing the fact. The individual has learned something beyond the merely factual. Take, for example, a news item. In this case, the individual is enlightened about the nature of reality in a situation. The person has come to know a truth or to possess some knowledge. The person is not merely informed; rather, he or she is *instructed*. Communication has educated, enriched, and enlightened this individual, for communication brings knowledge, not just information.

Finally, we come to the third mode of communication, which leads to understanding between persons. This is the hermeneutical or integrative mode of communication, the content of which I shall call values. The term "values" is specifically chosen here to mark a distinction between concepts that fuse with the deep experiences and feelings of an individual and the concepts that are independent of the subjective standpoint of the individual. I will call those concepts that fuse with deep experience and feelings of an individual, "values." Values, therefore, are concepts that guide an individual's choice, mold an individual's life and conduct, and determine the action and direction of an individual. This implies that values are practically motivated principles, but this does not imply that values are simply practical beliefs. On the contrary, they are basic categorical concepts which define the ontological metaphysical outlook or orientation of an individual.

When I describe values as feeling-fused concepts or action-directed concepts, I wish to underscore their conceptual nature—their ability to apply to reality. In this sense, they are ontological in intent but they are, at the same time, entrenched or ingrained in the subjective belief-system of the individual as a whole. They are integrated with the subject and become part of the individual. That is why they are fused with experiences and feelings, which are the ingredients of the individual's subjectivity that is involved in the communication process. In contrast, concepts independent of the individual subjectivity are capable of objective representation or being rooted in objective reality, and in this sense, they are more akin to facts than to values.

For convenience, we would call concepts in the conceptual mode of communication objective concepts and call values subjective concepts. Now it can be noted that whereas objective concepts are a matter of knowledge *via* communication, because they can impress themselves into the rational understanding of persons, values or subjective concepts are not a matter of knowledge. Instead, they are a matter of deep, whole, and integrative understanding, which integrates the objective with the subjective, the rational (cognitive) with the volitional in a person. The process of communication that yields this deep-whole integrative understanding is, therefore, called the integrative mode of communication. The primary paradigm for such a mode of communication is, "I understand." What I understand is values, not simply concepts or facts. Here I intend the term "understanding" to be more than *being informed of facts*, and *acquiring knowledge*, but to mean organizing *oneself* and transforming *oneself* in terms of values. But, values become values through a process of communication sometimes intended, sometimes unintended, for this *becoming*. Hence, the communication of values is an autonomous genre or type of communication in deference to the first two types of communication. In this mode of communication, the recipient *understands* things in virtue of the communication. What he *understands* are values for him; therefore, this understanding is not any ordinary form of understanding but is an understanding that generates values, for it is an understanding that transforms individual beliefs and sets standards for behaving. One also may describe *understanding* as a creative source of meanings in the process of communication. In fact, when the process of communication is intended to generate meanings that an individual understands and therefore acts in accord with, that process of communication stands alone as a significant way of defining values or understanding values.

Meanings here are used to designate something more than facts and concepts or objects: they are intended to be frame-setting or worldmaking perspectives or views. But how can they set frames and make worldviews if they are not derived from an integration of concepts with ingrained beliefs and views of an individual? We may even say that meanings are ingrained views or beliefs occasioned to arise by a surface symbol used in a communication process: they are ingrained views or beliefs that are now symbolically linked to a situation and a system of concepts. Hence, we may simply assert that understanding is the source of meanings. Communication that yields understanding, and hence understanding of meanings, is indeed a subtle process of its own, which can be characterized by two aspects. In one aspect, understanding integrates concepts with objective reality so that they have a truth-content. In another aspect, understanding integrates with personal subjectivity (assertiveness and beliefs or perspective) so that it becomes a basis for action, choice, and incorporating a form of life. Hence, we may characterize this process of communication as both integrative and hermeneutical. Understanding, then, is a process that interprets the objective to the subjective and organizes the objective in view of the subjective.

To sum up, the three types of communication we have described above suggest three definitions of communication. The informational mode of communication defines communication as presentation of facts. The conceptual mode of communication defines communication as transmission of knowledge, and the hermeneutical mode of communication defines communication as establishment of understanding. As knowledge presupposes facts and understanding presupposes knowledge, communication can be said to involve many levels. As such, the three types or modes of communication are indeed three levels of communication. Presentation of facts is the rudimentary level of communication not because it is involved in the common information exchange, but because it is intended as purely objective, devoid of any interpretation or evaluation from a communicating individual. Transmission of knowledge is the next higher level of communication because it requires interpretation and organization of facts into a systematic meaningful whole, which nevertheless applies to the objective, and therefore depends on the objective as a validating principle.

Understanding in the sense of integrating one's belief and values, finally, represents the most complex level that presupposes the first two levels as a basis. For the purpose of understanding communication, presentation or acceptance of facts is not enough, nor is a scientific investigation that results in systematic knowledge, for neither can bring forth a sense of subjective relevance that revolutionizes and transforms one's views and *perspectives* as well as determines one's action and beliefs. For a rational person, the first two levels—knowing facts and knowing their why—are necessary for a genuine understanding, an understanding that defines one's own identity and one's own form of *life* (to use a Wittgensteinian expression). For it is only on the basis of the first two levels that one may fully *link* the subjective to the objective and integrate the objective into the subjective so that one can behave uniquely in one's unique circumstances of life, find one's place in the scheme of things, and see meanings of things in a uniquely significant way.

With the above theory of the levels of communication, we may now come to see how the tradition-honored, age-old book of the *Yijing* functions as a rich source of understanding, and consequently as an enduring mode of communication that gives rise to meanings and values. We shall explain why the *Yijing* is so appealing on the basis of its communicative nature, which combines the three types of communication outlined above. The *Yijing* provides a basis for integrating facts, concepts, and values into three levels of communication, and, therefore, provides a basis for producing understanding *par excellence*, which is vitally essential for the development of the individual mind. We shall see that the reason the *Yijing* is capable of doing this is that it is symbolically structured and metaphysically organized in such a way that presentation of facts, transfer of knowledge, and transformation through understanding become possible. In this sense, we can speak of the *Yijing* as a symbolic system of communication and understanding.

Three Subsystems of the *Yijing*: Forms, Judgments, and Numbers

The *Yijing*, as traditionally conceived, is composed of two parts: the original text of forms (*xiang*) and judgments (*ci*), which date back to the antiquity of twelfth century BCE, and the Confucian *Ten Commentaries* or *Ten Wings* (*Shiyi*), which were written in the third or fourth century BCE. The *Ten Commentaries* is an attempt to philosophize about the original texts of *xiang* and *ci*. About this philosophizing there have been two views. First, there is the view that the philosophy of the *Yijing* developed in the *Ten Commentaries* is independent of text as the latter is intended only for practical use in divination. Second, there is the view that this philosophizing is an explicit manifestation of the implicit metaphysics in the original text. I agree with the latter view, for as we shall see, the neatness of the symbolic structure of the original texts requires or presupposes a profound, albeit unformulated, understanding of reality and life in order that it can be used for a divinatory purpose. Taking this position will enable us to utilize insights and illustrations from the *Ten Commentaries* for the understanding of the *Yijing* system as a system of integrated communication that is conducive to a hermeneutical mode of understanding. In the following I shall explain and explore the *Yijing* system in light of both the original texts of forms and judgments and the philosophizing of the *Ten Commentaries*.

On closer investigation, the *Yijing* system may be said to be comprised of three subsystems: the subsystem of forms, the subsystem of meanings, and the subsystem of numbers. To distinguish forms and numbers from meanings is not to say that forms and numbers do not have meanings. They do have meanings, but their meanings are not explicitly specified in words or judgments; therefore, they are distinct and separate from the system of meanings, which come from judgments on the forms. The subsystem of meanings is the system of judgments that formulate meanings from observations on the forms and numbers in the *Yijing*.

The distinction between the subsystems of forms and that of numbers also needs an explanation. The presence of numbers in the *Yijing* original texts is not conspicuous, yet numbers are very much involved in the formation and transformation of the forms (trigrams and hexagrams), in the determination of the nature of lines in a form (*gua*), in the divinatory process of applying the *Yijing*, and in particular in the interpretation of the relations of the *gua* in the *Luo Diagram* (*Luoshu*) and the *River Chart* (*Hetu*) from which some meanings of the eight hexagrams are supposedly derived. Insofar as numbers are an integral part of the whole *Yijing* system and play a dominating role in generating meanings, we have to recognize numbers as subsystems of the *Yijing*.

The importance of the recognition of the three subsystems in the *Yijing* is not that each is independent of the other two, but that all three are interdependent and form a creative unity which generates meanings and support for each other. As we shall see, the three subsystems are basic systems of interpretation, which impart meanings to individual phenomena and inspire personal actions once they are internalized in a person as a system of understanding. They enable a person to see things in a certain perspective and therefore generate meanings for a certain thing. In this sense, they can be considered the matrix of meaning. If we examine how this meaning is generated, we shall see that the system functions both as an identifier or indicator, that is, as a device that can identify or indicate an object or situation with regard to its nature, and as a background or context against which a meaning will emerge with regard to a given object.

That each system has this potency of meaning generation is due to two important features of the system:

1. The system is a closely developed network of interrelating position-forces or place-forces, which will generate meanings through the relationships among themselves: relationships such as balance, symmetry, polarity, opposition, and conjunction. The reason I use the term "position-force" is that each form, number, or judgment (decision) can be analyzed into both a static structure and a dynamic process. The static structure is determined by the position/place it occupies in the system, and the dynamic process is determined by the power and direction of movement in the system. The whole system thereby becomes a structure of related positions and a field of moving forces. By virtue of its internal contextualization of meaning, the system is a highly sensitized inter-textual matrix of meaning in its application all by itself.

2. Each system is closely linked to experience and highly disposed to apply to experience. This applicability or adaptability to experience is due to its arising from broad syntheses of experiences and its capturing experiences in a paradigmatic way. For the *ci* (judgment) system, each *ci* actually records an experience that is subject to many interpretations. The numbers in the number system also have experiential meaning as one may witness in, for example, pairs of animals, or quintets of fingers. The forms (trigrams and hexagrams) no doubt to some extent symbolize or even iconize actual objects and are ascribed meanings from direct observations of the world.

312   The Primary Way

The principle of the ready applicability of the system as explained in (2) above is presentation of concrete episodes and situations that are always subject to interpretation and reinterpretation. When this principle is combined with the principle of *a priori*, determinate interrelationships of position-forces, which is abstract and universal in nature, as enunciated in (1), there is naturally generated meaning for the applied instance of interpretation.

To further explain these two important principles, we may formulate the mechanics of meaning generation in terms of the following basic ingredients: (a) the form system; (b) the number system; (c) the judgment (meaning) system; (d) a given form; (e) a given number; (f) a given meaning (or description). Any object x could have a form, a number, and a description, either from experience, convention, or from the form system, the number system and the judgment system functioning as identifiers. Then the meaning of x is generated by respective considerations of:

(a) + (d)
(b) + (e)
(c) + (f).

Or the meaning of x is generated by the combination of these:

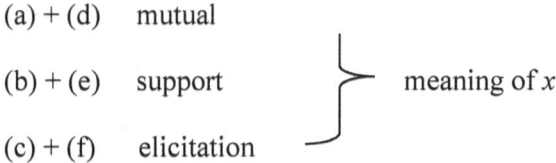

How do we understand the contents of the three subsystems as described? The form system (or the subsystem of forms) is made of forms that are either made of three or six lines (broken or solid): the trigrams and hexagrams, respectively. These forms form a well-knit relationship that makes structuring of places or moving of forces possible. The judgment system is composed of explicit statements of meanings of the forms, in this sense, it is composed of naming, describing and evaluating the forms coupled with the achieved imagery and meaning of forms, where potent meanings are pregnant. They attach to historical occasions of divination and embody practical solutions or admonitions for action and life, and therefore can be said to form an autonomous body of ideas or thoughts already linked to experience and readily applicable to future and possible experiences.

Finally, the number system is formed of numbers ranging from 1 to 10, their sums, and products. Each integer has a meaning from the primary model of experiences of *yin* and *yang*, as well as some sum and product of them. For example, 6, 7, 8, 9 acquires specific meaning in terms of the generation of the *yin-yang* forces or positions/forces. Because of a very old legend of the *River Chart* (*Hetu*) and *Luo Diagram*, numbers are given even deeper cosmological or onto-cosmological meanings and have been interpreted as the basis for generating the other two systems.

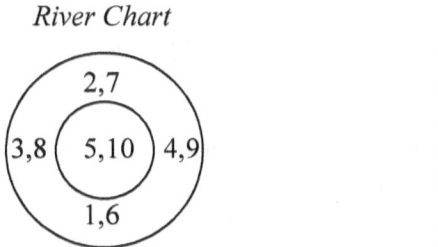

For a deeper and thorough understanding of the three systems we should see these three systems as interrelated and interpenetrating, and in principle as capable of mutual generation and mutual support. But in order to appreciate the very origin-source of meaning generation and understanding, we should see them as originating from a base-structure proto-ontology, which defines and produces both the symbolism and the primal meaning of the symbolism in form, number, and judgment. This is the foundation of the *Yijing* thinking and the source of understanding, which creates a system of meaning generation and a system of understanding.

Change and Generative Onto-Cosmology and Dialectical Methodology of the *Yijing*

The proto-model and base of the three subsystems of the *Yijing* is the generative ontology of the *Changes* (*Yi*). The notion of changes (*Yi*) is the ultimate notion in the *Yijing*; it summarizes a fundamental experience of the reality, a primal vision of the world and a direct perception of the creative force in the making and change of things. "Changes" refers to actual becoming (*bianyi*) of things, the constancy of change and principles of change (*buyi*), and the simplicity (*Qianyi*) all at the same time. "Changes," therefore, describes some primordial experience of change, which is simple and which embodies the constant principles of change. This experience is considered the ultimate experience of reality and as revealing the true nature of the world in terms of which all things and processes in the world can be explained and understood. The reality is constantly changing according to simple and constant principles. But these principles are not deterministic. They are realized and implicit in the processes of change and are not separable from processes of change. This means that the constancy of principles of change is not separate from the change. To say this is to say that changes are not chaotic, but can be cognized by reason, which implies again that rationality and creativity can go together. The onto-logical-cosmological experience of reality in the *Yijing* combines rationality and creativity in a simple primordial unity. Truth and understanding are derived from a sense of this unity and application of this sense to all things.

On the basis of this simple unity of rationality and creativity, the fundamental onto-cosmological conception of reality as the *taiji* (The Great Ultimate) of the unity of the *yin-yang* polarity becomes possible and significant. According to this conception, the world is conceived as an interpenetration of two opposite forces: *yin* or the receptive (female) force and *yang* or the creative (male) force. Change is produced by movement from *yin* to *yang* and *yang* to *yin*. Although *yin* and *yang* are opposite, they are never independent. The unity of the two is what causes or makes the change and hence the creativity of the unity of the *yin-yang*. It is in this sense that *yin* and *yang* are dependent on each other and complement each other. Furthermore, it must be noted that the mutual movement from *yin* to *yang* and *yang* to *yin* is not a mechanical repetition. Instead it is an organic dialectical process by which differentiation and production of new things become possible. This process explains why many come from one and why there is always novelty in the world. The mutual reversion between *yin* and *yang* is what in the final analysis defines creativity or creative change productive of ever new things.

In order to articulate this onto-cosmological understanding of the real, a generative ontology of *yin-yang* is naturally formulated in the *Yijing*.

On the Yijing as a Symbolic System of Integrated Communication 315

The Great Ultimate (*taiji*) of oneness gives rise to *yin-yang* activities, which in turn give rise to basic cosmological activities, and eventually proceeds to generate ten thousand things through the generation of the basic forms or phenomena such as eight trigrams and sixty-four hexagrams. The *Yijing* evolves a cogent system of representation, which formulates this generative ontology very successfully. We can let 0 represent the *taiji*, and we can represent *yang* by 1 and *yin* by 2. We can even represent the *yang* by —— and the *yin* by — —. Then the *taiji* could be represented by ——/— —. In other words, when the *taiji* begins creative movement, it can be represented by the symbol ——/— —. Then, through a process of binomial expansion, change can be said to involve a sequence of stages or levels: each of which has its rationality, shows its creativity, and therefore preserves the basic vision of the unity of the *yin-yang* places/forces.

Level/Stage 1: The Great Ultimate (*taiji*)

Level/Stage 2: two norms (*liang yi*)

Level/Stage 3: four phenomena (*si xiang*)

Level/Stage 4: eight trigrams (*bagua*)

Level/Stage 5: sixty-four hexagrams (*liushisi zhonggua*)

Each level/stage is a complete representation of reality. With the exception of the level/stage 1, each level/stage is a representation of a differentiated state of the world. The differentiation of the world as represented at each level/stage is a sequence of mutually exclusive and yet interdependent forms that symbolize natural phenomena or the human situation. For example, the eight diagrams in level/stage 4 represent eight basic natural phenomena: heaven, wind, fire, lake, mountain, water, thunder, and earth, which in turn can be generalized into eight modalities of natural forces of either basic *yin* or *yang* nature. These eight forces are correspondingly: creativity (*Qian*), entering (*Xun*), brightness (*Li*), joy (*Dui*), stillness (*Gen*), depth (*Kan*), arousing (*Zhen*), and receptivity (*Kun*).

As each form is a combination of *yin-yang* forces/places, the eight modalities acquire *yin* or *yang* nature, depending on whether *yin* or *yang* force/place rules. The rule of ruling is generally understood in the *Yijing* in such a way that if there is a single line of *yang* or *yin*, the single line rules. Therefore, *Qian*, *Zhen*, *Kan*, *Gen* belong to the *yang* camp, whereas *Kun*, *Xun*, *Dui* belong to the *yin* camp.

Apart from the characteristic that each form of change is made from the *yang* in its simplest form, there are several other characteristics of a form in any totality of forces. First, each form in the sequence is symbiotically related to the other forms by way of *a priori structural* relationships or by way of *a priori genetic* relationships. The structural relationships are those of opposition of lines, (such as *Qian* and *Kun*), reversion of lines (such as *Gen* and *Zhen*), replacement of upper and lower trigrams for hexagrams (such as *Pi* and *Tai*); and other less obvious structurally determinable relations. The genetic relationships are those of generation by way of gradual inception of a different line in a given form such as *Qian* gives rise to *Dui* by inception of - - in place of — in the *Qian*. For the *Yijing*, the convention for forming a form is to "grow" *line* by *line* upward from the bottom. Another convention for genetic relationship is set by the results of *divination* as stipulated in the tradition. Both relationships enable us to see that each form interpenetrates with all other forms and can be logically or temporally derived from other forms by transformation, and that they equally contribute to an organic unity of totality. Therefore, there are individuality, totality, and mutually transformable relationships of forms at the same time, which together define and present an image of reality as we live and experience it.

Second, whether structural or genetic, the above relationships among forms are linear or horizontal in the sense that they all belong to the same level/stage of reality. These relationships also define a sense of development and growth, a sense of a decline and decay, a sense of simplification and complication for the changing process within a level/stage. But as we can see from the potential expansion of reality from level to level, or from stage to stage, we have another sense of development and growth, another sense of decline and decay, another sense of simplification and complication. This is the vertical sense of expansion or contraction as opposed to the horizontal one. In this sense, the *taiji* gives rise to the two-form level/stage, and the two-form level/stage gives rise to the four-form level/stage, and so on. Looking backward, one can see that the sixty-four-form hexagrams can retract into the eight-form trigrams, which can finally retract into the one-form *taiji*. In this fashion one can understand how reality is both one and many, both static and dynamic. The unity of one and many, static and dynamic is what makes the *Yijing* symbolism and what it symbolizes dialectical.

The above characterizes the ontogenesis of the real or the world. This ontogenesis not only preserves organic unity on each level/stage of the world, but also logically generates new levels/stages from receding levels/stages to accommodate or range over things of larger and larger scope. In this way, the system simultaneously achieves more and more detailed differentiation and individuation of things. Hence, we have the generative nature of the onto-cosmology or ontology. This generative ontology is not intended simply as descriptive, it is intended as regulative as well. In fact, it is more regulative than descriptive in its application to the world (the real). This means that one can always look at the world or a situation from the point of view of the forms in a given level/stage and see things in the order of the change according to whichever level/stage of reality one chooses. This is possible because the Yi forms *a priori* represent reality *in toto*, and because all things are basically analyzable into *yin-yang* forces/places. The Yi forms, therefore, will only introduce certain *relationships*, whether structural or genetic, which are identifiable by the forms in the system. This is how new meanings are generated, from relationships revealed by the order of forms in a level/stage of the world as articulated by the symbolism of the change. The generative ontology is generative of meanings from an ontological determination of the level/stage of being and consequently the identification of constituent forms. This leads to the next characteristic of the *Yijing* system.

Third, in light of the above, once can see that the generative ontology of the *Yijing* goes hand in hand with a dialectical methodology. This dialectical methodology consists in viewing any form of reality as basically a *yin-yang* polarity in which two opposite forces/places are co-present and an internal development from *yin* and *yang* or *yang* to *yin* takes place. This internal opposition of *yin-yang* and their development is *natural* and *spontaneous* (in an ontological sense). The conditions for complementarity and reversion—*yin* and *yang*—though opposite in nature, complement each other adequately for any form of reality. Though the development may appear to be linearly forward, in actuality it entails an eventual reversion of development so that a total balance of change will remain. Thus, too much *yin* leads to the inception of the *yang* and too much *yang* leads to the inception of the *yin* and hence the reversion. But reversion need not be considered repetition, because in terms of the individual things or situations, there are always novelties or uniqueness for the individual things or circumstances. The reversion may be conceived as a way of forever bringing out creative differences among infinite different things. Since the *Yijing* ontological view is to see things as maintained or changing for the maintenance or production of harmony in individual things or in the overall totality of things on any level/stage, the dialectical way of analyzing things and their relationships may be said to be the exploration of actual or potential (unrealized) harmony among things. This dialectical way of thinking can be called dialectics of harmonization,[3] as harmonization is the ultimate goal of the understanding of reality and the solving of problems.

Not only can one see the generative ontology of the *Yijing* as embodying the dialectical way of thinking, but also one can see that the application of the generative ontology of the *Yijing* to the world involves dialectical considerations that are made possible by the generative ontology itself. What I mean is that one has to identify *forms* in things or situations and choose a description of the world at a certain level/stage. One's choice and identification very much depend on how one understands or evaluates a problem. Thus, it is both a practical and a dialectical decision: a decision that will formulate one's problem relevant for the generative ontology and for the solution in terms of the generative ontology of polaristic opposites.

From the above demonstration, it is clear that the generative ontology of the *Yijing* and the dialectical methodology of the *Yijing* are two sides of the same thing. The base model of the *Yijing* is methodological just as it is ontological, and the generativeness of the *Yijing* ontology consists precisely in the dialectics of its methodological thinking. That is why the *Yijing* ontology does not lend itself to a rigid system of *concepts* for description of the real, nor prescribe a closed system of determinations of the real. Instead, it allows for subjective elements to play a role in understanding the real. In this sense, it is not an objective system like science, but this does not mean that it is merely a subjective system of intentional symbols (symbols with intentional meanings). Instead, it is something between, which forges the objective and the subjective together, and provides an active function of the mind and experience to enrich the meanings of the objective and the subjective at the same time. Hence, it is open to creative insights into the unseen and hidden aspects of both reality and mind.

The *Yijing* as Matrix of Meaning and Onto-Hermeneutics of Communication

The above generative ontology base model of the *Yijing*—along with its dialectical methodology—forms a system of concepts or categories that satisfies the following conditions:

1. It is powerful enough to generate a manifold and simple enough to reduce or return to oneness.

2. It is capable of adducing similarity among things and yet capable of accounting for rise of differences among things.

3. It is capable of comprehending an infinity and presenting a unified totality of the infinite.

4. It is capable of preserving our sense of reality (concrete yet general and nontransitional) and our sense of transition to one and many at the same time.

5. It is capable of identifying all individual things as individuals and relating them to reality and all other things, to allow each individual thing to contribute meaning to other things.

6. It allows meaning to be related to truth (in the objective sense) and understanding (in the subjective sense) at the same time.

Such a system of concepts or categories is a matrix of meaning from which all meanings of a symbol can be derived because a symbol in such a system is given meaning through the system no matter what original meaning the symbol may have. Insofar as the system integrates generative ontology and dialectical methodology, it applies to reality as a whole so that it can be regarded as reflecting the generative structure of reality. In actuality, it is this integrative system that gives rise to our abstract *view* of reality as a structured whole, and this, in turn, gives meaning to a symbol in the system in terms of its underlying ontology and methodology.[4] Onto-hermeneutical systems enable one to interpret symbols or anything that has symbolic value in terms of a given ontology and methodology. This technique and method of derivation of meaning can be called onto-hermeneutics. Onto-hermeneutics in reference to the *Yijing* symbolic system determines the meanings of the number system and the judgment system from the form system, or one may hypothesize that the primary form system onto-hermeneutically gives rise to the system of numbers and judgments. These latter clearly can be explained in terms of properties of *yin-yang* as they are either ontologically or methodologically explained. This of course is not to deny that both number system and judgment system in their formations may contribute to the meaning of the forms.

Many have noted that the *Yijing* is readily applicable to life or world in order to generate meanings. The reason why the *Yijing* is so applicable is that the base system (the generative ontology and dialectical methodology) of the *Yijing* is closely knit and tied to reality as widely observed and deeply experienced by persons. The system is in fact rooted in such an experience of reality so that it becomes a generalized reflection of experience and reality. In the *Great Appendix* of the *Yijing*, the formulation of the form system of the *Yijing* is said to arise from deep reflection on the nature of heaven and earth, beginning and end of things, substances (of things), and changes. Thus it is said:

> The *Yijing* matches heaven and earth, and therefore is capable of uniting and organizing the way of heaven and earth. The sages who devised the *Yijing* looked up to heaven and inspected the earth, and therefore came to know the causes of darkness and light; [who] traced the origins of things and their ends, and therefore came to the reasons of death and life; [who] observed the condensations of *yin* and *yang* forces into things and the dissipation of things into the *yin-yang* forces, knew the configurations of stretching and return [of *yin-yang* forces].[5]

It also says:

> The sages, seeing the assemblage of things in the world, describe their forms and symbolize them in proper forms; these symbols are called the *xiang* (resembling forms such as trigrams and hexagrams); the sages, seeing the movements of things, observe their interfacing relationships and exchanges so that they will act according to paradigms and properties

(as derived from their observation), and therefore attach judgments in order to judge what is good to pursue and what is bad. This is the origin of the lines (yao).[6]

These passages testify to the wide experiential basis of the base form system of the *Yijing*. In fact, the embodiment of experience in the *forms* of the *Yijing* is even more direct: it begins with the basic yin-yang symbols. Both yin and yang are direct experiences of different aspects of reality: yin is the shady, the weak, the soft, the hidden, the negative, the receptive, the passive, the feminine, the quiet, the resting; whereas yang is the bright, the strong, the hard, the manifest, the positive, the creative, the active, the masculine, the moving, and the initiating. The original etymological meanings of yin and yang perhaps have to do with the common natural phenomenon of the light, of the sun observed on the sides of mountain and river. Hence, the ancient dictionary *Shuowen* suggests that the southern side of a mountain is yang and the northern side is yin, reflecting the experience of sunlight in northern China. One experiences yin and yang, as two aspects of nature, together with one's experience of nature. Here, the nature of Nature is aptly conceived as a force, place, or process, which can undergo subtle change and transformation.

The reality of nature is later explicitly described as the vital force (qi). Qi is fluid, formless and yet very active and real; it forms the material-energy base of all things. In this sense, a unified conception of qi clearly reflects a unified experience of the nature of reality. The yin-yang forces can be easily conceived as a unity of qi with the negative and positive aspects. Not only yin-yang forces are experienced as a unity of qi, but all the interpenetrability, opposition, complementarity, reversibility and mutual generativeness of yin-yang are deeply experienced together with the experience of the yin-yang unity of qi. This unity then gives rise to the potentially complex and yet basically simple system of generative ontology and dialectical methodology articulated in the symbols of the *Yijing*. This system can be called a system of symbolic empiricism: empiricism based on symbolic relationships and symbolism based on intricate and basic experience of life and world.

There are two levels of experiential meanings associated with the forms of the base *Yijing* system: the natural level and the human level. On the natural level, as we have seen, the forms such as trigrams have naturalistic meanings of natural phenomena; on the human level, the eight trigrams are assigned the symbolization of father ☰, mother ☷, first son ☳, second son ☵, third son ☶, first daughter ☴, second daughter ☲ and third daughter ☱.

Moreover, in the system of sixty-four hexagrams, most of the hexagrams have personal-human or social-human meanings and references. Those that have not been assigned explicit human meanings can be easily assigned such meanings in light of the judgments (*ci*) attached to the forms. This is just as in the cases of those hexagrams that may not be assigned naturalistic meanings, they can be easily given such meanings, for they are all composed of trigrams that already have naturalistic meanings. One may say that the base forms (whether eight trigrams or sixty-four hexagrams) have two basic models: the naturalistic one and the humanistic one, which can be regarded as manifesting two levels of meanings or two sorts of meanings. These two levels of meanings can be regarded not only as two models of experience-reality, but also as two systems of interpretation, in which interpretation of the meaning of a given human phenomenon or rational phenomenon can be made.

Further, one may regard two models of the base system of the *Yijing* as particular derivations of a general character symbolized by the base forms, or conversely one may generalize on the two models to arrive at a general character of the symbolic forms. This is precisely what takes place for the eight trigrams of the *Yijing*. The eight trigrams are given universal properties such as these: the creative ☰, the receptive ☷, the arousing ☳, the deep ☵, the still ☶, the entering ☴, the bright ☲, and the joy ☱. In terms of these universal properties, which need not be considered abstract, not only the two above models can be said to be their illustrations, other models of reality and experience can be derived from them. In actuality, this universal interpretation and the two particular interpretations (two models) will interact and interpenetrate to reinforce each other, leading to more and more enriched instances of the base system of generative ontology and dialectical methodology. This is called symbolic reference by Whitehead, which I have discussed previously.[7] We can represent this symbolic reference or interplay of properties and instances (models) in the following diagram:

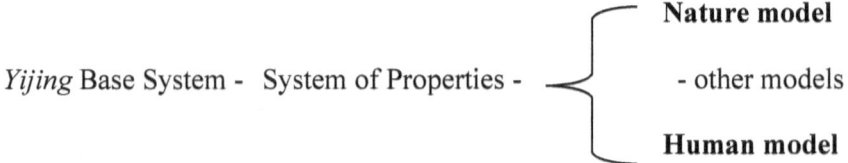

If we incorporate the independent subsystems of the Yijing discussed in the earlier section in the diagram, we will have the following structure of symbolic reference:

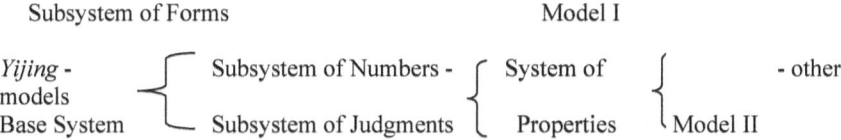

Coordination and Assimilation of Other Systems

The Yijing system is enriched not only in its mechanism of meaning generation by symbolic reference, but also by coordination with other systems of cosmology or cosmological meaning generation, which evolved from ancient times like the Yijing system of trigrams and hexagrams. This coordination sometimes can be seen as assimilation of other systems into the Yijing in the sense that other systems are given meanings by the Yijing, rather than the Yijing system being given meaning by other systems. In this sense, other systems are subordinate to the Yijing system. A good example of this is the assimilation of the Celestial Stems (*tian gan*) and Earthly Branches (*di zhi*) into the Yijing systems of trigrams and hexagrams. A genuine case of coordination for the Yijing is the coordination of the Yijing with the system of the *wuxing* (five powers), an ancient cosmo-morphological theory developed by the third century BCE thinkers into an elaborate cosmo-genetic theory.

The system of the *wuxing* has five basic tenets: (1) The world is composed of five basic materials, vital powers, properties or phases of a process: metal, wood, water, fire, and earth. (2) All concrete things in the world are composed of these five powers in different proportions, even things of the same kind can differ because of the degrees of combinations of the five powers. (3) The differences of kinds of things are also accounted for on the basis of the qualitative differences within each of the five powers. (4) The five powers can be ordered according to their relations of generation and production: water generates wood, wood generates fire, fire gives rise to earth, earth to metal, and metal to water. (5) They also can be ordered according to their relations of destruction: fire destroys metal, metal wood, wood earth, earth water, water fire. These two orders of relations can be diagrammed as follows:

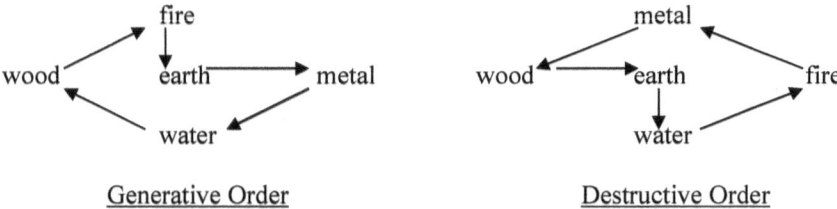

Generative Order   Destructive Order

This system of natural phylogenesis has been fully explored and has accrued an enrichment of meanings in terms of incorporating properties and phenomena that are distinguished in different areas of natural and human experiences. Thus, for example, there are five directions: the south (fire), the west (metal), the north (water), the east (wood), the middle (earth); five seasons: spring (wood), summer (fire), midsummer (earth), autumn (metal), and winter (water); five colors; five organs, and so on. In light of these sets of coordination and assimilation, the five powers system functions as an interpreting procedure that classifies phenomena and experiences and identifies their relations in accordance with the five powers. The concepts of the five powers function as criteria and paradigms for selecting phenomenologically similar phenomena and experiences and give meanings to them. This, in turn, enriches the meanings of the concepts of five powers by broadening their scope of application. This then enables us to meaningfully apply these concepts of five powers to various kinds of things in the world through negotiation between meanings of those concepts and our experiences of things in the world. This is again a process of symbolic reference, which finally makes the *wuxing* system a powerful means of interpretation. When this system is finally coordinated and integrated with the base system of the *Yijing*, one can immediately see how much more powerful each system becomes in functioning both as a system of interpretation (meaning, order and relation giving) and as a system of cross-reference. In this way, we establish an isomorphic relationship between the system of *Yijing* and what is regarded as the world of things.

The interesting fact is that while the *Yijing* is made powerful in its interpretative capability by the *wuxing* theory, it preserves its primary identity as a generative ontology and dialectical methodology. Perhaps

On the Yijing as a Symbolic System of Integrated Communication   325

because of this onto-generative and dialectical nature, it can be said that the Yijing system finally *subsumes* the five powers theory and makes it more or less a system exclusively applicable to the differentiated world of the yin-yang or the qi as indicated in the Diagram of the Great Ultimate preserved by Zhou Dunyi. The five powers (wuxing) are explained as products and also as activities of differentiation of the yin-yang; they derive their vitality and meaningfulness as active constituting elements of things from the Great Ultimate. The principles of the formation of things in terms of the wuxing are therefore to be found in the creativity of the Great Ultimate (taiji), not in the wuxing themselves.

That the wuxing system enriches the Yijing system is further seen in the production of the after-heaven diagram as contrasted with the before-heaven diagram. The latter is formed on the principles of complementation of opposites and of generative unity of organic change (see diagram A); the former is on the contrary formed on the principles of the mutual generation of the five Powers (see diagram B).

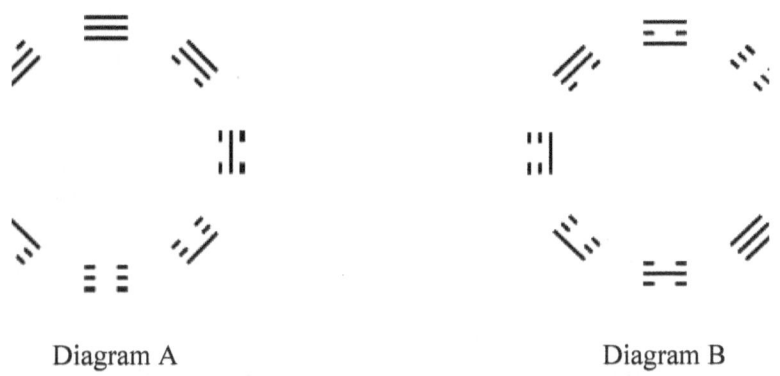

Diagram A   Diagram B

In the after-heaven diagram (diagram B), it can be seen that the diagram is formed on the identification of the (arousing) Zhen ☳ and Xun ☴ (entering) as wood, Li ☲ (the brightness) as fire, Kun ☷ (the receptive) and Gen ☶ (the still) as hill, Dui ☱ (joy) and Qian ☰ (the creative) as metal, and the Kan ☵ (the abysmal) as water. The diagram indicates a flow of the five powers in their generative order.

With regard to the incorporation of the wuxing system into the Yijing system, three fundamental observations can be made. First, the Yijing system can be readily applied to reality for interpretation, and it can now be explained partially as a result of the incorporation of the *wuxing* system, which concretely describes reality in its ordered ramification and partially as a result of its primary process-reality descriptive force. Second, the incorporation of the *wuxing* into the *Yijing* is highly significant in that it represents an act of symbolic extension through symbolic reference and unity of feeling. That this is possible must be explained not as a matter of factual objective similarity, but as a matter of subjective understanding. The mind that symbolizes it in terms of natural symbols must already see things in an organically interrelated way, which gives a web of meaning to the symbols in the first place. The basic insight and experience of mind initiates the symbolic process of extension and reference of one system to another, or one set to another set. This means that underlying the affinity and assimilability of the *Yijing* system and the *wuxing* system or any other system, there is the primary affinity and a similarity between the world and the mind of the experiencing self. This leads to the creation of the *Yijing* system in the first place. In this sense, we can readily see that the *Yijing* is a creation of the understanding, not a creation of knowledge-formulation or factual information-gathering. This leads to a final insight into the nature of the *Yijing* as a system of symbolic communication.

Finally, the base system of the *Yijing* and its coordination schema or interpretative procedure as exemplified in the subsumption of the *wuxing* system quickly lend themselves to the field of values and norms and practical judgments of good and bad, as related to the interpretive agent, that is, the individual who experiences or accepts the system and its extension. This means that the extension of meanings is not merely ontological or cosmological but necessarily axiological. Thus, one can see how the *ci* (judgment) subsystem arises within the *Yijing* tradition. The *ci* subsystem deals with values such as fortune and misfortune, good and bad, all being humanly relevant and practically directed. This possible practice shows clearly that the *Yijing* system is closely linked and applicable to the human world of psychological needs and spiritual ideals. This shows a dimension of the *Yijing* system that deeply reflects the human experience of one's involvement and confrontation with oneself, not just with the world. Indeed, Confucians have pointed this out in the *Ten Commentaries*. When it is said that the authors of the *Yijing* have "profound misgivings (about persons and) times" (*Xici*). This explains why the *Yijing* is de facto rooted in the ultimate creativity of persons. The meaningfulness of its symbols thrives on this understanding and indeed reveals its deep link to the ultimate creativity of persons that is explicitly embodied in the *ci* (judgment) subsystem of the *Yijing*.

Thus, to conclude, the *Yijing* system can now be seen as an integrative link and therefore a communicative bridge or vehicle between the mind (subject) and the world. This communicative vehicle in terms of the symbolic nature also can be seen as an ongoing and open process that makes mind (subject) and the world interchange and exchange for a more meaningful and richer interpretation of the world for the self. In addition, the communicative vehicle, as such a process, provides for more meaningful and richer articulation of the self in the world. This means that the *Yijing* succeeds as a system of understanding due to its symbolic nature; even more directly, it succeeds due to what makes this symbolic system possible and what makes its open and assimilating capacity possible. There exist two aspects of the symbolic reference to the external symbols the mind of the world Yijing the symbolic reference to the internal Yijing system, the external one to the world and the internal one to the self, which verifies the system as a vehicle of understanding and a means of organizing and integrating the self and the world together for coherent action and interpretation of every thing.

Concluding Remarks

In the above, we have explored the nature of the *Yijing* as a symbolic system, a system of reference, and a system of symbolic extension. We also have analyzed how this system is organized and composed and we revealed that the three subsystems of the *Yijing* system are interrelated by reinforcement of mutual meaning-giving, and sharing of an underlying base structure of generative ontology and dialectical methodology. This base structure or base-system of the *Yijing* formulates the most basic insight of an individual into reality and thus reflects reality and the individual. The base system, besides being generative and dialectical, is readily applicable to reality because of its being deeply rooted in human experience and because of its wide and open coordination and incorporation of other cosmogenetic systems such as the *wuxing*. This coordinative and incorporative textuality of the *Yijing* again reflects not only that objective reality is open to synthetic categorical line-up, but also that the subjective mind or self of the human being is actively inclined to seek organic unity among the multitude of things as well as among a multitude of systems of categories. Both mind and world thereby converge and agree in terms of and in virtue of the symbolic system of the *Yijing*.

Now in light of our distinction between the three kinds and levels of communication in the beginning section of this paper, we can easily see that the *Yijing* system is a system for understanding, for it contributes to activity of understanding or a system of understanding, and paves the way for the taking place of understanding. In this sense, it belongs to and contributes to the type and level of communication called understanding. In fact, the *Yijing* can be said to define a paradigm for communication of understanding. It aims at understanding the self and the world as well as the relation between the two by way of its symbols, which makes this understanding possible. This means that in terms of the generative ontology and dialectical methodology the *Yijing* system together with its coordination and assimilation of other systems defines the understanding itself and therefore the consequent communication on the level of understanding. To understand is to see things in the base system of the *Yijing* system. Communication becomes a matter of subsuming concepts and facts in the base system of the *Yijing*. If any system has properties isomorphic to or equivalent to those of the *Yijing*, that system would be naturally a system for understanding and therefore a system of understanding, or a system for communication and therefore a system of communication on the level of understanding.

That the *Yijing* is a system for and of understanding and that it is a system for and of communication on the understanding level can be further explained as follows. First, the *Yijing* provides a symbolic system that interprets experiences and things in light of its base ontology and methodology and thereby confers meanings on them. In this sense, the *Yijing*, because of its generative and dialectical nature, is an unlimited source and matrix of meaning and is, therefore, an interpretative system. Second, the *Yijing* is capable of functioning and in fact has functioned to organize peoples' perceptions and categories of things in both their genesis and constitution. This is amply shown in its coordination and subsumption of the *wuxing* system. One can see that there is no limit to such coordinating and subsumption of meaning in virtue of the base system it possesses and in virtue of the pristine insights it reveals into self and reality. In this sense, the *Yijing* is an integrative system because

On the Yijing as a Symbolic System of Integrated Communication 329

it integrates experiences and concepts into an organic unity and enriched order. Third, the Yijing no doubt is highly and readily applicable to reality, and this reality should include self, the world, and the relation between the two. This is because the symbolic system with its symbolic reference and extension is intimately linked to reality as experienced, that is, reality revealed as a relation between the self and the world. This explains why the Yijing has homologous models of different kinds of things and on different levels of things: psychological, personal, social, political, historical, cosmological, or simply naturalistic. These modes manifest the practicality and applicability of the Yijing system in virtue of its symbolic reference and extension. Hence, the Yijing is a practical or practically motivated system for action and purposeful application. Fourth, the Yijing system, as we have seen, is deeply ingrained in a self's experience of reality and in its practicality and applicability. This clearly indicates that it involves an irreducible reference to self or subjectivity; for it is the subjectivity of self which gives rise to the perception and symbolization of reality *qua* reality. This is shown in the development of the value and norm systems of the Yijing: the ci subsystem. The interpretive and the integrative nature of the system necessarily and naturally interprets and integrates the values and norms in terms of the base system and creates a fusion or unity of feelings among the values and other categories or concepts and perceptions of things.

That the Yijing system is capable of doing this is due to its symbolic empiricism, which embodies a primary symbolic reference to the self and a primary symbolic reference to the world. In this sense, the symbolic system of the Yijing provides a paradigmatic study and formulation of communication in the sense of and on the level of understanding. The co-presence and unity of double reference, internal and external reference, also points to a demonstrative presence of the self in the formulation of the system, which, being needed together with the demonstrated presence of the self, makes genuine understanding possible. To sum up, the *interpretative*, *integrative*, the *practical*, and the *ingraining* function of the Yijing system defines what a system for and of understanding and communication is. A system for and of understanding and communication is simultaneously interpretative (meaning-conferring), integrative (meaning-assimilating), practical (action-inspiring) and ingraining (self-referring). Nothing else is. Therefore, the Yijing system cannot be seen as a system for or of information or informational communication, as it does not embody a system of information for transfer or for communication of such. Nor is it a system of knowledge or for knowledge, and therefore cannot be used to communicate knowledge or concepts and theories of things as science does.

CHAPTER 11

On Zhu Xi's Integration of *Yili* (义理) and *Xiangshu* (象数) in the Study of the *Yijing*

Two Aspects of the *Yi*: *Xiangshu* and *Yili*

Although Zhu Xi argues strongly for the *divinatory* nature of the *Yijing* Texts,[1] his methodological starting point is historical fact. With regard to the *Yijing*, however, to recognize the divinatory nature of the original *Yi* Text, which consists in making judgments of fortune and misfortune according to forms (*xiang*) and numbers (*shu*), is not to affirm that the *Yijing* consists only of divinatory judgments based on *xiang* and *shu*. In fact, according to Zhu Xi, earlier Confucian scholars overdo their *Xiangshu* study, which leads to artificial constructions. Thus, Zhu Xi is not simply for numerology and formology (*xiang* studies). Neither is he simply for discovering meaning and reason (principle) (*Yili*) in the *Yijing*. This tradition of *Yili* approach to the *Yijing* is again overplayed, as exemplified in the *Yizhuan* of the Cheng Yichuan. Zhu Xi is critical of the *Yizhuan* in this sense.[2] In fact, he is even not quite satisfied with his own *Yi benyi* (original meanings of the *Yijing*) for this reason.[3] Even in his own *Yi benyi*, he has not given sufficient attention to the *Xiangshu* as recognized in the *Xici* and other classical works, which is why seven years later he began writing the *Yixue Qimeng*.

In sum, Zhu Xi does not wish to see one overdo the *Xiangshu* nor overdo the *Yili*; instead, he argues, one should recognize the *Xiangshu* base of the *Yi* system and develop the *Yili* as a compatible extension. At the same time, one must go beyond the *Xiangshu*. In a certain sense, the ultimate goal of Zhu Xi is to integrate the *Yili* and *Xiangshu* in a comprehensive system of understanding and meaningfulness in which both *Xiangshu* and *Yili* receive new significance from each other. In this sense, Zhu Xi is truly a synthetic and objective-minded creative thinker.

Zhu Xi's main argument for the original divinatory nature of the *Yi* against the *Yili* masters is this: if the *Yijing* is intended as an explanation of philosophical principles (*Yili*), then why does the sage not simply write a separate book to speak explicitly of the philosophical principles instead of developing the *gua* forms and making judgments that are so difficult and obscure for us to understand?[4] This is indeed a powerful argument. But this argument is rooted in Zhu Xi's insight into the nature of the *gua* forms and their practical usefulness by way of divination. With this insight, Zhu Xi explains why those scholars who speak of *Yili* or *Wen Yi* without looking into the practical divinatory contexts of the *gua* forms become "scattered, dissipated, and without roots" (*zhi li san man er wusuo genju*), and therefore become arbitrary, prejudiced, narrow, (*jian he wei zhu*) and incapable of comprehension, penetration and unobstructed understanding (*bao han hai guan, qu chang pang tong*).

The lesson Zhu Xi obtains from this is not simply to embrace the *gua* forms as *gua* forms and see them only as meaningful for divination, but to look into the *gua* forms and their practical contexts in order to see what they mean and what the associated judgments refer to. In this way, one can understand the meaning as well as the rightness or wrongness of the judgment on fortune and misfortune.[5] This means that we should attempt to enliven and recapture the vital perception of the sage, and understand the forms in their original practical contexts. The meanings of *forms* are therefore not artificial but are well-rooted in real concrete life. From this, then, we can move to investigate and obtain the principles and reasons of the forms in a more generalized way.

Zhu Xi says:

> Therefore, today if any one wants to read one *gua* and one *yao* (line), one must read them as results of actual divination, and with an objective mind seek out the references of the words and judgments (associated with the forms and lines) so that one can see how (the sage) reaches the judgments of fortune/misfortune and permission/non-permission. Then one will look into what the *forms* actually stand for and inquire into what their justifiable principles are. Finally, one will

apply (these principles to) cultivation of self and government of state so that they become practically useful.[6]

Thus, we can see that Zhu Xi argues for recognition of the divinatory nature of the *gua* forms and *gua* judgments not simply because we have to recognize a historical fact, but because we can derive living reasons and meanings from the divinatory contexts. We also can see that Zhu Xi does not want to reject the *Yili* as such, but wants only to reject *Yili* as not related to the concrete practical contexts of the *forms* and *lines* and their judgments. In fact, he wants to see *Yili* as developed out of the *forms* and *lines* in the divinatory contexts and then extended and applied to basic situations of life and government. This is a most profound methodological position, which implies a deep understanding of the process of meaning-extension and concept-application in a symbolic process. I have attempted to describe this process in an article, which is independent of Zhu Xi's methodological concern here.[7]

To describe Zhu Xi's methodological insight here concisely, one may say that Zhu Xi recognizes, first, that symbols such as *gua* forms and judgments such as *gua*-judgments acquire their primary meanings from their concrete uses, which in fact dictate their originating. Second, these meanings can be extended and given rational justification as a result of rational inquiry into reasons and meanings and, therefore, generalized over given experiences. Third, these new meanings can be applied to new situations and experiences to generate further practical results or understanding or reality. Finally, Zhu Xi recognizes that this process of extension and application is capable of indefinitely organizing, discovering, and developing new meanings and new principles organized or discovered, which will enrich the original symbolism of the forms and judgments. This understanding is what I describe as an onto-hermeneutical understanding of the symbols.[8] We can in fact diagnose this process as follows:

Stage 1	Stage 2	Stage 3
Gua forms and judgments in divinatory contexts	*Yili* (meanings and principles) Abstraction and generalization toward philosophical explanations	Extension and application toward new affairs and practical situations

The three stages of the understanding of the *Yijing* are interdependent, and are rooted in some primary vision of the reality that makes the original *gua*-judgments and *gua* forms possible. For this reason, I have myself pointed out that even divination presupposes a philosophy of understanding the world so that we can speak of the philosophy of divination. If we take divination by the *Yijing* to be in some way similar to the method as prescribed by the *Xici*, then divination clearly presupposes some understanding of the systems of *numbers*. This also means that the systems of the *Hetu* and *Luoshu* are quite possibly used as bases of a world-picture as well as the bases of divination. Zhu Xi has not quite recognized this; but he does give a very realistic account of the origin of the *gua* forms as instruments of divination. He says:

> The *Zhouyi* only comprehends the divination and in general speaks of *yin-yang*. Because of the decline and growth of the *yin-yang*, there are some principles amidst them. At the time of Fuxi, somehow by accident he sees one as *yang* and two as *yin* and consequently draws (forms) to represent them and lay them aside. At the time no person seems to recognize either one or the two, either the *yin* or the *yang*. But Fuxi somehow pointed these out to them. Then there exists the one/two, and consequently, many ideas about the *forms* and *numbers* come about. The way this develops, he is not able to prevent. But even at the time what people understand are things like nets and traps, and there were no sophisticated inventions and elaborations such as found in the books of applications in later times. Today people speak of Fuxi as if he is a deity who knows everything. But in fact Fuxi is simple by himself, knowing not so many things. It is since he provides an insight into the nature of reality (*di gai zhe yi ge ji*) that people in later times develop so many things *after* him, but he could not help it, and he might not necessarily want this to happen.[9]

From this quotation, it is clear that Zhu Xi does recognize the original insight of the author of the *Yi*-forms, namely the insight into the *yin-yang* nature of reality. But he also recognizes the importance of this insight, for it opens up the opportunity (*ji*) for future development of the meaning and use systems of the *Yijing*. He is quite correct in pointing out that Fuxi is simple by himself. Although he acquired the insight into reality and started the *Yi*-thinking, he is no god, nor does he know everything.

The development of meaning takes time, and only in time does the *Yijing* gradually become a sophisticated book of forms, judgments, meanings, and principles. Yet, we should not forget its simple beginnings, as these are important and their later developments are natural. When one recognizes this, one can put the study of the *Yijing* in the correct context and approach the *Yijing* from a proper perspective. In this regard, Zhu Xi is quite logically, historically, and philosophically minded. He has respect for facts, and allows development; he is interested in philosophical principles, and is concerned with practical uses. He is particularly keen in linking practicality with concreteness and philosophical thinking with practicality. For this reason, one can quite agree with him in holding the following:

> There are many levels of meaning and principle (*Yili*) regarding the positions of *gua* in the *Yijing*, which are naturally ordered in sequence. Each level shows a phase and a world of its own (*zhu ceng ge shi yi ge de mian*), and one should not combine them into one view by force. The student should understand level by level. When one understands the upper level, one should not disturb the lower level. Only when one understands this upper level thoroughly, then one can softly uncover the lower level for understanding. Even though one may not feel good about being slow, yet when doing this for long, and understanding every level, then one can see many patterns of reason, with all differences belonging to their proper places. Is this not quite satisfying?[10]

Zhu Xi says this is his general methodology in reading books, which is not simply applied to the study of the *Yijing*. But perhaps he cannot deny that this study of the *Yijing* has provided him an important occasion for seeing clearly how one should proceed to understand the origin, meaning, and principle of a classic level by level, and one may of course suggest that it is at the same time due to the methodological mind of Zhu Xi that he is able to analyze the *Yijing* in the way he does.

By using this methodological analysis of understanding the *Yijing*, one can see how Zhu Xi identifies the levels of understanding in the *Yi* study. He suggests analyzing the *Yijing* into three levels: the *Yi* of the Fuxi, the *Yi* of King Wen, and the *Yi* of Confucius.[11] The *forms* and *numbers* used in divination belong to the level of the *Yi* of Fuxi; the *gua* and *yao*-judgments belong to the level of the *Yi* of King Wen; and finally the *Ten Wings* (*Commentaries*) belong to the level of the *Yi* of Confucius. Whether Zhu Xi is historically accurate on this distinction and identification of the levels and their authors, we need not determine here. What is important, however, is to recognize that these identifications and distinctions represent a methodological effort to get things in order and introduce a rationale of understanding for the understanding of the *Yi*. The above supports a finding that Zhu Xi would allow many interpretations of the *Yi* and does not see the study of the *Yi* stopping at the three levels, for he speaks strongly for the approach of Shao Yong and shows great interest in the *Can Dong Ji*. Of course, he would still hold that any such new developments must be traced to the beginning of the *Yi* insight found in the forms and numbers or in the commentaries of the *Ten Wings* attributed to Confucius.[12]

At this point, it is pertinent to suggest that Zhu Xi sees the possibility of further inquiry into meaning and principle on the basis of seeing the *Yi* forms, numbers, and judgments as containing the *Li* (principles). In fact, on many occasions Zhu Xi speaks of the *Yijing* as a book speaking of *li*. He says: "The sage creates the *Yi*, only to speak of one *Li*, and there are not many things attached to it, and they are not created for many things to attach to them."[13] He also says "*Yi* is a vacuous thing; before there is this thing, one must speak of this *Li*, and therefore (the *Yi*) can comprise many *daoli*. Whatever one does, fits into it."[14] Therefore he is able to distinguish the *Yijing* from the *Chun Qiu* (*Spring and Autumn Annals*), for "The *Yi* is to proceed from the above-form to the under-form; whereas the *Chun Qiu* is to proceed from the under-form to the above form."[15] This distinction is similar to the Aristotelian distinction between philosophy and history. As a philosopher, Zhu Xi recognizes the *Yijing* as a book of philosophy.

Is there any contradiction between his insistence on the *Yi* as originally rooted in the divinatory art and his seeing the *Yijing* as a philosophical book of *Li*? From our discussion of Zhu Xi's view and his distinction of the levels of the *Yi*, it is obvious that there is no contradiction whatsoever. The *Yijing* is rooted in practice and is capable of being developed and indeed has been developed as a work of *Li*. What is missing in earlier scholars is the recognition that there is indeed a dialectical and dynamical link between the two—practice and principle—in a continuous process of development. The great contribution of Zhu Xi lies in his insight into this link. From this insight, one can also see that Zhu Xi would strongly link the principles and meanings with the forms-numbers not externally but internally, namely, by way of insisting there is *Li* in the forms and numbers because they are most able to express *Li*. This implies that without *Xiangshu* there could be no discovery of subtle and elaborate *Li*. Although Zhu Xi did not argue explicitly for this, it seems evident that if he had not subscribed to this view, he would not have developed and refined the diagram and sequence of changes of the sixty-four *gua* in the last part of the *Qimeng*, and he would not have discussed the meanings of numbers of the *Luoshu* and *Hetu*.

Importance of *Qi* Considerations toward *Li*

If we are allowed to speculate a bit on behalf of Zhu Xi, in reference to his philosophy of *Li* and *Qi*, we can say that the *Xiangshu* and judgments in their original divinatory contexts are all directed toward concrete representation of *Li* in terms of *Qi*, for they refer to objective things, situations, affairs, and relations of nature and man. Then it is the *Li* implicit in the numbers, forms, and judgments that *unifies* the numbers, forms, and judgments; moreover, it is the same *Li* that leads to other discoveries of *Li* and their applications. If we consider forms and numbers as first given, and judgments as based on the contemplation of forms and numbers, we can say that *Li* results from contemplation of forms, numbers, and judgments. Since there are many levels of *Li*, and *Li* are organically interrelated and highly applicable to things, one *Li* can lead to other *Li*, and one can develop the *Yijing* in terms of *Li*. But if this is to prove fruitful, one must develop the *Li* in light of the concrete things or the *Qi*, and alternatively in reference to the forms and numbers of things. We may indeed present an integrated theory of Zhu Xi's view on the *Yijing*, which, on the one side, reflects his methodology of approach, and on the other, his actual understanding and analysis of the meanings of the *Yijing* in terms of his *Li-Qi* philosophy.

Taiji (the Great Ultimate)

Li (principle)   *Qi* (vital force)
Functions in   Corresponding to
Xiang (forms)   things, relations, situations
shu (numbers), *ci* (judgments)

We must see *li* and *qi* as two poles not separated from each other but interpenetrating each other from respective directions to form different kinds of things on different levels, with the level of forms, numbers, and judgments corresponding to and inhering in things, relations, and situations as well. This shows that the *Yili* and *Xiangshu* cannot be separated as independent pursuits or representation systems. It is a mistake to do the separation in the traditional denominations of schools of the *Yijing* scholars or scholarship.

As the above demonstrates, we cannot abandon one level at the expense of the other in the study of *Qi*. Only when we can preserve all levels and preserve them in good order and distinction are we able to integrate them in a unified understanding of the *Yijing* with a consequent integrated understanding of the reality for which the *Yijing* stands.

Zhu Xi wrote his *Zhouyi benyi* (1117) before he wrote his *Yixue Jimeng*, which he wrote when he was fifty-seven years old, ten years after he wrote the former. We have reason to believe that he wrote the later book to complement or even to correct his earlier book, for his earlier book was written in an effort to expound the meaning and principles (*Yili*) of the *Yijing* without paying adequate attention to the forms and numbers. Qian Mu has pointed out that as in the *Benyi* there are references to *Qimeng*; the *Benyi* was therefore revised after the *Qimeng* was composed.[16] This shows that Zhu Xi definitely moved away from his pro-*Yili* position of the *Benyi* to his pro-*Xiangshu* position of the *Qimeng* seven years later.

Creative Functions of the *Taiji*

In the contemporary period, Chinese scholar Zhang Liwen has done wide research on Zhu Xi's position on the *Yijing*.[17] His writing is highly informative on Zhu Xi's position on the *Zhouyi*, and he correctly points out that Zhu Xi synthesized the two major schools on the *Yijing*: the Form Number (*Xiangshu*) School and the Meaning Principle (*Yili*) School. This synthesis of course is more immediately based on Zhu Xi's wish and effort to bring the *Yi* thoughts of Cheng Yi, which represent the *Yili* School, and the *Yi* thoughts of Shao Yong, which represent the *Xiangshu* school, together into a harmony and a unity. Insofar as Zhu Xi has made efforts to synthesize and integrate the Neo-Confucian thoughts of his predecessors, his interest in attempting to unify the two schools of the *Yi* tradition is not surprising. Indeed, it should be expected that he would develop a system of the *Yi* that would function as the foundation or at least as a model for his integrative thinking. In this sense, Zhu Xi's position on the *Yijing* has a peculiar methodological significance: it is a manifestation of his *li* (principle) and *qi* (vital force) metaphysics and therefore should throw light on his overall philosophy of *li* and *qi*. Zhang has correctly stressed the importance of Zhu Xi's approach. Yet, he did not give reasons why this approach of Zhu Xi is important. For myself, I believe that this importance is to be found internally in Zhu Xi's system, and externally in Zhu Xi's influence on later scholars. However, we will not be able to understand this twofold importance until we understand Zhu Xi's position on the *Yijing* and its metaphysical and historical significances. In the following I shall make some observations that I regard as essential and fundamental to understanding Zhu Xi's position and its significances.

First, Zhu Xi's concept of *taiji* has long been a controversial one. Is the *taiji* purely *li* or is it inseparable from *qi*? Zhang has focused on *taiji* as a still, formless, or imageless entity without location. He comes to conclude that it is a *spirit* that transcends time and space and yet must manifest itself in terms of *yin-yang* activities. This may be considered an idealistic interpretation, which leads to a dualism based on a bifurcation between *li* and *qi*. However, from a deeper reading of Zhu Xi, we may suggest that such an interpretation need not be warranted by Zhu Xi's overall philosophy. As I have pointed out,[18] *taiji* is not an Aristotelian unmoved mover, but must embody the *qi* even for its own being: the *li* of the *qi* is the *qi* of the *li*. There is a dialectical unity between *li* and *qi* so that the world of *li* can be said to exist as the world of *qi* exists. The priority of *li* over *qi*, as indicated by Zhu Xi, is an epistemological or rational priority. That presupposes a context where *li* and *qi* are united. There simply cannot be a context of pure *li* in which *li* alone exists. I believe that Zhu Xi speaks of the *taiji* in this sense, although he may fail to indicate where his position exactly lies. In fact, he refers to *li* in the *Yixue Qimeng* in these words: "The *taiji* is where forms and numbers have not yet emerged and there are *li* to them."[19] This statement, however, only leads to the position that *li* is an indeterminate state of *li-qi* identity in which the *yin-yang* forms and numbers through the internal dynamics of *qi* would emerge and interact to form all determinate things.

By "*yin-yang* form," I mean a form composed of a configuration of individuated forces of *yin* and *yang* as indicated in the *gua* (trigrams and hexagrams). But even before the trigrams are formed, you could have two norms and four images as composed of the *yin-yang* forces represented by the broken line and solid line. The formation of these forms presents both an inherent structure of a concrete situation and a potential process of development. As these forms are composed of lines of *yin-yang*, the positions of *yin-yang* lines can be identified with numbers such as 6, 7, 8, 9, which signify their relative positions and propensities toward change or nonchange. The numbers of *yin-yang* also come from the odd and even numbers of the first digital system of numbers. The even and odd numbers can be assigned to different positions of the *gua* (trigrams or hexagrams) or assigned to different trigrams in a system of five powers (*wuxing*) such as the *Hetu* and *Luoshu*. Hence, numbers are given metaphysical meanings in terms of *yin-yang* relationships. The process of formation and transformation of things of course could therefore be understood in terms of the forms and numbers of the *gua*, which results from a dialectical division of one (namely, the *taiji*) into two (namely, the *yin-yang*) as described by Zhang.

The notion of *taiji*, it should not be forgotten, does not occur in the original texts of the *Yijing*, but was introduced in the *Xici*.[20] If we look carefully into the way and context in which this notion is introduced, one can see that *taiji* is intended as the source of creativity of all things, and this creativity also embodies an order that explains the rise of differentiation and multiplicity as shown in the eight trigrams. In reference to a statement made by Confucius, the following is said: "Therefore, the Yi symbols have the Great Ultimate (*taiji*), from which are generated the two norms; the two norms generate four images and the four images generate eight trigrams."[21] The statement attributed to Confucius is as follows: "What does the Yi study do? The Yi is to open up all things and accomplish all affairs of the world and comprehend the way of the world. That is all. Therefore, the sage uses the Yi to relate to the mind of the people, to found the great deed in the world, and resolve all the doubts of the world."[22] Thus, *taiji* is the dynamic foundation of all things and a dialectical matrix of all things. It cannot be simply meant in its original context as a passive and receptive principle devoid of dynamics and vitality. Even when it is conceived as *li*, it is to explain the *li* of all things, which have formed from the *qi*, and therefore should function as a unifying force of both *li* and *qi* in things as well as *li* and *qi* in a generalized sense.

In stressing the importance of *li*, Zhu Xi may unwittingly lend himself to the impression of dualism by failing to distinguish between logical and ontological priorities and between the logical and ontological nature of the *li*. Instead of viewing *li* and *qi* as two separate entities, it would be more germane to the intention of Zhu Xi that they be regarded as two aspects of the *taiji*, the primordial unity of which, in a logical sense, transcends *li-qi* and *yin-yang* and yet at the same time comprehends both.

Moreover, it is beyond question that the fundamental principle of creativity of the *taiji* is unity of polar opposites, which means division of one into two without losing the one. That the one divides into two and yet also *unites* after division makes it possible for the one to continue serving as basis of further division and re-division. This again means that the universe is indeed infinitely creative and yet always maintains oneness of totality; there is interpenetration of one and many on different levels. This, of course, can be mathematically or logically formulated as a law of binomial expansion, as often pointed out by scholars. In this notion of division and unity lies the *Yi* authors' pristine insight into the change-nature of reality—that is, seeing reality as creative *change* that is yet rational and understandable. This insight also leads the authors of the *Yi* to marvel at the wonder of the natural numbers' sequence and endow special meanings to the odd and even numbers. The use of number system for the *Yi* is, therefore, not accidental, but is linked closely to the rise of forms and understanding of change. The relation of odd and even numbers is the relation of *yin* and *yang*: when they combine they form larger and different things (numbers). The generative (recursive) nature of natural numbers to an extent sheds light on the generative nature of *yin* and *yang*: *Yin* gives rise to *yang* and vice versa, just as odd number gives rise to even number and vice versa. As such, there is no cause for wonder that the integers 1, 3, 5, 7, 9 are used to signify *yang*, and integers 2, 4, 6, 8 are used to signify *yin*.

Further, one may note that an even number and an odd number, when put together, even though they are opposite to each other, yield an odd number, which, as a *yang* force, is in turn creative of an even number. A natural number, whether odd or even, contains an odd or an even number. This again symbolizes how *yin* and *yang* form a creative unity that leads to other *yin-yang* divisions. The number "1" is unique in that it generates every other number and is contained in every number but contains explicitly no other number. In this sense, it is like the *taiji* as the formless matrix of creativity that potentially contains the *yin-yang* activities and their capability for unfolding. The *taiji*, insofar as it is conceived as only a model of quietude (*jing*), may appear to be only *li*, as *li* is conceived as quiescent. One should not forget, however, that *taiji* also has a dynamical aspect, and with regard to this dynamical aspect, the *taiji* is vital and creative. Therefore, it is functionally identifiable with the *yin-yang* activities to which the *taiji* gives rise. Thus the natural number system forms a model of *yin-yang* just as the *yin-yang* system, conceived as a unity of opposites, forms a model of the natural numbers. They reinforce each other and lend their own meaning to each other to enrich the significance of the other. In this sense, there exists mutual support and interdependence of the two systems. As such, *yin-yang* as forms and odd-even as numbers go hand in hand in the development of the *Xiangshu* interpretation of the *Yijing*.

Generative Functions of Numbers

In this connection, we also can observe that number serves two functions in the development of the *Yijing* metaphysics: a calculative function and a symbolic function. Both functions thrive on the generative nature of the natural numbers. Thus $3 \times 3 = 9$ resulting from the maximum productivity of the 3, and therefore symbolizes the *yang* at the strongest. But $2 \times 3 = 6$ resulting from maximum productivity of the *yin*, represented by 2, factored into the three levels of the world, namely, heaven, earth, and man. Therefore, 6 symbolizes the *yin* at the strongest. $1 + 6 = 7$, as the first odd number after 6 symbolizes the young *yang*, and $9 - 1 = 8$, as the first even number in the retrogression of 9, symbolizes the young *yin*. Other numbers in the *Xici*—such as the numbers of heaven (*tian*), earth (*di*), heaven-earth (*tian-di*), and great evolution (*da-yan*), 25, 30, 50, 55—are all produced as sums or products of the odd and even numbers, and they acquire symbolic meanings in terms of *yin-yang* metaphysics; that is, they symbolize creativity, totality, and a well-ordered world of *yin-yang* relationships. Thus $1 + 3 + 5 + 7 + 9 = 25$; $2 + 4 + 6 + 8 + 10 = 30$; $25 + 30 = 55$; 5 (heaven number in the *Hetu*) × 10 (earth number in the *Hetu*) = 50. There are also the "generating numbers" (*sheng shu*) 1, 2, 3, 4, 5 and the "completing numbers" (*cheng shu*) 6, 7, 8, 9, 10. Together they also make 55. $1 + 2 + 3 + 4 + 5 = 15$; $6 + 7 + 8 + 9 + 10 = 40$; $40 + 15 = 55$. Therefore, the "heaven-earth number" (*tiandi zhi shu*) is the same as the sum of "generating numbers" and "completing numbers." The symbolic function of numbers is fully displayed in the *Hetu* and the *Luoshu*, and it is with this symbolic significance that the *Hetu* and the *Luoshu* should be understood.

Mutual Transformability of *Hetu* and *Luoshu*

Introduction of the *Hetu* and the *Luoshu* leads us to discuss how these two concepts relate to the *Yijing*. Zhu Xi does not seem to directly answer this question; but he does believe that the *Hetu* and *Luoshu* are genuine documents from antiquity that elucidate and symbolize the *yin-yang* interchange philosophy of the *Yijing*. For Zhu Xi, these two concepts *show*, in a Wittgensteinian sense, the onto-generative relationship and creative process of the reality in a concrete yet abstract way. According to Zhu Xi, the evidence for the existence and origin of the *Hetu* and the *Luoshu* is found in the *Book of History* (*Gu Ming* chapter), the *Xici*, the *Analects*, and the *Da Dai Li* (*Ming Dang* chapter). Zhu Xi also points out that the number presentation of both *Hetu* and *Luoshu*, transcribed from ancient times in different versions, remains basically consistent and identical. From this and other statements of Zhu Xi, one can see that he is a fair and open minded, logical scholar, for, as there is no sufficient reason to reject the authenticity of the *Hetu* and the *Luoshu*, Zhu Xi is interested in finding a rational and empirical explanation of these two charts, rather than pushing them aside. Now the question is how to account for their origin and meaning? Here I wish to quote a most significant statement from Zhu Xi's "Reply to Yuan Shu,"

> Although the *Xici* does not speak of Fuxi's creating the *Yi* (system) by receiving the *Hetu*, but in speaking of his observing heaven and looking over earth, seeking afar and taking in what is near, who knows but that the *Hetu* is one of the things [that Fuxi found]? In fact there need not have been a single cause for the sage to create the *Yijing*. But the norm and form (*fa xiang*) of things must have their most appealing aspects. As in the case of the beginning of the world, between heaven and earth, even though there are forms for the *qi* of *yin-yang*, *there are not yet numbers*. Only when the *Hetu* appears, then the odd and even numbers generate 55 numbers [there are odd and even numbers in the number 55]. This can be made conspicuously visible. This reveals the unique insight of the sage which is not to be located in the general natures of things.[23]

Thus according to Zhu Xi, the *Hetu* is one cardinal factor that sets a determinate pattern on the *Yi*, if not causing it. The *Hetu* is of divine origin and if we trust the words of Gong Anguo, which Zhu Xi quotes in the *Qimeng*, it is believed to give rise to the eight trigrams. By the same token, the *Luoshu* is accepted by Zhu Xi as of divine origin as it is believed to give rise to the Nine Fields (*jiu dao*). Now the question is how does the *Hetu* give rise to the eight trigrams? It is said in the *Xici*:

> Thus, the heaven generates miraculous things, then the sage follows it as a principle; the heaven and earth change and transform, then the sage imitates them; heaven discloses forms so that good fortune or ill fortune can be displayed, then the sage represents them. When the [Yellow] River produces the map [*Hetu*] and the Luo [River] produces the script [*Luoshu*], the sage patterns (principles) them (*shengren ze zhi*).[24]

Zhu Xi comments in the *Zhouyi benyi*: "These four things are what caused the sage to create the *Yi* Text (symbols)." But Zhu Xi nowhere explains exactly how these four things cause the sage to create the *Yi* symbols, not to mention how specifically the *Hetu* and the *Luoshu* lead to the sage's creation of the eight trigrams. To decide independently of this textual reference whether the principles for generating the trigrams are linked to the *Hetu* is a difficult issue to settle. If they are linked, however, an even more difficult problem arises: namely, how exactly the trigrams and the *Hetu* are related.

Insofar as the *Hetu* and the *Luoshu* are made of highly suggestive numbers in highly suggestive configuration, their relations to the *Yi*-forms could be speculated on. However, the "*ze*" from the above *Xici* quotation does not mean simply patterning or copying the chart and the script, but it may mean an active evaluation of what one is to follow up. Commenting on the heaven numbers and the earth numbers, Zhu Xi says:

> Heaven generates water by one and earth completes it by six; the earth generates fire by two and heaven completes it by seven. The heaven generates wood by three and the earth completes by eight; earth generates metal by four and heaven completes by nine; heaven generates earth by five and earth completes by ten.[25]

This may explain the *Xici*'s reference to the *Hetu* numbers, and may even explain the positions of the numbers in the *Hetu*, but only at the expense of introducing the *wuxing* (five powers) theory. Yet still, nowhere does it explain the rise of the eight trigrams as we know them.

2, 7
3, 8 5, 5 4, 9
1, 6

The *Xici* does not even mention its numbers, and therefore Zhu Xi rules out that it can be the basis for the production of the *Yi* (as trigrams).[26]

The Qing scholar Li Guangdi of *Zhouyi Zhezhong* points out that Zhu Xi only follows early Confucians (apparently meaning the Confucians of the Han) in interpreting the *Hetu* and the *Luoshu* in terms of the *wuxing* in the *Qimeng*. In other places, Zhu Xi acknowledges that it is not clear how the *Hetu* and the *Luoshu* are related to the eight trigrams and the nine fields.[27] In light of this remark, the only possible explanation of the statement, "The sage follows [the *Hetu/Luoshu*] as paradigms in creating the *Yi*," is that the numbers of the two charts inspire the sage to relate *forms* in some onto-generative and counter-onto-generative order. This means the sage must relate the independently produced *gua* system to the *wuxing* theory, which evolved independently. Zhu Xi simply fails to account for the origin and meaningfulness of the *Hetu* and the *Luoshu*. Further, he does not explain how the *wuxing* are generated ontogenetically or how the *wuxing* theory is developed. Apparently, he accepts the view that the *wuxing* theory is one of the fields of the *Hong Fan*, and *wuxing* results from the *yin-yang* activities as indicated in Zhou Dunyi's *Taiji tu shuo*.

Regarding the question why 5 is centered in both the *Hetu* and the *Luoshu*, Zhang illustrates Zhu Xi's answer from the *Qimeng* in terms of the geometry of squares and circles. Zhu Xi's answer is that "The beginning of numbers is the alternation of one *yin* and one *yang*. The symbol for *yang* is the circle. For the circle the diameter is 1 and the periphery is 3; that is, the proportion is 1:3. The symbol for *yin* is the square. For the square, one side is 1 and the periphery is 4; that is, the proportion is 1:4."[28] But for the periphery of the circle Zhu Xi takes 1 to be 1 and therefore triples the one *yang* to get the 3 of the periphery. For the periphery of the square, he takes 2 to be 1, and therefore divides the one *yin* to get 2. This is called "triple heaven and double earth (*santian liangdi*). The union of 3 and 2 is 5." From this statement, it appears that 5 stands for the union of heaven and earth. Since 5 is in the middle of both charts, the question is then how both charts represent the union of heaven and earth, or symbolically the union of circle and square. Zhang's explanation of this relationship is not clear to me. Notably, the outer number of the *Hetu* sums up to 30 (6 + 7 + 8 + 9 = 30), and if the diameter of the circle is 10, then there is the rough proportion of 1:3. This, of course, falls short of the known mathematical ratio 3.1416 between diameter and periphery in a circle. For the square we have the inner numbers totaling to 10 (on the second layer 1 + 2 + 3 + 4) and to another 10 on the third layer (5 + 5) in the *Hetu* of the following structure:

```
7
2
8 3 5 + 5 4 9
1
6
```

This does not fit with the proportion of 1:4 in the square if the side is 5. Therefore, one must see the two layers of the *Hetu* as forming a single square instead of two squares. Thus we have the following:

```
7
5
8 (2 + 3) 5 (1 + 4) 9
5
6
```

This explains what Zhu Xi means by "take one to be two" (*Yi yi wei er*) and further explains why there are two layers of the inside in that it is a way to "double the one *yin* and form twoness" (*gu liang qi yi yin er wei er*). From this we can see how the *Hetu* represents the union of heaven and earth, the circle and the square, and why 5 is symbolically important and central.

The next question is whether this same theory holds for the *Luoshu*? The answer is: apparently not. The *Luoshu* seems to only reflect the square with 5 as the side length either by the linking of the odd numbers 1 + 3 + 7 + 9 = 20 or by the linking of the even numbers 2 + 4 + 6 + 8 = 20.

```
4 9 2
3 5 7
8 1 6
```

The circle must be developed as the *Luoshu* changes into the *Hetu* in some way. One may indeed regard the *Luoshu* as a result of the change from the *Hetu*.

Zhu Xi does attempt to explain how the *Hetu* and the *Luoshu* are related. He shows how the *Luoshu* can evolve the *Yi* (forms) and how the *Hetu* may represent the *wuxing*. Because of this he says: "How do we know that the *Hetu* is not for the *Luoshu* and the *Luoshu* not for the *Hetu*?"[29] He wants to demonstrate that they are interchangeable and should not be discriminated on the basis of later and earlier discovery as it was traditionally believed that the Hetu was first discovered and the Luoshu was later discovered.

Zhang correctly explains how Zhu Xi regards the *Hetu* as representing the order of the generation of the five powers and the *Luoshu* as representing the order of destruction of the five powers. Upon closer scrutiny and much labor, I have found the following results. If the *Hetu* represents the mutual generation of the five powers, then the *Luoshu* should represent the mutual destruction of the five powers by natural inference. The mutual generation order of the five powers can be expressed as the sequence of 1, 3, 7, 5, 9, which means 1 is water, 3 wood, 7 fire, 5 earth, and 9 metal. And the mutual destruction order is 1, 7, 9, 3, 5. If we group the generating numbers 1, 2, 3, 4, 5 respectively with the completing numbers 6, 7, 8, 9, 10, then we can see that (1, 6), (3, 8), (2, 7), (5, 10), (4, 9) can be diagrammed as

```
    7
    +
    2
8 + 3 5 + 10 4 + 9
    1
    +
    6
```

This is precisely the *Hetu* diagram. On the other hand, (1, 6), (2, 7), (4, 9), (3, 8), (5, 10) can be diagrammed as

```
4 9 2
3 5 7
8 1 6
```

which is precisely the *Luoshu*.

This shows that not only the *Hetu* and the *Luoshu* represent the different order of the *wuxing*, but that the *Hetu* may be said to generate the *Luoshu* via the *wuxing* relationships. That is, given the *Hetu* and given the *wuxing* generative order introduced into the *Hetu*, then by the destructive order of *wuxing* the *Luoshu* can be generated.[30] What is even more amazing is that one need not regard the *Luoshu* as only representing the destructive order of *wuxing*, but instead can interpret it as representing the generative order of *wuxing*; thus we have the sequence (1, 6), (3, 8), (4, 9), (5, 2), (2, 7):

```
4, 9
3, 8   5, 10   2, 7
1, 6
```

The destructive order sequence would then be (1, 6), (4, 9), (2, 7), (3, 8), (5, 10). The diagram organized according to this sequence would then be

```
2 + 7
3 + 8   5 + 10   4 + 9
1 + 6
```

which of course is the *Hetu*.

From this analysis, it appears that the *Hetu* and the *Luoshu* are mutually transformative and generative of each other and their mutual transformation and generation must be based on the *wuxing* theory. In other words, they can transform into each other with reference to the generation order and destruction order of the *wuxing*. Insofar as the generation-order and destruction-order of the *wuxing* are intimately related, the *Hetu* and *Luoshu* are equally intimately related and they naturally presuppose that the *wuxing* are *interpreted into* the *Hetu* and the *Luoshu*. This interpretation is partly based on the theory of the *wuxing* and partly based on the theory of the directions and positions (*fang wei*) of the numbers in the *Hetu* and the *Luoshu*. For the *wuxing* theory, it is important that the *wuxing* are given meanings or directions just as directions are given meanings of the *wuxing*. Thus, water stands for North, fire for South, wood for East, and metal for West, and earth stands for the middle. Similarly, for the number theory of the *Hetu* and the *Luoshu*, it is important that the numbers are given meanings of directions just as directions are given meanings of the numbers. Thus (1, 6) stands for north; (2, 7) for south; (3, 8) for east; (4, 9) for west, and (5, 10) for the middle. With this common ground of direction, the *Hetu* and the *Luoshu* can be said to map onto the *wuxing* system in its generative order or in its destructive order, and vice versa.

Mapping of Independent Systems as a Way of Interpretation

On the basis of these relationships, the following conclusions can be drawn.

1. Since the *Hetu/Luoshu* have no apparent intrinsic number-theoretic properties that correspond to the sequences of *wuxing* generation/destruction, the number sequences (1, 6), (3, 8), (4, 9), (5, 10), (2, 7); (1, 6), (4, 9), (2, 7), (3, 8), (5, 10); (1, 6), (3, 8), (2, 7), (5, 10), (4, 9); (1, 6), (2, 7), (4, 9), (3, 8), (5, 10) do not seem to possess a logically necessary connection. They must be considered a system independent of the *wuxing*. Similarly, the *wuxing* system is independent of *Hetu* and the *Luoshu* as the *wuxing* theory carries no number-theoretical implications. This is a logical point of which earlier scholars including Zhu Xi failed to take note. Because of this failure, they jumped to the conclusion that the *Luoshu* or the *Hetu* are disguised systems of *wuxing*, which they, in fact, are not. Yet one also must recognize that there are logical and arithmetic properties in the *Hetu* and the *Luoshu* themselves that enable them to be mutually transformable *via* the *wuxing* model. These properties are those that can be discerned in the relationships of numbers in the two charts, which need not be considered mystical.

2. Because of the logical independence of the *Hetu*, the *Luoshu*, and the *wuxing* systems, one must account for the origin of these systems on independent grounds. Although the *Hetu* and the *Luoshu* are *a priori* discoveries, their discoveries still need not be considered divine or mystical. The *wuxing* system is no doubt based on empirical observations and generalization, later systematized with symbolic extension of meaning.[31] To bring them together may require a similar natural mentality that sees both as manifestations of the same underlying truth, but this also may be a result of careful coordination and constructive categorizing. The latter can be explained on the basis of the Whiteheadian theory of symbolic reference and unity of feeling.[32]

3. For similar reasons, we also may suggest that the eight-trigram system is logically independent of the *Hetu/Luoshu*, as well as logically independent of the *wuxing* and vice versa. Yet again through widening experience and deepening observation, the eight-trigram system is mapped onto or assimilated into the *Hetu/Luoshu* system and into the *wuxing* system as well. The eight-trigram system has its own principle of organization as observed by Shao Yong, which not only gives rise to the generation of the sixty-four hexagrams, but also gives rise to the before-heaven diagram. The before-heaven diagram is based on the principle of polar opposition (*dui zhi*) and the principle of *yin-yang* coordination and needs no external interpretation from the other systems. Upon analyzing the after-heaven diagram, we see that the relationships of the trigrams are such that they must be induced by the *wuxing* theory. This shows not only that the two systems mutually transform one another, but also that the two systems mutually assimilate or integrate through reinterpretation or assignment of meanings. The rise of the after-heaven diagram of the eight-trigrams is a good example.

As for the relation between the before-heaven diagram and the after-heaven diagram, it might be said that the before-heaven diagram represents a structural orientation of forms, whereas the after-heaven diagram represents a process of circulation (*liu xing*) of *qi*. Both are present in the actual configurations of things and one determines the other; they are two aspects of reality. But what makes the process of circulation of *qi* possible is the *wuxing* theory already formulated. Zhu Xi has not distinguished the three systems clearly nor explained how they work together. An investigation into the *wuxing* theory is meaningful for explaining the integration of the three systems together.

4. One may raise the question whether there is a criterion for judging the validity of the three systems (the eight-trigrams, the *Hetu/Luoshu*, the *wuxing*) and the objective correctness of integration of the three systems as representations or symbolic manifestations of reality. The answer is that there is such a criterion as suggested, but not necessarily precisely formulated by Zhu Xi. Zhu Xi notes in his reply to Lin Shu that the generation of sixty-four hexagrams by rotation of eight trigrams against another eight trigrams "forms the natural movement of the heavenly principle" (*tianli zhi ziran*), which is different from the artificiality of the manmade.[33] He also notes in his reply to Yuan Shu that in seeing the order and clarity of their positions, "One sees the sixty-four hexagrams as naturally arranged according to heavenly principle (*quan shi tianli ziran anpai chulai*) and there is no aid from intelligence to make it so, for it is due to the sage's seeing them clearly that they are drawn out accordingly."[34] From this it is clear that Zhu Xi sees "the naturalness of order and principle" as intrinsically validating a system. If we explain this "naturalness of order" as naturalness, consistency, and logical cogency, then it is clear that Zhu Xi would regard the three systems as embodying principle (*li*) for their validity. Indeed, it is based on this appeal to *li* that the three systems are accepted and integrated as showing and unfolding the significance of the *Yijing*. Zhu Xi notes in the same context (i.e., "Reply to Yuan Shu"), that after the hexagrams are formed then their vertical-horizontal, direct and reverse relationships will all become meaningful and logical (*du*

zheng yi li)." Thus they can be studied and further refined as a natural result.

The principle of "naturalness of order" and the principle of "meaningful relationships" bring the three systems into a unity and lead them to further meaningful enrichment by one another. In this light, Zhu Xi synthesized the diverse traditions of *xiang*, *shu*, and *wuxing* into the philosophy of *li* and *qi*. For, *xiang*, *shu*, and *wuxing* will become understandable only in terms of *li* and *qi*, and yet one does not abolish the *Xiangshu* and *wuxing* because of the *li*. The *li* integrates the three systems and presents a manifold unity. This is the spirit of Zhu Xi's philosophy of the *Yijing*. In this spirit, Zhu Xi is able to design an improved arrangement of each of the sixty-four hexagrams, which respectively generates sixty-four hexagrams in the *Qimeng*. This is an arrangement that commands logical clarity and logical-analytical insights together with a penetrating metaphysical mind. For, it is by this *gua*-change arrangement that Zhu Xi shows how one hexagram can yield all sixty-four hexagrams and sixty-four hexagrams can yield 4,096 hexagrams, and therefore how an infinity is potentially present in a single form. This understanding finally informs Zhu Xi's effort to interpret the *Zhouyi* text in terms of *li*, while at the same time acknowledging the practical basis and origin of the *Yi* forms, numbers, and judgments (*ci*) in divination.

CHAPTER 12

On Timeliness (*Shizhong* 时中) in the *Analects* and the *Yijing*

An Inquiry into the Philosophical Relationship between Confucius and the *Yijing*

Historical Heritage and Conceptual Link: A Methodological Issue

Both the *Analects* and the *Yijing* occupy unique and supremely important positions in the grand tradition of the Confucian school. The *Analects*, being the authenticated record of sayings of Confucius by his immediate disciples, acts as a pivotal point of Confucian insight and wisdom. Thus, it forms the ever-fresh and ever-lively source of Confucian philosophy of life and morality. The *Analects* also is unquestionably the starting point for the subsequent philosophical development of Confucianism in the works of the *Liji*, Mencius, and Xunzi. As a profound thinker, Confucius speaks his views and convictions based on his reflections and his observations on his times, past history, and the nature of things. His thought may be said to crystallize out of his concern for society and the tradition together with his desire to uncover universal principles.

Besides being a thinker, throughout most of his life Confucius also played the role of a humanist, teacher, and educator. Although he mainly taught of the way (*dao*), the universal principle of humanity and virtue, he also taught the traditional learning such as the "six arts" (*liu yi*). Confucius's teaching of the traditional learning implicitly links him to past tradition and thus he says: "I transmit and do not innovate"

(*Analects* 7.1). But in light of the creative insight and wisdom found in the *Analects*, the correct interpretation of this statement is that Confucius has identified with the tradition by drawing inspiration from the tradition, and thereby kept the tradition alive by giving it a new life and a new meaning. Hence, his teaching is historically rooted while at the same time being philosophically amplified by his own life wisdom. He has been nurtured inside the tradition and has developed out of it a new perspective that bears his name. To use Karl Jasper's expression, Confucius is an *axial* thinker, elevating humanity and the human mind from history and tradition to a higher level of civilization and value. He has revolutionized history by providing it as a corner stone for people to further build upon. In this sense, Confucius transmits the *dao* (universal principle) by purifying it from historicity and articulating it in terms of universal and universally learnable truth.

The whole point of understanding Confucius in the *Analects* is to underline the fact that there is both a dimension of history and a dimension of philosophy in the *Analects*, just as there is in the personal self-realization of Confucius himself. Confucius, speaking of his own self-development, says:

> I devoted [myself to] learning at fifteen and established myself at thirty. At forty I became immune from temptations. At fifty I came to know the mandate of heaven. At sixty my ears became pliable to the world. At seventy I do what my heart wishes without trespassing the bounds of right. (2.4)

On the other hand, he shows his own historical preference by saying:

> The rites of Xia I can speak about, but one cannot confirm them at Ji; the rites of Yin I can speak about, but one cannot confirm them at Song. It is because the historical documents are not sufficient. If the historical documents were sufficient, I could certainly confirm what I know . . . (3.14). The rites of Zhou were derived from the revision of the rites in two dynasties. They are indeed highly cultivated. I follow Zhou. (8.18, 18.9)

Confucius spoke of the way in which Yao and Shun govern (8.18) and identified Zhou as having the supreme virtue (8.20), and praised the virtue of Yu (8.21). The *Analects* is thus a reflection of the Confucian learning and Confucian wisdom, which inherits a past tradition and paves the way for a new tradition—the tradition of *humanity* and *virtue*. With this understanding, it is quite significant to raise the question as to how Confucius's thought and the Confucian *Analects* are related specifically to the intellectual contents of the tradition as represented by the *Classics*, which he edited for transmission and teaching. As is well known, Confucius is said to have edited the *Six Classics (Liu Jing): Shi, Shu, Li, Yi, Yue,* and *Chun Qiu*. Through his editing and teaching of these classics, he made them part of tradition. He transmitted and yet at the same time created. His efforts in editing and teaching assimilated and transformed the tradition of the past by preserving it and reorganizing it. The preservation and organization, or reorganization, inevitably acquire a meaning in relation to his own teachings and learning just as his own teachings acquire meaning in light of his editing and presentation of the classics.

The networking of Confucian teaching and his interwoven efforts in editing and teaching inevitably form a rich matrix and context for understanding Confucian insight and wisdom in the *Analects*. The *Analects* and the classics also illuminate each other. In order to understand Confucius correctly and adequately, we must be aware of this interwoven context imbued with rich latent meanings, and we must also open our eyes to the interrelationships of the *Classics* and the *Analects* in light of the historical role Confucius played in forming a new tradition by amplifying and purifying the old tradition. This understanding is a basis for understanding how Confucianism could develop creatively from the master and reach new heights of philosophical thinking in various periods of Chinese history, particularly in the Song-Ming period. It might be said that it is in the Song-Ming period that the interwoven context of tradition and wisdom in Confucianism was made fully clear, perhaps through the incentive of Buddhist systematic and theoretical thinking.

This understanding of the interwoven context of history and philosophy in Confucius, more significantly, leads to a recognition of a new methodology for creatively interpreting the Confucian works such as the *Analects* and evaluating their relation to the earlier classics. We should also uncover, evaluate, and organize insights and meanings of Confucian thought in relation to the history-philosophy unity in Confucian thought, and develop new paradigms of understanding through examining both the historical heritage and the conceptual link. We should let history illuminate thought, but we also should let thought illuminate history. We should especially let thought develop in light of conceptual organization, comparison and assimilations in light of the original thought-history matrix and context in which interrelationships of concepts become visible. Establishing conceptual links is a task that is as important as establishing the historical heritage, particularly when the former will strengthen the latter. We will call this method "creative hermeneutical analysis."

It is in view of the above history-philosophy unity in the Confucian *Analects* and in reference to the above methodological concept of creative hermeneutical analysis that we may now raise the question as to how the *Analects* historically relates to the *Yijing*, and derivatively, how the philosophy of Confucius conceptually relates to the philosophy of the *Yijing*. This question is of momentous importance because of the importance the *Analects* has and because of the importance the *Yijing* has in the whole tradition of Confucian philosophy. We have already described the importance of the *Analects* in terms of its being the source and pivotal point for the development of Confucian thought. Now we may see how the *Yijing* (or simply, *Yi*) is equally important in the whole architectonic structure of Confucianism.

In the first place, the *Yi* (for that matter, the *Zhouyi*), as the art of divination, is the oldest tradition in the Chinese civilization, which dates back to the second millennium BCE. It reflects the earliest stratum of Chinese experience in daily life and has served the practical purpose of guiding and influencing Chinese community life and civilized living. In the second place, the *Yi* contains a well-developed code of conduct and an orderly understanding of reality and life. (More will be said on this later.) In this sense the *Yi* presents the basic Chinese view of the world and life and carries an implicit theory of the origin of the universe and an explanation of things and their places. It is holistic and organic in outlook and therefore represents the total vision of life and reality for the Chinese tradition. In this perspective, the *Yi Text* embodies an important part of tradition, which Confucius would feel obligated to transmit.

In the third place, the *Yi* Text has since the Shang Period gradually penetrated to the core of Chinese life and implicitly shaped the common people. By the time of Confucius, one may say that the *Yi* tradition had been assimilated into the popular culture and become part and parcel of the Chinese practical living. Again, the *Yi* can be said to represent a tradition that widely and enduringly persists to the present.

In the fourth place, the *Yi* Text has been philosophically inspiring throughout its history. Beginning with the so-called *Ten Wings* (*Shiyi*), which are traditionally considered to be commentaries on the Yi Text by Confucius and his disciples, there is an unbroken tradition of commenting on the Yi Text. Such a tradition is to philosophize, theorize, systemize, and elucidate the ideas, principles, views, and insights into life and world implicit in the Yi Texts and in the Confucian commentaries of the Yi Texts such as the *Ten Wings*. Why is the Yi Text so philosophically inspiring? It is not because it is useful for divination, nor because it has been widely used in ancient times. It is inspiring because there is a philosophical wisdom implicit in the divinatory text. As we shall see, the Yi Text exhibits a structure and an understanding of reality, which makes the Confucian interpretation and synthesis possible and indeed occasioned the Confucian interpretation and synthesis. The Confucian interpretation and synthesis is the first great philosophical theorization and systematization of the Yi Text.

After approximately a period of sixteen centuries, a second great philosophical theorization and systematization took place. This time, the theorization and systematization took place in terms of the *Taiji tu shuo* of Zhou Dunyi and the *li-qi* theories of Cheng Yi and Zhu Xi. During the interval between these two great syntheses, there had been a rich sequence of philosophical theorization on the Yi Text. The Yi Text: the Yi-symbolism (trigrams and hexagrams) and the *Yizhuan* (*Ten Wings*). This sequence extends far beyond the second great synthesis. Perhaps we have now reached a point where a third great synthesis in a new attempt to theorize and systematize the Yi Text can be made.

This chapter represents an effort to clear the ground for such a new synthesis and to set the stage and framework for such a new systematization. What this tradition of commentaries suggests is that the Yi Text provides a metaphysical picture for understanding the world and life, which one does not find in the *Analects*. In this way, the former complements what is lacking in the latter. Perhaps the *Ten Wings* may be regarded as a statement and a formulation of the Confucian metaphysics, and, therefore, provide a metaphysical basis and ground for the Confucian philosophy of life and morality.

For the four major reasons given above, the importance of the *Yijing* in the Confucian tradition should not be underestimated. The *Analects* needs the Yi Text to provide a metaphysical description of the world and life. At the same time, the Yi Text needs the *Analects* for rational justification and moral interpretation of its practical guidance and advice. Indeed, it needs the Confucian insight to transform its divinatory practicality into principled philosophical views of reason and humanity. The

Analects, with its historical reference, must be anchored to historical roots, and must have a source for making its insights historically relevant, just as the Yi Text, with its profound philosophical import, must be articulated in philosophical consciousness making it explicitly philosophically relevant. In plain words, the *Analects*, for all its concern with moral development and cultivation of humanity, needs a metaphysical grounding and basis, whereas the Yi Text needs an explicit statement of its implicit ontology and cosmology and a moral justification or elucidation of its moral significance to make it relevant to human beings.

Considered in its entirety, one can easily see how the *Analects* could be said to be without metaphysical basis and without historical origins. Similarly, one may easily see how the Yi Text can be said to be *merely* a manual of divination devoid of moral and metaphysical significance. However, neither statement is true. Indeed, when we see the *Analects* and the Yi Text as mutually complementary and reciprocally fulfilling a potentiality in relation to and in reference to each other, we do not have to lament the lack of Confucian metaphysics in the *Analects*.[1] On the other hand, we do not have to conceive the Yi Text as merely a manual of divination. What I wish to stress is that there is natural mutual or reciprocal relevance of the Yi Text and the *Analects* for each other, which has not been sufficiently recognized, and which can be adequately recognized only in the context and matrix of the double unity-ambiguity of history and philosophy in the *Analects* and the Yi Text.

The efforts to provide the Confucian morality of the *Analects* with a metaphysics of the *dao* or of heaven and earth (*tiandi*) have been made, especially in the Song Neo-Confucian systems, but seldom is the need for making a moral justification of the Yi-metaphysics fully felt. For this reason, the Confucian contributions in the *Ten Wings* to understanding the Yi Text has not been fully appreciated, and the need for such a work has not been recognized. This results from a superficial understanding of the meaning of both classics, and from an impoverished sense of appreciation of the unity and ambiguity of history and philosophy in both. When one sees the *Analects* as simply philosophy or as simply history, or sees the Yi Text as simply philosophy or as simply history, one will understand less of the reality of the Yi or the *Analects*. One will consequently see each as independent by itself, and therefore, insufficient for both philosophical and historical explanations. This is the result of what Whitehead refers to as the fallacy of simple location: the fallacy of locating the existence of an entity in a fixed isolated locality, losing sight of the underlying continuum of relational meaning and reciprocal needs.

On Timeliness (Shizhong) in the Analects and the Yijing 359

We must have the methodological insight into the relational meaning and reciprocal need of a classic text as generated by the context of unity-ambiguity of history-philosophy, so that we will be able to have adequate understanding of, and give proper evaluation of, the Yi Text and the Analects. It is only in light of this methodological insight that the relation of the Analects to the Yi Text can be fully understood and answered. This methodology of generating meaning from the context of the unity-ambiguity of history-philosophy can be also called the methodology of holistic, dialectical, and hermeneutical analysis. It is holistic because it places the relation of two forms of text and thought in the whole context of relational meanings. It is dialectical because it traces the relation in question from the generative-developmental-evolutionary point of view. It is hermeneutical because it requires insight into the language of the two to rethink a problem and to reorganize a solution to the problem.

One may now point out that it is due to the lack of such a methodological training that very often arguments against treating the Yi Text as philosophical and as having a Confucian significance or against relating the Analects to the Yijing have been raised. This is quite true in the writings of the May 4th Period: Gu Jigang is a good example. More recently, scholars such as H. G. Creel have also questioned the relation of the Yijing to the Confucian Analects.[2] This is most unfortunate for understanding Confucian Philosophy. Confucian philosophy was understood as lacking a historical source and as lacking a metaphysical foundation. At the same time, the Yi Text is thereby deprived of its philosophical or metaphysical significance. This tendency must now be corrected. Although reasons for a more comprehensive view have been articulated, there are not thorough arguments for making the relation of the Analects to the Yi Text and, vice versa, clear and meaningful. It is because scholars lack an adequate methodology, and lacking this, lack a way to justify and formulate such relationship.

Now in this chapter, my purpose is to formulate and justify an intimate relationship between the Analects and the Yi Text, so that we can regard the Yi Text as a source, a basis, and an occasion for the development of Confucian metaphysics. We can simultaneously regard the Analects as an incentive and a starting point for synthesizing and transforming metaphysics into ethics or morality. Our arguments will establish both a relation of historical heritage and a philosophical or conceptual link beyond reasonable doubt. We will not show that we have new evidence for the historical heritage. We shall only note that a conceptual understanding of the *Ten Wings* against the background of the unity-ambiguity of the *Analects* and the *Yi* Text will suffice to give support to the belief that Confucius and his disciples have derived a metaphysical system from the original *Yi* Text and that they are warranted in doing so because the *Yi* Text is by its own nature suggestive of such a metaphysics. In this sense an argument for the historical relation is again conceptual and is based on the logic of explanation. We shall see what our arguments establish when we see what system of thought the *Yi* Text even on its divinatory level displays and what system of thought the *Analects* displays. We will discuss these two systems of thought in regard to some, but not all, prominent points so that their problematic relation can be clarified and a natural answer to such a problem can be introduced.

In this light that we shall see the moral significance of the *Yi*-metaphysics as well as the metaphysical significance of the Confucian morality in the *Analects*. We shall specifically discuss the problem of "*ji*" (good fortune) and *xiong* (ill-fortune) in the *Yijing*, and see how they can be related to the virtues of self-cultivation in the *Analects*' system of thought. A consideration of this relation will lead to another and perhaps more specific argument for the historical continuity and philosophical link between the *Yi* Text and the *Analects*. This is in regard to the essential concept of timeliness (*shi* or *shizhong*) found in both the *Yijing* and Confucian texts such as the *Zhongyong*. It will be shown that although the *Analects* does not directly refer to the concept of timeliness, it can be shown that timeliness is the very essence of the Confucian teaching in light of the *Zhongyong*. It can also be shown that timeliness, in light of the *Ten Wings*, can be said to be a noble natural goal and standard of conduct in the *Yi* Text. A comparative study of the *Yi* Text (including *Yizhuan*) on the one hand and the *Analects* on the other will serve the purpose of establishing the conceptual link between the *Analects* and the *Yi* Text.

If timeliness is the essence of the teaching in the *Analects*, and at the same time is the essence of the teaching in the *Yi* Text, the conceptual link between the *Analects* and the *Yijing* will become crystal clear. We will then have achieved a more accurate and rich understanding of the *Analects* and the *Yijing* themselves in light of an understanding of their relationship. When Mencius says that "Confucius is the sage of timeliness" (5B1), he may have already perceived the relevance of the *Yijing* tradition for the Confucian view of a moral life of self-cultivation as we have already perceived the essence of the Confucian philosophical teaching.

The Intended System of the *Analects*

How do we understand the *Analects* as a philosophical system? By "philosophical system" here, I do not mean a formalized and fully elaborated system of ideas; I mean generally salient philosophical points that reveal a framework for understanding human beings and reality and that mutually support one another. In other words, I am speaking of a system in a potential sense, which is indicated in terms of some main issues and concepts. It is from this point of view that I shall take the philosophical content and significance of the *Analects* to be relevant to the *Yijing*, which, however, has not been discussed in this fashion before.

There are five points of philosophical significance in the *Analects* that I believe represent the intended system of the *Analects*. These five points seem to provide a picture of the world and persons from the point of view of Confucius. The first point concerns human nature, in terms of free ability and *free will* to do good; the second concerns the limitations of human life and human destiny that one should recognize, accept, and even transcend in view of one's self-realization in practicing virtues; the third point concerns the constant and universal virtues a person should uphold at all times; the fourth concerns the application of one's virtues in the real world and the problem of appropriateness of the application; finally, the fifth point concerns how Confucius actually feels toward the tradition of the *Yi* Text. All these points are important for understanding thoroughly the concept of timeliness in Confucius and how Confucius relates to the *Yi* Text. I shall discuss the first four points under six headings in this section. I shall discuss the fifth point in a separate section.

Affirmation of Self-creative Power in the Human Being

Although Confucius speaks of limitations and inevitabilities of the human being (conveyed by the notion of *ming*), he spoke even more vigorously of the self-creative and free power in humans that enables them to develop, grow, and fulfill themselves. This self-creative and free power in fact defines a person as it defines the goal, the function, and the ultimate value of a person. He points out: "It is man who can expand the *dao*, not the *dao*, which can expand man" (*Analects* 15.29). But the expansion of the *dao* by persons is intrinsic in persons and thus implies the cultivation of virtues in persons so that they can achieve moral perfection in their lives. This moral perfection is called *ren*—the virtue of benevolence and love to be realized in different human relationships. The self-creative and free power in human beings is precisely this power to achieve moral perfection. Confucius says: "Is *ren* far away? If I desire *ren*, *ren* arrives forthwith!" (7.30)

To achieve the moral perfection of *ren* is self-fulfillment for a person; it is not for any extrinsic purpose, and it defines the ultimate value of human existence. Thus, Confucius further affirms: "To discipline oneself and restore rites (*li*) is *ren*. If for one day one disciplines oneself and restores *li*, the whole world will return to *ren*. To achieve *ren* is through oneself, is it through other people?" (12.1). It is in one's power to discipline oneself, to restore *li*, and to achieve *ren*. We see that Confucius believes one can be the master of one's own fate and can transform oneself. In this sense, we see human beings are free, morally free.

Moral freedom is a fundamental freedom of human beings, for it is the freedom that brings ultimate fulfillment and satisfaction to one's life as a whole. The recognition of this freedom is also indicated in Confucius's frequent reference to "wish and will." He asked his disciples two times to speak of their "wish and will" (*ge yan qizhi*). This "*zhi*" is free will in that it enables one to do things and to achieve a goal. In particular if this *zhi* is directed toward the *dao* and *ren*, one will achieve the *dao* and *ren*. This means that *zhi* as an expression of free will and also implies the self-creative power of a person, which will transform and fulfill that person's life. Confucius illustrates this self-creative power of self-transformation: "It is like heaping up a hill; if there is a shortage of one bucket of earth and one stops, this is because I stop (doing the heaping); it is also like heaping up a hill on level ground; even if I heap up one bucket of earth, this is progress and I am making progress" (9.19).

To build up one's moral character and determine to achieve moral perfection is a matter of one's free choice and is totally within one's self-creative power. It is on this ground that Confucius could blame his disciple, Zai Yu, for sleeping in the daytime: Zai Yu has failed to exercise his own will to discipline himself and let sheer laziness take hold of him. Confucius also rebuts his disciple Ran Qiu for finding an excuse for not following the *dao*, namely, by claiming to have no ability to do so. Thus, Confucius says, "But in your case you have confined yourself [without even beginning to try]" (6.12). One may say that Confucius staunchly believed that if one makes effort to do a certain thing, one can always make progress in attaining it. If one has not made progress in obtaining a goal, it is simply that one has not tried to do so. As he says in reference to a poem, "It is simply that one has not thought of someone; if one does, is the distance a problem" (9.31)?

Confucius has expressed a free-will philosophy and a belief in the self-control and self-transformation of a person independently of any external circumstances. This is the ultimate and unlimited freedom of a person *qua* person. Although Confucius has not named this ultimate and unlimited freedom of human beings to pursue good and achieve moral perfection, this ultimate freedom is no doubt what is called the *nature* (*xing*) in a person. It is indeed the ability and power of the nature in a person to enable that person to reach for the heaven (ultimate reality) and achieve unity and participation in the works of heaven and earth: this much is indicated in the *Zhongyong*.

The Limitations of Life

Although the nature of a person is such that he has freedom to aim at moral perfection, a person's life is limited by his existence as an entity in the world. Thus, a person is destined to die, and he cannot totally control and transform the circumstances of his birth and his fortune. Many things affecting the well-being of a person only happen to him, but are not dictated by his will. Thus, one person may be poor and another may be rich. One person may have an opportunity to realize his ambition, another may not and may instead suffer from adversity and hardship. One person may die early and another may live longer. All these illustrate what Confucius calls "*ming*" in the *Analects*.

As the *ming* constitutes the limitations of life, it may simply be referred to as limitations and contingencies of life beyond one's power of free choice and self-making. Thus, Zi Xia says: "The matters of death and life is a matter of *ming*; whether one becomes rich and powerful depends upon heaven" (12.5). When his disciple Bo Niu was seriously ill, Confucius lamented: "In losing you, it is *ming*! This good man has little illness; this good man has this illness" (6.10)! On both occasions, some contingency beyond one's ability encumbers one. When the best of his disciples, Yan Yuan, passed away, Confucius said: "Heaven wants to destroy me! Heaven wants to destroy me" (11.9)! In this expression, as in the expression of Zi Xia, heaven is also cited as a source of limitation. One may thus conjecture that *ming* is another aspect of heaven even as heaven shows itself in the unlimited freedom of a person for moral transformation.

This reference to heaven in regard to limitations of life throws light on heaven. It shows that heaven is the ultimate source of order and the necessity of things, on the one hand, and the source of value, freedom, creativity of life in human beings, on the other. To understand heaven in this twofold respect is for Confucius to recognize the "mandate of heaven" (*tianming*). *Tianming* is not simply *ming*, but what heaven ordains for the total order and total creative transformation of things. In this sense even the freedom one has and the moral perfectibility of human beings are matters of *tianming*. Life for Confucius, therefore, does possess a meaning because it is destined to fulfill itself in the *dao* and *ren* even though one has to freely choose and make ample effort to attain this goal. One may also speak of two levels of the ultimate reality: the ultimate reality as the higher level is referred to as *tian* (heaven) and the lower level is referred to as *ming*. The purpose of life is to strive for realization of oneself on the level of *tian*, and this is the only way to transcend *ming*, even while accepting *ming*.

As we see, *tian* and *ming* both belong to the ultimate reality; thus, we will also understand how Confucius speaks of the same thing in the following statements. Besieged at Guang, Confucius says: "After the death of King Wen, does the culture of the *dao* reside here? If heaven wants to lose this culture, it would not let me who came later participate in this culture. If heaven has no wish to lose the culture, what can the people of Kuang do to me" (9.5)? Referring to an incident concerning his disciple, Zi Lu, Confucius says: "If the *dao* will prevail in the world, it is a matter of *ming*; if the *dao* is to be abolished in the world, it is also a matter of *ming*. What can Gongbo Liao do to change *ming*" (14.36)? *Tian* and *ming* are one, and it is important to know that they are one so that one can strive for good and moral perfection according to one's nature and yet without complaint against the misfortunes or limitations one encounters in the form of one's *ming*. Thus, Confucius teaches: "Do not complain about heaven and do not resent others" (14.35). To understand this and to have the right attitude toward life is to know the *mandate of heaven*.

Understanding this is indeed of supreme importance for a human being. Thus, Confucius says: "At fifty I came to know the *mandate of heaven* (*tianming*)" (2.4). That Confucius came to know the *tianming* relatively late in life is clearly a sign that it takes much experience of life in order for one to see the limitations of life and to see that limitations exist as if they are mandated by heaven: their sanction and justification come from a deeper understanding of the ultimate reality (the *dao* of heaven), which gives rise to life and order. It takes a superior person, a person of much moral self-cultivation, to acquire this deeper understanding of the ultimate reality. Thus, Confucius remarks: "A person who does not know the *ming* cannot be a superior person" (20.3).

To know *ming* is to know the context, the background, and the process of self-development for a person; it is to demarcate a plan for oneself so that one knows one's purpose in life, and make pertinent effort to pursue one's purpose in life. This knowing of *ming* no doubt has metaphysical significance, for it presupposes as well as implies knowing the whole reality, knowing how one relates to it, and knowing what one can do and what one cannot do.

The desirability of knowledge of *ming* should make it clear that a superior person should look into the nature of reality, into how it presents itself in life, what one can do to relate to it and how one can do so. As a superior person, one has the need to fulfill oneself in any situation independent of the external influence, even though one has to learn to respond and adjust to any difficult situation. This knowledge of *ming* enables one to accept circumstance; to adjust and to strive for one's best. Only a superior person does this: without such knowledge a person would live in darkness and lose sight of himself too. Thus, Confucius points out that, while the "Superior man fears the mandate of heaven; the small man does not even know it" (16.8). To fear *tianming* is to respect life as it is given to us and as we strive to make it morally perfect. It is to engage one's life with a sense of destiny and a sense of purpose. Since the small person does not have a sense of destiny and a sense of purpose, that person cannot be said to know *tianming*; consequently, the small person leads a less meaningful life, a life with no sense of purpose and no sense of destiny.

Earlier I mentioned that in order to know *tianming* one has to have a deeper understanding of the ultimate reality. What then is this deeper understanding? Since Confucius seldom makes metaphysical statements, can we not conjecture from relevant statements in the *Analects* regarding what this ultimate reality is supposed to be? In this connection two statements by Confucius are quite relevant and revealing: "Heaven has not spoken of anything, yet the ten thousand things grow; heaven has not spoken anything, yet the four seasons rotate!" (17.19)! On looking over a creek, Confucius remarks: "It goes so fast—it goes in spite of day and night" (9.17)! From this statement, one can see that Confucius has experienced the ultimate reality as a flow of time. The ultimate reality is not a substance statically fixed; it is seen as movement and life shown in all changes and transformation of things. This reality of life-force is also highly creative and order-preserving so that the whole universe may be said to exhibit a creative process of change and production. It is clear that in reference to this process one can understand the limitations of life (*ming*) (as the latter is required to produce new life) and to value assertion and acquisition of freedom.

In the *Analects*, Confucius seldom speaks of profit, but instead gives himself to participating in both *ming* and *ren* (9.1). This parallelism between *ming* and *ren* is highly significant, for it shows that, while one can passively accept *ming*, one can still develop an active pursuit of *ren*. This means that in this description of Confucius, Confucius has shown how one may actively and freely seek education, self-cultivation and self-fulfillment in *ren*, which is a process totally within one's choice and fulfillment. Confucius has also shown how one can still accept the *ming* in different situations of life.

Ming and *Ren* as Two Aspects of Confucian Wisdom

Although it is not the place to review Confucius's life regarding his disappointments and setbacks, it is clear that one of the contingencies of life for Confucius is that he did not secure a lasting official position to bring about his life-dreams to put the world into order and harmony through virtuous influence and exemplary action. In his travel to many states, he failed to make his teachings heard by the rulers of the state. He had to recognize that in his lifetime he might not see the *dao* prevail and the world return to order and propriety.

In the *Analects* there are many expressions of the sage's feelings toward disappointing the world. Although Confucius could not but feel that the *dao* may not prevail in his time, he had abundant faith that it would prevail in the long run. This justified his making efforts to make the prevailing of the *dao* possible through teaching and transmitting the *dao* from the past. He was called, "The one who knows that one cannot succeed (in bringing about the *dao*) and yet who still persists in trying" (14.38). He was also sarcastically criticized by the hermits, who saw him as either seeking a position or as engaging in fruitless pursuit without understanding the world.

From my analysis of the notion of *ming* in the *Analects*, it is clear that Confucius understood the limitations of life. He could see in the later part of his life that the world remaining callous to his teaching is one of the limitations of the world and his own life. It is a matter of *ming* just like being rich or poor. One cannot but accept it, and yet, one has to do one's best to bring about what belongs to the nature of things. What belongs to the nature of things is a matter of moral cultivation and preservation of the *dao*. With this understanding, Confucius did not abandon his pursuit of moral perfection in himself and in the world, although he did come to suggest a modification of his own adjustment to the social reality. He says: "If I cannot find people to follow the principle of the mean (*zhong xing*), must I take those who are eccentric and wild? The wild are active and forward-looking, the eccentric have at least something they will not do (13.21) . . . If the *dao* does not prevail, [I] will ride on a boat and float in the ocean (5.7)." These expressions suggest that he accepted the chaos of the world as a matter of *ming*, and he did his best to live with it.

To recognize the limitations of life and world helps one recognize how it is more valuable to develop one's moral powers of *ren*. It encourages one to appreciate the importance of one's moral freedom. One still can fulfill one's life and bring about good in his life by exercising his moral freedom and making full efforts at self-cultivation. It is in this light that Confucius speaks of the superior man as "persisting in his poverty" and the small man as "losing principles because of poverty" (15.2). Also, in this light one can see how in the *Analects* Confucius persists in upholding many basic constant principles of virtues independent of consideration of limitations of life and world. These constant principles of virtue are based on and derived from consideration of the self-creative nature and the free power of human beings, which warrants human moral perfectibility.

Constant Virtues and Principles for Moral Perfection

By constant virtues (*chang de*) and principles, I mean virtues and principles a person will cultivate and uphold for his moral perfection under any circumstances of life and in spite of limitations or contingencies one confronts in one's life. As a creative thinker, Confucius focused and formulated constant virtues and principles from his understanding of human beings and their nature. He has in a way defined the value and worth of persons by defining the constant virtues and principles of humanity. In fact, it is precisely on the basis of deepened understanding of humanity that these virtues and principles are founded. Among all the virtues, as is well known, *ren* is the foremost and the perfect virtue as well as the foundation of all virtues. The following quotation will explicitly state how virtues and principles should remain constant and independent of the vicissitudes of life and how a person should abide by them under changing and difficult conditions in life:

> Wealth and power are what men desire. But if one does not gain wealth and power in the right way, one will not have them. Poverty and lowness are what men dislike; but if one does not remove them the right way, [(*sic*), here I substitute "remove" (*qu*) for "gain" (*de*)], one will not remove them. If a superior man removes *ren*, how can he have the name of a superior man? The superior man will not violate *ren* for a single moment even at meal time. In haste he abides by *ren* and in difficulty and hardship he abides by *ren*. (4.5)

This statement of Confucius demonstrates the constancy of virtues and shows that persons devoted to their own moral perfection (the *junzi*) should always remain steadfast to the virtues. Virtues are not wealth and power, which one can dispense with. They are essential for one's moral growth and self-fulfillment in life. The justification of virtue comes from the intrinsic worth of the human being. To recognize the constancy of virtue is to affirm and recognize the intrinsic worth of the human being independent of his being wealthy and powerful or being poor and lowly. This of course is not to say that Confucius rejects wealth and power. He is no ascetic and recognizes a comfortable good life as desirable. But virtues and principles of virtue must overrule the desire for power and wealth. If one acquires wealth and power without violating virtues, then there is no harm in having power and wealth. How one acquires wealth and power is a matter of principle and the principle must be conducive to the practice of virtue toward moral perfection of a person.

To see how Confucius comes to formulate principles of virtue is highly important. To uphold and practice virtues is an expression of one's intrinsic worth. It shows the self-consciousness of one's intrinsic worth as a person. It may be said to be both an expression of one's ontological existence as a person and an expression of one's total freedom as limited by nothing external. In this regard we can see that there is implicit in Confucius's notion of virtue (*de*) a Kantian element of moral autonomy—moral actions are dictates of one's free will and are subject to no external authority or force of circumstances. The moral action of a person comes from moral cultivation of the person, and virtues are ways of making this moral cultivation possible. They are essential ways of moral cultivation.

What are the principles of virtue and moral cultivation that Confucius formulates for the moral life? We have mentioned the virtue of *ren*. *Ren* as a principle is expressed as follows:

1. "Do not do to others what you do not wish others to do to you" (12.2).

2. "Love people" (12.22).

3. "Discipline yourself and restore the rites" (12.1).

4. "Establish others in order that you yourself become established; perfect others in order that you yourself become perfected" (6.30).

Without elaborating on the individual significance of each formulation of the *ren* principle, it suffices to note that each formulation embodies an aspect of the all comprehensive *ren* principle. As *ren* represents the ultimate ideal moral perfection, it has many meanings in many regards even though it remains a unified notion. Confucius says that his *dao* is penetrated with unity. One finds such unity precisely in the principle of *ren*.

Apart from *ren*, there are other principles of virtue; it suffices to briefly mention two more. One of the other important virtues is that of *yi* (rightness or righteousness). There is no explicit explanation of *yi* in the *Analects*. But from the contexts of its use one can see *yi* as a principle of achieving appropriateness and propriety in a situation. *Yi* also is a principle of observing principles rather than pursuing profit, a principle of conforming to public well-being rather than to selfish self-interest. In virtue of the *yi*-principle, one maintains one's moral dignity and moral autonomy despite hardships and adversity. Yi is a principle of preserving one's moral integrity and one's moral purity, to contrast with ren being a principle of giving to others one's care and consideration and love. Yi is such a basic principle that the understanding of it depends on one's understanding of what is *right* at a right time and in a right place; there is no uniformity of yi for all circumstances. The application of yi and in fact, the concrete evaluation as to what is Yi in a given circumstance depends on one's understanding of concrete circumstances and situations of life. In this sense, yi presupposes knowing and understanding the *ming* (*zhi ming* 知命), understanding proper form (*zhi li* 知礼), understanding benevolence (*zhi ren* 知仁), and understanding people (*zhi ren* 知人). Perhaps it is in this spirit of recognizing need for specific appraisal that Yi is not defined or fully explained by Confucius. It is also in this spirit in reference to concrete circumstances that Confucius says the following: "In the case of a superior man [there is no fixed way for acting toward things in the world], there is no 'absolute yes,' and there is no 'absolute no.' There is only Yi to follow" (*Analects* 4.10). But what is this yi 义? It is the righteousness embodied in a concrete situation. Hence, we may as well interpret yi 义 as capability to adapt to time and hence as change and transformation, namely Yi 易. Thus, Confucius would consider seeking office in times of order a desirable action so that one would be able to benefit the world whereas in times of disorder one would seek to only benefit oneself alone and even escape from the world by wondering in the sea. We shall see that it is through consideration of Yi that a superior person develops a sense of timeliness, which constitutes *virtue* in *action*, and direct application of virtue.

Regarding *li* as a principle of virtue, Confucius treated it as an expression of one's self-creative power and free will. It is a matter of demonstrating one's self-understanding of one's station in life and place in the world. Therefore, in *li*, there is presupposed a required understanding and knowing of the world and other people so that correct relationships can be established and observed. Insofar as ren 仁 and yi 义 can be fully realized by oneself, *li* can be fully realized by oneself. Confucius made *li* a basic principle of moral life as it stems from the free will of the human being to order and preserve his life in a context of human relationships. Thus, he lays down the following principle: "If a superior man devotes himself to learning human letters and disciplines himself to *li*, his conduct will not then deviate from the right path" (6.27).

There are many other virtues and principles that Confucius suggests for the cultivation of one's moral integrity and moral life. They may be said to be both practical guiding principles for maintaining one's independence of will and mind, as well as constituting principles defining the moral essence and moral life of a human being. It is clear that without these virtues and principles one will become a slave of circumstance, and one will lose whatever autonomy and freedom one has. It was recorded in the *Analects* that Confucius teaches human arts, the practice of virtue, loyalty and faithfulness (7.25). The *Analects* also notes many sayings of the sage on many things in perfecting life and conducting good government. Confucius even suggests the ideal form of a moral and good life: To be a person of wisdom, benevolence and courage (9.28). Do not be stubborn, prejudiced, bigoted, and selfish (9.4). "Devote yourself to the *dao*; reside in virtue; depend on *ren* and rest in the arts" (7.6). "Inspire oneself with poetry; establish oneself in *li*, and fulfill oneself in arts" (8.8).

The significance of this ideal form of moral life consists in a person's potential for fulfilling himself by achieving the ideal form of moral life; moreover, this potential is completely independent of the limitations of life and constitutes an inner dimension of human existence.

Timeliness, Persistence and Application of Virtues and Principles

In the *Analects*, there are two categories of statements and expressions by Confucius and his disciples that have not been carefully distinguished in earlier studies. One category of statements and expressions by Confucius marks out generally constant principles and virtues that a person must observe independent of, and under, all circumstance. This category of statements we have discussed already in the preceding section. The second category of statements and expressions, on the other hand, consists of those pertaining to how one applies one's virtue to some particular and specific sort of situation or how one preserves and persists in one's moral cultivation in a specific and particular sort of circumstance. There are statements expressing Confucius's perception that the way may not prevail, and he could achieve the reform of the world he aspired to.

Apart from what I have cited earlier about Confucius's recognition of *ming* for his teaching, the following statements also clearly represent a recognition of *ming*: "The phoenix does not come, the river does not produce the chart. I have no hope of fulfilling the way in the world" (*Analects*, 9.9). "I must be very old. I have not dreamt of Duke Zhou for a long time" (7.5). This type of statement indicates that one's way to benefit the world may not have the requisite *timeliness* for its recognition and acceptance because of *ming*. The statement also implies that it is because one has the option of persisting in one's way of virtue that one must feel disappointed in the face of *ming*. In these cases, we may say that there is no *timeliness* for one's way and virtue, not that one's virtue and way of being a morally cultivated a morally self-fulfilled person is untimely. Always, there is a timely use of one's virtue and principle in one's moral cultivation. What is important is to recognize the timeliness of one's persistence and the insistence of the virtue and moral principle.

What is timely use (*shiyong*) of one's virtue and moral principle? The notion of "timely use" does not appear in the *Analects*, but appears in the *Tuan Commentary* on the hexagrams of *Kui* and *Qian*. Such a notion obviously refers to use or application of a principle or virtue or an understanding (knowledge) in view of the changes of time and circumstances. As there is no time separable from concrete situations of change and change of situations in the *Yijing* (as we shall explain), "timely use" can therefore refer to any restriction of circumstances that one must observe in order to exercise one's virtue and principle and bring one's virtue and principle to bear.

In this light we may distinguish a broad sense of "timely use" from a narrow sense of "timely use" in the *Analects* that respectively characterize two types of statements in the second category of statements. In the narrow sense, "timely use" of a virtue and principle for a morally cultivated person (implicitly) refers to the exercise of one's virtue and principle relative to a certain period of time or life situation. Thus, consider Confucius's saying:

> A person (should) have sincere faith and devotion to learning and be determined to enlarge on the way until death. Do not enter a country of disorder and do not reside in a country of chaos. If the *dao* prevails in the world, one shows oneself; if the *dao* does not prevail in the world, one hides oneself. If the country follows the way, being poor and lonely should make one ashamed of oneself; but if the country does not follow the way, being rich and powerful should make one ashamed of oneself. (*Analects* 8.13)

Order and disorder, the prevailing or failure of prevailing of the *dao* in the world and the country, implies a specific time-period. One can easily see that Confucius could refer to times of order and disorder in the world or in a state. Thus, the statement can be said to refer to recognition of time for one's exercise of virtues and principles. The essence of this saying is that one has to live according to one's time, and there are different forms of showing one's virtues and principles in different times, such as, "not staying in poverty and lowliness during a time of order" and "not staying in power and wealth during a time of disorder." The person of moral cultivation (*junzi*) must know how to befit himself to his times so that he can always preserve his state of moral cultivation and keep his virtues and principles intact.

The advice from Confucius seems to be simply that one should not compromise one's virtues and principle to unsuitable times and situations, and one should fulfill and employ one's virtues and principles to the maximum degree in suitable times and situations. This, of course, coincides with his wish to withdraw from the world as was indicated in some statements quoted earlier. This also need not be incompatible with the determination of Confucius to do what he knows he cannot do: namely spread *dao* in a wayward world. He says, "Birds and beasts cannot be associated with. If I do not [associate] with man, who shall I associate with? If the *dao* prevails in the world, I will not seek to change it" (18.6). This positive attitude toward a negative world exhibits again a *timely* persistence and insistence on one's virtue and principle as one's virtue and principle is to change the *time*.

Thus, we can see that the timely use of one's virtue and principle depends on one's perception of the world, the time, and how one can relate to such world to generate purposeful and meaningful activities or to attain meaningful values and ends. What is timely and what is both timely and useful is what is useful in time, and this is what one can do in time.

We can clearly distinguish two modes of timely use: (1) to modify one's effort in some way in order to befit one's time, and (2) to creatively engage in changing one's time or make contribution to such a change. In the *Analects* we see that Confucius has suggested these two attitudes. Similar statements are "If a country follows the *dao*, one can get a position. If not, when one gets a position, it is shameful" (14.1; see also 14.3).

Involved in this timely application of one's virtue and principle is clearly the affirmation that one is the master of one's own life and moral commitment. This implies that timely application of one's virtue and principle presupposes as well as requires free will and assertion of free choice of one's moral commitment. It is in such free choice of one's value and one's moral commitment to virtue and principle that one becomes morally independent of the fluctuations of times and inevitably of *ming* and exhibits thereby moral strength and moral courage.

On commenting whether Bo Yi and Shu Qi feels resentful regarding their positions, Confucius remarks: "If one seeks *ren* and gets *ren*, what resentment does one feel?" (7.15) The life of moral cultivation itself is intrinsically satisfying and intrinsically justifying, and being so one need not feel subject to judgment by vulgar standards of success and failure. Confucius speaks of the free will and self-contentment at the same time when he says to Yan Yuan: "If I am put to use, I can let my *dao* benefit the world; if I am not put to use, I can hide my *dao* in myself" (7.11).

The broad sense of "timely use" permeates all other statements pertaining to exercise of and abiding by virtue and principle relative to positions, human relationships, and human situations. To illustrate, Confucius says: "If one is not in the position, one will not plan how to govern" (8.14) Zeng Zi also says: "The superior man does not let his thought go beyond his position" (14.26). To observe one's position in one's behavior is itself a virtue and principle; it is a virtue of timeliness or timely application. Statements illustrating relativity to human relationships and circumstances are as follows: "One may share in study [of things with another person] but may not settle in the *dao*. One may settle in the *dao* with another person, yet one may not establish oneself together with the other. Even if we may establish ourselves together in the *dao*, we may not discuss the *dao* with the other person in regard to its creative use" (9.30).

In the tenth chapter of the *Analects*, where the life style and manners of Confucius are described, we can also see that Confucius demonstrated a timely application of his virtues and principles. He responds to daily life situations with considerateness and propriety, and his response results from considerations of position, relationship and time. Thus, he says that he would not eat if the seat is not in the right position and if the time for eating is not right. He also says that, when he sleeps, he would not straighten out like a dead body, and at home he would not look so solemn. When he sees people in mourning, even though they are not close to him, he would show grief. When he sees officials in formal dress, even though they are close to him, he would treat them with courtesy, and so on and so forth. All these records show not only that Confucius was a courteous, considerate, cultured person, and not only that Confucius cared for *li* 礼 (propriety), but that he would act in a way befitting the position, the time and the relationship. This implies that he has a strong sense of timeliness in what he says and what he does even with regard to the minutest details of his daily life. These small incidents of daily life also illustrate what *timeliness* (*shizhong* 时中) means in the broad sense. As everything has a unique time-aspect and can be said to be manifested in a time interval, to act in a way according to considerations of time and what time contains in an interval is precisely what gives meaning to timeliness.

Timeliness is thus simply the comportment of a person, his facility and action according to individual situations. But this comportment should nevertheless exhibit the virtue and principle of having a timely quality. Only when one's action according to considerations of an individual situation embodies virtue and principle, will the timeliness of the action embody and illustrate a virtue and a principle. The virtues and principles Confucius exhibits in daily life are *li, ren, Yi, zhi* and a sense of harmony and beauty. It can be seen when any one of these virtues and principles is exhibited, in a real daily life situation, there is *timeliness*: *timeliness* also becomes virtue and principle. The virtue and principle of timeliness may be said to consist in exhibiting any virtue and principle of a person in any situation. Taking into consideration the daily life of Confucius, there is little doubt he is indeed a sage of *timeliness* and is aptly called so by Mencius.

To extend our insight into Confucius's sense of timeliness, we may point out that the majority of statements made by Confucius in the *Analects* can be understood better as statements of timely application of virtue and principle intended by the sage to have timely application in life. Even universal principles and virtues such as *ren, yi* and *li, zhong,* and *xiao* carry with them an implicit reference to concrete life situations. This explains why the concept of *ren* has been given different explanations by Confucius and why *yi* is a principle not restricted *a priori* to a particular form (of particular), and why *li* has to be both historically relevant and relationally appropriate. Even in the method of teaching, Confucius reserves discretion to do what is appropriate for the learning disciple. Thus, he could say: "Qiu is timid, therefore I encourage him; You is aggressive, therefore I restrain him" (11.22). This provides another example of the virtue of timeliness in Confucius: the timely application of wisdom (*zhi*).

Further Exposition of Timeliness in Confucius

As we discussed above, there is no explicit mention of "timeliness" (*shi* or *shiyong*) or "timely application" of virtue in the Analects. Yet as we demonstrated, there is every illustration of "timeliness" or "timely application" in Confucius's formulation of virtue and principle as well as in his daily life activities. This means that timeliness, as a concept, is very much prominent and yet implicit in the text of the Analects. Although in the Analects the term "*shiyong*" does not appear, the term "*shi*" does occur ten times. "*Shi*" by itself of course means "time." When the term "*shi*" is used, most of the time it is not time as such that is spoken of. In fact, the only time "time" as such is referred to is when Confucius speaks of the time when he was young. He says: "When I was young, I knew many lowly skills" (16.7).

When Confucius refers to "four seasons" (*si shi*), we have time as time-processes or time periods. A similar use occurs in describing Confucius: "If the time is not appropriate, he would not eat (10.6)," and when Gongshu Wenzi was described, "He would not speak until the time is appropriate (14.13)." But on both these occasions a judgment regarding "when is appropriate" is required by the actor or observer. Confucius himself had to determine, perceive or judge the appropriateness of time for his eating, and Gongshu Wenzi has to do the same for his speaking. This personal judgment or perception, however, must also be objectively fitting so that others may see how fitting it is with the time and the circumstances. So, on those occasions the concept of timeliness or timely application of virtue is implied.

In the first chapter of the Analects, Confucius speaks of the joy of "learning and yet frequently reviewing what one learns" (1.1). The term "*shi*" is used here to mean "frequently," a use of "*shi*" that connotes no concept of timeliness. Even though one may argue that how frequent is frequent depends on judgment of fitting with circumstances and time, it is not obvious at all that this judgment is intended by Confucius. "*Shi*" is also used to mean "calendar" as in "Follow the calendar of Xia" (15.11) or as a verb to mean "to find a time" or "to find the chance," as in "Confucius finds the time when (Yang Huo) is not home" (17.1). "*Shi*" obviously does not mean timeliness in the first case. In the second case there is an element of timeliness as can be seen, but this timeliness does not apparently exhibit a virtue or principle, so it is not timeliness in the strict sense.

We might say "timeliness" in the strict sense requires four components: (1) It requires a personal perception of circumstances and time, as well as a judgment or determination on how one is related to or placed in a given time and circumstances. (2) It requires an appropriate decision or action of the person to meet or to respond to the time and circumstances as a result of one's personal understanding of the time. (3) It requires that a person's perception and action *fit* with the time and circumstances in an objective way. This means that a person must know correctly and act appropriately at a given time and in a given circumstances not only in a subjective, but in an objective sense. (4) Finally, it requires that the judgment and the action of the person exhibit or exemplify a virtue or a principle of virtue.

Three more uses of "*shi*" remain to be analyzed. Two uses are in relation to the statement "to order people according to time," and the statement, "one likes to do things and yet does not find the right time." The first statement refers to finding "right time" and the second to losing "right time." A judgment of timeliness is involved in both uses of the term, "*shi*," and can therefore be said to refer to timeliness as a virtue. For to order people according to time is to do something appropriate in right time and right circumstances, and this exhibits the great virtue of *ren*. To lose "right time" of course means lacking judgment regarding timeliness and timely action, contrary to the virtue of *zhi* (wisdom).

Finally, there is the description of an incident involving the use of "*shi*": "The pheasants are alarmed and they gathered again after flying apart." Confucius says: "[You grab] the female pheasant resting on the mountain bridge. How timely is your action! How timely is your action! (*shi cai! shi cai!*) Zi Lu puts down the pheasant carefully. The pheasant looks around three times and then flies away" (10.18; 10.27). If this record is correct, then Confucius is blaming Zi Lu for lacking timeliness in his grabbing the resting female pheasant. The inappropriateness of Zi Lu's action is obvious and Confucius's utterance shows his disapproval of such an inappropriate action.

At this juncture, we may ask where is timeliness explicitly conceptualized by Confucius as a virtue and principle if not in the *Analects*? The answer is that Confucius comes to a full statement of the virtue and principle of timeliness in the doctrine of the *Zhongyong*. In the second chapter of the *Zhongyong*, Confucius is quoted as saying: "The superior man follows the principles of *zhong* and *yong* in his actions, the small man violates the principles of *zhong* and *yong*. In following the principles of *zhong* and *yong*, the superior man remains in the right at all times (*shizhong*); in violating the principles of *zhong* and *yong* the small man has no fear about [doing wrong things]" (*Zhongyong*, chapter 2).

In this passage the idea of "*shizhong*" is introduced. "*Shizhong*" means "*zhongshi* 中时," fitting in with time. But as explained by Cheng Yi in Zhu Xi's *Collected Commentaries on the Four Books*, "Not deviating is called '*zhong*' (in the middle), not changing is called '*yong*'; to be in the middle is the right path under heaven and to be unchanging is the constant principle under heaven." We may also mention Confucius's statement, "Excess is like deficiency in not being in the right" (11.16) as an implicit definition of the *zhong*. In light of this explanation, *zhong* is the right way to do things and clearly this presupposes that there is always a right way to do things in all situations. To do things right or to do things according to the right path in a given time and circumstance is to exemplify the virtue of "*shizhong*." A person who can always try to do things right under all times and circumstances, is a superior person (*junzi*).

The principle and virtue of "*shizhong*" or "*zhongshi*" is not difficult to understand. Since a virtue or principle is basically constant, and a superior person, in doing the right thing at all times and in all circumstances, exemplifies a constant principle and virtue, he has also the virtue of *yong* in Cheng Yi's sense. In fact, a person who can follow the constant principle in doing the right thing at a given time and circumstance is a person who knows how to apply the right virtue to a time and circumstance and actually applies the right virtue to a time or circumstance. In this sense the principle of *Zhongyong* implies the principle of "*shizhong*." Thus, we may even conclude that the doctrine of *Zhongyong* is equivalent to, or is the same as, the principle of *shizhong*. It follows also that the treatise on the *Zhongyong* can be said to be one devoted to exposing and making explicit the meaning and truth of the virtue and principle of timeliness or *shizhong*.

Although the term "*shiyong*" is not used in the *Zhongyong*, "*shiyong*" can be said to mean the same as "*shizhong*," for both mean that one will exemplify a virtue and principle in a given time and circumstance. The meaning given to "*shizhong*," through its relation to the *Zhongyong*, in fact elucidates and illuminates the meaning of "*shiyong*" as we have explained it above. The reverse is also true, particularly when we see "*shiyong*" in the context of the *Yi Texts*. It is instructive to see how Zhu Xi explains the principles of "*shizhong*" in his *Jizhu*: "The superior man remains in the right at all times," Zhu Xi says: "The superior man can abide in his virtue, and can stay in the right (*zhu zhong*) at all times." "The small man has no fear (of doing wrong things)," Zhu Xi says: "The small man, because of having the mind of a small man, has no fear [of doing wrong things]." "*Shizhong*" here is clearly understood as a timely application of virtue and principle to a situation or a time and consequently regarded as a virtue by itself.

Without making a full elaboration of the doctrine of the *Zhongyong*, we can briefly discuss some important points in the *Zhongyong* for the illumination of the *shizhong* principle. First, the observation of one's position (*wei*) in the world for right action is emphasized in the *Zhongyong*. This is consistent with Confucius's statement that "The superior man does not think beyond what he should think befitting his position" (14.26). This position principle is in fact fully formulated as follows: The superior person only acts according to his or her present position and will not crave for things beyond that position. If one is in the position of a rich and powerful person, one does what one should do in such a position. If one stays in the position of being poor and lowly, one will do what one should do in such a position. If one finds oneself in the circumstances of a barbarian country, one does what one should do in such circumstances. If one stays in circumstances of adversity, one does what one should do in such circumstances. Thus, the superior person can always find himself self-contented [with the *dao*] (*zide*) under any circumstances. Zheng Xuan explains the idea of *zide* as, "What one desires does not lose sight of the *dao*." This clearly indicates that the superior person can always embrace the *dao* and exercise virtue under any circumstances even though the person does different things according to different circumstances. The superior person exhibits a constancy of virtue and principle together with a flexibility of timely adjustment. This is precisely implied in the notion of "*shizhong*" or "*shiyong*": timeliness.

Second, the *Zhongyong* goes further to illustrate this principle of acting according to one's place:

> In a high position (the superior man) would not oppress those below; in a low position (the superior man) would not try to flatter those above. Rectify oneself and not ask favors from others, then there is no complaint; one will not complain about heaven above and will not resent others below. Thus the superior man acts according to his position and waits for the mandate of heaven. The small man takes risks in order to seek what he does not deserve. (*Zhongyong*, chapter 14)

The important point here is that superior persons will correct themselves first in order to meet the demands of external circumstances, and they make efforts to stay always in the right and accept what comes from the circumstances in which they find themselves. They recognize their conditions as a matter of *ming* or *tianming*, what is beyond their capacities and yet rightly sanctions their actions. Zisi even quotes Confucius to make this Confucian point: "Archery is like the way of being a superior man, if one does not hit the target, one tries to correct oneself." (*Zhongyong*, chapter 15). Following this, Mencius says: "A benevolent man sees himself as an archer: An archer has to straighten himself before he shoots his arrow. If he does not hit the target, he should [have] no gri[e]vance against the victor[;] instead he should reflect on himself and find the reason for missing the target" (Mencius 2A7).

Third, as to how one can always maintain oneself in the right and also remain assured that one is following the right path: the *Zhongyong* has developed the notion of "the way of heaven and earth" (*Zhongyong*, chapter 26) into a metaphysics of boundless creativity of life of heaven and earth; further, it indicates how a person may aspire to the way of heaven and earth, and eventually strive to participate in the way. This is the doctrine of "*jin xing*" (fulfilling nature). We will not enter into this doctrine here. Suffice to say that to fulfill nature begins with "being sincere or true to oneself" (*cheng*). With sincerity one can reach the state of fulfilling one's nature, the nature of other people, and the nature of all things; finally, [one may] participate in the creative activities of heaven and earth" (chapter 22). When one reaches this stage of fulfilling nature, one can be said to have "utmost sincerity." "The utmost sincerity can transform." This means that one can then achieve creativity and freedom not dominated by any circumstances or limitations (*ming*). All manifest heaven's or one's own nature. This is also the state where true harmony (*he*) obtains.

The best passage to describe this process of achieving, and the resulting achievement, is as follows:

> To be sincere, is the condition for perfecting oneself. The way is the right path to follow. Sincerity is the beginning and end of all things. If there is no sincerity, there are no things. Thus, the superior person always values most making himself sincere. To make oneself sincere is not just to perfect oneself, it is to perfect others according to their nature. To

perfect oneself is *ren*; to perfect others is *zhi* (wisdom). *Ren* and *zhi* are within the nature of a person and are virtues of this nature. They unify the way inside and outside, therefore is it appropriate to follow and practice them at all times (*shi zhe zhi yi*). (chapter 25)

Upon reaching this stage, one is naturally both free and right: "In being sincere, one will remain in the right without effort and will attain (*dao*) without thought" (20). Importantly, "*shi zhe zhi yi*" can be used to interpret the essence of "*shi yong*" or "*shizhong*": to maintain timeliness is to remain right at a given a time and circumstance. It is further important to note that *ren* and *zhi* as described by Zisi are the suggested way to achieve the virtue of timeliness. Zisi also makes it clear that *ren* and *zhi* require a process of cultivation in oneself in order to reach a state where one can remain right at all times and also participate in the creative transformation of things-where the obstacle of *ming* can be said to be overcome and be transformed into the nature of heaven. This also means that to have timeliness as a virtue is to emulate and follow the way of heaven and earth. This gives a metaphysical meaning to *shizhong*.

Given the above explication and discussion of the intended system of the *Analects*, we may now organize some of the salient and dominating ideas of Confucius. These ideas include *zhi* (free self-creative nature of the human being), *de* (constant virtues and principles for the human being), *ming* (*tianming*, limitations on one's life and restricting conditions/situations), and *shi* (*shiyong*, timeliness and appropriate application of one's virtue and principle according to time and circumstances). These ideas are interrelated in order to generate a picture of the destiny and station of human beings in the world and what they can hope to achieve.

First, a person is free to cultivate *de* (virtues such as *ren* and *zhi* and *yi*), but is not free to choose a life of poverty or wealth: this is a matter of *ming*. Thus, his inner virtue (nature) is confronted with a world of *ming* (external determination). Second, a person can perceive the world of *ming* as given and exercise virtues according to the time and circumstances to achieve an appropriate relation between the person and the *ming*; at the same time, the person can exemplify the constancy of virtue and principle. This is the virtue of timeliness, or appropriate application of virtue according to time and circumstances. Third, extending into the *Zhongyong*, if a person develops his virtues to the utmost, he will reach a state of transformation of all things, not only transformation of himself. In this sense he can transform *ming* into nature. Metaphysically speaking, timeliness becomes an ultimate virtue, like the creative virtue of heaven and earth, exhibiting perfect order and life. The following diagram should illustrate these major points as found in the *Analects* and as extended in the *Zhongyong*.

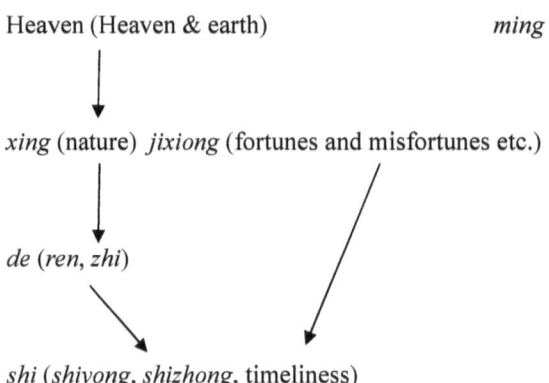

1. right action at any time and in any circumstances

2. perfect freedom and harmony when *de* becomes perfect and *ming* becomes *xing*

From the *Analects* to the *Yijing*: The Confucian Testimony

How does the system of the *Analects* relate to the *Yijing*? I indicated earlier that we can establish the relation between the Confucius of the *Analects* and the *Yijing* by examining the system of the *Analects* (SA) and the system of the *Yijing* (SY). One of my arguments above is intended to show that the philosophical picture of the human being in the SA easily leads into the philosophical picture of the human being in the SY and Confucius in the *Analects* creates a natural need and place for the SY. Another argument is intended to show specifically that the idea of timeliness implicit in the *Analects* finds an expression not only in the *Zhongyong* but in the *Yizhuan* (*Commentaries of the Yi*) insofar as the original *Yi* Text is understood as both presenting a tradition and a philosophy of the world to Confucius. It is natural to reach the position of timeliness as an essential philosophical moral of reading the *Yi* Text. Before we embark on illuminating the SY for this purpose, we may first point out that Confucius in the *Analects* relates himself to *Yi*, although not as conspicuously as one might hope. This shows it is more than plausible that Confucius undertook study of *Yi* very seriously.

There is only one occasion where Confucius speaks of studying the *Yi* (*Yijing*). He says: "Give me a few years, and I will study the *Book of Changes* at fifty, then I will not make major mistakes" (7.17). Although Zhu Xi suggests the term "*wushi*" (fifty) should be written as "finally" (*chu*), there is no good reason to accept Zhu Xi's suggestion. In fact, one may treat this statement as made by Confucius several years before he was fifty. His desire to study the *Yi* at fifty is quite consistent with his later statement, "At fifty I come to know the mandate of heaven." The *Yi* can be regarded as a book of mandate of heaven—certainly, it can be so interpreted, as we shall see. The mandate of heaven reveals what one's limitations in life are and what one should do to be in the right, and this is precisely what the *Yi* can be interpreted as. It is reasonable and natural for Confucius to interpret the *Yi* in this way, as we understand the system of the *Yi* has been constructed.

In accordance with the above, the two major points about Confucius's statement regarding studying *Yi* at fifty are even more significant. In the first place, it explains that before fifty, Confucius knew little about the *Yi* and what it represents and thus he seldom talked about things related to the *Yi*. Thus, we have statements such as made by Zi Gong: "We have heard the teacher speak about the Classics of Poetry, Documents, Rites and Music [to educate us]. But for nature (*xing*) and the way of heaven (*tiandao*), we seldom hear anything" (5.13). Many scholars quote this statement as evidence that Confucius has shown no interest in metaphysics and has no metaphysical views. This is not to take the evidence in its totality and results from a partial view. Those who take this view fail to see that Confucius developed his own life stage by stage as testified by himself. He might not have studied so important a classic as the *Yi* in the early stages of his life, but this was not so in the later stages. In fact, on the strength of his statement about his study of the *Yi* and his statement about knowing "*tianming*" at fifty, we may also infer that by fifty he already knew the *Yi* and had studied it. This gives reason to believe that the *Yizhuan*—if not all of it, at least a good part of it—is the result of the study of the *Yi* by Confucius. This immediately links Confucian philosophy to the *Yi* and establishes the system of the *Yizhuan* as an extension and/or ground of the *Analects*. We will understand this after we see how the initial system of the *Yi* Text (not the *Yizhuan*) can be interpreted by Confucius using the *Analects* system. We may further conclude that the SA represents Confucian thought and philosophy before he was fifty, whereas the *Yizhuan* system of *Yi* represents Confucian thought and philosophy after he was fifty. For the completion of Confucian philosophy, the system of *Yizhuan* is as equally as important as the system of the *Analects*.

Even in the *Analects*, Confucius made reference to a passage of the *Yi* Text. Commenting on the importance of constancy of virtues, Confucius quoted the *yao*-judgment of 9-3 of the hexagram *Han* from the *Yi* Text. "If a person does not have constant virtue, insult will ensue." He adds: "This kind of person is not worthy of being divined" (13.22). The specific message of this statement is significant for Confucius's stress on the constancy of virtues in a person. But more than this, this statement of Confucius shows that he has gotten quite well acquainted with the *Yi* Text, and that he approaches the *Yi* by giving an interpretation of the *Yi*-judgment in support of his philosophical observation. In other words, he is not using *Yi* only for the purpose of divination but rather sees it in a philosophical light. This should underscore the high probability that he could well be the originator of the *Tuanzhuan, Xiangzhuan, Wenyan*, and *Xici Dazhuan* of the *Yijing*, if not all the *Yizhuan* commentaries.

The Intended System of the *Yijing*

As in the case of describing the system of the *Analects*, one purpose in describing the system of the *Yi* is to single out the dominant and hitherto unnoticed points about the *Yi* for a better understanding of its philosophical significance. Specifically, we are interested in several facets of the *Yi* that make the Confucianization of the original *Yi* Text possible. By Confucianization, I mean the Confucian interpretation of the *Yi* Text made possible by Confucius's understanding of *Yi* (change) itself, which contributes to the formation of the *Yi*-metaphysics in the *Yizhuan* and its future philosophical growth as a fountainhead of philosophical inspiration and insight. We will discuss the system of the *Yi* in light of the following themes: (1) distinction between implicit and explicit meaning in the *Yi* Text; (2) metaphysics of the dialectics of the *Yi*-symbolism as a map of life and world; (3) the world of *ming* in the *Yi* Text; and (4) timeliness in the *Yizhuan*, which is a Confucian insight.

On Timeliness (*Shizhong*) in the *Analects* and the *Yijing*   385

The *Yi* Text is the original stratum of the *Yijing*, which is composed of the sixty-four hexagrams (derived from the eight trigrams) and their respective judgments (or decisions) plus the judgments attached to each line (*yao*) of the hexagram. Whether or not the body of the *Yijing* was authored by Fuxi, King Wen, and Duke Zhou, as mentioned in Zhu Xi's *Zhouyi benyi*, is not our concern here. Our concern is how this original stratum of the *Yijing* gives rise to the *Yizhuan* (commentaries) and takes on the philosophy of the *taiji* as described in the *Xici*. It is clear that the *Yi* Text is basically used as a tool of divination (*bushi*), and perhaps begins as a record of the divinatory findings. But once we conceive the *Yi* Text in the divinatory context, we will also see that more than divinatory use is implied by the system of ideas and images, which can independently function as a meaningful structure. In fact, only when the images and ideas of the *Yi* Text function independently as a descriptive picture do they become useful not only for making correct divinations on the one hand but for understanding the world on the other. The symbolism and the going interpretation of the symbolism therefore carry different meanings: meaning in the implicit and meaning in the explicit.

The explicit meaning of the *Yi* Text consists in the primary divinatory use of the text. The divinatory use that has been associated with the *Yi* Text from antiquity defines the explicit meaning of the text, for it constitutes a context in light of which the text is understood. It is possible that the *Yi* Text from antiquity defines the explicit meaning of the text, for it constitutes a context in light of which the text is understood. It is possible that the *Yi*-symbolism was first invented for the use of divination. When practice of divination was instituted, the meaning of the symbolism could be confined to the divinatory practice. The symbols of the *Yi* became an indicator of good fortune, ill fortune, and other life situations as determined by the judgments on the *gua* (hexagrams) and *yao* (lines of the hexagrams). Take for example the hexagram of *daguo*, the judgment for which says:

> "*Daguo*: beams of the house; intertwining; advantageous to go somewhere; prosperity."

This judgment clearly gives the meaning of the given hexagram to the effect that the hexagram means a good omen conducive to prosperity. Consider the *Yao* 9-2 of this hexagram: "The withered willow grows its roots. The old husband has his [young] wife. There is nothing there which is not disadvantageous." This judgment, again, clearly gives a meaning to the 9-2 of the hexagram to the effect that the 9-2 *Yao* signifies good omen conducive to prosperity. The explicit meanings of the symbolism therefore are generated by the divinatory judgments associated with the symbolism. We also should note that in the divinatory context, the symbolism or its representative, iconic image confers a meaning on the judgments that are thereby reinforced. In other words, the explicit meanings of the *Yi* Text are the result of reciprocal interaction between the *Yi*-symbolism and the *Yi*-judgments in the divinatory context. Even the naming of a hexagram may reflect the explicit meaning of the text and symbolism to some extent, for the names of the symbolism do not come into being by accident.

What then is the implicit meaning of the *Yi* Text? This meaning is derived from at least the following two considerations. In the first place, insofar as the divination practice makes sense, it must presuppose a certain systematic view of the world and life so that the divinatory meaning of good fortune and ill fortune would ensue. In fact, if we look carefully into the divinatory practice whereby milfoil stalks are sorted out to generate a "hexagram" (*zhonggua*), we must already see how the world and life are to be pictured so that a hexagram will present a given section of the world and life rather than another one. To divine is to identify a section of the world and life and read its meaning for the future. Thus, divination must presuppose not only a world-picture about the whole world, but a method of classifying the world sections for divination to identity. Both the world-picture and the method of classifying the world sections can be a subject of study and understanding, and they must have been previously developed in order for divination to proceed. This is conspicuously clear if we consider the *Yi*-symbolism of the hexagrams. For any symbol generated to pertain to a situation in the divination, a whole system of symbolism must exist in order to represent the whole set of possible situations. A method of classifying the possible situations must also be established with reason. Thus, we may conclude that the very practice of divination presupposes a rational scheme of categorization for understanding the world.

The implicit meaning of the *Yi* Text may be said to consist precisely of the rational scheme of categorization for describing the world and the method of sectioning the world or reality. In other words, the symbolism of the *Yi* Text presupposes a metaphysics, a dialectics of world sectioning (sectioning the world into possible situations). We may call the world-picture "the descriptive metaphysics of reality." We may call the method of classifying the world into possible situations, or the method of sectioning the world into sections, "the dialectics of world-development." I shall discuss later the structure of the Yi-symbolism as a metaphysics and a dialectics.

In the second place, the implicit meaning of the Yi Text derives from a context of understanding versus a context of divination. Although divination with the Yi-symbolism, as we indicated, presupposes a metaphysical description of the world, divination itself shows a special dimension of a person's need in life: the anxiety toward the given place of a person in the given world. This anxiety is not simply an apprehension about the future of one's destiny; it is involved with ascertaining the meaningfulness of one's existence and action in the scheme of changing things. Perhaps it is time (in an ontological sense) that causes this anxiety and at the same time inspires life-creativity and in fact brings about life. But time in this sense is reality itself, the total reality underlying life as well as underlying the meaning of life. This anxiety gives rise to the art and practice of divination so that divination can serve as a mirroring of one's position in the world and as a counsel for what is best to do.[3]

The *Yizhuan* calls this anxiety the "grave misgivings" (*you huan*). Thus, Confucius says in the *Dazhuan*: "Must not the rise of the Yi have been in medieval antiquity? Must not the author of the Yi have had grave misgivings?" (*Xici Xia* 7). The divinatory system was designed and utilized to search for a deeper meaning. The divination embodies the "grave misgiving" of one's mind toward the reality as a changing process. But there is no reason we may not simply treat the Yi-symbolism and its judgment system as a metaphysics and a view of morality without involving the anxiety shown in its application in divination. In other words, we may study and understand the Yi-symbolism as a source of explanation and object of knowledge. To treat Yi-symbolism in this manner is to create the context of rational understanding versus the context of personal misgiving and concern created by the author of divination. It is with this rational understanding that Confucius and his disciples transformed the Yi Text into a text of metaphysical significance by producing the *Yizhuan* (commentaries) on the Yi Text.

The *Yizhuan*, specifically composed of the *Tuanzhuan*, *Xiangzhuan*, *Wenyan*, *Xici* (*Dazhuan*), *Shuoguazhuan*, *Xuguazhuan*, and *Zaguazhuan*, may be said to be the result of such a transformation. They are inspired by the insight of Confucius and the Confucian spirit of learning. It seems quite reasonable to assume that Confucius and his disciples approach the Yi Text from this rational point of view. They already have a rational mentality and a rational, yet humanistic methodology for understanding the human person and the human world. They especially value the process of learning as an integral part of self-cultivation and self-realization in the *dao*. This is clearly evidenced in the *Analects*. (The term "*xue*" appears sixty-five times in the *Analects* and appears in many sentences requiring "*xue*" as a restrictive condition of the virtues.) This emphasis on *xue* may be said to be conducive to the formation of the rational-intellectual approach to the Yi Text, and it explains the evolution of the Yi Text from being a manual of divination to being depository of metaphysical wisdom.

Through the above perspective that the implicit meaning of the Yi-symbolism and Yi-judgments become explicit. The divination practice assumes a metaphysical and moral importance, and finally the divination practice transforms into a philosophical system justifying morality. The Confucian spirit of inquiring and learning makes this transformation definitely possible, and it is directly guided by the searching soul of Confucius. It is only in this light that the transformation of the Yi Text becomes intelligible and plausible.

We may say, as a final note, that the implicit meaning of the Yi-symbolism consists in what can be produced by objective, cognitive, and rational understanding, which is made possible by the inquiring spirit, such as that of Confucius. Confucius related himself to the Yi Text not by way of inheriting the Yi Text as a divination book, but by way of transforming it into a book of moral and metaphysical meaning. This is because the book itself has metaphysical depth and moral import. It took Confucius and his disciples to apply their rational methodology to the study of the Yi Text so that the transformation in question finally took place. It is only natural that such a transformation should take place because the subjectivity of anxiety and misgiving of divination finally gives way to the objectivity of reason and understanding of philosophy. In this process of transformation, not only does the implicit meaning of the Yi Text become explicit, it also provides a metaphysical foundation for divination. The practicality of divination leads to practicality on a higher plane: the moral practicality produced by a rational and humanly holistic understanding of world and humankind as suggested by Confucius.

On Timeliness (*Shizhong*) in the *Analects* and the *Yijing* 389

Metaphysics of *Yi*-symbolism and Dialectics of the *Yi*-symbolic Transformation

Although this is not the right place or time to elaborate on the explicit meaning of the *Yi* Text in terms of a complete metaphysical system, I shall, nevertheless, indicate how this system can be generated from a careful reading of the symbolism and note the salient points about that system that leads to my conclusion about the conceptual link between the *Yijing* and the Confucian *Analects*.

The Rise of the *Xiang* (Images)

The *Yi*-symbolism can be said to originate from a desire to symbolize the total reality as one experience. The very term "*Yi*" may be said to indicate an experience of change, process, development, growth and integration, decline and disintegration. But this *Yi* experience must have a comprehensive scope of heaven, earth, life, things, and human beings in order to claim universal validity. From this experience we also note the unchanging in the changing, the simple in the complex. *Yi* is therefore said to combine the meaning of change, unchanging, and simple. These three meanings of change attributed to the term must be derived from a deep and wide experience of reality such as indicated in section 4 of *Xici Shang* and section 2 of *Xici Xia*:

> The *Yi* matches with heaven and earth. Thus it can unite and order the way of heaven and earth. Above [the sage] observes the patterns of the heaven; below [the sage] discerns the patterns of the earth. Thus [the sage] knows the reason and causes of the dark and the bright. The *Yi* also traces the origins [of things] and reflects on their endings, thus knowing the theory of birth and death [of things]. The essential *qi* becomes things and floating *qi* (from death) constitutes change, thus (the sage) knows the situation of returning (*gui*) and stretching (*sheng*). (*Xici Shang* 4 in *Zhouyi benyi* of Zhu Xi)

> In antiquity when Bo Xi ruled the world, he observed the forms of heaven above and the laws of earth below. He saw

the patterns of birds and beasts and what environment suited them. He took lessons from what was close at hand and from things afar, and consequently invented the *bagua* (eight trigrams). (*Xici Xia* 2)

The *Yi*-symbolism, which is composed of the sixty-four hexagrams, is perceived to derive from the original eight trigrams. The eight trigrams, on the other hand, are clearly seen to represent directly the comprehensive phenomena of nature and things based on wide and close observation and experience. Hence, "*Yi*" can be said to originate from the symbolic representation of nature and life as carefully observed. The term "*xiang*," as used in the *Yizhuan*, thus has a double meaning. It means at once the phenomena of nature as well as the symbolic representation of these phenomena; as such, an empirical basis of the *Yi*-symbolism is exhibited. Thus it is said, "Thus the *Yi* are forms (*xiang*). Form is representation (*xiang*)" (section 3).

In light of the empirical basis of the *Yi*, we may further note that the *xiang* of the *Yi* has two aspects: the spatial aspect of correlation of things, and the temporal aspect of succession of things. The symbolic representation of nature must exhibit both aspects of reality, and this is aptly done by the invention of the trigrams where changes are exhibited together with the forms of things. We may note that there are two forms of change. First, each trigram representing a natural form represents the movements within the form, which is called the *yao* (lines of change), and determines the internal nature of the form. This internal nature of the form is the internal movement within the form that makes the relation of the form to other forms possible. Thus, one form can relate to other forms not only because of their constituent structures, but also because of the internal changes within the form itself. This is the change from one trigram to another. This is the second form of change. Given the total system of forms, every form acquires a position in the system. Thus, each trigram not only represents a natural form but also represents a position of the form in the total system. Each trigram indicates the change between forms or the possibility of such change.

The Meaning of the *Yao*

At this point it is noteworthy that the *xiang* of things is basically the *xiang* of change, for the *xiang* is composed of change, as indicated in

On Timeliness (Shizhong) in the Analects and the Yijing   391

the composition of the *gua* (symbol) from the *yao*-lines of movement. Hence, the explanation given in the *Xici* on the *yao* constitutes a most basic insight of the *Yi*-symbolism: "When the eight trigrams are arranged, there are forms of things within them. Thereby the trigrams are doubled, the *yao* are found there" (*Xici Xia* 1).

The doubling of the trigrams merely explains why there are six *yao*-lines in one hexagram. The important thing is that the *yao* symbolizes movement and change. As the *dao* has *yin* and *yang* types, it is clear that the basic unit of change for the symbolism is that of *yin* changing into *yang* and vice versa. The *Yi*-symbolism does not speak of *yin* and *yang* as understood by later philosophers. But the composition of the trigrams and hexagrams leaves no doubt that *yin* and *yang* are basic constituents of change, which are explicitly displayed in the *Yi*-symbolism of "—" and – –."

Notably, although *yin* and *yang* may have etymological meanings related to natural phenomena of shining and shading, the meaning of the *yin* and *yang* basically pertains to the movement inside or outside a form: "In the mutual movement of the solid (*gang*) and the soft (*rou*), there is change (*bian*). When judgments are appended to judge (this change), there is movement (*dong*). . . . Thus, the solid and the soft mutually push each other. The eight trigrams mutually push each other" (*Xici Shang* 1). These passages and others clearly indicate that the *yin* and the *yang* movements are movements of the solid and the soft. The *yao* is used to represent these movements.

As the judgments of the form (hexagram) is called *Tuan*, referring to the material context and meaning of the form, the *yao*-lines in the *gua* are said to represent and release the movements within the *gua* (*Xici Shang* 5). The existence of the *yao* therefore indicates that there is a simplest way of representing the change. It is simply the binary change between the *yin* and the *yang*. Again, this is deeply verified with reference to change in reality. We may title this experience of change that of *yao* movement as opposed to the experience of change of the *xiang*.

The Derivation of the Great Ultimate (*Taiji*)

From the recognition of the *yao* movement, there is no difficulty in understanding the derivation of an onto-cosmology of *yin-yang* exchange and the concept of the great ultimate (*taiji*) from the very symbolism of the *Yi*. Thus, it is said: "One *yin* and one *yang*, there is the *dao*, what follows (from the *dao*) is good. What completes (the movement) is the nature" (*Xici Shang* 5). The trigram and hexagram belong to the cosmological topology of change, whereas change by itself can be explained as the simple exchange of *yin* and *yang* in a cosmological ontology of the great ultimate. "Thus closing is called *Kun* and opening is called *Qian*. One closing and one opening is called change (*bian*)." "Thus the *Yi* has the great ultimate; from this, two norms (of *yin* and *yang*) are generated. The two norms generate four forms. The four forms generate the *bagua*" (*Xici Shang* 11).

The formation of the concept of the great ultimate must be understood through the dynamics and dialectics of the *yin-yang* as exchange and interchange. The *yin* must change into the *yang* and vice versa. One is the condition for the other and vice versa. They are opposite and yet complement each other to form a unitary whole. To see the unity of opposition and complementation is to see how change takes place in a context of wholeness. It is also to see how change can be ceaseless and unceasing even if it is always bounded by configurations of *yin* and *yang*. This is the meaning of the "*taiji*": it is a concept based on considerations of the unity of *yin-yang* movement and its unceasing creativity. *Taiji*, therefore, is derived from a deeper reflection on change and simplicity and hence on basic posture of change and its representation in the *Yi*-symbolism. As the hexagram is more complex than the trigram and the trigram more complex than the two-*yao* diagram and the two-*yao* diagram more complete than the one-*yao* exchange, the *taiji* as the simple source of all changes and complexities of things (*xiang*) is a natural concept to be formed; as such, it serves the good purpose of cosmological explanation. Thus, we have a complete cosmology of the great ultimate derived from the understanding of the *xiang* and the *yao* in the essays of the *Xici*.

Although we may make a distinction between the descriptive metaphysics of *xiang* and *yao* and the speculative metaphysics of the *taiji*, we may still grant that the *taiji*, like the *yin-yang* movements, need not be conceived as mere speculation in *abstracto*. It is in fact something that can be experienced in terms of the totality of reality or the experience of reality as a whole. The symbolism of hexagrams forms a holistic system of interrelated units and that each unit depends upon the other units for its meaningfulness and possible change. The position and change of each unit are defined in the system as a whole. To see the wholeness of the system is to see the great ultimate.

Furthermore, in the process of change one can observe and experience the unity of *yin* and *yang* as nothing purely *yin* or *yang* in actuality, but *yin* and *yang* are only limiting cases represented by *Qian* and *Kun*. Thus, even though there is a speculative side to the philosophy underlying the *Yi*-symbolism, this side is always complemented by actual experience and observation of reality. To recognize this enables us to see that there is no conflict between the generation of the hexagrams from doubling the *bagua* and the derivation of the hexagrams from the *taiji*. The *Yi*-symbolism allows the interplay between the practical method of representation and a theoretical method of derivation.[4]

The Organic Dialectics of Change

A dialectics of change and development can be said to evolve due to the possibility of derivation of the hexagrams from the single source of the *taiji*. This dialectics thrives on the fact that the change, the nonchange, and the simplest form of change are basically a unity that explains and comprehends all changes. In other words, in any change there is an aspect of nonchange, namely, the *xiang*, and an aspect of simplicity, viz., the *yao*. Whereas the change is presently represented by the sixty-four hexagrams, a careful scrutiny of the symbolism in light of the generation reveals that change can be exhibited on levels that embody more forms. The dynamical way of generating forms will follow the binary law of expansion of 2^n for any n. This reveals again that reality may have many levels of organization. On each level there is a systematic wholeness of interrelated forms, which inclusively represent the reality. This shows the organic structure of reality and its potentially infinite possibility.

Since each level of representation is holistic and organic, changes can be understood as transformations relative to each level; moreover, changes can here be understood in terms of increased complexity, relative to each system of organization. The movement in fact was observed and developed by the diagram of the *Yi* in the works of the Song philosopher Shao Yong. For the movement of the forms on each level, however, we do not have a uniform way of representation and explanation. It seems that the development of the schools of the *Yi* from the Han period centers on formulation of rules of transformation on the level, say, of sixty-four hexagrams.

Here we are apt to note that in Confucius's reflections on the *Yi*-symbolism and its judgments (*ci*) some basic principles of interrelationships and transformations are revealed. Again, this seems quite natural and reasonable when we contemplate the nature and form of the hexagrams in a systematic wholeness. Thus we may suggest that the compositions of the *Tuanzhuan* (commentary on the material content of the *gua*) and the *Xiangzhuan* (commentary on the form of the *gua*) were carried out by Confucius and his disciples to make some basic principle of interrelating and transforming the hexagrams explicit; so, new meanings of metaphysical and moral significances could be explicitly generated. In the *Tuanzhuan* and *Xiangzhuan*, as Professor Qu Wanli has noted, the meaning of the form is almost explained on the principle of opposition. Thus, as the hexagram of *Song* ䷅ is related to the *Xun* ䷸ by opposition, the meaning of *Song* 2-9 is indicated as opposite to the *Xun* 5-9 in the *Tuan* statement: "The solid comes and obtains the centrality." This means that the changing line in the second position of *Song-gua*, which represents the strength of the *yang*, ascends to the ruling and hence central position in the *Xun-gua*. Similarly, the generation of meaning by opposition holds for all other hexagrams, as it is obvious that many hexagrams follow each other by opposition. This principle pertains to the generation of meanings in the *yao*-lines in a hexagram.

Regarding the form of representation (*gua xiang*), the principle of opposition also clearly serves as the guiding principle of explanation of meaning. This is amply illustrated in the *Xiangzhuan*. Thus, the form of heaven is opposed to that of earth, that of thunder to that of wind, etc. Without going into detail here, we note that the *Tuanzhuan* and *Xiangzhuan* serve to relate all forms of things in light of their relations of opposition, which derive their meanings from the *yin-yang* exchange. This indicates recognition of totality and unity in the system of *Yi* transformation.

Apart from the principle of opposition, there are other principles being expounded and shown in the *Tuanzhuan* and *Xiangzhuan*. There is the principle of decline and growth (e.g., line 19, "The solid invades and grows"). There is the principle of positional correlation and support (fitting, or *zhong*, e.g., line 2 and line 5 are called "fitting" [*ying*]), which operates to correlate a line in a beginning *gua* with a line in an ending *gua*, so that it will generate a meaning for each line. If a *yang* possesses position 5 and a *yin* possesses position 2, we have a case of "exact fitting" (*zheng zhong*). This positional principle often determines meanings of good and ill fortunes. From this principle, the concepts of obtaining position, having an appropriate position, and their opposites arise to give further meaning to the hexagrams and their *yao*-lines. Further considerations involve the relative positions of the two trigrams in a hexagram, which gives a correlation or noncorrelation between the inner and the outer as well as the tendentious movements implicit in this correlation or noncorrelation of positions and lines with *yin* and *yang* properties.[5]

In the *Wenyanzhuan* on *Qian* and *Kun* the principle of opposition and related distinctions are singularly appropriated for generating meaning and explanation. In the *Xici*, apart from the principle of opposition, a principle of mutual generation and relative exchange (*xiang dui* or *xiang yi*) is recognized. It is indicated in the idea of the mutual development (*xiang tui*) of the solid and soft (*gang* and *rou*), as quoted earlier. From this, the *Xici* goes on to say: "The change does rest in one place but circulates in all six void positions. There is no constancy of the above and below, and there is mutual exchange of the solid and soft."

The inconstancy of the above and below refers to the opposition principle, whereas the mutual exchange of solid and soft refers to the relative substitutability of *yao*-lines regarding their *yin* and *yang* properties. For the relative substitution, examples of the hexagrams are *Qian* ☰ / *Kun* ☷, *Kan* ☵ / *Li* ☲, *Yi* ䷚ / *Daguo* ䷛, *Zhongfu* ䷼ / *Xiaoguo* ䷽. The *Xici* is of course noted for its elaboration on the change through generation across levels of reality, as we have noted. In the case of the *Shuoguazhuan*, the discussion centers on correlation with the doctrine of five-powers (*wuxing*) for generating meaning and an image of the *gua*, as noted by Qu Wanli and other scholars. In the *Xuguazhuan*, the principles of opposition and mutual generation are followed. In the *Zaguazhuan*, the principle of opposition alone is followed. Whatever conclusion we may draw from these commentaries regarding generation and explanation of meaning in the *Yi*-symbolism, it is clear that *Xici* has the most comprehensive coverage on the horizontal and the vertical generative processes in terms of the metaphysics of the great ultimate and the principles of opposition and eventual generation. These principles are evidently germane and intrinsic to the symbolism of the *Yi* as it shows properties leading to the formulation of the metaphysics and principles. This is also true of the *Tuanzhuan* and *Xiangzhuan*. In this sense, the *Xici*, the *Tuanzhuan*, and the *Xiangzhuan* can be regarded as an outcome of reflection on the *Yi* Text by Confucius and his disciples.

The *Wenyan* is an elaboration on the fundamental opposites and relatives, *Qian* and *Kun*. The *Xu* and *Za* can be conceived as summary and supplementary statements of the relation of the hexagrams based on the *Tuan*, the *Xiang* and the *Xici*. The *Shuo*, on the other hand, must be judged as a later addition or attempt to relate the *Yi*-symbolism to the *wuxing* for more expansion of the meaning of the *Yi*-symbolism. This may have started a new trend in the *Yi*-thinking. But as it is extrinsic to the structure of the *Yi*-symbolism, it may be questioned whether it bears relation to Confucius and his immediate teaching and reflection.[6]

One more important thing to note is that all the principles of explanations of meaning are formulated in reference to the concepts of the solid and the soft, the inner and the outer. This means that a positional metaphysics is presupposed. This also means that the *Xici* perhaps should be construed as the very basis of the ideas in all other commentaries, as it is in the *Xici* that such a positional metaphysics is outlined.[7]

Perhaps it is in following the spirit of these Confucian commentaries that further principles of transformation were invented or discovered by later commentators, particularly by the Han period scholars of the *Yi*.[8] But we need not concern ourselves with these elaborations, as many of these are extraneous to the symbolism of the *Yi*. We may simply mention that in any analysis there are three main principles dominating the transformation of hexagrams and their mutual generation of meaning: (1) the principle of opposition; (2) the principle of relative exchange; and (3) the principle of transposition. The third principle is not explicitly formulated in the *Yizhuan*. But it is nevertheless obviously present in the distinction between the inner and the outer body of the hexagram as indicated. We may note that the combined use of these three principles enables anyone to derive many hexagrams from a given one, and they suffice to relate all hexagrams into a unitary sequence of generation. The *Zagua* does this relating through extrapolatory explanation of images and other metaphysical and cosmological associations, not by way of the formal principles of opposition, exchange and transportation. For this reason, we may note that the mutual transformation of all hexagrams must come from the natural and creative change of the *yin* and the *yang* in the lines (*yao*) of the hexagram. Thus, we can see that for any given hexagram the different changes of the *yao*-lines in that hexagram can produce any other hexagram. This shows how change can be universal and also creative in all directions. This is basically the principle embodied in the idea of *bian gua* (changing *gua*). I have referred to this change as the fundamental theorem of *Yi* transformation.[9]

The possibility of creative transformation from one form to all other forms not only shows that change is unitary, but shows that change is unlimited in potentiality. What is even more interesting to note is that these possible changes must be brought about by the divinatory moves or essentially by a process of orderly and yet creative relating, which to a large extent reflect the real nature of change in the real world. Change follows a pattern and yet allows a creative relating and reorganization.

Taking into consideration what has been said above, it is clear that apart from a descriptive metaphysics of change there is a dialectics of change on each level of reality-representation and across such levels. The principles of transformation in this dialectic are revealed by the *Yizhuan* to be highly self-evident. Nevertheless, they embody a richness to be explored by later commentators on the *Yi* Text. The richness of change testifies to the reality of change; at the same time, however, it demonstrates organic patterns of three proprieties of change and forms the basis of a fuller metaphysical description of reality, that is, the basic structure and picture of which the dialectics presuppose. There is therefore a creative interplay of the metaphysics and dialectics in the Confucian reflections on the *Yi* Text.

The World of *Ming* (Inevitabilities and Limitations in the *Yi* Text)

Take any *gua*: one finds that following the hexagram-symbol, the judgment normally names the *gua* and assesses the general value of the *gua*. The judgment states the *gua*'s general meaning pertaining to a categorical or hypothetical state of affairs; it appraises the value of the categorical or hypothetical state of affairs. The judgment further describes the trend of the *gua*-situation and reconsiders or indicates the advantageous course of action, or it indicates merely the disadvantageous course of action. Good examples are the following:

(*Qian* ☰ below, and *Gen* ☶ above)

Da Xu: Advantageous to be correct. Not to eat at home (eat from one's official appointment). Good fortune. Advantageous to cross the great river.

(Kan ☵ below, and Qian ☰ above)

> *Song*: Faith blocked. Alertness inside entails good fortune.
> Eventual misfortune. Advantageous to see the great person.
> Not advantageous to cross the great river.

Here, our purpose is not to analyze the language of the judgment and its ordering, but merely to note that the language of the judgment of a *gua* involves statement of valuation such as good fortune, misfortune, and so on. Although not every *gua* judgment makes explicit statement of such valuations, such valuation is an integral part of the judgment, even implicit and unstated as in many cases. As part of the judgment, this valuation pertains, on the one hand, to the relation of the divining subject to the place and to any situation in which he finds himself; on the other hand, the valuation pertains to the subject's action of tracing the situation. This means that the valuation in the judgment of a *gua* presupposes the understanding (including knowing) of a situation and entails a practical recommendation:

Knowledge ← valuation → n action

This also means that the valuations in the judgments follow from the knowing of the situation, or equivalently the situation represented in a *gua* gives rise to a practical value relative to the divining subject. With this background we may now pose the question: How does a value or a situation bearing that value, such as good fortune and misfortune, take place? Or, how does reality produce practical recognition of situations as represented by the *gua*?

To answer this question, we may first recognize that the system of practical value in the Yi Text of judgments represents a scale of advantage and disadvantage ranging from good fortune (*ji*), to no blame (*wu jiu*), to having regret (*you hui*), to small fault (*ling*), to danger (*li*), and to misfortune (*xiong*). These grades of practical valuation, which represent a scale of advantages and their converse to be applied to various situations, apparently have both an objective side and a subjective side. On the objective side, they pertain to qualities in an objective situation; on the subjective side, they pertain to the feelings and psychological responses of the individual involved. But both sides should reciprocate and therefore indicate a real problem or a real circumstance for the individual in a situation.

Now the question is how this circumstance or problem takes place, and what is its basis for existing. It is indeed a common experience that life situations have such practical value attached to them, and these have been recognized, classified, and given attention even in such writings as the *Hongfan* chapter of the *Shujing*. One may say that the misgivings that gave rise to the formation of the *Yi* Text are precisely worries and anxieties about the practical values of one's personal situation—or even more seriously, situations involving more than one person, such as the situation of power, the situation of war, or the situation of famine. Therefore, it is important to know the situation and its ensuing practical valuation and relation to life, as well as possible courses or options of action and choice.

The original *Yi* Text does not give any explanation of the basis of practical valuations of *gua* or reality. It is not until Confucius and his school formulate a philosophy of reality in light of the system of the *gua* that the explanations of *ji* and *xiong* are given. That explanation should indicate how Confucius's notion of *ming* comes into play and how knowing and acting are important for an individual of free will in a situation external to and limiting his action and influence.

In the *Xici*, the good fortune, misfortune, and other practical values in a situation are said to come from the grouping and separation of things and affairs, and the purpose of judgments in the *Yi* Text is in clarifying the fortune and misfortune of a situation. The first statement of the *Xici Shang* is significant:

> Heaven is noble and earth is low; thus the forms of *yin* and *yang* are fixed. The low and high are displayed. The noble and low are positioned. Movement and rest have constancy and thus the solid and soft are decided. Things are grouped according to their orientations and are separated according to their grouping. Thus fortune and misfortune are generated. In heaven there are heavenly forms and on earth earthly things. Thus change and transformation are manifested. (*Xici Shang* 1)

From this one may say that fortune and misfortune are matters resulting from the positioning of things and their change and transformation. They result from configuration or ordering of elements of things and affairs. Certain configurations and orderings of things and affairs are beneficial and advantageous for a person; certain others are not beneficial and advantageous, and may be even harmful and disadvantageous for a person. To talk about benefit, harm, advantage and disadvantage is to talk about things, their effects and influences in processes of change producing or promoting well-being or ill-being of a person or a group of persons. These practical values must be understood relative to the self-interest of a person or a group of persons. They need not be understood on a short-term basis. The important thing to recognize is that what determines the fortune and misfortune of a person is the circumstances surrounding him, and therefore, the fortune and misfortune are conditioned by the limiting external forces.

From the above, we can immediately see that fortune and misfortune belong to the world of the *ming* as experienced and spoken of by Confucius. One's *ming* is something beyond one's control and one must recognize its existence even if one may lament the *ming*. As we have seen, for Confucius, *ming* consists of such things as being born rich or poor, to live long or to live short. *Ming* also circumscribes things that happen to us, confining our activities in spite of our wishes and will. *Ming* is a world of inevitabilities and limitations of one's capacities as well as conditioning circumstances. In this sense, the fortune and misfortune in the *Yi*-judgments are precisely matters of *ming*. As *ming*, they are to be known and accepted; yet, at the same time, they are to be confronted with the right attitude, right actions, and a commitment to virtues. In doing so, the *ming* can be transformed into one's nature (*xing*), or one's nature will come into full play independent of the *ming* and will achieve self-realization and self-fulfillment.

Confucius may have recognized the world of *ming* in the organization of the *Yi* Text. He studied and valued the *Yi*-symbolism and *Yi*-judgment as a *model for situations* with built-in limitations and inevitabilities; he undertook this study to demonstrate that one can face life and reality with calm, courageous and harmonious adjustment. This leads to his consideration of *timeliness* as a supreme virtue for meeting the *ming* with commitment to nature and virtue. For as we have seen, one has free agency or will to develop and realize one's nature in terms of virtuous actions in spite of adverse circumstances.

In the *Xici*, we have other statements referring to fortune, misfortune, regret, fault, and the like as belonging to the practical dimension of a situation. It is said: "The sage creates *gua*, observes phenomena and appends judgment so that fortune and misfortune can be changed. The mutual push of the solid and soft generates change and transformation. Thus, fortune and misfortune are forms of *gain* and *loss*. Regret and small fault are images of anxiety" (*Xici Shang* 2).

The *Xici* continues to say: "The fortune and misfortune (of a situation) refer to gain and loss. Regret and shame refer to small imperfection. 'No blame' refers to facility to make up 'faults'" (section 3). Further, it is said, "Fortune, misfortune, regret and shame are generated amidst movement (of the *yao*-lines in the *gua*-situation)" (*Xici Xia* 1). "The *yao*-lines are to imitate the movement in the world. Thus, fortune and misfortune are generated; and regret and shame are manifested" (section 3). "The *dao* has movement; thus, there are *yao*-changes. The *yao*-lines have different variations—thus there are things. Things mix, thus there are patterns. Patterns may be appropriate or inappropriate. Thus fortune and misfortune are produced" (*Xici Xia* 10). All these indicate that practical values such as fortune and misfortune are inherent in a situation; they are brought in by the internal structure and change of a situation. For this reason, they are matters of *ming* to be forewarned about and correctly treated by a superior person.

In section 12 of the *Xici Xia*, a new aspect of the practical values (namely, fortune and misfortune, etc.) is mentioned, an aspect that reflects a state of harmony of the individual with the circumstances:

> The *bagua* tells about forms (of things). *Yao*-lines and *yao*-judgments speak of affairs in change (*jing*); the mixing of the solid and soft gives rise to fortune and misfortune which can be seen. The changes can be evaluated in terms of advantages. Fortune and misfortune can *shift* because of change of circumstance. Thus, when love and hate mutually attack each other, there are fortune and misfortune. When there is mutual possession of far and near there is regret and shame. The mutual influence of circumstances and efforts gives rise to consideration of advantage and disadvantage. For all changes of affairs entailing unfitting things, there will then be misfortune, which will be harmful and [the person] may feel regret and be ashamed (*ling*).

This passage clearly indicates that practical valuations result from how one relates to a situation and how one responds. The inherent values of the situation may shift just as the reality-representation of the *gua* may change into some other situation. A correct assessment of a situation and its potential transformation will prove as important as a correct maintenance of a correct attitude for confronting the world of *ming*, in which practical values such as fortune and misfortune may occur. The superior person would have much to learn from such a situation. Such a person can achieve practical adjustment to a situation as well as achieve a self-fulfillment and self-cultivation independent of and yet stimulated by the world of *ming*. The superior person may further make efforts to avoid falling into situations where inevitabilities and imitations will reign. In this light, the study of the *Yi*-symbolism and judgments is most meaningful and sufficient. For they would provide guidance for one's action and enhance knowledge of oneself and efforts to cultivate oneself. This point is not only consistent with Confucius's attitude toward *ming* in the *Analects* but actually constitutes a position Confucius would take for justifying study of the *Yi*.

In the *Xici Shang*, section 12, it is said, "The superior man observes the *forms* (of the *Yi*) and contemplates the judgments when at rest, and observes the changes and plays with the practice of divination. Thus he will be blessed by heaven; there will be fortune, and there is nothing disadvantageous." This attitude toward study of the *Yi* Text is perfectly consistent with the position of Confucius. Again, it may indeed be generated by Confucius's own considerations on the *Yi*. In fact, it is through one's understanding of the meaning of the *gua* as *models of life situations* that one may avoid misfortune and induce fortune beforehand by making better adjustment to one's life and by making better decisions on action as well as by cultivating oneself in virtue to achieve goodness.

By carefully and closely analyzing the section of the *Xici Shang* and sections five through seven of the *Xici Xia* we can easily see how Confucius relates his wisdom and views to the *Yi*. Through Confucius's interpretation the *Yi*, one's understanding of life may be enlightened, and one's pursuit of goodness and virtue may be enhanced. After all, what Confucius does in his reflection on the *Yi* Text is look into the meaning the *Yi*-judgment as a description of a life situation. He shows that a life situation ensues from one's lack of prudence, virtue and knowledge, or he shows how a realization of benevolence, knowledge and goodness may produce a life situation of well-being and fortune. It is natural to expect that Confucius wished to draw moral conclusions from or delineate moral premises for life situations of fortune and misfortune as described, or judged by the Yi Text. He was able to do so because the Yi Text provides a rich ground for drawing moral lessons.

If a life situation is momentous, as the Yi Text shows, how can it avoid having moral significance? On the other hand, how could Confucius avoid making his own moral vision of life relevant for a metaphysical and yet practical description of life situations and their transformation, while the Yi-judgments and even the Yi-symbolism need a moral evaluation? Confucian moral understanding needs an ontological application. One may therefore conjecture that it is in view of both the need for moral evaluation in the Yi, and the need for ontological application in the Analects that Confucius took the Yi Text very seriously, pursued a close study of it, and reached important conclusions about it as indicated in the commentaries of the Yi Text—predominantly the commentaries of the Tuan and the Xici.

The Confucian methodology of seeking moral conclusions and premises from the Yi-judgments on fortune and misfortune on a life situation, and grounding a moral vision and view of persons in the general metaphysics of change (to be actually formulated by Confucius) can be called a hermeneutical interpretation centered on merging moral and metaphysical insights of life. It is a methodology of unifying truths of moral reason and truths of cosmological-ontological understanding and experience. It is hermeneutical in the sense that it reflects an interpretation of the given Yi Text and the process of generating a philosophical position from the interpretation. This methodology is highly creative as it also effects a philosophical transformation of the original text to yield a more coherent and mere explicit picture of reality and life. This is precisely how Confucius related to the Yi Text.

In carrying out his hermeneutical interpretation of the Yi-judgments, we may point out that Confucius generally assumed that virtues such as benevolence, righteousness, and propriety are efficacious in two important senses. First, one realizes one's *nature* independent of *ming* (limitations of life). This is the intrinsic significance of virtue—virtue by way of self-realization and self-fulfillment. Second, virtues are ways to ensure and produce harmony and order in the world, if not in the short run, at least in the long run. This is clearly agreed upon by Confucius in his social and political philosophy of governing a state. How could a ruler reach order and harmony in the state without embodying virtues of love and righteousness? For the individual self, even though virtues do not guard against *ming*, virtues command respect and empathy and can be seen to eliminate undesirable feelings and desires in both oneself and others. Since virtues include also the virtue of knowing and being wise and prudent, one will achieve a better understanding of oneself and one's environment so that a better adjustment can be planned and implemented.

Decisions and actions produce consequences. When decisions and actions assume a moral significance, they are made with regard to life as a whole and thus aim at the potential well-being of an age as a whole. Thus, morality in Confucius's system as presented in the *Analects* should be regarded as efficacious: as inducing and achieving harmony and order in one's life. Confucius would separate harmony and order from considerations of advantage (*li*) and disadvantage; the latter is short-term and selfishly motivated. In light of this general assumption of moral efficacy in Confucius, we can see that the Confucian interest in making a moral transformation of the metaphysics of the *Yi* lies in providing a moral foundation for the *Yi*-inspired concepts of fortune and misfortune. For Confucius, fortune and misfortune can be considered the limiting cases of *ming*. They are circumstances no one and no virtues can change: they are simply external limitations and inevitabilities. But fortune and misfortune can also be considered results and consequences of one's behavior and one's comportment in life. In this sense, fortune and misfortune are self-made acts suggested by the ancient motto: "If others did something to give rise to misery, there is something to say about it; if one does something to give rise to misery, one simply cannot survive.[10]

This aspect of *moral efficacy* is an important aspect of Confucian morality apart from the aspect of *moral autonomy*—one is free to realize one's nature and one has the power to do so. It is in regarding fortune and misfortune as results of moral efficacy that Confucius gives a new meaning to fortune and misfortune and thus defines a new type of fortune and misfortune: fortune as harmony and order, and misfortune as disharmony and disorder from which other disadvantages and harms may ensue. In this light, the *Yi*-judgment about fortune and misfortune then becomes the judgment about harmony (order) and disharmony (disorder) requiring moral wisdom and understanding of life. It is perhaps with this moral understanding that this is said in section 8 of the *Xici Shang*.

To illustrate the above analysis of fortune and misfortune in a diagram, we have the following:

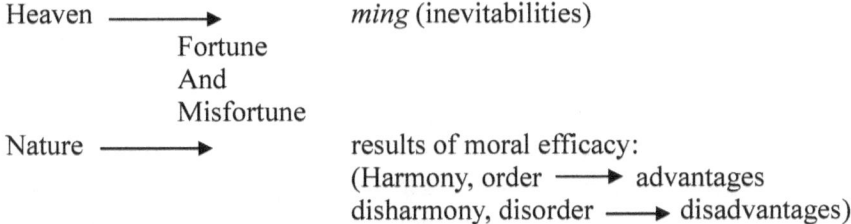

In the *Xici* there are nineteen cases of the Confucian interpretation of the *yao*-judgments in the *Yi* Text. Although we have no direct proof that the quotation from Confucius must be Confucius's own, there is no contrary proof, either. In view of the total coherence of the Confucian moral philosophy with his professed interest in the *Yi* and the nature of the *Yi* System, it is more likely than not that Confucius actually made those remarks on the *yao*-judgments, which are indeed directly attributed to him. For the nineteen cases of his interpretation, the general rule is to draw a moral conclusion from each *Yi* passage; moreover, in his interpretation, moral premises are also formed for each *Yi* passage. These illustrate the application of his hermeneutical methodology described above. Without going into every one of them, I shall present five such examples for illustration. "The sage sees something in the movements under heaven and contemplates their influence and interrelating, and thus performs proprieties (appropriate to these movements) and appends statements in order to judge the fortune and misfortune (of these movements). These are called the *yao*-statements." This clearly shows the moral transformation of the *Yi* Text by which a moral interpretation of the formation of the *Yi*-judgments is made. Fortune and misfortune are not a matter of objective perception of external circumstances, but a matter of moral insight relating to the sage's moral wisdom.

Qian ䷉ (Humility) 9-3 *yao*-judgment says: "The superior man (ruler) who works industriously and with humility has good result-fortune." Confucius interprets this passage as follows:

> Work industriously and do not exercise expedition. Achieve and do not gain. This is the utmost of virtue. This means that the ruler's achievement (*gong*) has reached people below. Virtue bespeaks the flourishing [of one's achievements]. Propriety bespeaks the respect [in which he is held by people].

> Humility is a matter of reaching respect and preserving his position [as a ruler]. (*Xici Shang* 8)

The net meaning of this interpretation is to show that fortune is brought by virtue of hard work and humility.

Qian ☰ top-9 *yao*-judgment says: "The dragon on high has regret." Confucius reasons: "Have noble honor and yet have no proper position. Stay high and yet have no people [follow him]. The good man is in low position and therefore there is no support of the above. Thus, there is regret in one's movement." This clearly indicates how a ruler without the virtue of knowledge, proper action and love for his people and the good will fail as a consequence (*Xici Xia* 8).

With regard to *Bi* ䷇ 9-5 *yao*-judgment, "Whether one will perish depends on mulberry blossoming," Confucius has this to say:

> [Remembering] danger one will be secure in one's position. [Remember] perishability, one will preserve what one has. [Remembering] cause for disorder, one will achieve ordering. Thus the superior man does not forget danger when being secure, doesn't forget perishability when prospering; does not forget disorder when ordering. Thus one can achieve safety for oneself and peace for the country. (section 8)

Again, the interpretation stresses the importance of comprehensive *wisdom* of understanding reality and one's self-cultivation and self-control.

With regard to *Kun* ䷮ 6-3 *yao*-judgment: "Being stuck in the stone and relying on the high grass (*ji li*), one enters one's house and does not see one's wife." "Misfortune," Confucius comments, "It is not the right thing to be stuck with and yet one is stuck with it. Thus, his name will be insulted. It is not the right thing to rely on. Thus, his person will be endangered. When one person has been insulted and exposes himself to danger, his day of death will come close. How could he see his wife?" The stress in this comment is that the person in question has done something that should not have been done. The desperation he has is self-made by his moral stupor, but not a matter of *ming* (*Xici Xia* 5).

Regard the *Yu* ䷏ 6-2 *yao*-judgment: "To lie between stones, without waiting for the ending of a day, good fortune will arrive." On this, Confucius states: "If one person lies between stones, why should he even wait for the ending of that day to [receive fortune]? This can be clearly seen. A superior man knows the beginnings of things so that he sees them manifest. He knows the soft and the solid and [can reach] what all people wish" (*Xici Xia* 5). In this comment, Confucius draws the conclusion of fortune from a moral attitude of fortitude.

In light of these illustrations it is not difficult to see how the *gua*-judgments and meanings of the whole *Tuanzhuan* may provide a moral guide and moral counsel to a superior person, who is concentrating on fulfilling life virtuously and inducing order and harmony in the state and the world. It is not surprising to see, therefore, that the nine forms of the *Yi*-symbolism are regarded and interpreted as representing nine aspects of virtue and reason. This understanding is said to come from a deep metaphysical reflection on life and a moral insight into forms of life situations as models and bases for producing goodness in the sense of order and harmony. Thus it is said: "Therefore *Lü* (treading) is the basis of virtue (*de*); *Qian* (modesty) is the handle of virtue; *Fu* (return) is the root of virtue; *Heng* (duration) is the solidity of virtue; *Sun* (decrease) is the cultivation of virtue; *Yi* is the prosperity of virtue; *Kun* (depression) is the clarification of virtue; *Jing* (the well) is the ground of virtue; *Xun* (the gentle) is the measure of virtue" (*Xici Xia* 7).

The reason for these moral interpretations is the moral efficacy found in these *gua* forms: "*Lü* yields harmony and reaches the goal; *Qian* yields respect and lightens up; *Fu* discerns small differences in things; *Heng* persists even amidst confusion; *Sun* reaches easiness by starting with difficulties: *Yi* lasts and prospers and yet is not imposing: *Kun* penetrates from hardship; *Jing* moves and yet stays in one place; *Xun* becomes known and yet remains in obscurity" (*Xici Xia* 7). From these qualities of life situations, virtues will follow or will be presupposed: "*Fu* acts by harmony: *Qian* is used to institute propriety; *Fu* gives rise to self-knowledge; *Heng* brings unity to virtue; *Sun* removes harm; *Yi* promotes advantage; *Kun* reduces resentment; *Jing* senses righteousness; *Xun* follows concrete understanding." These explanations indicate how in general the *Yi* Text receives a moral analysis and moral meaning in light of the Confucian methodology suggested earlier.

Timeliness in the *Yi*-judgments

According to the *Xici*, it is change that produces fortune and misfortune. The implication of such a view is twofold. In the first place, fortune and misfortune are now external circumstances that affect the human being. In this sense fortune and misfortune are matters of *ming*. On the other hand, one's action and attitude make a difference to the fortune and misfortune of one's life. We have seen that Confucius basically conceived of a person as a free agent, and he thought that a person's action is just as efficacious as any happening of the world. Not only does one's action make a difference to the fortune and misfortune of one's life or life of others, but whether one's actions are moral or *not* also makes an efficacious difference. Thus, it follows that it is totally within a person's locus of control and determination of oneself as to how fortune and misfortune are to be brought about, particularly when we consider fortune and misfortune as a matter of harmony and order based on adjustment and understanding. No one, of course, is born to be so free as to be able to create all circumstances of his or her life. One is often placed in a situation extraneous and impervious to one's decision or action. This may happen through no fault of one's own. Even though one can be held responsible for some partial circumstances coming into existence, and in spite of the fact that one may mold or modify one's future through one's fresh decision and action, one is indeed subject to what is given externally.

With this said, one's knowledge of what is within one's capacity to transform and what is not—what one can do and what one cannot—is highly important for making actual adjustments in a given situation. In other words, *zhi* (knowing) is equally as important as *zhi* (wisdom or prudence). The basic maxim for both *zhi*, as was indicated earlier, is to maximize harmony and order as much as possible and to minimize disorder and conflict as much as possible (and indeed as early as possible).

The considerations of knowing life, self-responsibility, and moral efficacy will enable us to understand timeliness in the *Yijing* better, for such considerations will give more substantial meaning to the concept of timeliness (*zhi*). But we should note that when we speak of *shi* (time or timeliness) in the *Yijing*, we have already introduced a relatively later, explicit concept in the *Yizhuan* for something only implicit in the Yi-symbolism and the Yi-judgments. We must recognize that there is no explicit mention of *shi* in the original Yi Text. Apparently, the idea of *shi* suggests itself in virtue of the correlation of things and the happening of special events in nature: the virtue of the correlation of things and the happening of special events in nature: the term "*shi*" not only will have a descriptive meaning, but an ontological and a moral meaning.

The introduction of *shi* as a concept may be necessary for developing a metaphysical theory of change. It is required to stimulate an understanding about how one can adjust and fit with a live eye-situation in virtue of one's self-knowledge and knowledge of the world in change. It is in the *Xici* that *shi* has been given much use for explanatory purpose, and it is in the *Tuanzhuan* that the implicit message and meaning of *shi* in a given *gua* is made explicit.

When the term "*Yi*" is used in the *Yizhuan*, sometimes it refers to the original text of *Yi*-symbolism, sometimes to that of *Yi*-judgments, and sometimes to the totality of symbolism and judgments of the *Yi*. But in the *Xici*, it is apparent that the *Yi* has been elucidated into a unified philosophy and can be said to refer to the metaphysics and dialectics of change as explained in an earlier section above. More accurately, it is the way of change, as understood in the metaphysics and dialectics of change, that is being referred to as the *Yi*. *Yi* is described as comprehensive and vast, becoming and penetrating, having the creative potentiality for exchange of *yin-yang* polarity, as well as being simple and easeful. Then it is said, "The comprehension and vastness [of the *Yi*] matches heaven and earth; the becoming and penetrating match the four seasons; the *yin-yang* principle matches sun and moon; the goodness of 'easefulness' and simplicity matches ultimate virtue" (*Xici Shang* 6).

The reference to four seasons (or four times) makes it clear that *timely change* such as the change of seasons shows the virtue of becoming and penetrating of the change. By inference, for the Confucian commentators, time is not some entity independent of the change or change's transforming and creative power. *Time* is simply the form or phenomena of change—the becoming and penetrating (*bian tong*) of reality. It is concretely shown in the change of four seasons. Thus, in order to understand *time*, it is best to understand the four seasons and their evolution. As *change* is ultimately reality, reality functions according to the way of *yin-yang* alternation, and it is essentially a creative power of ever-new production and transformation: *time* must be similarly conceived. *Time* must be conceived as an aspect of the productive process of life, as well as the formative and transformative process of reality (which is understood in terms of the *yin-yang* alternation and its rich productivity). To be brief, *time* is the quality of becoming and penetrating (productivity) in things and is concretely embodied in the evolution of the seasons, which shows both alternation of the *yin* and *yang* and productivity of life.

The *Xici* further stresses: "To discover principles of things, there is nothing greater than observing heaven and earth; to discover the principle of becoming and penetrating nothing is greater than observing the four times (four seasons)" (*Xici Shang* 11). In the time of four seasons we not only find time but timeliness, namely, changes according to principles of *yin* and *yang* and the principle of vital productivity-production of life and virtue (section 5). Thus, any change of becoming and penetration (transformation and production) can also be said to be a matter of time and timeliness, for it is time that is appropriately displayed. Thus, it is said, "the solid and the soft are what establish the roots," and to become and penetrate is "to fit with time (*qu shi*)" (*Xici Xia* 1). The formation of heaven and earth, the production of human civilization, and the invention of the *Yi*-symbolism for divination by the ancient sages can all be said to represent a paradigm of timeliness, for they are events of "becoming and penetrating" (*bian tong*). They produce or enhance life and virtue, and they result from forces the *yin* and *yang*.

In this sense, time is both an ordering and a producing principle; as such, it is timeliness. What this means is, timeliness is time as embodied in concrete events of ordering and creating. To understand time depends on understanding timeliness and thus on understanding the way of *change* (*Yi*).

With the above interpretation of time and timeliness, we can clearly see how Confucius could develop notions such as the following from the *Tuan Commentary* on the judgments of the *Yi gua* and *Yi yao*: "meaning of time" (*shi yi*), "the function of time" (*shi yong*) "moving together with time" (*shi xing*) "following time" (*sui shi*), "the budding of time" (*shi fa*), "fitting with time" (*shizhong*), "the becoming of time" (*shibian*), "understanding time" (*ming shi*), "responding to time" (*dui shi*), "completion in accordance with time" (*shi cheng*), "not fitting with time" (*shi shi*), and "going with time" (*shi xing*). Before we examine and verify the meaning of time and timeliness in these various paradigms in light of what is said above, we may first point out that it is apparently from reflection on the metaphysical significance of the *Yi*-judgment in light of the total underlying metaphysical system of the *Yi*-symbolism that time and timeliness find their application for interpretation of the judgments. Thus, these time-related notions already presuppose or at least suggest a philosophy of change, which is quite consistent with the metaphysical view of change in the *Xici*. This point does not and cannot indicate whether the *Xici* or the *Tuanzhuan* appears first. But it does suggest that both works support each other and may appear at approximately the same time and from the same source, which we take to be Confucius and his school.

Let us elucidate the meanings of time and timeliness in the *Tuanzhuan* on individual judgments of the *gua*:

(a) On *Dun* (Retreat ䷠), *Yu* (Enthusiasm ䷏), *Gou* (Coming to meet ䷫), and *Lü* (Wandering ䷷), it is said,

"The meaning of time for *Dun* ䷠ is great indeed"

"The meaning of time for *Yu* ䷏ is great indeed!"

"The meaning of time for *Gou* ䷫ is great indeed!"

"The meaning of time for *Lü* ䷷ is great indeed!"

If we look into each *gua*-symbol and judgment, we shall see that "the meaning of time" clearly refers to the position of the forces (in the *yao*) and potential movements and influences in the *gua*. These positions, movements, and influences should command an appropriate correlative action or response on the part of the individual agent in the situation. "The meaning of time" for each *gua* thus depends on an understanding of the cosmological or metaphysical meaning of the *gua*. It is the latter meaning that exhibits "the meaning of time," and each different structure of the *gua* of course exhibits a different "meaning of time." Thus, for *Dun*, "the meaning of time" lies in recognizing the growth of the *yin*-force and the difficulty of positive advancement; hence, it lies in the consequent adjustment of action and response of individual in such a situation. This "meaning of time" enables the individual to achieve a better harmony and ordering of events and a better cultivation of himself. Thus, this "meaning of time" enables the individual to avoid any misfortune resulting from unenlightened action out of time with the situation.

Similarly, for *Lü*, "the meaning of time" is such that the soft obtains the middle position of the outer trigram and yet remains subject to the solid on the top. This may suggest a difficult situation; consequently, it commands attention to the balance of forces and an action to preserve or induce the best order and harmony for the individual agent. This is done to avoid unnecessary misfortune based on wrong action. For *Gou*, "the meaning of time" is to be careful over the subtle beginning of reverse change in the situation. For *Gou*, however, the *gua* form indicates an order and harmony in itself; its "meaning of time" lies in recognizing this and endeavoring to emulate it.

These examples should indicate how "the meaning of time" varies with each *gua*-situation, and how fortune and misfortune (in terms of difficulty and lack of difficulty, order and disorder, harmony and disharmony) obtain in different *gua*-situations. To discern these is to see "the meaning of time" in each situation. To respond appropriately is to act in *timeliness*, which should enhance order and harmony and avoid worsening the situation and resultant misfortune. Where misfortune already dominates, we shall see, one should hold oneself in virtue and bear through until the situation changes; the changes are always possible by way of principled alternation of the *yin-yang* forces as the underlying way of change and the underlying nature of reality.

(b) On *Kui* (Opposition ☷), *Jian* (Obstruction ☷), and *Kan* (The Abysmal ☷), it is said,

"The function of time (*shiyong*) for *Kui* is great indeed!"

"The function of time for *Jian* is great indeed!"

"The function of time for danger in the *Kan* is great indeed!"

The *shiyong* in fact differs not from the *shiyi* discussed above. The meaning of time is precisely the function of time, but this function of time is basically the function of change as represented in a situation indicated by the *gua* in question. To recognize the *shiyong* of the *Kui*, for example, is to recognize that opposition sometimes means complementation and positive communication. One must see the structure of the situation and its change-potential in order to see its *potential use*. The potential use of a situation is implicit in the process and result of change, which should be carefully discussed. To understand this and act accordingly is to act in accordance with time and hence to achieve timeliness. Similarly, for *Qian*, the understanding of the child-situation reveals the right course to take. The *Tuan Commentary* says: "*Qian* is difficulty. Danger is ahead. To see danger is to be able to stop in a matter of knowing (wisdom)." It is in fact a matter of timeliness. *Timeliness* thus means thoroughly knowing a situation and acting according to what is suggested in such knowing for the purpose of achieving order and harmony and consequently avoiding unnecessary misfortune. Similar explanation holds for danger in the *Kan*:

> (c) On *Qian* (The Creative ☰), it is said:
>
> "[*Qian*] is the beginning and ending of the great illumination (in the world). The six positions (of *yao*) are 'formed according to time,' like six dragons riding on heaven in accordance with time."
>
> On *Heng* (Duration ䷟), it is said: "The four seasons change and complete perpetually (*jiu cheng*)."
>
> On *Ge* (Revolution ䷰), it is said, "The time for *ge* is great indeed." "The heaven and earth change, and the four seasons form [according to time]."
>
> On *Jie* (Limitation ䷻), it is said, "The heaven and earth restrain, and the four seasons form (according to time)."
>
> On *Yi* (Nourishing ䷚), it is said, "The time for *Yi* is great indeed.
>
> On *Daguo* (Preponderance of the great ䷛), it is said, "The time for *daguo* is great indeed!"
>
> On *Xie* (Deliverance ䷧), it is said that "The time for *xie* is great indeed."

The formation of the six positions and four seasons are a matter of timely creativity of heaven and earth; thus, they can be regarded as a paradigm of timeliness in action—action thus being productive of order and harmony. In this perspective, the time for *Ge*, *Yi*, *Daguo* and *Xie* is also timeliness, which has its meaning and function for us so that we may follow and act accordingly.

(d) On *Meng* (Youthful folly ䷃), it is said that the prosperity of the *meng* derives from the timely action (or action fitting with time) (*shizhong*).

On *Dayou* (Possession in great measure ䷍), it is said, "Respond to heaven and God with time (*shi xing*)."

On *Xun* (Decrease ䷨), it is said, "To lose, to add, to fill and to void, one should go with time" (*yu shi jie xing*).

On *Yi* (Increase ䷩), it is said, "All the way of Yi is such that it goes with time."

On *Xiao guo* (Preponderance of the small ䷽), it is said, "to exceed in order to hold to the right is a matter of going with time."

On *Sui* (Following ䷐), it is said that "This is great property and firmness. No blame. All things under heaven take place according to time (*sui shi*). The meaning of *sui shi* is great indeed!"

On *Sheng* (Arising ䷭), it is said that the soft rises according to time (*shi sheng*).

On *Feng* (Abundance ䷶), it is said, "The fullness and voidness of heaven and earth grow and diminish with time (*yu shi xiao xi*)."

On *Dun* (Retreat ䷠), again it is said, "The solid stays in position and should go with time."

All these indicate how things themselves change by way of increasing and decreasing in accordance with time. This means that change of things has its rhythm and pattern, and time is the inner rhythm and pattern inherent in things and change of things. These also indicate how a person should follow the pattern and rhythm of changes in order to achieve order and harmony.

(e) In the *Xiang* commentary it is said regarding *Jie* (Limitation ䷻), "Even not going out of the door there is misfortune. This is the ultimate of 'not fitting with time' (*shi shi*)."

On *Ge* (Revolution ䷰), the *Xiang* says: "The superior man studies the calendar in order to understand time (*ming shi*)."

On *Wuwang* (Innocence ䷘), the *Xiang* says: "The former Kings nourished all things by 'correlating with time' (*dui shi*) to make them prosper."

On *Kun* (The Receptive ䷁), the *Xiang* says: "The implicit pattern can be preserved, but it can be developed in (appropriate) time" (*shi fa*). It is also said in *Wenyan*, "Receive heaven and go with time (*cheng tian er shi xing*)."

On *Bi* (Grace ䷕), the *Tuan* says, "observe the heaven-pattern in order to discern the change of time (*shibian*); observe the human-pattern in order to transform the world."

The natural course of things always has an inner order of time and thus fits with time. For human beings it is necessary to know the natural course of things and understand a situation in order to find the right course of action to go with the right course of things. Thus, the notion of "correlating with time" (*dui shi*) indicates an effort on the part of the sage to seek the right time for right action to achieve good results for all. Similarly, in the *Kun* case, one has to make an effort to realize and develop a potential capacity and quality in a situation. This effort must be coordinated with all forces in a situation and must be based on the ultimate reality (heaven) in order to be efficacious. The goodness or rightness of an action comes from correlation and coordination with all forces in a situation. This *timeliness* is to correlate, coordinate, and follow time, and this requires understanding and knowledge. Thus, we have a recommendation of the *Ge* and the *Feng*.

The actual timing by calendar and the discerning of time-changes (*shibian*) is also important for attaining the goal of ordering, harmonizing, and making virtue efficacious. "*Shibian*" refers, in fact, to the change of things in the process of change. Refusing to act according to time is to invite misfortune, and this is called "not fitting with time" (*shi shi*). It is not fitting with a situation, and it indicates an absence of virtue.

It is significant to go back to *Qian* ☰ for the insights into time and timeliness in the *Wenyan Commentary*. It is in regard to *Qian* that more remarks on time and timeliness are made by the Confucian commentators in the *Wenyanzhuan*. In fact, it is by quoting Confucius that the lessons on timeliness are given. In regard to interpreting *yao* 9-3, Confucius is quoted as saying:

> The superior man advances virtue and ultimate goodness. To be loyal and faithful is to advance virtue. To cultivate language and establish sincerity is to abide by goodness. To try to reach knowledge and reach it, one can participate in knowing the subtlety (of the way); to know the ending of a thing and to end it, one can preserve righteousness. Thus one can stay in high position without being arrogant and can stay in low position without anxiety. Thus the *yao* says, "One must diligently work and continuously alter oneself at all times (*ying qi shi*). Thus even if there is danger, there is no blame.

Confucius has seen that a person may be placed in an adverse situation, but how does he act? Knowing that action makes a difference for fortune and misfortune, one should carefully understand the situation and be alert to time for changes in order to act correctly. That Confucius mentions knowing and alertness to time is significant. For knowing is the basis of action and to be alert to time is to be alert to change of things. To act according to knowledge of the change and to be prepared for this is a high mark of timeliness. It is where the Confucian answer to the world of inevitabilities and indeterminable lies. One cultivates one's virtue and one alerts oneself to changes by making necessary adjustments without losing one's virtue. For example, a person can be amicable and soft in peace time, and then become courageous and hard in war time; that adjustment from softness to courageousness is due to a response to change in environment, but that does not deprive the person of his virtue. This means, also, there is internal relatedness of virtues mediated by changes of time. In this way one may face any adversity and misfortune. Again quoting from Confucius: "To advance virtue and cultivate goodness is to desire to act according to time (*zhi shi*)."

If one asks why advancing virtue and cultivating goodness is to desire to act in accordance with time, the answer is that only when one advances virtues such as *ren*, *yi*, *li*, and *zhi*, and cultivates goodness in practice, will one be capable of seeing the subtleties of change, adjust oneself carefully to act accordingly, and have the self-discipline and self-control to so act. Thus, a superior person should be always prepared for such a situation. In this preparation one should develop a deep understanding of the ways of change and a great sense of alertness for right action at the right time to achieve the right goal. In this manner, not only can one avoid misfortune, even danger, but one can develop and realize oneself to the extent that one can avoid all adverse situations and reach a state of perfection. This state of perfection for a sage is of course ideal and perhaps idealistic; thus, it is described by the *Wenyanzhuan*: "The great man unifies virtue with heaven and earth; unifies brightness with sun and moon, unifies the order with four seasons, and unifies [agencies of] fortune and misfortune with spirits. In the case of heaven, heaven would not violate the order of heaven and yet would also follow the course of time of heaven (*tian shi*). Even heaven makes no violation, not to mention human beings. Not to mention spirits." This means that heaven is to be understood by its own order and its immanence in the course of time. Therefore, nothing within below or within heaven could deviate from the heavenly order and heavenly time. This, then, describes how a sage with deep and perfect knowledge and virtue can act together with change of season in precision, and thus there should be no fault resulting, as there is perfect order and harmony in his life and the effects of his actions. This would be a perfect example of timeliness—indeed a perfect model and ideal for timeliness as a virtue.

The virtue of timeliness can be perhaps stated as follows: it is the virtue of acting toward time (change), as recognized by the individual, to achieve order and harmony. It is also best expressed by the *Tuan Commentary* on Gen ䷳: "Gen means stop. If stopping according to time, then stop; if proceeding according to time, then proceed. If one does not miss out on time (*shi shi*), then the way [of one's action] is bright." To stop and proceed according to time is to stop and proceed according to one's correct knowledge of changes and things in a situation: this ability requires a virtue of knowing and a virtue of acting. It further requires a constancy of alertness and a subtlety of discernment. If one has all these virtues, then one will not act out of time. One will always act in accordance with things and act to bring about order and harmony. One's way of action will always be right, and there should be no anxiety (*you*) on his part, even in time of influence (namely, adversity and misfortune are not of one's own making). Such a person would then be a Sage. Thus, the *Wenyan* on *Kun* concludes: "It is only the sage who can do this: know when and how to move backward, when and how to preserve, and when and how to relinquish without missing the right course. Is it merely the sage who can do this?" It is interesting to note: the notion of sage in terms of embodying timeliness is no doubt one highly comparable to the idea of a sage in the Confucian *Analects*.

In connection with the notion of timeliness (*shi*), the notion of centrality (*zhong*) is well developed in the *Tuan Commentary*, closely followed by the *Xiang* and *Wenyan* commentaries and equally emphasized in the *Xici*. In the *Tuan Commentary* "centrality" is so basic a notion that one may say that whether "centrality" obtains determines the state of fortune and misfortune for a situation, and therefore determines the timeliness or lack of such for an action. What, then, is "centrality"? To understand this notion for the *Tuan Commentary*, one must recall how the *gua* form is perceived to represent a structured order and a hierarchy of forces in which right position, right force and right correspondence are essential for understanding the meaning of the *gua* form. But what is right about a position or a force, is a right correspondence. All depends on how positions in the *gua* and the *yin-yang* forces are combined and related.[11] For the convention of the *Tuan Commentary*, the second position and the fifth position are respectively positions of centrality as is apparent form the configuration of the *gua*. As the *yin-yang* forces may each occupy the second and fifth position, *yin* and *yang* can be said to obtain centrality if this happens.

When the *yang* force obtains the fifth position and the *yin*-force obtains the second position, we have the case of having "exact centrality" (*zhengzhong, zhongzheng*). Since, this notion of centrality fulfills the requirement of the positional concept of "occupying a right position" (*dangwei*) understood as the *yang* occupying the first, third and fifth position or the *yin* occupying the second, fourth and top position, the case of having "exact centrality" is a case of "occupying a right position."

There also is the notion of correspondence (*ying*). When first and fourth, second and fifth, and third and sixth positions are respectively occupied by the opposite forces of *yin* and *yang*, we have correspondence. It is clear that the *gua* form may exhibit the obtainment of exact centrality without or with obtaining correspondence. If there are correspondence and exact centrality at the same time, we have forms of good fortune. Opposite to these notions of position, centrality, and correspondence, there are notions of "missing the right positions" (*shi wei*), "not having the right position" (*bu dang wei*), "missing the centrality" (*shi zhong* or *bu zhong*), and "lacking correspondence" (*di ying*). If we add more positional and qualitative distinctions such as above (*shang*) and below (*xia*), solid (*gang*) and soft (*rou*), we will have the concept of overriding (*sheng*), where the solid (*yang*) occupies the above position and the soft (*yin*) occupies the low position. In terms of valuation, the above is high and noble, and the below is low and lowly. We will be able to see which configurations of forces and positions produce more coherence, order, harmony and concordance (*shun*), and which other configuration of forces display less or lack of coherence, order, harmony and concordance.

In terms of such possible configurations we can obtain the concept of centrality in a broad sense. We can see "centrality" (*zhong*) as the right combination of positions and forces, which answer to all requirements of coherence, order, harmony, and concordance in positional, qualitative as well as evaluative aspects. If we further add dynamic considerations such as tendentious moving up and moving down, possible transformations to (or transformational relationships to) other related configurations, as we should if *gua* form is to represent a situation as a sector of process of change in a total context of co-relational structures as we have discussed, then we have to further define centrality in a larger dynamical framework. *Zhong* is the right configuration of position and forces that move and develop in the right relationships to other configurations. This means that *zhong* is a structure of harmony, order, and coherence as well as a concordance and process of producing and maintaining more order, harmony, coherence, and concordance.

With these three senses of *zhong* understood, we may easily see how timeliness can be related to *zhong*: as time is a dimension of things always integral to positions and their combinations with *yin-yang* qualities, timeliness is therefore the obtaining of centrality (in whatever manner or broader sense of centrality) in right time. But to say that centrality obtains in right time is to say no more than that centrality obtains in actuality, for time is displayed in the actual process of combination of positions and forces. Therefore, timeliness is in fact equivalent to obtaining centrality in actuality: namely, *shi* is *zhong*.

Now two aspects of *timeliness* must be pointed out that make it a more dynamic concept than *zhong*. First, the obtaining of *zhong* can be a matter of dynamic movement in the larger framework of interrelationships of configuration. Timeliness can be said to refer to a potential harmony or order apart from referring to the actual obtaining of such. Relative to such potential state, a situation may be untimely in one sense and yet timely in another. Second, timeliness is a feature of action to make obtaining *zhong* possible. It takes account of the individual agent in the total situation; thus, it requires the agent to know and understand the situation in order to act toward centrality—which is productive of coherence, order, harmony, and concordance.

In the above dynamic sense of timeliness, which is implicit in the Confucian *Analects*, *shi* not only is more dynamic a concept than *zhong*, but actually presupposes understanding *zhong* as an integral part of its understanding. Timeliness hence is to befit time to produce centrality, and any befitting (through natural course or action) is a matter of befitting time. For Confucius in the *Analects* as well as in the *Xici*, only the superior person who cultivates the virtues of moral wisdom, incorporating knowledge, love and righteousness can achieve timeliness and hence centrality. Confucius himself exhibited this virtue of timeliness in his own life and is aptly called by Mencius "the sage of timeliness." In light of the *Tuan* and the *Zhongyong*, which expounds both timeliness and centrality, the Confucian sagehood and the Confucian relevance for the *Tuan* and *Zhongyong* can be easily understood.

Concluding Remarks: Reciprocal Transformation Between Confucius and the *Yi* Text

Without explanation and analysis of notions of time and timeliness in the *Yizhuan* (*Xiang* and *Wenyan* primarily), we have shown the following: although notions of time and timeliness are implicit in the *Yi*-symbolism and *Yi*-judgments, they require a reflective understanding to reveal and make them explicit as well as to give them a correct formulation. This can take place only when a deeper understanding of reality, as presupposed in the *Yi* Text, is developed and hence the metaphysics of change and its dialectical methodology revealed. Insofar as notions of time and timeliness do logically cohere with the Confucian view of reality and timeliness as seen in the *Analects*, it is quite plausible that it is Confucius and his followers in his later life who introduced considerations of time and timeliness into the study of *Yi* Text and produced the *Yi* commentaries.

Moreover, it is further natural and reasonable for Confucius to have developed his views on the Yi Text as he contemplated and reflected on it. In this sense, the *Yizhuan* is a natural and reasonable extension of the Confucian philosophy of human beings, which is not only consistent with the metaphysics and dialectics of the *Yi*, but in fact supports this metaphysics and dialectics. In this vein, we can see that Confucius has the notion of *ming*, which clearly corresponds to the world of fortune and misfortune in the *Yi* Text. But Confucius proposes his solution to the problem of *ming* by advancing the concept of timeliness. The problem of *ming*, as the study of the *Yi* Text shows, is that when we are placed in a situation beyond our capacity of modification and transformation, we have to know what is the best way to act in such a situation.

Based on our distinction between *ming* as inevitabilities and limitations on our capacities, and *ming* as simply a given configuration of forces and positions, the Confucian solution to the problem of *ming* can be stated as follows:

1. Regarding inevitabilities one will have to accept them. This is reflected in Confucius's statement on poverty, wealth, length of life and death.

2. Regarding configurations of positions and forces, to act with knowledge and to act toward order and harmony, is necessary for one's action to have desirable efficacy. It is clear that Confucius recommends abiding by moral cultivation of oneself that will make one's action morally efficacious.

3. The individual person, *qua* person, however, should cultivate himself (or his nature) in order to achieve moral autonomy, self-fulfillment, and ontological transformation, independent of practical considerations of preserving fortune and avoiding misfortune.

4. Hence, the study of the *Yi* should be a study of the metaphysics and dialectics of the *Yi*, which can be morally efficacious for oneself on a higher level, which rules out fortune and misfortune as central considerations for the completion of a life of virtue. This is because it is

recognized that the value of a person comes from having a free will and from his applying his free will to self-cultivation according to the way.

Confucius's views in the *Analects* are compatible with and conducive to the Yi metaphysics and Yi dialectics or Yi methodology. Apart from the argument from the notion of timeliness in the *Yizhuan*, this is clear also from the following:

1. Confucius stresses importance of learning.
2. Confucius stresses the importance of knowing the mandate of heaven.
3. The Yi Text can be an object of profound learning; at the same time, it reveals a picture of the mandate of heaven. Thus, for Confucius, to study the Yi is like studying and getting to know the mandate of heaven.

The Confucian solution by way of timeliness to the problem of *ming* perhaps can be expressed as follows:

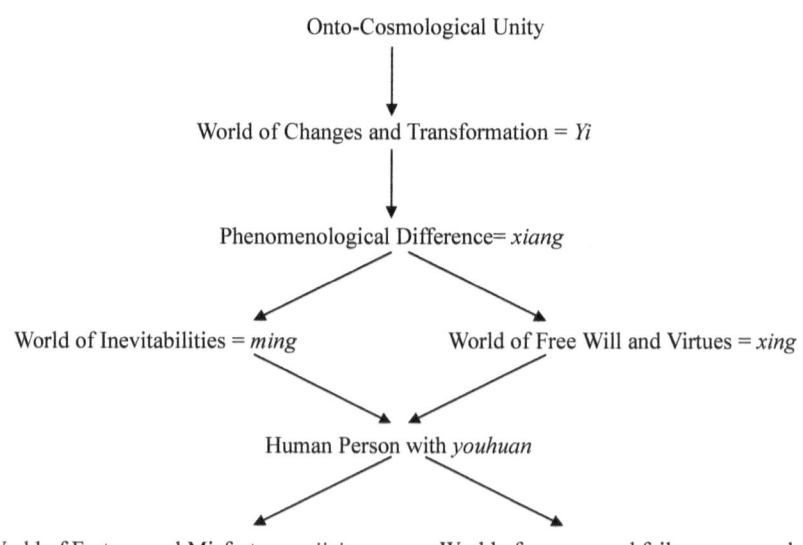

The individual person can develop virtue (and nature) and carefully act only from the self-cultivation of virtue. One can do this if one understands the principle of Yi and perceives the world of Yi as a meaningful whole of life-production and transformation. One would better understand the world of fortune and misfortune and would adjust and act on a higher level than in an earlier period: this is one form of timeliness. One can also act in a situation to preserve order and harmony already obtained or to be obtained: this is another form of timeliness. In both forms of timeliness, the individual person can apply morality to real life so that he or she can always follow the right. This of course presupposes self-knowledge, knowledge of one's situation, and knowledge of the situation of Yi.

Although the Yizhuan may not be Confucius's own writing, the quotations from Confucius, which abound in the Xici, seem to testify that Confucius does play an important role in the forming of the commentaries of the Xici, Tuan, Xiang, and Wenyan, as these commentaries do appear to support each other. The impact of the Confucian view is basically twofold.

First, it creates a new context for a metaphysical and philosophical understanding of the Yi as an experience and as a system. In fact, in the Xici and Wenyan we see that the Yi Text is conceived as a system of metaphysics and as a dialectical methodology for understanding reality. The idea of the ultimate reality and its nature emerges from the experience of change, whereas the latter reinforces correct class for formulation of the metaphysics and the dialectics of the Yi as we have shown.

In the Xici Shang, section 10, it is mentioned that the Yi has many aspects: "The judgments of the Yi manifest the principles of fortune and misfortune; the movements of things manifest the direction for action; the forms manifest ways for inventions and institutions; the divination manifests ways to make decisions or inquiries." Confucius basically eliminated the last aspect from the study of the Yi; in fact, he has developed and elaborated an understanding of the Yi in terms of reason and experience. This can be said to be the rationalization of the Yi, which leads to the formation of the Yi System by which the sage "inquires into profundity and studies subtleties (*ji shen yan ji* 极深研几)" (see section 10).

Second, Confucius transforms the divinatory context of the Yi Text into a moral context in which actions of individuals follow knowledge, wisdom and virtues. This is the context where virtue and knowledge can apply to a world of change and a world of inevitabilities. In this regard, the understanding of the *Yi* leads to perception of what is right to do and what is not right to do; thus, it leads to the understanding and practice of the virtue of *timeliness*. *Timeliness* is the wisdom and the virtue of applying wisdom and virtue to a given situation to generate harmony, goodness, and order. It is also to make oneself morally efficacious, as discussed. With respect to Confucian philosophy of human beings or persons, a person has a free will and is capable of achieving virtue and self-realization of his nature. In this capacity of efficacious agency, one can create one's own well-being and fortune. A person can even advance to identify with the creative source—heaven and the way of *yin* and *yang*, so that he or she can become supremely efficacious and transcend the bounds of *ming*.

All these indicate a moral transformation of the *Yi* Text and give rise to a moral dimension to the understanding of the *Yi*. Our exposition of time and timeliness in the *Analects* and the *Yizhuan* are intended to demonstrate and elucidate this moral transformation of the *Yi*. This in turn shows how important the notion of timeliness is in the practical-moral philosophy of Confucius as synthesized from the *Yizhuan* and the *Analects*. Our discussion also gives many reasons why timeliness becomes a dominant consideration in the *Yizhuan* under Confucian influence.

The twofold impact of the Confucian view on the *Yi* can thus be described as making the metaphysical and the moral transformations of the *Yi* Text (symbolism and judgments) possible. These two transformations are in fact complementary to each other and form a unity as theory and practice; along these lines, metaphysics and morality are to be considered complementary to each other and form a unity. The *Yi* Text assumes a totally new holistic, systematic and unitary meaning, which is best revealed in our analysis and formulation of the metaphysics and dialectics of the *Yi*. The image of the *Yi* as a text has also become transformed. For the *Yi* is not presented merely in a text, or in symbolism or a set of judgments; it is the ultimate reality embodied in all things and underlying all changes, and yet through the changes and things in the world it reveals its creative vitality through its transforming and ordering power. The *Yi* in fact becomes a power to be understood and imitated by the sage. This is how the term "*Yi*" was eventually used in the *Xici*. Thus, the quotation of Confucius runs: "*Yi*, what is it used for? It is used to open all things and achieve all values. It comprehends all principles and reasons. [By way of the *Yi*] the sage can unite the wills of all people and set the great work [of well-being] for all and will resolve all doubts" (section 11). It is not that the mere study of the Yi has this power by itself; rather, it is through the understanding and action of Yi resulting from the study of the Yi, that one obtains the power to make a difference of oneself and then to make a difference in reality and the world.

Now the Confucian impact has transformed the Yi Text, one may also see that this transformation of the Yi also gives a new depth to the Analects so as to make it more coherent and more profoundly significant. Not only do the Confucian virtues receive a metaphysical foundation, they become metaphysically efficacious and practically useful. The concept of *ming* and the implicit notion of nature, and the like, also receive explication in light of the Confucian transformation of the Yi. When Confucius says, "My way is penetrated with unity," (*Analects* 4.15) we know that it is not a unity of moral virtues as such but a larger unity founded on profound experience of Yi and the wisdom of timeliness as a comprehensive and supreme virtue.

To conclude, I cannot deny that my arguments for the historical continuity and conceptual link between Confucius in the *Analects* and the Yi Text are basically holistic, hermeneutical, and conceptually analytical. But they are nevertheless not totally nonempirically grounded. The holistic, hermeneutical, and conceptual approach cannot be avoided if we wish to make good sense of the relationship as well as to resolve difficult issues. Further, if we wish to understand reality and value of the human being as revealed by Confucius in his *Analects*, there does not seem to exist a better approach than to see reality and value of the human being in a holistic, hermeneutical and conceptual context. The cogency of my arguments from historical reference, from rational need, from formation and comparability of the notion of *timeliness*, and from explaining the conceptual unity and complementarities between the *Analects* and the *Yijing* should then be sufficiently self-evident from my lengthy presentation.

Chinese Glossary

Bagua 八卦—eight trigrams
baohe taihe 保合太和—cherish and embrace primal harmony
bao han hai guan, zhu zhang pang dong—comprehension, penetration, and unobstructed understanding from chapter 11
benti 本體—root body
bi 比—pair, match
bian 变—change
biantong 变通—to change and penetrate
bianyi 变易—transformation change
bianhua 变化—transformation
bu 卜—divination
buci 卜辞—divinatory judgment
burenrenzhixin 不忍人之心—heart and mind that cannot bear to withstand the suffering of others
buyi 不易—constancy
buzheng 不正—nonrightness
cha 察—inspection
chang 常—constancy
chen—movement
cheng 成—succeed, inherit
cheng 乘—ride, override
cheng shu 成數—completing numbers
qu shi 趋时—follow time
ci 辞—judgments
da guan 大觀—great overview
dasheng 大生—enhancing life
dang wei 當位—obtaining a proper position

dao 道—way
de 德—virtue
de 得—obtain
de wei 得位—obtaining a proper position
de zhong 得中—obtaining centrality
di gai zhe Yi ge ji—insight into the nature of reality
dingwei 定位—fixed in positions
diwei 地位—positions on earth
dong 動—movement, activity
dongjing 動靜—movement and rest
Tuanci 彖辭—divinatory judgments
dui 兌—joy
er 而—general conjunction: and, and then, then, but, etc.
erhou 而後—and then; afterward
fa xiang 法相—form
fangwei 方位—directed positions
feichangming 非常名—unnamable
feng 風—wind
fuyou 富有—virtues of great abundance of life
gan 感—feeling
gang 剛—firmness
gangrou 剛柔—hard-soft
ganyin 感应—feeling and response
ge yan qi zhi 各言其志—wish and will
gen 艮—resting: stopping, earth
Gua 卦—trigram, hexagram
guan 观—contemplative and comprehensive observation
guanyu—see over
guan hu tian wen Yi za shi bian 观乎天文以察时变—to observe the order of heaven and discern the changes of time
guangsheng 广生—expanding life
gui 归—return
gui 鬼—estrangement
Han 漢—Han Dynasty
Hetu 河图—River Chart
he 和—harmony
he hu—gate-closing
hongdao 弘道—enlarging the way
hua 化—transformation

hui 悔—resentment
huitong 会通—interpenetrations
ji 吉—beneficial, good fortune
ji 机—opportunity
jiji 既济—form of completion
jian 见—seeing: radical component of *guan* 观
jian he wei zhu—arbitrary, prejudiced, narrow
jianyi 簡易—simplicity
jiaren 家人—family
jie 解—resolution
jin de xiu ye, yu zhi shi ye—For advancing virtue and organizing one's deed, it is desirable to do things in time.
jing 经—book (i.e., classic)
jing 靜—rest
jingjie—world infused with a level of projective understanding
jiu 咎—blame
jiu dao—nine fields
Kan 坎—falling
ke—themes, as in "nine themes"
keguan 可观—worthy of being seen
keji fuli wei ren—To overcome oneself and restore the practice of proprieties is benevolent love.
kong 空—empty
Kun 坤—receiving
Kun yuan 坤元—receptivity
lei 类—types
li 礼—propriety
li 理—principle
li 厉—danger
li 骊—travel in pairs
Li 离—brightening
Liji 禮記—*Book of Rites*
liang yi 兩儀—two norms
liangzhi 良知—innate knowledge of good
liu wei shi cheng 六位時成—The six positions are accomplished in time.
lin 吝—difficulty
liu xing—process of circulation
lu—measures, as in "six measures"

Luoshu 洛書—*Luo Script*
ming 命—mandate, unchanging way
ming 明—clarity, luminosity
ming 名—name
nai ruo qi qing 乃若其情—to think of others in terms of others' feelings
pi 辟—opening
pi hu—gate-opening
qi 气—vital force, energy, dynamic and actualizing force bringing things and events into concretion
Qian 乾—creating, firmness, power of strength
Qian yuan 乾元—origin of creativity
qinqinzhisha, zunxianzhideng 亲亲 之杀, 尊贤之等—the grading of love according to kinship and the ranking of respect according to virtue
qing 清—purity
qiong 窮—deadlock difficulty
qiong 穷—exhaust
qizhi 气质—vital faculties
qizhi zhi xing 气质之性—irrational nature
ren 仁—benevolence
rixin 日新—ever-refreshing vitality
ren 人—person
rou 柔—softness
rou yi shi sheng 柔以时升—The soft arises because of *time*.
shen 身—self, lived-body, I
sheng 声—sounds
shengren 聖人—sage
shengren ze zhi 圣人择之—patterns them as a principle
sheng 生—birth, life, growing, creativity
sheng sheng 生生—creative creativity
shengsheng zhi wei Yi 生生之谓易—two moments of a process of creative productivity
sheng shu 生數—generating number
sheng wu feng, Yi wu ti—Subtleties of change have no limit and the change, or creativity, has no substance.
shi—representation
shi 蓍—milfoil stalks
shiwei 失位—losing positions
shi 時—time
shizhong 時中—timeliness

Chinese Glossary

shi she ye 时舍也—The time, forsake it.
shi yu wan wu 时育万物—The time nourishes all things.
shi zhi ze zhi shi xing ze xing 时止则止, 时行则行.—Stop when time requires stop; advance when time requires advance.
shu 書—writing
shu 恕—like-mindedness
shun 順—movement
shuzi gua—numerical hexagrams
chun cui jing 纯粹精—pure and quintessential essence
Shuo Gua 說卦—*Shuo Commentary*
sixiang 四象—four images
suoguan 所觀—that which is viewed
taihe 太和—great harmony
taiji 太極—the great ultimate
Taixu 太虛—great void
taiyi 太易—ultimate simplicity
ti 体—body
tian 天—heaven
tiandi 天地—heaven and earth; hence, the world
tiandi zhi shu 天地之數—heaven-earth number
tianli zhi ziran 天理之自然—natural movement of the heavenly principle
tianming 天命—mandate of heaven
tianxia sui shi 天下隨時—The world follows time at any time.
tianzhi 天志—will of heaven
Tuanzhuan 彖傳—two parts
dui—enjoying
tong 同—identity, sameness
tong 通—a penetrating understanding or comprehension
wanlai wusheng—the ten thousand sounds are quiet
wei 位—positioning
wei bian suo shi—changing at what is suitable
weiji—state of incompletion
wu 无—nonbeing, nothingness, nothing, there is no, not having
wu 物—instruments
Wuji 无極—ultimateless
wuwei 无爲—nonactivity
wuwei 无位—no positions
wuxing 五行—five phases, five elements, five processes

wuyi—positions and relations
xue 学—learning
xian—presentation
xian zhi shi yong da yi cai—how great is the function (use of time in danger)
xiang—as in *qian*, *xiang*
xiang 象—image, form
xiao ren 小人—small person, small man
Xiangshu 象數—image-number
Xiangzhuan 象傳—Xiang Commentary
Xici—*xia/shang*, 系辞—下/上—*appended judgments*
xin 心—heart-mind
xing 形—physical form
xing 性—nature
xing 行—act, do, travel, navigate
xing er shang 形而上—above physical form
xing er xia 形而下—below physical form
xiong 兇—harmful, ill fortune
xiusheng 修生—self cultivation
Xu Gua 序卦—Xu Commentary
xun 巽—entering
yan 言—language
yang 陽—light, opposite of *yin*
yaoci—divinatory judgment
youhuan—profound feeling of anxiety
Yi 易—change, *Yijing*
Yi 異—difference
Yi 义—righteousness, norm
Yi liang zhi yi yin er wei er—divide the one *yin* which is square into two
Yi yi wei er 以一為二—take one to be two
Yi zhi shi da yicai—how great is the *time* in Yi
Yijing 易经—Book of Changes
Yijing—world infused with an element of projected understanding
Yili 义理—*meaning-principle*
yili zhi xing 義理之性—rational nature
yin 陰—darkness, opposite of *yang* notes
yin—notes, as in "seven notes"
yin chi shi er ti—become cautioned because of time

ying—respond, answer to
yiwei qianzuodu
Yizhuan 易传—commentaries on the *Yi*, *Ten Wings*
yu shi jie xing—to advance with time
yu shi jie chi—to reach the ultimate with time
youhuan 憂患—profound anxiety
yunzhijue zhong 允執厥中—hold steadfast to the middle
yong 用—function, use, application
Za Gua 雜卦—*Za Commentary*
zhan 占—turtle shell divination
zhen 震—arising
zheng 正—positivity, correctness, rectitude
zhen guan 贞观—authentic overview
zhengming 正名—rectifying names
zhi 智—wisdom
zhi—balanced
zhi li san man er wusuo gen zhu—scattered, dissipated, without roots
Zhongyong 中庸—*Doctrine of the Mean*
Zhouyi 周易—*Yijing: Zhou Classic of Change*
zhuan shi tian li zhi ran ai pei zhu lei—naturally arranged according to heavenly principle
zhucong—initiating and following
zhu zheng ge shi yi ge di mian—Each level shows a phase and a world of its own.
zhuan 传—commentary
zong 综—converse

English Key Terms

being (*you* 有)
Book of Changes (*Yijing* 易经)
change (*Yi* 易)
complimentarity (*hubuxing* 互補性)
Confucianism (*rujia* 儒家)
constancy (*chang* 常)
Daoism (*daojiao* 道教)
dialectic (*bianzhengfa* 辩证法)
Great Appendix (*Xici* 系辞 *Shang*/ *Xia* 上/下)
great Ultimate (great ultimate 太极)
harmony (*he* 和)
heart-mind (*xin* 心)
heaven (*tian* 天)
hexagram (*zhonggua* 重卦)
horizontal transformation (*hengxiang* 橫向)
image (*xiang* 像)
image-number (*Xiangshu* 象數)
judgment (*ci* 辞)
logos
mandate of heaven (*tianming* 天命)
Mawangdui Silk Manuscripts (*mawangdui boshu* 馬王堆帛書)
meaning-principle (*Yili* 義理)
Neo-Confucianism (*lixue* 理學)
no-change (*buyi* 不易)
non-being (*wu* 無)
observation (comprehensive, contemplative observation) (*guan* 觀)

onto-cosmology (cosmology) (*benti yuzhoulun* 本体宇宙论)
onto-hermeneutics (hermeneutics) *benti quanshi xue* 本体诠释学 (*quanshi xue* 诠释学)
ontology (*bentilun* 本体论)
pattern, principle (*li* 理)
positioning (*wei* 位)
primacy (primary unity) (*yuan* 元) (*yuanyi* 元一)
sage (*shengren* 圣人)
superior person (*junzi* 君子)
symbolization (*xiangzheng* 象徵)
Ten Wings (*shiyi* 十翼)
time (timeliness, and timelessness) (*shi* 時, *shizhong* 時中)
transformation (*hua* 化, *bian* 变)
trigram, hexagram (*gua* 卦)
ultimateless (*wuji* 无极)
vertical transformation (*zongxiang* 縱向)
virtue (*de* 德)
way (*dao* 道)

Notes

Foreword

1. Chung-ying Cheng, *New Dimensions of Confucian and Neo-Confucian Philosophy* (Albany: State University of New York Press, 1991).

Preface

1. I do not use the title "Philosophy of the *Yijing*," which is different from "Philosophy of the *Yi*" in that the former refers to the classic text of change, whereas the latter among other things has a special focus on thinking and observation that gives rise to the formation of the classic text (*jing* 经). It is to philosophically identify an epistemological and onto-cosmological base and source that would characterize the indefinable *Dao* (道, the way) and define the creative humanity (*ren* 仁) in the context of heaven and earth.

2. I have made a distinction between the *dao* of the *Yi* (易之道) and the *Yi* of the *dao* (道之易). Before we come to know the *dao*, we must know the *Yi* (change), hence the *dao* that is primary is the *dao* of the *Yi*, which is revealed in the change; then we can speak of the *Dao*, as Laozi does in the *Daodejing* (道德经).

3. Confer Zhuangzi's *"Tianxia"* chapter and Sima Qian's statement on the essential points of Six Schools in the Classical Period in his *Shiji*.

4. By Chinese philosophy I mean philosophical issues and concepts derived primarily from Chinese thinkers and philosophers from the history of China, whereas by general philosophy I refer to common philosophical issues and concepts without specific reference to Chinese philosophy. I do not take it to be simply Western philosophy, either, for it is based on some consensus on philosophical issues of reality, human existence, and morality such as the problem of good and evil of human action and the problem of true or false knowledge.

5. See the Chan Master Ouyizhixu's 藕益智旭 (1559–1655) work *Zhouyi Chanjie* 周易禅解 in which he interprets the practical wisdom of *Zhouyi* in terms of and from the point of view of Chan Buddhism.

6. Professor Yang's first book is titled in Chinese 《太极哲学》 (Shanghai: Xuelin Publishing House, 2003). The title "*taiji zhexue*" comes from my work on the *taiji*.

7. This latter book is titled in Chinese 《成中英太极创化论》 (Hangzhou: Zhejiang University Press, 2013). This work now has two editions.

8. The term "*Yili*" as the name of the school is also translated herein as "Meaning-Principle."

9. Part 1 is traditionally referred to as *Shang* (Upper), and Part 2 is referred to as *Xia* (Lower). I have used these conventions of *Shang* and *Xia* throughout this work.

Chapter 1

1. It was called the *Boshi* (Scholar of Broad Learning), from which the Chinese translation of Doctor or PhD derives. The official chair of teaching of the Classic of *Yijing* begins with Han Emperor in the time of Shusun Tong (?–194 BCE). Zichuan Tiansheng 淄川田生 was the first *Yijing* Boshi (易经博士).

2. Even the best historical account of an event cannot be said to be an objective depiction but rather a picture or story to be projected on proper use of imagination. It is clear that our cognition of the past has to be supplemented by imagination and reasonable abduction from the present experience of the world. That is what often makes history a great piece of literature to be read with both understanding and feelings. We see in Sima Qian's biographical account of the life of Confucius or his account of Xiang Yu's loss of war in his last battle with Liu Bei so vividly that we cannot but be moved. The same can be said of Thucydides's account of the *History of the Peloponnesian War* in fifth-century BCE Greece because he witnesses the war and he has to write the history from both his understanding and feeling toward objective facts and events. He is not piling up documents and reports like a modern historian.

3. We should distinguish *bu* 卜 from *shi* 筮 in this tradition: generally, *bu* refers to divination by burning a tortoise backbone or an ox shoulder bone and reading the cracks of the burning. The writing of judgments on the bones are now known as Oracle bone inscriptions (甲骨文); on the other hand, starting with Zhou, divination is performed in using milfoil stalks eventually regulated by a method simulating a process of cosmogenesis in reference to a system of sixty-four hexagrams. The judgments are known as *gua* (卦 form) judgments with *yao* (爻 line) comments. Together they form the resources for formation of the *Book of Changes* (*Yijing* or *Zhouyi*) as attributed to the hands of King Wen of the Zhou.

4. One might question whether nomadic people may have started divination. The answer is that for early people, nomadic or not, their method of divination is

relatively simple as they tend to base their divination on beliefs in deities. They may not have yet developed a naturalistic or rationalistic system for explanation and interpretation. It is only when a people become well-settled that they would accumulate knowledge to a point that they could use their knowledge to identify and predict situations in light of what they have learned. The point is that unless a people has achieved some coherent experience of nature, it is difficult for them to significantly identify features and their significant changes in nature.

5. I have explained what I mean by "comprehensive observation" as a corresponding term to the Chinese concept of *guan* in a later chapter.

6. Recent archeological finds have dated the earliest ancient Chinese settlement to no later than 6000 BCE.

7. I do not intend to trace the rise of distinction between good and bad or evil in a community of people in such brief and speedy language. What is intended is to give a sense and direction how for early Chinese people the use of divination is related to formation of a system of values leading to distinction between good and bad dispositions and powers in a situation or in characters of people. Hence the distinction between good virtues and bad virtues were made where virtues in the sense of *de* 德 merely mean dispositions or powers. Later the word *de* comes to mean only good virtues or virtues which are good, and bad virtues are to mean simply badness or evil, *e* 恶.

8. These statements are made on the basis of an epistemological phenomenology of perception and feeling in which elemental distinctions relating to seeing and feeling such as the *yin-yang* distinction, motion-rest distinction and firm-soft distinction are made. As they have their own logical explanatory power, they are not intended as an historical account or record.

9. I take this to be the simplest explanation based on the natural feel of the human mind, similar to notions set forth by David Hume.

10. Regarding the formation of number signs in the *Yijing*, see chapter 4 of my book *Yixue bentilun* 易学本体论 (*Ontocosmology of Yi Learning*).

11. This is because the third position is a position of striving at a critical point, as it may be suppressed by the fourth position, whereas the fifth position is the power position that is high enough without yet becoming pushed to the limit.

12. Quine has made this important distinction between observation and perception in his book *Word and Object* and later in his book *Pursuit of Truth*. It is on the basis of this distinction that Quine is able to assert observation sentences as the basis for intersubjectivity and objectivity of knowledge based on observation.

13. The *Zuozhuan* is the earliest work of narrative history of China and covers the period of 772 BCE to 468 BCE.

14. I have said that there could be primitive divination since even earlier times after Fuxi, as people may wish to know about the future or about what to do in a future with regard to a special end. It is in the Shang that we come to see the results of divination in *buci* 卜辞 or judgment of divination.

15. I introduced the term "onto-cosmology" to refer to our understanding of a reality that is not only ontologically real but cosmologically lively. In other words, I wish to combine the notion of reality as a structure and the notion of reality as a process into a unity of process-reality or reality-process in order to avoid the abstractness of ontology and the rootlessness of a cosmology. I wish also to stress that the real has its constantly sustaining source that continuously gives rise to a system of things and events in the world. This term should correspond to the Chinese notion of "root-body" (*benti* 本体) or "rooted (grounded) world of whole reality." The term "onto-cosmological" is used to refer to such an understanding of the source-reality and whole-reality, which also is explained in the second section.

16. As we see in both Silk Manuscripts and Bamboo Inscriptions, Confucius in his old age has settled in the state of Lu, and evidently devoted much time to the study and interpretation of the *Yi* Text with his disciples.

17. See my 2004 article, "Dimensions of the Dao and Onto-Ethics in Light of the DDJ," in *Journal of Chinese Philosophy*, vol. 31, no. 2: 143–182.

18. Leibniz received the Fuxi diagram of the sixty-four hexagrams of the *Yijing* from Father Bouvet in 1701.

19. Richard Smith has written a wonderful book on many aspects of applications of *Yijing* in both East and West. See his *Fathoming the Cosmos and Ordering the World* (University of Virginia Press, 2008).

Chapter 2

1. In 1987, I was invited to speak on the origin of *Yijing* at the University of Shandong. I first brought out the thesis on the comprehensive observation and deep experience of nature and reality as the sources for understanding the meaning and principles of change (*Yi*). See my Chinese article "*Lun Yi zhi yuanshi ji qi weilai*" (On the Origin of the *Yi* and its Future) in the anthology *Dayi Jicheng* (Collected Articles on Great *Yi*), edited by Liu Dajun (Beijing: Xinhua Book Company, 1991), pp. 18–30. In 1995, I further developed the Comprehensive Observation thesis in my article "Philosophical Significances of *Guan* (Contemplative Observation): On *Guan* as Onto-Hermeneutical Unity of Methodology and Ontology," in *Guoji Yixue Yanjiu* (International *Yi* Studies), no. 1: 156–203, Beijing, 1995. This latter thesis is revised and reprinted herein.

2. See my article "作为宇宙教育的易经: 语言和哲学" (*On Yijing as Cosmic Education:Language and Philosophy*), in 哲学门 (*Philosophy Gate*), vol. 6, no. 1.

3. It is said in the *Xici* that "[It is by means of *Yi*] the sage comes to understand the desires and wills of people, becomes capable of finding the right direction of action, and is able to resolve the doubts of mind" (*Xici Shang* 11).

There are many relevant passages indicating the nature and *telos* of the *Yi* Text as a book of philosophical wisdom.

4. See my article "Inquiring into the Primary Model: *Yijing* and the Onto-Hermeneutical Tradition in Chinese Philosophy," in *Journal of Chinese Philosophy*, vol. 30, no. 2: 289–312, 2003. The article is revised and reprinted here as chapter 4.

5. It is in the sense that Heidegger and Gadamer have described the "*Sache*" or the subject matter of the text.

6. For the actual process and method of divination, see Richard Lynn's Introduction to *The Classic of Changes: A New Translation of the I Ching: As Interpreted by Wang Bi*. Translated by Richard Lynn. New York, Columbia Press, 1994, pp. 19–22. Originally, the method of divination is given in *Xici Xia* of the *Yizhuan*.

7. As this is a primary form of hermeneutics, a rule of reciprocity or recursion is already incorporated; from this point of view, onto-hermeneutics is a reciprocal and recursive system in which the onto-hermeneutical circle embodies reciprocal interaction.

8. I have described in detail the relation of *yin* and *yang* as an opposite and complementary pair that functions in a process of development, formation, and transformation in some of my earlier essays. It is conceived as vehicle and modus operandi for the creative act of the *taiji*. Cf. my 1989 article "On Harmony as Transformation: Paradigms from the I Ching," in the *Journal of Chinese Philosophy*, vol. 16, no. 2: 125–158; and my 2007 article "*Yijing zhexue zhong de Yi and qi: shicun de benzhi he cunzai de wuge chixu*" ("Change and Vitality in Philosophy of *Yijing*: Truth of Actual Existence and its Five Orders") in the *Zhexuemen Journal*, vol. 7, no. 2: 1–12.

9. In Xu Shen's 许慎 (circa 58–147 CE) *Shuowen jiezi* 说文解字 (*Discourse on Language and Explanation on Words*), the earliest Chinese dictionary of words in beginning of first century CE, it is said that *ben* is the underneath of a tree (*mu* 木). Similarly, the end of a tree is called *mo* 末, also written as 未, which has its own meaning of "not yet happening" or "yet to happen." If we understand the root of a tree in light of the growth of the tree, it is clear that the *ben* is the source of life of the tree and makes the tree the tree. The *ben* gives rise to a body of the tree where the body is the *ti* 体, again an iconic complex as shown in its original form 體. One needs to see also how the source of a water is referred as the *yuan* 源 (origin) or *yuantou* 源头 (origin-head).

10. In original *Shuowen jiezi* of Xu Shen, this word is not listed. But it is identified as an ancient oracle bone word, signifying the ultimate reality above the head of a man and has the similar indexic meaning of *tian* 天 heaven, namely what is above man. To combine *ben* and *yuan* we have *benyuan* 本元, which again suggests ultimate source.

11. In Xu Shen's dictionary, *Shuowen jiezi*, "*sheng* 生" is said to be "advance (*jin* 進)," signifying grass and wood coming out from earth, a combined meaning of earth, *tu* 土, and coming out, *chu* 出. (象艸木生出土上. 下象土. 上象出.) By extension, any life generation and birth of life is indicated by this powerful word, "*sheng* 生." In the *Xici*, the idea of *shengsheng* 生生 is formed to describe the permanent and ceaseless generating of life in the universe. This is referred as *shengsheng buxi* 生生不息 (the ceaseless generationing of life).

12. Cf. the fifth diagram in Zhu Xi's *Zhouyi benyi* ("Source Meanings of Zhouyi") for any standard edition.

13. See *Zhongyong*, section 25, where it is said that by being onto-cosmologically genuine (*cheng* 诚) by virtue of one's nature that one is to combine benevolence and wisdom as the way of unifying the inner and the outer.

14. I use the term *benti*-ontology or *benti*-cosmology in the sense of generative onto-cosmology.

15. In the occult interpretation of the meaning of *Yi* (the change), the anonymous work *Yiwei Qianzuodu* at the turn of first century CE has mentioned the three senses of the *Yi*. It is not clear what these three senses of *Yi* refer to and how they are related. Zheng Xuan suggested in his commentary on these three senses that *Yi* as simplicity means the natures of *Qian* and *Kun* as firmness and softness etc., *Yi* as *bianyi* means the change in terms of *yin* and *yang*, and finally *Yi* as *buyi* means the structure of organization in cosmos and reality in which changes take place. In my opinion, we may also suggest that these three senses apparently indicates three levels of understanding change: language of change as presented in the bamboo text of change that refers to the symbolic system of the *Yi* in the ordered *Yi* symbols and their divinatory judgments; the reality of change (*bianyi* 变易) that gives rise to the representations in the *Yi* Text (*yijian*); finally, the underlying reality that remains unchanged. We may even suggest that this understanding is actualized in Zheng Xuan's commentary on this: Zheng suggests a spontaneous process of creation of being (*you*) from nonbeing (*wu*) in which there is the beginning of heaven and earth. From them comes the four forms, five powers, nine palaces, and twelve times. To bring these changes in terms of eight trigrams and sixty-four hexagrams is what is intended by the concept of *jianyi*. Apparently, we can see two processes here: from the *Yi* Text to changes in actual world and then to a reality beyond reality, the *wu*-source of *you*; from the source of nonchange came the changes of things and from these comes the way of description in the system of symbols. The two interpretations in Zheng Xuan needs not to be in conflict: the virtues of basic changes in nonchanges are given as principles (*li*) that may be conceived to exist before *qi* is stirred.

16. For these two principles and their relations to the first three principles of *Yi*, see my book 《易學本體論》 (*On the Benti of Yixue*) (Beijing: Peking University Press, 2006) (in Chinese).

Chapter 3

1. See *Qiwulun* 齐物论 in Zhuangzi. Zhuangzi has described the state of reality in change even in more vivid language: "This is that, that is this. This is one state of right against wrong. That is another state of right against wrong. Is there really distinction between that and this? Or is there really no such distinction? In truth, that and this cannot find their opposites. This is called the axis of the *dao*." For Zhuangzi, the *dao* is not to identify this or that but only to reach out to all that and this in equality and equanimity.

2. He says, "To separate is to form in success, to form in success is to destruct. All things have no successful formation and no destruction, all things again interpenetrated in oneness." This is how Zhuangzi regards the *dao* as principle of transformation through opposition and mutual strife, a similar point made by Heraclitus.

3. See *Fragments* of Heraclitus as translated in *The Pre-Socratic Philosophers*, second edition by G. S. Kirk, J. E. Raven, and M. Schoenfied (Cambridge, England: Cambridge University Press, 2004), pp. 181–212. In Fr. 12 it is said that "Upon those that step into the same river different and different waters flow . . . They scatter and . . . gather . . . come together and flow away . . . approach and depart" (195). It is apparent that it is from this original statement of Heraclitus that different later versions of the river image of the change are formulated. Dewey is said to have remarked that we cannot step in the same river even once. This implies that our conception of "same river" is ambiguous.

4. Just as *yang* would naturally give rise to *yin* which in its turn gives rise to *yang* in a continuous and sustainable process of production and transformation, so being as individual or collection of individuals would naturally lead to an emptying state of being which would in turn lead to a substantiating state of being. Whitehead regards this process of continuous innovation, which is also described by the *Xici* of the *Yijing* as "the daily innovation is the flourishing of virtue of the change" (*Xici* Shang 5).

5. In this chapter I shall not give any detailed description of how the *Yijing* system of *gua* symbols is constructed in a period between the early period of animal tamers and agriculture settlers (in this regard highly different from the marine voyagers of the Greek world), but I shall note the basic principles of construction on the basis of long time processes of *guan*, 观 which provide opportunities of interrelation, correlation, integration, and revision (on the basis of checking against experience, confirmation and disconfirmation of divinatory forecasts and advices). We may see how the formation of *gua* system in original texts of the *Yi* with both descriptive content and prescriptive reasons tells a long history of development over a long period of time from 2000 BCE to 1200 BCE.

6. *Guan* is not gazing, but viewing, or overviewing or overseeing. It leads to a view in which things are images or resemblances called *xiang* 象. But I use

the term *guan* 观 (comprehensive observation) in order to stress its scope and depth that the term "overview" may not signify.

7. See Richard Wilhelm and Cary F. Baynes's translation of the *Yijing* text known as *The I Ching* (Princeton, NJ: Princeton University Press, 1950, 1967). This translation was done in light of Richard Wilhelm's understanding of these two primary *gua* in a system of *gua* in the Confucian *Yizhuan* as provided by Zhu Xi in the long tradition of *Yijing* studies in Chinese history.

8. See chapter 11 of the *Xici Shang* from the very beginning by quoting from Confucius.

9. In Chinese, the term is "*bentixue* 本体学," which is rendered as "onto-generative learning" or "generative ontology."

10. It may be useful to point out that one great difference between the Heraclitean approach to change and the *Yijing* approach to change is that the former has not developed a symbolic way of presenting change whereas the latter did successfully develop such a symbolic system of both presenting and representing change so that change can be better understood and therefore better utilized for the practical purpose of human action and human transformation. This difference makes a world of difference in one's attitude toward reality of change and certainly is a differentiating factor for distinction between the Chinese and the Western traditions of culture and philosophy. It is interesting to note that in modern times when algebra and calculus are developed and applied in science such as physics, a brand new worldview comes into being, a world of forces and entities in theory which changes our life forms through mediated application and technology, not through direct confrontation as in the worldview of the *Yijing*. This testifies to how our symbolizing ability and its actual development in symbolic systems could change our views of what is and what will become.

11. In this context, the individual may still have misgivings for knowing the future, but he can turn to divination in order to interpret his present situation as a guide for the future, but will not become consumed by anxiety toward the contingency of reality as experienced by Heraclitus in ancient Greece and by Heidegger in modern times.

12. See John Dewey's *Experience and Nature*, 1925. Dewey's view comes very close to the philosophy of *Yijing* in which the "precarious" could be revealed to contain deeper harmony which man could cultivate for his practical ends of developing himself.

13. Insofar as they can. But animals may normally respond to immediate environments and may not have abilities to assess the whole situation unless they have learned what a fuller situation is by experience. In this sense, we speak of instinctive response and learned response. The response based on assessment of the whole understanding is an ideal response which only the human species could approach with the use of reason.

14. See my articles "Inquiring into the Primary Model: *Yijing* and Chinese Ontological Hermeneutics"; "The *Yijing* as Creative Inception of Chinese Philosophy"; "*Yin-Yang* Way of Cosmic Thinking and the Philosophy of the *Yi*" (see chapter 6 of this book); also see my book *Onto-Cosmology of the Yixue* (易学本体论 in Chinese) (Beijing: Peking University Press, 2006).

15. Of course, in most difficult times one still could come to consult divination in order to achieve insights and decisions, as in many historical examples from the time of *Zuozhuan* to the time of Zhu Xi.

16. This is not to say that we can change the world as we wish. Our changing power must depend on our understanding of the world of changes as well as on understanding of our own selves as morally constrained human persons. If we lose control and discipline over our own selves and exploit nature as if it is our own private possession, we are to face reaction which will bring an end of our own being as part of the whole. The world stands in the role of both *yang* and *yin* to us and we need to see that we as human beings stand in corresponding *yin* and *yang* positions to the nature or the world.

17. Thus, one would become a self-ruling person, namely the *junzi* 君子.

18. See *Tuan Commentary* for *Qian* in any received text of the *Yijing*.

19. One must distinguish between two states of disharmony: the disharmony causing destruction without productivity and the disharmony as creative destruction which leads to productivity and positive works.

20. This is true in both Western languages and Chinese. The Chinese concept of good (*shan* 善) can have both moral and nonmoral sense. In the moral sense, good does not equate with one's happiness but with some ultimate well-being that would include well-being of individuals and communities of which individuals are members. Thus, good could allow self-sacrifice for others and community. If there is no life-meaningful end to that which one sacrifices oneself for, there is no good for such sacrifice. Hence, the intrinsic good of good will must induce a sense of ultimate good which is to be caused by the intrinsic good. To say that the good will is intrinsically good is to say that there is a good to be experienced by all as real, which we know by analysis of our notion of good and recognize as *a priori*.

21. In all uses of *yü* (欲) as verb in the *Analects*, the meaning of the term as "will" is connoted. For example, in all expressions of *ren*, *yü* is will: "What one does not will to happen to oneself do not will it to happen to others" (12.2, 15.24); "When one wills oneself to establish one's deed, one wills others to establish their deeds. When one wills oneself to arrive at one's end, then one should also wish others to arrive at their ends" (6.30).

22. Whether Hegel's dialectics has anything to do with Laozi's idea of *dao* and its dialectics of *wu* and *you* is not known, although one may make a closer analogy out of the two.

Chapter 4

1. Ast (1778–1841) was a German philosopher and philologist. For a survey of the rise of modern Western hermeneutics, see Gayle L. Ormiston and Alan D. Schrief, *The Hermeneutic Tradition* (Albany: State University of New York Press, 1990).

2. See Gadamer's article, "Universality of Hermeneutical Problem," written in the 1960s and made available in his 1976 book in German titled *Philosophische Hermeneutik* (Tuebingen: J.C.B. Mohr). This article is translated into English and presented in the book *The Hermeneutic Tradition*, 147–158. Habermas's critique is found in his article "The Hermeneutic Claim to Universality," written in 1971, translated into English and presented in the same Ormiston and Schrief volume, 245–272.

3. The *Yiwei Qianzuodu* is a late Han Dynasty text dealing with the sophisticated meanings of the *Yi*. It offers numerological insights into the major hexagrams of the *Yijing*. Since the authors are unknown, and the texts are considered unorthodox, the texts are said to be *yiwei*, informal, or side commentaries of the *Yi*. In this important passage, called *Qianzuodu* (Penetrating-gauging into *Qian*), the nature of change is defined as combining change and nonchange.

4. It is not clear as to what these three senses of *Yi* actually refer and how they are related. The famous Eastern Han scholar Zheng Xuan 郑玄 (127–200) suggested in his commentary on these three senses that *Yi* as *jianyi* 简易 or simplicity means the natures of *Qian* 乾 and *Kun* 坤 as firmness and softness etc.; *Yi* as *bianyi* 变易 means the change in terms of *yin* and *yang*; and finally *Yi* as *buyi* 不易 means the structure of organization in the cosmos and reality in which changes take place. In my opinion, we may also suggest that these three senses indicate three levels of understanding change: (1) language of change, as presented in the bamboo text of change that refers to the symbolic system of the *Yi* in the ordered *Yi* symbols and their divinatory judgments (*jianyi*); (2) the reality of change (*bianyi*) which gives rise to the representations in the *Yi* Text; and finally (3) the underlying reality which remains unchanged (*buyi*). We may even suggest that this understanding is actualized in Zheng Xuan's commentary. Zheng suggests a spontaneous process of creation of being (*you*) from nonbeing (*wu*) in which there is the beginning of heaven and earth. From these come the four forms, five powers, nine palaces, and twelve times. To bring these changes into terms of eight trigrams and sixty-four hexagrams is what is intended by the concept of *jianyi* (simple change). We can see two processes here: from the *Yi* Text to changes in actual world and then to a reality beyond reality, the *wu* source of *you*. From the source of nonchange comes the changes of things and from the change of things comes the way of description in the system of symbols. The two interpretations in Zheng Xuan need not need be in conflict: the virtues of basic changes in nonchanges are

given as principles of ordering (*li* 理), which may be conceived to exist before *qi* 气 (vital force) is stirred.

    5. A question could be raised whether this onto-hermeneutic is transcendental. My argument certainly implies a transcendental presupposition of an ability to form percepts and concepts of a given range of experiences of things, even if no specific onto-hermeneutical framework with content is historically formed. However, this does not imply that the transcendental structure of understanding is Kantian in the sense that fixed principles and categories are inherent in some transcendental mind of ours. It simply means that our mind can apply its imaginative and judgmental powers to adduce images and ideas or even rules from experiences of our life, so that we can apply them to any new situation. The process is similar to the situation in which we must make a description of a novel experience in our own language; we may struggle for new expressions, and we may not reach adequate descriptions at a given time, but a good observer can always come to some expression to indicate what he has experienced, so that people can come to some understanding. The point is that the minimum ontological presupposition is that my understanding can come with something I can share with others.

    6. Yet in Zhu Xi (1130–1200 CE) we find an example of Chinese hermeneutics in the commentarial tradition, which consists in identifying some believed relevant meanings of texts through multiple intertextual readings of the Confucian Classics. However, Gardner does stress the hermeneutical circle of the effectiveness of the multiple, layered, intertextual reading. See Daniel Gardner's *Zhu Xi's Reading of the Analects: Canon, Commentary, and Classical Tradition* (New York: Columbia University Press, 2003), especially translator's introduction. Apart from that we need also to see how a picture of a reference emerges with such reading that makes a hermeneutical reading an onto-hermeneutical reading. See Schliemacher for hermeneutical circle.

    7. See Tang Yijie's article, "Lun zhuangjian zhongguo jieshixue wenti" in *Collection of Essays in Celebration of the 80th Anniversary of Professor Wang Yuanhua*, Shanghai, 1999, 52–64. In this essay, Tang suggests that one cannot talk of a Chinese hermeneutics until one knows well Western hermeneutics and until one comes to a firm understanding of the nature of the commentarial tradition in the studies of Chinese classics. This is indeed a correct observation. But one need not doubt the legitimacy of a theoretical reconstruction or construction of hermeneutical understanding in the Chinese classics. This hermeneutical understanding would reflect the understanding of the subject matter in the Classics according to ways of understanding that come to define the content and form of thinking in the Classics. That is the reason why any hermeneutical understanding is ultimately onto-hermeneutical understanding because understanding must reflect a reality, and Chinese understanding must reflect a lifeworld of reality open to the Chinese experiences of reality.

8. Another reason for my skeptical criticism regarding the lack of a Chinese hermeneutics is this: there does exist a good deal of poetic criticism (such as we can find in works like *Shi Fu, Wen Fu, Wenxin Diaolong*, etc.) that could be organized as part of a formal theory of language and interpretation.

9. Plato has developed a metaphysics of idea-forms as the standard of reality that has influenced the Western tradition of hermeneutical thinking over the last 2,300 years. Heidegger rejected this approach and focused on the individual as source of metaphysical insights. The insights, however, are then limited to finite persons. The *Book of Yi* (*Yijing*) gives rise to the concept of *benti* (translated as "original substance," "origin-body," or better "rooted world-reality"), in which the world-reality comes from a source of creativity. From this source the individual arises and can fully participate as a co-creative force. I used the term *"Benti-Quanshi Xue"* (Learning of Interpretation from *Benti*) as early as the late 1980s in my lectures at Beijing University. Initial exposition of this learning has been presented in my book *Zhongxi Zhexue de Huitong yu Ronghe* (Integration and Fusion of Eastern and Western Philosophies), published by Knowledge Press, Shanghai in 1991, later reprinted under the title *On Philosophic Spirits of East and West* in 1995. The term "Onto-Hermeneutics," which I also adopted in 1991, stands for my term *"Benti-Quanshi Xue."* I intend to leave the term "onto-" or "ontology" open for possible integration or interrelation of Western being and Chinese "origin-body."

10. Note that there are levels, dimensions, or stages of our understanding of the *Yi* as a world reality of change and transformation of things, as indicated in other discussions.

11. I have advanced the theory of the meaning of the word "Yi 易" in light of overshadowing of sunlight by cloud vapor (*yunqi* 云气) and the emerging out of the sun from the cloud vapors. Hence, Xu Shen speaks of *qi* as *yunqi* in his *Shuowen*. This may have to do with many examples of how the original word "Yi" was written in bones and bronze inscriptions:

The shape makes it easy to see how the word "易" is actually derived from the observable phenomenon of the clouding and unclouding of a bright sun. The *Xici* statement "One *yin* and one *yang* is called the *dao*" could be even explained on this basis.

12. See my article on *Guan* "Philosophical Significances of *Guan* (Contemplative Observation): On *Guan* as Onto-Hermeneutical Unity of Methodology and Ontology," in *International Studies of I Ching Theory*, No. 1, edited by Zhu

Baikun (Bejing: Huaxia Publishing, 1995), 156–203. Now this article is incorporated as chapter 5 of this book.

13. See *Xici Shang* 9. "*Ke yu you shen yi*" is the same as "*Ke yu shen you yi*." It is intended here that if one is fully virtuous, spirits may come to one's help in revealing what reality is presented now.

14. But this does not mean that I subscribe to the theory of the origins of the *Yi* in *Hetu* (*River Chart* 河图) and *Luoshu* (*Luo Script* 洛书). On the contrary, both *Hetu* and *Luoshu* are capable of being interpreted in light of this totalistic image / understanding theory. Confer chapter 11 of this book.

15. I do not intend to give a thorough explanation of these two diagrams. One can notice the opposition of triagrams in the *Pre-Heaven Diagram* (also known as *Fuxi Pre-Heaven Diagram*) in four pairs of trigrams which forms a symmetry in a circle conforming to a logic of binary numbers, whereas there is a hidden process of five-power generation and destruction in the *Post-Heaven Diagram* (also known as *Wen Wang Post-Heaven Diagram*). The former suggests harmony and symmetric balances of natural forces whereas the latter suggests mutual generation and mutual destruction among natural processes of things and events. Each captures an essential aspect of the cosmos and life world and together they reflect a complex system of interpenetration of change and nonchange.

16. In *Analects* 13.22 Confucius says: "南人有言曰:'人而无恒, 不可以作巫医。'善夫。" "不恒其德, 或承之羞。" 子曰: "不占而已矣。" (see 杨伯峻, 论语译注. Beijing: China Book Co, 1980), page 145. In this passage Confucius wishes to convey the meaning that the hexagram of *Heng* brings out the importance of the virtue of *heng* 恒 (constancy) or constant heart (*hengxin* 恒心). Thus, if one does not have constant heart, he could not even be a medical doctor. This is because that one may not be trusted for his devotion to the same principles or ideas of treatment as well as his values to treat his patients. In light of this remark, it is clear that one need not to do divination to see how the virtue of constant heart is important. As a general principle Confucius wishes to make the moral meaning of a *gua* as for him each *gua* brings out a virtue, a virtue for us to observe in dealing with a given situation of life whether the name of the *gua* suggests the name of the virtue (such as the *Qian* and *Kun*) or implicitly suggests a virtue to deal with a *gua* as named in a situation. This further means that what Confucius says is that one needs not do divination for understanding the relevance and importance of a situation such as *hengxin* 恒. But this nevertheless does not imply that we need do divination in general. For it is logically compatible with one doing divination to bring out a relevant virtue which may not be made manifest by simply engaging a situation. On the other hand, one could have enough background knowledge and information so that given a situation one recognizes the situation and knows which virtue is required to deal with the situation. If one can do this, one would dispense with divination for one has a moral perception which functions as well or even

better than divination. This is perhaps the ultimate meaning of not seeking wisdom in divination but by engaging the world and cultivation of one's nature by self-cultivation and self-reflection.

Chapter 5

1. See *Yijing*, *Xici Xia* 1.
2. See my essay on *zheng*, "Zhanbu de guanshi yuzheng zhi wuyi" (Interpretation of Divination and the Five Meanings of Zheng), in *Zhongguo Wenhua* (Hong Kong: Ching Book Co., 1994), 29–38.
3. This is called *"dangming bianwu, zhengyan tuanshi"* in *Xici Xia* 6.
4. To understand onto-hermeneutics, see my book *Shijizhijiaodejueze: zhongxizhexue dehuitong yuronghe* (*Choice at the Cross of the Centuries: Convergence and Integration Between Chinese Philosophy and Western Philosophy*) (Shanghai: Knowledge Publishing Co., 1991).
5. We shall see later that a full, yet concise, description of *guan* would be "comprehensive, contemplative, and creative observation."
6. See Edmund Husserl's book *Cartesian Meditations* (The Hague, 1960).
7. See Martin Heidegger, *Being and Time*, translated by John Macquarrie and Edward Robinson (New York: Harper & Row, 1962) (*Sein und Zeit*, 1927), H.38. Heidegger says that "Philosophy is universal phenomenological ontology, and takes its departure from the hermeneutic of *Dasein*, which, as an analytic of *existence*, has made fast the guiding-line for all philosophical inquiry at the point where it *arises* and to which it *returns*." For a contrast of Heidegger with Husserl, see Hubert Dreyfus and John Haugeland's article "Husserl and Heidegger: Philosophy's Last Stand," in *Heidegger and Modern Philosophy*, edited by Michael Murray (New Haven, CT: Yale University Press, 1978), 222–238.
8. We are not to follow an epistemology of simple location and misplaced concreteness such as represented by the foundationalist theory of sense perception in Descartes, Locke, Hume, and modern-day phenomenalists such as H. H. Price and C. D. Broad. Contemporary philosophers in America such as Roderick Chisholm and others may strive to save this sense perception theory even after critique of Kant and criticism by Whitehead and the logical pragmatist, W. V. Quine. See Chisholm's book *Theory of Knowledge* (New York: Prentice Hall, 1986).
9. For discussion of *jingjie* or *Yijing*, see Wang Guowei, *Renjian Cihua* (*Discourse on Poetic Verses in the Human World*), annotated edition (Beijing: Zhonghua Book Co., 1955).
10. "*Lai*" has the meaning of a sound, and yet there are times all sounds become quiet because we can hear that the sounds are quiet. Cheng Yi has this to say: "In the vast stillness without life-stirring, the ten thousand forms

are already present. Not yet responding is not prior, having responded is not posterior" (quoted in Zhu Xi's *Jinsilu*, chapter 1).

11. See Zhu Xi's *Jinsilu*, *Zhuan* 4. Cheng Hao also speaks of "observing in contemplation (*guan*) the manner and air of the ten thousand things in heaven and earth" (*Jinsilu*, *Zhuan* 1). Mingdao says: "The stirring of life of the ten thousand things is most *keguan* (worthy of being observed). This source of life is where goodness comes from, this is what is called *ren* (sharing and feeling of life)" (see also *Jinsilu*, *Zhuan* 1).

12. D. T. Suzuki offers a good explanation of *jian* in the following, which may contribute to our understanding of *guan*:

> *Chien* [*jian*], composed of an eye alone on two outstretched legs, signifies the pure act of seeing. When it is coupled with *hsing* [*xing*], Nature, essence, or Mind, it is seeing into the ultimate nature of things, and not watching. . . . The seeing is not reflecting on an object as if the seer had nothing to do with it. The seeing, on the contrary brings the seer and the object seen together, not in mere identification but the becoming conscious of itself, or rather its working. The seeing is an active deed, involving the dynamic conception of self-being, that is of the Mind. (Suzuki, "Zen and the Unconscious/The Zen Doctrine of No-mind" in *Zen Buddhism/ Selected Writings of D.T. Suzuki*. William Barrett, ed. [New York: Doubleday, 1996], 160–161)

However, *guan* is still different from Suzuki's understanding of seeing because *guan* is comprehensive seeing with neither subjectivity nor objectivity stressed.

13. For the philosophical nature of Chinese language, see my article "Chinese language and the mode of thinking in traditional Chinese philosophy" in *Zhongguosiwei Bianxiang* (*Proclivities of Chinese Thinking*) (Beijing: Xinhua Publishing, 1991), 190–200.

14. See Heidegger's article "On the Essence of Truth," in Martin Heidegger *Basic Writings*, ed. by David Farrell Krell (New York: Harper & Row, 1977), 113–142. The original essay appeared in the 1930s and links to *Being and Time* (section 44) in chapter 6, H. 212–230.

15. See *Being and Time*, H. 25–26, where Heidegger explains the Greek notion of *legein* and epistemic core *noein* as "that simple awareness of something present-at-hand in its sheer presence-at-hand, which Parmenides had already taken to guide him in his own interpretation of Being—has the Temporal structure of a pure 'making-present' of something." He continues: "Those entities which show themselves in this and for it, and which are understood as entities in the most authentic sense, thus get interpreted with regard to the Present; that is, they are conceived as presence (*ousia*)." I quote this paragraph to illustrate

that the sense in which Heidegger speaks of "presence" or "presencing of the Present" is perhaps the same as the meaning of *guan* in the sense of showing (*shi*) and displaying or presentation (*xian*). This would make *guan* a matter of onto-cosmological happening, which has the structure of being understood by a mind in *guan*, which would then make *guan* an onto-epistemological event.

16. From Aristotle's *Metaphysics*, 993b-9–11, explained in Heidegger's *Being and Time* (section 32) and other places.

17. See *Zhengzhou linji huizaochansi yulu* in *Buzunxu yulu* (Recorded Sayings of Ancient Reverend Masters). The *Siliaojian* is also called *Sizaoyong* (Four Shining-Applications).

18. See *Being and Time*, H.52ff (from chapter 2 on), H.180ff (from chapter 6 on).

19. See Heidegger's *Discourse on Thinking*, translated by John M. Anderson and E. Hans Freund (New York: Harper & Row, 1966) (*Gelassenheit*, 1959).

20. See my 1989 article "On Harmony as Transformation: Paradigms from the *I Ching* (*Yijing*)," in *Journal of Chinese Philosophy*, vol. 16, no. 2: 125–158. This article is revised and reprinted herein as chapter 7.

21. See Shao Yong's *Jirangji* where some of his poems are collected. In stressing "viewing things from the viewpoint of things" (*yiwuguanwu*) is to detach feelings and emotions of the heart/mind from viewing the things so that heart/mind would not affect our viewing of things, and things would not affect our feelings and emotions in the heart/mind. This approaches on one hand Husserl's method of "*epoché*," which results in a study of what Shao Yong calls "theory of the *a priori* (*xiantianxue*)" based on pure intellectual intuitions. On the other hand, he comes to identify the *dao* of *taiji* (*daoweitaiji*) with heart/mind (*xinweitaiji*), which makes his *xiantianxue* a matter of "laws of mind" (*xinfa*). In this regard Shao Yong shares with Husserl the same tendency toward subjective idealism. See also his "*Guanwu Waipian*" in *Huangji Jingshi*.

22. See Heidegger's *Early Greek Thinking*, translated by David Farrell Krell and Frank A. Capuzzi (New York: Harper & Row, 1975). German originals dated back to 1950s.

23. Cf. also Heidegger's *An Introduction to Metaphysics*, translated by Ralph Manheim (New York: Doubleday-Anchor, 1961). Original published in 1953.

24. Cf. my essay "Chinese Metaphysics as Non-Metaphysics, an Inquiry into the Nature of Reality in Chinese Philosophy," in *Understanding Chinese Mind*, Robert Allinson Ed. (Hong Kong: Oxford University Press, 1989), 167–268.

25. Although Cheng Yi and Zhu Xi differ in their interpretations of the details of the *Yi* Texts, they basically agree that *li* represents the ultimate source of everything, including even the *qi*. On the other hand, Zhang Zai has no scruples in identifying *qi* 氣 as the primordial origin of everything. See his writing *Zhengmeng*.

26. See Heidegger's *On Time and Being*, translated by Joan Stambaugh (New York: Harper & Row, 1972). For Alfred Whitehead, see his *Process and Reality*, corrected edition (New York: The Free Press, 1978), 21, 348, where creativity is explained as the category of the ultimate and the principle of novelty as well as the principle of unity that transforms the polarities of World and God into concrescent unity.

27. Whitehead used the term "unity of feeling" to describe a relationship of accord and satisfaction in concrescence of actual occasions or events in the world. See his *Process and Reality*, 220.

28. The notion of *ganying* is derived from the following passage in the *Xici Shang* 10, where it is said, "The state of *Yi* is without thought and without action. It is quiet and nonmoving and thus feels [about the world] and penetrates into the causes and reasons of things in the world." Both Cheng Hao and Cheng Yi spoke of *ganying* and recognized their *onto-cosmological* significance. Yichuan says: "If there is feeling [of reality], there is response [to reality]." Mingdao says: "There is only feeling and response between heaven and earth." See *Jinsilu* 近思录, chapter 1. Yichuan speaks of *ganying* in connection with the *Xian gua* #9-4.

29. Etymologically speaking, both *zhong* and *zheng* are depictions of physical positions that mark out a center of power (for *zhong*) and a posture of natural balance (for *zheng*). Even in their ideographic forms they convey the basic ideas of centrality and rectitude. Specifically, *zheng* suggests iconically and indexically a balanced posture which is able to sustain stress and disturbance. Hence, we see that *Xici Shang* 6 refers to the *dao* of change as being infinite in distance and being "resting and well-positioned" (*jing er zheng* 静而正).

30. See *Zhuzi yu lei*, *Zhuan* 1 and other parts on the term "*taiji*." The basic idea comes from Zhou Dunyi's *Taiji tu shuo*, where everything can be considered to come into being from the nonultimate (*wuji*) because everything is uniquely determined and the nonultimate gives rise to the *taiji*.

31. For more concretely understanding meaning and significance of my making reference to the *yin* and *yang* lines or lines #9–5, for those unfamiliar with the *Yijing*, see my explanation of *Guan gua* later where one sees how *yang* forces and *yin* forces balanced creatively to generate a central point of judgment as to what to expect and what to do.

32. In the *Yijing*, *zheng* 正 is almost always—with the exception of the *Wuwang gua* 无妄卦 judgment—mentioned in the *Tuan* or *Xiang Commentaries* as comments on how a person could overcome his circumstances by maintaining or following rectitude in his own person. See specifically, for example, the *Tuan* for *Meng gua* 蒙, *Lin gua* 临, *Ge gua* 革. A similar point can be made for the notion of *zhong* 中 in the texts of the *Yijing*. It is mostly in *Tuan* and *Xiang* that centrality as being centrally placed is remarked on as an asset of the occupying individual. In the Neo-Confucian writings of the Cheng Brothers and

Zhu Xi, *jing* 敬 (serious-mindedness) is always considered as the beginning of virtuousness. This comes from the *Yijing* text *Wenyan* commentary on the *Kun* 坤 hexagram: "The superior man uses reverence to straighten his inside and uses righteousness to square with the outside." It might be said that all Confucian virtues are proposed for the undertaking of *zheng*.

33. One may note that one finds in the *Great Learning*, or *Daxue* 大学, more discussion of *zheng*, and *zheng* clearly plays a central role in the *Daxue*.

34. See Zhu Xi's comments on this line in his *Zhouyi benyi*. Jesse Fleming suggests that to observe people is to observe where their needs and hopes lie so that a ruler could learn how to take care of them. This is a good suggestion, which need not contradict the intent to examine oneself on the part of the ruler for the purpose of improving his rule.

Chapter 6

1. It is said that during the twelfth Century BCE when Jichang of Zhou was imprisoned by King Zhou 纣 of Shang he was able to systematize the divination records by ordering them in a certain way that reflects and also subtly reveals a cosmic outlook underlying and required by divination.

2. The term "*benti*" (本体) literally means origin-body, which suggests the presentation of the ultimate source and its integrated reality from a process of development as recognized by a deep experience of observation and reflection of the human person. This term has been used in vogue in Chinese philosophy from the time of the *Yi* scholar Xun Shuang (荀爽 128–190) in the East Han Period in the beginning of CE. I have argued for this point of view in my forthcoming book *Yixue benti lun* (易学本体论 Benti-Ontology of the *Yi* Philosophy; Peking University Press).

3. "Living force" is intended to capture the meaning of the Chinese term "*qi*," which has been also translated as vital force or material force in early translations of terms in Chinese philosophy. See Wing-Tsit Chan's *A Source Book in Chinese Philosophy* (Princeton, NJ: University of Princeton Press, 1963). The term "living force" (*vis viva*) has been used by Kant in his early writings on dynamics under the influence of Leibniz, who learned Chinese philosophy from Jesuits of his time. Henceforth, I shall refer to *yin* and *yang* as living or vital forces of the *qi*, which onto-cosmologically is a substance of no substance but a power of creativity informed by its intrinsic order called the principle or orderliness (*li*).

4. See *Xici Shang* 5.

5. *Daodejing* 42.

6. We see here that the concept of the *dao* becomes more definitely articulated as emergence of *yin* and *yang* rather than as something indefinite and unarticulated, as suggested by Laozi.

7. It is not the ultimate of void (*wu*), as the ultimate of void cannot have an ultimate something, which is the emergence of the ultimate (*ji*) as the starting point of becoming and transformation.

8. See my article on *guan*, "On the Philosophical Significance of *Guan* and Onto-Hermeneutical Interpretation of Change (*Yi*)," in my book *Yixue benti lun* (Beijing: Peking University Press, 2006), 77–106. This article is also chapter 5 of this book.

9. See the *Tuan* statement of the twentieth hexagram *Guan* in the *Yijing* Text.

10. See *Xici Shang* 10.

11. See *Xici Shang* 4.

12. It is perhaps because of this principle that Confucius comes to realize a depth of humanity as a matter of caring for all people and all things under heaven. His teaching on *ren* (feeling of care) inspired the Zisi-Mencius School of Heart-Mind, which defines human nature in terms of basic feelings and emotions in response to people and things in the world. See Guodian 郭店 Bamboo Text "性自命出" ("The Nature originates from the Mandate") and the Shanghai Museum Bamboo Text "性情論" (On Human Nature and Human Emotions). In both texts it is claimed that human nature ensues as an endowment of heaven and human emotions derive from human nature. This is precisely the position *Zhongyong* 中庸 articulates.

13. One must stress that the objective of *gua* is not to expound sexual love and intimacy but to reveal the deep affection and love that makes the advance toward physical intimacy possible. Hence, it is said in the *Tuan Commentary* of the *Xian* that "It is in the felt accord between heaven and earth that all things arise and transform. The sage who is capable of moving the hearts of people will make the world peaceful. If we look objectively at what has been felt, one would come to see the genuine state of heaven and earth and the ten thousand of things." Two short remarks could be made: First, that the sage can move the hearts of people is because he feels the hearts of the people and can respond in an effective and deep way to this feeling and thus to the needs and hopes of the people. Second, one needs to have not only feelings toward something but reflection on these feelings and feelings of others in order to see the genuine states of things. This means that it takes both feelings and observations on feelings of oneself and others in order to realize what is true of a situation. One needs to take one's feeling seriously, not lightly. One needs to be guided by an understanding of reality together with one's reflective scrutiny of one's feeling and the resultant deeper feelings.

14. Quoted from Zheng Xuan's *Zhouyi zhu* (郑玄周易注, mentioned in Li Dingzuo's *Zhouyi jishi* 李鼎祚周易集释.

15. See *Xici Shang* 1.

16. See *Xici Shang* 6.

17. In the English translation of Richard Wilhelm's book on the *I Ching* the four words are rendered as "sublime," "success," "furthering," and "perseverance."

See pp. 4–6. My translation of the four words has the advantage of showing the process of nature of change more vividly.

18. See *Zhouyi benyi* 周易本义, in his commentary on the *Shang*-11.

19. Whitehead may have this notion in his *Process and Reality*.

20. It is said in the *Xici Shang* 1 that "Heaven is noble and earth is lowly, and the positions are thus determined."

21. See the first chapter of my book, *Yixue benti lun* (*On the Origin-Body Ontology of the Yi Philosophy*) (Beijing: Peking University Press, 2006), 4–34. In this chapter I proposed a theory of five worlds in overlapping circles that incorporates all the traditional diagrams of *Yi* cosmography but that characterizes the emergent unity of identity and difference of the human world from objective reference to the ultimate source to natural and intentional actions of the human person, including moral action.

22. I have argued for the formation of the *Yi* thinking as the very beginning of Chinese philosophy. The *Yi* Texts of *gua* and *yao* were formed as early as the beginning of the twelfth century BCE, which is the time of the founding of the Zhou Dynasty (twelfth century–256 BCE) by King Wen 文王 and King Wu 武王. Hence, the term *Zhouyi* (*Yi* of Zhou) may be said to start with the editing of the *Yi* judgments from divinations based on a symbolic system of observations of the changes of the heaven and earth. Our received standard texts of *Yi* have been dated to former Han. Contemporary excavations in China have updated our known versions of the *Yi* to the fourth century BCE (in the Zhu Tomb Bamboo Inscriptions Version 1993) and first century BCE (in Mawangdui Silk Manuscripts 马王堆帛书 Version in 1976). Earlier fragments of symbols of *Yi* pertaining to the Yin in the sixteenth to twelfth century BCE have also been found in recent years. Reference to Xia Yi in the twentieth to sixteenth century BCE has been recorded as early as Han, but relics have yet to be found. Archeological cultural remains point to the development of a Sheep Culture (羊文化) as early as the end of the Neolithic Period whereby the culture hero Fuxi as the tamer of sheep is said to have designed the eight trigrams of the *Yi* based on what I have called *comprehensive observation* (*guan*).

23. One may indeed define and identify the *benti* of the world: reality as the *dao* or the *taiji* to indicate the originating power and organic unity of the *dao* or the *taiji* as deeply experienced by the human person.

24. I have argued for this point of view in my book *Yixue benti lun* (*Benti-Ontology of the Yi Philosophy*), as referred to above.

25. This is again an important thesis that I have suggested and defended in my interpretation of the *Yizhuan*. This interpretation has two parts: first, the *Yizhuan* can be regarded as faithfully reflecting later Confucian thought on reality based on his reading and reflection on the *Yi* Text since he came to devote himself to the study of the ancient *Yi* Texts after age of 50. Although the recording and editing of the *Yi* Text could come much later, as these thoughts

from Confucius might occur as late as after the birth of his grandson, Zisi, it is still very close to Confucius's own lifetime. This may not have to exclude Confucius's own cosmologizing the *dao* in interaction with the Daoists such as Laozi. But the *dao* in the *Yizhuan* is more worked out as a structured process of cosmological process of creativity than in *Daodejing*. Second, the Confucian philosophy of Yi in *Yizhuan* is both an intuitive and a logical recognition of the philosophy of cosmogony and cosmic change underlying the symbolic configuration of the becoming of world and time in the *Yi* Text. This can be clearly seen from how the sixty-four hexagrams and eight trigrams are conceived and integrated / interrelated into a system of images and concepts. The system forms a holistic picture or presentation / representation of cosmic reality in constant change patterned with observable patterns, which are open to interpretation for prediction and action.

26. Cf. my 2003 article "Inquiring into the Primary Model: *Yijing* and Onto-Hermeneutical Understanding," in *Journal of Chinese Philosophy*, 30, no. 3: 289–312. Revised and reprinted herein.

27. In speaking of the *yin* and *yang* in the deployment of the *dao* from the *taiji*, one may introduce the idea of *qi* (vital force) as the substance or the forces described as the *yin* and the *yang*. This is because the *yin* and *yang* are to be identified with concrete things in their subtle constitution and minute movement that we may describe as *qi*. *Qi* must be conceived to explain constitution and movement of all material things and hence conceived as moving forces and states of becoming that we may also describe as energies. But we need not confine *qi* to material forces alone—all inner feelings and mindings of a human person can be *qi* too. In this sense *qi* is conceived as cross-level and cross-stage energy—force that enables formation and transformation, constitution and destruction of things. To know the *dao* is to know the *qi* eventually. The *taiji* realizes its change and differentiation and integration by way of becoming the *qi*. Hence *qi* is the constitution and actualization principle of the *taiji* and the *dao*.

28. We may also speak of *zhong* as centralization and *he* as harmonization to emphasize the inner dynamics of the inner state and outer state of a human mind. But this way of talk no doubt can be extended to all things in the world and the whole world itself. It is because a thing must maintain itself by having a center for balance of all forces or vitalities and by trying or having to establish a harmony with external forces of the world. The same holds for the whole world as a whole albeit dynamically changing and open entity. The 中庸 *Zhongyong* speaks of the well-positing (位 *wei*) of the heaven and earth and the well-nourishedness (育 *yu*) of all the ten thousand things in the world.

29. Transcendence is often understood ambiguously. Strictly speaking, transcendence is separable, independent, and external existence relative to that which it transcends, whereas immanence is intrinsic and nonseparable form of existence related to a thing or nature of a thing. But we must also take a dynamic

approach to problems of transcendence and immanence and see both terms sometimes as contrasting each other and at other times intrinsically connected to each other. In the case of God as a wholly other in Christian theology, God is no doubt transcendent to humanity whereas human aspiration for God is immanent. But in the case of *tian* (天 heaven) in Chinese classical philosophy, heaven can exist in the form of the way of heaven that is embodied in all things and in the nature of the human person, and in this sense one may say that Heaven exists in man even though Heaven could be considered a transcendent but nonseparable source for humanity and human creativity. Thus, when we say here that there is no thing beyond this world of *taiji* and the *dao*, there is no transcendence in the contrastive sense. But there is nothing to prevent us from saying that there is still transcendence in a connected sense, namely the heaven or *taiji* as the source of the ultimate reality and the *dao* as the overall process of transformation are not to be identified with each individual thing or person, although they can be said to be within their existence or nature. This also means that one can strive for the *dao* and return to the origin of things in a process of transformation and self-cultivation.

30. Hence, we must speak of the structure of each *gua* in terms of how one line relates to another. For example, one may see in a *gua* how the first line responds to the fourth line, the second line responds to the fifth line and the third line responds to the top line. Then there is the relation of close support of one line over another, again depending on the position of the line.

31. In a sense, *shenming* 神明 becomes internalized as part of my wisdom and innate understanding as a human person.

32. In my counting, there are about over sixty comments touching on either the *gua* or the line of a *gua* in the *Yi* Text. This I would call Confucius's *Yizhuan*, which I distinguish from the Confucian *Yizhuan* and which is the primary source for the Confucian *Yizhuan* commonly known as the *Yizhuan*.

33. See *Boshu zhouyi xiaoshi* 帛书周易校釋, by Deng Qiubai (Changsha: Hunan Publishing, 1987, 1996), 481.

34. Although it was reputed that it is Zixia (子夏) who inherited the Confucian philosophy of the *Yi*, we do not have authentic works of Zixia preserved. We may therefore tread the whole *Yizhuan* as a miscellany of many contributions to the interpretation of the *Yi* Text and also the formulation of the *Yi* onto-cosmology as inspired by Confucius. It is in the texts of the *Yizhuan* that we find mainly what I have referred to as the Confucius commentary on the *Yi* Texts.

35. The *Rulin Zhuan* 儒林传 in *Shiji* records that Zixia received *Yi* understanding from Confucius and then after six generations it was transmitted to Tian He 田何 in Qi in about 300 BCE. Tian He has influenced many scholars (such as Ding Kuan 丁寬, Zhouwang Sun 周王孙, Qi Fusheng 齐服生) of *Yi* at the beginning of the Han about 200 BCE. It takes another 200 years to reach the time of

Meng Xi 孟喜 and then Jing Fang 京房, whereby the *Xiangshu* come to flourish and enjoy a high time of popularity within both the court and the populace.

Chapter 7

1. Even this meaning of musical harmony need not be the oldest one in the Greek etymology of *harmonia*, as noted by G. S. Kirk in his book *Heraclitus, The Cosmic Fragments* (Cambridge: Cambridge University Press, 1954). However, Heraclitus obviously did use the word in the sense of musical harmony.

2. One may point to some rigorously defined concepts of harmony in such phrases as "harmonic mean" in mathematics, "harmonic motion" in physics and "harmonic tones," or "harmonic progression" in music composition.

3. Kirk, G. S., *Heraclitus, The Cosmic Fragments* (Cambridge: Cambridge University Press, 1954), fragment 26.

4. See the fragments of Heraclitus's sayings; fragments 116 and 117 in Philip Wheelwright, *Heraclitus* (New York: Atheneum, 1964), 102.

5. The etymology of the Chinese character *he* represents the union of a mouth with grain, which suggests becomingness and fittingness.

6. *Zuozhuan, Duke Zhao 20th year*. Yan Ying on harmony and identity.

7. *Zuozhuan, Duke Zhao 20th year*. Yan Ying on harmony and identity.

8. There are many qualities that things have but mind does not have. There are other qualities that mind has but things lack. Yet, it must be recognized that harmony is one of the unique qualities which things and mind can both share, and there is an intrinsic relationship of interlinking and inter-causation between the two.

9. *Zuozhuan, Duke Zhao 20th year*. Yan Ying on harmony and identity.

10. See my 1972 essay "On *Yi* as a Universal Principle of Specific Application in Confucian Morality," *Philosophy East and West*, vol. 22, no. 3: 269–280.

11. *Analects* 13.23.

12. *Analects* 1.12.

13. *Analects* 1.12.

14. *Mencius* 2B1.

15. *Mencius* 2B1.

16. *Zhongyong*, Section 1.

17. *Zhongyong*, Section 1.

18. See the Neo-Moist Canons in Sun Yijang, *Mo-tzu xian ku* (Taipei: World Book Co., 1967), edition 0065; 65–66.

19. See the Neo-Moist Canons in Sun Yijang, *Mo-tzu xian ku*, edition 0065; 65–66.

20. For example, in the hexagram *Jian* ䷴ (progress 漸), the *Tuan* says: "The position is such that the firm (line) acquires a centrality" (*de zhong* 得中).

21. See the *Hong Fan* chapter of the *Shang Shu*.
22. *Analects* 11.16.
23. See the *Shang Shu*, *Lüxing* chapter. King Mu of Zhou (Zhoumu Wang) also clearly states in the same document: "One must be in the court with pity, and use the codes of criminal law with caution, for the purpose of attaining fairness [*zhong*] and rectitude [*zheng*]."
24. *Analects* 9.8.
25. *Mencius* 4B20.
26. *Zhongde* is the virtue of the *zhong*, or the "way of the *zhong*," *zhongdao*. The term *zhongde* was used in the *Shang Shu* proclamation on wine, *Jiu Gao* chapter. In the *Analects*, Confucius refers to the *zhong xing* (middle course of action), 13.21; Mencius is the first one to use the term *zhongdao* in reference to the vision and philosophy of Confucius. *Mencius* 7B37, 7A41. Mencius also discusses the nature of "hold steadfast to the *zhong*" by making a distinction between *zhizhong*"("holding steadfast to the *zhong*") and "*hiyi*"("holding steadfast to the oneness") *Mencius* 7A21.
27. The Chinese character for "difference" is also pronounced "*yi*," like the "*yi*" for the character signifying oneness or unity. See glossary.
28. Modern-day physics and biology manifest a new trend in interpreting the physical/biological sciences in terms of a philosophy of a higher reality called the *dao* or the "implicate order," which is holographic or hologram-like in nature. Cf. David Bohm, *Wholeness and the Implicate Order* (London: Routledge & Kegan Paul, Ltd., 1980).
29. Although there are major differences between Huayan, Zhu Xi, and Wang Yangming, the metaphysical principle of "one in all and all in one" is accepted by all three systems beyond a reasonable doubt.
30. *Analects* 4.15.
31. *Mencius* 1A6.
32. *Mencius* 1A6.
33. *Daodejing*, 42.
34. *Daodejing*, 39.
35. *Daodejing*, 81.
36. Perhaps all existent things, no matter how they appear to be irrelevant to one another, are materially related in one way or another from considerations of modern physics and modern ecology. In the light of the organic metaphysics of Whitehead, everything is "materially" related to everything else.
37. In modern physics, various categories of interactions between elementary particles are recognized, such as strong interactions and electromagnetic interactions.
38. Fragment 22 from the Kirk edition.
39. Fragment 26; also see fragment 25.
40. Fragment 27.

41. Bian 变 (change) is distinguished from *hua* (transformation) in the *Xici* of the *Yijing*. It is said there "To transform and order the transformation is called change;" "To transform and order the transformation consists in change" (*Xici Shang* 12). *Bian* is the result of mutual interaction between *yin* and *yang*, firm (*gang* 刚) and soft (*rou* 柔); but the very often subtle, gradual and imperceptible minute changes in things are transformation (*hua* 化). Hence, the concept of "transformation of heaven and earth" (*tiandizhihua* 天地之化) is the nourishing and life-giving process of gradual evolution and development such as in rotation of seasons, in contrast with sudden conspicuous changes of weather and other conditions to be connoted by the term "changes of heaven and earth" (*tiandizhibian* 天地之变).

42. To support this position, one need only mention the works of Whitehead and Bergson in philosophy, those of Heisenberg, Bohr, and David Bohm in physics, those of Pribram in physiology, and those of William James and Gestalt theory in psychology.

43. Hegel has a similar idea. He speaks of "union of union and nonunion" (*Early Theological Writings*, pg. 312), and "the identity of identity and non-identity" (*Jenaer Schriften*, pp. 35–41).

44. The *taiji*, usually translated as the great ultimate, is the primary unity and primary creativity from which all things arise. The *Xici* of the *Yijing* says, "The process of change and transformation (*Yi*) has the great ultimate as its foundation; [the *taiji*] gives rise to two norms; two norms gives rise to four forms; four forms give rise to eight trigrams" (*Xici Shang* 11).

45. Professor Thomé Fang (Fang Tung-mei) first suggested this term, "the creative creativity," for the life-creative power and process of *shengsheng* in the *Yijing*, where it is said that "The *shengsheng* is called the change (*Yi*)" and "The great virtue of heaven and earth is life-creativity (*sheng*)." See the *Xici Shang* of the *Yijing*, section 5. For reference to Thomé Fang, see his book *The Chinese View of Life* (Hong Kong: The Union Press, 1957), ch. 2.

46. The five meanings of *yi* as five unities discussed here in fact implicitly coincide with the five aspects of *yi* (change) in different grades of harmonization.

47. See the *Xici Shang*, section 5, in the *Yijing* for how shade/soft/rest and light/firm/motion are aligned generatively. See also my 1977 essay "Chinese Philosophy and Symbolic Reference" in *Philosophy East and West*, vol. 27, no. 3: 307–322, for an understanding the nature of correlative/coordinative thinking in Chinese philosophy.

48. Professor Thomé Fang refers to this as "creative creativity," which is the essence of change and transformation.

49. My interpretation of the *taiji* as "primary unity" underscores more clearly the fundamental nature of what the *taiji* refers to. But the *taiji* also was referred to as *taiyi* in the Daoist literature. We have seen the *Daodejing* speaking of oneness in a primary sense. In the *Qi wulun* of *Zhuangzi* it is said that "The

dao is penetrated with oneness. Its division is its completion; its completion is its extinction. All things have no division and no completion and are again penetrated with oneness." In the *Liezi*, chapter *Tianrui*, it is said that "There are the "primary change" (*taiyi*), the "primary beginning" (*taichu*) of *qi*; the "primary origin" (*taishi*) of forms; the "primary quality of matter" (*taisu*). But the "primary oneness" should contain and underlie all of these "primaries." The term "*taiyi*" ("primary unity" or "primary oneness") is actually first used in the *Tianxia* Chapter of the *Zhuangzi*: "[The world is] ruled by the 'primary unity' (*zhuzhiyitaiyi*)." The term also is used in the *Lu Lan* and *Gongzi Jia Lu*.

50. A trigram or a hexagram is a symbol for the whole phenomenon in nature or a relationship in the world. This symbol belongs to a system of symbolism in which all symbols are *internally interrelated* and hence are capable of articulating change and transformation between phenomena and between relationships in the world.

51. *Xici Shang* 11.

52. *Tuan Commentary* on the *Qian* hexagram.

53. See the *Tuan Commentary* on the *Kun* hexagram.

54. For until a harmony becomes a unity of opposites it can always be said to comprehend disharmonious elements that are not yet fully integrated into a unity.

55. The *Fuxi Diagram* of eight trigrams is as follows:

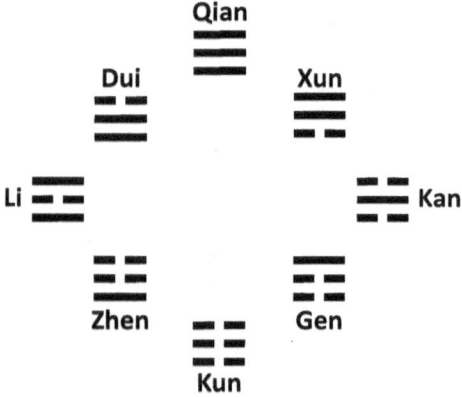

This diagram shows how the unities of opposites on different levels organize into a unity of totality of unities. From the three-branch presentation of creative division of the *taiji*, one can see the following groupings into the opposites: (*Qian, Kun*); (*Xun, Zhen*); (*Li, Kan*); (*Gen, Dui*).

56. *Xici Shang* 1.

57. The line-up of high/firm/movement and the qualities such as light and masculine on the one hand and the line-up of low/soft/rest and other qualities

such as dark and feminine on the other also suggests a phenomenological experience deeply rooted in the ontology of things and human existence. This is fundamentally how the distinction between *yin* and *yang* is made and understood in both the *Yijing* text and the *Daodejing* of Laozi.

58. The goodness or good fortune (*ji*) or badness or ill-fortune (*xiong*) of a line is very much a function of its placement, with regard to the propriety, centrality, or responsive correspondence of its positioning in its contexts and other structural relationships and hence is to be correspondingly interpreted. The goodness or badness is never seen as a subjective projection of one's mind, contrary to many misconceived interpretations. It is emphasized in the *Xici* that the *ji/xiong* in a state of affairs derived from differentiation, movements, and relationships of things. See the *Xici Shang* 1, 3, 8, 11, and *Xici Xia* 1, 9, 12.

59. For disharmonious opposition in the placement, one can cite the hexagrams of *Song* (conflict) and *Bi* (indifference) for illustration; for harmonious complementation in the placement, one can cite the hexagrams *Zhongfu* ䷼ (truth) and *Xian* ䷞ (union) for illustration. For mediating interaction in placement, one can cite the hexagrams *Sheng* ䷭ (decrease) and *Yi* ䷩ (increase) for illustration.

60. See my 1997 article, "Toward Constructing a Dialectics of Harmonization: Harmony and Conflict in Chinese Philosophy," *Journal of Chinese Philosophy*, vol. 4, no. 3: 209–245.

61. Both statements are found in section 12 of the *Xici Shang*. I translate the verb "*cai*" (order, control, restrain) in the Chinese as "order" to express the order introduced in the transformation of things.

62. The former is found in section 11 and the latter in section 12 of the *Xici Shang*.

63. *Xici Xia* 8.

64. Cf. *Xici Xia* 2.

65. The *Kun gua* (difficulty) may be said to symbolize this deadlock situation, whereas the *Song gua* (litigation) symbolizes conflict and the *Shihe gua* (biting) symbolizes strife. On the other end, the *Qian gua* (resolution) could symbolize penetration (*tong*) and duration (*jiu*), whereas the *Ge gua* (revolution) symbolizes change (*bian*) through a deadlock (*jiong*), and *Jiji gua* (already completed) symbolizes a state of completion in transformation and thus the beginning of a new creative change. It is also clear that all other *gua* could be interpreted as different modes in different situations of conflict, strife and deadlock or as different modes in different situations of change, penetration, and duration.

66. Here, *yi*, as in other relevant contexts in the *Yijing*, comprehends the meanings of both change and transformation as well as meaning of change (*bianyi*), preserving "the constant" (*buyi*) in "the simplest" (*jianyi*) manner.

67. *Xici Shang* 1, 7.

68. The interaction of opposites can be called *jiaoyi* (transaction).

69. The interaction of opposites can be called *jiaoyi* (transaction).

70. As in our discussion of the primariness of unity of opposites in the primary unity of the *taiji*.

71. This can be seen as an exemplification of the unity of truth and method in spite of Hans-Georg Gadamer to the contrary. See the introduction and part 3 of his book *Truth and Method* (New York: Continuum, 1975).

72. One may also point out that the *metaphysics of harmony* and the *dialectics of harmonization* are more than implicitly present. They are indeed well disclosed in the formulation of the judgments (*tuan*) and images (*xiang*) pertaining to each *gua*, and become fully articulated in the *Xici* and *Shuogua* commentaries. Our efforts are to analyze and systemize this system of philosophy and method of thinking in an intelligible language of reason and understanding.

73. *Zhongyong*, paragraph 3.

74. See the last chapter of the book *On Timeliness* (shizhong) *in the Analects and the* Yijing: *An Inquiry into the Philosophical Relationship between Confucius and the* Yijing.

75. For a detailed analysis of time and temporality, see my article "Confucius, Heidegger and the Philosophy of the *I Ching*," presented at the International Conference for Asian and Comparative Philosophy, August 13–17, 1984, Honolulu; forthcoming in a book edited by Graham Parkes, to be published by the University Press of Hawaii.

76. *Xici Xia* 1.

77. *Xici Xia* 8.

78. For illustrations of these formulations and their functions in forging unity and harmony between man and his world, see my essay on timeliness. *op. cit.* One also can see how the following *gua* clearly provide such illustrations: Qian, Ding, Ge, Yi, Li, Kun, Bo, Gan, Jian, Gu. These *gua* also illustrate the principle of right positioning (*zhengwei*) and centralization (*dezhong*).

79. In the *Zhongyong*, the concepts and doctrines of trinity (*san*) and creativity (*sheng*) of heaven, earth, and man have been developed. These doctrines are clearly consistent with and at the same time also enrich the *dialectics of harmonization* discussed on the basis of paradigms from the *Yijing*.

80. See my 1997 article, "Toward Constructing a Dialectics of Harmonization: Harmony and Conflict in Chinese Philosophy," *Journal of Chinese Philosophy*, vol. 4, no. 3: 209–245.

Chapter 8

1. I introduced the term "onto-cosmology" to refer to our understanding of a reality that is not only ontologically real but also cosmologically lively. In other words, I wish to combine the notion of reality as a structure and the notion of reality as a process into a unity of process-reality or reality-process

in order to avoid the abstractness of ontology and the rootlessness of a cosmology. I wish also to stress that the real has its constantly sustaining source that continuously gives rise to a system of things and events in the world. This term should correspond to the Chinese notion of "root-body" (*benti*) or "rooted (grounded) world of whole reality." The term "onto-cosmological" is also used to refer to an understanding of source-reality and whole-reality.

2. Namely, the reality in process or the process of reality as reality is conceived as a process of change and a process of change is conceived as reality, to borrow paradigms from Alfred Whitehead. See *Process and Reality: An Essay in Cosmology; Gifford Lectures Delivered in the University of Edinburgh During the Session 1927–28* (New York: The Free Press, 1978).

3. We can also speak of *fangwei* (directed positions) with regard to positions that are identified by the directions in a system of local places with directions and other features determined by a locale.

4. Although a few scholars have argued for the Daoist influence of the *Laozi* on the *Yizhuan*, it is likely that both Confucianism and Daoism shared a common onto-cosmological worldview (or world vision) that is derived from the same time-worn tradition of the *Yi* view of the world as presupposed in the use of divination. For this, see my article "Onto-hermeneutics of the *Guan*: Comprehensive/Contemplative Observation Presupposed in the *Zhouyi* Tradition," in the *International Journal for Yijing Studies*, vol. 1, no. 1: 79–110 (reprinted herein as chapter 5). Although Confucianism and Daoism shared the same philosophical origin in such an onto-cosmological worldview, this does not imply that their ethical and political attitudes must be the same. On the contrary, many factors could influence the ways in which the Confucian and the Daoist interpreted the same onto-cosmology differently and thus gave rise to their different specific approaches to life and government. Besides, it could be the internal "ontological" difference in the *Yi* Text that leads to the difference between the Confucian and the Daoist ethics and politics.

5. In Zhuangzi's *Tiandi* chapter it is said, "When virtue [*de*] is accomplished it is called establishment [*li*]."

6. "To form things is called the *Qian*; to follow through is called the *Kun*" (*Shang* 5).

7. That *qi* did not appear in *Zhouyi* but did appear in the *Laozi* suggests that the *Laozi*'s view is developed later than the *Yizhuan*, for any reification must come after observation without ontological commitment. See Quine's book *From Stimulus to Science* (Cambridge, MA: Harvard University Press, 1995), chapters 2 and 3.

8. This map must be more like a meteorological chart that changes as the world weather changes.

9. Zhou Dunyi has taken the *taiji* as the source of all changes and transformations that are to take place in the process of generating *yin* and *yang* polarities from a simple level to a complex level.

10. Mencius says, "What is desirable is called the good [*shan*]" (*Mencius* 7B25). In fact, the term *shan* is etymologically derived from the desired tasty mutton, which also gave rise to many cognate words of value, such as "beauty" (*mei*) and "righteousness" (*yi*).

11. The *Zhongyong* (section 22) says: "It is the utmost sincere [person] who can fulfill his own nature. Once capable of fulfilling his own nature, he is capable of fulfilling the natures of others. Once capable of fulfilling the natures of others, he is capable of fulfilling the natures of things. Once capable of fulfilling the natures of things, he is then capable of participating in and supporting the formation and transformation of things. Once capable of participating in and supporting the formation and transformation of all things, he is capable of forming a trinity with heaven and earth." Also see my essay, "Trinity of Cosmology, Ecology and Ethics in Confucian Personhood."

12. Quoted from Zhuxi, *Zhouyi benyi*, commentary on *Xici Shang*.

13. Noticeably, the hierarchical ordering of forms is the reverse of the Shao Yong presentation of what is known as "*Fuxi Bagua Circle*," where the *taiji* is placed underneath to represent the foundation of all beings, whereas the eight forms would represent the surface manifestations of the differentiation of levels and forms. Logically speaking, there is no difference between my ordering and Shao Yong's. Onto-cosmologically, I stress heaven's function of bestowing its vitality downwards whereas Shao Yong stresses the earth's function of growing life forms upwards. It could also mean that the way Shao Yong presents suggests an immanence in contrast with the way of transcendence suggested by my diagram. But again there is no real logical difference because there is not any breach between the source and the world developed from the source. The immanence has an upward movement and the transcendence has a downward movement. Thus, we could speak of the transcendence of immanence and the immanence of transcendence to enrich the meaning of both immanence and transcendence. In fact, the interlinking of the two forms of presentation, mine and Shao Yong's, for the purpose of stressing the need for parallel movements in two directions, the upward and the downward, would amply justify such an enrichment of meaning.

14. See the chapter "On Mutual Transformability Between the *Hetu* and the *Luoshu* in the Philosophy of the *Yijing*." I have shown how the *Luo Script* could be understood as a disguised diagram of the five powers (*wuxing*) in mutual generative order and how the *Luo Script* can be mapped onto *Hetu* by way of changing the order of mutual generation of five powers into the order of the mutual destruction of five powers.

15. *Laozi* clearly stressed the *fan* and *fu* processes of creative change, which need to be distinguished as mentioned, as pertaining to both vertical and horizontal changes on the last diagram.

16. This indicates, no doubt, that positions on a given level could be mutually transformed into each other through certain basic forms of transformation, which could be dynamically or topologically understood. To make these transformations possible would require an understanding of the nature of things in reality and their natural causal or long-term evolutionary linkages. But in the human world of actions it is clear that positions could be effectively transformed through strategic management, maneuvering or simply a matter of recognition such as in the Gestalt perception of a picture as an image of a rabbit or as an image of a duck.

17. In the *Xiang Commentary* on *gua* there are two references to *wei*, one in *Ding* and one in *Gen*.

18. We may in fact consider the *yao* position as analogous to an atomic proposition and the *gua* as analogous to a molecular proposition formed out of the atomic propositions of *yao* by way of developmental entailment á la Wittgenstein in his work *Tractatus Logico-Philosophicus* (1921).

19. The present ordering of the *gua* is one of many possible orders and perhaps is one which describes best both the natural and political changes of a human community life as suggested in the *Xu Commentary* and the *Za Commentary*. I shall not enter into discussion of this, as it forms another important topic.

20. There is a widespread confusion among scholars or students of *Yijing* from ancient times up to the present, namely, the *Yijing* as a manual of divination or a Zhou method of divination is conflated with the *Yijing* as a symbolic system of *gua* that has slowly evolved from the earliest period when divination was practiced. Although there could be a philosophy of the method of divination, the philosophy of the contemplated picture of the world and its changes in the symbolism are developed independently of the method and are not to be identified with the method of divination.

21. Given the understanding of the *bianyao*, we can see that a *Qian* could have all its *yao* lines changed into their opposites and therefore we have a resulting *gua* called the *Kun*. In such a case the *Zhouyi* has a special name and judgement reserved, namely the situation called "*yongjiu*" (nine being used). The description of this new situation is that "See group of dragons having no leader. Fortune." Why fortune? Because there is no pressure for leadership and there is no competition for power: there would be complete relaxation, freedom and tolerance. The *gua* position is that of the *Kun*, a position for softness and comprehensive love and patience like the great earth. Perhaps, because of the nature of this change, there is no special prescription for action. This perhaps suggests that no action is better than any action, a Daoist insight. In the case of the whole changeover from all the *yinyao* to all the *yangyao* in the *yongjiu* in the *Kun gua*, there is the admonition that it is advantageous for a person to remain firm and constant.

22. Some recent Chinese research has focused on the Daoist influence on the formation of the *Yizhuan*, but no arguments have shown any substantial evidence of such influence. There is the problem of what essential criterion (or criteria) to use. The essential criterion of *wei* clearly makes *Yizhuan* a work of the second-generation Confucians, not a work of Daoists. For disputing the Confucian nature of the *Yizhuan*, see Chen Guying's article, *Lun Xicizhuan shi jixiadaojiazhizhuo—Wulun Yizhuan fei Rujia Dianji*" (On *Xici Commentary* as Work from *Jixia* Daoists: Fifth Discussion on *Yizhuan* as Not a Confucian Classic), in *Daojia Wenhua Yanjiu*, II, edited by Chen Guying, Shanghai, 1992, 355–365.

Chapter 9

1. This has been the view of many commentators on the *Yijing*, including the noted commentary on the *Yijing* by Zhu Xi and the recent work *Zhouyi gu jing chu* by Gao Heng. Many Western translators also subscribe to this view.

2. There is no account of the logic and philosophy of divination; it is simply regarded as a primitive irrational form of mystic or superstitious belief.

3. To project one's values into the objective world and to recognize a life situation as objectively meaningful is subject-objectification; to infer meaning and assimilate values from a given situation so that one might act on it is object-subjectification.

4. For an explanation of basic dialectics of the *Yijing*, see also my 1977 article "Toward a Dialectics of Harmonization and Conflict in Chinese Philosophy," *Journal of Chinese Philosophy*, vol. 4, no. 3: 209–245.

5. For discussion of another criticism of the *li-qi* scheme in Neo-Confucian philosophy, see my 1975 essay, "Reason, Substance and Desires in 17th Century Neo-Confucianism" in *The Unfolding of Neo-Confucianism*, edited by William deBary (New York: Columbia University Press, 1975), 469–509.

6. See *Jinsilu*.

7. "*Li*" for principle/reason and "*li*" for "propriety/ritual" are homonyms, but they are two different Chinese characters. In both *Liji* and *Xunzi*, *li* for propriety/ritual is often explained and justified in terms of *li* for principle and reason.

8. See Zhou Dunyi's *Tongshu*.

9. See *Jinsilu*, chapter 1.

10. See *Jinsilu*, chapter 1.

11. See *Jinsilu*, chapter 1.

12. See *Jinsilu*, chapter 1.

13. See *Jinsilu*, chapter 1.

14. See *Jinsilu*, chapter 1.

15. See *Jinsilu*, chapter 1.

16. See Zhang Zai's *Zheng Meng*, *Taihe* chapter.

17. See Zhang Zai's *Zheng Meng*, *Taihe* chapter.
18. See Zhu Xi's *Zhouyi benyi*, Preface.
19. These quotations are all from *Zhuzi quan shu*.
20. Quotations from *Zhuzi quan shu*.
21. For Zhu Xi's defense of Zhou Dunyi, see *Taiji tu shuo jie*.
22. See Zhu Xi's *Daxue Huo Wen*.
23. See Zhu Xi's *Wenji*, 46.
24. See Zhu Xi's *Yulei*, 1.
25. See Zhu Xi's *Yulei*, 1.
26. See Zhu Xi's *Yulei*, 1.
27. Op. cit. p. 103.
28. See Wan Menglong *Zhuzi Bian Bu*. Zhu Xi's philosophical thought came to maturity around the time he was forty years of age.
29. See Zheng Kangcheng's work *Zhouyi jizhu* where he says that the meaning of *Yi* is threefold: namely, creativity, constancy, and simplicity. Actually, this suggestion was first mentioned in one of the unauthored texts on *Yi* (*Yiweiqianzuodu*) prevailing in the later part of Late Han period.
30. See Zhou Dunyi's *Taiji tu shuo*.
31. The translation is mine based on a consultation of translations by Richard Wilhelm and James Legge.
32. This translation follows that of James Legge, *The Book of Change*.
33. This translation follows that of James Legge, op. cit., 304.
34. All translations are mine after consulting translations by Richard Wilhelm and James Legge.
35. This translation follows James Legge.
36. See Zhu Xi's *Zhouyi benyi* 周易本义.
37. This alternation of *yin* and *yang* leads to a form of dialectics of affirmation and negation which could be seen as giving support or inspiration to modern dialectics beginning with Hegel. Hegel has a discussion of the dialectic of force in his *Phenomenology of Spirit*, which may come from the philosophy of Kant and Leibniz, which in turn are influenced by the *yin-yang* idea of the *Yijing*. For Hegel, see the chapter "Force and Understanding" in *Phenomenology of Spirit*, translated by A. V. Miller (Oxford University Press: 1977), 79–103. For Leibniz, see his "Monadology" and his final monograph on natural theology in Zhu Xi in *Writings on China*, translated by Daniel J. Cook and Henry Rosemont, Jr. (Chicago and Lasalle, IL: Open Court, 1994). For Kant, see his early work on the dynamics of force and his last work: *Opus Postumuum/The Cambridge Edition of the Works of Immanuel Kant*, edited by Eckart Forster and Michael Rosen, translated by Eckart Forster (Cambridge University Press, 1993), 23–61.

For Hegel, force is a kind of dynamic, unifying interchange between two seemingly antithetical factors. In the case of force, one finds that it actualizes itself by splitting into two forces (a positive and negative, or a soliciting and solicited) (*Phenomenology*, 85). "These two Forces exist as independent essences; but their existence is a movement of each towards the other, such that their being is rather a pure positedness or a being that is posited by an other, i.e. their being has really the significance of a sheer vanishing" (*Phenomenology*, 85). "They [antithetical forces] do not exist as extremes which retain for themselves something fixed and substantial" (*Phenomenology*, 85). "The interplay of two Forces thus consists in their being determined as mutually opposed in their being for one another in this determination, and in the absolute immediate alternation of the determinations" (*Phenomenology*, 84). "These two moments [positive and negative force, or solicited and soliciting] are not divided into two independent extremes offering each other only an opposite extreme: their essence rather consists simply and solely in this, that each is solely through the other, and what each thus is it immediately no longer is, since it is the other. They have thus, in fact, no substances of their own which might support and maintain them" (*Phenomenology*, 86).

38. See Zheng Xuan's *Zhouyi zhu*.
39. See Kong Yingda's *Zhouyi zheng yi*.
40. Kant in his *Critique of Judgment* spoke of indeterminate concepts that reflect the activity of understanding in conjunction with imagination toward identifying the object of aesthetic feelings (of pleasure). Here, the indeterminate concept can be regarded as process or activity of the mind, as it searches to provide a unified, harmonious pattern for the manifold of intuition present before it. (See *Critique of Judgment*, especially Introduction, sections 6 & 7, also §1, §2, and §9.) In our current discussion, the indeterminate *li* would be an onto-cosmological counterpart (or analogue) to Kant's epistemologically oriented notion of the indeterminate concept.
41. See Zhu Xi's *Taiji tu shuo jie*.
42. Translation is mine after consulting James Legge's translation.
43. See *Zhouyi, Xici*.
44. I borrow these two names from the 63rd and 64th hexagrams of the *Yijing* to underscore not only the main difference of two situations, but the difference of underlying principles inherent in these two situations.
45. There is a "great chain of being" in Western philosophy, as suggested by Arthur O. Lovejoy.
46. See Zhang Zai's *Zheng Meng*, chapter 1.
47. See *Daodejing*, chapter 40.
48. See *Jinsilu*, chapter 1 (all translations are mine).
49. See *Jinsilu*, chapter 1.
50. See *Jinsilu*, chapter 1.
51. Translation is mine.

Chapter 10

1. To criticize the *Yijing* from a scientific point of view is to mistake it for what it is not. But to say that the *Yijing* system is neither informational nor scientific is not to say that, as an autonomous system of and for understanding, it may not organize factual information for factual communication or integrate scientific knowledge for scientific communication. The *Yijing* can be used to do these jobs, but it is not intended just to be used to do these jobs. Instead, it is intended primarily to provide understanding and communication on the understanding level. If to organize facts and to integrate concepts are parts of what a complete communication does involve, then the *Yijing* system no doubt can be regarded as a supreme vehicle of complete communication for it is capable of doing communication on all three levels. One must not forget that for the *Yijing* system the organization of facts for information and the integration of concepts for knowledge are all eventually directed toward the goal of communication for understanding or simply toward the goal of understanding itself.1. J. L. Austin, *How to do Things with Words* (New York: Oxford University Press, 1962).

2. Gottlob Frege distinguished between object and concept, the former being saturated in meaning and therefore nameable, and the latter not being so saturated in meaning, and therefore only capable of predicative function in a sentence. See *Translations of the Philosophical Writings of Gottlob Frege*, edited by Peter Geach and Max Black (Oxford: Blackwell, 1952).

3. See my 1977 article "Harmony and Conflict in Chinese Philosophy," *Journal of Chinese Philosophy*, vol. 4, no. 3: 209–246 (also incorporated in this volume).

4. What is regarded as reality need not be reality in itself. A system may represent an underlying view of reality rather than reality itself.

5. See the *Great Appendix* of the *Yijing*. For translations of some passages see Richard Wilhelm, *The I Ching; or Book of Changes*, translated by Cary F. Barnes (New York: Pantheon Books 1950); 2 vols. Bollingen Series, 19, and James Legge, *The I Ching* (New York: Dover Publications, 1963).

6. See the *Great Appendix* of the *Yijing*.

7. "Chinese Philosophy and Symbolic Reference," *Philosophy East and West*, vol. 27, no. 3: 307–322.

Chapter 11

1. See *Yulei*, *Zhuan* 67, and *Wenji*, *Zhuan* 60, Reply to Liu Chun Fang.
2. See *Wenji*, *Zhuan* 72, *yihejin suobipian*.
3. See *Yulei*, *Zhuan* 67.

4. See *Wenji, Zhuan* 33, Reply to Lu Bei Gong.
5. See *Wenji, Zhuan* 33.
6. See *Wenji, Zhuan* 33.
7. See chapter 10. Also see my 1977 article, "Chinese Philosophy and Symbolic Reference" in *Philosophy East and West*, vol. 27, no. 3: 307–323.
8. See my article "On Zhu Xi's Theory of Understanding and Knowledge: An Onto-hermeneutical Analysis." In *Chu Hsi and Neo-Confucianism*, eds. Wing Tsit-chan (Honolulu: University of Hawai'i Press). Presented at the International Zhu Xi Conference at the University of Hawai'i, Honolulu, July 6–13, 1982.
9. *Yulei, Zhuan* 66.
10. *Wenji. Zhuan* 38, "Reply to Yuan Zhizhong."
11. See *Yulei, Zhuan* 67.
12. See *Wenji, Zhuan* 38, "Reply to Yuan Zhizhong."
13. *Yulei, Zhuan* 67.
14. *Yulei, Zhuan* 34.
15. *Yulei, Zhuan* 67.
16. See *Jian Mu, Zhuzi Xinxue an*, vol. 4, p. 31.
17. See Zhang Liwen's article in the book, *Chu Hsi and Neo Confucianism*, ed. Wing Tsit Chan (Honolulu: University of Hawai'i Press, 1986).
18. See my article "Chu Hsi's Methodology and Theory of Understanding."
19. See the preface in my "Chu Hsi's Methodology and Theory of Understanding."
20. *Shang*, section 11.
21. *Shang*, section 11.
22. *Shang*, section 11.
23. Attached to *Yi Xueh Qimeng, Beng Du Shu*, in *Zhouyi Zhe Zhong*, p. 87, 1980 Taipei edition; my emphasis.
24. *Shang*, section 12.
25. *Shang*, section 12, chapter 1.
26. Regarding the number 55 and the number 50, one might say that the method of divination is very much linked to these numbers, and these numbers also give a philosophical significance to the divinatory process formed. But note hexagrams are not trigrams and it is far more far-reaching and detoured to make this suggestion even plausible.
27. *Hong Fan*, in the *Book of Documents*.
28. *Hong Fan*, in the *Book of Documents*.
29. *Hong Fan*, in the *Book of Documents*, chapter 1.
30. Of course, there is one condition to satisfy: namely, that the display of individual numbers from groups of two numbers must be such as to preserve the number 15 in the middle.
31. See chapter 10.
32. See my essay "Chinese Philosophy and Symbolic Reference."

33. *Qimeng*, chapter 1.
34. *Zhuzi yu lei*, section on the *Yi*.

Chapter 12

1. It often occurs that one may even reduce the *Analects* to a mere manual of ethical code and common sense, as it is conceived by Bertrand Russell in his book *Problems of China*. This is because Russell lacks an in-depth understanding of the intellectual tradition in China.

2. See H. G. Creel: "Comments on Harmony and Conflict," in the *Journal of Chinese Philosophy*, vol. 4, no. 3 (October, 1977): 275–278. See also my lead article, "Toward Constructing a Dialectics of Harmonization: Harmony and Conflict in Chinese Philosophy," and my responses to Creel's comments in the same issue at 209–246 and 279–286.

3. The meaning of life in a situation revealed by divination may be said to be more significant than the meaning of good fortune and ill fortune. For as we shall see, a man holding a good and right attitude (*zheng*) may still suffer from ill fortune, but one can reconcile to it by recognizing the meaning of fullness of one's suffering and bearing through.

4. Qu Wanli mentioned these two methods in his scholarly work *Hsienjin Han-wei I li-ping, shu ping*, vol. 1 (Taipei, 1969) 1.

5. See Qu Wanli, op. cit., pp. 1–46.

6. Qu Wanli indicates that the *Shuogua* must appear very late because of the evidence of relating to the *wuxing*. See Qu Wanli, op. cit., p. 58.

7. The first line of the *Xici* is "The Heaven is noble, the earth low, thus the *Qian* and *Kun* are fixed [in positions]."

8. For a review of this see Kao Huaimin, *Xianqin Yixue Shi* (History of the *Yi* in the Pre-Qin Period) (Taipei, 1975). See also Qu Wanli., op. cit.

9. See Daniel S. Goldenburg, "The Algebra of the *I Ching* and its Philosophical Implications," in the *Journal of Chinese Philosophy*, vol. 2, no. 2 (March 1975): 149–180, for the exact formulation of the fundamental theorem under as originally proposed by me.

10. See quotation from the *Mencius*, 2A4, 4A9 in the Harvard Yenching Index to the *Mencius* (Cambridge, 1941).

11. For the following discussion, see Qu Wanli, op. cit., pp. 1–60.

A Bibliography of the *Yijing* in Chinese

1 (西汉) 京房.京氏易传[M].《汉学堂经解》本
2 (西汉) 郑玄. 宋王应麟编, 清惠栋辑考, 增补郑氏周易[M].上海: 上海古籍出版社, 1987.
3 (汉) 郑玄.周易郑注[M].北京: 中华书局, 1985.
4 (汉) 毛亨.毛诗注疏[M].上海: 上海古籍出版社, 2013.
5 (汉) 毛氏传、(汉) 郑氏笺《毛诗》[M].济南: 山东友谊出版社, 1990.
6 (汉) 河上公等 注, 老子, 上海: 上海古籍出版社, 2013.
7 (晋) 郭象.庄子注, 北京: 北京大学出版社, 2010.
8 (战国) 左丘明撰 (西晋) 杜预集解[M].上海: 上海古籍出版社, 1997.
[汉]刘安、点 著；陈广忠 校；[汉]许慎 注, 淮南子, 上海: 上海古籍出版社, 2016.
9 (魏) 王弼、(晋) 韩康伯, (唐) 孔颖达疏.周易正义[M].阮元校《十三经注疏》本, 中华书局影印, 1979.
10 (东汉) 许慎撰 (清) 段玉裁注.说文解字注[M].上海: 上海古籍出版社, 1981.
11 (晋) 郭璞注, (宋) 邢昺疏.尔雅注疏[M].十三经注疏本.北京: 中华书局, 1980.
12 (唐) 陆德明.经典释文[M].北京: 中华书局, 1983.
13 (唐) 瞿昙悉.唐开元占经[M]. 北京: 中国书店, 1989.
14 (唐) 魏徵, 褚亮, 虞世南合编.群书治要译注[M]. 北京: 中国书店, 2013.
15 (唐) 孔颖达.尚书正义[M].北京: 北京大学出版社, 2015.
16 (唐) 李鼎祚撰.周易集解[M].上海: 上海古籍出版社, 1989.
17 (宋) 欧阳修.易童子问[M].中国书店据世界书局影印, 1986.
18 (宋) 程颐.伊川易傳 [M].王孝鱼点校, 中华书局, 1978.
19 程颢, 程颐. 二程集.《周易程氏传》卷第四[M].北京: 中华书局, 1981.
20 (宋) 朱熹.周易本义[M].上海: 上海古籍出版社, 1989.
21 (宋) 朱熹、吕祖谦撰. 近思录[M].上海: 上海古籍出版社, 2010.
22 (宋) 黄士毅.朱子语类汇校[M].上海: 上海古籍出版社, 2014.
23 (宋) 苏轼.东坡易传[M].上海: 上海古籍出版社, 1987.
24 (宋) 张根.吴园周易解[M].文渊阁四库全书本.上海: 上海古籍出版社, 1987.
25 (宋) 耿南仲.周易新讲义[M].文渊阁四库全书本.上海: 上海古籍出版社, 1987.
26 (宋) 朱震.汉上易傳[M].通志堂经解本.

27 (宋) 郭雍.郭氏传家易说[M].文渊阁四库全书本.上海: 上海古籍出版社, 1987.
28 (宋) 沈该.易小傳[M].通志堂经解本.
29 (宋) 林栗.周易经传集解[M]. 文渊阁四库全书本.上海: 上海古籍出版社, 1987.
30 (宋) 邵雍, 邵雍全集, 上海: 上海古籍出版社, 2016.
31 (宋) 邵雍, 皇极经世, 北京: 九州图书出版社, 2005.
32 (宋) 邵雍著, 郭彧整理[M].北京: 中华书局, 2013.
33 (宋) 周敦颐著, 太极图说 通书, 上海: 上海古籍出版社, 1992.
34 (宋) 周敦颐, 周子通书, 上海: 上海古籍出版社, 2000.
35 (宋) 朱熹.周易本义[M].上海: 上海古籍出版社, 1987.
36 (宋) 张栻.南轩易說[M]. 文渊阁四库全书本.上海: 上海古籍出版社, 1987.
37 (宋) 杨简.杨氏易传[M]. 文渊阁四库全书本.上海: 上海古籍出版社, 1987.
38 (宋) 张载.横渠易说[M].张载集[Z].北京: 中华书局, 1978.
39 (宋) 胡瑗.周易口义[M].上海: 上海古籍出版社, 1987.
40 (宋) 項安世述.周易玩辞[M]. 文渊阁四库全书本.上海: 上海古籍出版社, 1987.
41 (宋) 杨万里.诚斋易传[M]. 上海: 上海古籍出版社影印四库全书本, 1990.
42 (宋) 易祓.周易总义[M]. 文渊阁四库全书本.上海: 上海古籍出版社, 1987.
43 (宋) 魏了翁.周易要义[M].四库全书本.
44 (宋) 俞琰.周易集说[M].通堂志经解本.
45 (元) 吴澄撰 《易纂言外翼[M].文渊阁四库全书本.上海: 上海古籍出版社, 1987.
46 (元) 保巴.周易繋辭述[M].影印本.
47 (元) 赵采.周易程朱義折衷[M]. 文渊阁四库全书本.上海: 上海古籍出版社, 1987.
48 (元) 胡一桂.周易启明启蒙翼傳[M].通堂志经解本
49 (元) 胡炳文.周易本義通釋[M].通堂志经解本
50 (元) 熊良辅.周易本義集成[M].文渊阁四库全书本.上海: 上海古籍出版社, 1987.
51 (元) 龍仁夫.周易集传[M]. 文渊阁四库全书本.上海: 上海古籍出版社, 1987.
52 (元) 陈应润.周易爻变易蕴[M].文渊阁四库全书本.上海: 上海古籍出版社, 1987.
53 (元) 梁寅.周易参义[M].通堂志经解本
54 (明) 来知德.周易集注[M]. 北京: 九州出版社, 2004.
55 (明) 潘士藻.讀易述[M].文渊阁四库全书本.上海: 上海古籍出版社, 1987.
56 (明) 林希元.易经存疑[M].文渊阁四库全书本.上海: 上海古籍出版社, 1987.
57 (明) 逯中立.周易劄记[M].文渊阁四库全书本.上海: 上海古籍出版社, 1987.
58 (明) 高攀龙. 周易简说[M].四库全书本
59 (明) 蕅益智旭.周易禅解[M].方向东、谢秉洪校注, 广陵书社, 2006.
60 (明) 何楷.古周易订诂[M].四库全书本
61 (清) 黄宗羲.易学象数论[M].上海: 上海古籍出版社, 1987.
62 (清)王夫之.周易稗疏[M].文渊阁四库全书本.上海: 上海古籍出版社, 1987.
63 (清)王夫之.周易外传.周易内传.船山易学[M].武汉: 岳麓书社, 1996.
64 (清) 毛奇齡.易小帖[M].文渊阁四库全书本.上海: 上海古籍出版社, 1987.
65 (清) 马其昶.重定周易费氏学[M].上海: 上海古籍出版社, 2002.
66 (清) 陈梦雷.周易浅述[M].九州出版社, 2004.
67 (清) 李光地.周易折中[M].成都: 巴蜀书社, 2008.
68 (清) 刘沅.周易恒解[M].长春: 吉林大学出版社, 1996.

69 (清) 胡煦.周易函书[M]. 北京: 中华书局, 2008.
70 (清) 王引之.经义述闻(卷二)[M].南京: 江苏古籍出版社, 1985.
71 (清)秦朴散人刘一明 周易阐真[M].西安: 三秦出版社, 1989.
72 (清) 尚秉和.周易尚氏学[M].北京: 中华书局, 1980.
73 (清) 尚秉和.周易古筮考[M].北京: 光明日报出版社, 2006.
74 (清) 严可均辑《全后汉文》(卷四十四) [M].北京: 商务印书馆, 1999.
75 (清)惠栋.周易述[M].上海: 上海古籍出版社, 1987.
76 (清) 李道平.周易集解纂疏[M].北京: 中华书局, 1994.
77 (清) 焦循.焦循文集[M].北京: 九州出版社, 2016.
78 (清) 戴震.原善 孟子字义疏证[M].古籍出版社, 1956.
79 (清) 张惠言.周易虞氏义[M].北京: 北京大学出版社, 2012.
80 (清) 朱骏声.六十四卦经解[M].北京: 中华书局, 2013.
81 (清) 杭辛斋 学易笔谈[M].北京: 中华书局, 2017.

近现代专著
1 李镜池.周易通义[M]. 北京: 中华书局, 2007.
2 李镜池.周易探源[M].北京: 中华书局, 1984.
3 胡朴安.周易古史观[M].上海: 上海古籍出版社, 2005.
4 高亨.周易大传今注[M].北京: 清华大学出本社, 2010.
5 屈万里.汉石经周易残字集证[M].台北: 联经出版事业有限公司, 1984.
6 杨伯峻.春秋左传注[M].北京: 中华书局, 1983.
7 杨伯峻.论语译注[M].北京: 中华书局, 1980.
8 黄寿祺、张善文.周易译注[M].上海: 上海古籍出版社, 2007.
9 金景芳, 吕绍纲. 周易全解[M].上海: 上海古籍出版社, 2005.
10 闻一多.周易与庄子研究[M].成都: 巴蜀书社, 2003.
11 Zhu Boqun, *Yixue Zhexue Shi* (History of Philosophy of Yi Learning), 4 Volumes, Taipei: Landun Culture Enterprise, 1991. 朱伯昆, 易学哲学史, 四卷, 台北篮灯文化实业公司出版, 1991年
12 刘大钧.今、帛、竹书〈周易〉综考[M].上海: 上海古籍出版社, 2005.
13 Liu Dajun, edited, *Xiangshu Yixue Yanjiu* (Studies in Images and Numbers of the Yi Learning), Jinan: Qilu Book Company, 1997. 刘大钧主编, 象数易学研究, 济南: 齐鲁书社, 1997.
14 Liu Dajun, edited, *Dayi Jiyi* (Collected Meanings of the Great Yi), Shanghai: Ancient Texts Publishers, 2002. 刘大钧主编, 大易集义, 上海古籍出版社, 2002。
15 Gao Huaimin, *Xianqin Yixueshi* (Pre-Qin History of Yi Study) Taipei: Dongwu University, 1965. 高怀民, 先秦易学史, 台北东吴大学出版社, 1965.
16 Yan Zheng, *Wujing Zhexue jiqi Wenhuaxue de Chanshi* (Philosophy in the Five Confucian Classics and their Cultural Interpretations), Jinan: Qilu Book Company, 2001. Chapter 4. 严正, 五经哲学及其文化学的阐释, 济南: 齐鲁书社, 2001 第四章.
17 成中英.中西哲学精神[M].上海: 东方出版中心, 1991.

18 Chung-ying Cheng, *Yixue Benti Lun* (Benti-Ontology of the *Yi* Philosophy), Beijing: Peking University Press, 2006. 成中英, 易学本体论, 北京大学出版社, 2006.

———. "*Chanpu de quanshi yu hen zhi wuyi: lun yichan yuanzhu sixiang de zhexue yansheng*" (Interpretation of Divination and Five Meanings of Zhen: on the philosophical extension of the primary idea of divination in the *Yijing*), in *Zhongguo Wenhua*, Issue 9, February 1994, 29–36.

———. *C Lilun: Yijing Guanli Zhexue* (C Theory: *Yijing* Management Philosophy), Sanmin Publishing House, Taipei, 1995.

———. "Inquiry into the Primary Way: *Yijing* and the Onto-Hermeneutical Understanding, in vol. 30, no. 3 and 4, *Journal of Chinese Philosophy* 289–312, 2003. Also in *Zhouyi Yanjiu* (Studies in Zhouyi), Additional Issue, April 2003, 150–180. 周易研究 增刊 2003 四月, 150–180.

19 Lou Yulie, *Wang Bi Xiaoshi* (Emendations and Annotations of Wang Bi), Two Volumes, Beijing: China Book Company, 1999. 樓宇烈, 王弼校釋, 兩卷。 北京 中華書局出版, 1999.

20 Duan Changshan, edited, *Guizang Yi Kao* (Archaelogical Inquiries into the *Yi* of Guizang), Hong Kong: China Philosophy and Culture Press, 2002, 585–607. 段长山主编, 归藏易考, 香港 中国哲学文化出版社, 2002。"关于归藏易的几个问题," 585–607.

21 濮茅左.楚竹书周易研究[M].上海：上海古籍出版社, 2006.

22 Li Xueqin, *Zhouyi Jingzhuan Suyuan* (On Origins of Zhouyi Text and Commentary), Gaoxiong: Liwen Culture Press, 1995. 李学勤, 周易经传溯源, 高雄 丽文文化出版公司, 1995.

23 Guo Yi, *Guodian Zhujian yu Xianqin Xueshu Sixiang*, Shanghai: Shanghai Education Press, 2001. 郭沂, 郭店竹简于先秦学术思想,上海教育出版社, 2001.

24 徐志锐.《周易大传新注》[M].济南: 齐鲁书社.1988.

25 潘雨廷.易学史发微[M].上海: 复旦大学出版社, 2001.

26 余敦康. 汉宋易学解读[M].北京: 华夏出版社, 2006.

27 曾凡朝.易经[M].武汉: 崇文书局, 2012.

28 鲁洪生.细读易经 [M].北京: 研究出版社, 2017.

29 林忠军.易学源流与现代阐释[M].上海: 上海古籍出版社, 2012.

30 林忠军.象数易学发展史[M].济南: 齐鲁书社1998.

31 廖名春.帛书周易论集[M].上海: 上海古籍出版社, 2008.

32 李尚信.卦序与解卦理路[M].成都: 巴蜀书社, 2008.

33 张其成 象数易学 北京: 中国书店, 2003.

34 邓球柏, 帛书周易校释, 长沙湖南出版社, 1987, 1996。 要篇, 第三章480481.

35 杨庆中.从中西会通到本体诠释[M].北京: 中国人民大学出版社, 2013.

36 丁四新.楚竹书与汉帛书〈周易〉校注[M].上海: 上海古籍出版社, 2011.

37 杨伯峻编著.春秋左传注[M].北京: 中华书局, 2011.

38 李学勤.李学勤讲演录[M].长春: 长春出版社, 2012.

39 陈来. 仁学本体论[M].北京: 三联书店, 2014.

40 张政烺.马王堆帛书《周易》经传校读[M].北京: 中华书局, 2008.
41 张克宾.朱熹易学思想研究[M].北京: 人民出版社, 2015.
42 裘锡圭.裘锡圭学术文集[M].上海: 复旦大学出版社, 2015.
43 冯友兰.中国哲学史[M].上海: 华东师范大学出版社, 2000.
44 (美) 史华兹著, 程钢译.古代中国的思想世界[M].南京: 江苏人民出版社, 2004.
45 杨成寅.成中英太极创化论[M].杭州: 浙江大学出版社, 2012.
46 李翔海编, 知识与价值——成中英新儒学论著辑要[M].北京: 中国广播电视出版社, 1996.
47 张岱年.中国哲学大纲[M].北京: 中华书局, 2017.
48 成中英.成中英文集（十册）[M].北京: 中国人民大学出版社, 2017.

研究论文

1 萧汉明.论《周易》的哲学思想与爻性爻位的关系[J].武汉大学学报（社会科学版), 1985, (5).
2 黄沛荣.马王堆帛书《系辞传》校读[J].周易研究, 1992, (4).
3 陈德述.《周易·易传》中的治国理论与德治思想[J].中华文化论坛, 2003, (3).
4 陈来.马王堆帛书《易传》的政治思想——以《缪和》《昭力》二篇之义为中心[J]. 北京大学学报（哲学社会科学版), 2008, (2).
5 Shi Shangang, "Numner Hexagrams and the Yijing," in Qi-Lu Academic Journal, No. 6, 2006, 5–6. 史善刚, "数字易卦与易经," 齐鲁学刊, 2006, 第六期, 5–9.
6 金春峰.《周易》卦及卦爻辞的诠释方法——《大象》对《周易》解读的启示[J]. 陕西师范大学学报（哲学社会科学版), 2010, (3).
7 成中英.论象数互生: 对朱熹易学中义理与象数整合问题再商榷[J]. 第六届中国国际易道论坛——易经哲学学术专题研讨论文集（上), 2015.
8 林忠军.《易传》符号解释视域下的儒道互补会通[J].山西大学学报(哲学社会科学版), 2009, (3).
9 林忠军.论王念孙、王引之父子的易学解释[J].周易研究, 2013, (1).
10 郑万耕.三陈九卦章考释[J].周易研究, 2007, (3).
11 郭沂.从自然易到道德易而形上易——试论三代文化及周易成书[J].周易研究, 2013 (5).
12 胡治洪.帛书《易传》四篇天人道德观析论[J].周易研究, 2001, (2).
13 张涛, 陈婉莹.《周易》经传与先秦阴阳家[J].理论学刊, 2015, (11).
14 刘大钧.再读帛书《缪和》篇[J].周易研究, 2007, (5).
15 王新春.哲学视野下的京房八宫易学[J].周易研究, 2007, (6).
16 张文智.从出土文献看京房六十律及纳甲说之渊源[J].周易研究, 2015, (5).
17 余敦康.京房易学的象数模式与义理内涵[J].周易研究, 1992, (2).
18 徐强.海外汉学视域中的易学哲学——史华慈的《周易》研究[J].孔子研究, 2013, (4).
19 刘震.清华简筮法与左传国语筮例比较研究[J].周易研究, 2015, (1).
20 蒙培元.孔子是怎样解释周易的[J].周易研究, 2012, (1).
21 李尚信.论今帛本《周易》卦序的先后问题[J].哲学研究, 2008 (6).

A Bibliography of the *Yijing* in Western Languages

The following abbreviations will be employed in the Works Cited list that follows.

A	*Antaios*
AIHS	*Archives Internationales D'Histoire Des Sciences*
APQCSA	*Asia and Pacific Quarterly of Cultural and Social Affairs* (Seoul)
ATS	*Asian Thought and Society* (Oneida, New York)
BMFE	*Bulletin of the Museum of Far Eastern Antiquities* (Stockholm)
BSOS	*Bulletin of the (London) School of Oriental Studies*
BUA	*Bulletetin de Université L 'Aurore*
C	*China*
CC	*Chinese Culture*
CCS	*Collectanea Commissionis Synodalis* (Beijing)
CDA	*Chinesisch-Deutscher Almanach* (Frankfurt am Main)
CJSA	*China Journal of Science and Art*
CR	*China Review*
CRec	*Chinese Recorder*
CRep	*Chinese Repository*
CSP	*Chinese Studies in Philosophy*
EH	*Eastern Horizon*
EJ	*Eranos Jahrbuch*
FA	*France-Asie*
FCR	*Free China Review*
H	*Harvest*
HJAS	*Harvard Journal of Asiatic Studies* (Cambridge)
HR	*History of Religions*
IRM	*International Review of Missions*
JA	*Journal Asiatique*
JAF	*Journal of American Folklore*

JAOS	Journal of The American Oriental Society (New Haven)
JCP	Journal of Chinese Philosophy
JCS	Journal of The China Society (Taipei)
JES	Journal of Ecumenical Studies (Temple University)
JHI	Journal of the History of Ideas
JOS	Journal of Oriental Studies
JPS	Journal of the Polynesian Society
JRAS	Journal of the Royal Asiatic Society
JRT	Journal of Religious Thought
MCMT	Main Currents in Modern Thought
MEO	Message D'Extreme Orient
MS	Monumenta Serica
N	Numen
NCR	New China Review
NY	New Yorker
PEW	Philosophy East and West
Qcc	Quaderni di Civilta Chinese (Milan)
R	Reflections
SIN	Sinica
SA	Scientific American
SL	Studia Leibniziana
SM	Scripta Mathematica
SP SY	Spring
SYS	Systematics
T	Tohogaku
TICOJ	Transactions of the International Congress of Orientalists in Japan (Tokyo)
TP	T'oung Pao (Leiden)
TR	Tamkang Review (Taipei)
VI	Le Voile d'Isis
WZKMU	Wissenschaftliche Zeitsclrrift D'er Karl Marx Univeristat
ZDMG	Zeitschrift Der Deutschen Morgenlandischen Gesellschaft (Wiesbaden)
ZMR	Zeitschrift Fur Missionswissenschaft Und Religionswissenschaft (Munster, West Germany)

Works Cited

"A Student." "A Study of the *Yih King*." *CRep* (1883): 18–32.
Adler, Joseph, trans. "Introduction to the Study of the Classic of Change." A translation of Zhu Xi's *Yixue qimeng*, with Adler's own useful "Introduction" to Zhu's "Introduction." www2.kenyon.edu/depts/religion/fac/adler/Writings/Chimeng.htm
Aiton, E. J. "Gorai Kinzo's Study of Leibniz and the *I ching* Hexagrams." *Annals of Science* 38 (1981): 71–92.
Alabaster, Chaloner. "The Doctrine of the *Chi*." CR 18 (1889–1890): 299–307.
Anders, Allan W. "On the Concept of Freedom in the *I Ching*: A Deconstructionist View of Self-Cultivation." *JCP* 17, no. 3 (1990): 275–288.
———. "Approaches to the Meaning of *Ming* in the *I Ching* with Particular Reference to Self-Cultivation." *JCP* 9 (June 1982): 169–195.
Anthony, Carol K. *A Guide to the I Ching*. Stow, MA: Anthony Publishing Co., 1980.
———. *The Philosophy of the I Ching*. Stow, MA: Anthony Publishing Co., 1981.
Arguelles, Jose. "Compute and Evolve: Some Reflections on the *I Ching* as a Prelude to a Post-Scientific System." *MCMT* 25 (Jan/Feb 1969): 63–67.
The Astrology of the I Ching. Translated by W. K Chu. Edited by W. A. Sherrill. London: Routledge and Kegan Paul, 1976.
Avitus. "Quelques notes sur le *Yi-king*." VI 37 (Aug/Sept 1932): 152–153, 573–583.
Barde, Rene. "La Divination par le *Yi-King*." Unpublished manuscript.
———. "Recherches sur les origines arithmétiques du *Yi-king (I-Ching)*."*Archive internationales d'histoire des sciences*. Continuation of *Archeion*, 1952.
Baruch, Jacques. "Le *Yi-King* et son interpretatione divinatoire." MEO 3, no. 10 (1973): 731–742.
———. "Introduction a la symbolique chinoise. A propos de 'Yin' et 'Yang.'" MEO 1, no. 4 (1971): 277–285.
———. "Introduction à la symbolique chinoise: Les nombres." MEO 2, no. 7 (1972): 501–512.

———. "Introduction à la symbolique chinoise: Les nombres." MEO 2, no. 8 (1972): 587–596.

———. "L'interpretation des presages dans la Chine ancienne." MEO 1, no. 2 (1971): 127–132.

Baruzi, Jean. *Leibniz et l'organisation religieuse de la terre d'apres des documents inédits*. Paris: Alcan, 1907.

Bascom, William. *If a Divination: Communication between Gods and Men in West Africa*. Bloomington: Indiana University Press, 1969.

———. "The Relationship of Yoruba Folklore to Divining." JAF 56 (1943): 27–131.

Bauer, Wolfgang. *China Und Die Hoffnung Auf Gluck; Paradies, Utopien, Idealvorstellungen*. Munchen: Darl Hanser Verlag, 1971.

Bemstein, Jeremy. "A Question of Parity." NY (May 12, 1962): 49–96.

Bernard, Henri, S. J. "A l'occasion d'etudes recentes sur l'*I King*: Comment Leibniz decouvert le Livre des Mutations." BUA 3, no. 5 (1945): 432–445.

Blofield, John. *I Ching: The Chinese Book of Change*. London: Unwin Paperbacks, 1976.

Bodde, Derk. *Chinese Thought, Society and Science*. Honolulu: University of Hawai'i Press, 1991.

Bogun, Zhu. *Zhouyi Zhexue Shi* (*History of Philosophy of Zhouyi*) (4 vols.). Taipei, 1991.

Bol, Peter K., with Kidder Smith, Joseph A. Adler, and Don J. Wyatt. *Sung Dynasty Uses of the I Ching*. Princeton, NJ: Princeton University Press, 1990.

The Book of Changes (Zhouyi). Translated by Richard Rutt. Richmond, England: Curzon Press, 1996.

Bourdieu, Pierre. *Language and Symbolic Power*. Translated by Gino Raymond and Matthew Adamson. Cambridge: Polity Press, 1994.

Boyle, Veolita Parke. *The Fundamental Principles of Yi-King, Tao, the Cabalas of Egypt and the Hebrews*. Chicago: Occult Publishing Co., 1929.

Brasovan, Nicholas S. "An Exploration into Neo-Confucian Ecology." JCP 43, no. 3–4 (September 2016): 203–220.

Brown, Chappell. "The Tetrahedron as an Archetype for the Concept of Change in the *I Ching*." JCP 9, no. 2 (June 1982): 159–168.

———. "Inner Truth and the Origin of the Yarrow Stalk Oracle." JCP 9, no. 2 (June 1982): 197–210.

Burke, Kenneth. *Permanence and Change*. Los Altos, CA: Hermes, 1954.

Cadiere, Leopold. *Religious Beliefs and Practices of the Vietnamese*. Translated by Ian W. Mabbett. Clayton, Australia: Centre of Southeast Asian Studies Working Papers, 1989.

Cage, John. *Silence: Lectures and Writings*. Middletown, CT: Wesleyan University Press, 1961.

Camman, Schuyler. "The Magic Square of Three in Old Chinese Philosophy." HR 1 (1961): 37–80.

Carroll, Thomas D. "The Hidden Significance of the *I-Ching* Diagrams." *JCS* 2 (1962): 31–49.
Cassien-Bernard, F. "*Pa-kua* et l'origine des nombres." *FA* 6 (1950): 848–856.
Chang, Chi-Yun. "The Book of Changes (*I Ching*)—A Philosophical Masterpiece Mirroring the Zeit-Geist of the Western Chou Dynasty." *CC* 6, no. 4 (Oct. 1965): 1–41.
Chang, Hao. "The Expression *hsu*, 'Void,' in the *I-Ching, Lao-Tzu*, and *Chuang-Tzu*, and Its Implications in the Chinese Way of Life and Culture." 29th International Congress of Orientalists. Paris, 1973.
———. "Chine Ancienne: Section organisee par Michel Soyrnie." Paris: L'Asiatheque, 1977.
Chang, Tsung-gung. *Der Kult Der Shang-Dynastie Im Spiegel Der Orake-linscriften: Eine Pakrographische Studie Zur Religion In ArchaisehenChina*. Wiesbaden: 1970.
Divination et rationalité en Chine ancienne. Extrême-Orient/Extrême-Occident: Cahiers de recherches comparatives Vol. 21. Edited by Karine Chemla, with Donald Harper and Marc Kalinowski. Saint-Denis: Presses Universitaires de Vincennes, 1999.
Chen, Shih-Chuan. "How to Form a Hexagram and Consult the *I Ching*." *JAOS* 92, no. 2 (1972): 237–249.
Cheng, Chung-ying. "On the Same Substance and Common Origin of *xiang* (image), *shu* (number), *yi* (meaning), *li* (principle) in the Philosophy of the *Yijing*." *Zhouyi Studies*, no. 1 (1990) 1–14.
———. "On the Origin and the Futurity of the Yi Philosophy." In *Da Yi Collected Papers*, edited by Liu Dajun. Jinan, 1991: 18–30.
———. "Onto-Hermeneutical Paradigm in 20th-Century Chinese Philosophy." In *Twentieth-Century Chinese Philosophy*. Edited by Nick Bunnin and Cheng Chung-ying. Boston and Oxford: Blackwell Publishing, 2002.
———. *shijizhijiaodejueze: zhongxizhexue dehuitong yuronghe* (*Choice at the Cross of the Centuries: Convergence and Integration between Chinese Philosophy and Western Philosophy*). Shanghai: Knowledge Publishing Co., 1991.
———. "Confucius, Heidegger, and the Philosophy of the *I Ching*." *PEW* 37, no. 1 (January, 1987): 51–70.
———. *New Dimensions of Confucian and Neo-Confucian Philosophy*. Albany: State University of New York Press, 1991.
Cheng, Yung-Hsiao. "*I Ching*: A Survey of Criticism in English." *TR* 8, no. 1 (April 1977): 207–225.
Choain, Jean. *Introduction au Yi-King*. Monaco: Editions du Rocher, 1991.
Chou, Philip. "7000 Years of Prognostication." *FCR* 14 (June 1964): 24–35.
Chow, Kai-wing, On-cho Ng, and John B. Henderson, eds. *Imagining Boundaries: Changing Confucian Doctrines, Texts and Hermeneutics*. Albany: State University of New York Press, 1999.

Chih-Hsu, Ou-I. *The Buddhist I Ching*. Translated by Thomas Cleary. Boston and London: Shambala Press, 1987.
Chu, Pingyi. "Ch'eng-Chu Orthodoxy, Evidential Studies and Correlative Cosmology: Chiang Yung and Western Astronomy." *Philosophy and the History of Science* 4, no. 2 (October, 1995).
Chung, Chang-Soo. *The I Ching on Man and Society: An Exploration into its Theoretical Implications in Social Sciences*. Lanham, MD and Oxford: University Press of America, 2000.
Clark, J. J. *The Tao of the West: Western Transformations of Taoist Thought*. London and New York: Routledge, 2000.
———. *Jung and Eastern Thought: A Dialogue with the Orient*. London and New York: Routledge, 1994.
———. *C. G. Jung on the East*. London and New York: Routledge, 1995. Aleister Crowley Foundation webpage. www.thelemicgoldendawn.org/acf
Clarke, A. G. "Probability Theory Applied to the *I Ching*." *JCP* 14, no. 1 (March 1987).
The Classic of Changes. Translated by Richard John Lynn. New York: Columbia University Press, 1994.
Cobb, John B. "Post-Conference Reflections on *Yin* and *Yang*." *JCP* 6, no. 4 (December 1979): 421–426.
Collani, Claudia von. "Gottfried Wilhelm Leibniz and the China Mission of the Jesuits." In *Das Neueste uber China: G. W. Leibnizens Novissima Sinica von 1697*. Studia Leibnitiana Supplementa 33. Edited by Wenchao Li and Hans Poser. Stuttgart: Franz Steiner, 2000.
———. *P. Joachim Bouvet S. L. Sein Leben und sein werk*. Nettetal: Steyler Verlag, 1985.
———. Chinese Figurism in the Eyes of European Contemporaries. *China Mission Studies (1550–1800) Bulletin*, 4 (1982): 12–23.
———. *Die Figuristen in der Chinamission*. Frankfort and Bern: Peter Lang, 1981.
Collins, Roy. *The Fu Hsi I Ching: The Early Heaven Sequence*. New York and London: University Press of America, 1993.
The Complete I Ching. Translated by Alfred Huang Huang. Rochester. VT: Inner Traditions, 1998.
Conrady, August. "*Yih–king* Studien." *AM* 7. Edited by Eduard Erkes (1931–1932): 409–468.
Cook, Daniel J., and Henry Rosemont, Jr. *Gottfried Wilhelm Leibniz, Writings on China*. Chicago: Open Court, 1994.
Copleston, Frederick. *Philosophies and Cultures*. New York: Oxford University Press, 1980.
Cornelius, J. Edward and Marlene, eds. "*Yi King*: A Beastly Book of Changes." *Red Flame: A Thelemic Research Journal* 5 (1998): 1–234.

Cornu, Phillipe. *Tibetan Astrology*. Boston and London: Shambala, 1997. Translated from the French by Hamish Gregor.
Culling, Louis T. *The Incredible I Ching*. Helios, 1965. Crowley, Aleister, 777. London: Neptune Press, 1955.
———. *Magick in Theory and Practice*. New York: Castle Books, 1960.
Davis, Scott. "Operating the *Yijing* Apparatus: A Compositional Analysis. *The Oracle: The Journal of Yijing Studies* 2, no. 7 (Summer, 1998).
de Harlez, Ch. *Le Yih-King: Terte Primitif Retabli, Traduit et Commente, par Ch. Harlez*. Brussels: F. Hayez, 1889.
———. "Le Texte originaire du *Yih-king*, sa nature et son interpretation." JA 8, no. 9 (April/June, 1887): 424–456.
———. "Les Figures symboliques de *Yih-King*." JA (1897): 223–287.
———. *The Yih-King: A New Translation from the Original Chinese by Magr. de Harlez*. D.L.L. Translated from the French by J. P. Val d'Eremao. Wo King: Publication of the Oriental University Institute.
———. "L'Interpretation du *Yi-king*." TP 7 (1897): 197–222.
———. *Le livre des mutations. Texte primitif traduit du Chinois*. Annotated by Raymond de Becker. Paris: Editions Denoel, 1959.
de Fancourt, William. *Warp and Weft: In Search of the I-Ching*. Freshfields, Chieveley, Berks, England: Capall Bann Publishing, 1997.
De Lacouperie, Terri. *The Oldest Book of the Chinese: The Yih-King and its Authors. Volume I: History and Method*. London: Nutt, 1892.
De Saussure, Leopold. "On the Antiquity of the *Yin-Yang* Theory," NCR 4 (1922): 457–463.
Desderi, Paolo. "Il Libro delle Mutazioni," QCC 4 (February 1956): 253–264.
Dhiegh, Khig Alx. *The Eleventh Wing: An Exposition of the Dynamics of the I Ching for Now*. Los Angeles: Nash, 1973.
———. *I Ching: Taoist Book of Days, Calendar-Diary 1975*. Berkeley, CA: Shambala, 1974.
Dickinson, Gary, and Steve Moore. "Trigrams and Tortoises: Sino-Tibetan Divination." *Oracle* (special issue) 1, no. 5 (Summer, 1997): 1–48.
Dilworth, David. *Philosophy in World Perspective: The Hermeneutics of the Major Themes*. New Haven, CT: Yale University Press, 1989.
Doeringer, F. M. "Oracle and Symbol in the Deduction of the *I Ching*." PEW 30, no. 2 (April 1980): 195–209.
Doniger, Wendy. *The Implied Spider: Politics and Theology in Myth*. New York: Columbia University Press, 1998, 33–34.
Dubs, Homer H. "Did Confucius Study the Book of Changes?" TP 24 (1927): 82–90.
Eason, Cassandra. *I Ching Divination for Today's Woman*. Sonoma, CA: Foulsham and Co., 1994.

Edkins, Joseph. "The *Yi King*, with Notes on the 64 *Kwa*." CR 12 (1883–1884): 77–88, 412–432.

———. "The *Yi King* and its Appendices." CR 14 (1885–1886): 305–322.

Eitel, E. J. "Chinese Philosophy before Confucius." CR 7 (1878, 1879): 388.

The Elemental Changes: The Ancient Chinese Companion to the I Ching. Translated by Michael Nylan. Albany: State University of New York Press, 1994. [On the *Taixuan jing*.]

Erkes, Eduard. "Eine P'an-Ku Mythe des Hsia-Zeit." TP 35 (1942): 159–173.

Fang, Tung-Mei. "The Creative Spirit of Confucius as Seen in the *Book of Changes*." CSP 7 (Spring 1976).

Farquhar, Judith. " 'Medicine and the *Changes* are One.' An Essay on Divination Healing with Commentary." *Chinese Science* 13 (1996): 107–134.

Fendos Jr., Paul G. *"Book of Changes* Studies in Korea." *Asian Studies Review* 23, no. 1 (March 1999): 49–68.

Feng, Gia-Fu, and Jerome Kirk. *Tai Chi, a Way of Centering, and I Ching*. London: Collier, 1970.

Fleming, Jess. "Categories and Meta-Categories in the *I Ching*." JCP 20, no. 4 (1993): 425–434.

Franke, Otto. "Leibniz und China." ZDMG 7 (1928): 155–178.

Frawley, David. "The Cosmic Language of the *I Ching*." CC 20, no. 4 (December 1979): 45–51.

Fujino, Junko. "The *I Ching* and the Philosophy of Fortune." E 8, no. 8 (September 1972): 19–28.

Fung, Yu-Lan. "The Appendices of the Book of Changes and the Cosmology of the *Huai Nan Tzu*." *A History of Chinese Philosophy*. Translated by Derk Bodde. Princeton, NJ: Princeton University Press, 1952.

Gall, Michel. *Le Yi-King, La Bible Des Chinois*. Paris: R. Laffont, 1980.

Gardner, Martin. "Mathematic Games: The Combinatorial Basis of the *I Ching*, the Chinese Book of Divination and Wisdom." SA (January1974): 108–113.

Gernet, Jacques. "Pratiques divinatoires et conceptions scientifiques dans la civilisation Chinoise." T 45 (January 1973): 1–11.

Goldenberg, Daniel S. "The Algebra of the *I Ching* and its Philosophical Implications." JCP 2, no. 2 (1975): 149–180.

Goodman, Howard L., and Anthony Grafton. "Ricci, the Chinese, and the Toolkits of Textualists." *Asia Major*, 3.2 (1990).

Gottshalk, Richard. *Divination, Order and the Zhouyi*. Lanham, MD: University Press of America, 1999.

Govinda, Anagarika Brahmacari. *The Inner Structure of the I Ching, The Book of Transformations*. New York: Weatherhill, 1981.

Gräfe, E. H. *I Ging: Buch des Stetigen und der Wandlung*. Oberstedten: Hugo Gräfe Verlag, 1967.

———. *Di Acht Urbilder des I Ging*. Oberstedten: Hugo Grafe Verlag, 1967.

———. *Die Weltformel: Das Geheimnis des I Ging Entdeckt.* Oberursel: Hugo Gräfe Verlag, 1974.
Graham, A. C. *Disputers of the Tao: Philosophical Argument in Ancient China.* La Salle, IL: Open Court, 1989.
Groupe de travail du Centre Djohi. *Le Yi King mot a mot.* Paris: Editions Albin Michel, 1994.
Guowei, Wang. *Renjian Cihua (Discourse on Poetic Verses in the Human World),* annotated edition. Beijing: Zhonghua Book Co., 1955.
Guying, Chen. "On *Xici* Commentary as Work from *Jixia* Daoists: Fifth Discussion on *Yizhuan* as Not a Confucian Classic." *Daojia Wenhua Yanjiu* II (1992): 355–365.
Hacker, Edward A. "Temperature and the Assignment of the Hexagrams of the *I Ching* to the Calendar." *JCP* 9, no. 4 (December 1982): 395–400.
———. "Order in the Textual Sequence of the Hexagrams of the *I Ching.*" *JCP* 14, no. 1 (March 1987).
Hall, David, and Roger T. Ames. *Anticipating China: Thinking Through the Narratives of Chinese and Western Culture.* Albany: State University of New York Press, 1995.
———. *Thinking from the Han: Self, Truth and Transcendence in Chinese and Western Culture.* Albany: State University of New York Press, 1998.
Hauer, Erich. "*I Ging,* Das Budh cer Wandlungen, aus dem Chinesischen verdeutscht und erläutert, von Richard Wilhelm . . . 1924 (Review)." *Ostasiatische Zeitschrift.* Berlin, Lipzig, 1925.
Hayashi, Y. *I-Ching: Fortune Telling and the Book of Changes, a Game.* San Francisco: Japan Publishing, 1972.
Henderson, John B. *The Development and Decline of Chinese Cosmology.* New York: Columbia University Press, 1984.
———. *Scripture, Canon and Commentary: A Comparison of Confucian and Western Exegesis.* Princeton, NJ: Princeton University Press, 1991.
———. *The Construction of Orthodoxy and Heresy: Neo-Confucian, Islamic, Jewish, and Early Christian Patterns.* Albany: State University of New York Press, 1998.
Higgins, Charlie. "The Hexagram and the Kabbalah" (1997). www.mension.com/del 3.htm
Ho, Peng Yoke. "The System of the *Book of Changes* and Chinese Science." *Japanese Studies in the History of Science* 11 (1972).
Hook, Diana Farrington. *The I Ching and its Associations.* London and Boston: Routledge and Kegan Paul, 1980.
———. *The I Ching and Mankind.* London: Routledge and Kegan Paul, 1975.
———. *The I Ching and You.* London: Routledge and Kegan Paul, 1973.
Ho Lo Li Shu: The Astrology of I Ching. Translated from the "Ho map lo map rational number" manuscript. Edited and Commentaries by W. A. Sherrill. New York: S. Weiser: 1980.

Hu, Shih. *The Development of the Logical Method in Ancient China.* New York: Paragon Books, 1928.
Huang, Alfred. *The Numerology of the I Ching.* Rochester, VT: Inner Traditions, 2000.
Huang, WenShan. "*T'ai Chi Ch'uan* and the *I Ching*, or the Book of Changes." CC 10 (March 1969): 1–20.
Hui, Li, and Samuel Beal. *The Life of Hiuen-Tsiang, by the Shaman Hwui Li.* London: Kegan Paul, Trench, Trubner, 1911.
I Ching: A Philosophical Prophecy. Edited by Ken White. Anaheim, CA: Dynamic Design, Inc., 1972.
I Ching: An Annotated Bibliography. Edited by Edward A. Hacker and Lorraine Patsco. London and New York: Taylor and Francis, 2002.
I Ching: Het Boek Der Veranderingen. Translated by Peter Ten Hopen. The Hague: Bert Baker, 1971.
I Ching, The Book of Changes. Translated by Frank J. MacHovec. New York: Peter Pauper Press, 1971.
I Ching: The Classic Chinese Oracle of Change. Translated by Rudolf Ritsema and Stephen Karcher. Rockport, MA: Element Books, 1994.
I Ching: The Shamanic Oracle of Change. Translated by Martin Palmer and Jay Ramsay with Zhao Xiaomin. London and San Francisco: Thorsons, 1995.
I Ching. Translated by Stephen Karcher. London: Sterling Publications, 2002.
The I Ching or the Book of Changes. Translated by Richard Wilhelm. Princeton, NJ: Princeton University Press, 1968.
The I Ching: Text and Annotated Translation. Translated from classical Chinese to modern Chinese by Liu Dajun and Lin Zhongjun. Translated into English by Fu Youde. Jinan: Shandong Friendship Publishing House, 1995.
Interpreting across Boundaries: New Essays in Comparative Philosophy. Edited by Eliot Deutsch and Gerald Larson. Princeton, NJ: Princeton University Press, 1988.
Jao, Tsung-I. "On the Divinatory Diagram *(I-kua)* in the Shang Dynasty." *TICOJ* 25 (1980): 145–146.
Javary, Cyrille. *Les Rouages du Yi Jing.* Paris: Javary, Phillipe Picquier, 2001.
———. *Understanding the I Ching.* Translated from the French by Kirk McElhearn. Boston: Shambhala, 1997.
Javary, Geneviève. "Traduction du conflit et conflits de traduction." *Hexagrammes* 6 (1991): 64–112.
———. "Le Père Bouvet, a-t-il retrouvé Pythagore en Chine?" *Hexagrammes* 6 (1991): 113–122.
Johnson, O. S. *A Study of Chinese Alchemy.* Eastford, CT: Martino Publishing, 2009. First published in 1928.
Johnson, Willard. *I Ching: An Introduction to the Book of Changes.* Berkeley, CA: Shambala, 1969.

Julien, François. *Figures de l'immanence: pour une lecture philosophique du Yi King, Le classique du changement*. Paris: Grasset, 1993.

———. *The Propensity of Things: Toward a History of Efficacy in China*. Translated from the French by Janet Lloyd. New York: Zone Books, 1995.

Kaplan, Charles David. "Method as Phenomenon: The Case of the *I Ching*." Master's Thesis, University of California at Los Angeles.

Karcher, Stephen. *How to Use the I Ching*. Rockport, MA: Element, 1997.

Kegan, Frank R. *I Ching Primer: An Introduction to the Relevant Process Perspective upon the Occult in General and Flux Time (I Ching) in Particular*. Chicago: Aries Press, 1979.

Keightley, David N. "*Shih Cheng*: A New Hypothesis about the Nature of Shang Divination." Paper presented at the "Asian Studies on the Pacific Coast" conference, June 17, 1972, Monterey, California.

———. "Was the *Chou Yi* a Legacy of Shang?" Paper presented to the panel "Early Chinese Divination: The *Yijing* and its Context," 34th Annual Meeting of the Association for Asian Studies, April 3, 1982, Chicago.

———. "Shang Divination and Metaphysics." *PEW* 38, no. 4 (October 1988): 367–397.

Kiang, Kang-Hu. "The *Yi Ching* or The Book of Changes." *CJSA* 3 (1925): 259–264.

Kingsmill, Thomas W. "The Construction of the *Yih King*." *CR* 21 (1894–1895): 272–275.

Kunst, Richard F. "The Original *Yijing*: A Text, Phonetic Transcription, Translation, and Glosses based on Recent Scholarship." PhD dissertation, University of California, Berkeley, 1982.

Kupperman, Joel J. "Confucius and the Problem of Naturalness." *PEW* 18 (1968): 275–285.

Lach, Donald F. "Leibniz and China." *JHI* 14 (1945): 437–455.

———. *The Preface to Leibniz Novissima Sinica*. Honolulu: University of Hawai'i Press, 1957.

Lackner, Michael. "Jesuit Figurism" in *China and Europe: Images and Influences in Sixteenth to Eighteenth Centuries*. Edited by Thomas H. C. Lee. Hong Kong: Hong Kong University Press, 1991.

———. "Richard Wilhelm: A 'Sinicized' German Translator." In *De l'Un au Multiple. La traduction du chinois dans les langues européennes*. Edited by Viviane Alleton and Michael Lackner. Paris: Maison des Sciences de l'Homme, 1998.

LaCouperie, Terrien de. "The Oldest Book of the Chinese (the *Yi-King*) and its Authors." *Journal of the Royal Asiatic Society* New Series 14 (1882): 781–815 and New Series 15 (1883): 237–289.

Lai, Whalen. "The *I-Ching* and the Formation of the Hua-Yen Philosophy." *JCP* 7, no. 1 (March 1980): 245–258.

Landry-Deron, Isabelle. *Les leçons des sciences occidentales de l'empereur de Chinese Kangxi (1662–1722): Texte des journals des Pères Bouvet et Gerbillion.* Paris: E.H.E.S.S., 1995.
Lavier, Jacques. *Le Livre de la terre et du ciel: les secrets du Yi King.* Paris: Tchou, 1969.
Lee, Jung Young. "The *I Ching* as a Framework for Self-Therapy and a Practical Instrument for the Self-Healing Process." APQCSA 10, no. 2 (Winter 1978): 13–21.
———. "The *I Ching* and Its Basic Philosophy of Inner Process." CC 16, no. 2 (June 1975): 63–70.
———. *The I Ching and Modern Man: Essays on Metaphysical Implications of Change.* Secaucus, NJ: University Books, 1975.
———. "*Yin-yang* Way of Thinking: A Possible Way for Ecumenical Theology." IRM 60 (July 1971): 363–370.
———. *The Principles of Changes: Understanding the I Ching.* New Hyde Park, NY: University Books, 1971.
———. "Some Reflections on the Authorship of the *I Ching*." N 17 (December 1980): 200–210.
———. *Patterns of Inner Process. The Rediscovery of Jesus' Teachings in the I Ching and Preston Harold* (Secaucus, NJ: The Citadel Press, 1976).
———. "Death is Birth and Birth is Death: The Parascientific Understanding of Death and Birth." SYS 9, no 4 (1972): 188–200.
———. "Can God be Change Itself!" JES 10, no. 4 (1973): 752–770.
———. "The Origin and Significance of the *Chongyok* or the Book of Correct Changes." JCP 9, no. 2 (June 1982): 211–242.
———. "The *I Ching* and Its Basic Philosophy of Inner Process." CC 16, no. 2 (June 1975): 63–70.
———. "The *I Ching* as a Framework for Self-Therapy and a Practical Instrument for the Self Healing Process." APQCSA 10:2 (Winter 1978): 13–21.
———. "The *Book of Change* and Korean Thought." In *Religions in Korea: Beliefs and Cultural Values.* Edited by Earl Phillips and Eui Young Yu. Los Angeles: Center for Korean American and Korean Studies, California State University, Los Angeles, 1982.
Lessa, William A. "The Chinese Trigrams in Micronesia." JAF 56 (1943): 27–131.
———. "Divining Knots in the Carolines." JPS 68 (1959): 188–204.
Leung, Koon-Loon. "An Algebraic Truth in Divination." JCP 9, no. 2 (June 1982): 243–258.
Lewis, Mark Edward. *Writing and Authority in Early China.* Albany: State University of New York Press, 1999, esp. Chapter 6.
Liebniz, Gottfried Wilhelm. *Discourse on the Natural Theology of the Chinese.* Translated by Henry Rosemont, Jr., and Daniel J. Cook. Honolulu: University Press of Hawai'i, 1977.

———. *Zwei Briefe über das binäre Zahlensystem und die chinesische Philosophie*. Edited and translated by Renate Loosen and Franz Von Essen. Stuttgart: Belser Verlag, 1968.

Lim, Kim-Anh. *Practical Guide to the I Ching*. Havelte, Holland: Binkey Kok Publications, 1998.

———, trans. *Practical Guide to the I Ching*. Translated from the French by Valerie Cooper. Havelte, Holland: Binkey Kok Publications, 1998.

The Literary Mind and the Carving of Dragons: A Study of Thought and Pattern in Chinese Literature. Translated by Vincent Yu-chung Shih. Hong Kong: Chinese University Press, 1983.

Liou, Tse-Houa. *La Cosmologie des Pa Koua et l'astronomie moderne*. Paris: Jouve, 1940.

Liu, Zheng. "The Dilemma Facing Contemporary Research in the *I-Ching*." *Chinese Studies in Philosophy*, 24, no. 4 (Summer, 1993).

Liu, Da. *I Ching Numerology: Based on Shao Yung's Classic Plum Blossom Numerology*. San Francisco: Harper and Row, 1979.

———. *I Ching Coin Prediction*. New York and Evanston, IL: Harper and Row, 1975.

———. *T'ai Chi Ch'uan And I Ching: A Choreography of Body and Mind*. New York: Harper and Row Publishers, 1972.

Loewe, Michael, and Carmen Blacker, eds. *Oracles and Divination*. Boulder, CO: Shambala, 1981.

Loosen, Renate. "Leibniz und China." A8, no. 2 (July 1966): 134–143.

Loy, David. "On the Meaning of the *I Ching*." *JCP* 14, no. 1 (March 1987).

Lui, I-Ming. *The Taoist I Ching*. Translated by Thomas Cleary. Boston and London: Shambala Press, 1986.

MacGillivray, D. "A New Interpretation of the Book of Changes." *CRec* 49 (1918): 310–316.

Mair, Victor H. "A Reordering of the Hexagrams of the *I Ching*." *PEW* 29 (October 1979): 421–442.

Marshall, S. J. *The Mandate of Heaven: Hidden History in the I Ching*. New York: Columbia University Press, 2001.

McCaffree, Joe E. *Divination and the Historical and Allegorical Sources of the I Ching, The Chinese Classic or Book of Changes*. Los Angeles: Miniverse Services, 1967.

———. *Bible and I Ching Relationships*. Hong Kong and Seattle: South Sky Book Co, 1982.

McClatchie, Rev. Canon. *A Translation of the Confucian Yih King or the "Classic of Change" with Notes and Appendix*. Shanghai: American Presbyterian Mission Press, and London: Trubner, 1876.

McClatchie, Thomas. "The Symbols of the *Yih-King*." *CR* 1 (1872–1873): 151–163.

McEvilly, Wayne. "Synchronicity and the *I Ching*." *PEW* 18, vol. 3 (July 1968): 137–149.

McKenna, Terrence, and Dennis McKenna. *The Invisible Landscape: Mind, Hallucinogens and the I Ching.* San Francisco: Harper Collins Publishers, 1993.

McKenna, Stephen, and Victor Mair. "A Reordering of the Hexagrams of the I Ching." *PEW* 29, no. 4 (October, 1979): 421–41.

Mears, Isabella, and Louisa E. Mears. *Creative Energy: Being an Introduction to the Study of the Yih King, Or Book of Changes.* London: Murray, 1931.

Meeting of Minds: Intellectual and Religious Interaction in East Asian Traditions of Thought. Edited by Irene Bloom and Joshua Fogel. *Meeting of Minds: Intellectual and Religious Interaction in East Asian Traditions of Thought.* New York: Columbia University Press, 1997.

Melyan, Gary G., and Wen-Kuang Chu. *I Ching: The Hexagrams Revealed.* Rutland, VT: C. E. Tuttle Co., 1977.

Merkel, Franz Rudolph. *G. W. von Leibniz und die China Mission.* Leipzig: J. C. Hinrichs, 1920.

Metzner, Ralph. *Maps of Consciousness.* New York: Collier Books, 1971.

Moore, Steve. *The Trigrams of Han: Inner Structures of the I Ching.* Chatham, KT: The Aquarian Press, 1989.

Morel, Hector V. *Yi Ching. Las Enigmaticas Lineas Del Y Ching Develadas Con Criterio Eminentemente Occidental. Col, Pronostic.* Buenos Aires: Kier, 1972.

Morris, Elanor B. *Information Puzzles and the I-Ching* (Taipei: Cheng Chung Book Co., 1978).

———. *Information Puzzles and Astronomical Prediction in the I Ching.* Taipei: Cheng Chung Book Co., 1978.

Mou, Bo. "An Analysis of the Ideographic Nature and Structure of the Hexagram in *Yijing*: From the Perspective of Philosophy of Language." *JCP* 25, no. 3 (September, 1998): 305–320.

Müller, R. *I Ging: Das Buch der Wandlungen, aus dem Chinesischen verdeutscht un erläutert.* Jena, 1937.

Mungello, David E. "Leibniz's Interpretation of Neo-Confucianism." *PEW* 21, no. 1 (January 1971): 13–22.

Murphey, Joseph, and Ken Irving. *Secrets of the I Ching.* Paramus, NJ: Reward Books, 2000.

Needham, Joseph. "The System of the Book of Changes," in Joseph Needham and Wang Ling, *Science and Civilization in China,* Vol. 2. Cambridge: Cambridge University Press (1956): 304–345.

Neilsen, Bent. *A Companion to Yi jing Numerology and Cosmology.* London: RoutledgeCurzon, 2003.

Ng, Benjamin Wai-ming. "I Ching Scholarship in Ch'ing China: A Historical and Comparative Study." *Chinese Culture* 37, no. 1 (March, 1996): 57–68.

———. "The I Ching in Late Choson Thought." *Korean Studies* 24 (2000).

———. *The I Ching in Tokugawa Thought and Culture.* Honolulu: University of Hawai'i Press, 2000.

———. "The *I Ching* in Tokugawa Medical Thought." *East Asian Library Journal*, 1 (Spring, 1998).

———. "The *Yijing* in Buddhist-Confucian Relations in Tokugawa Japan." *Studies in Central and East Asian Religions*, 10 (1998).

———. "The *I Ching* in Shinto Thought of Tokugawa Japan." *Philosophy East and West* 48, no. 4 (October, 1998).

———. "The *I Ching* in the Adaptation of Western Science in Tokugawa Japan." *Chinese Science*, 15 (1998).

———. "Study and the Uses of the *I Ching* in Tokugawa Japan." *Sino-Japanese Studies* 9, no. 2 (April, 1997): 24–44.

———. "The History of the *I Ching* in Medieval Japan." *Journal of Asian History* 31, no. 1 (July, 1997): 25–46.

———. "The *I Ching* in Ancient Japan." *Asian Culture Quarterly* 26, no. 2 (Summer, 1996): 73–76.

———. "The *I Ching* in the Military Thought of Tokugawa Japan." *Journal of Asian Martial Arts* 5, no. 1 (April, 1996): 11–29.

Ng, On-cho. *Cheng-Zhu Confucianism in the Early Qing: Li Guangdi (1642–1718) and Qing Learning*. Albany: State University of New York Press, 2001.

Ngo, Van Xuyet. *Divination, magie et politique dans la Chine ancienne*. Paris: Presses Universitaires de France, 1976.

Nylan, Michael. *The Five "Confucian" Classics*. New Haven, CT and London: Yale University Press, 2001.

Olivier, Roy. *Leibniz et la Chine*. Paris: Librarie Philosophique J. Vrin, 1972.

Olsvanger, Immanuel. *Fu-Hsi: The Sage of Ancient China*. Jerusalem: Massadah Ltd., 1948.

Ong, Hean-Tatt. *The Chinese Pakua*. Selangor Darul Ehsan, Malaysia: Pelanduk Publications, 1991.

Pailoux, Jacques. *Le diamant chauve ou la tradition des évidences: Théorie générale de l'énergétique fondée sur le Yi King*. Erde: Foundation Cornelius, 1976, 2002.

Peterson, Willard. "Making Connections: "Commentary on the Attached Verbalizations of the *Book of Changes*." *Harvard Journal of Asiatic Studies* 42 (1982): 67–116.

Phelan, Timothy S. "Chu Hsi's *I-hsueh Ch'i-meng* and the Neo-Confucianism of Yi T'oegye." *Korea Journal* 18:9 (September, 1978): 12–17.

Philippe Couplet, S. L (1623–1693): The Man Who Brought China to Europe. Edited by Jerome Heyndrickx. Nettetal: Steyler Verlag, 1990.

Piper, Gottfried Otto. "Ueber das I-King. Die verschiedenen Bestandtheile des Buches und ihre Verständlichkeit." *ZDMG* 5, no. 2 (1851): 195–220.

———. "Uber das *I-King:* Die Texte des Konfucius, welche sich auf die verschiedenen Reihenfolgen der *Kua* beziehen." *ZDMG* 7 (1853): 187–214.

Plaks, Andrew. *Archetype and Allegory in the Dream of the Red Chamber*. Princeton, NJ: Princeton University Press, 1976.

Ponce, Charles. *The Nature of the I Ching, its Visage and Interpretation.* New York: Award Books, 1970.

Praag, Henri van. *Slentel Tot De I Tjing.* Deventer: N. Kluner, 1972.

Progoff, Ira. *Jung, Synchronocity, and Human Destiny: Noncausal Dimensions of Human Experience.* New York: Julian Press, 1973.

Redmond, Geoffrey, and Tze-ki Hon. *Teaching the I Ching (Book of Changes).* New York: Oxford University Press, 2014.

Reifler, Sam, and Alan Ravage. *I Ching: A New Interpretation for Modern Times.* New York: Bantam Books, 1974.

Reisinger, Leo. *Das "I ging.": Eine formalwissenschaftl. Untersuchung des chinesischen Orakels Acta ethnologica et lin 25.* Vienna: Inst. f. Völkerkunde d. Univ. Wein, 1972.

Reitsma, J. "De I-Ging," C 2 (1926–1927): 156–170.

Riegal, Jeffrey. "A Textual Note on the *I Ching.*" *Journal of the American Oriental Society* 103, no. 3 (July–September, 1983): 601–605.

Ritsema, Rudolf. "Notes for Differentiating Some Terms in the *I Ching.*" S (1970): 111–125; (1971): 141–152.

———. "The Corrupted: A Study of the 18th Hexagram in the *I Ching.*" S (1972): 90–109.

———. "The Pit and the Brilliance: A Study of the 29th and the 30th Hexagrams in the *I Ching.*" S (1973): 142–170.

Roberts, Moss Pensak. "The Metaphysical Context of the *Analects* and the Metaphysical Theme in Late Chou Confucianism." PhD dissertation, Columbia University, 1966.

Rouselle, Erwin. "*Yin* und *Yang* vor ihrem Auftreten in der Philosophie." S 8 (1933): 41–46.

———. "Drache und Stute: Gestalten der mythischen Welt." *CDA* (1935): 6–17.

Rump, Arianne. "Die Verwundung des Hellen als Aspekt des Bösen im I ching." PhD dissertation, University of Zurich, 1967.

———. "The Darkening of the Light as an Aspect of Evil in the *I Ching.*" Columbia University, University Seminar on Traditional China, April 25, 1972. Mimeographed paper.

Ryan, James A. "Leibniz's Binary System and Shao Yong's *Yijing.*" *PEW* 46, no. 1 (January, 1996): 59–90.

Sadler, William. *The I Ching of Management: An Age-Old Study for New Age Managers.* Atlanta: Humanics Publishing Group, 1996.

Scharfstein, Ben-Ami, et al. *Philosophy East/Philosophy West.* New York: Oxford University Press, 1978.

———. *A Comparative History of World Philosophy: From the Upanishads to Kant.* Albany: State University of New York Press, 1998.

Schlegel, Gustave. *Uranographie Chinoise* (3 vols.). Leiden: Brill, 1875.

Schlumberger, Jean-Phillipe. *Yi king: Principes, pratique et interpretation.* Paris: Éditions Dangles, 1987.
Schmitt, Gerhard. *Sprüche der Wandlungen auf ihrem geistesgeschichtlichen Hintergrund.* Deutsche Akademie der Wissenschafen, Berlin, Institut fur Orientforschung 76. Berlin: Akademie Verlag, 1970.
Schönberger, Martin. *The I Ching and the Genetic Code.* New York: ASI Publishers, 1979.
———. *Verborgener Schlussel Zum Leben: Welt-Fonnel I Ching Im Genetischen Code.* Munchen: Barth, 1973.
Schoter, Andreas. "Boolean Algebra and the *Yijing.*" *Oracle: The Journal of Yijing Studies* 2, no. 7 (Summer, 1998): 19–34.
Schubert, Johannes. "Das *I-Ching* und seine Probleme." *WZKMU* 9, no. 3 (1959–1960): 453–460.
Schwartz, Howard. "On the Creation of a Poem," *R* 16, no. 1 (Winter 1967): 22–36.
Secret, François. "Quand la Kabbale expliquait le 'Yi king,' ou un aspect oublié du figuratisme du P. Joachim Bouvet." *Revue de l'histoire des religions* 195 (1979): 35–53.
Secter, Mondo. *The I Ching Handbook: Decision-Making with and without Divination.* Berkeley: North Atlantic Books, 2002.
———. *I Ching Clarified: A Practical Guide.* Boston: Charles E. Tuttle Company, 1993.
Seiwert, Hubert. "Orakelwessen im altesten China: Shang und westliche Chou dynastie." *ZMR* 64 (July 1980).
Shaughnessy, Edward L., "The Composition of the *Zhouyi.*" PhD dissertation Stanford University, 1983.
———. "I ching (Chou I)" *Early Chinese Texts: A Bibliographical Guide.* Edited by Michael Loewe. Berkeley, CA: Institute of East Asian Studies, 1993.
———. *I Ching: The Classic of Change,* English translation of Mawangdui Silk Manuscript of the *Yijing.* New York: Ballantine Books, 1997.
———. *Before Confucius: Studies in the Creation of the Chinese Classics.* Albany: State University of New York Press, 1997.
Shchutskii, Iulian K. *Researches on the I Ching.* Translated by W. L. MacDonald, Tsuyoshi Hasegawa, and Hellmut Wilhelm. Princeton, NJ: Princeton University Press, 1979.
Sherrill, Wallace Andrew. *Heritage of Change: A Background to Chinese Culture.* Edited by W. A. Sherrill and W. K. Chu. Taipei: East-West Eclectic Society, 1972.
Sherrill, W. A., and W. K. Chu. *An Anthology of I Ching.* London, Henley and Boston: Routledge & Kegan Paul, 1983.
Simbriger, Heinrich. *Geheimnis der Mitte: aus dem geistigen Vermächtnis des alten China.* Dusseldorf-Koln: Eugen Diederichs Verlag, 1961.

Simmons, Jayne F. *I Ching: A Philosophical Prophecy*. Anaheim: Dynamic Design, 1972.

Siu, R. G. H. *The Man of Many Qualities: A Legacy of the I Ching*. Cambridge, Massachusetts: M.I.T. Press, 1968.

———. *The Portable Dragon: The Western Man's Guide to the I Ching*. Cambridge, Massachusetts: MIT Press, 1968.

Smart, Ninian, and Richard Hecht, eds. *Sacred Texts of the World: A Universal Anthology*. New York: Crossroad, 1982.

Smith, Kidder. "Cheng Yi's (1033–1107) Commentary on the *Yijing*." PhD dissertation, University of California, Berkeley, 1979.

———. "The Difficulty of the *Yijing*." *Chinese Literature: Essays, Articles, Reviews*, 15 (1993): 1–15.

Smith, Richard J. "The Place of the *Yijing* in the World Culture: Some Historical and Contemporary Perspectives." *JCP* 25, no. 4 (1998): 391–422.

———. "The Languages of the *Yijing* and the Representation of Reality." *Oracle: The Journal of the Yijing* (Summer 1998): 35–50.

———. "The Book of Changes." In *Great Literature of the Eastern World*. Edited by Ian McGreal. New York: Harper Collins, 1996.

———. *Fortune-tellers and Philosophers: Divination in Traditional Chinese Society*. Boulder, CO and Oxford: Westview Press, 1991.

———. "Divination in Ch'ing China." In *Cosmology, Ontology and Human Efficacy: Essays in Chinese Thought*. Edited by Richard J. Smith and D. Y. Y. Kwok. Honolulu: University of Hawai'i Press, 1993.

———. "The Jesuits and Evidential Research in Late Imperial China: Some Reflections." *Ex/Change* (February 2002). www.cityu.edu.hk/cityu/about/exchange.htm

———. "Some Western Language Works on the *Yi Jing*, Topically Organized: A Guide for Students." Rice University, Houston, Texas, November 10, 2002.

Stein, Sherman K. "The Mathematician as an Explorer." *SA* (May 1961): 149–158.

Sterling, Marysol Gonzalez. *I-Ching and Transpersonal Psychology*. York Beach, ME: Samuel Weiser, 1995.

Sun, Xiaoli. "A Wrong Statement about Leibniz and his Interpretation of Chinese *I Ching* Figure." *Historia scientiarum* 8 (1999): 239–247.

Sung, Z. D. *The Symbols of Yi King or the Symbols of the Chinese Logic*. Shanghai: The China Modern Education Co., 1934. (Reprinted, New York: Paragon, 1969.)

———. *The Text of Yi King (and its Appendices)*. Shanghai: The China Modern Education Co., 1935.

Swanson, Gerald William. "The Great Treatise: Commentary Tradition to the *Book of Changes*." PhD dissertation, University of Washington, 1974.

Sze, Mai-Mai. *The Tao of Painting: A Study of the Ritual Disposition of Chinese Painting*. New York: Pantheon Books, 1956.

Tang, Mingbang. "Recent Developments in Studies of the *Book of Changes*." *Chinese Studies in Philosophy* (Fall, 1987).
Thang, Yung-Thung. "Wang Pi's New Interpretation of the *I Ching and Lun Yu*." *HJAS* 10 (1947): 124–161.
Tong, Lik-Kuen. "The Concept of Time in Whitehead and the *I Ching*." *JCP* 1, no. 3–4 (June/September 1974): 373–393.
———. "The Appropriation of Significance: The Concept of Kang-T'ung in the *I Ching*." *JCP* 17, no. 3 (1990): 315–344.
Tong, Paul K. K., "A Cross Cultural Study of the *I-Ching*." *JCP* 3, no. 1 (December 1975): 73–84.
Tsheou Yi: Le Yi king ou Livre des changements de la dynastie des Tsheou. Translated by P. L. F. Philastre. Paris: Peroux, Vol. I, 1883; Vol. II, 1893. Republished by Maisonneuve (Paris 1982) and reissued in a single volume by Éditions Zulma (Paris, 1992; preface by François Jullien).
Tung, Gea. "A Conceptual Model for the Understanding of Opposites: Some Reflections on the *I Ching*." *ATS* 4, no. 10 (April 1979).
Van der Blij, F. "Combinational Aspects of the Hexagrams in the Chinese *Book of Changes*." *SM* 28, no. 1 (1966): 37–49.
Van Praag, H. *Sagesse de la Chine* (Verviers: Gerard and Co., 1966): 75–100.
Vinkenoong, Simon. *Tussen wit en zwart: Een persoonlijke benadering van het Chinese boek der veranderingen (De I Ching)*. The Hague: Bert Baker, 1971.
Vinogradoff, Michel. *Yi Jing: la marche du destin*. Paris: Éditions Dangles, 1995.
Visdelou, Claude. "*Notice du livre chinois nomme Yi-King*." In Gaubil de Guignes' *Le Chou-King*. Paris: Tilliard, 1770.
Von Delius, Rudolf. *Das ewige China: Von den Symbol der Seele*. Dresden: Reissner, 1926.
Von Franz, Marie-Louise. *Zahl und Zeit: Psychologische Überlegungen zu einer Annaherung von Tiefenpsyehologie und Physik*. Stuttgart: Klett, 1970.
Wagner, Rudolf G. *The Craft of a Chinese Commentator: Wang Bi on the Laozi*. Albany: State University of New York Press, 2000.
Waley, Arthur. "Leibniz and Fu Hsi," *BSOS* 2, no. 1 (1921): 165–167.
———. "The Book of Changes," *BMFEA* 5 (1933): 121–142.
Walter, Derek, *The T'ai Hsuan Ching: The Hidden Classic* (Wellingborough, Northamptonshire: The Aquarian Press, 1983).
Wang, Dongliang. *Les signes et les mutations*. Paris: L'asiatheque, 1995.
Wei, Henry. *The Authentic I-Ching*. North Hollywood, CA: Newcastle Publishing Company, 1987.
Wei, Tat. *An Exposition of the I-Ching or Book of Changes*. Hong Kong: Dai Nippon Printing Co., 1977.
———. *An Exposition of the I-Ching or Book of Changes*. Taipei: Institute of Cultural Studies, 1970.

Wilhelm, Hellmut. *Heaven, Earth and Man in The Book of Changes: Seven Eranos Lectures*. Seattle: University of Washington Press, 1977.

———. *The Book of Changes in the Western Tradition: A Selective Bibliography*. Seattle: University of Washington Press, 1972.

———. "Leibniz and the *I Ching*." CCS 16, no. 3–4 (March–April 1943): 205–219.

———. *Die Wandlung: Acht Vorträge zum I-Ging*. Peking: Editions Henril Vetch, 1944.

———. *Change: Eight Lectures on the I Ching*. Translated by Cary F. Baynes. New York: Pantheon Books, 1960. Bollingen Series 62.

———. "Das Schopferische Prinzip im Buch der Wandlungen." *EJ* 25 (1956): 455–475,

———. "Der Sinn des Geschehens nach dem Buch der Wandlungen." *EJ* 26 (1957): 351–386.

———. "The Sacrifice, Idea and Attitude; Thoughts from the *Book of Changes*." H4 (1957).

———. "*I-Ching* Oracles in the *Tso-Chuan* and the *Kuo-Yu*." JAOS 79 (1959): 275–280.

———. "Das Zusammenwirken von Himmel, Erde und Mensch." *EJ* 31 (1962): 317–350.

———. "Wanderungen des Geistes." *EJ* 33 (1964): 178–200.

———. "The Interplay of Image and Concept in the Book of Changes." *EJ* 36 (1967): 31–57.

———. *Sinn Des I Ging*. Düsseldorf-Koln: Eugen Diederichs Verlag, 1972.

Wilhelm, Richard, "Das *Buch der Wandlungen*." In *Chinesische Lebensweisheit*, 65–107. Darmstadt: Otto Reichl Verlag, 1922.

———. "Der Geist der Kunst nach dem *Buch der Wandlungen*." CDA (1927–1928): 25–50.

———. "Dauer im Wechsel: Vorträge über Zeichen aus dem *Buch der Wandlungen*." CDA (1928–1929): 24–54.

———. "Gegensatz und Bemeinschaft: zwei Vorträge gehalten wahrend der Herbsttagung des China-Instituts in Frankfurt aM. am 25. und 26. November 1929," CDA (1930), pp. 36–60.

———. *I Ging, das Buch der Wandlungen, aus dem Chinesischen verdeutscht und erläutert* (2 vols.). Jena: Eugen DiederichsVerlag, 1924.

Wilson, Colin. *The Occult: A History*. New York: Random House, 1971.

Witek, John. *Controversial Ideas in China and Europe: A Biography of Jean-François Foucquet S. J. (1665–1741)*. Rome: Institutum Historicum S.I., 1982.

Wong, S. Y. "The Book of Change: A New Interpretation." EH 2 (1962): 11–18.

Woo, Catherine Yi-yu Cho. *Characters of the Hexagrams of the I Ching*. San Diego: California State University Press.

Wu, Wei. *The I Ching: The Book of Changes and How to Use It*. Los Angeles: Power Press, 1995.

Yan, Johnson. *DNA and the I Ching*. Berkeley, CA: North Atlantic Books, 1991.
Yang, Samuel. *Book of Changes, with Biblical References*. Adelphi, MD: Advanced Technology and Research, 1973.
Yang, Zu-hui, and Hiria Ottino. *Le livre de la simplicité*. Paris: Éditions Trédaniel, 1998.
Yi-Ching: A Concordance to the Yi Ching (in Chinese). Harvard Yenching Institute, Sinological Index Series, suppl. no. 10.
Yijie, Tang "*Lun zhuangjian zhongguo jieshixue wenti*" in Collection of Essays in Celebration of the 80th Anniversary of Professor Wang Yuanhua. Shanghai, 1999, 52–64.
Yi Jing: Le Livre des changements. Translated by Pierre Faure and Cyrille Javary, Éditions Albin Michel, 2002.
The Yi King (Part 2 of *The Sacred Books of China, the Texts of Confucianism*). In the *Sacred Books of The East* 16. Translated by James Legge. Edited by F. Max Muller. Oxford: Clarendon, 1882.
You, Jiyuan. "Virtue: Confucius and Aristotle." *PEW* 48, no. 2 (1998): 323–347.
Yüan, Kuang. *Méthode pratique de divination Chinoise par le Yi-king*. Paris: Vega, 1950.
Yuen, Ko, and Aleister Crowley. *Shih Yi: A Critical and Mneumonic Paraphrase of the Yi King*. Oceanside, CA: Thelema Publications, 1971.
Zelmpliner, Arthur. "Gedanken über die erste deutsche Übersetzung von Leibniz." Abhandlung über die chinesische Philosophie." *SL* 2 (1970): 223 ff.
Zenker, Ernst Viktor. *Der Taoismus der Frühzeif: Die alt-und gemein-chinesische Weltanschauung*. Leipzig: Hölder-Pichler Tempsky, 1943.
Zhang, Longxi. *Mighty Opposites: From Dichotomies to Differences in the Comparative Study of China*. Stanford, CA: Stanford University Press, 1999.
———. *The Tao and the Logos: Literary Hermeneutics, East and West*. Durham, NC: Duke University Press, 1992.
———. *Reflections on Things at Hand: The Neo-Confucian Anthology*. Translated by Wing-Tsit Chan. New York: Columbia University Press, 1967.

Index

Absolute Spirit, 61
action. *See* decision making; timeliness
agriculture
  divination and, 2
  livestock and, 98
aletheia (truth), 127–128, 135–136. *See also* truth
Analects (Confucius), 24–25, 196–197, 203, 252
  background on, 353–357
  dao in, 362, 366–367
  free will and, 361
  hermeneutics and, 356
  human situation and destiny in, 361
  intended system of, 361
  ming in, 371–372
  self-realization and, 106–107
  system of, 382–384
  virtue in, 361
  Yi Text and, 356–361
  Yijing and Confucian testimony, 382–384
Anaximander, 135, 136–137, 139–140
animals
  livestock and domestication of, 98
  tortoise shell readings, 5, 6, 37
Annals of Lu State, 32

archaeology
  archaeological findings, 179–180, 184–185, 187
  divination and, 2–3, 268
Aristotle, 61, 62–63, 127, 169, 299
Austin, J. L., 304

bagua system, 1, 42–43, 157, 256
  divination with, 6–7
  guan and, 120, 121
  heaven and earth in, 119–120
  natural elements and, 8–9
  number theory and, 6–7
  post-heaven diagram of, 109, 350–351
  pre-heaven diagram of, 109, 350–351
  symbols of, 13–14
Bamboo Inscriptions Manuscripts, 179, 187
becoming, 44
  change and, 314
  Dewey on, 55
  five stages of, 168
being
  in Buddhism, 127, 296–300
  creativity and, 51
  dao and, 86, 135, 296, 298, 300–301
  in Daoism, 299–301

503

being (continued)
  divination and, 168
  Greek, 134–137, 299
  guan and, 125, 128–132, 134–137
  Heidegger on, 125, 127–128, 130, 134–137, 139, 140
  as Human Existence, 128
  ill-being, 83
  language and, 134–136
  logos and, 135–136, 138
  metaphysics of, 294–301
  Neo-Confucianism on, 299–300
  nonbeing and, 47–48, 292, 294–301
  oneness and, 74
  onto-hermeneutics of, 128–132, 140
  perception and, 295
  point of view and, 131–132
  presence and, 129, 134, 140
  taiji and, 74–75, 127–128, 132–133, 138–139
  time and, 134–135, 138
  unifying nonbeing and, 294–301
  unthought and, 137
  Way of Transformation and, 129
  Whitehead on, 54
  world-being, 257
  yin-yang and, 138–139
  as *you*, 42, 47–48, 74–75, 86, 169, 294–301
  Zhang Zai on, 299–300
ben, 41, 44, 45
benefiting, 168
benevolence. See *ren*
benti, 43, 44–45
benti-cosmology, 46
Benti-Ontology, as onto-cosmology of Yi, 41–45
ben-ti-yong, 45–46
bianhua, 12, 172, 266
bianyi, 165, 168, 170–171, 172, 233
binomial expansion, 39–40
Bo Xi, 389–390

Bo Yi, 374
body, 42–43
  cosmic, 43–45
  feeling and, 159
  source-body, 43–44
  time and, 45
The Book of Documents (*Shang Shu*), 203
Book on Comprehending the Yi (*Tongshu*), 275
Boshu, 179–180, 187
buci (divinatory judgments), 6, 37, 78, 111–112, 268, 273, 279
Buddhism, 53, 208–209, 276
  being in, 127, 296–300
  Chan, 127, 296–297
  guan in, 15
  Madhyamika, 243
  nonbeing in, 296
  positioning in, 270–271
  Yijing and, 27–29

Can Dong Ji, 336
Celestial Stems (*tian gan*), 323
centrality (*zhong*), 176, 377–378
  in Confucianism, 144–145, 203–204
  harmony and, 144–145, 202–206, 224–228
  lines of, 142–147
  oneness and, 204–205
  positioning and, 202–203, 418–419
  rectitude and, 141–147
  timeliness and, 418–420
  in *Tuan Commentary*, 418
Chan Buddhism, 127, 296–297
change, 4. See also Yi change
  Aristotle on, 61, 62–63
  becoming and, 314
  as *bianyi*, 165, 168
  as closing and opening, 249
  Confucius and, 8–9, 48–49, 77–84, 164–165, 186–187, 393–397

contingency and, 48–49
cosmography of Yi, 11–15
creativity and, 39, 46–49, 62, 71–77, 151, 218–219, 248–251, 253–255, 262–264, 266–269
dao and, 60, 106–107
in *Daodejing*, 63, 85–87
Dewey on, 55, 62
dialectics of, 393–397
essential elements of, 48–49
five major points on, 63
forms of, 390
fortune and, 407–408
freedom and, 79–80
generative onto-cosmology and, 313–318
God and, 61, 62, 63
good and, 81–82
guan and, 68–71, 78
harmony and, 85
Heraclitus on, 54, 59–61
hermeneutics and, 93
in hexagrams, 12–13
human life and, 12–13, 33–34
human situation and, 80, 88–89
introduction and paradigm of, 59–63
large, 12
li and, 283
logos and, 59–60
macro-epistemic, 68–71
meaning of, 8–9
microscopic, 12
moralization of, 77–84
natural phenomena and, 14
natural world and, 64–66, 165
nonchange of, 46–47, 168–169, 233
number theory and, 75–76
observation and, 14, 33, 153, 159–160
onto-cosmology and, 313–318

penetration and, 231–232, 409–410
positioning and, 248–251, 253, 254–255, 260, 262–264, 266–269
power of, 249–250
PPFIC and, 282–283
qi and, 283
reality and, 106, 188–189, 281–282, 314
simplicity of, 49–51, 164–165
symbolism and, 99
taiji and, 72–73, 74, 250, 291
timeliness and, 409–410, 412, 416
transformation and, 48–49, 64–67, 74, 75, 88–89, 98, 170–171, 212, 224
trust in, 88–89
truth and, 88–89
in *Tuan Commentary*, 172, 394–395
universe and, 70
in *Wenyan Commentary*, 395, 396
Whitehead on, 54, 62–63
world-ordering and, 70–77
Xiang Commentary on, 394–395
Xici Commentary on, 48–49
as *yao*, 170
yin-yang and, 64–67, 159–172, 315–316
in *Yizhuan*, 63, 64
Cheng Brothers, 137
Cheng Mingdao, 275, 300
Cheng Yi, 20, 137, 274, 378
li and, 275–276
Cheng Yichuan, 331
Child's View, 145
Chinese ontological hermeneutics, 91–96. *See also* hermeneutics
Chinese philosophy. *See specific topics*
Christianity, 299
commentaries. *See specific commentaries*
Commentary on Zhouyi (Wang Bi), 188

communication
  conceptual mode of, 306
  content and goal of, 303–304
  coordination and assimilation of other systems, 323–327
  of facts, 304–306, 308–309
  hermeneutical mode of, 306–308
  language and, 304
  medium, 304
  onto-hermeneutics of, 319–323
  perception and, 308–309
  three subsystems of, 309–313
  three types of, 304–309, 328–330
  understanding and, 309, 329–330
  values and, 306–308
community and moral development, 5
completing numbers, 342
Completion, 87
Comprehensive Observation. See *guan*
conceptual mode of communication, 306
conflict
  from contradiction, 209
  dialectics of conflict, 243
  from disagreement, 195–196, 198
  hostility and, 209
  from resistance, 209
  strife and, 192–193, 194, 195–196, 207–212
Confucianism
  centrality in, 144–145, 203–204
  guan in, 15
  in Han Dynasty, 26
  positioning in, 246–247, 253–255, 270–271
  rise of, 52–53
  self-cultivational process in, 46, 197–198, 236–237, 252–253, 362–363
  on unity, 204–206

Yijing in, 23–27
  Zhu Xi and, 345
Confucius, 108, 326. See also *Analects*
  change and, 8–9, 48–49, 77–84, 164–165, 186–187, 393–397
  divination and, 17, 101, 113–114, 162–163, 183–188
  before and after fifty, 383–384
  on fortune, 405–407
  on harmony, 161, 195–202
  historical heritage and conceptual link to *Yijing*, 353–361
  humanity and, 24
  impact of Confucian view, 423–425
  on judgments, 405–406
  on learning, 376, 387–388
  on *li*, 370–371
  on life activities, 48–49
  on limitations of human life, 363–368
  metaphysics of, 358–360
  on *ming*, 363–367, 421–423
  morality and, 24, 81, 107, 367–371
  reciprocal transformation between *Yi* Text and, 420–425
  on *ren*, 362, 366–367, 368, 374
  on self-creative power in human being, 361–363
  on *taiji*, 340
  timeliness and, 371–382, 422–425
  on transformation, 370
  virtue and, 8–9, 24, 185, 197, 198, 361, 367–375, 423–425
  Yi Commentaries and, 3, 8, 34, 115
  Yijing and, 23–27, 382–384
consciousness
  post-divinatory rational, 183
  self-conscious and, 8, 41, 183, 188–189
constant *dao*, 86

constant virtues, 367–371
contingency
    change and, 48–49
    Dewey on, 55
    of life activities, 48–49
    perception and, 49
    universe and, 49
contradiction, 209
cosmic body, 43–45
cosmic creativity, 44–45, 81–83
cosmic gap, 15
cosmic reality, 44
cosmogony, 2
    Tuan Commentary and, 116
cosmography, 2
    guan and, 19
    of *Yi*, 11–15
cosmo-humanological system, 7–8
cosmology, 2, 22. *See also* onto-cosmology
    benti-cosmology, 46
    life activities in, 7–8
    natural, 3–4, 14–15
    symbols and, 6
    in *Xici Commentary*, 247
creation
    God and, 61, 62
    Laozi on, 85–87
    regeneration and, 46
creative action, 45–46
creative interpretation, 114–117
creative power, 83–84, 361–363
creative prosperity, 83
creativity, 25–26
    being and, 51
    change and, 39, 46–49, 62, 71–77, 151, 218–219, 248–251, 253–255, 262–264, 266–269
    cosmic, 44–45, 81–83
    creative co-creativity, 71–77, 161
    creative cultivation of humanity, 77–84

creative principles of onto-cosmology, 71–77
    of creativity, 218
    dao and, 83–84
    good and, 81–82
    harmony as, 76–77, 208, 215–220
    heaven and earth and, 82
    innovation and, 70
    Kun and *Qian* and, 219–220
    li and, 277–278
    life-creativity, 46–48
    moral, 81
    natural world and, 40–41, 62
    opposites and, 215–216
    as penetration, 218–219
    qi, 288, 289–293
    reality and, 62, 106, 314
    ren and, 83–84
    self-creative power and, 361–363
    taiji and, 47–48, 72–73, 74, 76–77, 174–175, 338–342
    unity and, 215–220
    world-ordering and, 70–77
    yin-yang and, 71, 155–156, 167–168

danger, 412–413
dao (way), 27–28, 39, 104, 153
    in *Analects*, 362, 366–367
    being and, 86, 135, 296, 298, 300–301
    change and, 60, 106–107
    constant, 86
    creativity and, 83–84
    harmony and, 196–198
    heaven and earth and, 85–86
    li and, 289–290
    ming and, 364
    oneness and, 206
    onto-cosmology and, 9–11, 74
    profound female and, 86
    as return to origin, 87

508 Index

dao (continued)
  taiji and, 173–179, 254–255, 391–392
  timeliness and, 372–373
  yin-yang and, 64–65, 81–82, 151, 169, 176, 249, 281, 287–288, 300
Daodejing (Laozi), 47–48, 89, 153, 161, 188, 207, 300
  change in, 63, 85–87
  unity in, 206
Daoism
  being in, 299–301
  guan in, 15
  positioning in, 246–247, 266, 270–271
  rise of, 52–53
  taiji and, 276–277
  Yijing and, 27–29
Daoist School of Laozi, 173–174
dark, in *yin-yang*, 153, 164, 248
Dasein, 134–135, 136, 140
death
  of God, 138
  ming and, 363–364
decision making
  creative action and, 45–46
  divination and, 33, 101–102
  feeling and, 102
  freedom and, 408
  interpretation as basis for, 23
  morality and, 404
  natural world and, 33
  self-cultivation and action, 236–237
  simplicity and, 50
  understanding and, 21
  valuation and, 22
desire, 278
  discipline and, 84
  freedom and, 84
  morality and, 294, 368
destructive order, 324

Dewey, John, 55, 62, 76
di, 8
di zhi (Earthly Branches), 323
"Diagram of Eight Palaces" (Jing Fang), 179–180
dialectical methodology, of *Yijing*, 313–323
dialectics of change, 393–397
dialectics of conflict, 243
dialectics of harmonization, 233–236, 237–239, 241–243, 318
dialectics of negation, 243
dialectics of *Yi*-symbolic transformation, 389
difference as opposites, 220–224
directions, 324
disagreement, 195–196, 198
discipline
  desire and, 84
  morality and, 362–363
Discourse Commentary, 65
Discourse on the Diagram of the Great Ultimate (*Taiji tu shuo*), 275, 357
disunity, 211–212
diversity, 43
divination
  agriculture and, 2
  archaeology and, 2–3, 268
  with *bagua* system, 6–7
  being and, 168
  Confucius and, 17, 101, 113–114, 162–163, 183–188
  decision making and, 33, 101–102
  ethical foundation of the practical and, 15–18
  feeling and, 102, 112–113
  fortune and, 5–6, 9, 78, 185
  future and, 78, 100–103
  gua and, 9, 18, 101
  in hexagrams, 2
  human civilization and, 356

human situation and, 100
Image-Number School and
  questions regarding, 181–183
interpretation and, 23, 37, 101–102, 109–110, 184–187
key concepts of, 37
li, *qi*, and, 283–284
logic of, 15–18, 273–274
meaning and, 100–101
metaphysics of, 279–280
number theory and, 101
origins of, 31–32, 99–104, 107–108, 273–274
positioning and, 268–270
practical and logical relevance of, 99–104
present relating to future and making, 4–6
restrictions of, 101–102
ritual, 103
self-development and, 107
self-realization and, 106–107
symbolism and, 99–104, 273
symbols, 2
systematization and, 38
understanding and, 46, 78, 102–103
valuation system of, 5
Xici Commentary and, 101, 103
Yi Commentaries and, 309–310
in *Yi* Text, 99–104, 385–387
Zhou method of, 268–269
Zhu Xi on, 331–334
divinatory creative interpretation, 114–115
divinatory judgments (*buci*), 6, 37, 78, 111–112, 268, 273, 279
divine spirit (*shenming*), 182, 184
diviner, 32, 101–102, 110–111, 183
Doctrine of the Mean (*Zhongyong*), 10, 26, 144–145, 177, 198, 260, 271, 363

harmony and, 200–201, 238
  positioning in, 247
  timeliness in, 378–379
dualism, 54–55, 80
  of *li*, *qi*, and Zhu Xi, 278, 290, 293, 339–341
duty, 5

Earthly Branches (*di zhi*), 323
eight primary principles, 110–117
enlightenment, 306
  self-realization and, 296–297
epistemological principles, 40–41
ethical foundation of the practical, 15–18
exchange and harmony, 171
experience
  reality and, 55–56
  of *yin-yang*, 151, 153–156, 160–161, 164–167
Experience and Nature (Dewey), 55, 62
external harmony, 194

facts, 304–306, 308–309
feeling
  body and, 159
  decision making and, 102
  divination and, 102, 112–113
  divinatory judgments and, 112
  guan and, 112–113, 142, 158
  PPFIC and, 282–283
  spiritual, 158
  understanding and, 13, 113
  yin-yang and, 158–161
feelings, spiritual, 158
fengdi, 8
five powers. See *wuxing*
folklore, 29
forms. See also *gua*
  of change, 390
  identity and, 318

forms (continued)
  as images, 121–122
  judgments, numbers, and, 309–313, 335–336
  subsystem of, 322–323
fortune and misfortune
  change and, 407–408
  Confucius on, 405–407
  divination and, 5–6, 9, 78, 185
  gua and, 398–400
  harmony and, 83
  human situation and, 402–403, 407–408
  judgments and, 398–407, 423
  ming and, 400–405, 421
  morality and, 403–407
  timeliness and, 412, 415–418, 423
  virtue and, 405–407, 416–418
  Xici Commentary on, 401–402
four-causes theory, 61
Fragments (Heraclitus), 59
freedom, 48–49, 366
  change and, 79–80
  decision making and, 408
  desire and, 84
  good and, 84
  harmony and, 381–382
  moral, 362–363, 369–370, 373–374, 380–382, 404
  self-creativity and, 361–362
  will and, 79–80, 84, 284, 361, 362
Fu, 79, 130
fulfilling nature, 380–381
function (yong), 377–378
  in guan, 137–141
  three meanings of Yi and ti-yong, 45–51
function/force of language, 304
future, 17. See also divination
  divination and, 78, 100–103
  in Image-Number School, 182–183
  observation and, 69, 119

present and, 4–6
uncertainty of, 100
Fuxi, 4, 13–14, 16, 28, 31–32, 68, 334, 343
  observation by, 98–99, 119, 157
Fuxi Circle, 257, 258–259
Fuxi Diagram, 256

Gadamer, Hans-Georg, 91–92
gan, 13, 156
Ge, 79
generating numbers, 342
generation
  of generation, 174
  process, 172–173
  reality and, 174–175
  regeneration and, 46, 177–178
generative functions of numbers, 342
generative onto-cosmology, 313–318
generative order, 324
geography, 4
God, 174
  change and, 61, 62, 63
  creation and, 61, 62
  death of, 138
  logos and, 61
Gong Anguo, 344
Gongshu Wenzi, 375
good, 206, 251–252
  change and, 81–82
  creativity and, 81–82
  freedom and, 84
  harmony and, 22, 82
  human situation and, 81–82
  morality and, 83
  supreme, 83
  unity and, 293–294
  will and, 84
good life, 371
governance, 195, 203, 206
great ultimate. See taiji
Great Yu, 4

Index 511

Greek philosophy, 53–54, 59–63, 67
  on being, 134–137, 299
  on harmony, 191–194, 207, 208
  on strife, 210–212
growth, 41
gua, 7–9
  divination and, 9, 18, 101
  five features of, 66–67
  fortune and, 398–400
  guan integrated with, 156–162
  in Image-Number School, 180–181
  interpretation of, 104–110, 180–181
  judgments and, 397–401
  li and, 284–286
  number theory and, 101, 180
  origins of, 31
  positioning in, 255–268
  in Shuogua Commentary, 109
  symbols of, 10, 36, 38
  systematization of, 104–110, 255–257
  Yi change in, 64–67
  Zhu Xi on, 332–334
guan (Comprehensive Observation), 6, 8, 40
  analysis of guan-gua, 141–147
  bagua system and, 120, 121
  being and, 125, 128–132, 134–137
  in Buddhism, 15
  change and, 68–71, 78
  characteristics of, 123–124
  in Confucianism, 15
  cosmography and, 19
  in Daoism, 15
  feeling and, 112–113, 142, 158
  function in, 137–141
  gua integrated with, 156–162
  Heidegger and, 124–125, 127–128
  images in, 121–122
  natural cosmology and, 3–4, 14–15
  natural world and, 14–15, 157–158

  onto-hermeneutics of, 125–126, 128–133
  onto-hermeneutics of being and, 128–132
  onto-hermeneutics of taiji and, 132–133
  in Shuogua Commentary, 122
  substance in, 137–141
  symbols and, 99
  in Tuan Commentary, 142, 157–158
  understanding, 119–126, 158
  in Xiang Commentary, 142
  Xici Commentary on, 120–122
  in Xugua Commentary, 109, 123
  Yi Text and, 96–99
  yin-yang and, 152–153
  in Yizhuan, 68
  in Zagua Commentary, 123
guanbian, 12

Habermas, Jürgen, 92
Han Dynasty, 1–2, 117, 396
  Confucianism in, 26
  Image-Number School in, 20
  standardization in, 9
  Yang Xiong in, 8
hardness, 153–154, 166, 290, 292
harmony
  centrality and, 144–145, 202–206, 224–228
  change and, 85
  Confucius on, 161, 195–202
  as creativity, 76–77, 208, 215–220
  dao and, 196–198
  dialectics of harmonization, 233–236, 237–239, 241–243, 318
  differences as opposites and, 220–224
  Doctrine of the Mean and, 200–201, 238
  exchange and, 171
  external and internal, 194

harmony (continued)
　fortune and, 83
　four grades of, 207–209
　freedom and, 381–382
　good and, 22, 82
　Greek, 191–194, 207, 208
　Heraclitus on, 192–193
　hiddenness of, 192–193
　human nature and, 200
　identity distinguished from, 195–202
　for individual thing, 229–230
　justice and, 59
　Laozi on, 85, 153, 161
　Liu Xiahui and, 199–200
　logical relationship of, 207–208
　material relationship of, 207–208
　Mencius on, 199
　metaphysics of, 233, 236–239
　of mind, 202–203
　Mo Di on, 201–202
　Moist view of, 195–202
　morality and, 22–23, 81, 83
　multi-interactive, 175–176
　musical, 191–194, 208
　nonchange and, 233
　positioning and, 202–203, 224–228
　as primary unity of opposites, 212–220
　primordial, 76, 82–83, 171–172
　qi as, 291
　reality and, 192
　ren and, 84
　six stages of, 234
　strife and, 192–193, 194, 195–196, 207–209
　supreme, 197
　timeliness and, 236–241, 413–418
　timely application of, 236–241
　time-space-quality relationships of, 229–230
　as transformation, 212, 228–233, 234, 242–243
　in *Tuan Commentary*, 171–172
　two types of, 216–217
　unity and, 202–206, 210–220, 224–228
　as unity of opposites, 210–212
　Yan Ying on, 193–196
　yin-yang and, 153, 161, 171–172
hearing, 126
heart-mind, 130, 158, 200
heaven (*tiandao*), 24–25
heaven and earth, 24–25, 38–39, 47, 201, 301, 389
　in *bagua* system, 119–120
　creativity and, 82
　dao and, 85–86
　diagrams, 51–52, 109, 350–351
　fulfilling nature and, 380–381
　heart-mind of, 130
　humanity and, 169
　li and, 275, 277–278
　mandate of heaven, 364–366
　numbers, 342
　positioning of, 252–254, 261–267
　understanding, 252–254
　in *yin-yang*, 163
Hegel, Georg Wilhelm Friedrich, 61
Heidegger, Martin, 95, 299
　on *aletheia* and truth, 127–128, 135–136
　on being, 125, 127–128, 130, 134–137, 139, 140
　guan and, 124–125, 127–128
heng, 168, 407
Heraclitus, 53–54, 139–140
　on change, 54, 59–61
　on harmony, 192–193
　on strife, 210–212
hermeneutical mode of communication, 306–308

Index 513

hermeneutics. *See also* onto-hermeneutics
  Analects and, 356
  change and, 93
  Chinese ontological, 91–96
  Gadamer on, 91–92
  Habermas on, 92
  interpretation, understanding, and, 91–96
  judgments and, 397–404
  onto-hermeneutic understanding, 38, 92–96, 113–117
  onto-hermeneutical interpretation, 19, 35–41, 92–96, 110–117
  overview of, 91
  Western, 91–92, 94–96
  of Yi Text, 96–117
Hetu (River Chart), 310, 334, 340
  mutual transformability of, 343–349
  number theory of, 347–349, 350
  origins of, 343
  trigrams and, 344
  wuxing of, 347–348, 350
hexagrams, 1–2, 3. See also *gua*
  assimilation and coordination of, 323–327
  binomial expansion of, 39–40
  change in, 12–13
  divination in, 2
  formation of, 6–7, 172–173
  hierarchy of forms, 48
  human situation and, 80
  meaning in, 322
  number theory and, 6–7, 18
  organization of, 64–66
  origins of, 31–32, 39–40
  systematization of, 97–99, 133, 256–257
  three main principles of, 396
  validity of, 351–352
  yin-yang in, 42–43
  Zhu Xi on, 351–352

heyi (Principle of Harmonization), 51
hiddenness, 145–146, 175
  of harmony, 192–193
historical background, of *Yijing*, 31–35
historical trends in Chinese philosophy, 57
history-recorders, 32
horizontal transformation, 228–232, 234–236, 243
hostility, 209
Huangdi (Yellow Emperor), 4–5, 100
human civilization, 70, 100, 117, 356
Human Existence, 128. *See also* being
human life
  change and, 12–13, 33–34
  good life, 371
  human-social processes and, 40
  interrelatedness of, 40
  life activities, 7–8, 48–49
  life-creativity, 46–48
  life-realization, 41
  limitations of, 363–368
  meaning and, 51
  mental dispositions and, 5
  natural elements and, 8–9
  natural world and, 32–33, 38–39, 70–71, 275
  Neo-Confucianism on, 26–27
  reality and, 356
  reflecting on human situation and, 7–8, 25
  self-cultivation in, 46
  universe and, 43–44, 70
human nature, 278
  harmony and, 200
human situation
  Analects and, 361
  change and, 80, 88–89
  divination and, 100
  fortune and, 402–403, 407–408
  good and, 81–82

human situation (continued)
  hexagrams and, 80
  li and, 283–284
  ming and, 363–365
  morality and, 81, 278, 402–403
  natural world and, 80–81
  onto-cosmology and, 80, 254
  qi and, 284
  reflecting on human life and, 7–8, 25
  self-creative power and human being, 361–363
humanity
  Confucius and, 24
  creative cultivation of, 77–84
  heaven and earth and, 169
  virtue and, 355
Husserl, Edmund, 68, 124

identity (tong), 13, 60–61, 219
  forms and, 318
  harmony distinguished from, 195–202
ill-being, 83
Image-Number School (Xiangshu), 19–21, 117
  diversification of Yi into Yili and, 51–52
  divination and questions posed for, 181–183
  failure of, 181–182
  future in, 182–183
  gua in, 180–181
  integration of Yili and, 179–188
  li and, 336–338
  qi and, 337–338
  reality in, 181–183
  Yi Text in, 331–337
  Zhu Xi and, 331–337
images, 150
  forms as, 121–122
  in guan, 121–122

numbers and, 51–52
reality and, 55–56
rise of xiang, 389–390
symbolism and, 389–390
Yi Text and xiang, 96–99
Incompletion, 87
indifference, 209
inexhaustible origination, 174–175
infinity, 267, 291
innovation, 70
instrumentalism, 55
internal harmony, 194
interpretation. *See also* understanding
  creative, 114–117
  decision making and action based on, 23
  divination and, 23, 37, 101–102, 109–110, 184–187
  of gua, 104–110, 180–181
  hermeneutics, understanding, and, 91–96
  judgments and, 6–19, 184
  key concepts of, 37
  onto-hermeneutical, 19, 35–41, 92–96, 110–117
  Origin of the Interpretation, 115–116
  of reality, 55–56
  systematization and, 349–532
  by Wang Bi, 107
  Xici Commentary on, 104–105
  Yi Commentaries and, 115–117
  of Yi Text, 104–117
  Yijing as symbolic system of, 18–23
interrelatedness
  of guan and gua, yin and yang, 156–162
  of human life, 40
  of trigrams, 283

Jasper, Karl, 354
ji, 83

jianyi (simplicity of change), 49–51, 164–165
Jiao Xun, 20
Jiao Yanshou, 187
jiaoyi (Principle of Exchange), 51
Jie Zhou, 32
Jing Fang, 20, 179–180, 187
Jirangji (Shao Yong), 131
judgments
  Confucius on, 405–406
  divinatory, 6, 37, 78, 111–112, 268, 273, 279
  forms, numbers, and, 309–313, 335–336
  fortune and, 398–407, 423
  gua and, 397–401
  hermeneutics and, 397–404
  interpretation and, 6–19, 184
  of *li* and *qi*, 284–286
  line, 6–7
  ming and, 400
  morality and, 402–409
  perception and, 195–196
  subsystem of, 326
  symbols and, 19–20, 109–110
  timeliness in, 407–420
  understanding and, 34
  validity of, 351–352
  virtue and, 403–409
justice, 59

Kantian morality, 369
King Wen Diagram, 258
Kun, 8, 50, 65, 151–152, 392
  divinatory judgments of, 111–112
  primary unity of opposites and, 219–220
  taiji and, 105
  Xici Commentary on, 292
  yin-yang in, 71–74, 165–166, 248, 249, 288

language, 176
  being and, 134–136
  communication and, 304
  function/force of, 304
  understanding and, 114–115
Laozi, 27, 42, 52, 60, 62, 178, 300. See also *Daodejing*
  on creation, 85–87
  Daoist School of, 173–174
  on harmony, 85, 153, 161
learning
  Confucius on, 376, 387–388
  self-development and, 186
Leibniz, Gottfried Wilhelm, 28
li, 24–25, 168, 197–198
  avoiding difficulties of, 286–294
  being, nonbeing, and, 294–301
  change and, 283
  Cheng Mingdao on, 275
  Cheng Yi on, 275–276
  Confucius on, 370–371
  creativity and, 277–278
  dao and, 289–290
  divination and, 283–284
  dualism of, 278, 290, 293, 339–341
  gua and, 284–286
  heaven and earth and, 275, 277–278
  human situation and, 283–284
  Image-Number School and, 336–338
  importance of *qi* considerations toward *li*, 337–338
  judgments, 284–286
  natural world and, 283
  Neo-Confucianism, *qi*, and, 274, 275–279, 286–301
  origins of, 275–278
  positioning of, 275
  reality and, 292–293
  reconceptualizing, with *Yijing*, 279–286

li (continued)
  in *Shuogua Commentary*, 288–289
  symbolism of, 282–283
  taiji and, 276–277, 291, 337–338, 339
  Tuan Commentary on, 285
  unity of *qi* and, 293–301
  as virtue, 370–371
  wuji and, 276–277
  wuxing and, 352
  Xiang Commentary on, 285–286
  Xici Commentary on, 287–288
  Yi change and, 282–283
  yin-yang and, 288, 289–290
  Zhou Dunyi on, 275
  Zhu Xi on, 276–279, 283, 290, 336–341
Li Guangdi, 345
Liangshan, 32
life activities, 7–8, 48–49
life-creativity, 46–48
life-realization, 41
light, in *yin-yang*, 153, 164, 248
limited and limitless reality, 177–178
Lin Shu, 351
line judgment, 6–7. See also judgments
Linji, 127
Liu Jing (Six Classics), 355
Liu Xiahui, 199–200
livestock, 98
logic of divination, 15–18, 273–274
logos
  being and, 135–136, 138
  change and, 59–60
  God and, 61
love, 24. See also *ren*
Lu Xiangshan, 277
Lu Xing, 203
Luoshu (Luo Diagram), 310, 334, 340
  mutual transformability of, 343–349

  number theory of, 344–349, 350
  origins of, 343–349
  wuxing of, 347–349, 350

macro-epistemic change, 68–71
Madhyamika Buddhism, 243
mandate of heaven (*tianming*), 364–366
mapping of independent systems, 349–532
matrix of meaning, 310–313, 319–323
Mawangdui Silk Manuscripts, 20, 106, 179–180, 184–185
meaning
  divination and, 100–101
  in hexagrams, 322
  human life and, 51
  matrix of, 310–313, 319–323
  of numbers, 313
  reality and, 319–323
  systematization and, 311–312
  in trigrams, 322–323
  understanding and, 33–34
  of *wuxing* (five powers), 323–326
  of *yao*, 390–391
  Yi, 171
  of *Yi* Text, 386–388
Meaning-Principle School (*Yili*), 19–21, 117
  diversification of *Yi* into *Xiangshu* and, 51–52
  integration of *Xiangshu* and, 179–188
  taiji and, 338–339
  Yi Text in, 331–337
medicine, 154
Mencius, 26, 49, 198, 203, 360–361, 375, 380, 420
  on harmony, 199
  on oneness, 206
Meng Xi, 20, 187
mental dispositions, 5

metaphysics, 136, 275, 293–294
  of being, 294–301
  of Commentaries, 279–280
  of Confucius and Yi Text, 358–360
  of divination, 279–280
  of harmony, 233, 236–239
  of symbolism, 279–280
  systematization and, 280–281
  of Yi-symbolism, 389
microscopic change, 12
mind
  harmony of, 202–203
  mental dispositions of, 5
  of person, 278
ming, 37
  in Analects, 371–372
  Confucius on, 363–367, 421–423
  dao and, 364
  death and, 363–364
  fortune and, 400–405, 421
  human situation and, 363–365
  judgments and, 400
  mandate of heaven and, 364–366
  reality and, 364
  timeliness and, 371–372, 422–423
  world of, 397–407
Ming period, 189
minister and ruler, 195
misfortune. See fortune and misfortune
Mo Di, 201–202, 203
modern sciences, 28
moira, 135–136, 139–140
Moist view, of harmony, 195–202
moon, 163
moral creativity, 81
moral development, 5
moral freedom, 362–363, 369–370, 373–374, 380–382, 404
morality
  Confucius and, 24, 81, 107, 367–371
  decision making and, 404
  desire and, 294, 368
  discipline and, 362–363
  fortune and, 403–407
  good and, 83
  harmony and, 22–23, 81, 83
  human situation and, 81, 278, 402–403
  judgments and, 402–409
  Kantian, 369
  moral perfection, 362, 367–371
  moralization of change, 77–84
  natural world and, 65–66
  self-cultivation and, 362–363, 370–371, 373
  timeliness and, 372–375
  understanding and, 370
  unity and, 293–294
  virtue and, 367–371, 381–382
  in Xiang Commentary, 105
motion, 153–154, 165–166, 290, 292
multi-interactive harmony, 175–176
multiplicity, unity in, 245–246
musical harmony, 191–194, 208

natural cosmology, 3–4, 14–15
natural cycles, 4
natural elements, 54, 323–324
  bagua and, 8–9
  human life and, 8–9
natural phenomena, 14, 27
  eight, 47, 96–97, 315–316
  in trigrams, 39, 96–97
natural world
  change and, 64–66, 165
  creativity and, 40–41, 62
  decision making and, 33
  fulfilling nature, 380–381
  guan and, 14–15, 157–158
  human life and, 32–33, 38–39, 70–71, 275
  human situation and, 80–81

natural world *(continued)*
  li and, 283
  modern science and, 28
  morality and, 65–66
  reality and, 39–41
  timeliness and, 413–414
  trigrams and, 96–97, 283
  world-ordering and, 70–77
  wuxing and, 323–324
  yin-yang and, 71, 150–151, 165, 321–322
Neo-Confucianism, 20, 107, 137
  on being, 299–300
  on human life, 26–27
  li, qi, and, 274, 275–279, 286–301
  rise of, 26–27
  Song, 143
Neo-Moist Canons, 202
New Text School, 187
Nietzsche, 138
nonaction (*wuwei*), 86–87
nonbeing
  being and, 47–48, 292, 294–301
  in Buddhism, 296
  unifying being and, 294–301
  wu as, 42, 47–48, 74–75, 86, 169, 178–179, 294–301
nonchange
  of change, 46–47, 233
  harmony and, 233
  yin-yang and, 168–169
nondivinatory creative interpretation, 114–115
nonultimate. See *wuji*
Northern Song period, 20
number theory
  bagua system and, 6–7
  change and, 75–76
  divination and, 101
  gua and, 101, 180
  of *Hetu* and *Luoshu*, 344–349, 350
  hexagrams and, 6–7, 18
  images and numbers, 51–52
  line judgment in, 6–7
  oneness in, 6–7
  symbols and, 51–52, 177, 342
  trigrams and, 6–7
  twoness in, 6–7
numbers
  completing, 342
  forms, judgments, and, 309–313, 335–336
  generating, 342
  generative functions of, 342
  heaven and earth, 342
  images and, 51–52
  meaning of, 313
  yin-yang and, 339–342, 345–347
  Zhu Xi on, 341, 342–349

observation, 23, 33. See also *guan*
  change and, 14, 33, 153, 159–160
  future and, 69, 119
  by Fuxi, 98–99, 119, 157
  key concepts of, 36
  perception and, 11–12
  of primary unity of opposites, 214–215
  symbolism and, 98–99, 108
omens, 5
oneness, 6–7
  being and, 74
  centrality and, 204–205
  dao and, 206
  Mencius on, 206
  unity and, 204–206
onto-cosmology, 26–27
  Benti-Ontology as, 41–45
  change and, 313–318
  creative principles of, 71–77
  dao and, 9–11, 74
  human situation and, 80, 254
  of positions as positioning, 246–255

reality and, 41–45, 105, 106–108, 255, 317
symbols and, 105
transcendence and, 74
in *Tuan Commentary*, 105, 171
world ordering and, 73–74
Yi as onto-cosmology of change and yin-yang, 162–172
of Yi change, 105–107, 162–172
yin-yang and onto-cosmic thinking, 149–156
onto-epistemology, 156–162
onto-generative cosmology
generative onto-cosmology and, 313–318
yin-yang and Yi as, 172–179
ontogenesis of reality, 317
onto-hermeneutic understanding, 38, 92–96, 113–117, 320
onto-hermeneutical interpretation, 19, 92–96
five levels of, 35–41
original position of, 110–117
onto-hermeneutics
of being, 128–132, 140
of communication, 319–323
of *guan*, 125–126, 128–133
overview of, 128
symbols and, 319–321
of *taiji*, 132–133
ontological phenomenology (OP), 128
opposites
creativity and, 215–216
differences as, 220–224
disunity and, 211–212
harmony as primary unity of, 212–220
harmony as unity of, 210–212
yin-yang contrast, 153–154, 163–166, 215, 220–223, 290, 291, 321–322, 419

oracle bones, 5, 6, 163
organic dialectics of change, 393–397
organismic totality, 178–179
Origin of the Interpretation, 115–116
Original Meanings of Zhouyi (Zhouyi benyi), 268–269, 276, 338, 344
origination, 167–168
Ouyang Xiu, 25

Parmenides, 63, 135, 136–137, 139–140, 299
Peeping View, 145–146
penetration
change and, 231–232, 409–410
creativity as, 218–219
perception
being and, 295
communication and, 308–309
contingency and, 49
judgments and, 195–196
observation and, 11–12
point of view and, 124, 131–132
positioning and, 214, 267–268
reality and, 55–56
philosophical phenomenology (PP), 128
Plato, 63, 95, 134, 299
point of view, 124, 131–132. *See also* perception
polar-generative process, 175
positioning (*wei*)
in Buddhism, 270–271
centrality and, 202–203, 418–419
change and, 248–251, 253, 254–255, 260, 262–264, 266–269
in Confucianism, 246–247, 253–255, 270–271
in Daoism, 246–247, 266, 270–271
divination and, 268–270
in *Doctrine of the Mean*, 247
in *gua*, 255–268
harmony and, 202–203, 224–228

positioning (*wei*) (*continued*)
  of heaven and earth, 252–254, 261–267
  of *li*, 275
  onto-cosmology of positions as, 246–255
  perception and, 214, 267–268
  power of, 249–250, 258, 261–267
  in *Qian*, 227, 264, 265
  in *Shuogua Commentary*, 258
  of superior person, 379–380
  of *taiji*, 258–259
  unity and, 225–228, 245–246, 250–252
  unity in multiplicity and, 245–246
  in *Wenyan Commentary*, 265–266
  Xici Commentary on, 269–270
  of *yao*, 259–264, 266–267, 269–270
  of *yin-yang*, 258–259, 261–262, 418–419
  Zhou method of, 268–269
post-divinatory rational consciousness, 183
Post-Heaven Diagram, 258
post-heaven diagram of *bagua*, 109, 350–351
power, 151, 247–248. *See also wuxing*
  of change, 249–250
  creative, 83–84, 361–363
  of positioning, 249–250, 258, 261–267
  self-creative, 361–363
  wealth and, 368
PP. *See* philosophical phenomenology
PPFIC. *See* primordial and profound feeling and insight into change
pre-heaven diagram of *bagua*, 109, 350–351
presence and being, 129, 134, 140
present and future, 4–6
pre-Socratics, 134–137, 139–140
Primary Model, 116–117

primary unity of opposites, 212–220
primordial and profound feeling and insight into change (PPFIC), 282–283
primordial harmony, 76, 82–83, 171–172
Principle of Comprehensive Observation, 40. *See also guan*
Principle of Creative Unfolding and Development, 41
Principle of Dialectical Development, 99
Principle of Exchange (*jiaoyi*), 51
Principle of Harmonization (*heyi*), 51
Principle of Organic Holism, 109
Principle of Polaristic Opposition and Complementation, 40–41
Principle of Simplicity, 97
Principle of Systematic Consistency and Simplicity, 40
Prior-Heaven Diagram of Hexagrams, 28
Process and Reality (Whitehead), 54, 62
profound female, 86, 301
proprieties, 24–25. *See also li*
prosperity, 83, 168
Pythagoras, 63

qi, 97, 150, 158, 163
  avoiding difficulties of, 286–294
  being, nonbeing, and, 294–301
  change and, 283
  creativity, 288, 289–293
  divination and, 283–284
  dualism of, 278, 290, 293, 339–341
  as harmony, 291
  human situation and, 284
  Image-Number School and, 337–338
  importance of *qi* considerations toward *li*, 337–338

judgments, 284–286
Neo-Confucianism, li, and, 274, 275–279, 286–301
  origins of, 275–278
  reality and, 292–293
  reconceptualizing, with Yijing, 279–286
  symbolism of, 282–283
  as taiji, 290–291, 337–338
  transformation of, 282–283, 290–291
  unity of li and, 293–301
  Xici Commentary on, 287–288
  Yi change and, 282–283
  yin-yang and, 248, 288, 289–290
  Zhang Zai on, 276, 291
  Zhu Xi on, 277–279, 290, 337–338
Qian, 8, 50, 65, 104, 151–152, 316, 392
  positioning in, 227, 264, 265
  primary unity of opposites and, 219–220
  taiji in, 76, 105, 143
  timeliness and, 412, 416
  Xici Commentary on, 292
  yin-yang in, 71–74, 165–166, 248, 249, 288
Qimeng, 344–346
Qing Dynasty, 20
Qu Wanli, 395

realism, 22–23
reality, 39–41, 285
  change and, 106, 188–189, 281–282, 314
  cosmic, 44
  creativity and, 62, 106, 314
  experience and, 55–56
  generation and, 174–175
  harmony and, 192
  human life and, 356
  in Image-Number School, 181–183

  images and, 55–56
  as inexhaustible origination, 174–175
  interpretation of, 55–56
  li and, 292–293
  limited and limitless, 177–178
  meaning and, 319–323
  ming and, 364
  as multi-interactive harmony, 175–176
  natural world and, 39–41
  onto-cosmology and, 41–45, 105, 106–108, 255, 317
  ontogenesis of, 317
  as organismic totality, 178–179
  perception and, 55–56
  as polar-generative process, 175
  qi and, 292–293
  as recursive but limitless regenerativity, 177–178
  symbols and, 319–323
  taiji and, 174–179, 297, 314, 316–317
  unity and, 314
  as virtual hierarchization, 176–177
  yin-yang and, 97, 150, 174–179, 314–318
  you, wu, and, 295
  Zhu Xi on, 334–335
receptivity, 151, 248
rectitude (zheng)
  centrality and, 141–147
  lines of, 142–147
recursive but limitless regenerativity, 177–178
regeneration
  creation and, 46
  recursive but limitless regenerativity, 177–178
  symbolism and, 177–178
relativism, 127
religion. See specific religions

ren (benevolence, love), 24–25, 65, 197
  Confucius on, 362, 366–367, 368, 374
  creativity and, 83–84
  harmony and, 84
  moral perfection of, 362, 367–368
resistance, 209
rest, 153–154, 165–166, 290, 292
rightness or righteousness, 369–370, 380–382
ritual divination, 103
River Chart. See *Hetu*
ruler, 195, 203, 206

SA. *See* system of *Analects*
sages, 13, 49, 110–111, 121, 140, 253, 320–321, 400–401
  understanding by, 102–103
seasons, 4, 47, 49, 68, 82, 238, 366, 376, 409–410, 413–416
seeing, 123–124, 126
self, 5
  unity and, 44
self-actualization, 46, 87
self-conscious, 8, 188–189
  post-divinatory rational consciousness, 183
  in Principle of Understanding in Human Consciousness and its Creative Self-Regulation, 41
self-creative power, 361–363
self-cultivational process, 46, 197–198, 236–237, 252–253
  morality and, 362–363, 370–371, 373
self-development, 79
  ben-ti-yong and, 45–46
  divination and, 107
  learning and, 186
self-fulfillment, 366, 380–381

self-realization, 44
  Analects and, 106–107
  divination and, 106–107
  enlightenment and, 296–297
  life-realization, 41
shamans, 32
Shang Dynasty, 7, 16, 356
Shang Shu (*The Book of Documents*), 203
Shangyi, 32
Shao Yong, 48, 131, 222, 257–258, 336, 350
  dominant concepts of, 275
shenming (divine spirit), 182, 184
shi and timeliness, 376–377
shizhong. See timeliness
Shouwen jiezi (Xu Shen), 162
showing, 146–147
Shu Qi, 374
Shuogua Commentary, 9, 108–109, 116, 256
  gua in, 109
  guan in, 122
  li in, 288–289
  positioning in, 258
  yin-yang in, 166–167, 289
shuzigua, 7
Silk Manuscripts, 179–180, 184–185. *See also* Mawangdui Silk Manuscripts
Sima Qian, 26, 31–32
simplicity, 40, 409
  decision making and, 50
  Principle of Simplicity, 97
  simplicity of change (*jianyi*), 49–51, 164–165
Six Classics (*Liu Jing*), 355
Socrates, 138
softness, 153–154, 166, 290, 292
Song Neo-Confucianism, 143
Song period, 25, 189

sounds, 126
  musical harmony and, 191–194, 208
source-body, 43–44
spirit
  Absolute Spirit, 61
  shenming, 182, 184
spirits, 49
spiritual feelings, 158
spontaneity (*ziran*), 86–87
Spring-Autumn Period, 16
stability, 168
standardization, 9
strife
  four grades of, 209
  Greek, 210–212
  harmony and, 192–193, 194, 195–196, 207–209
substance (*ti*), 42–44
  in *guan*, 137–141
  three meanings of *Yi* and *ti-yong*, 45–51
sun, 163
superior person
  positioning of, 379–380
  virtue and, 407, 416
supreme good, 83
supreme harmony, 197
SY. See system of *Yijing*
symbolism
  change and, 99
  divination and, 99–104, 273
  images and, 389–390
  key concepts of, 36
  of *li*, 282–283
  metaphysics of, 279–280
  observation and, 98–99, 108
  PPFIC and, 282–283
  of *qi*, 282–283
  regeneration and, 177–178
  of trigrams, 280–283

in *wuxing*, 325–326
of *yao*, 385–386
in *Yi* Text, 99, 104–110, 357, 389
yin-yang symbolic system, 66–67, 97, 320–322, 345–346
Yi-symbolism and dialectics of *Yi*-symbolic transformation, 389
symbols
  of *bagua* system, 13–14
  cosmology and, 6
  divination, 2
  of *gua*, 10, 36, 38
  guan and, 99
  judgments and, 19–20, 109–110
  matrix of meaning and, 310–313, 319–323
  number theory and, 51–52, 177, 342
  onto-cosmology and, 105
  onto-hermeneutics and, 319–321
  organization of, 3
  reality and, 319–323
  systematization of, 36–37, 133
  Yi Commentaries and, 3
  Yijing as symbolic system of interpretation, 18–23
system of *Analects* (SA), 382–384
system of *Yijing* (SY), 382–388
systematization
  coordination and assimilation of other systems, 323–327
  divination and, 38
  of *gua*, 104–110, 255–257
  of hexagrams, 97–99, 133, 256–257
  interpretation and, 349–532
  key concepts of, 36–37
  mapping of independent systems, 349–532
  meaning and, 311–312
  metaphysics and, 280–281
  of symbols, 36–37, 133

systematization *(continued)*
  of trigrams, 96–99, 133, 256–257, 280–283
  validity of, 351–352
  wuxing, 323–327
  of *Yi* Text, 104–110
  yin-yang symbolic system, 66–67, 97, 320–322, 345–346
  by Zhu Xi, 331–337, 351–352

taiji (great ultimate), 39, 41, 85, 104, 281
  being and, 74–75, 127–128, 132–133, 138–139
  change and, 72–73, 74, 250, 291
  Confucius on, 340
  creative functions of, 338–342
  creativity and, 47–48, 72–73, 74, 76–77, 174–175, 338–342
  dao and, 173–179, 254–255, 391–392
  Daoism and, 276–277
  derivation of, 391–393
  differences as opposites and, 221–222
  Kun and, 105
  li and, 276–277, 291, 337–338, 339
  life-creativity and, 47–48
  Meaning-Principle School and, 338–339
  onto-hermeneutics of, 132–133
  positioning of, 258–259
  as *qi*, 290–291, 337–338
  in *Qian*, 76, 105, 143
  reality and, 174–179, 297, 314, 316–317
  root source of, 174
  transcendence and, 74, 76
  transformation of, 229
  wuji and, 154–156, 170, 178–179, 291

  yin-yang and, 154–156, 169–170, 174–179, 282, 288, 314–315, 339–340, 391–393
  Zhou Dunyi on, 298
  Zhu Xi and, 338–342
Taiji tu shuo (Discourse on the Diagram of the Great Ultimate), 275, 357
taixu (ultimate void), 276
teleology, 62–63
Ten Wings. See *Yi Commentaries*
ti. See substance
tian, 8, 25
tian gan (Celestial Stems), 323
tiandao (heaven), 24–25
tianming (mandate of heaven), 364–366
time, 366
  being and, 134–135, 138
  body and, 45
  time-space-quality relationships of harmony, 229–230
  unity and, 293
timeliness (*shizhong*)
  centrality and, 418–420
  change and, 409–410, 412, 416
  Confucius and, 371–382, 422–425
  dao and, 372–373
  in *Doctrine of the Mean*, 378–379
  fortune and, 412, 415–418, 423
  four components of, 377
  further exposition of, 376–382
  harmony and, 236–241, 413–418
  idioms and paradigms of, 239–240
  in judgments, 407–420
  ming and, 371–372, 422–423
  morality and, 372–375
  natural world and, 413–414
  persistence and application of virtues and principles, 371–375
  Qian and, 412, 416

shi and, 376–377
Tuan Commentary on, 410–413
virtue of, 380–382, 416–418, 423–425
Zhu Xi on, 378–379
ti-yong, 45–51
togetherness, 50
tong. See identity
tongbian, 12, 37
Tongshu (Book on Comprehending the Yi), 275
tortoise shell readings, 5, 6, 37
transcendence
  onto-cosmology and, 74
  taiji and, 74, 76
transformation
  change and, 48–49, 64–67, 74, 75, 88–89, 98, 170–171, 212, 224
  Confucius on, 370
  harmony as, 212, 228–233, 234, 242–243
  horizontal, 228–232, 234–236, 243
  mutual transformability of Hetu and Luoshu, 343–349
  of qi, 282–283, 290–291
  of taiji, 229
  unity and, 212, 215
  vertical, 228–233, 235–236, 243
  Way of Transformation, 129
  yin-yang and, 129, 170–171
  Yi-symbolism and dialectics of Yi-symbolic transformation, 389
trigrams, 1–2, 3. See also gua
  assimilation and coordination of, 323–327
  formation of, 6–7, 9, 172–173
  Hetu and, 344
  interrelatedness of, 283
  meaning in, 322–323
  natural phenomena in, 39, 96–97
  natural world and, 96–97, 283

number theory and, 6–7
  origins of, 38–40
  representations and references of, 283
  symbolism of, 280–283
  systematization of, 96–99, 133, 256–257, 280–283
  validity of, 351–352
  yao and, 390–391
trust, in change, 88–89
truth, 37, 190
  change and, 88–89
  Heidegger's aletheia, 127–128, 135–136
  understanding and, 314
Truth and Method (Gadamer), 91
Tuan Commentary, 28, 37, 76, 80, 110, 144
  centrality in, 418
  change in, 172, 394–395
  cosmogony and, 116
  guan in, 142, 157–158
  harmony in, 171–172
  on li, 285
  onto-cosmology in, 105, 171
  on primary unity of opposites, 219–220
  on timeliness, 410–413
twoness, 6–7

Ultimate as the Same, 137
ultimate source, 41–42, 44
ultimate void (taixu), 276
understanding
  communication and, 309, 329–330
  decision making and, 21
  of differences of opposites, 222–223
  divination and, 46, 78, 102–103
  feeling and, 13, 113
  five stages of, 35–41
  guan, 119–126, 158

understanding *(continued)*
　heaven and earth, 252–254
　hermeneutics, interpretation, and, 91–96
　judgments and, 34
　language and, 114–115
　meaning and, 33–34
　morality and, 370
　onto-hermeneutic, 38, 92–96, 113–117, 320
　in Principle of Understanding in Human Consciousness and its Creative Self-Regulation, 41
　by sages, 102–103
　truth and, 314
unity
　of being and nonbeing, 294–301
　Confucianism on, 204–206
　creativity and, 215–220
　in *Daodejing*, 206
　in differences as opposites, 223–224
　disunity and, 211–212
　diversity and, 43
　good and, 293–294
　harmony and, 202–206, 210–220, 224–228
　harmony as unity of opposites, 210–212
　of *li* and *qi*, 293–301
　morality and, 293–294
　in multiplicity, 245–246
　oneness and, 204–206
　positioning and, 225–228, 245–246, 250–252
　reality and, 314
　self and, 44
　time and, 293
　timeliness of, 237–238
　transformation and, 212, 215
　yin-yang and, 160–161, 215, 314–316

universe
　change and, 70
　contingency and, 49
　cosmic body and, 43–45
　human life and, 43–44, 70
　world-ordering in, 70–77
unthought, 137

valuation, 22
values and communication, 306–308
vertical transformation, 228–233, 235–236, 243
vices, 5
viewing, 125, 140–142
virtual hierarchization, 176–177
virtue, 5, 39, 169
　in *Analects*, 361
　Confucius and, 8–9, 24, 185, 197, 198, 361, 367–375, 423–425
　constant virtues, 367–371
　fortune and, 405–407, 416–418
　humanity and, 355
　judgments and, 403–409
　li as, 370–371
　morality and, 367–371, 381–382
　persistence and application of virtues and principles, 371–375
　rightness or righteousness and, 369–370, 380–382
　superior person and, 407, 416
　of timeliness, 380–382, 416–418, 423–425

Wang Bi, 20, 42, 107, 188
Wang Yangming, 20
way. See *dao*
Way of Transformation, 129
wealth, 368
wei. See positioning
Wei-Jin Period, 20
weizhi, 151–152
well-being, 83–84, 400

Wen of Zhou (King), 2, 7, 8, 16, 31–32, 35, 36–37
Wenyan Commentary, 105, 116, 143, 161, 417
　change in, 395, 396
　positioning in, 265–266
Western hermeneutics, 91–92, 94–96
Western philosophy, 53–55, 134–137
Wheelwright, Philip, 192–193
Whitehead, Alfred North, 54–55, 62–63, 322, 358
will
　freedom and, 79–80, 84, 284, 361, 362
　good and, 84
world-being, 257
world-ordering, 70–77
wu. See also nonbeing
　as enlightenment, 296–297
　as nonbeing, 42, 47–48, 74–75, 86, 169, 178–179, 294–301
wuji (nonultimate), 282
　li and, 276–277
　taiji and, 154–156, 170, 178–179, 291
　Zhu Xi on, 291
wuwei (nonaction), 86–87
wuxing (five powers), 10, 282
　diagrams, 325
　of *Hetu* and *Luoshu*, 347–349, 350
　li and, 352
　meaning of, 323–326
　natural world and, 323–324
　symbolism in, 325–326
　systematization, 323–327
　yin-yang and, 325

Xia Dynasty, 4, 100
Xian, 13, 159
xiang. See images
Xiang (King), 206

Xiang Commentary, 28, 37, 80–81, 171
　on change, 394–395
　guan in, 142
　on *li*, 285–286
　morality in, 105
Xiangshu. See Image-Number School
Xici, 9, 19, 31
Xici Commentary, 11, 37, 46–47, 116, 119
　on change, 48–49
　on change-penetration, 231–232
　cosmology in, 247
　divination and, 101, 103
　on fortune, 401–402
　on *guan*, 120–122
　on interpretation, 104–105
　on *Kun*, 292
　on *li* and *qi*, 287–288
　on positioning, 269–270
　on *Qian*, 292
　Shang 1, 50, 247
　Shang 4, 389–390
　Shang 5, 64–65, 81–82, 151–152, 163
　Shang 10, 423
　Shang 11, 72
xiong (ill-being), 83
Xu Commentary, 116
Xu Shen, 162
Xugua Commentary, 109, 123

Yan Ying, 193–196
Yang Chu, 203
Yang Xiong, 8
yao, 1–2, 170, 281
　meaning of, 390–391
　positioning of, 259–264, 266–267, 269–270
　symbolism of, 385–386
　trigrams and, 390–391
　yin-yang and, 391

Yellow Emperor (Huangdi), 4–5, 100
Yi change. *See also* change
  Benti-Ontology as onto-cosmology of, 41–45
  cosmography of, 11–15
  diversification of Yi into Xiangshu and Yili, 51–52
  formation of, 19
  in *gua*, 64–67
  historical development of, 189–190
  li and, 282–283
  onto-cosmology of, 105–107, 162–172
  as onto-generative cosmology, 172–179
  philosophical reflection on development of, 188–190
  PPFIC and, 282–283
  qi and, 282–283
  ti-yong and three meanings of, 45–51
  Yi as onto-cosmology of change and *yin-yang*, 162–172
Yi Commentaries. *See also specific commentaries*
  Confucius and, 3, 8, 34, 115
  development of, 309–310
  Discourse Commentary, 65
  divination and, 309–310
  interpretation and, 115–117
  metaphysics of, 279–280
  philosophy of, 34–35, 273
  symbols and, 3
Yi meaning, 171
Yi Text
  Analects and, 356–361
  divination in, 99–104, 385–387
  guan and, 96–99
  hermeneutics of, 96–117
  in Image-Number School, 331–337
  as inspiration, 356–357
  interpretation of, 104–117
  meaning of, 386–388
  in Meaning-Principle School, 331–337
  metaphysics of Confucius and, 358–360
  original position of onto-interpretation and eight primary principles of, 110–117
  reciprocal transformation between Confucius and, 420–425
  rise of, 96–99, 107–108
  symbolism in, 99, 104–110, 357, 389
  systematization of, 104–110
  xiang and, 96–99
  yin-yang and principles of onto-epistemology of, 156–162
  Yi-symbolism and dialectics of Yi-symbolic transformation, 389
  Yizhuan and, 187, 387–388
yijian, 164–165
Yijing. *See also specific topics*
  Buddhism and, 27–29
  comprehensive origins of, 11–15
  in Confucianism, 23–27
  Confucius and, 23–27
  Daoism and, 27–29
  dialectical methodology of, 313–323
  folklore and, 29
  historical background and theoretical presupposition, 31–35
  intended system of, 384–388
  modern sciences and, 28
  new approach to, 189–190
  organization of, 3–10
  origins of, 1–2, 149–150
  rise of, 96–99
  six developmental stages of, 3–10
  six topics in primary philosophy of, 11–29
  standardization of, 3–10

as symbolic system of
    interpretation, 18–23
system of *Yijing*, 382–388
three strata of, 273–274, 279–280
Zhu Xi's three stages of, 333–334
Yili. See Meaning-Principle School
yin-yang, 10, 12, 18, 144
    activity, 287–288
    in *bagua* system, 6, 15
    being and, 138–139
    change and, 64–67, 159–172,
        315–316
    contrast, 153–154, 163–166, 215,
        220–223, 290, 291, 321–322,
        419
    creativity and, 71, 155–156,
        167–168
    dao and, 64–65, 81–82, 151, 169,
        176, 249, 281, 287–288, 300
    difference as opposites and,
        220–223
    experience of, 151, 153–156,
        160–161, 164–167
    feeling and, 158–161
    five principles of, 40–41
    guan and, 152–153
    as hard and soft, 153–154, 166,
        290, 292
    harmony and, 153, 161, 171–172
    heaven and earth in, 163
    in hexagrams, 42–43
    interrelatedness of, 156–162
    in *Kun*, 71–74, 165–166, 248, 249,
        288
    li and, 288, 289–290
    as light and dark, 153, 164, 248
    medicine and, 154
    as motion and rest, 153–154,
        165–166, 290, 292
    movements, 1–2, 391
    natural world and, 71, 150–151,
        165, 321–322

nonchange and, 168–169
numbers and, 339–342, 345–347
onto-cosmic thinking and, 149–156
onto-generative cosmology and,
    172–179
positioning of, 258–259, 261–262,
    418–419
principles of onto-epistemology of
    Yi Text and, 156–162
qi and, 248, 288, 289–290
in *Qian*, 71–74, 165–166, 248,
    249, 288
reality and, 97, 150, 174–179,
    314–318
in *Shuogua Commentary*, 166–167,
    289
symbolic system of, 66–67, 97,
    320–322, 345–346
taiji and, 154–156, 169–170,
    174–179, 282, 288, 314–315,
    339–340, 391–393
three main principles of, 167–168
transformation and, 129, 170–171
two dimensions of, 41–43
unity and, 160–161, 215, 314–316
wuxing and, 325
yao and, 391
Yi as onto-cosmology of change
    and, 162–172
Yi as school of *Yin* and *Yang*,
    162–172
in *Yizhuan*, 71
Yiwei Qianzuodu, 46, 93
Yixue Qimeng (Zhu Xi), 331
Yizhuan, 9, 27–28, 46, 85, 246, 271
    change in, 63, 64
    guan in, 68
    on self-cultivation, 252–253
    Yi Text and, 187, 387–388
    yin-yang in, 71
    Zhu Xi on, 331
yong. See function

you (being), 42, 47–48, 74–75, 86, 169, 294–301. *See also* being
yuan, 41, 168
Yuan Shu, 343

Zagua Commentary, 109, 116, 123
Zeng Shen, 205
Zeng Zi, 374
Zhang Zai, 137
 on being, 299–300
 on *li*, 276
 on *qi*, 276, 291
 Zhengmeng by, 76
zhen, 168
zheng. *See* rectitude
Zheng Kangcheng, 282
Zheng Xuan, 46, 379
Zhengmeng (Zhang Zai), 76
zhihua, 12
zhiwei, 151
zhong. *See* centrality
Zhongyong. *See Doctrine of the Mean*
Zhou (King), 7
Zhou Dunyi, 170, 178–179, 275, 276–277, 325
 on *taiji*, 298
 treatise by, 47–48
Zhou Dynasty, 2, 6, 268–269
Zhouyi benyi (*Original Meanings of Zhouyi*), 268–269, 276, 338, 344

Zhu Liangshan, 184–185
Zhu Xi, 16, 20, 27, 137, 143, 169, 268–269, 274, 383
 Confucianism and, 345
 on divination, 331–334
 dualism of, 278, 290, 293, 339–341
 on *gua*, 332–334
 on hexagrams, 351–352
 Image-Number School and, 331–337
 on *li*, 276–279, 283, 290, 336–341
 Lin Shu and, 351
 on numbers, 341, 342–349
 on *qi*, 277–279, 290, 337–338
 on reality, 334–335
 systematization by, 331–337, 351–352
 taiji and, 338–342
 on three stages of *Yijing*, 333–334
 on timeliness, 378–379
 on *wuji*, 291
 Yixue Qimeng by, 331
 on *Yizhuan*, 331
Zhuangzi, 60, 62, 162, 173–174
Zi Mo, 203
ziran (spontaneity), 86–87
Zisi, 380–381
Zuozhuan, 15–16

www.ingramcontent.com/pod-product-compliance
Lightning Source LLC
Chambersburg PA
CBHW030319020526
44117CB00029B/42